Children's Dreams

LONGITUDINAL STUDIES

Children's Dreams
LONGITUDINAL STUDIES

DAVID FOULKES

Emory University and
Georgia Mental Health Institute
Atlanta, Georgia

A WILEY-INTERSCIENCE PUBLICATION

JOHN WILEY & SONS New York Chichester Brisbane Toronto Singapore

Library of Congress Cataloging in Publication Data:

Foulkes, William David, 1935–
  Children's dreams.

  "A Wiley-Interscience publication."
  Bibliography: p.
  Includes indexes.
  1. Children's dreams.   I. Title.   [DNLM:
1. Dreams—In infancy and childhood. WS 105.5.D8
F767c]
BF1099.C55F68   155.4'1   81-11478
ISBN 0-471-08181-7   AACR2

Printed in the United States of America

10 9 8 7 6 5 4 3 2 1

*This book is dedicated with
appreciation to all of the children,
parents, and teachers who
participated in this research,
but, especially, to Bill Foulkes.*

Acknowledgments

No project of the scope described here could have been accomplished single-handedly. Many persons—besides the children, parents, and teachers who provided the primary data but who must remain anonymous—contributed substantially to whatever success the project has enjoyed. Rather than wave a general hand of thanks in their direction, I want to acknowledge their role in the project specifically and to thank them all once more for their expertise and for their personal support: Barbara Ahrens, Edward Belvedere, Constance Brizuela, Lawrence J. Brown, Sharon K. Brown, Terry Brubaker, David Bush, Stephen F. Butler, Marge Cruise, James Fitzgerald, Sharon Frost, Margaret R. Gabler, Scott Harris, Joel Humphrey, Kathy Irwin, Cindy Keneally, Nancy H. Kerr, James D. Larson, Monte Lopez, Peggy McConnell, John McMullen, Patricia L. Maykuth, Leonard Medoff, Sergio Molinari, Jean Petrik, Connie Ponder, Richard Pope, Joey Porter, Amy Prather, Steve Renfro, Beynon St. John, Marcella Schmidt, Elizabeth A. Scott, John Sindelar, Eric W. Trupin, Arthur L. Walker, Robert Weisz, Gerry L. Wilcove, and David Worley.

Whatever "we" 's appear in the text are not to be interpreted as majestic extensions of the author's self, but as recognition of the collaborative nature of the research on which this book is based. The drafting of this text, however, has been my sole responsibility, and none of the persons listed above should be held culpable for defects in it.

Acknowledgment also is gratefully offered to the organizations that supported the research described here: The National Science Foundation (1968–1970), The National Institute of Mental Health (1970–1974; 1978–1981), The National Institute of Child Health and Human Development (1970–1975), The Center for Advanced Study in the Behavioral Sciences (1974–1975), The Department of Human Resources, State of Georgia (1977–1981), and Emory University (1977–1981).

I also owe a debt of gratitude to the Department of Home Economics at the University of Wyoming for the use of its Home Management House in our nursery-school studies and to Louise Wesswick, who helped us adapt the facility to our use. Finally, I owe special debts of thanks to Nancy H. Kerr, for her patient and thorough reading of this book in manuscript form, to Peggy Plant, who skillfully transformed it into typescript, to Melanie Ross, who undertook the arduous task of typing our correlational results, and to Marcella Schmidt and Anne MacConochie, who helped in the preparation of the text's printed version.

The quotation in chapter 8 from Hermann Hesse's *Demian* is made with the kind permission of the copyright holder, Harper & Row, Publishers, Inc.

D.F.

Contents

Children's Dreams
LONGITUDINAL STUDIES

PART 1 ————————————————————

Why and How We Studied Children's Dreams

CHAPTER 1 _____

Introduction

What do children dream about? Do they have different kinds of dreams, or different symbols in their dreams, at different ages? Are their dreams more frightening than ours? More imaginative? When, in the course of human development, does dreaming begin? What are those first dreams like? Do boys and girls have different kinds of dreams? Is dreaming related to intelligence? What can young children's dreams tell us about their otherwise hidden private fantasy life? Do children's dreams reflect their waking behavior and personality, and if so, how?

There is practically no limit to the number of interesting questions one can ask about children's dreams. One would imagine, then, that these questions would have been the object of much systematic scientific study, and that such study would have yielded some reasonably definite answers to them. In fact, however, that has not been the case.

THE STUDY OF CHILDREN'S DREAMS

Over 40 years ago C. W. Kimmins (1937) subtitled his book on children's dreams *An Unexplored Land*. From the perspective of its rigorous empirical study, children's dreaming remains largely unexplored today. This state of affairs is a double surprise, because in the past several decades there has been a veritable explosion of scientific interest both in childhood and in dreaming. But somehow students of children's waking cognitive and social development have not paid much attention to the products or processes of the child's dreaming mind, and psychophysiologists, in the heady years following their discovery (Aserinsky & Kleitman, 1953) of rapid eye movement (REM) sleep and of its correlation with adults' reports of vivid dream activity, did little to extend their techniques to the study of children's dreams. The present book is an attempt to fill this substantial gap in our understanding of children and of dreams. By observation and interpretation I want to show that the systematic study of children's dreams has a great deal to tell us both about child development and about what our minds do during that substantial portion of our lives when we are asleep. I also want to take a stab at answering all of the questions of my introductory paragraph, and more besides.

There has, of course, been no lack of clinical speculation about children's dreams. But neither clinical observation nor the theory so loosely built on it has given us reliable, empirical knowledge. In fact, the net impact of clinical work on the scientific study of children's dreams no doubt has been negative: The clinical pretension to recondite knowledge probably has been a substantial deterrent to the entry into children's dream study of more scientifically oriented researchers. Moreover, since the discovery by psychophysiological researchers of how very much dreaming we do, and of how little of it we ordinarily remember (i.e., outside the sleep-laboratory setting that permits its representative sampling), it is clear that clinical observations have more to say about the selective remembering of dreams than about what and how children typically think during sleep. This book focuses on these latter problems.

Two concurrent longitudinal dream studies will be described in which children were studied in a sleep-laboratory setting periodically for 5 years. The children had their sleep monitored with electrophysiological recordings, were awakened on the basis of stages of sleep identified in these recordings, and were asked, "on the spot," to describe the dreams or other mental experiences that they were having just before having been awakened. For over 25 years now these methods have been employed productively in the study of the mental activity during sleep of adult subjects (e.g., Arkin, Antrobus, & Ellman, 1978; Cohen, 1979). Obviously there are some special problems in employing these techniques with children, particularly very young ones (several children began service in our studies before their third birthdays). Where potentially important effects of such problematic variables on children's dream reports might be imagined, or where real effects may have been apparent, I will discuss the methods of these studies with a greater eye to their influence on the results.

By and large, however, I will not go into elaborate detail on the methodology of the longitudinal studies whose results are discussed herein. My intention is to present data and to raise questions at a level somewhat more accessible than that of the scientific monograph or the professional-journal article. One of the advantages of the understandably long period separating the time in which our subjects were studied (1968–1973) and the date of this publication is that there has been much opportunity to analyze and think about our findings. We have written privately circulated project reports for each of the 5 years of the study, and have published some articles (Foulkes, 1971; Foulkes, Shepherd, & Scott, 1974; Foulkes, 1977; Foulkes, Petrik, & Scott, 1978; Foulkes, 1978a, 1979a, b). At my laboratory at the Georgia Mental Health Institute, we have been perusing and discussing the results of this study for the past several years. We think now that we have some sense not only of the many trees, but also of the larger shape of the forest that they make. It is my aim here to describe that shape and to spend no more time on lesser detail than seems absolutely essential to justify my perception of the larger pattern.

This means, in effect, that this is not a book addressed merely to those few professionals whose specialization is in the particular subject matter or methods under review. Rather the book is intended for a wider audience of those persons—professional or not—who are interested in child development, in how the human mind works, and in understanding the course of development that makes it possible for us to do all the amazing and wonderful things we do with our minds each night that we sleep. Professional readers whose interests require further documentation of method will need to consult the extant literature on our project in professional journals (and there no doubt will be additions to this literature) and to pay special attention to the technical appendixes to this book, in which there are extensive presentations of our primary research data (the reliability of our dream scoring procedures; year-by-year dream results; and results of correlational studies indicating, on a year-by-year basis, what sort of child was dreaming what sort of dream).

WHY STUDY CHILDREN'S DREAMS?

Why would one be seriously interested in—and want to spend many years studying—children's dreams? This is a question that both parents and children have asked me directly, and one that has been at least latent in the reaction of some of my colleagues to the amount of time I have devoted to the research reported here. It is a question that deserves an answer, and I shall now try to provide one—many, actually, for I think there are numerous reasons why an understanding of children's dreams is an essential part of understanding our children and ourselves.

The most obvious answer—but ultimately, perhaps, the least important one—is at an immediate, practical level. Parents want to know how to minister to children whose dreams have carried them past the boundaries of safety, and of sleep. How, knowledgeably, does one explain their dreams to children themselves?

But beyond the situation of the child who trembles before them, parents also must wonder why children have to dream at all, and why, if dream they must, it often seems to be in forms that disturb their waking well-being. Do these dreams reveal some fundamental maladjustment, some problem requiring further parental attention or, perhaps, even professional counseling? Even parents with minimal psychological sophistication are aware of the claims of therapists that they can determine (and perhaps alleviate) a person's conflicts or problems through dream analysis. Do all dreams reflect festering concerns that we have not been able to "work through" in wakefulness? Are children, with their lesser abilities to meaningfully organize their own experiences, particularly susceptible to having their dreamlife invaded by unresolved waking conflicts?

Underlying these last questions is a particular view of human nature, a position that, thanks to generations of psychiatric propagandizing, now has made its impact felt at every stratum of society. It is a venerable tradition that we look to children to find out who we really are. Here is the raw material of humanity, as yet incompletely touched (or contaminated) by social convention. We are told by "experts" who have made children's emotional lives their speciality that underneath the superficial placidity of much of the child's waking behavior lies a set of animalistic impulses and egotistical wishes that bode ill for the child's prospects for harmonious social adaptation and, ultimately, for our own as well, because inside each of us there also lies this same infantile irrationality.

It is an equally venerable tradition that we look to our dreams to find out who we really are. In our dreams we are, momentarily at least, cast adrift from social convention and ordinary social restraints. Mentally, if not (fortunately) behaviorally, we can express who we really are, what we really think, what we really want. Since the writing of Freud's (1900) *Interpretation of Dreams,* it has been impressed on us that our dreams form the royal road to this beast who is our other, less amiable self. Thus in the hands of clinical psychiatrists the confluence of speculations about dreams with those about children has given us an unflattering but persuasive way of thinking about ourselves.

But is this view substantially correct? What are its empirical supports? If we accept the proposition that the spontaneous mental life of the child, our own spontaneous mental life during sleep and, especially, the spontaneous mental life of the child during sleep may be key elements in understanding human nature, have Freudians, Jungians, and other theorists of that sort accurately apprehended the facts necessary to drawing the appropriate conclusions? There is reason to believe that they have not.

With the discovery of REM sleep and of its correlation at the adult level with vivid dreaming (Aserinsky & Kleitman, 1953), two conclusions soon were reached about adults' dreaming. First, we do a lot of dreaming, far more than we are aware of ordinarily. Even leaving aside the fact that much dreaming occurs in non-REM[1] sleep (Foulkes, 1966), approximately 25% of our total sleep time, say 1½ to 2 hours each night, is spent in the REM (vivid-dreaming) state. Evidently, ordinarily we are aware of only a small fraction of all the dreaming that we actually do. Second, when one samples representatively, through deliberate awakenings during sleep, all of the REM dreaming that we do experience, it becomes clear that ordinarily we are aware not only of a small fraction, but also of a highly biased fraction, of

---

[1]In this book "non-REM" sleep designates *both* sleep onset *and* ordinary non-REM ("NREM") sleep.

the dreams that we experience. Unlike "spontaneously recalled" home dream samples, laboratory REM dreams are most notable for their mundane quality and for their affective tranquility, rather than for bizarre scenarios or frightening contents (Snyder, 1970). Moreover, it has been demonstrated that most or all of this difference is attributable not to changes induced in the dream process by the method of study in the laboratory but to biased sampling in home recall (Weisz & Foulkes, 1970; Foulkes, 1979b). Thus clinical dream samples, which rely on "spontaneous recall," have given us an inherently biased view of what adults' dreams really are like.

In addition, clinical dreams have still another bias over and above that introduced by their method of sampling. It has been demonstrated, both for adults (e.g., Foulkes & Rechtschaffen, 1964; Pivik & Foulkes, 1966, 1968; Cartwright & Ratzel, 1972) and for adolescents (Foulkes, Larson, Swanson, & Rardin, 1969), that more disturbed persons have more disturbing dreams. That is, one cannot generalize from the dreams—however collected—of clinic patients to those of unselected ("normal") populations.

We have, then, considerable basis for doubting the adequacy of the empirical base on which most clinical or psychiatric speculation about adults' dreams has been based. We have equal reason to doubt the adequacy of extrapolations from adult psychopathology, or of observations of disturbed children, to tell us about the typical mental or emotional experience of childhood. We have special reason to doubt the general relevance of clinical impressions of children's dreamlife. If we believe that children's dreams may make a unique contribution to our understanding of human nature, no longer can we rely uncritically on clinical impressions. We need to study, empirically, in unselected ("normal") populations, and with the techniques of representative dream sampling now available to us, what children's dreams are like. We need to view "failures" of effective dream management—those dreams that our children spontaneously present to us as they come tumbling into our beds in the middle of the night—in the context of those far more typical dream experiences that children have but generally sleep through and spontaneously forget.

In the more limited contexts of dream psychology and of the study of waking cognitive development, children's dreams also have a unique role to play. As Freud realized, children's dreams may, by virtue of their relative simplicity, cast light on the many still obscure problems of adult dream psychology. What are the sources—physiological or mental—of dreams? What do dreams mean? How, if at all, do they contribute to waking adaptation? What functions do they serve? There is reason to believe that such questions can be addressed more feasibly at age levels where dreams themselves are relatively unadorned. The student of adult dreams still will have to consider later embellishments of the dreaming act in extending clues discovered at the child level to typical adult dreams, but the clues themselves may be more accessible in children's than in adults' dreams.

But the major import and impact of the study of children's dreams may well be on those disciplines that study children's waking mental development. Whatever may or may not *be read out of them* for purposes of personality assessment, dreams themselves *are* mental acts. It is easy to lose sight of the fact that dreaming is a form of thinking, that dreams are not experiences that "happen" *to* us but stories that we make up with our own minds. Herein lies a large part of the sense of mystery that so easily attaches itself to our perception of our dreams. How is it possible that, without deliberately trying, we construct so effortlessly imaginative yet internally coherent narratives during sleep, stories that seem never to hem or haw but that glide along with a rapidity that we would find it almost impossible to simulate in wakefulness? Doesn't this highly skilled act of cognitive construction promise to tell us a great deal about the capability of our minds? And, by the same token, won't an analysis of how children learn to master the skill of dream generation be terribly important in understanding how children pass from being stimulus-response machines into creatures who think, plan, and organize, and whose later behavior will be much more a function of internal "programs" than of environmental inputs (Cohen, 1979)?

Recent theorizing by experimentally oriented students has begun to stress the cognitive-skill component of adult dreaming (e.g., Foulkes, 1978b,c; Antrobus, 1978; Cohen, 1979). This is a much-needed corrective to the traditional placement of dreams as a subject matter fit only for students of psychopathology or, more recently, of exotic "altered states of consciousness." It may well be developmentally that dreams will be the most instructive indices of mental operations and organizations. How does mind develop? Extensive studies by Piaget (Gruber & Vonèche, 1977) and others have given us invaluable accounts of the unfolding of children's waking mental capabilities, but, to my knowledge, in the almost three decades since the discovery of REM sleep not a single developmental psychologist has studied systematically children's REM mentation from a comparable perspective.

This is a shame, for dreams are uniquely situated to complement the emerging picture of the ontogeny of waking mental operations. Dreams are spontaneous, rather than having to be elicited in artificially contrived experimental conditions. And yet, precisely because children do not recognize their own role in dream generation, they seem unlikely to be self-conscious about their dreams or reticent in sharing such impressive experiences with others. As "objectified" mental acts, dreams may be our best window on the inner mental life of children, who otherwise are neither interested in, nor competent at, introspection. Furthermore, unlike most of the waking cognitive acts developmental psychologists have studied, dreams are not "pure" cognition. That is, they engage the *whole* child: motive as well as skill, feeling as well as thought. As such they present developmentalists with a rare opportunity to integrate their models of *thought* development with more holistic models of *child* development.

These, then, are some of the reasons why one might be interested in children's dreams. But these reasons all are, to some degree or other, external—children's dreams are important because of their implications for something else (counseling children, understanding human nature, or studying adults' dreams or children's waking cognitive development). For the scientist there is another compelling reason to study children's dreams— because they are there, because they are a phenomenon of (human) nature. Dreams consume a surprisingly large part of our lives; they constitute a surprisingly large part of what we do with our minds. In these days when cries for "relevance" are inflicted ceaselessly on a small and greatly beleaguered research community, we do well to remind ourselves, as a society, that: (1) the need to understand persons—and that means children as well as adults—never has been greater; (2) the paths to such understanding rarely can be prescribed a priori and often start from observational contexts from which they are the least likely to have been expected; and (3) a society that is not fundamentally curious about human phenomena cannot provide a hospitable environment for the unfolding of the human potential of either children or adults. I would like to think that reasons such as these entered into the support by various governmental and private agencies of the research described herein, and that their confidence has not entirely been misplaced.

The Study

BACKGROUND

During the 1960s my laboratory at the University of Wyoming was engaged in a program of research on the determinants and correlates of laboratory-collected REM dreams. As a follow-up to an earlier study (Foulkes & Rechtschaffen, 1964), we decided to see if and how we could influence dreams by systematically manipulating dreamers' presleep experiences. The earlier study had exposed young adult dreamers, on separate nights, to a violent and a nonviolent episode of a popular television series. In the follow-up study, the subjects were to be boys, ages 6–12, a choice dictated by the fact that much of the social concern about mass-media violence is directed to its alleged effects on the fantasies of male children. In fact, the child study (Foulkes, Pivik, Steadman, Spear, & Symonds, 1967) did not reveal any striking effects of short-term exposure to film violence on children's dream content, and it did not suggest that children were made anxious or hostile by such content. The film effects we did observe proved to be inconsistent both with the adult findings (Foulkes & Rechtschaffen, 1964) and with findings of a subsequent study of children commissioned by the Surgeon General's Scientific Advisory Committee on Television and Social Behavior (Foulkes, Belvedere, & Brubaker, 1971). Our study did, however, introduce us to the possibility and the potential value of more extensive descriptive studies of children's dreams.

Our child subjects generally were willing, even enthusiastic, participants in laboratory dream research. They were able to report dreams on REM awakenings almost as often as were young adults. The boys' dreams were suggestive, even more than young adults' dreams had been, of a large degree of continuity between dreams and waking thoughts. The boys often dreamed, and dreamed in relatively direct and realistic ways, about major interests or concerns in their waking lives—of parents, siblings, and peers as characters, for instance, and of play, social-interactional, and achievement themes. Subsequent cross-sectional studies (Foulkes, Larson, Swanson, & Rardin, 1969) extended our observations both to older boys (ages 13–15) and to younger children (ages 3–5) of both sexes. Essentially, in these studies we replicated our observations of (1) the feasibility of studying children's dreams with REM awakening techniques and (2) the ordinariness and/or essential realism of the contents of most dreams collected in this manner.

As we attempted to understand just why particular children had the dreams that they did, however, we became increasingly aware of how few of the relevant data were at our disposal. We had the children's dream reports, but, aside from a few psychological test scores, we did not have sufficient basis for knowing who the children "really were" or what the particular textures of their waking lives were like. Like so many of the research subjects studied by psychologists, these children had passed into and out of our short-term laboratory studies without leaving behind many traces of their individual identities. Somewhat more extended and comprehensive case studies of four boys who had participated in our first study (Foulkes, 1967a) helped point us toward the obvious conclusion that we would be in a far better position to understand children's dreams if we collected extended dream samples from each child (in the cross-sectional studies mentioned above, children typically were studied for only two nights apiece) and if we obtained significantly more information about each child's waking-life situation. Breger's (1969) case study of a single boy, "Jake," later provided an even richer indication of the power of intensive, comprehensive case-study methods in analyzing children's REM dreams.

It was clear to us, then, that if further steps were to be taken to enhance our understanding of children's dreams, they would have to be part of a research design: (1) in which we studied each child over a long enough period of time to collect a meaningful "dream series"; (2) in which we gathered enough nondream (i.e., waking) data for each child so that we could, in principle, consider that child as "in-depth" case-study material; (3) yet in which we studied enough children at a sufficient number of different ages that we might also justifiably discuss children in general, rather than the mere handful we happened to be able to study. From 1968 to 1973 we conducted two studies faithful to this plan, and it is the results of those studies that are reported here and that provide the major empirical basis for our current knowledge of the ontogeny of dreaming.

DESIGN

Two concurrent longitudinal studies were conducted, in which the same children were examined repeatedly over 5-year periods beginning at, respectively, ages 3 or 4 and ages 9 or 10. Thus at the end of the project we had one 10-year series of dream observations extending, in two discrete sections, from the preschool years into early adolescence. In each of three major study years, Years 1, 3, and 5 of the project, we collected dreams from children in each group following exactly the same procedure. Children were studied for nine nonconsecutive nights, spaced at roughly equal intervals during each of these years. In each of these "normative" dream-collection years, the same awakening schedule was followed for the retrieval of dream reports (Table 2.1). Over the course of each such year, the schedule provided for 15 awakenings from REM sleep, nine awakenings from ordinary non-REM (NREM) sleep, and three awakenings at sleep onset. Each kind of awakening was made at representative points throughout the night, and ordinary NREM awakenings were balanced between "lighter" and "deeper" NREM stages. In addition, on two normative-year nights, attempts were made to influence children's dreams (to induce dreams that "incorporated" stimulation that we applied to the children shortly before awakening them).

These stimulus trials were doubly motivated. We wanted to see if we could "verify" children's reports by showing that preawakening stimuli

Table 2.1   **Normative-Year Awakening Schedule**

	Awakening Number[a]		
Night	1	2	3
1	R	R	R
2	RI	NRI	RI
3	NRL	R	NRD
4	R	SO	R
5	R	NRL	SO
6	SO	R	NRL
7	NRD	R	R
8	R	NRD	R
9	NRI	RI	NRI

Notes:

R   - Stage REM.

RI   - Stage REM, stimulus-incorporation trial.

NRL - NREM "light," stages 2 or 3, cyclically placed near a REM period.

NRD - NREM "deep," unbroken stages 3 or 4, cyclically placed midway between REM periods.

NRI - NREM, stimulus-incorporation trial ("light" or "deep").

SO   - Sleep onset, initial in ordinal position 1, following the prior arousal in ordinal positions 2 and 3. Descending EEG stage 1 or early descending stage 2.

[a] Awakening 1 is to be made approximately 11 p.m. to 1 a.m., awakening 2 at approximately 3 a.m., and awakening 3 at approximately 4 a.m. to 6 a.m. When scheduled for REM sleep, awakenings 1, 2, and 3 are to be made at eye-movement bursts approximately 5, 10, and 15 minutes, respectively, after REM onset. Incorporation trials were as follows: ordinal position 1, puff of cotton rubbed on subject's cheek; ordinal position 2, induced limb movement; ordinal position 3, spray of water on subject's face or scalp.

appeared in children's postawakening reports. Presumably the report then would have to have been of a preawakening dream rather than of some postawakening fabrication invented to please or appease the experimenter. But the stimulus trials also might indicate how the children's minds were working during sleep. By comparing the known stimulus with its dream representation, we hoped to be able to determine the kinds of transformations dreams effected more generally on their typical internal (memory) sources.

Our concern with report verification was dictated by the not unreasonable fear that children would prove to be less faithful reporters of their actual dream experiences than adults generally are assumed to be. This concern also dictated the choice of certain tests or observations we arranged to include in our daytime test sessions. These sessions, scheduled several times during each study year, were aimed at keeping us continually and comprehensively informed about the children's current intellectual, social, and emotional status and about their family-life situation (Table 2.2). Certain tests within our overall battery were designed to determine how well children understood what a dream was (Laurendeau-Pinard Dream Test) and how accurately children could describe known pictorial stimuli encountered in the waking state (Description Test, Fidelity of Report). Certain of our ratings also were relevant to how children might be performing on nocturnal dream interviews (e.g., ratings of how dependent children were upon adult support).

The most notable feature of our daytime test program was a "nursery school" that we ran for two-week periods in the summers of 1968, 1969, and 1970 for our younger group of subjects. Here children's behavior to adults and peers, and their imaginative ("pretend") play behavior, were systematically observed and rated. Family-life data were collected in several ways: Parents completed attitude and value questionnaires; children were given instruments (e.g., Cornell Parent Description Device) by which they directly could describe their fathers' and mothers' interactions with one another and with them; the younger children also were administered procedures (Emmerich Parental Identification Interview) in which indirectly, through doll play, conceptions of parental-child interaction might be observed. At the age level where our nursery-school observations ceased, we elicited the almost unfailingly good cooperation of regular schoolteachers in judging the academic and social-emotional status of our subjects.

Waking observations other than those listed in Table 2.2 were available for each child. Children were observed during the presleep period in the laboratory, and the experimenter rated the children's behavior quantitatively and kept a qualitative verbal account of that behavior for every dream-collection night in the study. In addition, from the third year of the study to its conclusion, the experimenter kept records, for each older-group child's laboratory visit, of physical development (height, weight). Thus by the time the study was completed, laboratory personnel had the sense of

Table 2.2   **Schedule for the Daytime Collection of Test/Observational Data**

	Test/Observational Procedure	
Time	**Older Group**	**Younger Group**
Screening interview (Spring 1968)	Demographic**/Sleep-Habits Questionnaire (completed by a parent)[1]	Demographic**/Sleep-Habits Questionnaire (completed by a parent)[1]
	Parent Attitude Research Instrument (completed separately by both parents at home)**	Parent Attitude Research Instrument (completed separately by both parents at home)**
	Traditional Family Ideology Scale (completed separately by both parents at home)**	Traditional Family Ideology Scale (completed separately by both parents at home)**
	Kohn Child-Rearing Value Index (completed separately by both parents at home)**	Kohn Child-Rearing Value Index (completed separately by both parents at home)**
	Description Test[10]	Description Test[10]
Year 1 Summer 1968	Pickford Projective Pictures, Set I[10]	Pickford Projective Pictures, Set I[10]
	Children's Personality Questionnaire, Part IA[10] Children's Personality Questionnaire, Part IIA[10]	Laurendeau-Pinard Dream, Life, and Night Tests of Precausal Thought[1] X[10] Nursery-school observations:
	Cornell Parent Description Device[10]	(1) Fels Nursery-School Rating Scales[1] K[10] (2) Time-sampled behavioral observations[6] (3) Sociometric Test[10]
Fall 1968		Wechsler Preschool Primary Scale of Intelligence[8] X[14]
Spring 1969	Wechsler Intelligence Scale for Children[8] Cornell Teacher Rating Scales (completed by child's teacher at school)	Napping Questionnaire (completed by a parent at home)

Table 2.2   (Continued)

	Test/Observational Procedure	
Time	**Older Group**	**Younger Group**
Year 2 Summer 1969	Children's Manifest Anxiety Scale[15] Coleman Fate Scale[15] Rosenberg Self-Esteem Scale[15] Vocational Preference Questionnaire[15] Douvan-Adelson Internalization-Externalization Scale[15] Fidelity of Report Experiment[15]*** Body height, weight[15]	Nursery-school observations: (1) Fels Nursery-School Rating Scales[4]K[10]* (2) Time-sampled behavioral observations[2]* (3) Sociometric Test[10]* (4) Adjective Check List[2]K[4]K[10] Emmerich Parental Identification Interview[2] IT Test of Sex-Role Preference[2]
(End of test file correlated with Year-1 dream data)		
Winter 1969/ Spring 1970	Symonds Picture Story Test, Set B[10] Cornell Teacher Rating Scales (completed by child's teacher at school)*	Description Test[10]* Body weight[10] Pickford Projective Pictures, Set II[10]*
Year 3 Summer 1970		Nursery-school observations: (1) Fels Nursery-School Rating Scales[2]K[10]* (2) Time-sampled behavioral observations[2]K[6]* (3) Sociometric Test[10]* (4) Adjective Check List[2]K[6]K[10]*
Fall 1970	Children's Personality Questionnaire, Form B[10]*	Wechsler Preschool Primary Scale of Intelligence or Wechsler Intelligence Scale for Children[9]*

(Continued)

Table 2.2 (Continued)

	Test/Observational Procedure	
Time	**Older Group**	**Younger Group**
Spring 1971	Wechsler Intelligence Scale for Children[9]* Loevinger Sentence-Completion (Ego Development)[10] Cornell Parent Description Device[10]* Cornell Teacher Rating Scales (completed by child's teacher at school)*	Laurendeau-Pinard Dream, Life, and Night Tests of Precausal Thought[5]* Fidelity of Report Experiment[5] Fels Nursery-School Rating Scales (completed by child's teacher at school)*
Year 4 Summer 1971	Rosenzweig Picture-Frustration Test[7] X[13]	
Fall 1971	P. Sears Self-Concept Scales[10] Crandall Social Desirability Scale[10] R. Sears Aggression Scales[10] Sleep Habits Questionnaire[10] Media Preference Questionnaire[10] Environmental Participation Index[10]	Kagan Matching Familiar Figures Test[11]**** Children's Embedded Figures Test[11]**** Stephens-Delys Reinforcement Contingency Interview (Locus of Control)[11]****

(End of test file correlated with Year-3 dream data)

Winter 1971– 1972	Reference tests for cognitive factors: (1) Fa-1 (associative fluency)[11] (2) Fi-2 (ideational fluency)[11] (3) Cs-1 (perceptual unification)[11] (4) P-3 (perceptual speed)[11] Embedded Figures Test[11]	Torrance Tests of Creative Thinking (Figural A)[11] Kagan-Lemkin Perception of Parental Attributes[11]

	Test/Observational Procedure	
Time	**Older Group**	**Younger Group**
Spring 1972	Symonds Picture Story Test, Set A[10]*	Torrance Tests of Creative Thinking (Verbal A)[11]
	Menstrual Questionnaire (girls)[10]	Body height/weight[11]*
	Reference tests for cognitive factors:	Young Children's Social Desirability Scale[11]
	(1) Ma-3 (rote memory)[10]	Fels Nursery-School Rating Scales (completed by child's teacher at school)*
	(2) Ms-2 (visual digit span)[10]	
	Cornell Teacher Rating Scales (completed by child's teacher[s] at school)*	
Year 5		
Summer 1972	Torrance Tests of Creative Thinking (Figural A, Verbal A)[11]	Pickford Projective Pictures, Set III[10]*
	Reference tests for cognitive factors:	Early School Personality Questionnaire, Form A1[10]
	Fe-3 (expressional fluency)[11]	Pickford Projective Pictures, Set I[10]*
	High School Personality Questionnaire[11]*	Early School Personality Questionnaire, Form A2[10]
Fall 1972	Wechsler Intelligence Scale for Children or Wechsler Adult Intelligence Scale[12]*	
	Rorschach Test[12]	
Winter 1972-1973	Loevinger Sentence-Completion (Ego-Development)[10]*	Wechsler Intelligence Scale for Children[3]×[12]*
	California Psychological Inventory[10]	Rorschach Test[12]
Spring 1973	Description Test[10]*	Description Test[10]*
	Cornell Parent Description Device[10]*	Body height/weight[10]*
	Cornell Teacher Rating Scales	Laurendeau-Pinard Dream,

(Continued)

Table 2.2 (Continued)

Time	Test/Observational Procedure	
	Older Group	**Younger Group**
	(completed by child's teacher[s] at school)* Autobiography[12]	Life, and Night Tests of Precausal Thought[10]* Cornell Teacher Rating Scales (completed by child's teacher at school) Autobiography[12]

(End of test file correlated with Year-5 dream data)

Notes:

A break between listed procedures within a given time period indicates that separate test sessions were scheduled within that period for the age group in question.

*Indicates a readministration of a procedure previously employed with this group or an administration of a comparable form of an earlier-administered procedure, permitting, in either case, the computation of "change" scores vis-à-vis earlier performance as well as of scores of current performance.

**Indicates variables also correlated with Year-3 and -5 dream data; ***indicates variables also correlated with Year-3 dream data; ****indicates variables also correlated with Year-5 dream data.

Numerals following procedures indicate the sleep laboratory personnel responsible for administering those procedures, according to the following key: [1]Barbara Ahrens; [2]Constance Brizuela; [3]Lawrence J. Brown; [4]Sharon K. Brown; [5]Sharon Frost; [6]Margaret R. Gabler; [7]Joel Humphrey; [8]James D. Larson; [9]Leonard Medoff; [10]Jean Petrik; [11]Elizabeth A. Scott; [12]Eric W. Trupin; [13]Arthur L. Walker; [14]Robert Weisz; [15]Gerry L. Wilcove. A notation [1]X[2] means either person 1 or person 2 administered a procedure; a notation [1]K[2] means both persons 1 and 2 independently made the ratings or observations in question.

Tests and, where applicable, test scoring procedures and scoring reliabilities, are discussed in Appendix C.

knowing particular children quite well, and an extensive folder of quantitative and qualitative waking observations had been collected for each child.

The second and fourth years of the study were devoted to collection of supplementary data that we hoped would both qualify and extend our normative-year observations. One major concern underlying our research in these years was to determine how our particular methods of dream study might be affecting our results. Most important, were dreams being "changed" by virtue of their collection away from children's usual home environments (Elkan, 1969)? This proved to be a somewhat more complex question than might at first be imagined. We had studied dreams in the laboratory precisely *because* we believed that they would be different from dreams remembered spontaneously at home. That is, we had strong reason to believe that we could, thanks to the REM-awakening strategy, sample children's dreamlife more representatively in the laboratory than at home. But we needed to show that this sampling advantage was not vitiated by effects of the somewhat "unnatural" features of the laboratory environment (the laboratory as a setting, the experimenter as a presleep stimulus, the presence of unfamiliar peers during the presleep period, the attachment and wearing of tiny metal disc electrodes for recording sleep patterns, etc.). To show this, we needed to establish that when dream *sampling* was comparable at home and in the laboratory, then dreams themselves also were comparable both in their accessibility and in their contents. In Year 2, in studies in which children's dreams were collected at 6:30 a.m. awakenings in each setting, we were able to demonstrate that these dreams were comparable both in availability and in nature. In studies conducted in Year 4, we were able to show further that whatever differences might be found between children's "spontaneously" remembered home dreams and their laboratory-elicited dreams could be attributed to biased sampling at home, rather than to influences of the environment on laboratory reports. These studies have been described in detail elsewhere (Foulkes, 1979b).

During nonnormative years we also were able to evaluate the effects of certain features of our normative-year experimental design.

1 We showed that the dream reporting of young children was not un-derestimated by our somewhat "laid-back" interviewing strategy (we did not insist that children *must* have been dreaming, even on REM awakenings, if the children thought otherwise). An experimental condition in which we increased subjects' arousal (making them sit up in bed to talk to the interviewer in a fully lighted room) and in which the interviewer was more insistent ("The machine said you were dreaming, so I want you to think real hard and see if you can remember a dream") did not produce either heightened dream recall or altered dream content as compared to our standard normative-year procedures (in which subjects lay prone in their beds in a dimly illuminated room and in which the experimenter more freely allowed children to decide whether or not they had been dreaming [Foulkes & Shepherd, 1972]).

2 We showed that other interviewers did not elicit dream reports from children at rates different from those obtained by the normative-year interviewer. This was true both for the older children, when graduate students interviewed them in the laboratory (Foulkes, Shepherd, Larson, Belvedere, & Frost, 1972) and for younger children, when the normative-year interviewer followed a dream-collection strategy in the laboratory comparable to that of the child's own parent at home (Foulkes, 1979b).

3 We showed that the only significant effect of laboratory-induced REM awakenings of children at actual bursts of eye-movement activity rather

than in the ocularly quiescent periods between such bursts was to heighten subjects' reporting of their own visual activity (watching, looking, etc.) within the dream (Foulkes, Shepherd, Larson, Belvedere, & Frost, 1972). Because this difference, found with 10- and 11-year-olds, is such a plausible correlate of the difference in preawakening physiology, it argues strongly for the truthfulness of these children's dream reports.

4 We demonstrated, as we switched the younger children from one interview strategy to the other (in Year 4), that it made no difference for either their rate of dream reporting or the kinds of dream content they reported whether they were interviewed at their bedside or over an intercom (Foulkes, 1979c). (Typically we interviewed subjects over an intercom, but we had decided that this procedure might be less comfortable and comprehensible for preschoolers than for school-age children.)

Other of our special projects during the nonnormative years of the longitudinal dream studies will be described later on. However, it should be noted here that our design included still other opportunities to evaluate how our procedures might have affected the children's dreams. A major concern in longitudinal studies is that repeated study itself may alter the phenomenon being investigated. One way to determine whether that, in fact, is the case is to supplement one's longitudinal observations with cross-sectional ones, that is, to add novice subjects comparable in age but not in prior experimental experience to subjects already participating in the entire longitudinal series. We did this twice in our study, adding older boys at ages 11–13 and younger girls at ages 7–9. In addition, of course, our regular design permits the comparison of younger children at the end of their five-year series of observation (ages 8–9) with older children at the beginning of their five-year series of observation (ages 9–10). Results of our observations for each of these kinds of comparison generally suggested that children's dreams were not greatly affected by the length of our prior study of them; these results also will be described in greater detail later in the text.

SUBJECTS

How does one get children to participate in a long-term laboratory study of dream content? What sort of children can one get to do so? How does one retain subjects in such a study?

As in our earlier research with children, we advertised for subjects, this time in the daily newspaper of Laramie, Wyoming, where the longitudinal studies were conducted. *The Daily Boomerang* (named for the mule of its first editor, the humorist Bill Nye) circulates widely in Laramie. Moreover, because the paper usually consists of only 10 or 12 pages, any item therein receives considerable attention. Our advertisement stressed these points: (1) that we were competent to conduct the research (we had support from the

National Science Foundation and had conducted a number of earlier studies of local children and college students); (2) that our studies would be long-term ones, in which children would sleep in our laboratory 8 to 10 nights a year for a 5-year period, hence that we wanted children of parents who were permanent residents of Laramie (rather than, for instance, children of university students); and (3) that children would be well paid for their participation, earning "as much as $500 over the next five years." Our advertisement ran for five consecutive days.

Eight boys and eight girls were volunteered by parents in the younger age range for which we had requested subjects (ages 3–4) and 16 boys and 19 girls were volunteered by parents in the older age range for which we had requested subjects (ages 9–10). When parents called the laboratory, we gave them a brief description of the project design and collected demographic information from them. Parents of all 3- and 4-year-old children and of the first eight boys and eight girls to be volunteered at ages 9 to 10 then were invited to come to the laboratory for an interview, along with the children. No parent who called requesting information about the project declined a laboratory interview. When the parent (generally, the mother) and child arrived for their appointment, they were taken on a tour of the laboratory and were acquainted with the equipment and the procedures to be employed in the nighttime study. Parent and child then were separated, as one assistant obtained background data on the child's sleep and dreams from the parent while another assistant administered our "Description Test" to the child. The Description Test was used at this time as a screening device, in that children unable or unwilling to describe simple pictorial stimuli to an unfamiliar adult seemed to us to be unlikely candidates for our study, in which dreams would have to be described to an initially unfamiliar adult. The parent was given a comprehensive written description of the project, including a full account of the child's responsibilities and rights, and then was asked to sign a form indicating her or his agreement to the arrangements contained in that description and permission for any subsequent anonymous uses by us of the child's dreams.

All 16 older-group children interviewed agreed to serve in the project. We declined one younger boy, who was highly distractible and almost totally unresponsive during the Description Test administration. After one night in the laboratory, one younger girl refused to return. The other 14 younger children agreed to serve in the project and, in fact, did participate throughout its 5-year duration. Each of the two children we interviewed who did not serve in the study had one or more older siblings who did participate. Eleven of the original 30 subjects had one or more siblings in the study (one threesome and two pairs of siblings in the older group, and two pairs in which a younger child had an older sister in the project). Two of the children had been studied by us before, and another child had two siblings who had participated in an earlier study.

The only children who left service in our study (other than the younger girl mentioned above) were those whose families moved out of town (two older boys—brothers—at the end of the first year, and an older boy and an older girl—brother and sister—at the end of the third year). All children who remained in Laramie also remained in our study.

At the start of the study's third year we added six older-group boys (ages 11–12), and at the start of the fifth year we recruited seven more younger-group girls (ages 7–8). To try to insure the comparability of these additional subjects to our continuing subjects in matters other than prior experimental experience, we solicited them, where possible, through the auspices of our continuing subjects or, failing that, through advertisements similar to those that had elicited the service of our continuing subjects. All supplemental subjects served from the point of their induction into the study until its termination at the end of Year 5. They were oriented to the study's procedures in the same manner as had been the continuing subjects. Among the boys recruited in Year 3 were two pairs of brothers, one pair of which was recruited from a family with a younger-group girl already serving in the study. Thus altogether 44 children participated in the dream project: 26 for all 5 years, 34 for at least 3 years, and 43 for at least 1 complete year.

This degree of subject retention no doubt in large measure reflects the financial incentives we arranged to insure children's continuing participation. For each night the child spent in the laboratory, he or she was credited with $10, and for each daytime test/observation session, with $6. However, only half of those sums was paid to children during the study itself; the other half was set aside for payment at the study's termination on the condition that the child participated in the study until it was completed. However, we believe that our degree of subject retention also reflects the extent to which we were successful in making children feel comfortable in the study itself and to which we treated the children with courtesy and dignity.

Data will be described on children's adaptation to our laboratory procedures. With respect to our attitudes to the children, parents were informed, in writing, that both they and their children retained the right to refuse to participate in any aspect of the study that was not to their liking, and that we would always answer questions about the rationale of whatever procedures were not immediately comprehensible. Refusals never occurred, and, although children and parents occasionally asked us questions about details of our methods, it never was on the basis that if they could not receive a satisfactory answer, then they would withhold their cooperation. It was our intention to be as open with the families as we possibly could about what we were doing and why. Since our goals generally were descriptive rather than manipulative, we never had to deliberately misstate our purposes or methods, and we tried to be as genuinely informative about these things as we could without, in certain cases (e.g., the stimulus-incorporation trials), compromising the scientific value of our data. We acknowledged our responsibility to parents and children to be honest, fair, and considerate in all of our dealings with them and strove to be faithful to that responsibility.

Who were these children and these families? Can they claim to be a *random* sample from any population of general interest? The answer to the latter question is no because "random" describes a method by which people are selected for observation, and we did not (and could not) randomly select subjects. Obviously there must have been selective variables at work that led some families to consider, and other equally eligible families not to consider, participating in our project. But this kind of selectivity is a feature of almost all psychological research and has not greatly hindered the search for reliable knowledge about psychological *processes* and their stages of developmental elaboration.

More to the point, perhaps, one can ask how *representative* our subjects were of children in the community and in the nation in which they were studied. Description of the children, and of their community, provides some answers to this question. Table 2.3 presents a description of the children we studied in terms of family social class (actually, occupational status on the revised scale of Warner, Meeker, & Eells, 1960) and their own intelligence quotient at intake. It is apparent that our samples were mainly of children with I.Q.'s that were somewhat higher than average but that only infrequently reached into the superior range. Our maximal I.Q. range was achieved within the sample of six boys added at the start of Year 3: one boy had an I.Q. of 145, another of 81. It also is evident from Table 2.3 that younger-, but not older-group, children predominantly came from high-status families (on a scale where 1 = professionals, large-scale entrepreneurs; 3 = salespersons; 5 = skilled blue-collar workers; and 7 = unskilled heavy labor or families on welfare). This probably is related to differences in how the samples were generated: Younger-group children were volunteered by parents (who most often seemed to believe that participating in our project would be an intellectually broadening experience for their children), whereas some older-group children initiated interest in the project themselves (and most often were attracted by our pay schedules) while others were volunteered by parents for the same reasons as were younger children.

With either age group, however, it is clear that high-status professional families were overrepresented in our sample and low-status, manual-labor families underrepresented. It should be borne in mind that Laramie is essentially a one-industry town, and that that "industry" is the state university. This fact no doubt skews its actual distribution of occupational status as compared to that which might be found in many other towns of its size in Wyoming or elsewhere in the United States. Still, judged even against the standards for a university town, we failed to obtain a proportionate representation of working-class children in our samples. We did not, for instance, obtain any children from the cross-the-tracks, Mexican-American section of West Laramie, despite the "affirmative action" wording of our advertisement. Thus neither this ethnic/racial minority group—Laramie's

Table 2.3 **Number of Children Studied, by Family Social Class and Own I.Q.**

Subjects	Occupational Status of Family's Primary Wage-Earner			Child's I.Q. (at Intake)				
	1–2	3–5	6–7	Below 91	91–100	101–110	111–120	Above 120
Younger group								
Girls								
Original sample	5	1	1	0	0	2	4	1
Supplemental sample	5	2	0	0	1	5	1	0
Boys	4	2	1	0	1	3	2	1
	14	5	2	0	2	10	7	2
Older group								
Girls	4	3	1	0	0	4	1	3
Boys								
Original sample	3	3	2	0	0	6	2	0
Supplemental sample	2	2	2	2	0	2	0	2
	9	8	5	2	0	12	3	5

major one—nor any other is represented in our sample, and it was only for the older boys' groups that we began to approximate the town's social-class composition.

Our subjects were, then, mostly somewhat brighter-than-average sons and daughters of upper middle-class families. In most cases the biological-mother/biological-father family unit was intact and the child we studied had one or more siblings. This begins to sound very much like the traditional America, now increasingly eclipsed in more urban and "progressive" areas of the country. In fact, however, three of our children came from father-absent families, and during the course of our study or subsequent to it, several more families were splintered by divorce. And the time is past when *any* American community can be imagined to approximate the sort of bucolic life portrayed in Norman Rockwell magazine covers. When we studied them, Laramie children were exposed to the same very mixed blessings of the fragmentation of American middle-class culture as were children elsewhere: television, drugs, sexual permissiveness, and so on. As older-group subjects have reached maturity since we studied them, they have provided their parents with the same causes for pride and disappointment familiar to parents living in more cosmopolitan areas of the country. It is my feeling, then, that whatever the other problems may be of generalizing from the children whom we studied, the community in which they lived may not be so potent a drawback as urban readers might imagine.

Still, there is no doubt but that it may be something of a problem to talk about our Laramie children as if they were the same as white middle-class children from Short Hills or Sherman Oaks, or Manhattan or Los Angeles. For an urban American moving to Laramie (1970 population: 23,000), there is a genuine sense of culture shock. Laramie is isolated—it is 50 miles to the nearest settlement of any magnitude at all, and between the two there is no continuous commercial strip, only rugged mountainous terrain broken by an occasional billboard or an off-ramp to someone's ranch. Winters are harsh and summers short. There are no shopping centers or malls on anything like the now-familiar suburban model. When we studied the children, there was not even a McDonald's hamburger restaurant! The nostalgic but reactionary culture of the cowboy remains a continuing symbolic presence in Laramie. The superimposition of a university environment on such a background produces an odd set of contrasts—and more than occasional conflicts, definitely felt by children at least by the time of their entry into junior high school. Laramie lies in a common American culture, then, but it also is distinctive. My belief is that while certain dream contents we observed—hunting and fishing themes for older boys, for instance—must be distinctive features of Laramie dreams more than of Manhattan dreams, the ontogenesis of the cognitive processes that make dreaming possible and permit its creative reconstruction of waking memory must be pretty much the same in Laramie as anywhere else in the United States. It remains for future research to demonstrate whether this plausible belief is, in fact, empirically justifiable.

PROCEDURES

So now the child is "signed up" and has made a commitment to her or his first laboratory session. With some mixture of anticipation and trepidation, she or he prepares for "the big night." Arrival at the laboratory, especially early in the study or for younger children, probably is in the company of one or both parents and, perhaps, of curious siblings or friends as well. Particularly early in their service in the study, children were permitted whatever degree of free exploration of the laboratory environment and whatever company they seemed to require to make them feel at ease there. There was no pressure for children to begin preparations (i.e., have electrodes attached) for the evening's task.

Until early in Year 3, the laboratory facility was on the third and top floor of the second oldest building on the university campus. Originally built as a dormitory, this building was not altogether unsuited for our purposes, but it was an old and somewhat dreary place. We attempted to spruce it up with colorful posters, rugs, and curtains, and outfitted it with a revolving collection of toys, games, puzzles, books, and magazines. Subjects slept in acoustically isolated separate bedrooms, of which there were at first two, and then three.

Early in the third year we moved to first-floor quarters in a brand-new, well-lighted research building, which we attempted to outfit much as we had the more homely but less antiseptic rooms of the earlier laboratory environment. We were concerned, of course, about the effects that the move might have on the children's sleep and dreams. So far as we could tell, there were no major or systematic effects of the move on children's presleep demeanor, on their sleep, or on their dreams.[1] By this time, of course, children were quite accustomed to our studying their sleep and dreams, and, except for the physical setting, most other interpersonal and technical details of the experiment remained constant.

I was the primary experimenter on all 1,347 subject nights of the study. At the beginning of the first year, there often was a co-experimenter who attached electrodes to one of the two children to be studied that night and who loosely supervised that child's behavior in the presleep period. Thereafter, for reasons of economics, I generally worked alone. I conducted all

---

[1]Specifically, presleep anxiety ratings did not significantly differentiate children's behavior in the two settings; there was no increase in laboratory-related dreams, which were infrequent in both settings (5.4% premove; 4.5% postmove); and sleep scorings showed no significant increase in time to fall asleep, time to achieve an initial REM period, or incidence of spontaneous awakenings in the two settings.

2,711 normative-year dream interviews and also many of the interviews during Years 2 and 4 (for the comparison of REM-burst and REM-quiescent awakenings in Year 2 and the determination of the effects of presleep television programming on older children's dreams during Year 4, an outside interviewer, "blind" to experimental condition, was employed). Thus there was a familiar (and, I hope, reassuring) presence on children's every return to the laboratory.

Also generally present during the presleep period was at least one other subject (often, but not always, from the same age group) and her or his retinue, if any. Parents were told that they were welcome to come and observe nocturnal sessions whenever they wished to (provided their child was agreeable), and, early in the study, they occasionally stayed for at least part of a night. Sometimes subjects would ask to be scheduled with particular children they knew before the study started, and, where feasible, we complied with their request. Siblings often but not invariably were scheduled together, for reasons of practical convenience to their parents and to us. Occasionally a parent or child would forget an appointment (although we sent out reminder notices a few days in advance of each scheduled session), and this left another child to be studied solo. It also sometimes happened that, when unrelated younger and older children were to be studied on the same night, the younger child would already be asleep when the older child arrived. Thus amid the constancy of experimenter and experimental procedure, the interpersonal aspects of the presleep period generally contained some elements of novelty as well, a novelty to which children soon seemed to adapt graciously.

Generally, seven electrodes, metal discs the approximate diameter of a pencil, were affixed to each subject: lateral to the right and left eyes (to record horizontal REMs); at the right and left mastoid process (reference electrodes); on the forehead (one as a ground, the other to record vertical REMs and a prefrontal electroencephalogram); and on the hairy portion of the scalp (a frontal/central EEG, between position $F4$ and $C4$, in the international "10−20" system of electrode placement). The latter EEG electrode, and a gauze pad that anchored the electrode chain to the subject's scalp midline, were secured with collodion-impregnated gauze pads. Other electrodes were affixed to the bare skin with hypoallergenic tape or double-side adhesive bandages adhering both to the electrode and to the child's skin. These attachments generally were completed in 10 to 15 minutes' time. They were in no way painful to the child, nor did children report discomfort from wearing the electrodes during the night.

The recording system permitted children considerable freedom of movement while in bed, since there was considerable "play" in the electrode chain connecting the child's head and a terminal box where the pin end of the electrode wire was attached. Cables led from the terminal box back to an adjacent control area where the experimenter would watch a continuous paper tracing of the subject's spontaneous electrical activity ("brain waves," eye-movement potentials) during the night. Next to the subject's bed was an intercom unit through which the child's activity was monitored throughout the night and through which (without having to activate it in any way) the child could signal the experimenter whenever she or he wished attention.

Children were put to bed at a time that was a compromise among parental desire (children were scheduled to arrive at the laboratory one-half hour before their reported "usual" bedtime), children's wishes, and my perception of when they were "ready" for bed. In general, there was no pressure for children to retire at some set time, and many children chose to play or read for some time following the attachment of their electrodes. My role during such play periods was essentially a passive one: I did not seek to direct children's activities, although I joined in them if invited.

When children were put to bed, they were reminded of their experimental task. They were told that they would be awakened several times during the night and asked if they could remember a dream, which, if they could, they were to tell to the experimenter. Further they were told that it was not expected that they would be able to remember dreams on every awakening, but that it was expected that they would try to do so. At the start of the study, not all younger children appeared to have a secure grasp of the concept "dream." Explanation was attempted in the case of such deficiencies, and interview questions were framed so as to avoid using the term "dream" (i.e., "What were you seeing?" "What was happening just before I woke you?"). All children in the younger group periodically were administered a test of the adequacy of their knowledge about "dreaming" (Laurendeau & Pinard, 1962), and dream correlates of their scores on this test will be described later.

Children generally slept until 6:30 a.m. Continuous brain-wave and eye-movement recordings were taken from "lights out" until completion of the scheduled awakenings or 6:00 a.m., whichever came later. I scored these records on the spot for: time to fall asleep after lights out; sleep time until REM onset; start and end of all REM periods; and number and duration of spontaneous awakenings. Most but not all scheduled awakenings were, in fact, made, and they generally were made at the times suggested in Table 2.1. As already mentioned, during early years of the study younger children were awakened and interviewed at their bedside, while later on they were interviewed, as were older children throughout the study, via an intercom. (On stimulus-incorporation nights, however, all interviews were at subjects' bedside.) With rare exceptions in cases of equipment (or experimenter) malfunction, all interviews were tape-recorded for later transcription.

In early interviews with the younger children, questioning beyond the initial inquiry ("What were you dreaming [seeing, doing] just before I called you?") was not systematic. I judged, correctly I think, that rigid adherence to a fixed interview format was inappropriate for eliciting information from children with widely varying understandings of the experimental task and degrees of willingness to be interrogated. The choice was made, then, to try to achieve standardization of effect (through varied questions and question sequences) rather than standardization of method. The risk in such an intuitive procedure, of course, is that there are going to be at least occasional lapses from an optimal (i.e., nondirective) interview strategy. I certainly committed some such lapses in early interviews with the 3- to 4-year-olds. One's intuition is not always a reliable instrument at three o'clock in the morning. In general, however, most interviews at this age level were in conformity with standard practice in information-gathering interviews (Kahn & Cannell, 1957). At later ages children were questioned systematically, with questions increasing only slightly in complexity at older age levels. A typical interview schedule is given in Table 2.4. At all ages, topics probed included: characters, settings, activities, dreamer's own role, feelings, and degree to which dream content was visualized.

The major decision I faced in interviewing children was how far to push when children quickly responded no, they remembered no dream. Our fear before initiating the study was that, if we exerted too much pressure on subjects to try to recall a dream, they would perceive that the way to cope with this pressure was to make one up just to please us. On the other hand, it soon became apparent that children also readily could perceive that a couple of simple no's would terminate the interview, get the light turned off, and let them go back to sleep quickly. The seductiveness of sleep's siren song surely is no less, and is probably greater, for children than for adults.

In interviewing the children, particularly the younger ones, therefore, a general problem was insuring that negative responses to the initial interview question (e.g., "I had no dream") were given after thoughtful reflection rather than from a disinclination to arouse oneself enough to try to remember one's dream. My strategy was to try to insure, through verbal or physical prodding, that children were, in fact, moderately alert before the opening interview question was asked. It was not always easy to initiate or sustain that level of arousal, and on rare instances it was impossible to get or keep a child awake long enough to question her or him. When less than optimal arousal was apparent or suspected, however, I did not directly challenge a child's negative responses (although on subsequent nights I would give particular emphasis during the presleep orientation period to the necessity that the child *try* to recall a dream when awakened).

The effects of this choice are not totally clear. It probably guarantees that many, if not most, of the dream reports that I did manage to collect are "real" ones, that is, bore some relationship to preawakening dream experience. In other words, the choice must have operated to reduce "false positives," claims of dreams in the absence of genuine remembrance of them. However, it also may well have resulted in an unknown number of "false negatives"—lazy claims of no dream when there was remembrance (or potential access to remembrance) of one. To the degree that this was the case, the recall rates reported below underestimate subjects' potential ability to recall dreams and may, in ways one cannot understand from our data, even have distorted our picture of the nature of young children's dreamlife. These

Table 2.4   **Nocturnal Interview Schedule: Year 5, Younger Subjects (Ages 7–9)**

E: (Child's name) (repeated until affirmative response given by subject)
↓

What were you dreaming about just before I woke you up?

↓   ↓   ↓

(If something is reported   (negative reply)
spontaneously)   ↓

↓   Would you think for just a while and
                                                             see if you can remember anything?
Could you see this dream, was it in   (Omitted if S has already given
pictures (were you watching this   evidence of same or a thoughtful
dream, etc.)?   pause.)

↓   ↓   ↓

What could you see?   (affirmative)   (negative)
↓   ↓

What people were in it?
↓   Would you say you had a dream but

Did you know them (who were they,   forgot it, or do you think you had no
etc.)?   dream at all?

↓

What were they doing?
↓

Were you in it?
↓

What were you doing?
↓

Where was the dream (where were . . .
[the characters], etc.)?
↓

Did you know this place?
↓

Did you have any feelings in the
dream? Were you sad or happy, calm
or worried, mad or excited, anything
like that, during the dream?
↓

Can you remember anything else?
↓

OK, thank you. You may go back to sleep now. (On third awakening, when it is
before time for subject to wake up for the morning: That is the last time I'm going
to wake you up and ask you about your dreams; you may sleep till morning now.)

issues will be discussed in more detail later, when we consider the dreams
young children did report to us. For now, however, two points are worth
considering:

1   The same lack of postawakening vigilance that results in no dream report
may indicate a preawakening lack of vigilance associated with no dream
experience.

2 If dreaming is viewed as a complex cognitive act *permitted* by the aroused conditions of REM sleep, that act may not, in fact, occur or occur very often until children have the cognitive repertoire to take advantage of REM sleep arousal to generate dreams. That is, the actual "making" of dreams may be too difficult a symbolic accomplishment to occur reliably until children reach a certain stage of mental development (Foulkes, 1978a, 1979b).

A problem of a different sort occasionally presented itself during dream-report interviews. As a child described a dream to me, I would get the distinct impression that what I was hearing was no dream at all, but a waking confabulation: The content was too stereotyped, adhering to a repetitive formula, and the dream was told with too much evident amusement and self-satisfaction (most dreams are reported quite matter-of-factly) for the account to be credible. Yet, ultimately, who is to say that the child did not have the dream precisely as described? The apparent confabulation problem was encountered most often with a 3-year-old, Colleen,[2] but it cannot be ruled out as an at least occasional difficulty for other children and ages as well.

When I heard a "dream" report that struck me as somewhat incredible, occasionally I would challenge the veracity of the report and remind the child that it was "OK" if she or he couldn't remember a dream; it was not necessary to make one up. Under mild challenge occasionally Colleen did admit confabulation (which does not necessarily mean that the original report was not truthful), but otherwise insisted that her reports were of real dreams (which does not necessarily mean that the original reports were truthful). We counted the former cases, nonetheless, as recall-failures and the latter ones as recall-successes. That is, we accepted the child's final word as to the status of her or his report. (Empirical data bearing on the credibility of children's dream reports will be discussed, along with the nature of those reports, in Chapters 3–8.)

In the case of Colleen, who, at age 3–4 seemed to have generated the most consistent series of suspect "dream" reports, there was clear parental pressure that she "test out" well in the laboratory. We had instructed parents, at the outset of the study as follows:

> It is probably best for all concerned, and particularly for our purposes, if your child does not feel under any particular pressure to report dreams while he is in the laboratory. We do not expect that all our subjects will always, or even very often, be able to report their dreams to us. All we ask is a conscientious try. We do want to avoid placing the child under such pressure that he feels compelled to make up dreams when he can't remember real ones. To this end, it will be best if you avoid making too much of a "big deal" about whether your child has been able to remember his dreams or not. It isn't really clear what not being able to recall dreams means, and we want to avoid bias in our

---

[2]All names used in this book are, of course, pseudonyms.

results by not seeming to reward the child for reporting them or to punish him for not being able to do so. We hope you will understand our reasons, and treat his performance in the laboratory—whatever happens—as matter-of-factly as we will try to do.

And yet at least two mothers—including Colleen's—seemed to treat each laboratory session as a school period and eagerly wanted to be certain that their children had "graded" out well. When I drove children home on the mornings following experimental sessions, I might encounter a mother's "bottom-line" question: "Well, did she have any dreams?" Besides threatening to compromise the integrity of our results, such attitudes also put children themselves in crossfire between parental demands and experimenter suspicions. Fortunately for us and for the children, these attitudes apparently were effective influences on the "dream" reporting of only one child.

ADAPTATION

How well did children adapt to our procedures of sleeping away from home, of being wired up for sleep recordings, and of having sleep interrupted by a would-be dream interrogator? In general, we think, quite well—surprisingly well. The adaptability of children to unusual sleeping arrangements would have to be listed among the primary results of our study. However, this general answer does not apply with equal force to all of the children studied, and, in fact, no simple answer applies to any child at every point during the study.

Psychologists sometimes talk of their experimental arrangements as existing apart from "real life" (and wonder how to generalize from experiment to world). In the case of our studies, it is quite clear that the laboratory regime became a significant part of our subjects' "real" lives. Our study superimposed on the children's other real-life relationships and involvements new sorts of interpersonal bonds and social roles. These bonds and roles acquired, over a 5-year period, a kind of continuity and intensity that could be matched by few others outside the domain of family life itself. It would be idle to pretend that, either on the children's side or on our own, we were not, at least in subtle ways, altered by new social patterns *within* our lives. A longitudinal study is an extended form of interpersonal relationship.

Thus when one asks about "adaptation" to a longitudinal study, one is asking no simple question. What, in a word or two, can one say that summarizes the state of any 5-year relationship? Probably the closest one can come to a truthful summary statement is: "It had its ups and downs." At the outset there may have been excitement and eager anticipation, later yielding to a stabilized level of relative comfort—or boredom—as procedures and personnel became familiar features of one's life. Or at the outset there may have been apprehension, only slowly yielding to feelings of comfort—or even of confidence and pride in one's mastery of a novel hurdle in social development. Or at the outset there may have been reluctance to commitment to this relationship, such as would be experienced by certain children in any other novel interpersonal situation, a reluctance never quite extinguished through years of acclimatization. Or there may have been a period of midstudy boredom, bounded on one side by initial enthusiasm and on the other by a sense of loss for relationships that have, in hitherto unappreciated ways, come to have an important role in one's life. We have seen all of these patterns, and many others besides.

On our side there is the sense that all of these children have become, in some sense, a part of our extended family. One reads the newspaper, or asks a friend, to find out what has happened to "our" children. They are children you knew "way back when," perhaps even children whose backs you have rhythmically patted or beside whom you have lain as you tried—veritably *in loco parentis*—to comfort them back to sleep after a disturbing mid-night spontaneous arousal. They are children—much like your own biological issue—about whom you have widely varying feelings but about all of whom you find yourself caring and wondering and—especially—hoping.

It is extraordinary, in these contexts, to imagine that the longitudinal study did not itself affect children's dreams. And yet the evidence of our home–laboratory comparisons, discussed earlier, and of our novice–veteran subject comparisons, to be discussed in detail in Chapters 5, 6, and 7, does not strongly suggest such effects. Perhaps the resolution of this paradox is precisely that we did not exist as influences outside the mainstream of our subjects' lives, but as influences within that mainstream, influences more "ordinary" than extraordinary in their import and effects. This is not to claim that we believe that there were *no* effects on children's dream reports of the way in which we collected them (longitudinal, psychophysiological, laboratory studies). We believe that there were some such effects about whose nature our data permit us to speculate. But we reject the idea that we have done something so exceptional in our study of these children that their dreams stand quite apart from "real-life" children's dreams. We were "merely" figures in their real lives, and they in ours.

On the session-by-session adaptation of children to sleeping in the laboratory, we have at least two sorts of relevant data. I made a number of ratings of children's behavior in each presleep period. One of these ratings was of children's apparent comfort–malaise, using a 5-point scale (5 = very anxious, 1 = very calm). In addition, the session's sleep scoring permits the assessment of whether children's sleep was disrupted in ways known to be associated with heightened anxiety (i.e., long latencies to sleep onset, long latencies to REM onset [Rechtschaffen & Verdone, 1964; Agnew, Webb, & Williams, 1966], and frequent incidence and lengthy duration of mid-night spontaneous awakenings).

For both of these experimenter-scored variables, there is the possibility of bias. Specifically, I might have underestimated the degree of presleep anxiety and of sleep disturbance to have made the children look better adapted than they were. In confessing to this possibility, I do not accept its plausibility. The very purpose of both the presleep and sleep observations was to differentiate subjects and nights, and to study how differences in presleep demeanor and sleep physiology were associated with dream differences. In this context, it would have made little sense for me to have portrayed all children as equally well relaxed.

Table 2.5 contains information on the typical incidence of signs of presleep anxiety and sleep disturbance. In general, the children seemed to be

Table 2.5 **Adaptation Measures**

A. Presleep Anxiety Ratings

	Nights on Which Child Is Rated				
Age (years)	Extremely Anxious (%)	Moderately Anxious (%)	Neither Anxious nor Relaxed (%)	Moderately Relaxed (%)	Extremely Relaxed (%)
3–5	5.4	15.4	8.5	45.4	25.4
5–7	.8	9.4	11.8	50.4	27.6
7–9	2.1	10.6	10.6	44.4	32.3
9–11	0.0	10.9	20.4	38.8	29.9
11–13	.6	9.4	12.2	45.9	32.0
13–15	.6	6.2	13.0	35.2	45.1

B. Sleep Variables

Age (years)	Median Time to Fall Asleep (min) [a]	Median Sleep Time to REM Onset (min) [a]	Spontaneous Awakenings		Experimental Awakening Time (min) [b]
			Median Number [a]	Median Duration (min) [a]	
3–5	20	122	1	8	4
5–7	12	132	0	5	4
7–9	16	135	1	4	5
9–11	18	154	1	6	6
11–13	18	121	1	4	6
13–15	20	110	1	4	6

[a]Median of individual subject medians.

[b] First two experimental awakenings: median time from the experimenter's awakening of subject to subject's return to sleep. No dreams were collected after the third experimental awakening, which generally was close to the subject's normal morning wake-up time.

relaxed in the laboratory before they went to sleep, to enjoy generally sound sleep apart from experimental awakenings, and to fall back to sleep quickly following such awakenings. These facts are important, for they establish that the representativeness of our children's dreams cannot be doubted either on the grounds of the children's uncharacteristic presleep distress or on the grounds of gross experimental distortions of their sleep patterns.

On only one night—the second scheduled study night for a 4-year-old girl—was a child's psychological distress such that the session was terminated. This child had required her mother's continuous presence during her first night in the laboratory, but her mother abruptly left her before "lights out" on her second night. In bed the girl cried hysterically, and she was taken home. (By her fifth year in the study, this same girl was so comfortable and competent an experimental subject that novice subjects inducted at ages 7–9 deliberately were scheduled to participate with her, in the hope that her attentive, matter-of-fact approach to the study might prove to be contagious.) Distress of the magnitude she showed during her first year in the laboratory was exceptional even then (and almost always—in six of seven instances of "extreme"-anxiety ratings—shown by girls). During our first study year, six of 14 3- to 5-year-olds and nine of 16 9- to 11-year-olds had not a single night (of nine) in which their presleep behavior was judged either extremely or moderately anxious. For only six children studied in this year (four in the younger group and two in the older) was presleep behavior judged extremely or moderately anxious even on their first study session. Whatever problems arose with the 3- to 5-year-olds seemed to reflect not positive fear of the laboratory environment as much as reluctance to be separated from their parents. As Table 2.5 indicates, younger children experienced no more nights of presleep distress by their third year in the project than did older children, and were, in fact, judged "relaxed" on over three of every four experimental sessions, on the average. This pattern probably is not greatly out of line with children's presleep mood variation when sleeping at home.

Novice boys studied at ages 11–13 were, by my ratings, as comfortable in the laboratory as veteran boy subjects of the same age. However, novice girls studied at ages 7–9 were considerably less at ease in the laboratory during the presleep period than were veteran girl subjects of the same age (judged extremely or moderately anxious on 27% vs. 11% of sessions, respectively). Veteran boys studied at ages 7–9 *never* were judged anxious during the presleep period. (It seems possible that the fact that the experimenter was male may have contributed to this boy vs. girl adaptation difference, although sex differences in presleep adaptation otherwise were not pronounced or consistent in direction.)

No child ever had an experimental night on which REM periods failed to occur, and, as successful adaptation also would predict, the typical child fell asleep relatively easily, showed no unusual retardation in the appearance of REM sleep, seldom woke up spontaneously, and returned to sleep quickly after experimental awakenings. Sleep patterns of novice and veteran boy subjects at ages 11–13 were not significantly different from one another, nor were sleep patterns of novice and veteran subjects studied at ages 7–9. Evidently, whatever discomfort the novice girls experienced in the presleep period did not adversely affect their sleep itself. The slight increase with age in time awake following experimental interruption of sleep reflects the greater likelihood that older children would have some dream, and a dream of less than minimal length, to report (see Chapters 3–8) when so interrupted.

Statistically significant[3] intragroup changes in sleep patterns over the course of our studies included the following: reduction in latency to the onset of REM sleep from ages 9–11 to 11–13 and from ages 11–13 to 13–15; reduction of *maximum* latency to sleep onset from ages 3–5 to 5–7 (indicating fewer nights on which it took children a considerable period of time to fall asleep initially, which might have been predicted from the children's lesser incidence of presleep anxiety at ages 5–7 than at 3–5); reduction in the frequency and duration of spontaneous awakenings from ages 3–5 to 5–7; reduction in the duration of spontaneous awakenings from ages 9–11 to 11–13; increased latency to sleep onset and increased incidence of spontaneous arousal from ages 5–7 to 7–9. All but the last pair of differences suggest increasingly sound and mature sleep as the study progressed; it is possible that the differences observed between ages 5–7 and 7–9 reflect children's increasing capacity for self-reflection (Flavell, 1963), which, in turn, may permit the increasing effect on sleep performance of anxieties or anticipations that are absent or unsustained at earlier ages. In this sense, certain forms of insomnia may depend on cognitive development.

But the most general conclusion that might be reached about age differences in the sleep data in Table 2.5 is how unremarkable they are. Despite the fact that the years at which we have studied children include major advances in social-emotional, waking-cognitive, physical, and even dream development, children's sleep rhythms, at least as indexed by the variables at our disposal, seemed reasonably comparable from ages 3 to 15 (cf. Williams, Karacan, & Hursch, 1974).

In summary, then, the *group* data on presleep demeanor and on sleep performance do not suggest general problems of adaptation to being, sleeping, or reporting dreams in the laboratory. We take these results as reflecting, in considerable measure, the resiliency of children and of persons more generally. We also believe, however, that they bear testimony to the care we took in structuring and executing our study so that the laboratory would be a familiar, reassuring, and supportive environment for the children.

Individual reactions to the laboratory were, of course, variable: Some

---

[3]Unless otherwise noted, a statistically significant difference, effect, or correlation noted is one with $p \leq .05$, 2-tail. Wilcoxon tests (matched pairs or rank sum for, respectively, intragroup and intergroup comparisons) were used to evaluate group differences, and the Pearson product-moment formula was used to describe correlated observations.

children were consistently relaxed and consistently slept well, some (few) others were fairly consistently ill at ease and/or fairly consistently had less than optimal sleep efficiency, while many others generally were relaxed and slept well, although they experienced occasional "off" sessions. The effects of these individual differences on dream reporting and dream content can, and will, be evaluated (in Chapters 3–8), in terms of how presleep or sleep variables were correlated with children's dream phenomena.[4]

ANALYSIS OF RESULTS

All nighttime interviews were transcribed by a typist and were evaluated by two judges using our Scoring System for Children's Dreams.[5] In the form in which they were judged, the interviews were identified by subject and night, but not by the stage of sleep from which the awakening had been made.

The scoring system includes three parts:

1 A content-analysis checklist on which the judge indicates which kinds of character, setting, activity, cognition, feeling, motive, and outcome were present in the child's report.

2 A series of rating scales through which the judge scores, on the basis of content-analysis results, the degree to which (a) the dream was unpleasant vs. pleasant (hedonic tone), (b) the child was an active participant vs. passive spectator of dream events (active participation), (c) dream characters were unfamiliar vs. familiar to the child (character distortion), (d) dream settings were unfamiliar vs. familiar to the child (setting distortion), or (e) the dream was experienced visually vs. non-visually (visualization).

3 Rules for counting the number of words in the child's report that actually describe the dream experience itself.

One judge scored the interviews for all three normative dream-collection years (Years 1, 3, and 5). It is her scorings that are reported in this book (in Appendix B), and which were correlated with waking test and observational measures (in Appendix C). The reliability of her scorings was evaluated by comparing her scorings with those of a second judge.[6] Reliability generally

---

[4]Among sleep variables available for such correlation are scorings by another judge, who never had met the children, of sleep records from two consecutive nights of uninterrupted sleep we recorded from all 34 Year-3 subjects during a special nondream study we ran during Year 4.

[5]The system has been described in abstract form (Foulkes & Shepherd, 1970). See also Winget and Kramer, 1979, pp. 174–77, for a brief description of the system. A detailed manual explaining the system is available from the author.

[6]Jean Petrik was the primary judge. Edward Belvedere was the secondary judge for Year-1 dreams, and Elizabeth A. Scott was the secondary judge for Year-3 and Year-5 dreams. For Year 3, the secondary judge was blind as to subject, study group, night, and stage of sleep.

was quite satisfactory for all frequently scored content-analysis categories, and for the dream ratings and word counts. Data on scoring reliability are presented in Appendix A.

For each year at which children's dreams were studied with identical methods—at ages 3–5, 5–7, 7–9, 9–11, 11–13, and 13–15—we tabulated, separately for boys and girls and for different stages of sleep, the rate at which dreams were reported, the overall frequency with which different contents appeared in these dreams, the mean group rating on the scoring system's rating scales, and the mean group word count for the children's dream reports. These data are presented in Appendix B. For each year we tested for statistically significant differences as a function of sex (boys vs. girls) and stage of sleep (REM vs. NREM, REM vs. sleep onset, NREM vs. sleep onset). Results of older and younger children studied in the same study year also were contrasted. In the third and fifth year in which subjects were studied, we also tested for statistically significant longitudinal changes in dream reporting and dream content.

For each normative dream year we also correlated all children's waking test or observational measures in that year's test file (see Table 2.2) with: their REM, NREM, and sleep-onset recall rates; their REM (and from age 7–9 on, NREM and sleep-onset) dream ratings and word counts; the relative frequency with which their REM dreams contained contents in as many as 62 frequently used scoring-system categories; (in Years 3 and 5 only) longitudinal changes in REM, NREM, and sleep-onset recall, in REM word counts, and in REM ratings; and (in Year 5 only) six additional ratios of one content class to another content class.

The numbers of dream and test variables entered into correlation with each other were as follows:

Age	Number of Dream Variables	Number of Test Variables
3–5	57	176
5–7	75	269
7–9	94	266
9–11	80	193
11–13	88	320
13–15	94	400

Details of the methods by which tests were scored (where that is not obvious) or waking observations were made are presented in Appendix C, along with a complete tabulation of the 6,995 correlations that attained significance at $p \leq .050$, 2-tail. Because of the large number of correlations that we calculated (136,411), these significance levels cannot be taken in any literal sense, but we feel (and the history of psychological research suggests) that the correlations we describe as significant are our best estimates of "true" waking–dreaming relationships for the children we studied, and our best basis for forming hypotheses to be tested in future research with other groups of children. In an area of psychology in which theory long has been richer than data, it seems reasonable to us to have taken advantage of the unparalleled opportunity afforded us to collect as many waking data as we could for each child, to have correlated these data with as many dream variables as possible, and to have attempted psychological interpretation of patterns of "significance" within those waking–dreaming correlations.

The following section is devoted to presenting our descriptive, comparative, and correlational results for each of the age levels at which we did normative studies of children's dreams. Not all findings can, or should, be discussed in these chapters. The appendixes permit interested readers to inspect the primary data and to draw their own conclusions. In Chapters 3–8, we attempt to summarize and integrate what we feel are the most important aspects of children's dreamlife from age 3 through 15: who dreams what when, and (through correlational data) why.

PART 2

Which Children Dream What, When, and Why

CHAPTER 3 _____

Ages 3 to 5

This chapter describes our results in studying 14 preschoolers during the first year of our project. At the start of this year, the children ranged in age from 2 years, 9 months, to 4 years, 8 months; half of the children were under 4 years of age (five girls, two boys) and half were 4 years old or more (five boys, two girls). The typical (median) girl studied was aged 3 years, 1 month; the typical boy was aged 4 years, 0 months. Only four of the children (two girls, two boys) were attending a nursery school.

To determine the children's stage of waking cognitive development, we examined scores from the only pertinent measure available in our test battery, the Laurendeau and Pinard (1962) interview in which children were questioned about their understanding of the concepts of "dream," "night," and "life." In these interviews children were asked a systematic series of questions concerning: the origin, location, organ, cause, and reality of dreams; the nature and origin of night; and what things are alive and what not, and why. By conventional scoring criteria, answers to each test are graded from stage 0 to stage 3, with only scores of 3 indicating a satisfactory ("operational") understanding of the phenomenon in question. If we grossly dichotomize children's summed scores such that total scores of 7 to 9 are considered "operational," then no child we studied at ages 3−5 was operational at the start of our study year. Summed scores ranged from 0 to 5, with a median score of 2.5. No child obtained an operational score on the dream or life subtests; two children (one boy, one girl) had scores of 3 on the night subtest.

To the extent that this classification system can be believed (and we often were later to regret our failure to collect more relevant data from the children, e.g., on "conservation" tasks), our children's waking cognition at ages 3−5 had the largely unsystematic character that other observers have found to be so common at these ages. The preoperational child is "symbolic" (uses linguistic and imaginal representations in her or his thinking), but her or his symbolic performances are largely externally driven rather than spontaneous and are highly distractible rather than planfully regulated. The child's thought also is largely egocentric, in the sense that it is difficult for the child to "center" thought around any perspective other than her or his own momentary situation, feelings, or prior thoughts.

THE REPORTING OF DREAMS

Remarkably few dreams were reported by our preschoolers. The facts may be laid out very simply: Only 27% of REM awakenings (18% of sleep-onset awakenings and 6% of NREM awakenings)[1] were associated with a reported dream. These figures are averaged across children and, therefore, are "inflated" by a few children who did report dreams relatively often: three children (all *under* 4 years at the start of the study) reported almost half (26 of 53) of the dreams that were obtained on REM awakenings. The *typical* (median) child reported dreams on only 15% of REM awakenings, and never on either NREM or sleep-onset awakenings. (Every child, however, reported at least one REM dream.)

It would be fair to say that initially we found these results to be quite disappointing. When one sets out to study children's dreams, one wants to have such dreams to study, particularly when so much effort has been expended to that end. Neither prior theory nor observation had prepared us for the results we obtained. Where was the vaunted imaginativeness of young children, expressed in the quintessential act of human imagination? How could the anecdotal observations of parents and clinicians lead to such definite characterizations of early-childhood dreaming, when our allegedly more systematic observations were so terribly meager? How, critics began to ask (Schwartz, Weinstein, & Arkin, 1978) had we missed all those other dreams the children had been having?

In the course of developing further data, and of rethinking how it must be that dreaming begins, we believe that we have developed a perspective on the ontogeny of dreaming that begins to answer some of these questions and that casts light as well on those dreams that the children *did* report at ages 3 to 5. The remainder of this chapter will be devoted to elaborating this perspective, and to supporting it with empirical data.

REPORTING, REMEMBERING, AND DREAMING DREAMS

One can, of course, think of many reasons why children might not report dreams on REM awakenings in the laboratory. Young children can be difficult to arouse from sleep, and our schedule often called for awakenings at times when the children had experienced relatively little of their usual quota of sleep and, therefore, might have been expected to be particularly groggy. Perhaps our children could not or would not awaken sufficiently well to be able to remember their dreams or to be able or willing to report them. There are several problems, however, with this line of explanation.

First, as noted in Chapter 2, children's arousal level on awakening from sleep may reflect their arousal level during the preceding sleep period.

---

[1]The REM/NREM difference was statistically significant; the REM/sleep-onset difference was not.

Specifically, children who cannot be sufficiently alerted on awakening may not have been sufficiently mentally "alert" during the prior sleep period to have been engaged in dreaming. Second, our observations on arousability on nocturnal awakenings (as judged by the nocturnal interviewer) did not suggest that low-rate dream reporters were habitually groggy and that high-rate dream reporters were habitually alert. Third, these same observations also failed to indicate that a given child's propensity to report a dream was strongly associated with how alert she or he was during experimental interviews: On REM awakenings when I judged children's alertness to be good, dreaming often was denied, while on REM awakenings when I judged children's arousal to be poor, dreaming sometimes was reported. Fourth, and perhaps most significant, our data indicate that in our children sleep onset, from which arousal of both children and adults is most effectively achieved and from which adults report dreams even more often than they do from REM sleep (Foulkes & Vogel, 1965), was associated with extremely few reports of dreaming. The absolute paucity of sleep-onset reports in 3- to 5-year-olds argues that it may well be the case not that these children have difficulty retrieving their dreams—for at sleep onset the conditions for retrieval are as optimal as they ever can be—but that they often simply are not having dreams.

A lack of "understanding" is another possible explanation of children's failure to report REM dreams. Perhaps even when well aroused and eager to cooperate the children simply did not understand the experimental task. Neither the concept "dream" nor the situation of describing one's mental experiences to others is likely to be well understood by preschoolers, particularly at one or three or six o'clock in the morning. Once again, however, one could hold that the children's failure to understand dreams reflected either a lack of a sufficient knowledge base (i.e., if they hadn't ever dreamed, or dreamed enough to know what a dream was, they surely *would* be confused during a "dream" interview) or an immature stage of cognitive development that also made dream construction during REM sleep relatively unlikely. Empirically, significant correlates of children's rates of REM recall at ages 3–5 did *not* include: the Piagetian measure (Laurendeau & Pinard, 1962) of stage of understanding of the concept "dream"; measures of waking descriptive or memory ability; *any* cognitive variable at all; or chronological age, which might be expected at least imperfectly to covary with absolute stage of cognitive development. (In fact, as we have seen, it was relatively younger children who were the most fecund reporters at ages 3–5). That our own waking index of children's ability to report a pictorial stimulus from memory was uncorrelated with REM recall ($r = .04$) indicates that differential dream reporting was *not* a function of demonstrated differences among children in understanding of, or accuracy in, reporting "visual" experience from memory.

Children's lack of motivation might serve to explain their failure to have reported dreams on REM awakenings. It often seemed to me that the children were relatively disinterested—or absolutely uninterested—in dis-

cussing dreams (or anything else) on their mid-night experimental awakenings. One clearly does not expect 3- or 4-year-olds to be as fascinated by
the research potential of such discussions as the experimenter would like
them to be, or that they will find their dreams as captivating as do adult
subjects who fully realize the dream's potential for self-revelation. However, the explanation of children's nonreporting in terms of poor motivation
also presents some difficulties. At least sometimes the children's disinterest
may have stemmed from the lack of a relevant dream to discuss, rather than
from a failure to appreciate the value of discussing a dream they could (or
might have been able to) remember. Empirically, differences in apparent
waking interest in dreams and in apparent motivation on experimental
arousals themselves (as judged by the experimenter) did not always seem
well correlated with differences among children in dream reporting or with
differences among REM awakenings in any given child's dream reporting.
Nonetheless, motivation clearly must have played some not insubstantial
role in mediating report rates for REM dreams at ages 3−5.

In fact, we have some correlational observations to precisely that effect.
Children who were judged talkative and spontaneously expressive and who
showed, at least at our nursery school, dependence on adults were the ones
most likely to claim dream experiences on REM awakenings. One imagines
these children to have been characterologically propelled toward talking
with the interviewer on their nighttime awakenings, whether or not they
actually had a dream to discuss. That is, these correlates suggest the
likelihood that our 3- to 5-year-olds' data include both false positives (the
garrulous, adult-oriented child has no remembered dream but describes a
"dream" anyway) and false negatives (the reticent, nondependent child has
a remembered or memorable dream but chooses not to discuss it with the
experimenter).

One cannot, of course, hazard much of a guess about the precise nature
of the dreams some children failed to describe to the experimenter.
However, it does not seem likely that they could have been vastly different
from the true dreams other children did describe. The main problem,
therefore, is how to determine which reports in our 3- to 5-year-old
collection bore some resemblance to actually experienced dreams and which
did not. I shall try to indicate below that there are some reasonable
procedures by which this problem can be resolved.

For the meantime, I would like to put this problem in some perspective.

1   All 3- to 5-year-olds reported dreams more often on REM than on NREM
    awakenings, a fact indicating that the children's reports might be
    accorded some degree of credibility.[2]

---

[2]Also, NREM "light" awakenings produced more recall (8.1%) than did NREM "deep"
awakenings (0%). However, it could be argued that both this difference and the REM vs.
NREM difference were artifacts of differences in arousal threshold. (But, in turn, those
differences could be related plausibly to mentational differences.) Another factor complicating
interpretation of the sleep-stage discrimination data is that I was not "blind" to awakening
condition during my interviews.

2 There was no suggestion in the correlational data that it was particularly dull or careless children who claimed most often to have dreamed—that is, the dream sample cannot, even on the correlational evidence, be portrayed as *generally* invalid.

3 That most children reported REM dreams so seldom suggests that both the inner impetus and the external reinforcement for false dream telling must, *in general*, have been fairly well controlled for the children we studied.

4 It might even be argued that, in early childhood, cognitive skills are particularly liable to be manifested overtly and that such skills are, therefore, as adequately assessed by what a child generally does as by her or his "latent capabilities," as indexed by responses to unfamiliar "mental test" items. Thus taking initiative behaviorally in wakefulness might have been a valid, and a "cognitive", correlate of mental "initiative taking" (dreaming) during REM sleep.

My feeling is that the major reason why children reported so few dreams on REM awakenings at ages 3–5 was that their REM periods often were wholly or largely "empty" of those organized mental experiences that we call dreams. From the perspective of what we know about children's waking mental development, it hardly would be surprising were a complex, integrative psychological process such as dreaming either to be absent or present only in rudimentary form during the REM sleep of preschoolers. REM sleep can only permit dreaming, not mandate it. Dreaming must depend on skills of imaginal representation and narrative organization, which develop rather slowly in early childhood and which perhaps even by age 3 or 4 have not reached that "critical mass" requisite to dreaming.

It does no good to fall back on the position that dreaming is a perceptual process (cf. Dement's [1965] chapter on dreams entitled "Perception during Sleep"), for it is not perception but imaging and imagination that are at issue during REM sleep, a state in which little or no sensory input is being processed. Observation (Kerr, Foulkes, & Jurkovic, 1978) suggests that dream representations are dependent not on how we *see* the world, but on how we are able to *think* about it. There is no reasonable ground for expecting that very young children should be able to think as often or as well as adults during REM sleep, however versatile their perceptual processing may be. There is much reason to believe that dreaming, as is the case with other sophisticated mental acts, requires certain cognitive preconditions which initially are absent in human development, whose appearance requires a predictably extended period of developmental elaboration, and whose "perfection" is a rather late developmental accomplishment.

THE CONTENT AND CORRELATES OF REM DREAMS

When the 3- to 5-year-olds *did* report REM dreams, those reports were exceedingly brief. Generally children's dream reports were only a sentence or two long. The typical girls' report was 14 words long, the boys', 13. No report ever exceeded 50 words. (By way of contrast, for the 9- to 11-year-olds being studied concurrently, typical lengths were 75.5 words for girls' reports and 60.5 words for boys' reports, and maximum report lengths were 443 words for girls' reports and 249 words for boys' reports.) Relatively longer REM reports at ages 3–5 came from children who, in one of our waking test sessions, gave more comprehensive reports of a known and physically present pictorial stimulus. The accuracy component of this test performance is noteworthy, because long reporters otherwise did not seem particularly garrulous and, in our nursery school, they were peer oriented rather than adult oriented. (There was, at ages 3–5, no significant correlation between children's REM recall rates and their mean REM word count: $r = -.11$; the word-count scores, however, had a highly restricted range, with 11 of 14 children reporting REM dreams with a mean count of 18 or fewer words.)

Even more remarkable than the brevity of the children's dream reports was the static and nonnarrative quality of the situations they described. While one could account for the brevity on the grounds of defective memory, descriptive vocabulary, or motivation, one would imagine that the children's limited skills and interest would have been attracted most strongly—as they are in wakefulness—by motion, action, and interaction. But social interactions, either pleasant or unpleasant, were quite rare, appearing, respectively, in only 4% and 6% of the children's reports. Overt motor activities also were rare. Only 26% of the children's reports described any locomotor or whole-body movement, and only 13% described self-movement of *any* sort. The most commonly reported dream theme ("motive") had, in fact, to do with sleep or fatigue: 25% of the children's reports contained such themes. All of these findings are quite unique, not merely against the standard of adult dreams, but also against that of children's dreams at all other ages at which we studied them, including these very same children's dreams two years later at ages 5–7.

Less surprisingly, but equally uniquely, the major characters in 3- to 5-year-olds' dreams were animals, which appeared in 45% of girls' dreams and in 33% of boys' dreams. Although animals continued to be highly represented in children's dreams at ages 5–7, only at ages 3–5 did they appear to the relative exclusion of human characters. Relatively few dreams (17%) contained family members, other known persons appeared even less often, and human strangers were almost totally absent.

There are several reasons why this animal predominance might be unsurprising. Nelson (1973) found that children's earliest verbal symbolizations often refer to animals. During early language acquisition, it may well be animal movement that is the major environmental property to catch the child's attention and to attract her or his interest. Later on, it has been suggested, it may be the relatively uncontrolled or impulsive nature of animal movements, real or fantasied, that makes animals such appealing objects of identification for young children (Bellak & Adelman, 1960).

Pitcher and Prelinger's (1963) data on stories children tell in wakefulness indicate more animal than human characters at age 3 and continuing high rates of animal characterization at age 5. These same data also indicate a very fluid relationship between animal characters and the self:

> Stories which name an animal as a character at the beginning may end by assuming that the child himself is the animal; the essential continuity seems to lie in the action rather than in the nature of the character. (pp. 168–169)

The extensive use of animals in fairy tales and other children's stories meant to convey messages about socialization depends on this linkage.

Our data indicate that children's dream animals most often came from the same repertory as animals appearing in fairy tales and cartoons. In general, these animals were neither highly familiar (pets, such as cats or dogs) nor highly exotic (zebras or polar bears). Rather, they tended to come from domesticated farm animals (horses, cows, pigs, chickens, etc.) or from various "untamed" but unaversive species indigenous to the area in which the children lived (frogs, birds, deer, etc.).

One of the most puzzling but potentially revealing questions that might be asked about the mind of young children is why animals are such significant symbols in the organization of their thoughts, both sleeping and waking. One simple answer is that many of the narratives to which children are exposed—in print, orally, and in the visual media—are animal narratives. Yet presumably the reason why adults present so many animal stories to children is that children find animals particularly interesting—more interesting, often, than people, and more fertile objects of identification than people. Why? From a Piagetian perspective, perhaps because there is as yet a failure to distinguish sharply between humans and other animate (and inanimate) forces. But even on this hypothesis of preoperational animism, it is not clear why children's dreams should contain animal figures at the rate that they do, a rate that surely exceeds the animals' importance, relative to humans, in the texture of children's waking experience.

From a Freudian perspective, the self-as-animal equation makes perhaps more sense, and, contextually, themes of impulsive containment vs. expulsion sometimes seem to be in accord with the tenets of this perspective (as when a 5-year-old boy dreamed that a buck broke a stock fence, freeing the pigs and horses contained therein). But such contextual evidence was by no means universal. What, on the Freudian hypothesis, is one to make of dreams simply of a bird singing, a horse running, frogs in the water, chickens eating corn, a dog barking, and a calf in a barn? A lot, clearly, if one is sufficiently inventive. But children's animal symbolism is too significant a feature of their early mental development to be left solely to the analysts. This symbolism must have as important implications for the ontogeny of thinking as it does for the ontogeny of conation (see Chapter 4).

The settings of the 3- to 5-year-olds' dreams often were ill-defined or unknown. In part, however, but not totally, this may reflect my initially insufficient probing of this aspect of dream experience (9- to 11-year-olds' dreams collected in the same year also were uncharacteristically high in judged vagueness of setting). Otherwise, reported settings most often were residential (more often than not the child's own home) or outdoors (in a field, in the mountains, or "just outdoors"). Only six of 53 REM reports (11%) contained characters or activities in the child's immediate setting, our laboratory.

The hypothesis that young children's dreams would be drenched with feeling, particularly unpleasant feeling, was disconfirmed by our data. In only 8% of reports were any feelings reported, and neither fear nor anger *ever* was reported (nor were events described that generally would seem to generate or accompany such feelings). However, fatigue states or activities were relatively often ascribed to the self-character. In addition, hunger "themes" were observed with some frequency in REM reports (11%). Overall, body-state themes were, uniquely at ages 3−5, more frequent than were themes of action or interaction in the external world. The hypothesis that young children would be traumatized or victimized in their REM dreams was disconfirmed. In only one report of 67 (from all sleep stages) was a 3- to 5-year-old the recipient of an unfavorable or unpleasant outcome. Given the context of the children's dreams, this is not surprising, for the self-character was, as such, rather minimally involved in most narratives (the relatively high Active Participation Scale rating of boys' dreams reflects, as we shall see, their "participation" in the quintessentially passive activity of sleep).

CONTENT AND CREDIBILITY

Having drawn these conclusions about the REM reports of 3- to 5-year-olds, one inevitably returns to the question of their validity. Do the summary characterizations above say something about the *dreamlife* of the children, or merely about waking fancies they have brought to bear on the experimental task of describing dreams? Like children's earliest waking stories, their reported REM dreams are terse and relatively static (Amen, 1941) and highly populated by animals (Pitcher & Prelinger, 1963). Cannot the similarities be viewed as a reflection of the circumstance that both sorts of narratives derive, in fact, from the same source—waking imagination?

Features of the children's REM reports suggest that this cannot, at least entirely, be the case. Children's stories, for example, would hardly be expected to be as devoid of social interaction and of physical activity as were our children's REM reports. Nor would they be expected to dwell so often on sleep-related themes. Still, in view of the absence of cognitive correlates for the reported occurrence of the skilled mental act of dreaming and of the presence of correlates that suggest the possibility of false-positive reports in our sample, it would be nice to know in precisely what kinds of REM contents reported at ages 3−5 one may place greatest credence.

Correlates of particular features of REM reports can, I think, be used to point toward resolution of this problem. The same credibility criteria can be applied to individual dream features as one would have liked to have employed regarding whole dream accounts—one places relatively greater belief in those dream features reported by children talented in ways that might contribute to effective dream construction, dream remembering, and dream reporting, and in children who do not seem otherwise to have been characteristically careless or highly dependent on adult (e.g., experimenter) approval.

Using such criteria, most of the unique qualities ascribed above to 3- to 5-year-olds' dreams prove to be somewhat credible. Correlates of children's rate of reporting *animal* dream characters were generally uninformative, except in indicating, by way of a positive association with social class, that actual exposure to relevant animals probably was a less important mediator of dreaming animal dreams than was exposure to stories about animals[3] and in suggesting that animal dreaming was associated more strongly with the receipt than with the initiation of hostility (reflecting an angry, impulsive world rather than an angry, impulsive self?). However, when one examines the correlates of reporting animals to the relative *exclusion* of reporting human characters (represented, since there were practically no human strangers reported at ages 3–5, in our Character Distortion ratings), then it is apparent that children who reported animal characters rather more than they did known human characters were cognitively skilled (high in Wechsler Comprehension and Geometric Design), and, although they cooperated with the experimenter in the presleep period, they were not particularly dependent on his approval. Interestingly, these children *were* vigorous, assertive, and aggressive. The difference between correlates of the rating and the frequency variables for dream animals rests on the fact that animal-plus-human dreamers score high on the latter (since, absolutely, they have many dreams with animals) but not on the former (since the dominant characterization of their particular dreams may be human rather than animal). The difference in correlates suggests that *the most reliable early-appearing other-representations in children's dreams are generic animal images of a familiar sort that possibly may reflect the children's own impulsiveness.*

However, there is an alternative hypothesis that I cannot rule out. This is that animal characters *never* are major figures in children's dreams, but rather are claimed as dream characters by children who confuse the question "What were you dreaming?" with the instruction "Tell me a story." Unlike the fatigue themes to be discussed below, animal characters did not tend to be reported by older children (correlation with age, $r = -.26$). Moreover,

---

[3]Not only were hunting and fishing associated more with "town" than "gown" culture in our sample, but our lower-class families also tended to live in areas of Laramie more closely bordering on the surrounding countryside.

two children were responsible in large measure for the high pooled incidence of animal characters at ages 3−5: Colleen, aged only 2 years, 10 months, at the start of the study and the highest rate overall REM reporter for her sex, reported five of the girls' nine animal dreams; Christopher, the youngest of the boys we studied, had the highest rate of REM recall in the whole age 3−5 group, and reported eight of the males' 11 animal dreams.[4] Both children were highly motivated on nocturnal interviews and during other test procedures, but perhaps in inappropriate ways. Colleen was the sometimes "self-admitted" REM-dream confabulator mentioned in Chapter 2; she also had her group's highest NREM recall rate, perhaps another sign (at least at her age) that she was "making up" her dream reports while awake; and she had no comprehension, on the Laurendeau-Pinard test, of what a dream was. Christopher's case is somewhat more ambiguous. He claimed no NREM dreams; he was the only child in his age group with a "definite incorporation" of an experimentally applied stimulus (and that incorporation was an animal dream); and he had a relatively mature dream concept ("mitigated realism"). Despite these positive signs, however, our data also indicate that he, alone, among our subjects, was highly prone to "elaborations" going beyond the actual stimulus in our waking Description Test (he had 13 confabulatory errors vs. an age 3−5 mean of 1.5 such errors), and this was not a function of his simply having described more details (accurate as well as inaccurate) in general. I also find it curious that both these children later were to show, rather uniquely for their group, precipitous *declines* in apparent REM recall (Colleen's recall dropped to 29% in Year 3; Christopher's from 73% in Year 3 to 20% in Year 5, although in his case there were extenuating family-life circumstances that might have adversely affected his motivation). Some caution, then, might be appropriate regarding children's earliest claims of animal dreaming. And yet there is the fact that, at ages 5−7, when children's dreams generally were more credible, they still claimed animal characterization frequently, which itself, by correlational criteria, seemed credible.

It might be thought (and I, for some time, did think) that the relatively high incidence of *fatigue or sleep* themes in 3- to 5-year-olds' dreams reflected children's confusion during nighttime interviews between their having been asleep and their having imagined, *in* their sleep, *that* they were asleep. Of course, it also could be that such themes were dream "incorporations" of the presumably most salient drive state active during REM sleep, the drive for sleep-maintenance. The correlational data strongly favor the latter alternative. The children who reported relatively many sleep/fatigue themes were those: skilled in Wechsler Block Design (which, as we shall see, was the earliest and most consistent Wechsler correlate of REM reporting in childhood); skilled in reporting from memory details of earlier-

---

[4]These children were, however, relatively "exclusive" animal dreamers, that is, they scored relatively high on Character Distortion ratings (ranks of 4.5 and 3, respectively).

seen stimuli; relatively advanced in Piagetian development; but *not* emotionally dependent on the experimenter.

Once again, the picture is even more clear when one concentrates on the relatively *exclusive* reporting of the phenomenon. At ages 3−5 there was relatively little dreamer motor activity or involvement in social interaction in REM dreams; consequently, our Active Participation rating of the children's dreams depended heavily on (and was highly intercorrelated with: $r = .76$) dreamer-ascribed sleep motivation. But, unlike the raw rate of reporting self-fatigue themes, high scores on the rating variable depended on dreaming much of self-fatigue *and* little of other characters' (motor) activity. Two children who claimed self-fatigue themes also claimed, relatively more often, motor activity by other characters; the rating variable gives them much lower scores, relative to peers, than does the frequency variable. Children high in Active Participation (i.e., in the reporting of self-fatigue to the relative exclusion of other dream activities) were: high in social comprehension; high in visuospatial construction skill (including Wechsler Block Design); advanced in Piagetian-stage development; cooperative with but not emotionally dependent on the experimenter; and older than their peers. Socially, they were active and involved with peers. Thus it was the most cognitively *and* socially competent children who dreamed of static-self themes to the relative exclusion of active-other themes. The sleep-self theme would not seem, a priori, to represent any grand achievement in dream development, but it lay within the competence of only the brightest, most ambitious, and oldest preschoolers. The implication is that *the best single conclusion as to the origin of self-involvement in REM dreaming is that it begins preoperationally with static scenes relating to the dreamer's own sleep activity rather than with stories in which other characters also are active.* That it is older children, and children less animistic than their peers, who mostly have such involvement suggests that the passive apprehension of static animal scenes may be a conceptually earlier achievement.

What exactly were these self-fatigue dreams like? One boy, in four of his five REM reports was: sleeping in the window of a barber shop; sleeping atop a "fire car"; sleeping in a banana tree in California (where he recently had vacationed); and sleeping in an unfamiliar house, without covers or blankets. (In the other dream, he merely was "thinking" about something.) Cognitively, there are two important features of these dream representations. First, they suggest egocentrism: an inability mentally to decenter from an ongoing body state of the self. That dream property conforms nicely with classical accounts of early preoperational thinking in the waking state. Second, these dream representations must have been static ones, a fact that also is consistent with waking research, indicating that preschoolers are not adept at creating kinematic imagery (Piaget & Inhelder, 1966; Kerr, Corbitt, & Jurkovic, 1980.) In fact, the dream data constitute a substantial independent replication, in the area of spontaneous mental activity, of Piagetian findings on experimentally evoked mental activity during the preoperational period. The Piagetian data sometimes have been considered suspect because of their dependence on particular kinds of motor outputs (e.g., drawing) and on somewhat atypical reporting situations; that our dream data conform to them suggests that both tasks (dream reporting, reconstructing object movement in wakefulness) correctly index the preoperational child's relative failure to be able to image movement.

The paucity of physical movement or social interaction in the dreams of 3- to 5-year-olds, then, may have depended on their failure to be able effectively to represent such activities symbolically. It would seem from the data (e.g., only two of 53 dreams included self-locomotion) that this difficulty was particularly salient for *self*-movement.

There are considerable waking data indicating that preoperational children are not highly skilled in symbolically representing movement, interaction, and, particularly, self-movement. Preschool-age children show defects in spatial role taking, that is, in being able to imagine what another, from her or his perspective, might see, and in how it might be seen (Flavell, 1968). Presumably these defects also would generalize to an imagined self moving about imagined space. Even at somewhat later ages children seem to find it particularly difficult to move the "self" symbolically (Huttenlocher & Presson, 1973). The preoperational child's "egocentrism" implies that no sharp differentiation is being made between self and other; presumably such a differentiation would be critical to the establishment of a distinctive self-character in dreams.

It may seem strange to propose that 3- to 5-year-olds cannot represent their own action in dream narratives. They certainly can act effectively on their world; surely they must be "aware" of these actions. In fact, however, children's self-awareness in the preoperational period is quite limited. Piaget (1974) has shown that cognizance of one's own actions is not a passive "illumination" of what those actions are, but an active conceptual reconstruction of what they are imagined to be. He further has shown that the preoperational reconstruction of self-action is quite imprecise, and probably even more imprecise than is the symbolic reconstruction of the acts of others.

We may say, then, that the dream reports of 3- to 5-year-olds strongly confirm the conceptual rather than the perceptual or motor nature of dreaming. It is not what such children are able to *see* or *do* that determines their dream content, but what they are able to *think*. The unique properties of dreams at ages 3–5—their static quality, their representation of salient body states rather than symbolization of social interaction, their lack of motoric self-involvement and most often of any effective form of self-representation—are dictated not by peculiarities in the child's waking experience but by immaturity in the child's ability to recreate such experience symbolically.

Another property of 3- to 5-year-olds' dreams (actually, as we shall see, of 3- to 7-year-olds' dreams) that must be viewed similarly is their relative lack of feeling-states (affect). There can be no doubt that such children can act "emotionally." Yet apparently what is critical to the appearance of affect in dreams is not whether one can behave emotionally but rather whether one can recreate symbolically circumstances in which feelings may be felt and can recreate symbolically those feelings themselves.

With respect to the representation of affect in dreams, the link with cognition must, in fact, be even more intimate than it is for the representation of action. Schachter and Singer's (1962) classic demonstration of the role of cognition in determining emotional experience suggests that feeling itself is a cognitive achievement. A strong implication of their research is that, as Piaget has insisted (Cowan, 1978), emotional development itself can proceed only within boundaries defined by concurrent stages of cognitive development and the understandings they permit of organismic states and of self-environment encounters. Although we have some sense of how it is that emotional responses differentiate in childhood (e.g., the classic account of Bridges [1932]) and we know from more recent research (reviewed by Shantz [1975]) something of the course of the child's development of the ability to identify emotions in others, we know practically nothing of how young children "feel" or of how they imagine others to "feel" in "emotion-provoking" situations or during "emotional behavior" episodes. Perhaps the very waking experience we are looking to find dream representations of is, in the case of affect, either absent or so primitive as to defy symbolic re-creation.

There is, in fact, still another symbolic impediment to the representation of feeling in dreams: the lack of effective means of self-representation more generally. It is one of the hallmarks of "being in" a dream, rather than passively observing dream events, that you feel the feelings of a participant in these events. If there is no "you" in the dream, there is not likely to be any feeling. In this sense the almost total absence of affect in 3- to 5-year-olds' dreams strongly supports my earlier contention that effective self-representation generally is absent as well.

Our data on dream affect in early childhood probably seem counterintuitive both to traditional dream psychologists (for whom the primacy of impulse or affect in dreams has been a matter of faith) and to those whose professions lead them to deal with disturbances in early human development (and who are aware of any number of instances in which children have been traumatized by the content of their own dreams). To the dream theorists, I simply want to suggest that our data strongly indicate that their faith has been misplaced. The practitioner (and the parent who can identify with her or him), however, is owed some explanation over the discrepancy in our respective observations of dream affect.

I think that it is important, in evaluating these observations, to distinguish between being frightened *by* a dream and being frightened *in* it. I believe it is likely that the former experience must be far more prevalent in early childhood than the latter. It is now commonly accepted that many "sleep disorders" are, in fact, disorders of arousal from sleep (Broughton, 1968). It seems quite possible that most or all of young children's spontaneously reported frightening dreams represent not anxiety experienced *in* sleep but anxiety experienced during slow and imperfect arousal *from* sleep, wherein the potentially frightening dream imagery and/or the external darkness and internal confusion in which it is recalled evoke characteristically waking sorts of emotional response. In the laboratory, where awakenings are externally enforced and relatively rapid, there is much less opportunity for the development of slowly festering and reality-uncorrected affect.

The absence of feeling in 3- to 5-year-olds' dreams, then, must depend not on some remarkable ability of children to *dissociate* situation and feeling (an ability we adults sometimes display, as Freud [1900] observed), but on the facts that children (1) may be deficient at *making the associations* requisite to experiencing affect in wakefulness and (2) certainly are deficient in symbolically recreating such affect, either in wakefulness or in sleep. It is instructive that children's laboratory-reported dreams, which seldom have been considered by students of affective development, may in fact provide observations highly relevant to those interests. Likewise, developmental psychologists with interests in children's representations of self and of extrapersonal reality should find a treasure-trove of germane data in children's laboratory dreams.

WHO DREAMED WHAT

Given the substantial constraints the children's cognitive immaturity must have imposed on the content of their dreams, what can be said, from our correlational data, about determinants of dream contents that the children did claim? I should emphasize the word "claim" because, other than in their animal representations and in their portrayal of sleep or fatigue themes, the reported dream contents generally did *not* have cognitive correlates supporting the credibility of their claims.

With respect to *characters* other than animals, no class appeared sufficiently often to permit much meaningful speculation about its determinants. Based on quite limited dream data, dreamers of parents or nuclear-family members had mothers whose attitudes to the child were authoritarian and distant and fathers whose attitudes were authoritarian. The children themselves tended not to associate with peers at the nursery school, clinging to their adult teachers instead. These children's parents, in other words, were dependency-fostering, and the children were dependent. Only one dream at ages 3−5 contained any human strangers, and correlates of the most frequently scored "known" character class (any male: five dreams) were such that relatively little credibility can be attached to the appearance in children's dreams of members of this class. Specifically, compared to their peers, reporters of known male characters were poorer at a waking description task, younger, and less intelligent. One is left, then, with the observation that children dreamed, when they dreamed of dream characters at all, of persons highly familiar to them (family members) or of animals interesting to them and highly familiar to them through waking pictures and fantasy representations, if not direct experience. Presumably this restriction of dream characterization to the familiar and the significant reflects not only the limited perspectives of the child's waking world but also her or his difficulty in being able to reconstruct that world symbolically.

It has been suggested (e.g., Morris, 1967) that children are especially interested in animals with humanoid features, but the fact that children with potentially problematic family environments could and did dream directly of family members refutes the idea that their dream animals must have been motivated distortions of other members of their family. Correlates of animal dreaming itself did not suggest that dream animals symbolized a particularly angry or impulsive "I," but, as we have seen, relatively exclusive dreaming of such animals was associated with waking impulsiveness. However, given the rudimentary cognition of the preoperational period, it probably would be a serious conceptual error to attribute dream "symbolism" in any adult sense to 3- to 5-year-olds. Perhaps animal characters are, at best, diffusely symbolic of a self *and* world that, preoperationally, cannot be sharply discriminated as to subject and object. They may portray phenomenal facts—perhaps, as has been suggested, "movement" or "impulsiveness"—rather than any particular person—even, as we understand it, the self.

Dream *settings,* too, when children managed to construct (or report) them, were generally of highly familiar sorts, whether or not children could identify their real-life counterparts. Within the cognitive constraint that settings be of this order of familiarity, there was some suggestion that dependent or passive children dreamed relatively often of home settings, particularly own-home settings. But this correlation may also be interpretable cognitively—socially inexperienced children may simply have a less adequate knowledge base from which to construct nonhomelike settings. Outdoors dreamers, on the other hand, were relatively "expansive" behaviorally, in the sense of having been judged relatively hostile at our year-end (1969) nursery school. Vague or unclassifiable settings were reported most often by children relatively deficient in waking knowledge, who also were judged anxious, hostile, depressed, and dependent during the presleep period in the laboratory. Unfamiliarity with, and discomfort in, the setting in which dreams were collected may therefore have contributed somewhat to generation of vague-setting dreams.

In interpreting the few sensory-dreamer *activities* in 3- to 5-year-olds' dreams, it should be noted that, uniquely at this age, sensory and motor acts were significantly intercorrelated ($r = .60$). This correlation largely depended on an association of sensory-dreamer and motor-other scores, suggesting that "sensory" activities reported for the self may simply have reflected children's confusion about the distinction between visually dreaming of motor acts and dreaming that, as a dream character, one performs a visual act. Interestingly, it was children judged relatively high in make-believe or pretend behavior at our nursery school who claimed their own motoric participation in dreams, which was, of course, a relatively rare dream accomplishment overall. Also interesting was the observation that motor-self dreamers were judged to be both frequent initiators and frequent receivers of hostility at the nursery school, while motor-other dreamers were judged only to be frequent recipients of hostility. What motor activity there was in 3- to 5-year-olds' reports was much more often "physical" than "verbal" (14 locomotor reports, for instance, but only one verbal report). The most consistent waking behavioral correlate of whole-body locomotion in dreams was initiation of aggression to peers at the nursery school.

Regarding *states* ascribed to dream characters, the major finding, of course, was how few of them there were. Dream characters never "thought" anything in the dreams, and they rarely felt any feelings. This is unsurprising from the perspective of the dream as a spontaneous narrative, for young children's waking narratizing (Flapan, 1968) is similarly devoid of the "psychological" perspective that endows characters with cognitions or feelings. It was older children with somewhat better raw cognitive aptitude, but who were relatively deficient for their age in verbal I.Q., who reported the few (mostly happy) feelings in REM dreams. Possibly these children were merely socially experienced enough to realize the latent demand of my feeling probe ("give the man a feeling") but insufficiently accomplished to realize that a glib reply of "happy" was inappropriate if it only meant "It pleases me now to think back on that dream I had."

The dominant dream *motives* at ages 3–5 were "organic." As we have seen, sleep, almost always dreamer sleep, was the most frequent and credible of these motives. Hunger, interestingly enough, was most often ascribed to other dream characters, another datum suggesting that, with the exception of an accurately "located" sleeping self, there is not a well-demarcated self-character in preoperational children's dreams. To the extent that hunger dreams are stimulus "incorporations," that is, dream responses to a salient drive stimulus, I now am inclined to revise downward my estimate of the cognitive skill implied by the fact that young children's dream incorporation of external stimuli often seems to involve assigning a dreamer-received stimulus to another dream character (cf. Foulkes, Larson, Swanson, & Rardin, 1969). Rather than representing a creative transformation (self-perception to other-representation in the dream), such findings may simply be a function of the children's failure to have established a sharp ego-alter differentiation and, hence, to have created a distinctive self-character in their dreams. Unlike sleep dreamers, hunger dreamers *were* judged to be dependent on adults. With respect to social-interactional motives, the main finding was how very few of them there were: two attack-social (other) reports, both from the same dreamer, and three approach-social (dreamer) reports, from two different children. Cognitive correlates of the latter, moreover, suggest the substantial possibility that claims of self-initiations of social interaction were erroneous.

The scoring of dream *outcomes* is largely a reflection of the scoring of social motives. For the recipient of these initiations, approach-social initiations routinely were scored as leading to a favorable outcome, and attack-social initiations routinely were scored as leading to an unfavorable outcome. Once again, the scarcity of social exchange was most striking. Since the preschool child's waking life must consist, to a substantial degree, of such exchange, the omission is noteworthy. It suggests once more that it is not what a child experiences or what interests a child, but how adequately a child can reconstruct reality symbolically that determines her or his dream content. The absence of a self-representation in children's dreams is further indicated by the finding that in only one of 53 dreams was it claimed that the self received an interaction initiation from another dream character. In the case of other characters' reception of initiation, there was no evidence suggesting that claims of such reception came from particularly credible children. In the case of favorable outcomes, there were indications to the contrary. The two children who reported other reception of antisocial interaction were high on self-reception of hostility at our nursery school and found their parents to be unsupportive.

In light of our overall findings on dream activities it is interesting to reconsider animal "models" of human dream experiencing. Sastre and Jouvet (1979) have described the behavior *during* REM sleep of cats whose brainstem mechanism of motor inhibition has been lesioned. These cats' "oneiric behavior" consisted of predatory attack, rage, fear, exploration, and so forth. The most frequently occurring REM behavior was attack. Extrapolating these observations to humans, one might assume that the substrate of human dreaming would be environmentally oriented drive states with a strong emotional component. Presumably this substrate might be most evident in the dream experiences of young children, whose cognitive repertoire for coping with such drive states would be least well developed. Our data indicate the total irrelevance of the Sastre-Jouvet animal model to the ontogeny of dream experiencing and suggest, instead, that it is to cognitive-symbolic developments largely if not totally unique to humans that one must look for "'explanations" of dreaming.

Since children reported so very little affective or interactive content at ages 3–5, *ratings* of hedonic tone (unpleasantness–pleasantness) could vary but little around our scale's neutral point and correlates of these ratings presented no compelling pattern. Setting-distortion ratings were significantly correlated ($r = .62$) with dream unpleasantness, however, perhaps suggesting again that children who were uncomfortable in the laboratory reflected their out-of-place feeling in their ill-formed dream settings. Contrary to the theory that dream distortion is motivated by anxiety, it is noteworthy that neither setting distortion nor character distortion (i.e., animal dreaming) was predicted by waking signs of anxiety or social incompetence. In fact, animal dreaming to the relative exclusion of (known) human dreaming was associated not only with cognitive skill, but also with an absence of anxiety in the laboratory and with social dominance in the nursery school.

SEX DIFFERENCES

REM dreams were reported on 21% of awakenings for girls (individual children varied in recall rate from 8% to 57%) and on 33% of awakenings for boys (a range from 8% to 73%). The difference was not statistically significant and should be viewed in light of the comparable magnitude of difference in average *age* of our girl and boy subjects, a difference of slightly less than one year. It seems likely that a year's difference in age at ages 3−5 would be associated with more important cognitive and behavioral differences than would a year's difference in age at any of the other age levels at which we studied these children.

There were no significant sex differences at ages 3−5 for any dream-content variable. However, one would not want to generalize from this empirical finding to the general proposition that there are no real differences between boys' and girls' earliest REM dreams. The problem is that recall was generally so limited, and our subject sample size sufficiently small, that it is not clear that we have adequate data to test hypotheses about sex differences in the *content* of REM dreams at very early ages. Perhaps the only kind of difference to which our test would have proven sensitive was an all-or-nothing, night-vs.-day order of difference. At that level, at least, there seemed to be no difference in the children's dreams as a function of their sex. Nor, of course, would it have been plausible to expect differences at that level. The relevant question regarding expectations of sex differences in dream content is how much difference there is in the course of boys' and girls' waking lives that might be reflected in their dream content.

In the area of cognitive variables, there is little evidence of significant sex differences in the 3−5 age range (Maccoby & Jacklin, 1974). In the area of "personality" behavior (e.g., aggressiveness, activity level), there are some indications of boy−girl differences at these same ages, but it is questionable whether they are of a magnitude and consistency that, in small samples of boys and girls, they would appear in the rather terse and limited samples of REM dreams that one can collect even from a substantially extended observation period. There is no question but that gender identity has been almost irrevocably established by ages 3−4 (Money & Ehrhardt, 1972; Green, 1974), and that there is sex-typing of behavior and differential parental socialization of boys and girls at these ages (Maccoby, 1975). However, in the recent fascination with sex *differences*, it probably is easy to lose sight of human communalities across the male−female dichotomy. One's reasonable expectations about sex differences in dream content, then, should be bounded not only by recognition of the difficulty in collecting adequate REM dream samples from young children but also by cognizance of broad similarities attributable to the fact that, by virtue of their common species and their common maturational and cultural status, one is studying subjects *all* of whom share much more than they experience discretely by virtue of their gender or gender role.

STIMULUS INCORPORATION

Results of our attempts to induce stimulus incorporation in Night-2 and Night-9 REM and NREM dreams during normative dream-study years generally were unproductive. In one sense this was a fortunate outcome, for it suggests that our "normative" dream data are not contaminated by atypical dreams attributable to our manipulations of the children during sleep. However, these results also are disappointing in two respects: (1) they failed to "validate" children's reports (by showing a link between a sleep stimulus and a postsleep report); and (2) they failed to convey much useful information about *how* dreams transform external stimuli—that is, they did not provide an experimental model for determining how dreams might transform their more usual mnemonic sources during the act of dream formation. I will consider shortly some reasons why I think our attempts at influencing dreams might have been relatively so unsuccessful.

First, however, let me describe our procedures and observations at ages 3–5. On Nights 2 and 9 of this year, I made, as usual, all awakenings at the child's bedside. When awakening criteria were satisfied, I entered the child's bedroom quietly, turned on the tape recorder at her or his bedside, and stimulated the child according to the schedule in Table 2.1, waited for 5 to 15 seconds, and then awoke the child, as usual, by calling her or his name, and attempted to solicit a dream report.

Throughout our studies, the children generally seemed unaware of the dream-influence attempts. When subjects awoke at the sound of my entering the bedroom, I initiated a dream interview at that point, and the awakening was not included in the incorporation analysis. Awakenings during stimulation were included in the analysis; on cotton and limb-manipulation awakenings, I acted as if my touching the child was a natural part of my trying to wake her or him up, and immediately proceeded to conduct the dream interview. On the water trials, there was no direct contact with the children; drops of water (at room temperature) were squeezed on their faces or scalps from a cotton ball hidden in my hand. After such trials, of course, children sometimes noticed dampness of their face or scalp, but I never was accused of responsibility therefor. One older boy once looked up at the ceiling quizzically, as if he thought there must be a leak somewhere. Water trials also were widely separated in time: 7–8 months between the REM and NREM trials within a normative dream-collection year, and more than a year separating one normative year's second trial from the next normative year's first one. No subject ever voiced the suspicion that attempts at dream influence were being made. Since the older children, at least, otherwise demonstrated little reticence in confronting me with procedural questions, it seems likely that few if any were aware of the nature or intent of our incorporation-trial methods.

The results at ages 3–5 were as follows. Of 42 REM awakenings, only 11 were associated with a dream report (26% REM recall); of 41 NREM awakenings, only four were associated with a dream report (10% NREM recall). These recall rates were highly similar to children's overall recall rates at this age, indicating that preawakening stimulation itself did not enhance reported dream activity. Transcripts of dream-bearing interviews later were given to two experienced judges (without information as to night, awakening, stimulus, subject, or age—transcripts were judged along with those of 9 to 11-year-olds serving in the same study year). The judges were told to "read the reports and attempt to judge from the nature of the report which stimulus [of the three experimentally employed manipulations] was applied before the awakening producing the report. If there seems to be no apparent connection with any of the stimuli, rate the report negative. *Don't hesitate to say there was no incorporation if you feel there was none.*" Judges further classified their positive "incorporation" judgments as "certain" or "uncertain." The judging procedure was similar to that of Foulkes and Rechtschaffen (1964) and permitted control for the baseline rate of occurrence of stimulus-related elements. Specifically, *net incorporation rate* was defined as the percentage of judgments of stimulus *A* when *A* was, in fact, the stimulus *minus* the percentage of judgments of stimulus *A* when *A* was not, in fact, the stimulus. Since "uncertain" judgments for the Year-1 data were more often wrong than right, analysis was limited to "certain" judgments.

Only one judge ever saw certain evidence of incorporation in *any* dream report collected at ages 3–5: She correctly identified water as the stimulus for Christopher's dream of fish floating in a bowl on the side of a river.[5] Net incorporation rates for two cotton-stimulus reports and seven limb-manipulation reports were 0% for both judges. For the six water-stimulus reports, Judge 1's net incorporation rate was 16.7% and Judge 2's was 0%. For all stimuli combined, Judge 1's net incorporation rate was 6.7%, Judge 2's was 0%. Regarding the *mode* of incorporation in our one "positive" case:

1   The stimulus almost seems to have "caused" the dream, that is, the dream looks like an "interpretation" of the stimulus rather than the stimulus having intruded on and been "incorporated" in, an already ongoing sequence of dream imagery.

[5]As he woke up, Christopher looked at the experimenter and told him, "It's starting to rain." During stimulation itself, his facial musculature twitched.

2   The "transformation" of water felt by the self to a dream of water external to the self may *not* be a defensively creative warding-off of the stimulus's noxious quality so much as it is a necessary consequence of the boy's having been unable more generally to construct effective self-representations in his dreams.

3   Yet the dream did not simply "reproduce" the stimulus; it gave it an imaginal context and, in that sense, demonstrated the possibility of cognitive elaboration during REM sleep, even during early childhood.

Why, otherwise, did our stimulation trials seem to be so ineffective? It might be held that the results indicate the essential invalidity of our children's reports at ages 3–5. I do not believe that this hypothesis explains our data satisfactorily, for incorporation attempts were, as we shall see, equally fruitless at later ages, when there was substantial independent evidence of report credibility. Evidently our overall results with the incorporation procedure say something more either about the genuine influencibility of children's dreams or about our judging procedure than they do about the "validity" of children's reports.

One inherent problem in using stimulus incorporation to validate very young children's dream reports is that it is difficult to obtain a sample of these reports substantial enough to determine incorporation rates with any reliability. Since such children report dreams on so relatively few REM awakenings and since they do *not* seem to rely more than adults do on external stimuli for dream content, one is, in effect, multiplying two very small numbers in trying to study stimulus incorporation (low REM recall *times* low incorporation rate when dreams are reported). If our judging procedures are judged adequate, perhaps the major point to be made about young children's use of external stimuli in dream formation is precisely that our limited dream samples do *not* suggest greater dependence of their dream content on external stimuli than is the case for adults. This is an interesting and important conclusion, for it suggests that, from its initial stage of development, dreaming is an autonomous, internally driven mental act. Dreaming does not begin as the processing of stray external stimuli present during REM sleep and only later become a truly self-regulated mental process.

There may be some question about these conclusions as they apply to our limb-movement stimulation. In general, effects of this stimulation may have been underestimated by our stimulation and judging procedure, since my stimulation of the child could be either of a leg *or* of an arm (the choice dictated by which limb was more exposed and, hence, accessible to direct manipulation). Thus it must have been difficult for judges to work with limb-reports, not knowing even which limb, in particular cases, was stimulated. In addition, at later ages (but not at ages 3–5), there was a substantial baseline rate of dream occurrence of manual and locomotor activity, the most obvious ways in which limb manipulations could be "incorporated" in dreams. At ages 3—5 the problem may have been that limb stimulation implied a dream response (movement) beyond the child's capability of representation in dreams. But *none* of these objections applies to water stimulation, which our data, overall, do not indicate to have been markedly more effective than limb movement at influencing children's dreams. Therefore, it does not seem that our judging or stimulation methods can explain the paucity of incorporations we observed.

Is there a suggestion in our data, at ages 3—5 and later, that children's dreams actually may be *less* susceptible to external influence than are adult dreams? Reports in the adult literature (e.g., Dement & Wolpert, 1958; Berger, 1963) seem to have shown substantially higher rates of REM stimulus incorporation than we *ever* were able to demonstrate for our children. But Dement and Wolpert's claim of 42% water-stimulus incorporation in REM reports must be spuriously high. It seems likely, from these authors' report, that their subjects were aware that they were being stimulated and either were aware or soon became aware that water was one of the stimuli being employed (water is not a stimulus that "goes away" when you stop applying it). Such knowledge, which we successfully kept from our children, may well sensitize a person to stimulus effects. In addition, their method of judgment neither was "blind" nor did it contain control for baseline appearance of water-related imagery.

Berger (1963) would seem to have demonstrated, in a much better controlled experiment, substantial incorporation of *verbal* stimuli in adults' dream reports. Dreamers themselves were correct 42% of the time, and an outside judge 38% of the time, in matching dream reports with the one name (out of four employed) that was played to the subject on tape during the REM sleep in which the dreams were dreamed. In a subsequent analysis 54% of reports were judged by Berger himself as having "a definite connection" with its associated stimulus. But Berger's 42% and 38% values are not *net* incorporation rates; where the probability of a correct match by chance is 25%, these values indicate a very modest 13—17% rate of incorporation in excess of chance matching. And his 54% figure not only does not correct for baseline effects, it also does not derive from a "blind" analysis and it includes "nonspecific" incorporations, that is, dreams of hearing names but no specific one. Thus at best, in our sense, Berger has demonstrated net incorporation of verbal stimuli in adult dreams at a rate of about 15%.

The difference between this last value and our own typical rates of net incorporation, although small, may be a real one. It might be due to his greater repetition of stimuli—he presented each name about 12 times, on the average, on each trial. More interesting theoretically is the possibility that the linguistic nature of his stimuli may have lent them some special effectiveness. (It seems unlikely that it was simply the auditory modality that was effective, since, even by their own generous judging procedures, Dement and Wolpert [1958] found little evidence of dream incorporation of a 1,000-Hertz tone.) If dream construction is largely a *verbal* process (Foulkes,

1978c), it may be that stimuli already coded in the dream's underlying language will affect dream content more than will stimuli received as tactile or kinesthetic sensations. In retrospect, I think I probably erred in designing our stimulus-incorporation experiments, at least from the point of view of achieving maximum incorporation and of learning thereby about typical *modalities* of incorporation. I chose stimuli I judged suitable from the point of view of their fit with the final stage of dream construction (the concrete sensorimotor elaboration of dream narratives) rather than with intermediate processes of dream construction (which may be verbal, even if the manifest dream generally is not experienced in words [Kerr & Foulkes, in press]).

A CHILD'S DREAMS: "DEAN"

While quantification is necessary in scientific analysis, numbers alone cannot convey an intimate feeling for phenomena such as dreams. Where I thought it useful, I have cited individual dreams to illustrate particular points. But these have been paraphrases rather than reports in the child's own words, and they have been citations in the context of making general points about dreams rather than of illuminating any individual child. To correct this sort of imbalance, which is characteristic of writings in which many statistical data must be summarized, I will close each chapter on dreams at a given age level with an extended citation of an individual child's dreams. To gain maximal usefulness from our *longitudinal* data, the same child will be followed through each of the years in which we studied him or her. The boy, whom I shall call Dean, was aged 4 years, 8 months, when first studied and was the oldest child in our "younger" longitudinal sample; the girl, whom I shall call Emily, was aged 10 years, 5 months, when first studied. Dean and Emily were brother and sister.

The reader naturally will wonder about the representativeness of these children and, most particularly, of their dreams. Why were these particular children's dreams selected for extended presentation here? I believe that inspection of these children's dreams will reveal that they are not unusual in that, generally, they well reflect certain statistical generalizations made about children in their age range. If these two children's dreams are atypical, it is in the sense that, as in most illustrative material in scientific presentations, they exemplify in rather sharper-than-average focus what can be said to be true more generally of the population from which they were drawn. This may be both because Dean and Emily were at the older extreme of their respective age groups in our study and because they were brighter than the average child in these same age groups (final study year I.Q.'s were 120 for Dean and 138 for Emily). Dean and Emily lived comfortably in a relatively affluent neighborhood, and their parents had clear "middle-class" aspirations for them. Both children were emotionally controlled, characterized more by quiet competence than by flamboyant impulsivity. Neither child, however, seemed to have sacrificed personal identity or emotional growth in the process of attempting to fulfill high parental ideals. In sum, Dean and Emily are most representative of intelligent, healthy, normally developing children who have a good sense of self, good self-control, a good family life, good relationships with their peers, and good academic achievement. In these respects, whatever bias has entered into their selection as specimen subjects here runs in directions generally quite contrary to those reflected in clinical literature on children's dreams, a contrast that should prove instructive.

One of the main reasons for selecting these two children for specimen dream analysis is that, in general, they impressed me as having been conscientious and credible dream reporters. Thus they meet perhaps the major criterion for extended data presentation here, namely that, in discussing dream reports, one has reasonable certainty that one is, in fact, also discussing dream experiences.

During his first year of dream study, Dean reported only two dreams, both on REM awakenings:

1-2[6] I was asleep and in the bathtub. [Was this in your bathtub at home?] Yes. [Was there anyone else in the dream besides you?] No. [Could you see yourself there?] Uhhh, no. [I mean, did you have like a picture of the bathtub and you could see your body inside the tub?] No. [How did you feel?] Happy.

7-3 I was dreaming I was sleeping at a co-co stand . . . where you get Coke from. [Was this some particular stand that you know, or was this just made-up in the dream?] Just made-up. [Was there anybody else in the dream besides you?] No. [Were you doing anything besides sleeping?] No.

Perhaps the most remarkable facet of Dean's first-year performance was that, despite his age and intelligence vis-à-vis his peers, he recalled so few REM dreams. On experimental nights I found him often difficult to awaken, but, once awakened, he generally appeared comprehending and motivated. It may be that his low recall rate was simply a function of his low arousability, but such a meager performance from such a relatively old, bright, and generally interested child surely gives one some pause in evaluating the reports of the much younger but much more prolific "dream" reporters about whose dream data I earlier have raised doubt. It is possible—we never will know—that, studied a year or two earlier, Dean also would have been a relatively fecund animal dreamer. But it seems equally possible that he

[6]The figure 1-2 means Night 1, Awakening 2; similar codes will be used to identify all individual dream reports subsequently discussed for Dean and Emily. In the interest of economy, entire interview transcripts will not be presented here. Although excerpted, all interview protocols presented are verbatim transcriptions of the major portions of the original nocturnal interview. The interviewer's questions are bracketed, and my current interpolations are parenthesized.

simply might never have claimed such a dream, or any other, and that he might have been correct in these dream-negative claims (cf. the discussion above). Dean's absence of sleep-onset reports, that is, dream claims in circumstances in which arousability was not a problem, is highly suggestive of the possibility that even cognitively talented children generally do *not* dream during REM sleep even relatively late in the preschool years.

The dreams Dean did report clearly fit many of the generalized descriptions given above of "preoperational dreaming":

1 They are static.
2 They are egocentric.
3 They draw heavily on organic/bodily sensations or states (sleep).
4 They are, however, proto-narratized and fictional—that is, they construct a situation neither currently true nor more generally totally plausible in which the body state is to be represented.[7]
5 They are not, on the other hand, terribly bizarre—there are no deviations from the physical laws characteristic of everyday reality and there are no fantastic characters or archetypical images. The evident sources of dream images are familiar pieces of the child's everyday world.
6 There is relatively little representation of feeling or impulse, certainly no indication of terrifying emotions or of childish rage or greed, and so forth, running helplessly out of control.

SUMMARY

There is no evidence in our sample of 3–5-year-olds' dream reports to support clinical, anecdotal, or retrospective observations to the effect that young children's dreams are particularly rich in their imagery or are particularly impulsive in content or frightening in quality. The deficiencies of clinical or anecdotal-home dream samples already have been noted, both earlier in this chapter (e.g., the possibility that many of children's frightening-dream claims are, in fact, reports of mental experiences conjured up during slow arousal from sleep or in frank wakefulness) and in Chapter 1, where the sampling problems associated with "spontaneously recalled" dream samples were highlighted. Our Year-2 home vs. laboratory dream comparison for the group of children studied in this chapter would seem to rule out the possibility that our dream-recall or dream-content findings are substantial artifacts of our own distinctive methods in implementing a more deliberate

---

[7]It appears possible that both sleeping-in-a-strange-place dreams may be dream elaborations of the perceived novelty of sleeping in the laboratory rather than at home. In this respect, their specific content may have been laboratory influenced, but what they have to say about dream development more generally still may be accurate and generalizable.

and representative sampling plan for studying preschoolers' typical dream experiences. If the children's dreams reported here do not match our own impressions of our own earliest dreamlife, we would do well to remind ourselves of how distant these experiences now are, and of how liable they were to misunderstanding at the time of their alleged occurrence and they have been to subsequent embellishment or reconstruction. If the children's dreams reported here do not jibe with our impression of how imaginative children are, we would do well also to ask ourselves how much of this "imaginativeness" derives from the odd effect that children's inappropriate responses or immature understandings have upon us, and how much really represents creative narrative or other integrative skill. Dean's dream reports, for instance, do not seem out of line with the "imagination" he revealed in telling waking stories to Pickford (1963) Projective Test cards. For instance, in card 12 of the Pickford series, an evidently contrite child stands by a doll whose head is severed from its body, as a woman points her finger scoldingly at the child. Dean's "story" was that:

> His head came off. [Can you tell me anything else that is happening?] Nothing else. That's all.

This "story" is quite typical of responses we received from 3- to 5-year-olds in tests of waking imagination.

The really interesting story told by 3- to 5-year-olds' dreams is not about their vivid fantasy life, fueled by their natural creativity and their polymorphous impulsivity, but about the way in which children's earliest dreamlife is constrained and impoverished by their cognitive immaturity. As we have seen, there is a strong "preoperational" quality in preschoolers' dreams, as well as the suggestion that the limitations of this level of thought organization not only affect what is dreamed but also seriously limit the likelihood of dream experiencing itself. Our preschoolers' dream content proved to be remarkably defective in inventiveness and in its ability to portray a symbolic and dynamic reconstruction of the children's waking social world. What "body" symbolism there was in these children's dreams, moreover, was not an intricate maze of Freudian body zones, but a straightforward, holistic source of rather simple wants and pleasures, such as sleeping and eating. Asleep, our children thought about as complexly as their cohorts generally have been shown, by careful empirical observation, to be able to think awake, and neither as complexly and diversely as they can act when awake nor as complexly and symbolically as many clinicians would have us believe they can think when awake.

CHAPTER 4 _____

Ages 5 to 7

The same children whose dream reports were the subject matter of the previous chapter were restudied, following nearly identical procedures, two years later, at ages 5–7. At the start of their third study year, the median girl's age was 5 years, 1 month, and the median boy's age was 6 years, 0 months. During their third study year, all 14 children were attending school, either half-day kindergarten (five girls, two boys) or full-day first grade (five boys, two girls).

By the same criteria mentioned in the previous chapter, three children (all boys) had achieved "operational" status on our scale of cognitive maturation, and many of the other children were not far behind (the median child's scale score now was 6.0 [vs. 2.5 at ages 3–5], with a range from 2 to 8 [vs. 0 to 5 at ages 3–5]). On retest, 12 of the 14 children had increased their summed scale-score on the Laurendeau-Pinard tests, while two children had maintained a constant placement. Four girls and six boys were operational on at least one of the three Laurendeau-Pinard subtests; four boys (and no girls) were operational on two subtests. Thus our 5- to 7-year-olds generally were in transition from preoperational to operational thinking.

The child who is in transition to operational thinking is beginning the coherent organization of inner representations (symbols) by means of self-initiated plans or programs. No longer does thought seem largely to be driven by, and largely to be at the whim of, momentary circumstance. While the contrast with preoperational thinking can be overstated—for it is not as if the child suddenly passes from mental chaos to mental structure—there is a qualitative difference between the fuzzy and somewhat ad hoc organizational principles of preoperational thought and the precise and systematized principles of operational thought. In the transition to operationalism, egocentrism declines as rational rules begin to replace self-references as dominant forces in thought organization. With this decentering from momentary mood states or circumstances of the self, there is increasing comprehension of the realm of the not-self, of both the material and the social worlds lying outside the child's own skin.

The operational thinking of early school years is, however, considered *concrete* in the sense that the child's mental programs "operate" only on sense data or palpable facts. The early operational child is less abstract philosopher and daydreamer, more pragmatist and tinkerer. Idle speculation or "what if" thinking runs against the grain. The child seems to want first to get a good sound grasp of empirical phenomena and to leave the theorizing to later or to others.

THE REPORTING OF DREAMS

As it turned out, the cognitive maturation of our children since their first study year proved to be associated not with more *frequent* dream reporting, but with more *extensive* dream reporting. That is, there was not a significant increase from ages 3−5 in the rate with which dreams were reported, but substantially more content was reported when dreams were described.

Pooling over all awakenings of all 5- to 7-year-olds, dreams were reported on 31% of REM awakenings, 31% of sleep-onset awakenings, and 8% of NREM awakenings. In each case these figures were larger, but not significantly so, than recall rates at ages 3−5. Also in each case the boys (who, of course, were somewhat older as a group than the girls) reported dreams more often than the girls. For REM sleep the difference was 38% vs. 25%; for sleep onset, 43% vs. 19%; and for NREM sleep, 10% vs. 6%. However, as it was based on a maximum of only three awakenings per child, even the largest difference for sleep-onset reporting was not statistically significant.

As also had been true at ages 3−5, sleep-onset and REM report rates were not significantly different one from the other, while both sleep-onset and REM report rates were significantly higher than NREM rates. These findings all are consistent with data from adult dreamers and suggest at least some measure of "accurate" discrimination of mentational properties of the different sleep states.[1]

Despite the failure of the group data to indicate it at a statistically reliable level, I feel that there were some signs at ages 5−7 of increased occurrence or accessibility of the fact of REM dreaming. First, the pooled reporting of sleep-onset mentation had increased considerably—up to REM levels, in fact. For adults sleep-onset dreaming is reported at least as frequently as is REM dreaming, and, because sleep-onset awakenings are associated with quickest arousal times and with the best comprehension during dream interviews, it also may be true for children that sleep-onset report rates set a kind of upper-bound for credible REM report rates. On this hypothesis: (1) even the modest pooled REM report rate at ages 3−5 (27%) must have been inflated by false positives; (2) the pooled REM report rate at ages 5−7 (31%) was much less susceptible to spurious inflation by false claims of dreams; and (3) our data must, therefore, underestimate the true rise in dream occurrence/accessibility between ages 3−5 and 5−7.

---

[1]Once again, too, the pooled NREM light-sleep report rate (10%) slightly exceeded the NREM deep-sleep report rate (7%).

Second, when one examines median-child rates of REM reporting, which, unlike pooled rates, are not liable to substantial fluctuation as a function of what one or two children are doing, there *was* a moderately substantial rise in REM dream reporting: from 15% to 31% (and in sleep-onset reporting: from 0% to 17%). At ages 5−7 it no longer was true, as it had been earlier, that pooled and median-child REM report rates were discrepant. Earlier the pooled rate reflected a report distribution containing a few high-rate and many low-rate reporters. By ages 5−7, however, REM reporting had become a hurdle that most children could pass more than once or twice a year. This was so, interestingly enough, despite the fact that one boy (with two first-year REM reports) and one girl (with one first-year REM report) reported *no* REM dreams at all at ages 5−7.

Third, several children about whose reports we had few doubts as to credibility showed dramatic rises in REM report rate from ages 3−5 to 5−7. One boy's rate increased from 8% to 60%, for example, and one girl's from 15% to 67%. These children were not, obviously, representative of their groups. In light of later data, however, showing a significant *group* increase in REM report rate from ages 5−7 to 7−9, such findings indicate the possibility of true increases in the occurrence/accessibility of REM dreaming for individual children as early as ages 6−7 (the boy was age 6 years, 0 months, and the girl, 6 years, 6 months, at the start of the third study year).

DREAM-REPORT CREDIBILITY

From the children's advances in age and general mental development since the first study year, and from the fact that they now were being trained at school to acquiesce to adult requests to report facts of less than immediate interest to them, one might have predicted both that the children would report more dreams and that they would report them better by their third study year. As we have seen, the former prediction was not supported in any unqualified way by our data. That fact in itself may have something interesting to say about the credibility of REM dreams reported at ages 5−7: Although a number of factors had altered in ways so as to have enhanced acquiescence to, and comprehension of, our experimental task, report rates did *not* increase significantly as a consequence. This observation would seem to indicate that: (1) report rates were not simply functions of children's comprehension of our task or of their experience with comparable tasks elsewhere, and (2) the continuingly low absolute rate at which the children reported REM dreams may have been a function of continuing relative absence of such experiences. Perhaps the cognitive maturational factors that would have permitted the frequent generation of well-formed dreams, factors that as such depend neither on age nor on socialization to extrafamilial influences, constituted the limiting influence. On this hypothesis, either by age or by "stage" criteria, one would have predicted that the expansion of REM dream frequency would have occurred between ages 5—7 and ages 7—9 (and that, as noted above, was our finding).

If one believes that 5- to 7-year-olds' REM reports might, prima facie, be considered more credible than 3- to 5-year-olds', then, given the fact that overall report rates had not increased significantly from ages 3—5 to 5—7, one would not have expected much individual consistency in report rate across this time span. Children who originally falsely claimed dreams should have shown reduced rates of REM reporting (and, as we have seen, that happened for the girl most strongly suspected of confabulation at age 3—5), while other children (such as the boy and the girl mentioned at the end of the last section) might honestly have been increasing theirs. In fact, there was not substantial or significant intercorrelation of recall rates at ages 3—5 and 5—7 ($r = .38$).

It would be nice, however, to have more direct evidence of enhanced report credibility at ages 5—7. Our correlational data provide such evidence. Among the other correlates of REM report rate at ages 5—7 (high social class, democratically organized family, increased self-control) were several cognitive measures. Specifically, children talented at Wechsler Block Design and another task (Matching Familiar Figures) requiring both effective cognitive self-regulation and visuospatial analysis were high-rate REM reporters. Increases in REM recall from ages 3—5 to 5—7 were associated with comparable family variables and with still another visuospatial (McGee, 1979) measure: Children's Embedded Figures Test.[2]

We believe that the cognitive correlates of REM report rates at ages 5—7 are important in two contexts. First, because they are positive, they help to establish the general credibility of the children's reports. Because dreaming is a cognitive skill, one would expect especially skilled children to be reporting dreams especially often. Second, because of the nature of the particular cognitive variables associated with REM report rates (i.e., "visuospatial" measures more plausibly implicated in the construction of dreams than in their remembrance or telling), it does not seem as likely that "smarter" children are telling dreams more often because they remember them better or have better verbal facility in describing them as it does that they are telling dreams more often because they are *having* them more often. This is a point for which, as we shall see in Chapters 7 and 8, we have even more impressive evidence.

In respect both to their bearing on report credibility and to their seeming indication that it is dream occurrence rather than dream remembering or dream describing that may be at issue, the cognitive correlates of REM report rates at ages 5—7 tended to be replicated at subsequent age levels. No

---

[2]Consistent with the false-negative hypothesis at ages 3—5 were correlations of increases in REM report rate between ages 3—5 and 5—7 with increases in expressive behavior in the laboratory over that same period and with nondependence on adults at ages 5—7.

cognitive correlate of REM report rate at later ages was ever negative in direction, and at every later age level, some cognitive variable was correlated with REM report rate. Among later-observed Wechsler subscale correlates of REM report rate, Block Design was most frequently represented. These convergences, too, enhance the credibility of the REM reports of the 5- to 7-year olds. To the extent that one wants to consider adolescents' reports credible, by reason of their comprehension of the reporting task and their ability and motivation to perform that task adequately, by virtue of commonly patterned correlates, it seems that 5- to 7-year-olds' reports must be accorded equal credibility. In fact, we believe that, from ages 5–7 on, report credibility is not a *general* problem attaching to our data. And, as we saw in Chapter 3, this early stabilization of adequate reporting behavior can be helpful in determining what might or might not have been adequate reporting behavior even *before* ages 5–7.

While we are discussing report credibility, there is another significant point to be made. Although NREM and sleep-onset reporting were not terribly extensive at ages 5–7, these generic non-REM reports were, by the correlational evidence, at least as credible as the children's REM reports. As was the case for REM reports, there was very little consistency between NREM reporting at ages 3–5 and 5–7 ($r = .20$), and it was at the latter age level that positive cognitive correlates emerged—much more strongly, in fact, for NREM than for REM reporting. Perhaps, as pooled recall-rate data suggest, "making" NREM dreams requires even more skill (because it goes against the grain of concurrent physiological passivity) than does "making" REM dreams (because of supporting physiological activation). The NREM correlates included Block Design and the Children's Embedded Figures Test. Measures of effective visuospatial analysis also were correlated with absolute levels and increases in sleep-onset recall. Children who "improved" in NREM reporting between ages 3–5 and 5–7 were those who had the most improved and the best absolute comprehension of what dreams are (the Laurendeau-Pinard Dream Measure); they also were among the older children in their age group.

These sorts of data (also, as we shall see, repeated at later age levels) argue strongly against the hypothesis that children were mistaken or confabulating when they claimed dreams outside of REM periods. They suggest instead that report credibility stabilizes not only for REM but also for non-REM reporting at ages 5–7. In one sense, the convergence of REM and non-REM correlates is not surprising, because it was statistically significant at ages 5–7 that high-rate REM reporters also were high-rate NREM reporters ($r = .63$) and high-rate sleep-onset reporters ($r = .77$). These findings (also generally repeated at later age levels) indicate that, to the degree one accepts children's REM reports as being credible from ages 5–7 on, one must perforce accept their non-REM reports as also being generally credible.

THE CHANGING CONTENT OF REM DREAMS

Between ages 3−5 and 5−7, reported dreams changed dramatically, as the children seemed to take major steps toward organizing their dream experiences in the same way that older children and adults do. One indication of their progress in this regard is that, comparing younger and older study groups for the same study years, 3- to 5-year-olds' REM dreams were judged significantly different from older-group REM dreams in 55 content categories, while 5- to 7-year-olds' REM dreams were judged significantly different from older-group REM dreams in only 15 content categories.

How, specifically, had the children's REM dreams changed? There was a significant reduction in themes relating to sleep or fatigue. In place of such themes were significant increases in social interaction and physical movement in dream imagery. In short, REM dreams had changed from static, self-centered imagery to a narrative format in which characters moved about and interacted in a dynamic dream "world." Befitting this change, the mean length of the typical child's report almost tripled (from 14 words of substantive content at ages 3−5 to 41 words at ages 5−7).[3] Table 4.1 displays those scoring-system variables that significantly differentiated the younger group's dreams at ages 3−5 and 5−7.

While the general trend of longitudinal difference was for age 5−7 dreams to be more "dreamlike," in our (adult) sense, several of the individual variables listed in the table require or deserve additional comment. The decrease in unclassifiable settings—that is, in settingless dreams or in dreams with very vague settings—is probably some unknown mixture of fact and artifact. The possibility of artifact is suggested by a parallel decrease in unclassifiable settings between ages 9−11 and 11−13, that is, for the older group in the same two study years. As suggested earlier, either I failed to probe settings as well in the first study year as later on or the fact of the children's *being* in an initially unfamiliar setting (the laboratory) contributed to the relatively high incidence in the first study year of settings judges deemed vague or unclassifiable. The probability of fact, as well as artifact, is suggested by observation that all other elements of dream content seem to be increasingly well-fleshed out by ages 5−7, and there seems to be no reason to imagine that settings would be an exception to this trend.

The increase in "recreational" settings largely reflects the increases in motoric and interactive content, for we defined such settings in terms of "play" activities rather than in terms of physical place (i.e., if a child was

[3]Interestingly, the median girls' report (50 words) was twice as long as the median boys' report (25 words). Because of high intrasex variability, however, the difference was not significant. (Also, only six boys and six girls reported REM dreams.) In evaluating the appreciable but nonsignificant sex difference in REM word count, it should be remembered that the boys reported *more* dreams and, hence, may have been creating or accessing fragmentary dreams at times when the younger girl sample may have been unable to do so.

Table 4.1 **Dream Variables Showing a Significant Difference in Magnitude or Frequency of Occurrence Between Ages 3–5 and 5–7**

Significantly Higher at Ages 3−5	Significantly Higher at Ages 5−7
Settings Unclassifiable	Word count
	Characters Male strangers

States
  Fatigue, dreamer
  Fatigue, either
	Settings
	  Recreational

	Activities
	  Vision, other
	  Manual, other
	  Manual, either
	  Locomotor, dreamer
	  Locomotor, other
	  Locomotor, either
	  Any motor, dreamer
	  Any motor, other
	  Any motor, either

	States
	  Approach social, other
	  Approach social, either
	  Approach object, other
	  Approach object, either
	  Attack social, other
	  Attack social, either

	Outcomes
	  Unfavorable, other mediated, other
	  Unfavorable, other mediated, either
	  Favorable, other mediated, other
	  Favorable, other mediated, either
	  Favorable, any, other
	  Favorable, any, either

playing a game in his front yard, the setting was designated "recreational"; if he merely was sitting there, it was designated "home, own").[4] The significant rise in the incidence of male strangers should be viewed in the context of a parallel, although nonsignificant, rise in the elaboration of female strangers. Also, throughout childhood boys consistently dreamed

[4]As the example indicates, our category of home settings included not merely "in-house" but also "by-house" locales. This makes it inappropriate to use our setting data to test Erikson's (1963) hypothesis about sex differences in the use of open vs. closed spaces.

more frequently of male than of female strangers,[5] and at ages 5−7, the boys were older and the more frequent reporters of dreams.

Perhaps the most significant pattern to be observed in Table 4.1 is how most activity or interaction-initiation/outcome increases from ages 3−5 to 5−7 are for dream characters other than the self. The dreamer herself or himself is relatively lacking as an active participant in children's earliest dream scenarios. This raises the interesting question as to whether 5- to 7-year olds even are generally *capable* of effective self-representation in their dreams, a question to which I shall return shortly.

THE CONTENT AND CORRELATES OF REM DREAMS

Having seen how 5- to 7-year-olds' dream reports had *changed* from those of ages 3−5, we now need to examine in more detail what children's dreams had *become* at ages 5−7, as indexed by the children's verbal reports of them.

Length

As we have seen, dreams became longer, although they were not yet as long as they would be at later ages. The intermediate length of the typical report suggests that, although children had moved to a true narrative format of dream experience—a sequencing of interrelated activities—their stories still lacked the structural complexity of adult or later-childhood dreaming. That the children at ages 5−7 were reporting not only longer dreams, but also dreams that were qualitatively different from "reliable" dream reports collected at ages 3−5, further suggests that the word-count increase cannot by any means be attributed entirely simply to better memories or descriptions of dreams. There must also have been some enhancement in dream construction itself.

Probably this enhancement was reflected, for different children, in different ways. At ages 3−5 children's REM word counts rarely lay outside a small range of low values: 11 of the 14 children had means of 18 words or less per REM dream, and the highest individual mean was 32 words. By ages 5−7 mean REM word counts varied considerably more from child to child—from 21 words to 76 words per dream. Interestingly, the former figure applied to the boy who increased his REM recall rate from 8% to 60%, as well as to Dean, whose REM recall rate increased from 13% to 33%. Superimposed on general increases in reported-dream length, then, was the fact that some children seemed to be either detecting or generating "additional" dreams of a more fragmentary character. Even where recall rate did not show much change over time, some children increased their mean REM word count

---

[5]Hall (1963) has noted comparable sex differences in self-reported home dreams as we have found in laboratory-monitored REM dreams. For male dreamers, strangers generally are male, while for female dreamers, strangers are equally likely to be female as male.

substantially while others did not. Were some children simply better describing comparably fragmentary dreams, while others were describing "better" dreams? Clearly, when, as at ages 5–7, different children are following different paths of dream-report development, it will be somewhat more difficult to talk of typical dream contents than at stabilized periods of dream manifestation.

Who told the longest REM dreams at ages 5–7? Only two waking variables correlated significantly with REM word counts, but their nature suggests other than chance relationship. Children who gave long, spontaneous descriptions of a known film stimulus, and who were judged high in language quality at our nursery school, gave longer REM reports. Increases from ages 3–5 in report length also correlated positively with children's judged language quality. These correlates are consistent with the hypothesis that longer reports come from more verbally skilled waking reporters, but they do not rule out the hypothesis of real differences in the quality of narrative generation during sleep. In either case, it is comforting that task-irrelevant garrulousness, as such[6] – the sheer force to talk, regardless of what one has to say or how well one says it—was *not* a correlate of differences in REM report rate.

Characters

Family members appeared considerably but not significantly more often in children's dreams at ages 5–7 than at 3–5. They were characters more often in girls' dreams than in boys' dreams, but (as we shall have to remind ourselves rather often) the girls were younger and less socially experienced outside the family world. As throughout childhood, it was the restricted nuclear family of American society that participated most often in dream characterization: aunts, uncles, cousins, and grandparents appeared relatively seldom in the children's dreams. Consistently positive Wechsler correlates of the appearance of such familiar figures argue, moreover, that in the early narrative dreaming of childhood it takes some skill to be able to represent in one's dreams even those persons one knows best. This suggestion has implications, to be discussed later, for claims of having dreamed of less-familiar known persons or of persons not known at all to the child (i.e., human strangers). It may be significant that cognitive correlates of family-member dream reporting (dream representation?) tended to be "performance" rather than "verbal." The particular Wechsler subtest most directly implicated was Geometric Design.

But our correlational data also suggest—as seemed more generally to be true during childhood—that the appearance of parents or other family members in children's dreams reflected the probable salience of the child's family-life situation. In answering the question "Whom do we dream

[6]For example, ratings for talkativeness at the nursery school or in the presleep period in the laboratory.

about?'' Calvin Hall (1966) replied: ''We dream about people who are associated in some way with our personal conflicts'' (p. 33). In support of this
postion, we seem to have found that the more potential there is for parent
salience, and parent–child conflict, by virtue of nonsupportive or inconsistent parental attitudes, the more often children dream of their parents. Specifically, at ages 5–7 paternal control and distance (a lack of comradely or
equalitarian attitudes) and maternal pushiness (reflected in the PARI ''Approval of Activity'' scale) were associated with frequent dreaming of parents.

These correlates were, however, relatively nondiscriminating as to the
age or sex of particular family members of whom the child dreamed, and this
suggests another important conclusion generally supported by all of our
longitudinal observations. In the ''decision tree'' in the dreaming child's
mind, the basic choice seems to be ''family'' vs. ''not,'' with little discrimination made among family members once the family branch is selected. In
dreams, as in waking life, if there is one family member, the others generally
seem to be present as well. Thus our correlates of any one family-member
subclass look about the same as those for any other such subclass. As judged
by the manifest content of the dreams, children do not seem to draw hard
and fast distinctions between male and female members of the family environment. Family is family: a unit, rather than a highly differentiated set of
social roles or a highly distinctive set of object choices in the Freudian
melodrama of early sexual development.

As might have been expected from the parental-attitude correlates of
family dreaming, family dreamers themselves were dependent children; at
our nursery school they initiated interaction and association with adults.
Whether as cause or effect, they also received relatively much, and increasing amounts of, hostile interaction from their peers. The three-way association, then, was: dependency-making parents, dependent children, and
dreaming relatively often of parents and other family members.[7]

In general, claims of known nonfamily human characters did not increase
appreciably from ages 3–5 to ages 5–7, while claims of unknown human
characters (''strangers'') did so increase. The employment of known peers
began, at ages 5–7, to show a trend which later would become statistically
significant: boys claimed to dream mostly of male peers, and girls of female
peers. There were negative cognitive correlates of claims of having dreamed
of known nonfamily peers, and of known nonfamily persons more generally,
however, which may cast some doubt on the credibility of those claims.
Claims of the most frequently reported stranger class (any male), however,
were associated with positive status on several cognitive measures, includ-

---

[7]That a comparable pattern was observed for the relatively much less frequent dreaming of
parents at ages 3–5 might be used to support the credibility of those earlier reports, at least to
the extent that the reports of the 5- to 7-year-olds are regarded as generally credibile. However,
family dreaming at ages 3–5 did not have positive cognitive correlates.

ing our test of the description from memory of pictorial stimuli. In conjunction with the already-mentioned findings of positive cognitive correlates of dream claims of family-member participation, these results form a somewhat curious pattern.

It seems to take skill to dream of highly familiar (family) and highly unfamiliar (stranger) persons—or, at least, intellectually skilled children dream of such persons relatively often—while the less gifted children seem most often to dream of friends and acquaintances. One would have imagined that the level of cognitive skill required to construct strangers—whole people never before encountered, or encountered so infrequently as to be unidentifiable—would be greater than that required to reconstruct relatively familiar persons. On this seemingly reasonable hypothesis, the growth of dreamworld human characterization past the family level might have been expected to proceed as follows: (1) known persons will show a substantial increase in incidence before strangers do; (2) initially, cognitive correlates of reporting such persons will be positive—only the more skilled children will be able symbolically to reconstruct persons less familiar than family members. But our data disconfirm both of these predictions.

We believe a slightly more complex hypothesis does encompass these data, as well as some character findings at later ages. It suggests that reports of "strangers" carry different meanings before and after the achievement of fully operational thinking. Specifically, before this stage strangers may represent construction failures—relatively familiar persons not imagined with sufficient veridicality to be imaged as such—while past this stage strangers may represent construction successes—the fulfillment of an attempt to create genuine, fully articulated imagery of persons one never personally has encountered. Thus at ages 5−7 we might expect that children would be attempting to broaden the characterization of their newly kinematic dream imagery. But it is not easy to "develop" versatile images of less frequently encountered persons or objects (Piaget & Inhelder, 1966); thus there is general failure at ages 5−7 to achieve this goal. We might assume, then, that children who are more accurate at describing and remembering pictured events (recall the Description Test correlations with the reported incidence of any male strangers) report, accurately, that they were not successful at imaging known nonfamily persons (i.e., they report construction-failure strangers; note that the fact that most strangers at ages 5−7 *cannot* be precisely identified as to age is consistent with a construction-failure hypothesis). Less talented and precise children (recall the negative cognitive correlates of the reported incidence of known persons) might, at this same age, gloss over their construction failures and, during their dream "reports," more readily assimilate ill-formed dream images to persons known to them in waking life.

If *this* hypothesis were correct, one might make the following predictions about known-person vs. stranger incidence at ages 7−9 (i.e., at the next stage of dream development): (1) known, nonfamily character claims will have positive cognitive correlates—that is, by this age the more talented children will be able, in fact, to represent acquaintances veridically in their dreams; and (2) stranger incidence now will have generally negative cognitive correlates—the less talented children will report, accurately, that they have not been able to image "real" people. An assumption underlying these predictions is that, with increased age and more years of school exposure, all children will describe with increasing accuracy the sorts of characters they, in fact, have been able to construct.[8] As we shall see, these predictions generally are borne out by our data.

This revised hypothesis of factors influencing nonfamily human characterization at ages 5–7 would lead one to expect that it must have been somewhat different children who were claiming to dream of known nonfamily members and of human strangers. The differential correlates of these two character classes suggest that this must have been the case. In fact, at ages 5–7 as well as more generally in our longitudinal series, the relative incidence of male or female known persons was not correlated either significantly or strongly with the corresponding relative incidence of male or female strangers.[9] This, in turn, suggests that, at least early in dream development when dream characterization is expanding, there is no general tendency to simply fill one's dreams with more people, regardless of their reported characteristics.

Clearly it would be erroneous to imply that it only is cognitive *skill* that is implicated in the early expansion of characterization in children's dreamlife. Across the years in which we studied the younger-group children, the *knowledge base* on which they would have to rely to create a wider range of human characters also must have been increasing tremendously. But our data do indicate that, in early dream development, having a knowledge base regarding classes of persons, defined simply in terms of contact hours with them is never a *sufficient* condition for using that base in constructing dream images. Necessary, yes; sufficient, no. This is where cognitive skill—the capability of symbolically re-creating what one has experienced—seems to be critical.

At ages 3–5, 38% of the children's REM reports included animal characters; at ages 5–7 the figure was 36%. Thus although animals no longer provided the dominant presence in dreams that generally lacked other characters, at ages 5–7 they were a continuingly important part of children's reported dream scenarios. As noted earlier, since children's dreams seemed generally credible at ages 5–7, the suggestion is that young children's dreams really *are* peculiarly prone to include animal characters. At ages 5–7 it was the (generally older) boys who more often reported dreams with

---

[8]Longitudinal data from our Description Test demonstrated consistent gains in descriptive accuracy for younger-group children across the years in which we studied them.

[9]Exceptions were for male characters at ages 11–13 ($r = .48$) and for female characters at ages 13–15 ($r = .53$, both correlations significant).

animals. If one accepts the children's earlier animal reports, it would seem that this higher usage of animals might be expressive of differences in the life situations of boys and girls at ages 5−7; if one does not accept those earlier reports, it may simply reflect the boys' greater skill at portraying animals at an age where all dream reports are first becoming generally credible.

One can read our correlational data either way. Two cognitive-skill variables *were* positively correlated with the relative incidence of animals at ages 5−7, and that observation, coupled with the fact that the boys were older than the girls, suggests the possibility that these animal reports—and not the children's earlier ones—should be considered the first truly credible general indications of high-rate animal characterization in children's dreams.[10] Behaviorally, on the other hand, impulsive and somewhat socially immature children reported dreams with animals relatively most often at ages 5−7. Thus one could see these reports as symbolizing children's problems of impulse control, and interpret the boys' greater use of animal characters (marginally significant, $p < .10$, 2-tail, for "indigenous"—locally distributed but undomesticated—animals) as reflecting the fact that, for whatever reasons of heredity or socialization, impulsivity is a greater problem for boys than for girls.

Several bits of evidence are consistent with the impulsivity hypothesis.

1   Boys' dreams were particularly low in self-participation at ages 5−7, and their longitudinally decreased self-participation was concomitant with an increase in animal characters. One might see these animals as portraying the (missing) self, objectified in an appropriate symbolic form.

2   Certain temporal shifts within the animal subcategories suggest that dream representations at ages 5−7 are increasingly of animals that children can control or manage, hence that might portray the real-life requirements of increased impulse control. Specifically, compared to ages 3−5, at ages 5−7 there are more pets but fewer barnyard animals (both differences marginally significant at $p < .10$, 2-tail).

3   The attitudes of the parents of high-rate animal dreamers at ages 5−7 were such that impulse regulation may have been a problem for these children: distant, controlling fathers yet mothers who were reluctant to discipline their children.

4   There was some support, but it was relatively weak, for Hall and Nordby's (1972) hypothesis of an association of animal dreaming with dream aggression. Aggression in dreams (Attack Social, either) and the overall rate of animal dreaming were, from the time at which aggression themes began to appear at least moderately often in children's dreams (i.e., ages 5−7) until ages 9−11, positively correlated (ages 5−7, $r = .31$; ages 7−9,

---

[10]Longitudinal correlational data, however, suggest that it might be difficult to accept children's animal reports at ages 5−7 but reject them at ages 3−5. It was, by and large, the same children claiming animal characters in both study years ($r = .66$, a significant correlation).

$r = .57$; ages $9-11$, $r = .40$; with the ages 7–9 correlation attaining significance).[11]

One might, of course, accept both hypotheses: The use of animal characters at ages 5–7 reflects *both* cognitive skill in being able symbolically to represent animals in images *and* the requirement that some appropriate not-self characters be found to portray one's current real-life concerns. Perhaps both supported by their relative cognitive competence *and* forced by their real-life conflicts, impulsive children invent their own "fairy tales," dreams that, like so many other of the fairy tales with which children are familiar, deal with the theme that impulsiveness must be bounded by control.

As an alternative interpretation of what animals might symbolize in young children's dreams, it might be proposed that they are disguised representations of the child's parents. However, at no age did we observe a significant negative correlation between relative animal incidence and the relative incidence of either mother or father figures (i.e., animals "replacing" parents). Nor did animal dreaming ever relate significantly to human-stranger dreaming, as might be expected if the child's dream animals were part of some more general motivated avoidance of significant real-life relationships.

My feeling about why young children dream (and think and identify) so much in animal terms is shaped by the observation that animals begin to assume less significant (and more representative, in a real-life sense) roles in children's dreams when, at ages 7–9, children begin to be able to construct effective symbolic representations of themselves as actors in a dreamworld. The answer to the riddle of early-childhood animal dreams may be partly that, as clinicians have pointed out, animal life offers many obvious and appealing parallels to childlife, but also that preoperational children *require* objectified and externalized self-models because they are as yet *unable* cognitively to represent to themselves who or what they really are. In this sense children's animal dreams probably are not playful (creative, imaginative, etc.) in the sense that their manifest contents are deliberately removed from the child's daily routines and concerns, so much as they are compensations for a symbolic defect, namely, the child's literal inability to use the pictorial language of dreams to portray directly what is first and foremost in her or his mind: the self. In this sense, if animals are the earliest reliable *extraself* dream characters in a manifest-content sense, it should be understood that these seeming animal-others are, in fact, apprehensions of the still highly egocentric child herself or himself.

---

[11]At subsequent ages these correlations were (nonsignificantly) negative: ages $11-13$, $r = -.26$; ages $13-15$, $r = -.39$. Evidently animal dreams carry somewhat different meanings at different ages and stages of development.

Settings

Major locales in children's newly dynamic dreamworlds were homes (often, but by no means always, the child's own home), "recreational" settings, or generalized outdoor locations ("in the mountains," "in a field," etc.). Vague or unclassifiable settings were at their nadir, at least for our two longitudinal series. Settings were neither vague-to-absent (as a function of representational immaturity) nor so highly imaginative that they were difficult for judges to classify in terms of familiar waking settings. They were, in short, reasonably concrete and realistic. Thus our data suggest that 5- to 7-year-olds generally are capable of providing some sort of setting— usually a reasonably familiar one—for their dream scenarios.

It was socially passive and dependent children, and more often girls than boys, who reported home or residential dream settings. Home dreamers had, apparently, little taste for or competence in peer play; interestingly, they were low in active imagination ("pretend" play) at our nursery school. Similar characterizations apply to children who dreamed relatively often of their *own* home.[12]

As noted earlier, our "recreational" setting category is something of a grab bag as far as actual *locales* are concerned. Theoretically, however, it is interesting because it is our best index of the occurrence of recreational *activities*. Since play, games, or other pleasurable interactions of a lawful sort have been viewed as integral components in the development of imagination and creativity, one might have expected correlates of recreational-setting incidence to have included signs of cognitive and social competence. In fact, however, at ages 5–7 (and at all subsequent ages) it seemed not to be particularly gifted or sociable children who dreamed most often of recreational activities (settings). At least in its dream manifestations, "play" activity seems to derive more from hostile competitiveness than from the relaxed comradeship or spontaneous creativity that is endorsed by more nostalgic and romantic theorists of children's play. The hostility correlates are especially interesting because at no age did boys have appreciably or significantly more play settings than did girls.

At ages 5–7 dreamers of outdoor settings were slightly more likely to be boys than girls. They were outgoing and expansive, and high in waking "pretend" play.

Activities

As we have seen, claims of activity within the dream (seeing, hearing, talking, manual acts, locomotion) were, at ages 5–7, largely ascribed to

---

[12]It is interesting that, even at ages 3–5, own-home (but not any-home) dreaming was related to dependency on adults and passivity in peer play. It also is interesting that parental variables assocated with home dreaming did not suggest a strong pattern of fostering dependency. It seemed to be poor peer adjustment, rather than poor parenting, that was more strongly related in early childhood to home-dream settings.

characters other than the dreamer herself or himself. We also have noted (see Chapter 3) that, at ages 3–5, claims of dream activity were rare, and that such claims as were made were of somewhat dubious credibility. What about the credibility of the much more frequent claims of other-action and of the beginning of signs of motoric participation by the self in the 5- to 7-year-olds' REM reports? And, more generally, which kind of child most often claimed which kind of dream activity?

First, we should note just what kinds of activities *did* characterize reports of 5- to 7-year-olds. Roughly one dream report in four ascribed sensory (largely visual) acts to dream characters; these "passive" acts were about equally often assigned to the self and to some other dream character. Self-participation in a more active motoric sense was claimed at the verbal level in roughly one of every 20 dreams, at the manual level in roughly one of every five dreams, and at the locomotor level in roughly one of every four dreams. Insofar as claims of others' activity or of overall activity were concerned, the more subtle and symbolic category of verbal acts still was reported relatively infrequently, while manual and locomotor activity both were claimed in a majority of dreams, and almost all dream reports included a claim of at least some form of motor activity.

At ages 5–7 sensory acts for the dreamer no longer were correlated as highly with motor acts for others ($r = .27$), suggesting less confusion on the children's part between seeing a dream and seeing in a dream. In fact, the higher correlation ($r = .45$) was with motor acts for the *self,* suggesting an enhanced likelihood of some genuine self-involvement in 5- to 7-year-olds' dreams. Both sensory and motor acts ascribed to the dreamer were associated with high language quality. This suggests the possibility that grammatical competence plays some role in the enhanced self-participation in the dreams of 5- to 7-year-olds. Such competence was, at any rate, also significantly and positively associated with the overall ascription to dream characters of passive, sensory acts, as was our composite Piagetian-stage measure. The latter correlation seemed to depend more on an association with self-ascribed sensory activities ($r = .55; p < .10$, 2-tail) than with other-ascribed sensory activities ($r = .18$). Thus it seems likely that: (1) children no longer are generally mistaken when they claim to have participated in their own dreams; (2) the representation of such participation may depend on the achievement of linguistic competence and/or operationality; and (3) the stronger possibility is that it is still passive (visual) participation, rather than active (motor) participation, that is genuinely occurring in children's earliest self-participatory dreams.

But personal style may also be involved in determining whether one's dream participation, in this sense, is passive or active. Sensory-self dreamers were more dependent on adults and had to expend relatively much attention in our nursery school to get their peers' attention. Motor-self dreamers were garrulous, aggressive, and dominant. Particularly passive in wakefulness were the sensory-other dreamers, children who reported dreams in which other characters saw rather than acted on their "world."

It seems possible, then, that at ages 3−5 and to some extent at ages 5−7 children are not, by adult criteria, fully participating actors in their own dreams. At ages 5−7 there are some reliable signs of the beginning of such involvement, but its final achievement must be a somewhat slow and arduous process.

Examining the particular kinds of motor activities children reported at ages 5−7, it was again true, as at ages 3−5, that locomotor activities, both as ascribed to dream characters *other* than the self and overall, were reported relatively most often by hostile children (perhaps because, at the ages in question, it is difficult to construct a "self" dream character who reflects the real-life self?). But at ages 5−7 dreaming of others' locomotion also was strongly associated with waking activity in a more general sense, including, interestingly enough, loquaciousness (suggesting that talkativeness is not, at this age, a particularized style of interpersonal interaction, but merely another expression of general activity level). Dreaming of others' verbal activity, on the other hand, was associated with dependence and with low assertiveness. Waking active imagination ("pretend" behavior) was positively associated with overt motor activity in dreams—locomotion—but negatively associated with the more passive activity of dream verbalization.

Self-ascriptions of verbal acts at ages 5−7 were, as we have seen, too rare for our correlational data to be able to suggest much about who was claiming self-verbalization, or why. Self-ascriptions of locomotion were more plentiful (although they were far less frequent than other-ascriptions), but our correlational data said little regarding their possible cognitive or personal-social determinants. That this was so, in conjunction with the rather strong and coherent continuity observed between self-behavior in wakefulness and "other"-behavior in dream reports, suggests to me that the first way in which one's own personality or style is reflected in dreams is in the behavior of nonself-characters. This is so because of an inherent limitation in the representational possibilities of preoperational or early-operational dreaming; that is, a self-character cannot be constructed adequate to the task of effectively representing the waking self. Relatively precocious genuine exceptions to this last generalization will exist (but other claims of a motorically active self may simply be mistaken). The lack of sensible personal correlates of self-participation in locomotion may reflect a particular representational problem in attempts to use a locomoting dream-self to represent the real-self; locomotion alone implies a substantial displacement of self-perspective within dream "space" (Piaget & Inhelder, 1966).

States

Endowing dream characters with either thoughts or feelings depends on taking an internal, psychological perspective toward those characters. We know from waking studies (e.g., Flapan, 1968) that very young children generally do not take such a perspective, focusing instead on externally observable behavior. Likewise, in our children's REM reports at ages 3–5, there were no claims of character cognition and only a bare handful of reports containing feelings.

By and large this relative scarcity of internal perspective taking continued in children's REM reports at ages 5–7. The sole exception to this generalization was the girls' tendency to claim fairly often (in 36% of their dreams) that they felt "happy." I am inclined to skepticism regarding this apparent exception; I find it difficult to believe that there should be a sudden surge of good feeling in girls' dreams at ages 5–7, only to have it disappear at ages 7–9 (where only 12% of the girls' REM reports described a happy self).

There are, I think, more plausible interpretations of the ages 5–7 "happy-self" dreams. Our interview questions at ages 5–7 contained, for the first time, the kind of feeling probe we used at all later ages: "Did you have any feelings in the dream—*were you, for instance, sad or happy, calm or worried, mad or excited, at any point in the dream?*" For relatively inexperienced children, the latent demand of this question may have seemed to be that they should choose one of those alternatives, and their choice, no doubt, would have been the most conventional and socially acceptable one: happy. And, as suggested earlier, there may have been continuing problems in discriminating between "I was happy in the dream" and "The dream [now] pleases me." Consistent with the idea that the "happy" data at ages 5–7 contain at least some false positives is the (nonsignificant) negative correlation ($r = -.40$) between happy reports and subject age. Socially, the givers of happy reports were passive and immature in their behavior with peers, unimaginative, and dependent on adults, a pattern also consistent with the hypothesis that these children were being compliant, rather than accurate, in answering our feeling question.[13] The compliance hypothesis also is consistent with the sex difference in claims of happy feelings. I would conclude, then, that many (but probably not all) of the happy-feeling claims made at ages 5–7 were mistaken insofar as those claims were meant to refer to feelings actually experienced *within* a REM dream.

Otherwise there were very few claims of character thought or feeling at ages 5–7. There were still no reports of dreamer anger. Two dreams were reported with fear content, but, at an age where Block Design raw scores correlated positively with REM report rate, there were strong *negative* correlations of Block Design with dreamer-fear and any-fear, suggesting that these dreams were erroneously reported. Interestingly, in terms of the hypothesis that scary dreams spontaneously reported in early childhood are arousal artifacts, the incidence of laboratory-fear reports was correlated

---

[13]Flapan (1968) reported that 6-year-olds, in giving generally consensually inaccurate accounts of emotions in a moving picture that they had seen, were prone to give highly stereotyped accounts of emotional experience, repeating over and over again, for example, phrases like "he felt good." At age 9, however, children's accounts of character emotions were unstereotyped and consensually accurate.

with the tendency to experience partial or total arousals during otherwise uninterrupted sleep. Perhaps children prone to such arousal are sensitized to fearful feelings on any arousal from sleep.

Overall, at ages 5–7 feelings were reported most often, suspiciously enough, by children low in Block Design, an index of abilities that I believe our data show to be critical to effective dream construction in general. Feeling reporters were more notable for their dependence and garrulousness than for any accuracy or speed in cognitive processing. Proneness to report feelings in general also was related to sleep disturbance (although most of the feelings reported were not unpleasant), as well as to waking verbal imagination. One can imagine, then, that feeling reporters were children with considerable prior opportunity in "filling in" feelings upon awakening from sleep for mental experiences that most likely originally did not contain them.[14] At any rate, our data do not suggest that, at ages 5–7, children very often reliably experience either feelings or cognitions in their dreams or, more generally, take an internalized psychological perspective within their dreams.

These data, I think, further suggest problems in effective self-representation in the dreams of 5- to 7-year-olds. If it is a distinguishing characteristic of being *in* your own dream that you think and feel along with a (self) character within the dream, then 5- to 7-year-olds give little evidence of self-involvement in their dreams. Perhaps it is not until you *can* get "inside" of dream characters that it makes much sense even to identify an actor who looks like you as being you. In this sense, it would be impossible to say children were in their dreams until they began thinking somewhat "psychologically."

Motives and Outcomes

In our analysis of motives and outcomes, essentially we put the foregoing categories of activity and state into a fuller dreamworld context. Motive and outcome scores deal with the *ends* to which character activities are directed and with the *interpersonal consequences* of these activities. As we have seen, at ages 5–7 there was a dramatic increase in the incidence of dream events permitting analysis in terms of behavioral sequence or social exchange.

Our scoring system discriminates two classes of motivated behavior, "organic" motives (behavior whose object is to change some internal, physiological, self-regulatory drive state) and "social" motives (behavior whose object is to effect some change in one's environment). At ages 3–5 more dreams were scored as containing organic than social motives, but at ages 5–7, and at all later ages, social activities were considerably more

---

[14]Our home–laboratory studies (Foulkes, 1979b) offer empirical support for the hypothesis that feeling contents are particularly likely to be "added onto" dream experiences when these experiences are not told by the child to another person immediately after their occurrence.

prominent in dreams than were organic ones. This was only in small part because of a decline in the incidence of organic motives (hunger themes, for instance, were slightly *more* frequent at ages 5−7 than at ages 3−5); the major cause of the shift was the substantial introduction into children's dreams of themes of activity directed to the external world, both social and material.

Considering first the residual cases of "organically driven" dream behavior, at ages 5−7 hunger continued to be an evident dream concern, as indicated by both eating behavior and the presence in dreams of food objects. In this sense, about one dream in six could be considered a hunger dream. However, eating or food objects themselves now were more likely to be in a social context: One boy dreamed, for instance, of a grocery store being robbed. He was not in the dream. As this example indicates, as at ages 3−5, hunger-related activities continued to be ascribed to characters other than the self. This is still another indication of the absence of a differentiated self-character in early childhood dreaming. Hunger-other dreamers were motorically awkward and socially passive. Those children still dreaming of fatigue themes now also put them into more of a social context; there was a nonsignificant *increase,* for instance, in ascriptions to other dream characters of fatigue-related behaviors. Fatigue dreamers no longer were intellectually precocious, as at ages 3−5. In fact, it was children with relatively *little* improvement in Block Design who still were claiming fatigue themes. These children also had an "external locus of control," suggesting that susceptibility to having immediate-drive stimuli influence their dreams is related, in the late preoperational period, to children's more general sense of being driven, rather than of being drivers, in their own lives.[15] Fatigue dreamers were verbally imaginative but did not prove to be particularly competent interpersonally. More generally, at an age when children were beginning symbolically to construct dreams with portrayals of social interaction, it seemed to be relatively unaggressive or passive children whose mentation remained most susceptible to influence by "nonsocial" drive stimuli.

What, finally, may we say about the newly socialized dream world of our

---

[15]Fatigue dreaming also was related to the presence of phasic REM activity during nights of uninterrupted sleep (i.e., to the frequency of actual bursts of eye movement during REM periods). Hobson and McCarley (1977) have proposed that phasic REM activity is responsible for the bizarreness and abrupt scene changes of REM dreams. Here the correlates of such activity seem to be a very passive, static, and familiar (albeit drive-related) activity. In general, at no age did we find many dream correlates of phasic REM activity, that is, any indication that the determination of particular kinds of dream content, or of dreaming at all, is related to those physiological characteristics of REM sleep that seem to have their basis in primitive neural systems in the brainstem. Indeed, it is the argument of this book, and we believe of our data, that dream experiencing depends developmentally on the maturation of cognitive/cerebral systems that at present best can be studied psychologically. The ability to perform well on block-design tests, for instance, surely has a cerebral basis, but it seems unlikely now that we shall learn as much about how this ability relates to dream generation by physiological as by psychological observation.

5- to 7-year-olds? What sorts of interactions took place there: Who did what to whom, and why? Roughly speaking, only one dream of four, either for boys or for girls, contained a hostile ("attack") initiation by one character to another. It was, with a sole exception, always some character other than the child herself or himself who initiated such aggressive behavior. The more frequent form of social interaction in children's dreams was "positive" in character, a nonhostile initiation to other persons or to objects (often toys or other recreational paraphernalia). For boys object-approaches over-shadowed person-approaches, while for girls the reverse was true. The girls reported considerably more dreams with nonhostile ("approach") social interaction (56%) than did the boys (21%). *Self*-initiations of social-approach activity were less frequent than *other*-initiations—only 14% of reports contained claims of dreamer-initiated social-approach behavior. Once more we see that the representation of the self as a participating dream character is relatively rare.

Given my discussion of the imbalance between the girls' and the boys' claims of happy feelings, it might be expected that the similar imbalance in their claims of nonhostile social interaction would also point toward the possibility of confusion or confabulation in the girls' accounts. In fact, cognitive correlates of claims of social-approach episodes in dreams were overwhelmingly negative, and specifically indicative both of poor memory and of low Piagetian-stage attainment. I would not want to conclude that all claims of such episodes were erroneous, but only point to the likelihood that a substantial number of them are suspect, as is the apparent boy–girl difference in their incidence. Perhaps the boys' figures should be taken as more generally representative, although it does make some sense, in terms of sex differences in wakefulness, that girls would have somewhat more pleasant social dream content than would boys. However, since the negative cognitive correlates include age-corrected ratios, as well as raw-skill mea-sures, it cannot be the case that they depend simply on the girls having been younger than the boys. There is the suspicion of genuine contamination attaching to at least some of the girls' claims of having dreamed "nice" dreams.[16]

In the scoring of dream "outcomes," focus is on the recipient rather than the initiator of social acts. In general, as I have already indicated (see Chapter 3), outcome scoring reflects motive scoring—one is looking at the same acts from different perspectives. However, it *is* informative to see whether it is the dreamer, or someone else, who generally received dream interaction. In the case of approach-social interaction, our data clearly indicate that at ages 5–7 it generally was someone else. The self generally

---

[16]We did not compute correlates of the other "positive" motive class (Approach Object) because of secular changes in scoring (the class apparently was underscored in Year-1 dreams). For this kind of behavioral sequence, though, there were only minimal sex differences in reported occurrence.

seems to be present neither as friendly initiator nor even as friendly recipient in 5- to 7-year-olds' dreams. Our data also confirm the dubious quality of at least some of the children's nonhostile interaction claims at ages 5–7; these claims came from cognitively untalented children who were, however, highly motivated to meet adult demands.

Because our "attack" category was more homogeneous than our "approach" category (any action explicitly neither an aggression nor a withdrawal was considered an approach), information from its scoring should generally prove to be more informative. Sex differences for this category at ages 5–7 were negligible. The most important observation, in the context of getting a "big picture" of children's dream life, is that only about one-quarter of children's dreams contained explicit aggression and that the self was only rarely either initiator *or* recipient of such aggression. Representative dream sampling yields quite a different impression of children's dream-life in this regard than does biased, home-based "spontaneous recall."

A sole Wechsler correlate (Information) of dreaming of aggressive initiations was negative, but there was no more general pattern indicating either cognitive competence or incompetence for social-attack dreamers. These children were: relatively prolific fantasizers about—or relatively acute perceivers of—aggression in projective-test cards; prone to sleep disturbance; and characterized by an external locus of control (consistent with their dream portrayal of a world where other people do unpleasant things).

Indices of poor sleep also proved to be the most striking correlates of dreaming of unfavorable outcomes (which, in addition to character-mediated outcomes, included simple misfortunes). One could see dream as cause, and poor sleep as effect, of course, but, as I have suggested earlier, the causation (if any) could be reversed: Frequent awakenings predispose children, in intermediate confusional states experienced while still in bed, to interpret their imagery as frightening or "bad." In this regard it is interesting to note that the least credible *dream* reports of aggression (negative correlation with Block Design), namely reports of self-receipt of aggression, were correlated with: frequent and *long* mid-night spontaneous awakenings from sleep and a waking apperceptive set to read hostility and unpleasantness into pictorial stimuli. More generally, dreaming "bad" dreams (unfavorable-outcome dreams) was a characteristic of children low in reality-knowledge, but high (and increasingly high) in inventive-aggressive-unpleasant apperceptive tendency as well as high in sleep disturbance. It is interesting to speculate that "bad" dreams, as most often spontaneously reported by children, not only are not genuine sleep-mentation reports but also may not even be psychogenic. Instead they may derive from poor body regulation of sleep. I note, for example, that our "bad-dream" dreamers were not particularly anxious, not overtly hostile in wakefulness (some evidence even to the contrary), and not children of parents whose attitudes or behavior would seem to justify the creation of unpleasant dream scenarios. Might not their fearful apperceptive tendencies have stemmed from the fact that, unlike other (more fortunate) children, they simply happened to wake up a lot at night and therefore had had much experience in trying to cope, with relatively meager informational resources and analytic skills, with the situation of being alone and confused and in the dark?

Overall, then, our report data may overestimate the occurrence both of good dreams—because of some mindlessly compliant confabulation—and of bad dreams—because of some reports of waking apperception rather than of dream "perception." In any event our data are totally inconsistent with any portrayal of children's earliest dreamworlds as being overrun by bogeymen and monsters and wild animals, all out to "get" the child. The facts of the case are that young children's REM dreams portray activities of the same *general* sort that children perform or observe in wakefulness, and probably about in the same proportion as they do so in wakefulness.

Global Ratings

Our scoring system includes five ratings that are meant to provide a more global picture of what dreams are like. These ratings generally depend on the balance or ratio of different elements present in the same dream. Thus *hedonic tone* ratings are high (dreams are unpleasant) if negative feelings and outcomes exceed positive ones in individual dreams, but low (dreams are pleasant) if positive feelings and outcomes exceed negative ones in individual dreams. Likewise *active participation* depends on the balance of self vs. other presence in the dream, *setting distortion* on the ratio of unfamiliar to familiar settings in the dream, and *character distortion* on the ratio of unfamiliar to familiar characters in the dream. A final rating—*visualization*—was meant to determine the visual-perceptual vs. more purely ideational quality of dream mentation, but since children's reports at all ages and from all sleep stages almost always were judged perceptual, we did not enter this scale into our correlational analysis.

At ages 5–7 (and thereafter) distortion seemed to be a *general* property of children's dreams; that is, if a child dreamed relatively often of unknown places, he or she also dreamed relatively often of unknown persons ($r = .84$). Distortion also was significantly related to dream unpleasantness at ages 5–7 (setting distortion, $r = .62$; character distortion, $r = .78$), and this association lingered also at later ages, although in diminished quality and only until ages 9–11. No rated dream property of REM reports at ages 3–5 was significantly correlated with that same property at ages 5–7, reflecting perhaps both intervening dream development and the likelihood that some ages 3–5 reports were bogus.

Girls' dreams at ages 5–7 were judged somewhat (but not significantly) more pleasant than boys' dreams, largely because of the girls' frequent claims of "happy" feelings. As discussed earlier my suspicion is that these claims often were mistaken. Correlates of the hedonic-tone scale support that suspicion: Children who reported pleasant dreams were low in social comprehension and in waking descriptive skill. Perhaps consistent with sex differences in hedonic-tone ratings, reporters of relatively less pleasant dreams had more aggressive and dysphoric waking fantasies. As would have been expected from my hypothesis about nonmentational sources of claims of unpleasant dream affect in early childhood, these children also showed some indications of sleep disturbance. *Increases* in dream pleasantness from ages 3−5 to 5−7, mostly for girls, were associated with relative incompetence in describing pictorial stimuli, with unaggressive and cheerful waking fantasies, and with a greater interest in pleasing adults than peers. All of these findings reinforce my skepticism about the girls' "happy" dreams at ages 5−7.

At ages 3−5 Active Participation, actually self-presence in static, sleep-theme dreams, was positively correlated with cognitive competence. At ages 5−7 other characters relatively often and seemingly reliably were present in children's dreams, and these characters seemed to have been at least somewhat physically active and socially interactive. The major question about the children's REM reports seemed to be whether children actually imagined their own participation as well in their newly formed dream narratives. Absolutely, claims of self-participation at ages 5−7 still were relatively rare, although more frequent than at ages 3−5. Correlates of *increases* in self-participation claims relative to other-participation claims, in fact, cast considerable doubt on the validity of the former: for example, poor vocabulary, inaccurate waking description of a movie, dependence on the experimenter, low chronological age, social immaturity. Once again it does not seem likely that children's dreams at ages 5−7 had much genuine self-participatory activity. And, since girls' reports seemed generally less credible than boys' reports at ages 5−7, the nonsignificant sex difference in active participation ratings (the girls' pooled mean rating was 1.76, the boys' was 1.51) also may well be spurious. *Absolutely*, ratings for both sexes were quite low.

Boys at ages 5−7 were higher, although not significantly so, than girls in rated dream distortion. In the area of characterization, the most marked difference in children's dreams between ages 3−5 and 5−7 was the large increase in "stranger" characters. As I have suggested, stranger-reports may, in fact, have represented accurate accounts by brighter children of their unsuccessful attempts to reconstruct symbolically somewhat familiar persons—that is, they may have been "construction failures." Reports of known (non-family) characters, on the other hand, may have represented inaccurate accounts of similarly unsuccessful attempts—they may have been waking assimilations of ill-formed images to familiar schemata. In this regard it is interesting that character distortion ratings at ages 5−7, newly weighted by the presence of stranger reports, had a substantial number of positive cognitive correlates, including variables presumably implicated in mediating comprehension of, and accuracy in, the dream-report task: social comprehension, waking descriptive skill, and composite Piagetian stage. *Increases* in REM character distortion from ages 3−5 to 5−7 also had numerous positive cognitive correlates, including waking report accuracy in a memory condition, which strongly suggests that the children's new claims of unfamiliar characters cannot be explained in terms of poor description of familiar character representations.

At ages 5−7 setting distortion also had substantial and positive cognitive correlates, including, again, social comprehension, waking descriptive accuracy, and composite Piagetian stage. Once again, also, waking descriptive adequacy (but here not from memory) predicted increases in claims of setting distortion.

While there were other correlates of dream distortion at ages 5−7, we think that the cognitive ones must be the crucial ones. It sometimes seems to be imagined that children "naturally" will conjure up bogeymen or monsters to symbolize their anxieties or will create all manner of strange settings to symbolize their feelings of being "lost" in an alien adult world. But unless one wishes to fall back on the preposterous notion of innate archetypal images, there can be nothing "natural" about symbolically constructing imaginal representations of persons or places rather different from those one has in fact seen. Such construction must depend on the attainment of a certain level of cognitive-representational skill. Our data suggest that this level is *not* attainable by 3- to 5-year-olds, who rely on highly familiar and significant waking symbols—family members and especially animals—to people the static, essentially nonnarrative imagery they are able to create.[17] Our data also suggest that, at ages 5−7, more cognitively competent children are for the first time able to construct—and accurately report—reasonably well-defined characters and settings that, perhaps unwittingly, transcend the familiar and can be recognized as having done so.

Contrary to the well-known position of psychoanalytic theory, our data indicate, then, that dream distortion arises developmentally not in response to anxieties or conflicts that one cannot manage directly and so must deal with in disguised form, but rather as a natural outgrowth of one's enhanced cognitive skill. That is, one first "distorts" in dreams (and is aware of this distortion) because one *can*, not because one *must*. Neither parental-attitude nor child-behavior correlates of dream distortion at ages 5−7 offer any convincing picture of children whose real-life situation drives them to dream distortion. One might think, rather, of unfamiliar dream symbols as being new toys that the children's cognitive development now gives them a chance to play with (even though some children will still think the toys to be old ones), and of what happens in dreams at ages 5−7 as being the same sort of outcome one would expect for any other new toy as attractive and versatile as unfamiliar symbolism must be.

---

[17]Presumably, by adult standards, even these images are not well constructed (even at ages 5−7, it still seems to take skill to portray family members accurately). But younger children's image approximations no doubt are met with assimilatory tendencies that, in the absence of much concern for accuracy, readily identify them as symbolizing what the dreamer knows from her or his waking experience.

SEX DIFFERENCES: OEDIPUS REVISITED

There were, as at ages 3–5, no *statistically significant* differences between boys' and girls' REM dreams at ages 5–7. However, the previous section's discussion has indicated several ways in which boys' and girls' dream reports did not seem strictly comparable, and the failure to demonstrate significance should be viewed in the context of attenuated like-sex sample sizes ($n = 6$), due to the fact that one boy and one girl failed to report any REM dreams. If, in view of low subject and low report numbers, one accepted boy–girl differences that met a more lenient criterion of significance ($p <$ .10, 2-tail), then the following variables would have discriminated boys' and girls' dreams at ages 5–7:

Higher for boys	Higher for girls
Incidence of male strangers	Incidence of social-approach initiations by nonself or any dream character
Incidence of indigenous animals	Incidence of favorable outcomes: other mediated, for other and any dream character; any mediated, for other and any dream character.

Until our waking test-file correlational data became available, I was struck with how well these differences might be subsumed by the hypothesis that, as psychoanalytic theory would have it, 5- to 7-year old boys are undergoing an "oedipal" crisis, while girls are not (Foulkes, 1977, 1979d). By "oedipal" crisis one need not mean the full-blown Freudian concept, in which fears for genital integrity drive the boy to identify, rather than to compete, with the father. Our dream findings in fact provide little or no data to support many of the fine-scaled particulars of Freud's Oedipus complex. For instance, the manifest dream content of young boys offers little direct evidence of the pregenital precursors or anatomical concerns that Freud would feel to be central to the oedipal situation. Rather, one can point to a more overtly observable and explicable crisis in boys' sex-role development, a crisis to which some empirical data do point.

With, by age 4 or 5, a moderately clear conception of their own gender identity, children often begin, in overt and sometimes flamboyant ways, to "try it out," as they understand it. A "seductive" interest in the opposite-sex parent will be stronger for boys than girls, since all children retain a primary affectional tie to the mother (Stoller, 1973). But it is less likely that the boys' precocious "sexual" behavior will be tolerated: It's OK to be a father's girl, but not a mother's boy (Sherman, 1971). Fathers, who by social-role assignment if not also by nature tend to be more physically distant and less nurturant to children than are mothers, are also guardians of the masculine heritage and are likely to reinforce their powerful-punitive image in boys' eyes by insisting on "masculine" behavior. This leaves the boy in something of a dilemma: He gets more satisfaction and attention from his mother, but he is supposed to partially disavow his tie to her and the values for which she stands in order that he may be more like his father, who is neither known nor understood very well and who often behaves in unlikable ways.

Thus one need not be "Freudian" in any strict sense to acknowledge that it probably is more difficult at this stage to be a boy than a girl. The basic fact of early childhood is a primary tie to the mother, a feminization of both girls and boys (Mitchell, 1974). While the girl can continue a "love" relationship with her mother as she experiments with cross-sex behavior, the boy is not permitted the same luxury. He must learn, early in his school years, to renounce tenderness, femininity, and heterosexual feelings. He must give up "childish" behavior, categorized as "feminine," sooner and more definitely than the girl (Bardwick, 1971). He finds less positive reinforcement at home—to be a man's boy is also to be something of a nuisance (Sherman, 1971)—and at school he encounters another institution bent on "feminizing" him to being a "nice" boy. There certainly are more males among the visible casualties of early development; boys far outnumber girls in referrals for behavioral disorders (Shaw, 1966; Eme, 1979), and males are more likely later to manifest gender pathology—transsexualism, transvestitism, and homosexuality (Money & Ehrhardt, 1972; Stoller, 1973; Person, 1974).

In this reasonably plausible context, it was tempting (and I was tempted) to see our boy–girl dream differences at ages 5–7 as reflecting the greater turmoil boys were undergoing in arriving at definition of their "appropriate" sex role. Male strangers would stand for the distant (oedipal; Hall, 1963) father, and untamed animals for the impulses boys are trying to cope with and manage. The lesser incidences of pleasant social interaction and outcomes would reflect the greater turmoil of the boys' lives. Other data, already reviewed, seemed to fit into the picture equally well. As compared to ages 3–5, at ages 5–7: Boys' dreams seemed to be becoming somewhat more unpleasant and girls' much more pleasant; character distortion was decreasing for girls, but increasing for boys; animal incidence was rising for boys, but falling for girls; and so forth. While recognizing that many of these findings were small and of dubious statistical value, I felt that together they formed a pattern suggestive of oedipal crisis, at least in the social-learning, if not in the quasi-biological-Freudian, sense.

Based on the fuller view afforded by the correlational data discussed in the previous section, I now think that I was wrong and that our sex-difference data do not reflect the plausible scenario sketched out above regarding differences between growing up male and growing up female. Specifically:

1 As discussed above, the more happy-pleasant nature of the girls' dreams, against which the boys' dreams were being contrasted, was probably largely artifactual.

2 That boys invented male strangers more frequently at an earlier age level
   than did girls—for girls did later catch up—seems, in our sample, to have
   reflected the fact that the boys were, in fact, older and more cognitively
   mature than the girls at the "same" age level. In other words, they were
   better *able* to do so, rather than more *compelled* to do so.

In the context of our correlational data, there is no reason to resort to
oedipal crisis as an explanation for the major differences we observed
between boys' and girls' dreams at ages 5−7. Other, more plausible and
empirically supportable, reasons lie closer at hand. And when one takes
artifactual components into account, even those minimal and marginally
significant sex differences that we did observe between boys' and girls'
dreams that set off the oedipal chase in the first place seem to have vanished.
One is left with what the data, strictly interpreted ($p < .05$, 2-tail), said all
along: By and large, boys and girls seemed to dream pretty much the same
kinds of dreams, within the sensitivity of our scoring procedure to detect
difference, at ages 5−7. Even in children's dreamlife, where one might most
have hoped to find it (it was in his own adult dreams, apparently, that Freud
himself "discovered" Oedipus), the Oedipus complex, in either its original
or modified form, proves to be elusive. Once again, as at ages 3−5, boys and
girls at ages 5−7 are together children rather than members of two vastly
different races. This is not to say that more extensive and intensive study
will not turn up sex differences in dreams as a function of differences in
maturation and/or socialization, only to point out that, at the first and most
obvious level of observation, it is similarities rather than differences that
catch one's eye.
      My need to revise my earlier position carries, I think, a more general
message of methodology for dream psychology. With its classical roots lying
in personality theory and psychopathology, dream psychology is prone, in
the absence of *comprehensive* information about persons, to interpret dream
differences as reflecting personality differences: traumas, conflicts, fixations, complexes, and the like. The data reported here, which come from an
attempt to put children's dreams in a context of comprehensive, empirical
observation of the dreamers who dreamed them, indicate that these "clinical" interpretations often will be wrong. What is seen clinically as a pathog-
nomonic sign may simply reflect ability factors. In asking what the dream is
saying, we need to consider those cognitive factors that dictate what it can or
cannot say. And, as we shall see later, this is not a caveat whose force
declines after early childhood; it applies equally well in adolescence and
perhaps throughout the human life span.

STIMULUS INCORPORATION

As was true at ages 3−5, the children did not produce much evidence at ages
5−7 of incorporating the stimulation performed on them in REM and NREM
sleep during their second and ninth nights of observation. Of 41 REM awak-

enings after stimulation (Table 2.1), 14 (34%) produced dream reports; of 41 NREM awakenings after stimulation, three (7%) produced dream reports. Nine children had at least one poststimulation dream. Again, recall rates after stimulation were quite close to those observed more generally, indicating that stimulation during sleep does not "produce" dreams or enhance the dreamlike quality of background levels of mentation or consciousness.

The 17 reports were submitted, along with 56 reports collected from 11- to 13-year olds in the same study year, to two judges. As before, transcripts were randomly numbered and unidentified by subject, night, awakening, or stimulus. Different judges were employed than for first-year reports. The new judges were allowed access to first-year transcripts, the first-year judges' evaluation of those transcripts, and to the actual correspondence of judgment and stimulus in the first-year data, so that they might better acquaint themselves with the kind of materials they would be judging, criteria employed by first-year judges, and the degree and manner in which children earlier seemed to have incorporated external stimuli into their dreams. Method of original judgment was as for reports collected at ages 3–5 (see Chapter 3). However, in addition, the third-year judges performed two judgments not attempted with first-year data.

1 They were given pairs of reports matched by subject and stage of sleep and asked to identify which stimulus (of two suggested—the one actually employed and another one) was associated with which report.[18]
2 Following completion of this task, judges were given pairs matched by subject and stimulus, but not for stage of sleep, and asked to judge, for each pair, "which report is *more clearly* related to the stimulus." All pairs meeting matching criteria were judged by both judges. Because of the very small number of eligible reports for both of these sets of forced-choice judgments (one cotton-limb contrast and two cotton-water and limb-water contrasts in the first task, and two NREM-REM pairs in the second one), results of the additional judging proved informative only for the older-group children whose reports were judged simultaneously with those of the 5- to 7-year-olds (see Chapter 7).

Because the judges' "certain" judgments were not consistently or strikingly better than their "uncertain" ones, both classes of judgment were pooled in our analysis of 5- to 7-year-olds' dreams (and also in those of 11- to 13-year-olds, 7- to 9-year-olds, and 13- to 15-year-olds, the other ages for which these same judges were used). Overall, Judge 1 was correct in 44% (four of nine) of stimulus assignments, and Judge 2 in 33% (four of 12) of hers.

---

[18]Report pairs were formed so as to have approximately equivalent numbers of pairs among the three possible contrasts: water-limb, water-cotton, and cotton-limb. No report, of course, appeared in more than one such contrast. The number of reports available was not sufficient to permit judges to receive nonrepeating items in all contrasts. Therefore, both judges received the limb-water pairs—to determine their comparability of judgment with common materials—but only one judge received the cotton-limb pairs, while the other judged the cotton-water pairs.

Against a "baseline" of 33% chance, these figures suggest little or no incorporation, although the first (and more conservative, i.e., less-likely-to-see-an-incorporation) judge did exceed chance. By stimulus, net incorporation rates (see Chapter 3) were as follows:

Stimulus	Judge 1 (%)	Judge 2 (%)
Cotton	15	7
Limb	32	23
Water	−10	−20
All	9	0

The negative figures for water are interesting; they suggest that the Dement-Wolpert (1958) water-incorporation figures for adults, arrived at without a correction for chance, may well have been spuriously inflated, for here one sees water dream elements quite often when water is not the pre-awakening stimulus. There is a suggestion in the above data that the limb stimulation was somewhat effective in inducing genuine incorporation (despite the problems my varied method of stimulation posed for the judges; see Chapter 3).

Table 4.2 presents results of the incorporation procedure in a somewhat

Table 4.2 **Judges' Consensually Correct and Consensually Certain Incorporation Judgments: Ages 5–7**

	Judges Both "Certain"	One/Both Judge(s) Not "Certain"
Judges Are Consensually Right	*Linda:* Night 2, Awakening 1. Her brother was making designs on her head (a cotton-REM stimulation). **M** [a]	*Matt:* Night 2, Awakening 1. His cat playing with a ball (a cotton-REM stimulation). **M** *Matt:* Night 9, Awakening 2. Kids batting at a baseball (a limb-REM stimulation). **M**
Judges Are Consensually Wrong		

Reports judged = 17
"Certain" and right = 6%

[a] **M** denotes some body *movement* noted by the experimenter in response to the stimulus. Strictly speaking, it is only in the absence of such movement (or other arousal response) that one could talk of a stimulus incorporation during sleep itself.

different way. Linda's incorporation seems quite straightforward, although it shows typical dreamlike elaboration—the cause of her facial/scalp sensations is her somewhat pesky brother. I saw two other reports that I thought might be incorporations: Sally dreamed (Night 9, Awakening 2) of girls dancing, following a dance-step-pattern stimulation of her feet (but judges could not know that that was the particular "limb" manipulation I had used). Douglas dreamed (Night 2, Awakening 3) of a cat drinking whiskey that a man had poured (but the judges apparently were more impressed by the cotton-softness of the cat than by the liquid element). Perhaps these too were incorporations, or perhaps these examples simply show that it is easier to *see* a relationship when you know what the stimulus has been (e.g., Dement & Wolpert, 1958) than it is to *determine* one when you don't know what the stimulus has been.

Overall, then, the incorporation data present hints of incorporative possibility, but in a strict quantitative sense the children's dream reports did not reliably index preawakening stimulation. As at ages 3–5, so too here it seems that: (1) children rely on external stimuli no more than adults do to either generate, or to guide the content of, their dreams; (2) occasional instances of undoubted incorporation can, however, be elicited; (3) when there is incorporation, it is almost in the nature of an *interpretation* of the stimulus, as if the dream were nothing more than the child's attempt to explain the stimulus; and (4) yet even such interpretation goes beyond the stimulus received, and elaborates some sort of imaginary context for it.

DEAN'S DREAMS

At the start of his third year in the study, Dean was aged 6 years, 8 months. During this year he reported dreams on five (33%) of his REM awakenings, on one (11%) of his NREM awakenings, and on two (67%) of his sleep-onset awakenings.

Dean's *REM reports* were as follows:

1-1 A cabin, it was little and I looked in it. Me and Freddie (a friend and fellow subject, whom he discussed with the experimenter before going to bed). [Where was it?] At Barbara Lake. [Did it look like Barbara Lake really does?] Yeah, kind of. [Is there really a cabin up there or was this just made-up in the dream?] Uh, there isn't really one up there. [What were you doing in the dream, you and Freddie?] Playing around . . . with a few toys and things. [Could you see this, was it like in pictures, like you were watching what was happening?] Yeah. [Did you have any feelings?] No.

2-1 Some guy swimming . . . swimming and baseball at high school. [Was this a man or boy, or how old was this person?] I don't know. [What was the guy doing?] Golfing. [Golfing? Were you telling me before about swimming?] I don't know. (S remained groggy throughout the interview.)

2-3   Cow . . . cows on the ranch . . . they were just mooing. [Could you see anything in your dream?] Not much. . . . I could see the ranchhouse . . . that's all, (cows) just running around. [Were there any people in your dream?] No. [Were you in the dream?] No. [Was this anyplace you've ever really seen?] No. [Did you have any feelings?] No. [Could you tell me a little more about what this house looked like?] No. One made out of logs.

8-1   A race . . . a running race . . . John and I [A boy you know from school?] Yes. [Is he in your class?] . . . He's older . . . he's eight. [Where were you running?] On the playground. [Was this your school or some other school?] My own. [Who was winning the race?] Johnny won. [Did you have any feelings?] No.

8-3   I was building a bridge. I made a car bridge, bridge. [What did you make them with?] Legoes ("Lego" blocks). [Where were you doing this?] My room. [At home?] Yes. [Did your room look the way it really does or did it look different?] Different . . . my bed was in a different place. [Was there anybody else in this dream besides you?] No. [Were you doing anything else in the dream besides building bridges?] I drove cars on them. [With your hands?] Yes. [Did you have any feelings?] No.

Dean's *sleep-onset reports* were:

4-2   A cowboy riding a horse . . . in the desert. . . . I was the cowboy. [Did you think that you were bigger than you are?] Yes. [Did you recognize the place?] It was just made-up. [Did you have any feelings?] No.

6-1   I was going to school and I didn't do my work so I went out for recess and then I went home. [Was there anybody else in it besides you?] Well, some friends . . . just my teacher and children. [Was the teacher the teacher that you really have in school?] No . . . Mrs.—I don't know what her name was. [What about the boys and girls?] Some were people that were my friends but they go to another school, like Freddie. . . . Most of them go to the school, my school. [What did you do in the dream?] Well, I just sat there and everybody else got work . . . math. . . . I didn't do any. . . . I didn't get a paper . . . . I went home (at recess). [Did the other boys and girls stay at school?] Yes, they stayed at school. I was just going toward (home).

The *NREM report* was:

9-3   People taking drugs. . . . There was this kid, and he took drugs . . . and he died. [How old was he?] About 18. They were all walking around and driving cars. . . . I saw a cupboard with drugs in it. [How was (the boy) "taking" them?] Just taking them out of a bottle . . . . He threw them away . . . . He swallowed them . . . . He died. [Where was this guy supposed to be?] In his house. [Is it any place you really know?] No. [Did you have any feelings?] No. [It didn't bother you that this guy took drugs and that he died?] No.

Dean's reports nicely indicate the qualitative changes in REM dream content between ages 3−5 and 5−7 that have been discussed in this chapter. His dreams no longer are static, ego-centered protonarratives reflecting body states. They now portray dynamic action sequences unfolding in a moderately well fleshed-out "dreamworld." The self-character, however, generally is not the hub of this dreamworld. Sometimes it is absent (2-1, 2-3). Recreational themes are dominant (1-1, 2-1, 8-1, 8-3), and they generally are "constructive" in quality (e.g., 8-3), but not invariably self-serving (e.g., the lost race of 8-1). Characterization, action, and settings generally are realistic or inherently plausible. Often the source of relatively unrealistic elements is not difficult to discern (e.g., the cabin of 1-1 may be attributable to Dean's presleep cabin building with Lincoln Logs). Dean's dream world is quite concrete and action centered: Characters are looking, playing, swimming, golfing, running, building, "driving," and so forth, rather than thinking, feeling, wondering, and so on. His outdoors/action themes reflect, of course, not only his sex-typed masculine interests but also the culture and physical setting of the community in which he lived.

Put in their full context, at least for this boy the male-stranger (2-1) and animal (2-3) images of the "oedipal" boy certainly seem tame enough. The male stranger seems to be a hyperactive male athlete/model, and the animals, also hyperactive, are familiar ones and seem to be neither the source nor the object of any imminent danger. Dean's newly activated dreamworld does not seem particularly more terrifying or malevolent than his more static dream scenarios two years earlier. Where there is the newly achieved possibility of portraying dynamic interaction, there also lurks the danger of its veering out of control. Dean, however, seems to have his third-year dream scenarios well under control.

Interestingly, Dean's two third-year sleep-onset reports seem rather closer to typical waking fantasies of boyhood than do his REM reports. He is grown-up, a masculine cowboy; he doesn't have to work at school as other children do. The NREM report came on a stimulus-incorporation trial (before waking Dean, the experimenter had applied water to his scalp). It may represent a nonspecific dream response to the fact that someone was, in fact, "messing around" with Dean's body. If so, the dream elaboration of the disturbing stimulus seems to have drawn rather heavily on stereotyped prefabricated (e.g., television) fantasies with which the subject must have been somewhat familiar in waking life. It is also possible, of course, that the entire report is a confabulation. Aware of that possibility, I recorded my judgment, on the spot, that the report did not *sound* like a confabulation.

SUMMARY

It is between ages 3−5 and 5−7 that the single most important developmental change in REM dream content seems to be taking place. While there are a considerable number of later quantitative and qualitative accretions to the

REM dream, its basic structural elements are beginning to fall into place as children progress toward operational thinking. By ages 5−7 children's dreams are beginning to be *stories* rather than static descriptions. Dreams now begin to construct a mini-world, closely modeled on the real one, in which characters perform activities, pursue goals, and even realize the consequences of their actions. The activities are recognizably like, but not identical to, activities the child performs or knows about in her or his waking life. Compared to those REM reports I believe to have been most reliable at ages 3−5, the ages 5−7 reports evince a genuine interest in the real world lying outside the child's own skin. They no longer simply seem to be responses to body states or diffuse symbols of the self. Symbolization now undertakes the vastly more complex task of world mastery. While Dean's dreams at ages 6 and 7 are different from our own, for his knowledge, interests, and representational competences also are different from ours, they are beginning to become recognizably like ours in their organization and in the basic nature of their contents. They start to speak our language. This is an enormous step forward.

It is a development that our data indicate depends on the child's waking cognitive maturation. Because dreaming seems to develop as part and parcel of cognitive growth more generally, one naturally wonders if it shares the same ends as waking cognition. How does dreaming foster adaptation? Does it permit the more orderly acquisition, storage, and utilization of information? If so, how, and in what areas of human experience? These are questions to which we still have no very good answers, but our dream developmental data certainly indicate that they are questions to which students of waking cognition, as well as dream aficionados, must turn their attention.

If there is a sense in which the dreams of 5- to 7-year-olds still seem strikingly unlike ours, it must be in their general failure to integrate an effective self-representation into dream scenarios. The turn from self to other has been so abrupt, it is almost as if self has been left behind. This defect, too, parallels trends in waking representational development. And it should come as no surprise even (especially?) to us to realize that self-knowledge is that form of understanding that always comes most reluctantly.

CHAPTER 5 ⸻⸻⸻⸻⸻⸻⸻⸻

Ages 7 to 9

The 14 children whose dreaming was discussed in the previous two chapters also were studied, during their fifth and final year of laboratory service, at ages 7−9. In addition, as mentioned in Chapter 2, we supplemented the original sample with seven additional girls who were studied for the first time at ages 7−9. Methods of the study year in which all of these 7- to 9-year-olds participated were almost identical to those employed at ages 5−7.[1]

Among the original subjects, the median girl's age was 7 years, 1 month, and the median boy's age was 8 years, 0 months, at the start of their final study year. At the start of their first and final study year, the novice girls had a median age of 7 years, 6 months (range: 7 years, 3 months, to 8 years, 4 months). All of the children were in either second or third grade during the portion of the study year that they spent in school.

As a group, the novice recruits proved to be significantly less bright for their age than were the veteran girl subjects: Median novice I.Q. in the fifth study year was 105, while that for veteran girls was 118.[2] Veteran and novice female subjects did not differ significantly in social-class background (Table 2.3), however, nor did novice and veteran younger children differ significantly on any sleep parameter during our fifth study year.

That, for their respective ages, the novice subjects proved to be less bright than the veteran-girl peers does not mean that the two groups differed absolutely in their cognitive attainments, for the novices also were older than the veteran girls. In fact, on our composite scale of cognitive maturation as assessed by the Laurendeau-Pinard instrument, the novices, the veteran girls, and the veteran boys all had median scale scores of 7. That is, the typical child in all three groups was "operational" by our criteria (see Chapter 3), but not fully so.

Overall, most of the 21 7- to 9-year-olds were operational by the end of our study year, including five of seven veteran girls, five of seven novice

---

[1]As already noted in Chapter 2, fifth-year interviews were conducted (except on stimulus-incorporation nights) via an intercom, rather than (as earlier) at children's bedsides. But, on evidence of a special fourth-year study, this difference was not reliably associated with any difference in dream reporting or dream content.

[2]The figure for veteran boys was 119, and veteran boys' I.Q.'s also were significantly higher than those of the novices.

girls, and six of seven veteran boys. One veteran girl, two novice girls, and one veteran boy were operational on all three Laurendeau-Pinard subtests that we administered. Only two children (one veteran girl and one novice girl) failed to attain operationality on any of the subtests. Among the veterans, 10 had improved their composite cognitive-maturation score since ages 5–7, while four had maintained a constant (but subceiling) position on our scale.

Thus if as 5- to 7-year-olds the children could be described as in "early transition" to concrete-operational thought, as 7- to 9-year-olds they must be characterized as in "late transition." Although only a few children seemed to have consolidated *fully* the achievements of operational reasoning by ages 7–9, there clearly had been marked movement toward operationality since ages 5–7. In our sense, most children had become and now were at least partly operational in their thinking. Eight of the 14 original children (including Dean) *became* operational between ages 5–7 and 7–9, and at the latter age level, 76% of all children (vs. 21% at ages 5–7) *were* operational. Clearly these changes suggest the likelihood of enhancements in dream generation, in dream reporting, and in the quality of the narratives so reported.

THE REPORTING OF DREAMS

Between ages 5–7 and 7–9 there were significant[3] increases in both REM and NREM report rates. In terms of pooled recall rates, REM recall increased from 31% to 48%, and NREM recall from 8% to 21%, while sleep-onset recall held steady at 31%. In terms of typical-subject values, REM recall increased from 31% to 43%, NREM recall from 6% to 22%, and sleep-onset recall from 17% to 33%. All but one child of 21 (the girl nonreporter at ages 5–7) had at least one REM report; 15 children had at least one NREM report; and 13 children had at least one sleep-onset report.

While (finally!) the REM report rate was beginning its move toward adult values, the 48% pooled figure indicates that much room for improvement still remained. In fact, the 7- to 9-year-olds' REM and sleep-onset report rates were significantly inferior even to those of our 9- to 11-year-olds, that is, to the older-group children studied in the first year of their longitudinal series.

There are, I think, at least two plausible reasons why, in absolute terms, the 7- to 9-year-olds' report rate may have remained relatively low. First, as noted above, although the children had made great strides since ages 5–7 in

---

[3]The REM increase was significant only marginally ($p < .10$) by a 2-tail test. However, in the absence of reasonable grounds for expecting developmental decreases in dream reporting, it seems appropriate to use a 1-tail test. By such a test both NREM *and* REM recall increased significantly ($p < .05$).

waking cognitive maturation, much room for improvement past ages 7–9 remained. With such improvement these children might well have gained in the capacity for effective dream generation and/or reporting to the point where their REM report rates would have been comparable to those of our 9- to 11-year-olds. Second, the 7- to 9-year-olds' relatively low rate of REM recall may have been an artifact of our (longitudinal) research design, as also may have been the substantial cross-sectional gap in REM recall between ages 7–9 and 9–11.

The first possibility is highly plausible and must account for at least some of the difference in report rate between ages 7–9 and 9–11. The question is, how much? Or, more directly, to what degree might our study methods also artificially have depressed our report-rate index of the true generativity and/or accessibility of REM dreaming at ages 7–9? Certain lines of evidence suggest the possibility of some long-term effects of our longitudinal study design upon recall rates. Our longitudinal study consistently produced lower pooled REM recall estimates than did our earlier cross-sectional (generally two-nights-per-child) studies of children's dreams at roughly comparable ages:

Age	Longitudinal Study (%)	Cross-Sectional Study (%)
Preschoolers	27	44[4]
Early grade-schoolers	48	75[5]
Preadolescent males	61	69[5]; 73[6]
Early adolescent males	57	75[4]

From a motivational perspective, these differences may reflect the contrast between getting "up" for a crucial series (cross-sectional designs) and adapting to the more repetitive circumstances of a season-long schedule (longitudinal designs). Over an extended series of nights, and particularly when those nights include some NREM awakenings on which the experimenter clearly "made a mistake" (there *was* no dream), children may learn to relax the standards that, in a briefer and more focused series of observations, they would have employed in searching out and describing their dreams. In the process they may establish their own personal value as to what is a fair rate of "return" to the experimenter, based both on their past performance and on how easy it now is to generate dream reports. Thus perhaps in the face of a considerable expansion of readily accessible dream experiences between ages 5–7 and 7–9, the children may have reported only some of them, both because they had previously "learned" that

[4]Foulkes, Larson, Swanson, & Rardin, 1969.
[5]Foulkes, Pivik, Steadman, Spear, & Symonds, 1967.
[6]Foulkes, Belvedere, & Brubaker, 1971.

relatively few awakenings are, in fact, associated with dreams and because only some of the "new" dreams are so insistent as to demand attention when the child otherwise is not inclined to grant it. Longitudinal dream research is just another form of extended social exchange in which performances must be affected by informally achieved standards of fair "rates" of output (Roethlisberger & Dickson, 1939). Therefore, its performance increases (e.g., in rates of recall from ages 5–7 to 7–9) may underestimate capability increases.

Effects of a similar sort have been reported by Antrobus, Fein, Jordan, Ellman, and Arkin (1978). They describe a "novelty" phenomenon in which adult subjects on early nights in a multinight experiment, and early in the *first* night of that experiment, report more "dreamlike" activity than they do on later nights and later in that first night. These effects are described as being "among the strongest effects of any kind observed in the sleep-mentation literature" (p. 24).

But, interpretively, what is one to make of these "novelty" effects? It is not quite clear how they should be understood. Were the later decreases a function of motivational decrement in the report situation (thus a steady dreaming capacity was better indexed by short-term observations than by long-term ones), or were the early figures, in fact, generally unrepresentative increases in actual dreaming capacity induced by one's extraordinarily high state of arousal-anticipation-anxiety on entering the dream study? Perhaps there is some truth in each position. If so, by implication neither cross-sectional nor longitudinal estimates of dreaming should be used as "true" reference points with which to evaluate the other.

In support of either the motivational-decrement (for veteran children) or novelty-enhancement (for novice children) arguments were findings that novice girls at ages 7–9 were consistently (although not significantly) better dream reporters than were veteran girls. For REM sleep the pooled difference was 54% vs. 33%; for NREM sleep it was 24% vs. 10%; and for sleep-onset it was 37% vs. 14%. In all cases the novices' performances were much like those of the veteran boys (55%, 30%, and 43%, respectively). One could read these figures as follows: Veteran girls'—young, bright, but questionably motivated—report figures are serious underestimates of experience occurrence but experience capacity is not yet near to identity with that of older veteran boys; novice girls'—intermediate age, not particularly bright, but highly motivated—report figures are close to potential experience capacity and may, in fact, reflect situationally induced expansion in typical experience capacity; veteran boys'—old, bright, and moderately well motivated —report figures are only slight-to-moderate underestimates of true experience/report capability. The hypothesized motivational differences between veteran boys and girls could be attributed either to an interaction of sex with longitudinal adaptation or to characterological differences that happened to appear in our small samples of boys and girls.

Because median- or typical-child REM report values are less subject to deflation by a few "poorly performing" children or to inflation by a few "highly motivated" ones, it may be instructive to present such values for the three groups of children mentioned above: veteran girls, 23% (clearly indicative, I think, of some generalized motivational problems in this group); novice girls, 57% (indicative of what the veteran girls *could* have achieved); veteran boys, 73% (suggesting that dream capability probably is at near-adult levels for relatively bright 8- to 9-year-olds). It cannot have been raw intellectual capability (such as might have entered into dream generation or memory) that accounted for the novice–veteran girl difference in REM recall: The veterans had higher I.Q.'s than did the novices. Nor can the small age difference between the two samples explain the REM report difference: Veteran girls' *late* fifth-year (December 1972 to May 1973) median-child REM report rate was 24%, while novice girls' *early* fifth-year (June to November 1972) median-child REM report rate was 67%. Together these last two figures suggest *both* motivational decrement for veteran girls *and* either some novelty-enhancement early in the fifth study year and/or some motivational decrement late in the fifth study year for the novice girls. The stronger evidence is for motivational decrement for the veteran girls, who, at ages 7–9, managed a pooled rate of REM recall (33%) identical to that achieved by the boys *at ages 3–5*!

Taking Block Design raw scores as our most relevant *ability* marker, the data seem to suggest that REM report-rate differences must have been motivational in the case of the veteran vs. novice girl comparison, for the two groups had nearly identical Block Design median scores (12 and 11, respectively), despite their wide difference in REM report rates. However, our boy–girl differences also must have been cognitively mediated–the boys had a Block Design median score of 31, significantly greater than that of the girls which was 11. The novice-girl data suggest that motivation can partly, but not entirely, compensate for ability differences of such magnitude. Because, we did not have age- and I.Q.-matched girls to compare with our boys, it cannot be clear that the Block Design and dream-reporting differences we observed between boys and girls were other than accidental, although Bergan, McManis, and Melchert (1971) did observe consistent male superiority on Wechsler Block Design at age 9, and Vandenberg and Kuse (1979) have reviewed data-indicating a consistent male superiority on Block Design from age 6 on. Further research is required to relate these differences to differences in the increase of REM dreaming and/or its accessibility.

The novice girls' relatively high REM recall rates (particularly in view of their relatively low Block Design performances) raise another possibility: Perhaps these recall rates are in *excess* of those reasonably to be expected of children of their ability. Maybe these girls were, at least occasionally, confabulating reports to please the researcher. Evidence against this possibility is that, among novice subjects, full-scale Wechsler I.Q. was strongly and significantly related to REM reporting ($r = .79$). That is, within the novice group, age-scaled mental competence was a powerful predictor of dream reporting. Interestingly, this was *not* true for either veteran males or females. Presumably the veteran groups were more likely to include bright but motivationally jaded children who could, but did not, report dreams often.

Once again, at ages 7−9 children reported significantly more dreams on REM than on NREM awakenings. However, sleep-onset report-rate contrasts did *not* produce comparable findings as at ages 5−7. Sleep-onset awakenings were only marginally ($p < .10$, 2-tail) more productive of reports than NREM awakenings, and, for the only time in our two longitudinal series, REM recall was significantly better than sleep-onset recall. Sleep-onset rates, it will be remembered, were *not* increasing significantly from ages 5−7 to 7−9, while both REM and (especially) NREM rates were.

These data suggest a somewhat different course of development for the more voluntary phenomenon of sleep-onset dreaming than for the more involuntary scenarios of REM dreams. The sleep-onset mental activity of young adults seems to be more intimately related with the waking mental activity *from* which it is transitional than to the sleeping mental activity *to* which it is transitional (Vogel, 1978). Its occurrence and/or elaboration seems to depend, in particular, on attitudes of receptiveness to one's own experience that do not influence true sleep mentation. Such attitudes might also influence children's sleep-onset dreaming. At any rate, those same accretions in cognitive skill that foster increases in sleep mentation seem not to be sufficient conditions of increases in sleep-onset mentation. However, our sleep-onset data are·relatively scanty, and the differential ontogeny of sleep vs. sleep-onset mentation is a problem requiring further and more intensive study.

As at earlier ages, but now significantly, the children reported more NREM dreaming on "light" (29%) than on "deep" (13%) NREM awakenings. In fact, it was in large measure the children's increased access to "light" (EEG Stage 2) mentation that was responsible for their overall significant improvement in NREM report rates. Likewise, it was the children's increased creation of or access to late-night dreaming that was largely responsible for their increases in both REM and NREM dream reporting. At ages 7−9 the children showed, for the first time, effects of the ordinal position of nocturnal awakenings (it will be recalled that three awakenings were scheduled each night: early, middle, and late). REM awakenings early in the night produced significantly fewer recall reports (40%) than did those late in the night (60%); middle-night NREM awakenings produced significantly fewer recall reports (16%) than did late-night NREM awakenings (31%). In addition, at marginal ($p < .10$, 2-tail) significance, there were fewer mid-night REM reports (43%) than late-night ones, and fewer early-night NREM reports (16%) than late-night ones. These data indicate that *general increases in REM and NREM reporting are initiated by specific increases in late-night dream reporting.* All of the data discussed here add to the credibility of the 7- to 9-year-olds' reports because they are consistent with observations made for adults (e.g., Pivik & Foulkes, 1968; Foulkes, 1966) and because they indicate that accretions in dream reporting follow an orderly and predictable pattern, rather than being haphazardly distributed.

Who was reporting dreams, and why, at ages 7–9? First it can be noted that there were indications, among veteran subjects, of some stabilization of report rates. Year-3 REM reporting was better correlated with Year-5 REM reporting ($r = .44$) than was Year-1 REM reporting ($r = .25$), although neither correlation was significant. Next it should be noted that, again, REM report rate was strongly and significantly correlated with both NREM report rate ($r = .63$) and sleep-onset report rate ($r = .73$).[7] Thus to some degree the age 7–9 REM reporters also had been the age 5–7 REM reporters, and, to a strong degree, age 7–9 REM reporters were children who described dreams relatively often from all awakening conditions rather than merely selectively from REM sleep.

Finally, in terms of their own personal characteristics, age 7–9 REM reporters were talented both at visuospatial analysis tasks (Block Design, Embedded Figures) and at more verbally mediated tests of knowledge. Memory measures (e.g., Wechsler Digit Span, Description Test performance with the stimulus absent) did not predict REM report rate. Behaviorally, high-rate REM reporters seemed to be responsible, well socialized, and somewhat independent of their peers. Parental correlates were neither as numerous nor as internally consistent as at ages 5–7.

Since the significant rise in group REM recall rates at least in part represented a "catching up" of somewhat less talented peers to levels more precocious children already had achieved at ages 5–7,[8] it is not surprising to note that individuals with large *increases* in REM recall were not particularly talented cognitively. In fact, on the Matching Familiar Figures test they gave indications of having impulsive rather than reflective cognitive styles. For the first time there was some suggestion that REM-sleep properties themselves (but *not* REM phasic activity) may have been playing some role in mediating REM report rates; children with increased REM recall had more REM sleep and briefer latencies to their initial REM periods than did children with stabilized or decreasing REM recall. Those findings raise the possibility that children with high REM-sleep propensities thereby were more likely to generate dreams or to experience "salient" (more readily retrievable) dreams within their REM periods. Dream psychophysiologists might well turn their attention from relatively stabilized adult dream phenomena to earlier periods of dream development where the flux of psychological variables could be correlated with sophisticated multivariate recordings of concomitant physiological variability.

---

[7]And NREM and sleep-onset rates also were significantly intercorrelated ($r = .71$).
[8]REM report rate at ages 5–7 was negatively ($r = -.43$) correlated with increases in REM report rate between ages 5–7 and 7–9.

NREM report rate correlates suggested that visuospatial-task ability was less important to occurrence or access of NREM dreaming than to that of REM dreaming. Positive correlates of NREM reporting at ages 7–9 included Wechsler Information and Rorschach indices of imaginative intelligence. Rorschach "movement" scores also predicted *increases* in NREM reporting, but, overall, correlates of such increases were remarkably uninformative. Several cognitive variables were positively correlated with sleep-onset report rates at ages 7–9 (including Block Design and Children's Embedded Figures Test scores). Most or all of these measures are more plausibly interpreted as implicated in dream construction than in dream retrieval. Sleep-onset reporters also were older than their nonreporting peers.

In general, at a time of significant expansion of children's experienced and/or reported dreamlife, there was relatively much evidence that this was *permitted* by cognitive maturation and ability and relatively little evidence that it was *impelled* by children's waking conflicts or anxieties. This was the case both for the relatively more peremptory dreaming of REM sleep and for the possibly more optional or voluntary forms of mental activity occurring in NREM sleep or at sleep onset. And it also seems that by ages 7–9 there is little or no reason to doubt that most of the children's reports from all stages of sleep are credible ones.

THE CHANGING CONTENT OF REM DREAMS

Basically two kinds of significant changes were observed in children's REM dream reports from ages 5–7 to 7–9. Reports were longer, and there was more participation by the dreamer character in the activities and interactions of the dream scenario.

Girls' REM dreams increased from a median length of 50 to 70 words, and boys' from a median length of 25 to 48 words. Once again, the boys' lower figures must be interpreted in the context of the fact that they were reporting dreams more often than were the girls. The *typical child's* mean REM report length increased from 41 words at ages 5–7 to 72 words at ages 7–9. The latter figure was *higher* than that noted for 9- to 11-year-olds, and not grossly out of line with that noted, under comparable awakening conditions, either for our 11- to 15-year-olds or for young adults (Foulkes, Spear, & Symonds, 1966). The suggestion is that, by ages 7–9, children have reached near-adult levels with respect to the length of dream experiences reported when they do generate and/or report dreams for individual REM periods, but that they have not yet come close to adult performance in their ability to generate and/or report dreams for as many REM periods.

There are two empirically distinct ways in which young children can show growth in their REM dreaming/reporting skill: They can increase the length of individual dream reports, and they can increase their likelihood of giving dream reports. Until ages 9−11 indices of these two kinds of REM-dreaming capability (i.e., recall rate and mean word count) were uncorrelated (ages 3−5, $r = -.11$; ages 5−7, $r = .08$; ages 7−9, $r = .11$).[9] And, as we have seen, there were significant increases in REM word counts from ages 3−5 to 5−7, while significant increases in REM report rate first were observed only from ages 5−7 to 7−9. Neither REM recall nor REM word counts were reliably stable intraindividually from ages 3−5 to 7−9; both *were* reliable child characteristics from ages 9−11 to 13−15.[10] Thus it was not until ages 9−11 that report-rate and word-count measures had stabilized intraindividually and seemed to tap some common factor of dream generation or reporting. Until then it seemed that children's increases in dream phenomena could be reflected in word counts or in report rates or in both.

Thus at ages 7−9, as at ages 5−7, one is observing children who are probably at quite different phases of dream (or dream-report) development. In this regard, age norms or other within-age-group statistical descriptions may be somewhat misleading, for a child is probably better described in terms of where he or she has been or is going than in terms of what his or her age-mates are doing. This, in turn, suggests the superiority of longitudinal to cross-sectional analysis in charting the course of early dream (dream-report) development.

An additional possible implication of the separation of word-count and report-rate measures in early childhood is that report-rate measures may be better indices of dream generation, and word-count measures may be better indices of the development of reporting skills. Unlike the report-rate variable, REM word count seems to have shown the kind of gradual and continuous increase in early childhood that suggests it reflects continuous functions such as increases in attention, memory, vocabulary, and so forth. Plausibly one might hold that actual increases in dream generation would be both more discontinuous and limited to periods associated with qualitative shifts in cognitive organization, such as the attainment of operational reasoning. On this hypothesis, report rate, which increased significantly and appreciably in our studies only from ages 5−7 to 7−9 (longitudinally) and from ages 7−9 to 9−11 (cross-sectionally), is the better index of underlying changes in the actual experiencing of dreams.[11]

Besides the significant increase in length of REM dream reports, the

---

[9]Thereafter they were significantly intercorrelated: ages 9−11, $r = .66$; ages 11−13, $r = .57$; ages 13−15, $r = .64$.

[10]For REM report rates, from ages 9−11 to 11−13, $r = .87$, and from ages 11−13 to 13−15, $r = .89$; for REM word counts, from ages 9−11 to 11−13, $r = .65$, and from ages 11−13 to 13−15, $r = .83$.

[11]It is noteworthy that such visuospatial measures as Block Design and Embedded Figures did not correlate significantly, at any age level, with the extensiveness of REM reports, although they often were significantly related to the incidence of such reports.

following REM variables significantly increased in relative incidence from ages 5–7 to 7–9:

Locomotion, by the dreamer

Hunger, for the dreamer

Approach social, by the dreamer

Approach object, by the dreamer

Other-mediated favorable outcomes, for the dreamer

Any favorable outcomes, for the dreamer

The common link among these categories obviously is that they indicate increased participation in the dream by the self-character. In the context of my summary of the 5- to 7-year-olds' reports, it appears that there *is* an increasingly well-articulated self-character in children's dreams by ages 7–9, a self who can move about within the dream, who can experience drive-states, and who can both initiate and receive interaction with other dream characters. Another generalization that may be made about the motive and outcome categories showing significant longitudinal increases is that they all refer to prosocial or pleasurable dream sequences, rather than to antisocial or unpleasant exchanges. It is a socialized self who is newly being inserted into a socialized dreamworld, rather than a self who is victim either of its own impulsivity or of others' malice.

THE CONTENT OF REM DREAMS

Length

As we have seen, the length of the typical child's typical REM report was beginning to approximate that of the typical adult's REM report collected under comparable conditions. Relatively longer reports were collected from children with higher rates of cognitive maturation, with high indices of figural creativity (the Torrance test), and with higher rates of development of waking narrative complexity. More strongly than at any other age level, this pattern of cognitive correlates suggests that, at ages 7–9, differences in word count may reflect differences in actual dream elaboration and complexity. That is, not only children's increases in report rates but also their increases in word counts may be reflecting genuine expansions of dream experiencing, rather than just continuing increases in the memory, attention, and descriptive skills children bring to bear on the task of dream reporting. REM word-count increases from ages 5–7 to 7–9 were, in fact, also significantly associated with rate of cognitive maturation and with originality in figural manipulation. Contrary to the hypothesis that dreams are elaborated in response to conflict, anxiety was a *negative* correlate of such increases, as well as of the length of both NREM and sleep-onset reports.

Longer sleep-onset reports also came from children especially adept at waking description of a stimulus from memory. Interestingly, from the perspective that non-REM mentation is more "optional" than REM mentation, both NREM and sleep-onset word counts, but not REM word counts, were positively correlated with signs of artistic imagination or "psychological-mindedness."

Characters

Although there were no significant changes in dream characterization from ages 5–7, the following trends in character incidence were noted at ages 7–9: (1) decreasing utilization of animal characters, particularly of undomesticated animals, by boy dreamers; (2) increasing elaboration of human strangers, particularly of reasonably well-articulated male-adult strangers, by girl dreamers; and (3) continuity in the levels of representation of family members and of other known persons, with girls dreaming more often than boys of female known peers and persons.

Overall, immediate family members continued to be dreamed of relatively often by children who were passive and whose family situation seemed less than optimal. Maternal and paternal irritability predicted dreaming of parents. Cognitive correlates were less clearly patterned than at ages 5–7, but the three cognitive variables associated with dreaming of family members all were negative in direction. In line with the argument developed in Chapter 4, possibly it was the case that less talented children only now were surmounting hurdles in dream characterization already scaled at ages 5–7 by their more talented peers.

As was suggested by that same argument, cognitive variables at ages 7–9 tended to be associated positively with known-person incidence, but negatively with stranger incidence. For instance, if one takes the three pertinent character categories with substantial rates of occurrence that do *not* show marked or significant sex differences, significant cognitive correlates were as follows:

Known, any male

Wechsler Block Design	.46
Laurendeau-Pinard Night subtest, increase	.70
Laurendeau-Pinard composite, increase	.73
Torrance Figural Originality	.81
Torrance Figural Originality/Fluency	.83
Torrance Figural Elaboration	.74

Stranger, adult male

Wechsler Full-Scale I.Q.	−.57
Wechsler Verbal I.Q.	−.59
Wechsler Full-Scale I.Q., increase	−.55

Description Test, whole responses	−.53
Description Test, whole responses, increase	−.68
Matching Familiar Figures, *errors*	.64
Torrance, Verbal Originality	−.63
Stranger, any male	
Wechsler Full-Scale I.Q.	−.49
Description Test, whole responses, increase	−.60
Laurendeau-Pinard, composite	−.45
Matching Familiar Figures, *errors*	.64
Torrance, Verbal Originality	−.58
Torrance, Verbal Originality/Fluency	−.60
Torrance, Figural Flexibility	−.62

These are precisely the sorts of results one might have expected if: (1) it now is possible for talented children to construct veridical mental images of known persons of an order of familiarity lower than that attaching to family members; (2) less talented children still are unable to image such persons veridically and report this failure to the experimenter in terms of being unable to identify the characters whom they have, in fact, constructed.[12]

Several additional bits of evidence are consistent with this hypothesized developmental progression in dream characterization. There was a moderately negative correlation at ages 7–9 between known-person and stranger relative incidences for the more frequently reported and less dreamer-sex-biased class of male characters: $r = -.35$, $p = .133$, 2-tail. On the other hand, there were significant positive associations at the same ages between dreaming relatively often of male and of female strangers ($r = .61$) and between dreaming relatively often of male and of female known persons ($r = .46$). This particular pattern (see Chapter 6) was observed at no other age level, and suggests that whether characters were known or were strangers was, at ages 7–9, a much more salient dimension in individual patterns of dream characterization than whether they were male or female. I want to suggest that the 7- to 9-year-old is operating under a stage-specific cognitive imperative to attempt the imaging of persons in her or his widening world of waking social experience, an imperative that is relatively unselective as to which persons in particular are so imaged and the success of whose outcomes is mediated by the child's current level of representational skill. (Note that the correlates presented above of the incidence of the least sex-biased

---

[12]As a reminder that one needs to consider children's knowledge base as well as their cognitive aptitude for symbolically reconstructing it during dreams, it should be noted that high-rate stranger dreamers at ages 7–9 were socially timid, suggesting inexperience with others. Known-person dreamers, on the other hand, did not seem to be particularly peer oriented or socially competent.

class of known persons deal either with figural aptitude or with Piagetian maturation.)

Not only were animal characters in a state of terminal decline at ages 7–9, at least in relation to their disproportionate role in the dreams of earlier childhood, the individual children still employing relatively many such characters were among the younger and less cognitively gifted ones in their age group. Animal dreamers were defective, in particular, in their understanding of the difference between the animate and the inanimate. Children's early failure to differentiate clearly between these two aspects of reality, and between humans and nonhumans, suggests, of course, a partial answer to the question of why children dream so often of animals. Why not, if they don't recognize the categorical distinctions in our minds as we ask that question?

It may be particularly revealing that the beginning decline of *animal* characterization occurs at that point in dream development when effective *self*-representation is increasing (cf. the longitudinal increases in self-participation mentioned earlier). As I stated in Chapter 4, it is my hypothesis that dream animals are not deliberate disguises of anyone or anything in the child's life, but are convenient fill-ins for self-representation when the child's cognitive immaturity makes it impossible for her or him to construct more literal self-approximations.

Settings

Residential, recreational, and general outdoor settings remained the most frequently portrayed locales of dream events. Despite the increasing hours children were spending in academic pursuits at school, nonrecreational school settings were relatively rare—and generally remained so at later ages. Evidently dream representations are formed on some other basis than the sheer number of hours of waking exposure to the situations they portray. Perhaps the principle of selection is the degree to which a waking situation actively stimulates the child's interest, imagination, or feelings.[13]

Considering children who dreamed relatively often of their own homes (uniquely at ages 7–9, more such dream settings were reported by boys than girls), one finds support for both the exposure and emotional-involvement hypotheses of setting determination. Shy, unstable, and tense children— those presumably spending relatively little time in satisfying peer relationships—dreamed most often of their own homes. But the exposure alternative seems weakened by the school data cited above. Dreamers of residential settings more generally (home, any) no longer seemed particularly immature socially, however. In line with observations at ages 5–7, frequent dreamers of play activities (i.e., recreational settings) did not seem particu-

---

[13]In that regard, it is interesting that television watching, which for many children can be at least as time-consuming as are classroom activities, also was quite infrequently portrayed in children's dreams.

larly imaginative or creative, and outgoing children were frequent dreamers of generalized outdoor settings.

Activities

The range and incidence of activities in REM dreams at ages 7−9 did not differ greatly from those at ages 5−7. As we have seen, dreamer locomotion increased significantly, and the normative data indicate that this increase and a general increase in dreamer motor activity were attributable to change by boy dreamers. At ages 5−7 boys' Active Participation in their dreams was rated (insignificantly) inferior to that of the girls; at ages 7−9, pooled rating means for the two sexes were practically identical. As suggested in the last chapter, however, some claims of dreamer participation at ages 5−7 probably were erroneous. Therefore, it may well have been that true increases in self-participation in REM dreams occurred for both boys *and* girls from ages 5−7 to 7−9. Also, it is important to note that the increases in dreamer participation were not to the point of relative parity with participation by other dream characters, which only was achieved by ages 11−13. The movement toward increased motoric participation by the self-character, both absolutely and relative to participation by other dream characters, was one of the steadiest trends observed in children's dreams from early childhood until late preadolescence.

At this time, quite a bit more clearly than at ages 5−7 (perhaps because some reports there still were "mistaken"), cognitive competency was positively correlated with dreamer participation at a sensory level (the self, in the dream, *sees* something). Comparable correlations did not exist with the equally frequently scored class of sensory acts for other characters (someone else, in the dream, *sees* something). The difference is reasonable, for it seems likely that the ascription of seeing to the self-character, which implies a constructed image of what the character sees, must be a greater cognitive achievement than is the ascription of seeing to another character, which does not carry that same implication. In the differential personality correlates of sensory-self dreaming at ages 5−7 and 7−9, there was clear evidence of a new meaning for sensory-self participation in dreams. Sensory-self dreamers at ages 5−7 were dependent on adults and socially ineffective; at ages 7−9, however, they were mischievous, socially dominant, and lacking in dependence! Nor were sensory-other dreamers socially passive any longer; at school they were judged particularly aggressive. Motor-self acts no longer correlated with dreamer assertiveness, and it proved to be passive children who now were dreaming dreams with high overall incidences of motor activity. It is difficult to know what to make of these reversals and inconsistencies, except to observe that new determinants evidently are active on the dream landscape. Perhaps this is because the cognitive-constructional possibilities within that landscape have been subject to radical transformation. For the first time, children are beginning to be able to insert "themselves" into their dreams to the degree that their reports of sensory-self activity now mean that they are identified with, and sense through the senses of, a self-character in the dreamworld. The self-character now is the camera. So long as this remains the major modality of dream production, it might be expected that sensory-self reports would characterize the most active of children. It was, in fact, from ages 7–9 to 11–13 (i.e., at three age levels across two separate groups of children) "mischievous" children who most often reported sensory-self dreams. And as we shall see in Chapter 8, this continuity, in turn, breaks down in what seems at ages 13–15 to be the possibility of a still more advanced form of dream construction.

At ages 7–9 the relative incidence of verbal-dreamer reports remained low, but there was substantial evidence that verbal-other and verbal-either dreaming was positively associated with general mental ability. Social sensitivity and a relative disinterest in gross motor-play activities also were associated with dreaming of verbal acts. Locomotor dreaming, on the other hand, no longer was associated with interpersonal hostility or dominance, but it did seem to be associated with a less finely calibrated cognitive style (an overall deficiency of Rorschach responses, and a preference for global rather than particular form [Dd] determinants). Locomotor dreamers also scored low on the same Piagetian-stage measure (the Laurendeau-Pinard Night test) on which verbal-activity dreamers scored high.

States

A handful of reports at ages 5–7 included dreamer cognitions (in the dream, the self-character was reported to have thought, reflected, wondered, etc.), but correlates of these reports included measures of waking wordiness rather than of waking cognitive skill. Since the adoption of a mentalistic perspective in dreams presumably depends on the development of cognitive sophistication, the cognitive elements in these early reports more likely were verbalisms added in describing dreams than properties of dream experiences themselves. By ages 7–9, however, cognitive activities in dreams had increased somewhat in incidence and had substantial cognitive correlates. It now seemed possible for children occasionally (less than one dream in 10) to endow dream characters—including, for the first time, nonself characters—with internalized, mentalistic states and acts. Although this dream cognition generally was verbal in form—characters had "thoughts," not "mental imagery"—its correlates included a number of nonverbal cognitive scores. This suggests that the initiation of intradream cognition does not depend on specifically verbal skills so much as it does on general conceptual ability.

Fear also first was reported (two dreams) at ages 5–7, but its correlates were even more suggestive of erroneous dream reporting than were those of cognitive acts at the same ages. Fear reporting, too, increased from ages 5–7 to 7—9. At the latter ages—and from then through to adolescence—about one dream in 10 contained the ascription of fear to some dream character, generally the self. High-rate fear reporters were unstable and tense children, which suggests waking–dreaming continuity. However, they also were unconscientious children of an imaginative frame of mind, which suggests the continuing possibility that claims of *dream fear* were, in fact, *waking-report* elaborations of dreams experienced without fear or other emotions. Sleep disturbance continued to be correlated with fear reports, suggesting once again (see Chapter 4) a possible nocturnal basis/reinforcement for waking apperceptive tendencies of a fearful sort that some children might bring to bear on their dream remembrances. For the first time at ages 7—9, a few (4%) dream reports contained the emotion of anger, but these reports were considerably less reliable than the fear reports (they had negative correlations with comprehension, memory, and conscientiousness). Thus overall there was relatively little reporting of "negative" emotion at ages 7—9, and from correlates of giving such reports, it is not clear that the children even yet could actually experience fear or, especially, anger during the act of dreaming itself.

Even if one accepts reports of fear and anger at ages 7—9 at face value, it is remarkable how few and how developmentally late appearing these contents are. And yet from a cognitive perspective, it is not entirely unaccountable. Studies in wakefulness (Shantz, 1975) indicate both that the recognition of happy feeling generally predates that of fear or anger and that it is not until middle childhood that children are effective in judging emotions displayed by unfamiliar persons in unfamiliar situations (i.e., have genuine emotional recognition, rather than the ability to project or guess from their own experience in like situations). Nor is it until middle childhood that children begin to think "psychologically" about others and themselves with sufficient frequency in wakefulness that they might be able, in their dreams, to endow dream characters with either reasons or feelings. As noted in Chapter 3, it is far more "natural" to act emotionally than to be able to recreate symbolically feeling states; *dream* emotions must depend on the latter ability, which may not develop until—or past—the early grade-school years.

From the waking evidence, one might expect happiness to be the earliest-appearing reliable intradream emotion. At ages 5—7, as we have seen (Chapter 4), girls produced a host of happy-self reports, but there was some question as to whether these reports always corresponded with happy-self dream experiences. At ages 7—9 happy-self reports were given less frequently (12% of the girls' REM dreams, 18% of the boys'), but they now seemed to be reliable (positive correlations with Wechsler I.Q., Information, Comprehension, and Block Design). That Wechsler and Torrance scores were shared as positive correlates by the dreamer-cognition and the dreamer-happiness categories suggests that the ability to endow the self with feelings is a cognitive achievement comparable to the ability to endow it with thought. In both cases one is thinking (dreaming) "psychologically," something that seems not to be reliably demonstrable before ages 7—9.

But can we be sure that even these reports reflect actual *dream* experiences? Some pause for thought is occasioned by two of the happy-self correlates: The Torrance variable is Figural Elaboration, going beyond the figures given, and the Rorschach correlate is movement scores (shared with afraid-self reports), which also means the children have added something to the Rorschach card that is in some sense not there or there only by imaginal inference. If this kind of addition also is present in the children's dream accounts, can we be sure that it occurred during the dream itself, rather than later, in telling it? Such questioning in the face of the positive cognitive correlates of happy-self dreaming may strike the reader as perverse. But from the perspective of the dream as cognitive construction, should we routinely assume that reports of dream feelings in early or mid-childhood actually reflect dream experiences? I doubt it. Having made that general point, however, I do interpret the overall pattern of happy-self correlates at ages 7−9 as indicating that it is at these ages that children first are able to experience feeling in dreams. That the feeling that occurs relatively most often at this time, and that has the greatest presumption of actually having been experienced during the dream, is *happiness* should help to put to rest notions that the dreams of early childhood are mainly unpleasant and that dreaming is initiated developmentally as a process of dealing with one's negative feelings or instincts.

By ages 7−9 enough different kinds of feelings were being reported so that it probably makes little sense to ask who, in general, was reporting the most dream feeling. Correlates of overall feeling ascription were a hodgepodge of those of different feeling-states considered separately. The positive cognitive correlates of happy feelings washed out, and feeling reporters were tense but unconscientious children who were high in Rorschach movement responses, which, as suggested above, might reflect either reportorial elaboration or dream constructional activity. The correlation with waking tenseness does suggest a continuity—at some level—between waking and dream-report emotionality.

Motives and Outcomes

As we have seen, it was the participation of the *dreamer character* in motivated behavioral sequences that showed significant longitudinal increases from ages 5−7 to 7−9. For practically the first time, for instance, hunger-related activities were ascribed to the self-character, a strong indication of new possibilities of genuine self-participation in dream scenarios. It is particularly revealing of earlier problems in self-representation that what one might imagine to be the prepotent waking drive of childhood did not achieve self-expression until ages 7−9. As might be expected for any new dream-constructional possibility, the initial incidence of self-hunger themes at ages 7−9 had positive cognitive correlates—intellectually talented children were most able to dream such themes. Cognitive correlates of self-hunger dreams were much more compelling than those of hunger dreams more generally.

Fatigue representations at ages 7−9 did not reach any new plateau, but here too effective waking cognition (the ubiquitous Block Design) predicted dream self-representation, although cognitive correlates were more compelling for overall fatigue-theme incidence than for self-fatigue themes. Given the developmental primitivity of self-fatigue themes (see Chapter 3), and their rather uncomplicated means of representation, it probably should not be surprising that the appearance of such themes at ages 7−9 implied less cognitive skill than did the ego-decentered ascription of fatigue motivation to other characters—something observed only rarely at ages 3−5. Fatigue-self dreamers at ages 7−9 seemed not to be particularly sleep deprived or sleep frustrated; rather, they generally seemed to be efficient sleepers. They were "tense," however (and fatigue-any dreamers were both "tense" and "excitable"), suggesting that fatigue dreaming may be related to a generally high susceptibility to having one's thoughts influenced by one's body states. Phasic REM variables no longer correlated with the incidence of fatigue themes, however.

There were very few positive cognitive correlates at ages 7−9 of representations, either self- or other-ascribed, of social-motive themes. Evidently there is neither anything particularly subtle (cf. cognitive acts in dreams) nor anything particularly difficult symbolically (cf. organic motives and happy feelings) about portraying social initiation during the "operational" reorganization of dreaming. Presumably children's waking minds have been working most assiduously in developing coherent representations of self vis-à-vis social reality, but have been less successful in evolving schemata for portraying mental life or body states.

Overall, social-approach themes were reported most often by friendly, unaggressive children. About four dreams in 10 contained such themes, with object-directed approaches occurring even more often, in over one-half of all reports. Themes of the initiation of social approaches by the self came from friendly but socially uncomprehending children; themes of social initiation by others came from socially sensitive but insecure, undependable, and emotionally unstable children. Thus dreaming−waking continuity probably was somewhat stronger at the level of social interest than at that of social competence.

Social-attack themes continued to occur at a rate of about one dream of four, and continued to be largely other initiated, although self-initiations now did occur (9% of girls' dreams, 4% of boys'). Self-initiators of aggression in dreams were high in unprovoked physical aggression to peers, were physically mature for their age, and had somewhat authoritarian parents. The overall incidence of aggression themes was associated with overt physical aggression to peers, with increases in fantasy aggression, and with physical maturation indices, but not with any particularly punitive style of parenting.

Thus in general by ages 7−9 the selection of particular kinds of social initiations for dream portrayal was related to children's own waking styles of interpersonal behavior and/or their own waking interpersonal interests. This predictable pattern, however, was less apparent at earlier ages, where one encountered lower dream-report rates, smaller percentages of dreams containing some of the relevant dream attributes (particularly self-initiations), and reports in whose credibility one does not always have perfect faith. Or one might say more broadly that it may be only when one has attained cognitive mastery of the dream medium that her or his dreams can begin to express "personality" (noncognitive) variables in any coherent way. For would-be "interpreters" of children's earliest dreams, the message should be clear: Don't read "personality" into observed dream differences until you are sure that these differences don't merely reflect differential mastery of the representational processes that underlie dreaming.[14]

As for initiation, so too for receipt; children's self-involvement in social interaction at ages 7–9 was more likely to be in an approach-favorable sequence than in an attack-unfavorable one. And, as we have seen, it was dreamer involvement only in prosocial-interaction sequences that had increased significantly since ages 5–7. Viewed from the receipt side, as from the initiation side, frequent dreamers of prosocial interaction sequences did not seem particularly competent socially; rather they gave signs of having reasons for concern about their interpersonal adjustment (instability, apprehension, dependency) and of being sensitive to others' opinions of them. Children relatively high in self-receipt of hostility (or, for the boys almost equally as often, of unmediated, "chance" misfortunes) had increasingly hostile apperceptive responses and were not very talkative, but otherwise seemed unexceptional. The more numerous reports of *other*-receipt of unfavorable outcomes, on the other hand, came from children who were creative and socially active. Behaviorally they did not seem particularly aggressive, and their waking fantasies were pleasant rather than dysphoric. However, the parental climate for children dreaming of unfavorable outcomes suggested the presence of family tension. No longer were unfavorable dream outcomes related to sleep disturbance, and, unlike social-attack themes at ages 7–9, unfavorable outcomes were not predicted by the dreamer's waking overt aggressivity. More generally it is interesting that our social-motive and social-outcome categories, which were meant largely to be overlapping, produced somewhat different patterns of correlates for initiation vs. receipt of both positive and negative encounter: Waking friendliness predicted prosocial initiation but not favorable outcome, and waking aggressiveness predicted antisocial initiation but not unfavorable outcome. In both instances

[14]An interesting clinical example is the dream reported to have occurred at age 4 for Freud's (1918) patient the "Wolf Man." The dream itself conforms to representational processes that our data indicate generally to be operative at age 4: The child is in bed (fatigue-self); a window opens to reveal white wolves (animal characters) sitting in a big walnut tree (static imagery). In attempting to interpret the dream, however, Freud saw these features as motivated disguises of other mental contents. For instance, he thought that the wolves' immobility must have been a transformation (reversal) of some scene of violent activity (primal scene) that dream-distorting mechanisms would not admit directly to conscious awareness.

the correlation with overall initiation depended on a correlation with specifically dreamer-initiated activity. Evidently at the point where the self enters the dream in a substantial way, who the dreamer is in wakefulness is more strongly related to what he or she does in the dream than to what happens to him or her in it.

Global Ratings

At ages 7–9 dreamers who more often were successful in inserting themselves in their dreams and in playing active roles there had significantly more pleasant and less distorted dreams. Once again character distortion and setting distortion were significantly intercorrelated ($r = .64$), but although correlations still were positive, dream unpleasantness no longer was significantly related to dream distortion.

There was a reduction in the magnitude of the previous sex difference in ratings of the hedonic quality of dreams (a difference that, as we have seen, probably rested on artifactually "happy" reports by girls at ages 5–7), but girls' REM reports still were judged somewhat more pleasant, on the average, than were boys'. Perhaps in consequence, dreamers of unpleasant themes at ages 7–9 were relatively low in social sensitivity, dependence, and talkativeness, but relatively high in mischievousness. Dream unpleasantness was not associated with waking apprehension or anxiety; in fact, *low* ratings (and increasingly low ratings) for anxiety were associated with increases in REM dream unpleasantness from ages 5–7 to 7–9. However, increased REM unpleasantness also was associated with aggressive (and increasingly aggressive) waking fantasies. It is particularly interesting to note that the longer it took a child to fall asleep, the more unpleasant her or his *sleep-onset* mentation was. Apparently early in the period of concrete-operational thinking, unpleasant and intrusive thoughts may serve to keep children from quickly passing from wakefulness to sleep (Vogel, Barrowclough, & Giesler, 1972).

Consistent with the hypothesis that genuine self-involvement in interpersonal contexts first becomes possible at ages 7–9 is the finding of positive cognitive correlates of REM Active Participation ratings. *Increases* in participation from ages 5–7 to 7–9 did not have such correlates, presumably because among subjects with such increases were less gifted children catching up with more precocious peers who already had experienced self-participation at ages 5–7.[15] Visuospatial-analysis measures (Block Design, Children's Embedded Figures Test) predicted *sleep-onset* self-participation at ages 7–9.

Correlates of REM-dream distortion were less sharply drawn at ages 7–9

---

[15]A factor complicating interpretation of these increases is the likelihood that some claims of participation at ages 5–7 were erroneous. It was relatively subdued children, unresponsive to adult approval, who showed longitudinal increases. Such children probably would *not* have confabulated self-participation at ages 5–7.

than at 5−7. Setting distortion was associated with lagging rates of cognitive growth, but not with low absolute levels of cognitive skill. Increases in setting distortion were associated both with lagging rates of cognitive growth and with low absolute achievement on two measures of creative or synthetic ability. These findings suggest "catch up," as do parallel observations that increased setting distortion was associated with physical and social immaturity. It also seemed, probably for the same reason, to be cognitively slowly developing and relatively untalented children who showed increases in character distortion from ages 5−7 to 7−9, which is consistent with the observation that our girls' dreams increased but our (older) boys' dreams decreased in mean character distortion over this time span.

REM Ratios

For fifth-year dreams in both study groups, we also calculated correlates of the *ratio* at which certain content classes appeared in relation to others, or of the *difference* in their rate of appearance (see Chapter 2). One such ratio was of the appearance of *verbal* acts in relation to that of *locomotor* acts, that is, of subtle-cognitive action to gross-physical action. Correlates of this REM ratio at ages 7−9 were much like those of its numerator, except that higher social-class children also had high verbal/locomotor ratios. In general, high ratios seemed to be associated not so much with "basic intelligence" (i.e., Wechsler scores) or with waking verbosity as a social style as with situation-specific effective utilization of language knowledge and skills (e.g., effective stimulus description, originality and fecundity of verbal productions).

Our *sensory/motor* ratio proved, in retrospect, to have been somewhat ill-conceived, for sensory acts in dreams generally were reciprocal with motor ones—one character *saw* another one *doing* something. Correlates at ages 7−9 generally were like those of sensory acts. Correlates of a *cognitive/motor* ratio were quite similar to those of its numerator and included numerous measures of cognitive skill.

A REM difference score indexed the degree to which *external-focus* (other persons, environmental objects) vs. *internal-focus* (body state) motives appeared in children's dreams. Correlates of the index indicated that it was not particularly socially competent or sociable children who dreamed more often of world than of self (cf. correlates of approach-social dreaming at ages 7−9).

We also determined correlates of the rate at which *male strangers* were generated in relation to *female strangers*. Although throughout our studies girl and boy dreamers were better matched in the production of male than of female strangers, correlates of the index seemed to reflect more than the dreamer's own gender. A male bias also seemed to index what we call a "tough-guy" orientation. Correlated with such a bias were the following variables: (1) lower social-class; (2) a lack of intellectual reflectivity and expansiveness; (3) relative disinterest in adult approval; (4) irresponsibility; (5) social insensitivity; and (6) a lack of interpersonal expressiveness. Such a style clearly is more normatively "masculine" than "feminine," but its overlap with actual gender identity must be relatively imperfect.

A final REM difference score considered the kind of familiar or known characters who appeared in children's reports: Were they *familial* or *extra-familial*? Consistent with our hypotheses about the expansion of dream characterization in early childhood, at ages 7−9 a relative preference for less-familiar known characters was related to visuospatial creativity and rate of Piagetian maturation.

NOVICE AND VETERAN GIRLS

In the preceding normative summaries and correlational analyses (but not, of course, in longitudinal comparisons), the newly inducted girl subjects at ages 7−9 were included along with children studied for the prior four years. Is this procedure justifiable? Or, more generally, when one studies children over time, do their dreams change as a result of one's own observational procedures, so that their later dreams no longer will be like those of another set of age-matched children without prior experimental experience?

Comparisons of the REM dreams of our seven experimental novices and of their six experimentally experienced but age- and sex-matched peers at ages 7−9[16] should permit one to draw some conclusions about such issues. However, as we shall see, the interpretation of differences emerging from these comparisons is made somewhat difficult by the presence of alternative explanatory hypotheses; such differences as emerge could be not *repeated-study* effects for the veterans but *initial-adaptation* effects for the novices, and/or they also could simply be a function of *unreliability in subject sampling*, that is, our comparison groups may differ on other relevant variables than length of prior experimental service.[17]

We already have considered in the context of novice−veteran differences in REM report rates at ages 7−9 (novices with 54% pooled REM recall, veterans with 33%, $p < .15$, 2-tail) the possibility of one repeated-testing effect: that the veteran girls stabilized their level of REM reporting at a level farther from their true age 7−9 capacity for REM reporting (and closer to their age 3−5 capacity) than did the novices. And, as we have seen, it is unlikely that this intergroup report-rate difference can be explained by differences in either age or I.Q. between the novices and the veterans, although it could, at least in part, be an initial adaptation enhancement effect for the novices.

---

[16]As already noted, one veteran girl reported no REM dreams in her fifth study year.
[17]For example, as noted earlier in this chapter, in age and I.Q.

The report-rate difference suggests the probability of comparable novice–veteran differences in REM content. In fact we observed four such differences that attained statistical significance:

Veterans Higher In	Novices Higher In
Locomotion, by the dreamer	Unfamiliar home settings
Active participation ratings	Setting distortion ratings

One way to determine which 7- to 9-year-old female group is more generally representative (i.e., whether veterans' dreams had been experimentally altered by repeated study or novices' dreams by initial adaptation) is to use the 7- to 9-year-old boys (who seemed to show less of a repeated-testing effect in recall rate) as a reference point. Another is to determine which 7- to 9-year-old female group provides the more reasonable point of interpolation between our observations at ages 5–7 and (from the older study group) at ages 9–11.

By such criteria, the novices seem deviant in *the unfamiliarity of their REM-dream home settings.* The typical novice girl had a 25% relative incidence of unfamiliar residential settings; the typical veteran girl *and* the typical veteran boy had a 0% relative incidence of unfamiliar home settings. It seems likely that the new experience of sleeping away from home in a simulated home setting—a place where one undresses, has a story read at bedtime, goes to the toilet, lies down to go to sleep, wakes up—has made unfamiliar "residential" settings a more salient issue for novices than for veterans. Their dreams are reactive to the experimental situation, while those of the veterans are not. The effect may, then, be one of initial adaptation, rather than of repeated testing.

However, neither novice boys nor novice girls first studied at ages 9–11 showed a comparable effect. The typical child of either sex at these ages had a 0% incidence of unfamiliar home settings, and no individual child ($n = 16$) had a relative incidence of over 13%. Data on presleep adaptation (see Chapter 2) suggest one reason for the difference: The novice girls studied at ages 7–9 seemed to be more ill at ease in the laboratory than their veteran peers or than 9- to 11-year-olds had been in their first study year.[18] And there was a moderate (but nonsignificant) positive correlation among ages 7–9 novices between the number of presleep periods in which they were judged moderately or extremely anxious and the incidence of unfamiliar home settings ($r = .44$).

For *rated Setting Distortion,* not all of the analyses applied above to the relative incidence of unfamiliar home settings can be repeated so confi-

---

[18]At marginal significance ($p < .10$, 2-tail), ages 7–9 novice girls also had more unpleasant dreams (hedonic tone rating) than did veteran girls.

dently. The usefulness of the 9- to 11-year-olds' data as a reference point is vitiated by the likelihood that setting-relevant information was probed in less detail at ages 9−11 than at ages 7−9 (see Chapter 4). The major relevant interpretive datum is that veteran girls' setting-distortion ratings were significantly lower at ages 7−9 not only than those of the novices but also than those of the veteran 7- to 9-year-old boys.

One might explain this aberrance in terms of the veteran girls' lower report rates. Perhaps they simply "missed" reporting dreams with contents more difficult to assimilate to familiar waking schemata. But this hypothesis presents difficulties because 9- to 11-year-olds, with much better REM report rates, reported settings that were *more* familiar than those of the 7- to 9-year-olds. General increases in dream accessibility in mid-childhood apparently are not associated with the reporting of dreams with less familiar setting contents.

Another more likely possibility is that the setting difference relates not so much to which kinds of dreams the veteran girls reported at ages 7−9 as to how well they were being reported. Setting-distortion scores were, in effect, earned via an expenditure of effort. The child must have responded negatively to a question as to whether the setting was a familiar one (see Table 2.4) and then have gone on to describe in what way the dream home (school, etc.) was different from the familiar one of wakefulness. From the veteran girls' overall rate of REM reporting, we believe that at ages 7−9 this group was generally lacking in willingness to expend such energy. Perhaps, then, they also were less scrupulous than either the boys or the novice girls in reporting background (but not focal) features of their REM dreams.

In terms of the difference these hypothesized effects on dream settings might have had on our normative data—the repeated-testing effect perhaps depressing setting unfamiliarity for veteran girls and an initial-adaptation effect more likely enhancing the occurrence of at least certain kinds of unfamiliar settings for the novices—it would have, I think, to be judged minor. Unfamiliar home settings were rarely scored, and we included them in neither our normative data summaries nor our correlational analyses. The setting distortion rating variable, however, is of more general significance. Here, though, it can be said that the novice and veteran differences have effectively counterweighted one another so that the pooled veteran-and-novice normative data probably are more representative than either data set would be considered separately. The close similarity of the veteran boys and the novice girls on this variable suggests that, corrected for report motivation, there is no sex difference in setting distortion at ages 7−9. Without that correction, one would have been forced to conclude otherwise.

The locomotion and self-participation differences between veterans and novices are suggestive more of initial-adaptation effects for the novices than of repeated-testing effects for the veterans. The typical novice had only 8% *self-locomotion*, vs. 58% for veteran girls and 36% for veteran boys. At ages 5−7 typical-subject incidence of self-locomotion for girls was 28% and, at ages 9−11 the figure was 40%. Possibly the veteran girls' age 7−9 incidence is "too high" (perhaps because self-active dreams are best recalled), but clearly the novice girls' incidence is much "too low." For *active participation* ratings, the typical novice had a mean of 1.50, compared to 2.00 for veteran girls and 1.67 for veteran boys. The veterans' figures fit, in both cases, into a coherent developmental series of steady increases in participation, but the novices' figure lies outside independent estimates of typical participation by girls at ages 5−7 (1.80) and 9−11 (2.10).[19]

Having documented some aberrance in the novices' dream participation, one still needs to understand it. We believe that it rests on the discomfort the novices felt in the novel laboratory setting, their genuine feeling of being not in control of their immediate environment while in the laboratory. This laboratory effect did not directly affect dream content, for "sleep-laboratory" settings were seldom scored at ages 7−9 and were scored *less* frequently for novices than for veterans. Indirectly (i.e., through creative elaboration), however, discomfort might have been translated both into unfamiliarity of dream settings and passivity within dream scenarios.

Thus our search for repeated-testing effects on veteran subjects, with the cross-sectionally recruited novices as "controls," seems to have ended up more with a demonstration of "novelty" effects for the novices than with any clear evidence of long-term effects of dream study on dream content. If this interpretation of observed novice−veteran differences is correct, it raises the possibility of comparable "novelty" effects for 9- to 11-year-old girls in their first year of dream study. Suppose, then, one turns the model previously proposed for evaluating 7- to 9-year-old girls' reports around, and now uses the 7- to 9-year-old veteran girls' data to evaluate the 9- to 11-year-old girls' reports. Then it may be the case not that 7- to 9-year-old girls are peculiarly low in setting distortion and high in self-initiated locomotion, but that the 9- to 11-year-old girls, because they are experiencing novelty effects such as those seen with the 7- to 9-year-old novices, are artifactually high in setting distortion and low in locomotion.

On this hypothesis: (1) girls, but not boys, will show initial adaptation effects in typically designed sleep-laboratory studies of sleep mentation; (2) there is practically *no* evidence of repeated-testing effects on dream-*content* variables; (3) differential initial-adaptation effects by sex may either mask (e.g., in setting distortion at ages 7−9 and possibly at 9−11) or spuriously generate (e.g., locomotor activity at ages 9−11) sex differences in dream content. But is there evidence for this hypothesis? Because of the previously indicated difficulty in using 9- to 11-year-olds' setting distortion ratings to

---

[19]However, if the veteran girls' claims of participation at ages 5−7 are judged at least partly bogus (Chapter 4 presents supporting evidence) and the veteran boys' ratings at ages 5−7 are used as a standard for evaluating reports of girls ages 7−9, then the novices' data are somewhat less aberrant.

test the hypothesis, we restrict our consideration to self-participation in locomotor activity.

The following relative incidences of self-locomotion were observed at ages 7–13:

Participants	Ages 7–9 (%)	Ages 9–11 (%)	Ages 11–13 (%)
Veteran boys	36		59
Novice boys		50	58
Veteran girls	58		60
Novice girls	8	40	

A "novice" subject here is any subject in his or her first study year. From these data, it is apparent that novice boys' dreams contain self-locomotion at rates consistent with series generated by veteran boys' dreams, while novice girls' dreams, in both instances, do not conform to a progression generated by veteran girls' dreams. Adapted (veteran) girls at ages 7–9 were more like adapted girls at ages 11–13 than like the same girls as novices at ages 9–11, who seemed discrepantly low in the incidence of locomotor activity in REM dreams. Because they were significantly lower than 9- to 11-year-old boys in such activity, the girls' data cannot be attributed to secular scoring changes or other procedural factors that *generally* affected ages 9–11 scorings.

Thus it seems likely that girls initially studied at ages 7–11, at least in a design where the experimenter is male, may be prone to dream-novelty effects (e.g., dream passivity or quietude) reflecting their relative discomfort in the laboratory. There are alternative interpretations of the relevant data, but none is as comprehensive or parsimonious as this one. If the interpretation is, in fact, correct, then it is not repeated-testing effects so much as initial-adaptation effects that should concern researchers studying children's dreams, and it should be borne in mind that, in short-term cross-sectional research, the interaction of adaptation with sex may either becloud or falsely reveal sex differences in REM content. Only the combination of longitudinal and cross-sectional comparisons implemented here could have sensitized us to this possibility.

As we shall see in Chapter 6, there is yet another way our data can be used to assess whether repeated observation of children's dreams in a laboratory setting changes those dreams: systematic comparison of 7- to 9-year-olds' REM dreams from their fifth study year with those of 9- to 11-year-olds in their first study year. As will be detailed below, these comparisons also suggested little if any effect of repeated testing on REM dream content.

However the data of novice–veteran comparisons at ages 7–9 are to be interpreted, the following points deserve highlighting:

1 Significant differences were restricted to two broad dimensions of dream experience: self-participation and setting distortion. Other variables of

major interpretive interest did *not* reliably discriminate the two sets of dreams or suggest repeated-testing or initial-adaptation effects.

2 Pooling together the results of novice and veteran girls generally produced statistics that were more sensible, in the context of concurrently collected data from the veteran boys and of adjacent age-group data for girl subjects, than were findings for either group considered separately.[20]

3 What differences were observed as a possible function of repeated testing or initial adaptation seemed, in our design, to be limited to girls (a veteran–novice comparison for boys at ages 11–13 [Chapter 7] showed *no* dream-content differences).

4 Sufficient data were available from other pertinent dream contrasts to permit evaluation of the relative plausibility of different explanations of novice–veteran differences (and we think those data, for the most part, refute the hypothesis of repeated-testing effects, but do suggest some novelty effects on initially collected dreams of 7- to 11-year-old girls).

SEX DIFFERENCES

The preceding discussion suggests a possible difficulty in using our veteran and novice pooled girl data to evaluate sex differences in REM content at ages 7–9. If these data included generally unrepresentative scores achieved by novice subjects due to initial-adaptation effects, then observed effects might be spurious and the absence of observed effects might lead us falsely to conclude an absence of true effects. Although the data to be reported here come, in fact, from a comparison of all girls ($n = 13$) and all boys ($n = 7$) with REM reports, we shall try to indicate whether or not the observed effects or noneffects in our analysis seem to have been genuine.

Basically, the situation at ages 7–9 seems only little different from that at ages 3–5 and 5–7: By and large, boys' and girls' dreams were more remarkable for their similarities than for their differences. However, the following significant sex differences were observed:

Girls higher in relative incidence of
  Known female age-mates
  Known female persons
  Manual activity, ascribed to others

The character differences, which were noticeable even at ages 5–7, are comparable to ones observed for our older study group at ages 9–11 and,

[20]However, it is possible that the pooled intergroup figure for Active Participation at ages 7–9 underestimates girls' true ability to participate in their own dream scenarios and that it may, therefore, mask true boy–girl differences along this dimension. In direct comparison, however, veteran girls' and boys' dreams at ages 7–9 did not differ, even at marginal significance, in self-participation.

especially, 11−13. In middle childhood children begin a pattern of significant sex differentiation in their selection of known peers and persons for dream representation. Girl dreamers dream significantly more often than do boy dreamers of female characters in these classes. That the age 7−9 sex differences also were observed in the older study group strongly suggests their reality, and also is but another line of evidence that our two separate longitudinal series can generally be interpreted as one continuous series extending from age 3 to age 15.

The observed difference in manual activity is rather more difficult to interpret and perhaps deserves no interpretation (i.e., it may well have arisen by chance). As noted above, (veteran) boys had significantly more setting distortion than *veteran* girls (but not than novice girls, or than all girls considered together), but this difference may well have been an artifact of subject motivation interacting with the particular way in which we assessed setting familiarity. Alternatively, it may simply have reflected (as likely also did the marginally significant sex difference in male strangers noted at ages 5−7) the boys' greater mean age and cognitive maturation. There was little indication that it was part of a larger package of differences suggestive of more "disturbed" (bizarre, unpleasant, impulsive) dreams for boys than for girls. More generally, one would be hard pressed to find evidence in the children's dream reports of vastly different routes by which boys and girls attain "psychosexual" maturity. Rather, the broad similarity of boys' and girls' dream contents suggests that children's dreams better reflect common paths to social and cognitive maturation.

DREAMING OUTSIDE REM SLEEP

Until ages 7−9 it is impossible to use our data to arrive at any general impression of mental activity occurring outside REM sleep—during ordinary NREM sleep or at sleep onset. At ages 3−5 we collected only seven NREM and seven sleep-onset reports (from a grand total of 159 awakenings), and at ages 5−7 there were only 10 NREM and 13 sleep-onset reports (from a total of 166 awakenings). Furthermore, at ages 3−5 there were no indications that non-REM reports were particularly credible. At ages 5−7, however, NREM and sleep-onset reports seemed equally credible as (i.e., had comparable positive cognitive correlates as) REM reports, and we have seen, in Dean's non-REM reports, some indications of the nature of the non-REM reports (mentation?) of early childhood. Generally such reports (mentation) did not seem to be *qualitatively* different from REM reports (mentation), although certain areas of differentiation among reports from different sleep stages were suggested (see Chapter 4).

By ages 7−9 children's NREM report rates had improved to such a degree that there now was basis for systematically comparing NREM reports with REM (and sleep-onset) reports. There was, again, reason to believe these reports to be generally credible. Sleep-onset recall did not show concomitant improvement (indicating that the significant NREM increase cannot be attributed simply to generally enhanced cooperativeness, comprehension, or suggestibility), but expansion of the subject sample did permit an increase in the total number of sleep-onset reports available for inspection. Specifically, at ages 7–9, 15 children contributed a total of 40 NREM reports, and 13 children contributed a total of 19 sleep-onset reports.

Table 5.1 lists significant differences that were observed among reports collected from different sleep stages. The finding that REM reports were significantly longer than NREM ones was replicated at all age levels in the older longitudinal study group, and agrees with adult observations (e.g., Foulkes & Rechtschaffen, 1964). Uniquely in our observational series, however, sleep-onset reports also were reliably longer than NREM reports, but this finding also might have been predicted from the adult literature (Foulkes, 1966). However, the major finding of REM vs. NREM comparisons would have to be that reports did not differ qualitatively along

Table 5.1 **Differences in Dream Reports as a Function of Stage of Sleep**

REM vs. NREM	REM vs. Sleep Onset	Sleep Onset vs. NREM
Higher incidence/score in REM	Higher incidence/score in REM	Higher incidence/score in sleep onset
Word Count	Characters	Word count
Characters	Known peer, female	
Known peer, male	Known person, female	
Settings	Stranger,	
Conveyance	indeterminate	
States	age/sex	
Cognitive activity by	Settings	
other dream	Home, own	
characters	Sleep lab setting	
Social attack by	States	
dreamer	Sadness, dreamer	
	Sadness, any	
	character	
	Hunger, dreamer	
	Thirst, other dream	
	characters	
	Thirst, any character	
	Social attack by other	
	Social attack, any	
	Outcomes	
	Unfavorable,	
	other-mediated	
	outcomes, for other	
	dream characters	
	and for any dream	
	character	

dimensions (affect, visualization, distortion, dramatic quality) that have been found to be present more often in adults' REM reports than in their NREM ones. There were only scattered indications of such differentiation in the 7- to 9-year-olds' reports (more self-initiated aggression and more settings implying movement [conveyances] in REM reports), while other data pointed in an opposite direction (more thought elements [albeit as ascribed to others] and a greater relative incidence of a familiar [i.e., undistorted] character class in REM reports). Our impression is that these quantitative data speak fairly of children's earliest NREM reports: The reports do not reflect qualitatively different forms of thought organization in NREM as compared to REM sleep, but rather are scaled-down versions of the same kinds of dramatic episodes that children report on REM awakenings. If the data are to be believed, NREM dreaming does *not* begin as the kind of fragmentary, thoughtlike process it sometimes (but not generally [Foulkes, 1967b]) seems to be for adults. Rather it begins in the form of dramatic episodes distinguishable from REM dramas more in their length or elaboration than in their overall form.

But are these data to be believed? We believe they are.

1   Older study-group children, particularly at ages 9–13, produced comparably unthoughtlike, dramatic NREM reports. We seem to be dealing with a property of early NREM reports, and probably experiences, not with findings peculiar to the children we happened to be able to study at ages 7–9.

2   By virtue of its cognitive correlates, NREM reporting seemed credible throughout this period.

3   We have data (see Chapter 8) suggesting that it only is in early adolescence that NREM mentation begins to acquire the distinctive qualities it sometimes has for adults. Moreover, conceptual analysis suggests that it should be only then that NREM mentation would begin to acquire the sophisticated, "secondary-process" quality it sometimes has for adults. In uncritically expecting children's NREM reports to be just like ours, we are overlooking the cognitive prerequisites underlying our own distinctive forms of NREM mentation, prerequisites that most likely are lacking in concrete-operational children. We conclude that *NREM mentation begins as drama, rather than as fragmentary verbal or imaginal realizations of a quasi-waking thought process.* Compared to REM dreams, the drama is reduced in scale, just as the psychophysiological arousal associated with NREM sleep is inferior to that of REM sleep.

Seemingly paradoxically, we found many content variables that discriminated REM and sleep-onset reports, while adult data indicate greater discriminability of NREM and REM reports (e.g., Monroe, Rechtschaffen, Foulkes, & Jensen, 1965) than of sleep-onset and REM reports (Vogel, Barrowclough, & Giesler, 1972). But there are reasonable grounds for thinking that the difference is more apparent than real. Most of the categories discriminating sleep-onset and REM reports were relatively infrequently scored for any sleep stage, and in a contrast of a maximum of 15 REM awakenings with a maximum of three sleep-onset awakenings (where, in addition, REM recall rates were significantly superior to sleep-onset ones), it seems likely that one generally would find higher REM incidences even where the true rate of category occurrence per dream was identical in the two conditions. Yet the relative absence of dysphoric affect and body drive-states in children's sleep-onset reports is consistent with some adult data (e.g., Foulkes & Vogel, 1965) as well as with the requirement that one not be disturbed by such contents as one tries to fall off to sleep.

STIMULUS INCORPORATION

With the children ages 7−9, methods of study were comparable to those at ages 5−7 (see Chapter 4). In REM sleep 62 awakenings were made after stimulation (Table 2.1), 36 of which (58%) were associated with dream reports; in NREM sleep 63 awakenings were made after stimulation, 14 of which (22%) resulted in dream reports. Once again stimulation did not seem to enhance dream reporting or to be responsible for generating dreams where they otherwise might not have been expected to occur. Nineteen children had at least one poststimulation dream. The 50 dream protocols were submitted to the same judges employed in the age 5−7 analysis, along with 61 dreams collected on fifth-year stimulation trials with 13- to 15-year-old children. Transcripts were, again, randomly numbered and edited to delete information as to subject, night, awakening, and stimulus. As for the age 5−7 analysis, judges successively: (1) tried to match reports with stimuli, on an essentially 3-point basis—certain relation to a particular stimulus, uncertain relation to a particular stimulus, and no relation to any stimulus; (2) judged, for report pairs matched by child and sleep stage (cotton-limb, $n = 4$; cotton-water, $n = 4$; limb-water, $n = 6$), which report went with which stimulus; and (3) judged, for report pairs matched by child and stimulus ($n = 13$), which report more clearly reflected the preawakening application of that stimulus. In analysis of the first task, "certain" and "uncertain" judgments again were combined (see Chapter 4).

Judge 1 was correct in only 28% of her certain or uncertain judgments in the first task (five of 18 guesses were right), and Judge 2 was correct in only 30% of her stimulus assignments (11 of 37 guesses were right). By the stimulus employed, net incorporation rates (see Chapter 3) were:

Stimulus	Judge 1 (%)	Judge 2 (%)
Cotton	4	−4
Limb	−4	14
Water	0	1
All	−3	−4

In the second test both judges were correct in 57% (eight of 14) of their forced-choice judgments (vs. 50% chance). In the third task both judges thought REM reports more clearly stimulus related than NREM reports (62% vs. 38%, eight reports vs. five).

Table 5.2 presents results from the first judging task in the same alternative manner introduced in Chapter 4. There were three reasonably unequivocal incorporations (both judges were right and "certain"), constituting the same small fraction (6%) of reports judged as at ages 5–7. My own judgments, "on the spot," included these three reports and, once again, several others as well: two limb-stimulation reports and three water-stimulation reports. But also, once again, I can see how the judges came to differ with me. In the limb-stimulation cases they lacked the precise information I had on what limb was stimulated how, and in the water-stimulation cases they focused on nonfluid elements where all I could see was creeks, boats, and Kool-Aid.

Table 5.2 **Judges' Consensually Correct and Consensually Certain Incorporation Judgments: Ages 7–9**

	Judges Both "Certain"	**One/Both Judge(s) Not "Certain"**
Judges Are Consensually Right	*Freddie:* Night 9, Awakening 2. Rolls out of bed and a friend steps on his arm (a limb-REM stimulation). **A** [a] *Karen:* Night 2, Awakening 3. Working at school. The teacher goes over to open the window, and rain starts to come in (a water-REM stimulation). **M** *Rachel:* Night 9, Awakening 2. "I was ringing the bell. You pull the string . . . lots of times" (a limb-REM stimulation). **N**	*Matt:* Night 9, Awakening 2. At McDonald's . . . lifting a bag (a limb-REM stimulation). **A**
Judges Are Consensually Wrong	*Debbie:* Night 9, Awakening 1. A little man with a white beard, pounding on the floor, getting down on the floor, and listening to the ground (a cotton-NREM stimulation, judged "limb"). **N**	

Reports judged = 50
"Certain" and right = 6%

[a] **A** = awakens during stimulation; (**M** = moves during stimulation but does not awaken; **N** = no visible response to stimulation).

Thus once again little evidence was collected to suggest a general effect of the experimental stimuli on the children's dreams, although, also once again, a few individual reports seemed unequivocally to have been stimulus influenced.

The most interesting observation from the stimulus-incorporation trials at ages 7–9 was an unanticipated one, tabulated long after the study itself had been concluded. As indicated in Tables 4.2 and 5.2, for each stimulation trial I made notes on whether the subjects made some visible response (limb movement, general body movement, tensing of a stimulated limb, sighing or vocalization, etc.) to stimulation and whether they awoke during stimulation. Over the course of the experiment, the most constantly delivered form of stimulation was water. This was the only stimulation that did not terminate when I ceased delivering it, and, to avoid sensitizing the children to the fact I was stimulating them, I was perforce limited to a small number of drops of water per trial. It would be fair to say that cotton and limb stimulation more often was terminated by the *child's* response—an indication that it somehow had "registered"—and that the water stimulation more often was terminated by what *I* did—how many drops of fluid I had delivered. This makes responses to water stimulation a suitable dependent variable for cross-age and cross-stage comparison.

It was interesting to observe that older children showed a visible response (movement or awakening) to water stimulation relatively seldom, despite the fact that water was always assigned to the third (late-morning) awakening position and that water stimulation was our most intrusive or "foreign" stimulus, the one least related to expectable acts one might perform or stimuli one might encounter during normal sleep. Before ages 7–9, however, it was a different story:

	Movement or Awakening to Water Stimulation (%)	
Age	REM	NREM
3–5	67	38
5–7	62	8
7–9	14	24
9–11	17	23
11–13	25	11
13–15	17	17

Evidently somewhere between ages 5–7 and 7–9 the children developed a new strategy for coping with disturbing stimuli during REM sleep. That strategy is not, our data suggest, to weave the stimulus into the dream. It is tempting to believe that the difference between ages 5–7 and 7–9 may reflect the fact that a potentially alert REM brain (as shown by response values at ages 3−7) now increasingly is distracted from attending to external stimuli by its own continuously autogenous mentational stimuli.[21]

It would be interesting in this regard to compare, say, auditory-evoked responses (AERs) of children in relation to age and concurrent levels or types of mentation reporting during REM and NREM sleep. Ornitz, Ritvo, Carr, Panman, and Walter (1967) have described AERs in children that are somewhat different from those in adults during sleep (a single positive component in "younger" children, a P_1-N_1-P_2 wave complex in older children and in adults), but they do not identify the precise ages involved or discuss the possibility that qualitative changes in AER with age may be related to the presence/nature of mentational distractors. More refined study with more sophisticated evoked-response indicators (e.g., Lehmann & Skrandies, 1980) might prove useful in tracking down points in early childhood where episodic spontaneous mental acts first occur and where they later begin to be replaced by a more or less continuous and internally programmed stream of coherent, visual-imaginal dream narratization. Our normative dream data, cognitive-developmental theory, and the water-response data cited above suggest that there may be a substantial shift from episodic mentation to strongly programmed and continuous spontaneous dream imagery with a "mind of its own" concomitant with the shift to concrete-operational thinking. Without expecting ultimate explanations, cognitive developmentalists with interests in either waking or sleep cognition surely might profit from correlative psychophysiological observations such as evoked-response methods have to offer.

DEAN'S DREAMS

At the start of his fifth year of study, Dean was 8 years, 8 months old. As was true for his age group more generally, he showed an increase in REM recall between years 3 and 5 of the study (33% to 73%). Uniquely for his age group at ages 7−9, he also had perfect (100%) sleep-onset recall, coupled with very high (78%) NREM recall.

Dean's 11 *REM reports* were as follows:

1-1   I think we were supposed to come here and sleep. Only when we came here, we had a party, and Freddie (not his fellow subject, but another Freddie who lives next door to him) got a bike. [Who all was at this party?] Freddie and John, Kate (Freddie's sister), and me and the other (sleep lab) Freddie. [How did you come over?] I got a ride. [Who brought you over?] I don't know . . . I think it was my mom. [Were there any big people in the dream or at the lab?] Yeah, you. You were

---

[21]By contrast, NREM sleep never presents a comparable potential for arousal by external stimuli. The alternative hypothesis for the REM findings of stimulus adaptation (or of procedural variation) is refuted by third-year vs. fifth-year REM data for the older study group.

in your office, putting on the wires. [Who was I putting them on?] I don't know. [What made it be like a party?] Well, they had a big cake and everybody was giving out gifts . . . . I got a weight-lift. [Did the sleep lab in the dream look pretty much the way it really does?] Yeah, it looked like it really does. [Did you have any feelings in the dream?] I was happy. [Because of the party?] Yeah.

1-3 We were on a mountain, hiking. [Who was with you?] . . . I think another boy . . . a made-up one. [Did you recognize where this was supposed to be or where you were hiking?] No. [Did you have any feelings?] No.

2-1 I went skiing at a place and I broke my leg. I went again and nothing happened, so I kept going, and then I broke it again so I finally quit and I started to take up another sport . . . swimming. [Was there anybody else in the dream besides you?] Yeah. . . . There were other skiers and swimmers. [Were they kids your own age or big people or what?] All kinds. [Where did it take place . . . anyplace you know?] No . . . (The swimming was at) an indoor pool. [Did you have any feelings in this?] I was sad when I broke my leg. [Any other feelings?] Glad to get my cast off. [You had a cast?] Yes. [Did this happen in the dream that somebody put a cast on?] Yeah . . . on my leg. [Who did that?] A doctor, Dr. V——— (a local surgeon).

2-3 We were tree planters and we went up to this place and we planted a tree. And the next day we came back and the tree was already grown. So we planted more and they all grew and there was a forest fire and they wouldn't burn down. So we made forests out of them, and then some men were chopping them down for firewood and when they chopped them down the fire wouldn't work. So they told it to the state police and (the mayor) said that they planted trees and they won't burn. [You said "we" were planting trees. Who was with you?] My friends and I . . . boys . . . about five of them. [Where was this place where you were planting trees?] I don't know. [No place that you've ever seen before?] No. [When you said you planted trees, how did you plant them?] We had tree seeds, and we planted them. [Did you talk with anybody or move around?] Yeah, we walked all around the forest. [Did you have any feelings in this dream?] I was excited . . . because those trees wouldn't burn and they grew every day.

3-2 One day my mom, she got my sister some skis and she got all three sisters some skis and I didn't get any skis. And she got a letter that we could go skiing up at Steamboat (Springs, Colorado—a nearby ski area) and I couldn't go 'cause I didn't have any skis. And so I didn't go and when they got back they had got me some skis and I got to go skiing up at . . . Happy Jack (a local ski area). . . . They went with me. There was other people up skiing (too). [Why didn't your mom buy you skis?] Oh, it took too long and she didn't get around to buying me some and they didn't have any small enough sizes. [Did you have any feelings in the dream?] No. [How did you feel when you couldn't go skiing?] I felt a little sad. [How about when you got to go skiing?] I felt happy then. [Did your mother tell you that you couldn't go?] Yeah. [What did you say?] I didn't say anything. [You didn't beg her to take you or anything like that?] Well, yeah.

4-3   There was this boy and he was in Africa and he had a parrot and a mouse and a lion. And he told the mouse to do something, I don't know what it was, and the mouse came back and he didn't do it. And then he went back and he died and all he (the boy) had was this parrot and this lion. He told them to stay there and he was going to go out and catch an elephant 'cause he had to pull logs to stop the water from coming in. . . . And he set up a pit and the elephant came and fell in the pit but the pit was too little and the elephant got out. And so he tried a sleeping pill and he stuck it in with some weeds and the elephant came along and ate it and he fell asleep. And the boy took him and (indistinct) him and got the whatever-you-call-it fixed and it all went pretty good. [Were you in this dream?] No. [Did you have any feelings in this dream?] No.

5-1   There was this hippo and he got out of the zoo. And he got into this big van and went to a far country in Africa and he was living there. And people were trying to hunt him and stuff so he went back to the zoo, and everything was peaceful again. [Who were these people that were trying to hunt him?] Just Indians . . . about five. [Was anybody else in the dream besides the hippo and these guys?] There was a guy driving the van. [Who was he?] I don't know. [Were you in the dream?] No. [Could you see the zoo part of the dream?] Yeah. [Was it any zoo that you know, or just a made-up place?] No, it's not any zoo that I know. [Did you have any feelings in the dream?] I think excited when they were trying to hunt him . . . I wanted him not to get caught. [Were you worried when they were chasing him that they might get him?] Yeah.

6-2   My family and I were going on a trip skiing. And we were flying there. And when I turned around I took the wrong plane and I went to the Olympics. [What could you see?] I could see the airplane and I could see the people and things . . . an airport. [Did it look like any place you really know?] No. [Did you see the Olympics?] Yeah . . . I could see it all . . . the skiing things, and the people. . . . They had a torch and people skiing and stuff. [Did you recognize any of the people in the dream besides your family?] No. [Did you have any feelings in the dream?] I got worried when I went to the Olympics . . . 'cause I missed the plane. [What were you doing in the Olympics part of the dream?] I was just watching. [When you say that your family was going skiing, this was your mother, father, and sisters?] My father doesn't ski. My mother doesn't, but my sisters do, and Mom would take them. [Have you ever really been on an airplane on a skiing trip?] No. [So the situation was kind of make-believe?] Yes.

7-3   I was dreaming about when I got a puppy, and we went to this place, and they asked me if I wanted to name it something else, and I didn't.

So we took it home and gave it a bath. [Where is it that you got the puppy?] I don't know. [What kind of place was it?] There was people around and then he'd look at the puppy. [Was it like a veterinarian's place or wasn't it like that?] (It was.) . . . [What was its (the dog's) name?] I don't know. [Who was it that was . . . giving the puppy a bath?] I was, outside in our front yard. [Is this a dog that you really have, or is it just a make-believe puppy?] It's a make-believe puppy in the dream. . . . He was a small dog and he was brown. [Do you have a dog at home?] Yeah . . . a grown dog . . . black and brown and a little white. [Who was the person that asked you if you wanted to change the dog's name?] I don't know. [Do you remember if it was male or female?] No. [Did you have any feelings?] I was happy when I was giving him a bath.

8-3 We were going to get a new dog . . . I saw a dog in the pet store so I went in and went home and asked my mom if I could buy it. [What did she say?] I don't know. . . . It didn't get that far. [Who was in the dream?] The store man and my mom and that's all. . . . [At the store, who was the man? Somebody you really know, or a made-up person?] Just made-up. [When you were in the store, what could you see?] . . . a whole bunch of animals; monkeys and birds and gerbils and that's all. [Did you see this dog that you wanted?] Yeah, (a) small (one). [When you were in the pet store, what were you doing?] I was just asking the clerk for the dog. [What did he say?] He said I could (have it). [Did you have any feelings?] I was happy when I got the dog. [You got him in the dream?] Yeah . . . my mom said I could and I went and got him. [Before you said you didn't remember your mother saying anything to you. And now you think that she said yes?] Well, she said yeah. [What was the last thing in the dream?] I was just getting the dog in the pet shop. [Did (it) look like any place that you really know?] No.

9-2 I found some balloons and I untied them from the tree. And I was hanging on to them and I floated into the air. And I couldn't get them down. [Was anybody else in this dream besides you?] No. [Where was the tree?] In a park, I think . . . a made-up kind of place. [What was happening just before I woke you up?] I was in the sky. . . . I was scared when I couldn't get down from the balloons. [When you found the balloons, did you think that you wanted to untie them so that you could go for a ride on them, or what were your original ideas about what you wanted to do?] I wanted to get one balloon . . . but I untied the thing that was tied to the tree and I floated in the air. [You didn't want to float in the air?] No. [You just wanted one balloon to keep?] Yeah.

Our statistical data would suggest that the major *qualitative* shift in children's dreams is between ages 3−5 and 5−7, when dreams change from imagery of static, body-related themes to dynamic imagery symbolizing a more genuine interest in external reality. These same data would suggest that there is a lesser qualitative change from ages 5–7 to 7–9—the beginnings of real involvement of the self-character in dream scenarios—along with more general quantitative increases in the amount of dreaming experienced and/or reported both across and within particular REM periods. But Dean's dreams at ages 8 and 9 suggest almost equally dramatic changes in the quality of REM dreaming late as early in children's accession to operational reasoning. His dreams are more frequent (in experiencing and/or reporting), they are longer, and they contain more self-activity than his dreams at ages 6 and 7. But the net impact of these differences seems to be a qualitative leap in dream development of almost the same magnitude as that observed between ages 3–5 and 5–7.

In the context of his 8- and 9-year-old REM dreams, Dean's 6- and 7-year-old REM dreams are not really well-fleshed-out stories. Unlike his 4- and 5-year-old dreams, they do portray dynamic ongoing activities, but they rarely have strong narrative properties. There seldom is any clear sense of beginnings, middles, and ends or of thematic concerns that tie together surface-disparate activities. Compared to his own Year-5 dreams, Dean's Year-3 REM dreams are vignettes, imaginary slices of life or moments in time, long enough for some single line of activity to become elaborated but not sufficiently developed for this activity to be interrelated with other activities in the service of some higher narrative goal. To pick a set of metaphors that generally catch the flavor of Dean's developing dreamlife, at ages 4 and 5 he dreamed imaginary "snapshots" (with the camera, in some sense, turned inward rather than outward); at ages 6 and 7, he dreamed imaginary "short subjects" of the home-movie variety, in which the camera, now facing outward, is turned on and left running but in which there is relatively little editing; at ages 8 and 9, he dreamed "feature films," which can be discriminated from his ages 6 and 7 dreams not only in their greater length but also in their greater purposefulness, in the editing that oversees the integration of disparate film clips into a coherent narrative.

The quantitative scoring system has proven rather more sensitive to the first of these qualitative shifts than to the second. It has missed, apparently, the fact that in going from unedited "short subjects" to carefully edited "feature films" there is not only just "more" dynamic activity but also that such activity is organized in a qualitatively superior fashion. As with most content-analysis systems, the one used here is better able to count component elements than it is to evaluate the integration of these elements, better at cutting the dream into pieces and assessing its separate parts than at reassembling these pieces to catch the wholeness of the dream. Dean's dreams at ages 8 and 9 clearly have a wholeness or narrative integration lacking in his dreams at ages 6 and 7. This change is not captured by the scoring system's assessment that approach-social motives, for instance, have increased their overall incidence from Year 3 to Year 5 from 20% to 45%—a simple "quantitative" increase.

In this context, then, it appears that children's dreams may undergo two stages of movement toward becoming adultlike (for Dean's dreams, at ages 8 and 9, are much like our own, while at ages 4 and 5 they are not). First, for most subjects at ages 5−7, the child accesses the dynamic, kinematic, quasi-narrative surface representations of adult dreams. Then, for most subjects at ages 7−9, the child begins to put these elements together in truly narrative fashion. Both stages represent movement toward "operational" dream thought, but such thought only can be considered to be "consolidated" nocturnally at the later stage. As Bruner (1966) has argued, it is as if, at the later stage, those syntactic and narrative capabilities that heretofore have been speech-specific now are generalized to all the forms in which thought finds representation. For the first time narrative intentions and, through them, enduring representations with personal "motivational" relevance come to organize the manifest dream in a complex, systematic, and personally meaningful fashion.

What do Dean's REM dreams suggest about the nature of these underlying motive structures? In general, as has been argued persistently in the literature on laboratory-monitored children's dreams (Foulkes, Pivik, Steadman, Spear, & Symonds, 1967; Foulkes, 1967a, 1971; Breger, 1969; Foulkes, Larson, Swanson, & Rardin, 1969; Foulkes, Shepherd, & Scott, 1974), they often seem to be related to developmental aspirations. As Freud (1900) suggested, "Children have no more ardent wish than to be big and grown-up and to get as much of things as grown-up people do" (p. 268, n. 1). These developmental wishes are sex linked, in that growing up means somewhat different things for boys and girls. Dean's enduring wishes, for example, most generally are portrayed in the outdoors or in athletic endeavors in his REM dreams (e.g., 1−3, 2−1, 2−3, 3−2, 4−3, 5−1, 6−2, 9−2). There are physical challenges for the dreamer and physical dangers to him. One can read into some of the dream imagery classical "latency-era" concerns about body integrity (the broken legs of 2−1, yielding to the rapidly growing and indestructible trees of 2−3 and the rising balloons of 9−2), containment of the pressure of "animal impulses"[22] (4−3, 5−1), and psychosexual identity (7−3, where a play of words involving his family name contextually indicates that he is the puppy). While such concerns can be read rather more clearly now than at earlier ages, they are, if in fact present, by no means peremptory conative forces thrusting themselves upon hapless cognition; the surface structures in which they seem to appear are thoroughly rationalized and affectively rather bland. With the possible exception of 9−2, none of Dean's dreams seemed particularly terrifying or out-of-control affectively. His dream imagery generally was neither grandiose (cf. 1−1) nor defeatist (cf. 2−1) in its portrayal of life's possibilities. Rather realistically, it contained its share of successes and failures, of realized and unrealized dreamer intentions.

While some of Dean's REM dreams contained familiar peer and family

---

[22]Or possibly "body tensions" such as bladder pressure (4-3).

characters or reasonably representative settings, others clearly expand quite imaginatively beyond the boundaries of the familiar (2–3, the magical trees; 4–3, the boy and the elephant; 5–1, the hippo; 9–2, the boy and the balloons). It is the imagery of these dreams that most plausibly can be related to psychodynamic developmental themes. Their degree of imaginativeness probably is susceptible to overstatement; the animal and tree dreams are, in general, of the same genre as stories children of this age are likely to read, and the Laramie *Daily Boomerang* featured a cartoon strip in which a boy often was portrayed as flying by holding onto a balloon. Nevertheless, these dreams do represent considerable progress in the elaboration of unworldly or "imaginative" narratives during sleep. It is significant that such narratives, which popular reasoning and some psychological theory would assign to very young children, in fact seem to occur only after the child's accession to operational thought. That is, such narratives can only be viewed as relatively advanced cognitive achievements; they do not represent the operations of some developmentally primitive form of prelogical thought. Children do not naturally, natively think imaginatively, either awake or asleep. Imaginative, or "crazy," or dreamlike thinking is a skill at which they get progressively better over time.

Dean's *sleep-onset reports* were as follows:

4-2 I was at school and I was walking and someone tripped me and I broke my leg. I went to the hospital and came back and he tripped me and broke my arm. And when I came back again I didn't go past him and he didn't trip me. And so he goes past me, and I tripped him. [Who is this guy you're talking about?] His name is M.A. [Is he really a boy like that at school? Would he do something like that?] No. I don't think so . . . he isn't very nice, but he's pretty good. [Did you actually picture yourself in the hospital or any of the things happening there?] I could see the hospital . . . a made-up place . . . . I saw the operating rooms. He took me into the X-ray room . . . a doctor . . . a made-up doctor, he took some X-rays on my leg and my arm . . . . He put a cast on them. [The part in school, where did this take place?] In the classroom. [Your own school?] Yeah. [Did you have any feelings in this dream?] No. [What about when he broke your leg and arm— how did you feel then?] I didn't feel . . . I felt hurt. [Were you mad at the guy that did it?] Yeah. [And when you were staying away from him, were you afraid of seeing him again?] Yeah.

5-3 There was this toenail and it was loose and I tried to get it off. And I pulled on it and pulled off my toe. [Where were you?] In bed at my house. . . . It (looked) pretty much like it really does. [Did you have any feelings in the dream?] I was excited when my toe fell off. [Was it a bad kind of excitement like you were afraid, or was it good, or what?] Yeah, I was afraid.

6-1 I was making a picture. [How do you mean you were making it? What were you making it with?] Paints. [Where were you doing it?] I don't know. [Can you tell me anything at all about what you were painting?] I think I was trying to do a picture of a coat . . . like a down-filled coat is, jacket . . . like my size. It was yellow. [Do you have a coat like this or do you know anybody who does?] My sister has a yellow coat. . . . Mine is black. [Did you have any feelings in this?] I was happy 'cause I made a good picture. . . . I just got through painting it and I set it down and I just walked off.

Once again there is some suggestion that Dean's sleep-onset fantasies are rather closer to typical boyhood waking fantasies than are his REM reports—there are fantasies of revenge against tormenting peers, of creative success, and a thinly disguised representation of the feared consequences of "playing with yourself." With the exception of 4-2, which seems to lean heavily on stereotyped and probably prefabricated waking fantasy, the narrative element is less strong in these reports than in Dean's REM reports. And in some sense the symbolism of these sleep-onset dreams seems more "reactive" and that of the same child's REM dreams more "creative." In the one case potentially disturbing motive structures are simply translated into a somewhat obscure symbolic language (e.g., 5-3) or are given a rather hackneyed contextual elaboration (4-2); in the other case, such structures provide the occasion for more highly elaborated and truly imaginative response.

Dean's *NREM reports* were as follows:

2-2 There was this cake that you could see through. And it's supposed to be a diet cake. It's not supposed to have any pounds on it, so you won't gain any. So this one guy ate a piece and he started getting fatter until he stopped getting fatter and started getting thinner, until he was back to his normal weight. And then he told the waitress that the cake was not right. And so they made it again and he tried it and that time started getting littler. And then bigger until he was his full size again. [Were you in the dream?] No. [Where was this happening?] In a restaurant . . . sort of like a place I know, Ramada Inn. [Did you know the guy or the waitress?] No. [Did you have any feelings in the dream?] I thought the dream was funny.

3-1 It was our summer vacation. We went to see the Jackson Five (musical group) and when we got there I got to have their autograph. And we went there again and he wouldn't let me have his autograph. [Did you really do this on your summer vacation, or was this just a make-believe thing that happened in your dream?] Just a make-believe thing. . . . They were in Los Angeles . . . inside a building. [Who was with you?] My family . . . they were just watching (them) too. [You said this happened twice: One time you got the autograph and then the other time you didn't?] Yeah. [What happened in between those times?] We stayed at a motel . . . make-believe place. [How did you get from the motel to where the Jackson Five were? Was it just like you were in one

place and then suddenly it flashed to the other place, or did you remember dreaming about how you went there?] We drove in a car. [Did
you have any feelings in the dream?] I was happy when we went on our
vacation. [How did you feel at the end when he wouldn't give (the
autograph) to you?] I felt mad. [Were the Jackson Five doing anything?] They were dancing and singing. [Was anybody else in it besides
you and your family watching it, or was it just you guys?] It was a lot of
people.

3-3   Christmas was in a week (the dream was reported on November 12)
and you didn't have any Christmas presents yet. And you couldn't go
downtown 'cause you didn't have a bike to ride. [Who couldn't, you
couldn't or somebody else?] I couldn't. [Who else was in the dream
besides you?] My friend Freddie. . . . He had his bike, and I didn't. He
was in our driveway. . . . We were talking about how we could get me a
bike, and what we were going to do. . . . We tried to borrow one but we
couldn't. We, Freddie asked his sister if we could use her bike. [Did
you have any feelings in the dream?] I was worried when I couldn't get
a bike.

5-2   There was this . . . we went to this place and we saw a bullfight . . .
and the bull almost killed the man but then they killed the bull because
they didn't want him to kill the man. So the man was OK and he went
out there and then he got killed from another bull. [This is a dream you
were having just before I woke you up?] Yeah. [Who was going to the
bullfight?] My family. [Where was the bullfight?] In Mexico. [Have you
ever been to a bullfight (or) to Mexico?] No. [Were there any other
people in the dream?] There were other people in the stand. [Did you
have any feelings in this?] No. [You weren't worried about what would
happen to the man, or concerned about the fact that the other bull got
him, or didn't you get that involved in it?] Yeah, I got a little (worried)
. . . when the bull started to charge the man.

6-3   I was dreaming about some cookies. . . . They were really big. . . .
They were shaped like flowers and they were really big. [Where were
they?] At our house . . . in the kitchen. [Were there any people that
were in the dream?] There were people eating the cookies. Some of my
family . . . all of them . . . and me. [Did your kitchen look pretty much
the way it is, or was it different?] It looked like it really does. [Did you
have any feelings in this dream?] I was happy we had the cookies.

7-1   It was mostly about the sleep lab and it was different and everything.
. . . You woke me up. [I did in fact wake you up. Are you just telling
me what was really happening, or did you have a dream before I woke
you up about the sleep lab?] I woke up and then I had the dream. Right
when you woke me up. [OK, tell me what you can remember of it.
What happened in it?] I was flying over a pond and (my sister) got on so
we were flying around. . . . She was flying around in a helicopter . . .

she had to climb aboard, so she did. [Who was driving or piloting the helicopter?] I was. [Where was this pond place? Is it any place you really know or is it just a made-up place?] I don't know. [How did you pick her up?] I was pretty close to the ground—with a rope. [When I first woke you up you said something about the sleep lab and being waked up. Do you think now that was part of your dream, or can't you remember now what that referred to?] I think it was two different dreams. [And one dream had to do with the lab?] Yeah. [Tell me all you can remember of that one.] That's all I could. . . . He was just shaking me. [Somebody was shaking you?] Yeah. . . . [Which dream do you think came last?] The helicopter. [Do you think both of these things happened before I did in fact wake you up, or did one or the other happen after I woke you up but before you got fully awake?] They both happened before you woke me up.

9-3 I was chewing on something. [Chewing on something. Like what?] I don't know. [Was it like a food thing or something other than that?] Yeah, it was like licorice. [Was this visual? Could you see something?] I could see what was in your mouth but I couldn't see what it was. [What was in whose mouth?] Something was in, I don't know whose mouth it was. [It wasn't yours?] No. [When you first talked to me you said that you were chewing something. Do you think somebody else was doing the chewing, or was it you?] It was both of us. [Where were you guys?] I don't know. [This other person, was this a boy, girl, man, woman?] It's a boy . . . my age. [Did you have any feelings in this?] No.

These reports amply illustrate the puzzling array of accounts one gets on NREM awakenings. There are some indications (e.g., 7–1) that hypnopompic (awakening) imagery may be, at least in part, what is being reported, and there are also indications of more disorientation or confusion during NREM than during REM nocturnal interviews (e.g., the second-person assertions in 3-3 and 9-3 and the consequent uncertainty as to who is performing dream actions). There seems to be more vagueness about dream details than in REM accounts, and thus one feels somewhat more hesitant to accept those details that are reported, particularly those not initially volunteered. There are "crazy" elements (the diet cake, the huge cookies) that seem better to reflect children's (and adults') waking stereotypes of what dreams are like than they do children's (and adults') typical REM-awakening accounts of what dreams are like. It is not difficult to perceive why, relative to REM reports, NREM reports have more often been interpreted as procedural artifacts.

And yet at the adult level relatively strong evidence suggests that NREM mentation does not "behave" as if it were an artifact. Foulkes, Scott, and Pope (1980), for example, reported that six young-adult volunteers awakened during nocturnal Stage-2 NREM sleep reported dreams on 92% of those occasions. They found that subjects' reports discriminated patterns of EMG maintenance[23] vs. EMG suppression accompanying the prearousal NREM EEG patterns in a way predicted from a previous study of the mental correlates of EMG suppression during NREM sleep (Larson & Foulkes, 1969). Subjects themselves, the interviewer, and the report judge all were blind as to conditions associated with arousals and reports. Thus it is difficult to imagine their replication under the hypothesis that the subjects fabricated reports or that the interviewer induced them. The study suggests, rather, that NREM mentation in the young adult is both substantial in its extent and "real"—that is, that postawakening NREM dream accounts are reliably related to prearousal NREM physiology. If these observations are correct, then it seems plausible that 7- to 9-year-old children, whose REM dream accounts are much like those of young adults, might also be experiencing NREM mentation much like that reported, apparently veridically, by young adults.

Thus the fact that there seems to be something "different" about NREM accounts—noted from the very outset of direct study of NREM/REM differences (e.g., Foulkes, 1962; Rechtschaffen, Verdone, & Wheaton, 1963)—cannot be used immediately to discredit them. The difference reflects as plausibly different patterns of mental organization in the two sleep states as it reflects veridical reporting vs. confabulation. In this context one can turn to Dean's NREM reports to try to understand how mentation might be differentially organized in the two sleep states at the first point in childhood where mentation is reported from both sufficiently often to permit such comparison.

There seems to be a sense in which Dean's NREM reports are "superficial" in a way his REM reports generally are not. The diet cake (2-2) and the large cookie (6-3) dreams do not seem, for example, as susceptible to deep interpretation as the tree planter (2-3) or boy-elephant (4-3) REM dreams. They could, of course, be interpreted psychodynamically, but not, I think, in a compelling way; contextual clues that support such interpretations in the REM case are relatively absent in the NREM case. More plausibly, these NREM dreams—as "bizarre" in their distinctive way as the REM dreams are in theirs—might be interpreted as the output of an imaginative mind working somewhat whimsically on rather superficial notions of the sort that sometimes pass along the fringe of waking consciousness (Rechtschaffen, Verdone, & Wheaton, 1963). The dreams may have no deep meaning, because enduring, personally significant motive structures have not been involved in their creation.[24] In a sense the reports may reflect the operation of

---

[23]EMG = electromyogram, a recording of the tonus of, in this case, muscles of the face and/or neck.

[24]Dean's NREM reports suggest a still further way in which NREM mentation is "superficial": Plot development, when present, is more by repetition or alternation (e.g., 2-2, 3-1, 5-2) than, as in REM mentation, by invention or elaboration.

relatively "pure-thought" mechanisms, rather than thought mechanisms working on personally significant contents. The "pure-thought" is not realistic or rational by waking standards, but, given the conditions sleep sets for thought—no external surveillance, no reality testing—there is little reason why it should be.

In this same regard, the relatively less implausible scenarios Dean reported on NREM arousals—for example, seeking the autographs of celebrities (3-1), not being able to ride downtown to buy Christmas presents (3-3), watching a Mexican bullfight (5-2), flying a helicopter (7-1)—seem to represent the intrusion of superficial motives, passing fancies as it were, rather than of deeply significant, recurring motive systems. It can be argued that each of these superficial motives reflects a more basic one—childish wishes for omnipotence, for example. In some sense that must be true, for no motive can exist in total isolation from its proper "semantic" class. But just as in daytime we can fantasize some great but implausible achievement without a simultaneous welling-up of a host of related childhood wishes, so too in sleep it may be possible to entertain relatively frivolous and momentary wishes without simultaneously evoking the more serious and lasting ones to which they are ontogenetically related. It can be argued that that, in fact, is precisely what may be happening during NREM sleep.

The argument that NREM mentation is "superficial," then, boils down to something like this. Where associations are collected, the "sources" of NREM dreams should prove to be less "deep" than those of REM dreams. They should lie in relatively superficial or digressive lines of waking thought rather than in more enduring, personally significant motives. The critical difference between NREM and REM mentation may lie not so much in their manifest contents as in their "latent contents" and in the transformational mechanisms these different sets of latent contents require. Interestingly enough, in some 20 years of controversy regarding NREM mentation and its differences from REM mentation, this hypothesis never has been put to an empirical test. Reliable tools now are available for such a test, however (Foulkes, 1978c), and I hope soon to perform it with young-adult subjects.

My hypothesis is that in REM sleep significant, personally relevant motive systems are activated (and at sleep onset they retain some degree of their waking level of activation), so that they provide deep semantic structures on which thought mechanisms necessarily must operate. In NREM sleep these deep structures are relatively silent. However, thought operations remain potentially elicitable by more superficial, "fringe"-type mentational elements that are disinhibited by the silence of deeper semantic structures. It is not clear that their relative activation should be considered either obligatory or continuous during NREM sleep. Those persons more accustomed to intrusive disruption of orderly thought processes in wakefulness, however, do seem to be more prone to such disruption in NREM sleep (Pivik & Foulkes, 1968; Cartwright & Ratzel, 1972). But it may be that an "acquired taste" for letting one's mind wander far afield, for playful digression, is a determinant of the degree to which there is, in fact, any substantial degree of ongoing NREM mentation. The "taste" would depend on "skill" in this way: Certain sorts of mental operations would be necessary but insufficient conditions of experiencing relatively continuous mentation in NREM sleep. Dean's results, and those of his subject group more generally, suggest that the skill appears with the consolidation of operational thought.

SUMMARY

By ages 8 and 9 cognitively talented children have completed most of the steps on their pathway toward adult-level competency in REM dreaming. Less talented children still may have important strides to make, and, as we shall see in Chapter 8, early adolescence and its formal-operational reasoning are associated with a final few developments inaccessible even to more gifted 8- and 9-year-olds. By and large, however, REM dreams of talented 8- and 9-year-olds (e.g., Dean) are indistinguishable from our own both in terms of their formal structure and of how they are influenced by enduring motives and by more superficial traits of character or behavior.

The main steps taken between ages 5−7 and 7−9 toward consolidating and extending earlier dream achievements seem to be these: (1) the representation of a self-character who can freely act in the dream environment and "through whose eyes" one senses dream events; (2) the association of more REM periods with reportable dream activity; (3) the capability of generating small-scale dream scenarios in (or, at least, reporting them after) NREM sleep; (4) a quantitative increase in the amount of REM dreaming (or, at least, reporting) per REM period, along with a heightened structural complexity of the dreams so experienced (or reported); and (5) the first appearance of reliable claims that dreams were accompanied by affective (generally pleasurable) experience. However, at ages 7−9 several forms of dream construction still were conspicuous by their relative absence (e.g., having the self-character speak or feel anger), or by the failure of our correlational data to indicate their reliable presence (e.g., deliberately constructing novel human characters). But these gaps in dream elaboration between 7- to 9-year-olds and older children or adults were relatively few in relation to continuities extending from ages 7−9 into adulthood.

In retrospect, it is fortunate that our younger-group's period of observation extended through to the children's ninth postnatal year, for by this time their dream reports had begun to stabilize in near-adult form. *Within* the five years in which we studied the younger group, on the other hand, there were momentous but (in retrospect) predictable changes in children's dream reports, changes we were able to observe longitudinally, that is, in comparison to levels of accomplishment that the same children had demonstrated earlier. We were able to document, moreover, that our repeated-observation design probably had little effect on children's REM reports and that the larger risks in laboratory studies of dream ontogeny probably attach, in fact, to cross-sectional designs where initial-adaptation effects are likely to be salient.

CHAPTER 6 _____

Ages 9 to 11

Past age 9 our observations on children's dreams came from a second group of children, who, as explained in Chapter 2, were studied at the same time as our group of younger children. There initially were 16 children, eight boys and eight girls, in this second group, and all 16 completed the first year of our study. At the start of this year these children ranged in age from 8 years, 8 months, to 11 years, 9 months. The typical (median) girl's age was 9 years, 8 months, and the typical boy's age was 10 years, 4 months. During the study year whose dream findings are reported below, the typical girl was in the fourth grade and the typical boy, in the fifth.

From the children's ages and mental status (Table 2.3), it seems fair to presume that they were fully "concrete-operational" (see Chapters 4 and 5) during their first study year. Unfortunately, however, they were not systematically examined for their Piagetian "stage" of cognitive development (Table 2.2), as were younger-group subjects.

The children were studied in the laboratory in almost exactly the same manner as the 7- to 9-year-olds, whose dream data were described in the last chapter, and the dreams were analyzed in almost exactly the same manner as the 7- to 9-year-olds' dreams. Slight discrepancies in interview technique and content analysis will be noted insofar as they seemed to contribute to artifactual differences in findings between the two study groups. These discrepancies arose because 9- to 11-year-olds were studied in the first year of the project and 7- to 9-year-olds in the fifth; it was inevitable that both data collection and data analysis techniques would be subject to slight modification as we gained experience in applying them. It should be emphasized, however, that such modification was quite minimal and that for almost all intents and purposes, methods of study at ages 7−9 and 9−11 were identical.

THE REPORTING OF DREAMS

The 9- to 11-year-olds reported dreams on 66% of their REM awakenings, on 32% of their NREM awakenings, and on 61% of their sleep-onset awakenings. The typical child reported dreams on 79% of REM awakenings, on 33% of NREM awakenings, and on 83% of sleep-onset awakenings. These figures, which generally approximated recall findings at later age levels

(11−13, 13−15), are noteworthy in two respects: (1) they considerably exceed dream report rates observed by us at ages 7−9, and (2) they still remain somewhat inferior to typical dream report values observed in studies of young-adult subjects.

There was a significant intergroup difference in REM report rates between ages 7−9 and 9−11.[1] As discussed in Chapter 5, the "increase" shown by the 9- to 11-year-olds may have reflected both their greater cognitive maturation (permitting more dream generation) and enhanced motivation (novelty effect and/or absence of motivational decrement) of subjects early, as opposed to late, in their term of service in our experiment (permitting better recall of dreams typically experienced and possibly even the experiencing of more dreams). With regard to the first alternative, it should be remembered that only four of our 21 7- to 9-year-olds were operational on all three of our Piagetian tasks. As a group, then, the 7- to 9-year-olds still had considerable room for further development of operational thought, development that presumably would have enhanced their skill in dream generation. With respect to the motivational alternative, we found no evidence of a short-run novelty effect for 9- to 11-year-olds. Of the 152 REM reports we collected, 77 were from Nights 1−4 (eight scheduled REM awakenings per child) and 75 were from Nights 5−9 (seven scheduled REM awakenings per child). From the fact that these children generally had stable and constant REM recall rates throughout their later years of service in our study, one would have to propose that whatever longitudinally generated motivational decrements affected their REM report rates must have been operative in later study years, keeping report rates constant while dream experiencing increased. At ages 9−11, however, there is little evidence for such a motivational decrement, while, as we have seen in Chapter 5, such an influence may artificially have depressed the REM reporting of 7- to 9-year-olds, particularly the girls.

Thus both cognitive immaturity and performance decrement may explain the relatively low REM report rates of our 7- to 9-year-olds and, hence, the relatively large gap between their performance and that of our 9- to 11-year-olds. But why didn't the 9- to 11-year-olds better approximate typical levels of adult performance in REM reporting? Part of the answer lies in a comparison of their pooled mean and median subject report rates cited above. The *typical child was* reporting both REM and sleep-onset dreams at an almost adult level and, with further cognitive maturation, no doubt would have been able to do so at later ages, presuming the absence of adverse motivational factors engendered by her or his longitudinal service. That the 9- to 11-year-olds' *pooled rates* of REM and sleep-onset reporting were so low relative to adult values must reflect the inclusion in the study group of a few children with very low rates of dream reporting, which seldom are encountered in studies of young adults. In fact, four of our 16 9- to 11-year-olds had REM report rates below 30%: two girls with rates, respectively, of 27% and

---

[1]The intergroup difference in sleep-onset recall also was statistically significant.

20% and two boys with rates, respectively, of 27% and 25%. The other 12 children had a typical REM report rate of 86%, a value in an expected range for adult research.

Why were these four children such poor REM reporters? All of them were of average overall intelligence (I.Q.). For the girls, however, cognitive immaturity is a possible answer: They were aged, respectively, 9 years, 5 months, and 8 years, 8 months, at the start of our study, and had Block Design raw scores of, respectively, 15 and 19 (ranking them 13th and 12th, respectively, among our 9- to 11-year-olds). The group median on Block Design at ages 9−11 was 27.5. Thus these two girls were younger than and inferior to their typical peer in cognitive skills that play some presumptive role in dream generation. However, children with still lower Block Design scores were able to report dreams considerably more often than they did. Possibly a certain level of Block Design skill is a necessary, but not a sufficient, condition of dream generation. Perhaps, contrary to my earlier presumption, these girls were *not* fully concrete-operational, and that was the missing condition. Clearly, our data do not resolve the issue, but they suggest the desirability of further study of waking cognitive correlates of individual differences in REM report rate across the transition to operational reasoning.

For at least one of the girls, motivation may also have been a factor: The girl who had 20% REM recall at age 8−9 had only 7% REM recall at age 10−11,[2] had been held back a year in school because of poor motivation, and did not seem to take our experiment terribly seriously. The other girl, however, did seem to be trying to remember dreams on experimental awakenings, and, as her Block Design score increased in later years (22 at age 11−12, 28 at age 13−14), so too did her REM report rate (47% at age 11−12, 57% at age 13−14).

For the two aberrant boy recallers, motivation seemed the more likely answer. They were, respectively, aged 11 years, 9 months, and 10 years, 2 months, at the start of our study and had relatively good Block Design performances (31 and 38, respectively, ranking them 5.5 and 2.5 in their group). Later neither was ever to achieve 50% REM recall. In the final study year, their REM report rates were, respectively, 27% and 43%. Both showed relative disinterest in the experiment.

Whatever the reasons might have been for these particular four children's low rates of REM dream reporting, more generally no doubt it will be likely that child samples will include more subjects with very low rates of REM reporting than will adult samples. Past the point where REM dreaming generally will be accessible to children on laboratory awakenings, there still may be some children whose lagging cognitive maturation makes them exceptions to the general rule, and there almost certainly will be some whose preadolescent or early-adolescent ideology makes it impossible for them to

---

[2]She left the study at this point. Her Block Design score in the third study year had not improved from her performance in the first study year.

comply with the essential conditions of dream-report experiments. Most adult research tends to be with persons of generally high cognitive aptitude who are self-selected for their interest in dreams. In this respect, so far as generalization to humanity at large is concerned, our older group's performance may be more representative than the performance of typically selected adult research subjects.

All 16 9- to 11-year-olds reported dreams at greater relative frequency from REM than from NREM awakenings. The children also reported dreams significantly more often on sleep-onset than on NREM awakenings, but sleep-onset and REM recall rates were not significantly different from one another. Once again "light" NREM-sleep awakenings produced more dreams (42% recall) than did "deep" NREM-sleep awakenings (26%). Although this pattern was shown by seven of nine children with a difference in recall rate between the two conditions, the group difference did not achieve significance. It is interesting to note, despite a comparable failure of the ages 7−9 vs. ages 9−11 NREM recall difference to achieve significance, that the 9- to 11-year-olds' *deep* NREM recall figure was at a level approximately equivalent to that (29%) for *light* NREM sleep at ages 7−9.

Consistent with the idea that increases in REM and NREM reporting are initiated by increases in late-night reports (see Chapter 5), the 9- to 11-year-olds had progressively higher report rates with later REM awakenings (54% on Awakening 1, 68% on Awakening 2, and 75% on Awakening 3; all possible contrasts were significant), and significantly higher NREM report rates on the third nightly awakening (45%) than on the second (24%; on the first awakening, the pooled report rate was 27%).

High-rate REM recallers at ages 9−11 showed high achievement and achievement orientation, assertiveness, self-esteem, and imaginativeness. Interestingly, "dreaminess," a flighty waking propensity to impractical thought assessed by the Children's Personality Questionnaire's "Tender-Minded" scale, was *negatively* correlated with REM report rate. High-rate REM reporters were bright in comparison to age-matched peers (i.e., in intelligence quotients), but were not, compared to other children in our sample (i.e., in raw scores) conspicuously bright. Uniquely among our observations from ages 5−7 to 13−15, no visuospatial or performance score successfully predicted REM recall. That fact, together with the other, noncognitive characteristics of high-rate REM reporters, suggests that by middle childhood most of the basic cognitive prerequisites of REM dreaming are in place, so that individual differences in REM report rates now may more plausibly be related to differences in personal style (e.g., motivation to perform well) than to actual differences in dream occurrence.[3]

---

[3]That we observed performance score correlates at ages 11−13 and 13−15 seems to have depended on the fact that only at those age levels did we have in our sample two children with uncharacteristically immature Block Design−type skills. Omitting those two children, neither Block Design correlation with REM report rate was significant. However, for a sample of seven working-class males aged 13−15 described elsewhere (Foulkes, Larson, Swanson, & Rardin, 1969), we did find a relatively large (although, in view of the sample size, insignificant) correlation between WISC Block Design raw scores and REM report rate: $r = .64$.

As at ages 5−7 and all age levels thereafter, REM, NREM, and sleep-onset recall were significantly intercorrelated: Children who were high in reporting mentation from one sleep stage typically were high in reporting it from other sleep stages. Thus correlates of NREM and sleep-onset reporting at ages 9−11 were generally similar to those of REM reporting: generally supportive family environments, high I.Q., self-esteem, and achievement-oriented life goals. A Wechsler verbal raw score (Comprehension) predicted NREM report rate. In refutation of a confabulation hypothesis for NREM reporting, a measure of waking dissimulation (a "Lie" scale) was *negatively* associated with NREM report rate.

THE CHANGING CONTENT OF REM DREAMS

It is at ages 9−11 that we can with least certainty discuss "the changing content" of children's dreams, because in addition to the age differences separating our data at ages 7−9 and 9−11, there is the confounding fact that different children were studied at these two levels—the younger-group sample in its final year and the older-group sample in its initial year. The hope underlying our research design was that the results of these two study years would be sufficiently similar so that we could consider our data as forming one continuous 10-year series of observations on the development of dreaming, to which the fact that these observations happened, in fact, to come from two different groups of children would contribute minimal error variance. Even ideally, of course, there would have to be *some* difference between reports we collected at ages 7−9 and 9−11, for some genuine changes in typical dream content surely would occur over that age span, but one could hope that such differences as emerged in our data would be sensibly interpretable as continuations of, or as logical extrapolations from, trends observed in adjacent longitudinal comparisons within one or both of the two study groups considered separately. These were large hopes—or gambles—but, as we shall see, ones our data served largely to justify.

Table 6.1 lists the dream-content variables that were scored significantly more or less often for 9- to 11-year-olds than for 7- to 9-year-olds. Some clarification of the table's data base is in order. First, because we also were interested in using comparisons of 7- to 9- and 9- to 11-year-olds' dreams to examine effects of repeated testing on dreams of younger children, only the 13 veteran 7- to 9-year-olds who reported dreams in their fifth year of study were included in the analysis. Second, the older-group dreams employed in the contrasts of the table came from the 12 older subjects who eventually completed a full five years of the study. The justification for omitting four children studied at ages 9−11 but not at all later ages was entirely pragmatic: Only data from continuing subjects were in the computer's memory at the time we were able to perform this analysis. Because older-group subjects who left the study at some time subsequent to Year 1 did so only because of moves by their families, there is no reason to believe that the omitted children were conspicuously different from their peers who remained behind.

Table 6.1 **Dream Variables Significantly Differentiating REM Dreams of 7- to 9- and 9- to 11-Year-Olds**

Variables Scored at Higher Values for 7- to 9-Year-Olds	Variables Scored at Higher Values for 9- to 11-Year-Olds
Characters	
Animals, any	Known person, any, of indeterminate sex
	Stranger, any, of indeterminate sex
Settings	
	School, any
	School, own
	Unclassifiable
Activities	
Locomotion, other initiated	
Locomotion, any initiated	
Feelings	
	Happiness, dreamer
Motives/Outcomes	
Approach object, dreamer	Unfavorable outcome, self-mediated for other character
Approach object, other	
Approach object, either	
Ratings	
Visualization	Active participation

Of 211 dream variables analyzed, only 15 revealed a significant difference between 7- to 9-year-old "veterans" (studied for four preceding years) and 9- to 11-year-old "novices" (studied in their first year of experimental service). Indeed, perusal of Appendix B will reveal that the dreams of these two groups were, in most major respects, remarkably similar. Moreover, at least half of those intergroup differences that did attain statistical significance are readily explicable in terms of procedural (interview, dream-scoring) changes over the course of the study and hence suggest neither repeated-testing effects nor true developmental changes.

Specifically, the greater relative incidence of known persons and strangers of indeterminate sex and of unclassifiable settings for 9- to 11-year-olds reflected my greater imprecision in interviewing in Year 1 than thereafter. Such secular changes were visible as differences that appeared between Year-1 and later-year data for *both* study groups. The self-mediated outcome difference also may have been procedural rather than real: Self-mediated outcomes were scored more than twice as often, relative to the number of dreams scored, for older-group subjects at ages 9–11 than at older ages.

(They could not, however, be scored for 3- to 5-year-olds studied in the same year as 9- to 11-year-olds, since the former group hardly ever dreamed any social-interactional content.) As noted in Chapter 4, the three approach-object differences (Year-5 younger-group dreams superior to Year-1 older-group dreams) also were procedural rather than substantive; apparently this category was underscored in Year-1 dreams. My failure to press for definitive statements of imagery modality in Year-1 interviews helps to explain the apparent discrepancy in dream "visualization" ratings between ages 7−9 and 9−11.

Of the seven remaining differences in Table 6.1, at least four can be viewed as plausible changes in the true nature of dream experiences between ages 7−9 and 9−11. There were reasonably steady trends at adjacent age levels toward decreases in animal characters (recall that at ages 7−9 it was only relatively immature children whose dreams frequently included animals) and increases in school settings. The significant "increase" in dreamer self-participation is entirely consistent with longitudinal changes earlier demonstrated within the younger group (see Chapter 5), and with increases in cognitive maturation between ages 7−9 and 9−11 that should facilitate effective self-representation in dreams.

The evidence of Table 6.2 suggests, then, that our cross-group end-of-study vs. start-of-study tests *were* sensitive to both minor procedural variations across the course of the study and true developmental changes for which there is some presumption from adjacent intragroup data. It also suggests, in the residuum not comprehended by the foregoing explanations, that there was little, if any, effect of repeated testing on the content of younger children's REM dream reports. Of three remaining intergroup differences, two suggest initial-adaptation effects for 9- to 11-year-olds rather than repeated-testing effects for 7- to 9-year-olds: The 9- to 11-year-olds (particularly the girls) appear to be discrepantly low in other-initiated and overall locomotor activity. The 7- to 9-year-olds were more "in series" with the older group at ages 11−13 than were the older-group children themselves at ages 9−11. If there was an initial-adaptation effect for these two variables at ages 9−11, it was somewhat like that occurring in novice subjects at ages 7−9: observed in female subjects and having to do with the activeness of (but not here self-activeness in) dream scenarios. (The "happiness" difference also may have been due to an adaptation effect for the older girls; it is discussed later in this chapter.)

In sum, the data of Table 6.1 suggest that our two separate longitudinal series of dream observations can be viewed in most respects as having continuity with one another. Repeated-testing effects on dream content seemed to have been surprisingly minimal, and a few potential effects of initial adaptation were quite limited in scope. If these conclusions seem surprising, it should be remembered (see Chapter 2) that the laboratory method of dream study itself, in controlled home vs. laboratory comparisons, proved to have remarkably little effect on children's dream reports. Evidently dreams, at least children's, are generated in conditions in which the dream construction apparatus of the mind is relatively shielded from the kinds of reactive effects that flaw the longitudinal study of other psychological/behavioral phenomena.

Substantively, then, children's dreams between ages 7−9 and 9−11 seem to change in ways that, unsurprisingly, are less dramatic than those observed in earlier development. The findings on which this conclusion rests were predictable ones precisely because, as the last chapter demonstrated, most children already have scaled most developmental hurdles in dream development by the time they are 8 or 9 years old. There is little room left for major change in the form or content of dreams past this point, at least until the new problems of psychosocial adaptation and the new possibilities of abstract thinking associated with adolescence begin to make their mark. On the other hand, for dreams as for other aspects of psychological development, middle childhood and preadolescence are periods more of consolidation and continuity than of cataclysmic change.

THE CONTENT AND CORRELATES OF REM DREAMS

Length

As an illustration of the preceding generalizations, one merely needs to consider the fact that increases in the length of REM reports observed between ages 3−5 and 5−7 and between ages 5−7 and 7−9 were *not* repeated at any subsequent age juncture in our study. By ages 7−9 children's (particularly girls') REM reports were about as lengthy, on the average, as they ever would be through ages 14 or 15. For the first time, at ages 9−11 REM word count was positively and significantly associated with REM report rate, indicating that one is justified in considering that both variables now measure some common and integrated factor of dream making or dream reporting. Presumably, the report-rate measure would be the more reliable of the two, because, short of "perfect recall," it would be based on more observation occasions (awakenings rather than reports).

Unlike the case for report rate, there were no strictly "cognitive" correlates of REM report length at ages 9−11. There was, however, an instructive continuity between report-length correlates here and at ages 7−9. At both ages children who gave long REM narratives gave independent waking evidence of imaginativeness and of an ability to construct fantasies around physical-aggression themes. This pattern suggests that the elaboration of REM fantasies may be favored both by imaginative abilities more generally and by the sense of self-assurance that permits one to apply these abilities to potentially self-threatening contents. Interestingly, at ages 9−11 children with such a pattern were judged to be low in *overt* hostility, which suggests in turn that the development of effective fantasy capabilities may serve functions of behavioral self-control. Children high in fantasy aggression (but *low* in overt anxiety) also had longer sleep-onset reports than did children low in fantasy aggression.

Characters

The cast of important dream characters was reasonably similar at ages 9–11 to that at ages 7–9. Consistent with the hypothesis of initial adaptation effects for girls, at ages 9–11 girls reported more parent characters than at adjacent ages, perhaps because initial experience in sleeping away from home potentiated their dependency needs. Overall, male and female family members each appeared in about one of every four dreams. A like-sex bias persisted from ages 7–9 in the selection of known persons for dream representation, and, as at ages 7–9, human strangers were more often male than female for both girl and boy dreamers. As from ages 5–7 on, dream strangers were most likely to be adults, while dream known persons were most likely to be peers. As we have seen, the major shift from ages 7–9 was a significant decrease in animal characters, which now (and hereafter) were reported more often by girl than by boy dreamers.

Once again, children with less than optimal parenting dreamed most often of parents and other family members. Paternal authoritarianism was associated with dreaming of male family members, and maternal authoritarianism with dreaming of female family members. Such attitudes no doubt make parents more salient figures in children's lives, as well as contributing to a closeness, if not cohesiveness, in family relationships more generally. Mothers of frequent dreamers of female family members also were love oriented, however, and the general picture that emerges is that family dreamers came from traditionally organized family units rather than from pathologically authoritarian ones. Neither children's own adjustment nor their cognitive aptitude seemed to play any consistent role in family dreaming.

In distinction to the case at ages 7–9, there were no *positive* cognitive correlates of dreaming of familiar extrafamily persons at ages 9–11. There were such correlates for dreaming of human strangers, however, which at ages 7–9 had dominantly *negative* cognitive correlates. Specifically, high Wechsler verbal scores predicted stranger dreaming at ages 9–11. In terms of the developmental hypothesis for character elaboration presented in earlier chapters, one might conclude that reconstructing familiar persons is a task that, by middle childhood, all children are able to perform reasonably well (hence there are no positive cognitive correlates), but that the "deliberate" construction of novel characters is only now beginning in earnest, and that it is talented children who are leading the way. While our character-elaboration hypothesis is generally consistent with our data, it clearly requires testing in future research, particularly in view of the facts that: (1) our data at critical points in the developmental scenario, ages 7–9 and 9–11, came from different groups of children; and (2) the hypothesis has required us to interpret claims of dream strangers at ages 5–9 as construction failures rather than as fulfillments of genuine intentions to extend dream characterization beyond familiar persons. This last interpretation, while not wholly implausible, is post factum and requires independent examination in research more clearly addressed to testing its validity.

Two additional respects in which our hypothesis is consistent with our data deserve mention:

1   As the hypothesis might have predicted, reports of strangers rise until ages 7−9 (increasing accuracy at reporting failures to image known persons?), then "fall" (across groups) at ages 9−11 (when there is sufficient skill to image known persons veridically, and the stranger reports represent the construction successes of only a talented minority who are able to dream of genuinely novel persons?), to rise again thereafter (as a majority of children attain the levels of representational skill held only by the talented minority at ages 9−11?).

2   Those who gave many stranger-male reports gave relatively many stranger-female reports at ages 9−11 ($r = .60$, $p = .015$, 2-tail), while those who gave many known-male reports did not tend to give many known-female reports ($r = −.13$; cf. Chapter 5). The suggestion is that, at ages 9−11, the reigning cognitive imperative is only to generate strangers in an unselective way, rather than, as at ages 7−9, to generate, well or poorly, known persons in an unselective way.

Residual animal dreaming at ages 9−11 was reported relatively most often by socially inexperienced children whose parents were seen as nonsupportive and capricious or lax in their supervision. The children themselves may have been prone to somewhat diffuse waking fantasy.

Settings

With the exception of a probably artifactual excess of "unclassifiable" settings, dream settings at ages 9−11 were quite similar to those at ages 7−9. The significant "increase" in school settings was, in fact, absolutely of low magnitude. Interestingly, there was a consistent pattern of negative correlation of Wechsler cognitive variables with the incidence of own-home settings (and of general residential settings, to which own-home was the major contributor). At a time when dream *characterization* was progressing beyond the merely familiar, it was relatively dull children who tended most to limit themselves to the most familiar of *settings,* their own homes. However, unlike the case for characterization, there was no less familiar setting class (on the model of dream strangers) whose incidence was positively associated with cognitive skill. This may, however, say more about our class of setting categories, which had rather wide and fuzzy boundaries, than about the children's dream maturation. There was, once again (as at ages 5−7), some suggestion of social incompetence for any-home dreamers and (as at ages 3−9) of social passivity for own-home dreamers. As at earlier ages, dreamers of outdoor settings seemed expansive and outgoing. That most of the vague or unclassifiable settings *scored* at ages 9−11 may not have reflected vague or unclassifiable settings *experienced* is suggested by the fact that neither cognitive incompetency nor anxiety predicted their relative incidence; in fact, anxiety was negatively correlated with it.

Activities

Activities within dreams also were quite similar at ages 7–9 and 9–11. As noted earlier, the apparent "decrease" in other- or any-locomotion may have been situational (adaptational) rather than developmental. Among nonsignificant differences between ages 7–9 and 9–11 were "increases" in self- vs. other-visualizing within the dream and "increases" in self- vs. other-locomotion (and overall motor activity) within the dream. These changes, taken together, contributed to the significant "increase" in the rating for dreamer self-participation, which again seems to reflect one of the more consistent developmental accomplishments of childhood dreaming, the placement of a self-character into an increasingly prominent role within dream scenarios.

As we already have noted, continuity from ages 7–9 to 9–11 extended to correlates as well as normative data. Specifically, for the increasingly important self-as-camera modality of dream experiencing (the self, within the dream scene, inspects its environment), as at ages 7–9 so also at ages 9–11 (and at 11–13)—it was mischievous, spunky children who most often managed this degree of dream involvement. The personality profile of sensory-other dreamers was somewhat more mixed. Cognitive variables now seemed to play no role in dreaming of sensory acts.

Uniquely in our entire longitudinal series, however, there was a consistently *negative* pattern of cognitive correlates with *motor* activity by the self. Bearing in mind the positive cognitive correlates of sensory-self acts at ages 7–9, and the interpretation we have given these correlates (the self now first appears as a significant character in children's dreams), the negative cognitive correlates of motor-self activity may be interpretable, if one is again willing to generalize across groups as well as age levels. Suppose that by ages 9–11 the ability to picture a dream through their "own" (i.e., the self-character's) eyes has become accessible to most children. Imagine, however, that less cognitively mature children find particular difficulty in decentering the dream from this newly enthroned self-character. On this hypothesis we explain not only the negative cognitive correlates of motor-self acts at ages 9–11, but (nonartifactually, now) the significant cross-sectional decline in locomotor acts by others since ages 7–9. Motor acts by others have, in fact, been in steady decline since ages 5–7, where presumably they provided the only viable focus for a passive omniscient-narrator mode of kinematic dream experiencing, while motor acts by the self have been steadily increasing. On the way to a new integration (achieved, our data say, at ages 11–13), in which self and other acts will be almost equally intermixed according to the logic of the particular dream narrative, it might be expected that there would be some point (at ages 9–11, our data suggest) where less gifted dream constructors would lag in decentering the dream from a newly exercised, camera-eyed self who would, perforce, be the major dream doer. Perhaps consistent with this interpretation (which obviously requires independent validation) is the observation that motor-self dreamers at ages 9–13 had authoritarian fathers, while motor-other dreamers clearly did not. Such fathering may have contributed to children's difficulties in conceptualizing the world beyond their own fingertips (or toes, in the instance of locomotion).

It also is consistent with this interpretation of the lingering, immature egocentrism of self-active dreaming at ages 9–11 that even such more "intelligent" acts as speaking, when ascribed to the self, had negative cognitive correlates (while speaking ascribed to others had positive cognitive correlates). That the negative correlates of self-speaking were performance, rather than verbal, measures (including Block Design) suggests a general dream-construction deficit, rather than a more specific lack of act-relevant representational aptitude. Dreamer locomotion also had negative cognitive correlates, but here the variables in question were *verbal*! One way of understanding this difference in pattern of cognitive skills in relation to dreamer verbalization vs. locomotion is that act-specific aptitudes *are* beginning to play a role in the selection of dreamers' activities. Children who were high in performance skills (such as might facilitate the visual representation of self-action) chose not to have the self merely speak, while those children who were high in verbal skills chose not to have the self merely move through imagined space. More generally, verbal I.Q. predicted the overall incidence of verbal, but not of locomotor, activity in the dream.

In an era in which children's social interaction presumably has become increasingly verbal-symbolic in quality, we find that it is self-confident and self-reliant children who are making others' dream actions verbal, while it is relatively unassertive children who are making them "physical" (locomotion). It is extremely interesting that the locomotor correlates now have completed a full circle from those at ages 5–7, namely from extroversion to social passivity. That is, in the face of new developments in waking social interaction, it is socially inexperienced children who in their dreams still rely most heavily on earlier-developed interactional forms. There is, additionally, some suggestion of richness of inner fantasy in the high locomotor-other dreamers' profiles, as if imagination were now serving as a substitute for behavioral initiative.

States

As already noted, there was a significantly greater incidence of happy-self reports at ages 9–11 than at ages 7–9. Because girls' claims of happiness were, however, out of series with those at ages 7–9 and 11–13, and because the cross-group increase was attributable to the girls, I think it possible that this apparent change may have been spurious. Specifically, this was the point where older girls were first introduced to our standard feeling question (see Chapter 4), and they too, along with the younger girls at ages 5–7, may have been led by the wording of that question to feel that they must choose the most socially acceptable alternative among the feelings listed: namely, happiness. Otherwise, in contrast to ages 7–9, at ages 9–11 there were increasing, but still absolutely low, incidences of dreamer cognition and of the emotion of anger (for boys, generally felt personally; for girls, expressed by other dream characters).

As an exception to findings at other ages between 7 and 15, at ages 9–11 it was not brighter children who endowed their dream characters with mentalistic acts. Neither cognitive nor behavioral-personality variables were associated with dreamer cognitions in the dream.

Question has been raised (cf. Chapters 3–5) about the reliability of children's earliest reports of the negative emotions of fear and anger. One would like to believe that, by ages 9–11, children must generally be able to recreate symbolically such primary feelings as these in their dreams. Our evidence, however, remained somewhat equivocal, at least for fear. The major correlate of fear reports was that their dreamers were kind and considerate children. One can conceive that such well-socialized children might also have been fearful, but there was no independent evidence of waking maladaptation, and there continued to be no evidence that the symbolic accomplishment of putting fear into dreams had positive cognitive correlates. I am particularly suspicious of children's early fear reports as claims about actual *dream* experience, because our home vs. laboratory studies showed, for the same group studied longitudinally by us at ages 9–11, that fear is the emotion most likely to be added to dream reports after their first telling (Foulkes, 1979b). Thus reports of this emotion, even on laboratory awakenings, may be inherently least reliable—although fear was not felt, we want to add it, because it is implied so compellingly by the events we have described. It is interesting to speculate that the occasional dissociation of feeling and imagined circumstance, which seems to be one of the more widely remarked peculiarities of dream experience (Freud, 1900), may reflect no motivated denial or displacement but only offer continuing testimony, even for adults, of the degree of skill required to generate dream feelings symbolically.[4]

For anger at ages 9–11, there *were* first signs of potential report credibility. There was a positive cognitive correlate (WISC Information) of both

---

[4]It may be objected that we frequently generate feelings symbolically: by recalling some past frustration, we feel angry again. But what is at issue in dreams generally is the creation of some novel experience and the creation, for the first time, of feelings peculiarly appropriate to that never-before-encountered situation. One also must bear in mind here the great speed and occasional unpredictability with which dreams are generated; one may have no time to "get into the mood."

anger-self and anger-any reports, as might be expected for the skilled act of symbolically generating feelings, and there were plausible life-style correlates of overall dream anger (heedlessness, excitability). Interestingly, self-anger in dreams was negatively correlated with physical aggression in waking fantasy; it was, however, favored by paternal punitiveness.

The questions raised by normative findings of increased self-happiness in 9- to 11-year-old girls' REM dreams are amplified by the correlates of self-happiness reports at ages 9–11: low WISC Comprehension, poor memorial accuracy, and several independent indications of high motivation for social compliance. In view of findings at ages 7–9, the suggestion now cannot be that *all* of the children's happiness reports are unreliable, but rather that social-compliance factors may have contributed to a spurious *excess* in the incidence of such reports. If this was, in fact, the case, then it is interesting to note how short-term cross-sectional comparisons might yield sex differences that depended more on differential adaptation (e.g., heightened compliance in early dream interviews) than on true dream differences. Our data suggest that girls are more prone to such adaptation effects, at least in the design that we employed, than are boys.

Once again, because dream affect-elaboration does not proceed uniformly, but at a different pace for different feelings, correlates of the overall ascription of dream feelings probably have relatively little psychological significance. As at ages 7–9, such correlates again included a creativity index, but here they were in the context of an otherwise somewhat negative pattern of cognitive skill, perhaps reflecting the presence of false-positive claims among self-happiness reports.

Motives and Outcomes

Here too normative data were surprisingly constant with those at ages 7–9, with the exception of object-approaches, where scoring criteria evidently had changed. Neither hunger nor fatigue themes any longer had positive cognitive correlates (as at ages 7–9), and the incidence of fatigue themes was somewhat reduced. There was a cross-group, cross-test replication of the finding at ages 7–9 of the association of excitability with fatigue dreaming (one is prone to excitation by one's own body states?). Also, at a time when the horizons of the make-believe social world of dreaming must have been expanding, at ages 9–11 it was the less intellectually effective children who dreamed of their sleepy selves most often.

As at ages 7–9, there were indications of some continuity between waking and dreaming social interests. Frequent dreamers of social-approach themes were judged kind and considerate in interpersonal relationships; in addition, themes of prosocial initiation by others and overall were associated with richness of waking fantasy. Dreamers of self-initiated antisocial interaction, on the other hand, presented a somewhat "harder" picture: They were well informed, shrewd, and calculating. Dreamers of antisocial initiations by others, however, did not seem particularly hostile, although they did describe their parents as not being particularly companionable.

In terms of receptions of initiations from other dream characters, children who dreamed relatively often of their own ill fortune were superficially pleasant but somewhat undersocialized (not conscientious); their mothers were authoritarian-controlling. Time spent with peers was a correlate of dreaming of ill fortune more generally (experience as the worst teacher?). In general, however, at ages 9−11, correlates of neither prosocial nor antisocial interaction were terribly revealing. It is interesting that it was only at this age level, of the six that we studied, that the overall observed number of dream-test file correlations (669) was less than 5% (772) of the total number of correlations computed (15,440). While cross-age comparisons must be inexact because test variables varied from year to year, this deficit of "significant" correlations may suggest either the absence of developmental movement in middle childhood (so that all children are more or less at the same levels of waking maturation/development) or the presence of adaptational effects (which, particularly if they affected some children [girls?] more than others, may have masked underlying relationships).

Global Ratings

The remarkable degee to which dream data at ages 9−11 were continuous with those at ages 7−9, despite the different samples on which they were based, is revealed by inspecting the REM intercorrelation matrices for global dream ratings at these two ages.

Rating Variable	Ages 7−9			Ages 9−11		
	AP	SD	CD	AP	SD	CD
Hedonic tone (HT)	−.51*	.37	.27	−.51*	.49	.37
Active participation (AP)		−.50*	−.70*		−.60*	−.41
Setting distortion (SD)			.64*			.49
Character distortion (CD)			—			—

Starred entries were significant. At both age levels, dream unpleasantness was moderately predictive of dream distortion and strongly predictive of self-passivity in the dream; self-passivity was strongly predictive of dream distortion; and distortion in one modality (characterization) was associated with distortion in another (setting). What is particularly interesting, in terms of one's concern about using different groups to estimate dream development, is that the matrices above from such groups are more similar to one another than either was to the matrix from the same study group at an adjacent age level:

	Ages 5–7			Ages 11–13		
Rating Variable	AP	SD	CD	AP	SD	CD
Hedonic tone (HT)	.39	.62*	.78*	−.03	−.08	.18
Active participation (AP)		.14	.26		−.31	−.42
Setting distortion (SD)			.84*			.48*
Character distortion (CD)			—			—

One of the most interesting findings from the older group of children was that there was significant longitudinal consistency in who dreamed (or reported) unpleasant dreams ($r = .63$ between ages 9–11 and 11–13, and $r = .55$ between ages 11–13 and 13–15). No other dream-rating variable demonstrated such long-term stability for older children (although setting distortion was constant—$r = .60$—between ages 11–13 and 13–15), and no dream-rating variable showed such consistency in the period of great dream flux in which the younger group was studied. One is particularly interested, then, in who is dreaming these characteristically unpleasant REM dreams (for the consistency did *not* generalize at any age level to NREM or sleep-onset reports), and why. Our correlational data at ages 9–11 provide few clues on this last point. High-unpleasantness dreamers were relatively bright, had generally supportive parents, and showed no signs of personal distress or maladjustment. It is possible that differential disturbance due to initial adaptation effects may again have masked underlying relationships; it is suggestive, for instance, that children's dreams were significantly less pleasant[5] at ages 9–11 than at later ages. But, as we shall see in Chapters 7 and 8, the correlational picture is not greatly clarified at later ages.

It was children low in verbal skill and general intellectual efficiency who were most active, vis-à-vis others, in their REM dreams at ages 9–11. The difference with ages 7–9, where cognitive correlates were positive, could rest on a difference in children studied (although data such as those presented at the beginning of this section suggest otherwise). It also is possible, as I have suggested earlier, that it would be less talented children who would take longer to decenter from a newly achieved self-character and to reestablish an equally active realm of other-action in their dreams. Perhaps consistent with this interpretation are other characteristics of high active–self-dreamers at ages 9–11: relatively much time spent alone, rather than with peers; a low sense of self-worth; and a tendency to experience unpleasant fantasy. Dullness, passivity, and low self-worth also characterized NREM dreamers with high active participation at ages 9–11, where REM and NREM ratings were, uniquely, significantly intercorrelated ($r = .85$). At sleep onset, interestingly, it was older, daring, outgoing children who most often played leading roles in their own dreams. Clearly in this key aspect of

---

[5]Although, absolutely, on the average, not unpleasant.

dream development, REM and NREM stand together, and both are apart from sleep onset.

The meaningfulness of setting distortion ratings at ages 9−11 is partly clouded by the ambiguous interpretation one has to assign to "vague" or "unclassifiable" setting scores (improperly probed or really sketchy?). That children high in REM setting distortion performed poorly at a waking description task suggests that the locus of distortion may, in fact, have been the dream interview rather than the dream. Poor memory and low cognitive skill also predicted, respectively, NREM and sleep-onset setting distortion. In those sleep stages, instability/apprehension also predicted setting distortion, but REM distortion was *not* associated with signs of personal distress.

In line with my earlier suggestions that, once the self is enthroned in the dream at ages 7−9, the next cognitive challenge in characterization is to endow extraself-characters with novelty features, we found that Block Design predicted REM character distortion at ages 9−11.

SEX DIFFERENCES

Another continuity with findings at earlier ages was the continuing paucity of sex differences in variables describing major aspects of the form and content of children's REM dreams. Precisely two variables significantly differentiated boys' and girls' REM reports at ages 9−11: Girls' dreams more often contained known female peers, and boys' dreams more often contained some gross locomotor activity. The former finding replicates a result observed for the younger group at ages 7−9, while the latter result, which could reflect genuine differences in the sex typing of motor behavior, deserves to be viewed with some caution. As suggested earlier, it may not reflect a genuine sex difference in dreaming so much as a sex difference in initial adaptation to our experiment. As a token of the continuity of REM and NREM mentation, and as another indication that NREM mentation may better index maladaptation stress than does REM mentation, it is interesting to observe that three NREM motor variables (dreamer locomotion, any locomotion, and any dreamer motor behavior) were scored significantly more often for boys than for girls at ages 9−11. There were no significant sex differences in sleep-onset mentation. Again, we must conclude that their dream data point to communalities rather than to divergences in our boys' and girls' development.

DREAMING OUTSIDE REM SLEEP

Both by virtue of the fact that non-REM dream reports came most often from high-rate REM reporters and that non-REM reporting had positive cognitive correlates, we must presume once again that non-REM reports are entitled to be treated as credible accounts of non-REM mental activity. How, in middle childhood, is such activity different from typical REM dreaming? As listed in Table 6.2, we observed significant differences among reports collected in different sleep stages.

This rich harvest of REM vs. non-REM differences, again greater for REM comparisons with sleep onset than for those with ordinary NREM sleep, must be viewed with some caution. As at ages 7–9, non-REM report

Table 6.2   Differences in Dream Reports as a Function of Stage of Sleep

REM vs. NREM	REM vs. Sleep Onset	Sleep Onset vs. NREM
Higher incidence/score in REM	Higher incidence/score in REM	Higher incidence in NREM
Word count	Word count	States
Characters	Characters	Approach social, dreamer
Father	Mother	
Known peer, M	Siblings, M/F	
Known adult, F	Family, M/F	
Known, any F	Stranger, any M	
Stranger, adult M		
Stranger, any M	Settings	
	Home, any	
Settings	Home, own	
Other outdoors	Other outdoors	
Activities	Activities	
Verbal, other	Verbal, other	
Verbal, either	Manual, other	
Manual, other	Any motor, other	
Manual, either	Any motor, either	
Any motor, either		
	States	
States	Cognitive, either	
Happy, dreamer	Any feelings, dreamer	
Happy, either	Any feelings, either	
Any feelings, other	Hunger, other	
Hunger, dreamer	Hunger, either	
Hunger, other	Approach social, dreamer	
Hunger, either	Approach social, other	
Attack social, other	Approach social, either	
Attack social, either	Approach object, dreamer	
Outcomes	Attack social, dreamer	
Unfavorable, other mediated, dreamer		
Unfavorable, other mediated, other	Outcomes	
Unfavorable, other mediated, either	Unfavorable, other mediated, dreamer	

Table 6.2 (Continued)

REM vs. NREM	REM vs. Sleep Onset	Sleep Onset vs. NREM
Unfavorable, any, other	Unfavorable, other mediated, either	
Unfavorable, any, either	Unfavorable, self mediated, other	
	Unfavorable, any, other	
	Favorable, other mediated, dreamer	
	Favorable, other mediated, other	
	Favorable, other mediated, either	
	Favorable, self-mediated, dreamer	
	Favorable, self-mediated, other	
	Favorable, any, dreamer	
	Favorable, any, other	
	Favorable, any, either	

samples often were small (due to the awakening schedule for sleep onset plus significantly inferior report rates for NREM sleep), not permitting attributes with equal but relatively low chances of occurrence per dream equal chances to appear in non-REM samples. There also is a correlated difference at ages 9–11 (newly appearing for REM vs. sleep onset) between REM and both ordinary NREM and sleep-onset reports that one may or may not want to consider a source of artifact in content-category comparisons: REM reports are longer. That is a genuine difference, but one that inevitably carries in its wake a host of content-category differences. Even where report samples might be equated in number, if individual report lengths varied systematically by stage, there would be differences as a function of the greater opportunity that longer reports afforded for the inclusion of different characters, settings, actions, states, and outcomes. If one is interested in sleep-stage differences per unit of dream, these would be artifactual; if one allowed that systematic differences in the number of dream units created in different sleep stages were real, then they might not be so viewed.

In evaluating Table 6.2, one also must bear in mind that both REM and sleep-onset report rates have "increased" since ages 7–9, enhancing the likelihood that the age 9–11 data, better than those of ages 7–9, will indicate the true magnitude of discriminability of mentation by sleep stage in middle childhood. Uncorrected for word count, that magnitude is considerable in

REM vs. non-REM comparisons. Twenty-five content categories significantly discriminated REM reports from NREM ones, and 33 categories discriminated REM reports from sleep-onset ones. However, as at ages 7–9, where discriminating variables were fewer in number, there still was not much evidence that REM and non-REM reports were qualitatively different from one another. For instance, *no* global rating dimension (dealing with the visual vs. conceptual quality of mentation, the relative degree of self-involvement, the affective polarity of dream content, and the realism-distortion of dream elements) discriminated REM from either NREM or sleep-onset reports. Once again one thinks of children's earliest non-REM experiences as REM dreams in miniature, rather than as a different sort of mental act.

In NREM reports, both known and unfamiliar characters appeared relatively less frequently than in REM reports (i.e., there was no apparent selectivity on the basis of realism vs. distortion in NREM characterization). Settings, in general, were comparable in REM and NREM reports. While NREM reports contained less physical movement than REM ones (cf. Foulkes, 1962), it was relatively subtle (manual, verbal) acts as performed by others that occurred, individually, less often than in REM reports. Gross locomotor activity, the most frequently scored REM motor act, also was the most frequently scored NREM motor act, and its relative incidence did not significantly discriminate the two sleep stages. While antisocial interaction occurred less often in NREM reports, so too did happy feelings: NREM reports were not generally more pleasant than were REM reports. Thus, as indicated in Chapter 5, our data suggest that whatever degree of *qualitative* difference there may be between adult REM and NREM reports (and that historically has been overestimated, despite contradictory evidence from the outset; Foulkes, 1962), that difference must be the outcome of relatively late branching off of a common trunk, in which mental experiences from *both* sleep stages are programmed to be narratives appearing in the form of sensory imagery.

If there is any difference at ages 9–11 between content variables that discriminated REM reports from sleep-onset as opposed to ordinary NREM reports, it might be said to have been manifest in a characteristic dampening of affect and of the portrayal of self-involving interactional sequences with affective implications at sleep onset. As noted earlier (Chapter 5), it has been suggested (Foulkes & Vogel, 1965) that this affect dampening also characterizes adult sleep-onset mentation, indeed that it almost is inevitable if sleep-onset mentation is to lead to sleep, rather than to arousal incompatible with sleep induction.

STIMULUS INCORPORATION

Success at experimentally influencing children's dreams reached an apparent high-water mark at ages 9–11, but the crest reached, even for the most successful water stimulus, wasn't all that high. Experimental methods were comparable to those in other study years, while methods of judging the effectiveness of my stimulation of the sleeping children were comparable to those at ages 3–5. As noted in Chapter 3, the reports of 3- to 5-year-olds were judged simultaneously with those of the 9- to 11-year-olds.

Of 42 REM awakenings after stimulation, 29 produced dream reports (69% REM recall); of 44 NREM awakenings after stimulation, 12 produced dream reports (27% NREM recall).[6] Once again these figures were comparable to children's REM and NREM recall more generally at this age level, suggesting that stimulation per se does not enhance dreaming or dream recalling.

Judge 1 (identical with the "Judge 1" of ages 3–5) made 11 estimates of "certain" incorporation; seven (64%) were correct. Judge 2 (identical with the "Judge 2" of ages 3–5) made seven estimates of "certain" incorporation; five (71%) were correct. Thus despite (or because of) the fact that neither judge saw many instances of what she or he took to be clearly stimulus-influenced dreams, when they did see that, generally they were correct. No certain guesses (successful or not) were hazarded for cotton-stimulation reports (0% net incorporation rate for both judges). Net incorporation rates for limb-stimulation reports were 15% (Judge 1) and 9% (Judge 2); for water-stimulation reports they were 15% (Judge 1) and 14% (Judge 2). Averaged over all stimuli, Judge 1 achieved a net incorporation rate of 12% and Judge 2, a rate of 10%. While modest, these figures may not be much different from values observed with adults in appropriate statistical analyses (see Chapter 3).

Do these figures suggest some real increase in middle childhood in the likelihood that stimuli of external origin can influence dreams? Unfortunately, we can't be sure. The difference in judges, and in the ways different judges apportioned guesses to "certain" vs. "uncertain" judgment categories,[7] is a potential confound in comparison with incorporation data at ages 7–9, the only younger age with a sufficient number of dream reports to permit meaningful comparison and an age where net incorporation rates were *negative* for both judges. But it is instructive that the only other age level at which two judges both produced positive rates of net incorporation was the immediately following one, ages 11–13; this, of course, despite the different judges employed. Age differences in whether and how the dreaming mind reacts to exogenous stimulation obviously require further and more systematic study.

Table 6.3 presents qualitative data on judges' "certain" incorporation judgments for dream reports collected at ages 9–11. By the two-judge,

---

[6]As in other study years, these figures do not include occasions on which children awakened as I entered their bedrooms. At ages 9–11 this happened 10 times, more frequently than at any other age level.

[7]At ages 9–11 both judges' "certain" judgments were markedly superior in accuracy to their "uncertain" judgments; this was not the case at ages 7–9, where Judge 2's uncertain judgments actually were more accurate (33%, i.e., chance) than were her certain ones (25%, below chance).

certain-and-right index also, incorporation was relatively highest but still very modest (10%) at these ages.

Several features of the data in Table 6.3 are noteworthy.

Table 6.3 **Judges' Consensually Correct and Consensually Certain Incorporation Judgments: Ages 9–11**

	Judges Both "Certain"	**One/Both Judge(s) Not "Certain"**
Judges Are Consensually Right	*Patty:* Night 2, Awakening 3. Water starts dripping beneath the sink; she puts a pan there to keep it off the floor (a water-REM stimulation). N[a] *Edgar:* Night 9, Awakening 2. A boy with a broken arm who, as he pulls his shirt down on one arm, finds it goes up on the other one (a limb-REM stimulation). N *Patrick:* Night 2, Awakening 3. Looking for his friends on a rainy day; on the next day, finds "him," who is hungry, and eats spaghetti (a water-REM stimulation). N *Patrick:* Night 9, Awakening 3. Rain, then a tornado, washing his house away (a water-NREM stimulation). N	*Charmane:* Night 9, Awakening 2. A strike at the supermarket; she is throwing dishes (a limb-REM stimulation). N *Al:* Night 9, Awakening 3. Camping at Casper Mountain; he couldn't find a lake to fish in (a water-NREM stimulation). N *Andy:* Night 2, Awakening 3. Two boats are shipwrecked, and the survivors go to two separate islands and form parties to wage war against one another; (unrelated) going by a Mobil station, whose pumps were as low as his bed is (a water-REM stimulation). N
Judges Are Consensually Wrong	*Teddy:* Night 9, Awakening 1. Looking at a volcano; sleeping in a stream (a cotton-NREM stimulation, judged "water"). M *Teddy:* Night 9, Awakening 2. At the beach with his family, running in the water (a limb-REM stimulation, judged "water"). N	

Reports judged = 41
"Certain" and right = 10%

[a] N = no visible response; (M = moves during stimulation but does not awaken).

1   Without exception, consensually correct judgments came from stimula-
    tions that did *not* produce visible motor responses. This suggests much
    more strongly than at earlier ages that children now can incorporate
    exogenous stimulation into their dreams while they still are fully asleep
    by behavioral criteria.

2   For the first time, at ages 9–11, consensually correct judgments include
    NREM reports, and in roughly the proportion in which NREM awak-
    enings more generally were associated with reports in contrast to REM
    awakenings.

3   In line with children's increasing narrative ability, it seems that "incor-
    poration" reports since ages 3–7 have become less sheerly interpretive
    and more openly elaborative of the stimulus whose presence they seem
    to reflect. Patty's report, like Karen's at ages 7–9 (cf. Table 5.2), has the
    property of not merely explaining water but of using it for narrative
    development. These dreams begin to sound very much like those Dement
    and Wolpert (1958) collected from adults following water stimulation:
    The water is recognized, but the story goes on. In both Patrick's and
    Andy's REM dreams, it seems to go on to someplace else entirely. Even
    Patrick's NREM dream carries us past the sheer fact of wetness to an
    imagined set of consequences of the water's presence. But Charmane's
    dream may best illustrate a mature direction in which stimulus-
    incorporation is moving. The story determines the fate of the stimulus,
    rather than vice-versa. If you're dreaming that you're in a supermarket
    where your mother has started a "strike" against the manager, and
    someone moves your hands as you're dreaming this, convert that
    stimulus to an act that fits the angry context: Throw something in protest.

But the major result, at ages 9–11 as elsewhere, may bear even stronger
testimony to the independence of dream elaboration from determination by
aperiodic exogenous stimulation. Most often, the ongoing dream is not
demonstrably affected *at all* by such stimulation.

EMILY'S DREAMS

We already have met Emily, briefly, in Chapter 3. She is Dean's older sister
and will be our specimen dreamer from ages 10 to 15. During her first year in
our study, Emily was in fifth grade. During this same year she reported 14
REM dreams (93% recall), five NREM dreams (56% recall), and three
sleep-onset dreams (100% recall).

Her *REM reports* were as follows:

1-2   I dreamed about the (sleep-lab's) nursery school and the little nursery-
      school kids. There were only three kids there. And then they were
      leaving and going up the stairs, and the nursery-school teacher said
      good-bye. [Were you in the dream, or were you just watching?] . . .

Just watching. [Did you recognize any of the people?] I recognized Dean, he's my little brother. [What about the teacher or any of the other children?] No. [Where did the dream seem to be taking place?] It looked like it was taking place in a gym or somewhere. It was made-up. [Did you have any feelings?] No, I don't think so.

1-3   There were some people walking down the hall, talking to each other. There was three people. Two people were walking together and one person was walking alone. [What sort of people were they?] Ladies. [Were you in the dream, or were you just watching?] I was just watching. [Where did this seem to take place?] It looked like it was in a school. [Did you have any feelings?] No, I don't remember anything.

2-1   It wasn't scary. There was a song in it. I was just listening to it. I don't know what kind. I don't think there was any people. [Did you have any feelings?] No, really.

2-3   There was a little boy and two girls and they lived in our house. And the little boy wanted to play, and so he came out into the kitchen, and he asked the mother if he could play with his blocks in his room. And so he went out and played and the two girls stayed in the kitchen . . . sitting at the table, eating. They were looking at the mail. [Did you recognize the girls or the boy?] No. The little boy was about five, and the girls were about eleven. [Were you in this dream?] No. [Do you remember any feelings?] No.

3-2   I dreamed I was playing with the two twins that live next door to me and my sister. We were playing something, on the driveway of our house. It was something with a rope . . . might have been jump rope. [Did it look like your driveway does, or was it changed at all?] No, it looked like our driveway. [Did you have any feelings?] Well, it was kind of . . . we were having fun playing.

4-1   I dreamed that there was a lady and she was on a TV show and in a commercial too. The TV show was *Gilligan's Island* and she was on a Josephine commercial with Comet (cleanser). She didn't do anything, playing on the show or anything. When she was doing the commercial, she was crying about her house, because it was so old and torn up. [Were you in this dream?] No. [Did you think that you were seeing this on television?] Yes. [This lady that you mentioned——is she really on *Gilligan's Island*?] She's really on *Gilligan's Island*. [In the dream you thought she was doing a Comet commercial?] Yes. [Was there anybody else in the dream besides the lady?] The plumber . . . Josephine. [Who was the person that was crying because of the house?] The lady that was on *Gilligan's Island*. [Do you recall any feelings?] No.

4-3   I was thinking about costumes there at a birthday party and you go and dress up like an animal. There was these two guys and they were ice-skating and they dressed up like bears. Some other guys were making a cake, and some guys were playing with trains, and I was in the dream. I don't remember what I was wearing. [Did you recognize any of the other people?] My next-door neighbor . . . she was playing with me. [A girl about your own age?] Yes. [Did you recognize any of the guys?] No. [Where did the dream seem to be taking place?] It was outside, but it was a skating rink, and it was up in the mountains somewhere . . . made-up. [Do you recall any feelings?] No. I don't think so.

5-1 I remember there was a rug. It was near Christmas and it was just about when it was now. . . . (People) were in a house, I don't know what the house was. [What were they doing?] I can't remember. [Where did the rug come into it?] . . . it was just there. [On the floor?] Yes. [How did you know that this was near Christmastime?] Well, somebody said that next year at Halloween we'd have to get another costume for Halloween before Christmas came. And then he said, "Well, it's after Halloween now!" [Did you recognize any of these people?] No . . . they were just about the age that I am. [Were you in the dream?] Yeah. I think so . . . just listening. [Did you have any feelings?] No. I don't think so.

6-2 I was dreaming about bears and snakes. I don't remember them doing anything. The bears were growling and they were outside someplace, but I don't know where it was. I wasn't in the dream. [What exactly could you see?] I saw the mountains. . . . I didn't know where it was . . . and then there were bears on the left side and then on the right sides were the snakes. [Any people?] No, there were just animals. . . . I wasn't in it at all. [The snakes . . . were they doing anything?] Well, they were moving around, they weren't standing still. [Did you have any feelings?] No.

7-2 I don't know how many, but there was some doctors looking down the hall. [Were you in the dream?] No. [Did you recognize these doctors?] No . . . there were about six, I guess. [Where did this seem to be taking place?] In the hall of a hospital. . . . It was made-up for the dream. [Did you have any feelings?] No.

7-3 I was in school and the teacher was up at the board talking and showing us something, writing on the board. We have some SRA (Science Research Associates) things in school and she was telling us we had to hand in one SRA thing and she was talking about how we'd have to do it. [Did you recognize any of (the people)?] No. [Was the teacher your teacher?] Yes. There were other kids there. I didn't really look at the other kids, though. [What exactly were you doing in the dream?] I was doing a "powerbuilder" in SRA. . . . It was my school. [Did you have any feelings?] No.

8-1 There was a guy and a thing. He was at a microphone, and I don't know what caused it. He moved, and the microphone fell down. When I woke up, the microphone fell off. [Did you recognize the man?] No. [Was there anyone else in the dream?] No. [Were you in the dream?] No. [Where did this seem to take place?] On a stage. [Did you have any feelings?] No.

8-3 It was a nice night before Easter and we had company over at our house and nobody would get in bed. There was a big fight and every-body was crying. There were two boys that were in the bedroom and they were throwing a bunny back and forth to each other. And then another girl was in the living room crying. And a girl popped another girl's balloon, and then she got mad at her, and they started having a fight. [What people are they?] Some neighbors that live next door to me on both sides and the rest of my family. And some people that live downtown that we know. [Your mom and dad?] They were in it, but they had already gone to bed. . . . I was in it. [Did your house look the way it really does, or was anything changed in the dream?] It didn't look the same. . . . The living room was in the wrong place. [Was it a real live bunny, or a . . . toy one?] It was a inflatable. . . . [Do you remember any feelings?] I was kind of mad. Nobody would go to bed and I was trying to get them to bed.

9-2   A crate of oranges and some were great big giant ones and some of them were real little ones. Somebody was picking up a big orange and then there was some brown paper stuck in between the little oranges. . . . It was a woman, I don't know who it was. . . . I was in the dream, watching him (sic) take the oranges out. . . . It was inside somewhere, but I don't know where it was. [Did you have any feelings?] No.

The possibility was raised earlier that, as a group, the older girls first studied at ages 9–11 may have had an initial-test effect in the direction of having less "active" dreams than would have been expected from the younger girls' age 7–9 data or the older girls' own age 11–13 data. Overall activity was somewhat less frequent in their dreams than in those of either comparison group, and gross locomotor activity was especially so, leading, uniquely at this age, to a significant boy–girl difference in locomotor activity. Emily's Year-1 dreams seem to support this possibility.

Emily had a passive role (just watching/listening) or no role at all in at least 10 of her 14 REM dreams (1-2, 1-3, 2-1, 2-3, 4-1, 5-1, 6-2, 7-2, 8-1, 9-2), and few of her REM dreams had the narrative complexity of, for example, her brother's REM dreams at ages 8 and 9. That this may in part be a reactive-testing effect is suggested by a relatively high incidence of possibly laboratory-related content (e.g., the sleep lab's nursery school—which Dean did, in fact, attend—in 1-2; the hallway setting in 1-3 [it was necessary for subjects to walk down a long corridor to reach the sleep lab, and the control area was, in fact, merely the end of the corridor]; the initial "it wasn't scary" comment in 2-1 [was she worried that she would have scary dreams in the laboratory?]; a 5-year-old boy and 11-year-old girls in 2-3 [her brother's and her current ages]; birthdays in 4-3 [the subject of an extensive discussion she'd had that evening with me]; Halloween and Christmas in 5-1 [also subjects of presleep conversation with me]; "doctors" looking down the hall in 7-2; microphones in 8-1; trying to get children to bed in 8-3). Rather more than her brother at ages 8 and 9, Emily at ages 10 and 11 seems to be attuned in her dreams to the observational setting in which they are being studied. Perhaps in consequence, her dreams seem less revealing of enduring thoughts, feelings, and motives, and seem to show less imaginal complexity, than her brother's REM dreams at ages 8 and 9. Her "dream generator" seems to be working in a generally cautious, somewhat inhibited fashion. Domhoff (1969) has insisted this generally is true in sleep-laboratory studies. Data from this project (Foulkes, 1979b) contradict that position but do not preclude that it sometimes is the case for some subjects.

But, of course, given only these data, it is impossible to rule out more genuine sex differences in explaining the apparent differences between Emily's Year-1 dreams and Dean's Year-5 ones. Using our older subjects' data, Trupin (1976) showed that boys' dreams at ages 11–13, were more "agentic" and girls' dreams were more "communal":

> Characteristics of agentic functions are libido, assertive behavior, aggression, danger, conquest, risk, self-sufficiency, and success. Communion is characterized by social consciousness, interpersonal concerns and interests, generosity, and receptivity. . . . (p. 171)

The hypothesis of a reactive effect for the older girl subjects studied in Year 1 might, in fact, be plausible in terms of these more general patterns of sex differentiation; girls *should* be more sensitive to social context than boys. The extent to which initial-testing effects versus more enduring sex differences were determinants of Emily's generally rather "quiet" Year-1 REM dreams might, of course, be estimable from her REM dreams from later years of the study.

However they are to be explained, Emily's dreams do have several features not generally possessed by those of her brother at age 8–9. Settings tend to be indoors (1-2, 1-3, 2-3, 5-1, 7-2, 7-3, 8-1, 8-3, 9-2) rather than clearly outdoors (3-2, 4-3, 6-2). Plots do, in fact, seem more communal than agentic. Revealingly, in 2-3 the boy goes off to play with objects, while the girls remain together, looking at the "mail." Social separation or isolation appear as themes in several dreams (e.g., 1-2, 1-3, 2-3); social niceties are observed (1-2); the state of one's home is a concern (4-1); recreation themes seem more interpersonal than object or skill centered (3-2, 4-3); social occasions and appropriate dress therefor are at issue (4-3, 5-1); etc.

Yet it would be incautious to conclude from these differences that Emily's Year-1 dreams revealed no motive structures or conflicts of comparable "depth" as the ones that plausibly could be read into Dean's dreams at ages 8 and 9. By no means all of her dream imagery is easily interpretable as situationally determined or as reflecting relatively superficial interpersonal interests. As did Dean's final-year dreams, her less realistic or plausible first-year dreams suggest rather more significant concerns related to psychosexual development (something wrong with the woman's "plumbing"? in 4-1; dressed like an animal, "bear" boys in 4-3; growling bears and wriggling snakes in 6-2; the man losing the top of his microphone when he moved in 8-1; a girl's balloon deflated and the boys tossing around an inflatable "bunny" in 8-3; the woman's [man's?] concern about globular sizes in 9-2). One wonders also whether the SRA "powerbuilder" on which Emily is working assiduously in 7-3 is meant to be taken in a purely intellective way. At least by Night 4, some of the kinds of determinants plausibly seen in her brother's dreams plausibly can be seen in hers. In this light, dream 8-3 might be interpreted as saying how difficult it is for Emily to stay the rowdy forces of her sleeping mental "house." But, as generally seems true in childhood, she in fact does a competent job of containing such forces even when there are surface dream representations possibly deriving from them. *All* of her REM dreams seem to be relatively well-controlled fantasy experiences.

Emily's *sleep-onset dreams* were as follows:

4-2   Something was happening at school, and it wasn't really true, but I can't remember what it was. I don't remember if I was in there or not. . . . I was in the school; well, I don't know if I was in it or not. Either I saw some people at school or I was in school. [What people were in this?] . . . I don't remember if I was, but that would be me and then the rest of the class and my teacher. [Did it seem to be in any particular school that you know about?] No. [Did you have any feelings?] No.

5-3   It was about some people going to college . . . kids that were going to college. [How old are the kids?] About 20. [Were you in (this)?] No. [Where did the setting seem to be?] It seemed to be outside somewhere, but I don't know where the college was. [Did you have any feelings?] No.

6-1   I was dreaming that I was at school and somebody asked me, the teacher asked me a question and I was answering it, but I forgot what the question was. I couldn't see the teacher. I could just hear her talking to me. I could see the desks. [Were there any other people in the dream?] The rest of the class. [People . . . actually in your class?] I couldn't tell. [What were you doing in the dream?] I was sitting at my desk and I was answering the question. [Did this school room look like your real school room?] It was just about the same. [Did you have any feelings?] No, I guess not.

Emily's sleep-onset mentation seems close to everyday situations in her waking life, rather than, as seemed to be the case for Dean's sleep-onset mentation, being close to typical waking fantasies or daydreams. Two of Emily's sleep-onset situations draw on her own daytime school experience; the third plausibly is related to the fact that, in coming to the laboratory, she also was in fact coming to a college campus. None of the situations seems at all affectively toned, and none seems as clearly drawn or vivid as were most of her REM reports.

Emily's Year-1 *NREM dreams* were as follows:

5-2   I was dreaming about some people, they were outside and they were playing something. I don't think I was in the dream. [Who were these people?] I don't know who they were, but there were some children and some grown-ups. . . . They were playing some kind of game. . . . I think it was something like tag. [Where did this seem to take place?] Outside somewhere, and when it was real hot. I mean there wasn't any snow on the ground and people weren't wearing coats. [Did you have any feelings?] No.

6-3   There was some water somewhere. [Could you see it?] Yes. [Were there any people in the dream?] I don't know. I think there might have been. [Were you in it?] No. [When you say water, do you mean a body of water, like a lake or river, or some other kind of water?] It was more like a swimming pool or a lake or something, it wasn't like a river. [Was this some place that you recognize, or was it made-up?] It was made-up. [Did you have any feelings?] No.

7-1   I was making out cards. I can't remember what kinds of cards they were. [Was this visual?] Yes. [What could you see?] Just some other people making the cards that I were. [Who were these people?] Some of them were people in my class. [And what were you doing in the dream?] I was sitting at my desk signing the cards. [Where did this seem to be taking place?] I don't know. I guess at school . . . my school. [Did you have any feelings?] No.

8-2   I dreamed I was in Paris and I was walking by that Eiffel Tower. I could see the Eiffel Tower and some cars going down the street. And some stores, and buildings. [What people were in this?] I just saw me, I didn't see anybody else. But there were people in the cars. [What exactly were you doing in the dream?] I was walking down the street. [Did the setting in this dream look realistic?] Yes. [Have you ever been to Paris?] No. [Did you have any feelings?] No.

9-3   We were swinging outside. Somewhere, I don't know where it was. Me, my neighbor (a girl), and my sister. [Where was this?] There's a swing set out in the neighbor's backyard and we were swinging on it. . . . I really couldn't see the backyard. [But you thought it was in the backyard?] Yes. [Did you have any feelings?] No. [Were you talking to one another, or were you just swinging?] We were talking, but I forgot what we said.

As also was true of Dean's final-year NREM reports, these reports seem "superficial," the kind of thought Rechtschaffen, Verdone, and Wheaton (1963) have likened to

> that large portion of our waking thought which wanders in seemingly disorganized, drifting, non-directed fashion whenever we are not attending to external stimuli or actively working out a problem or a daydream. (p. 411)

"Nondirected" may be the key term in this characterization. As suggested earlier, it may be the case that the regnant, personally significant motives that generally direct REM mentation and, to some degree, sleep-onset mentation are relatively silent in NREM sleep.

The interpreter always can, of course, see Eiffel Towers as penises, or swings as devices to generate pleasurable body sensations. But such interpretations seem somewhat overblown for mentation whose content otherwise is as bland and plausible as Emily's Year-1 NREM reports. It seems likely that these reports would generate only superficial kinds of associations, such as "Paris is a neat place; I've always wanted to go there" or "Swinging with my friends is a good way to spend an afternoon." If so, it could only be theory, theory that goes well beyond the evidence at hand, that pushes one into the position of demanding "deep" interpretations, when the dreamer-generated context for dream thoughts is "shallow" and that "shallow" context adequately encompasses the explicanda. Probably quite fortunately for the human mental economy, neither in wakefulness nor apparently in sleep are we always condemned to think "deep" thoughts. Emily's early REM reports suggest that even in REM sleep, there is the option of disengaging the motive systems more generally operative there: REM dream 3-2 is, for example, indistinguishable in quality from NREM dream 9-3. But there is nothing in Emily's NREM reports that compares in quality to her REM dreams 4-1, 4-3, 5-1, 6-2, and so forth. When motives come to knock, it is the REM door that swings open most fully.

SUMMARY

In general, the middle-childhood years from ages 9 to 11 seem to be years of quantitative growth (e.g., in the dreaming or remembering of dreams) and consolidation (e.g., in involvement of the self-character in narrative generation), rather than comprising an era in which dream-report phenomena undergo further qualitative change. Because for most children many of the major developmental hurdles in the accession of adultlike dream form have by now been surmounted, there seems to be somewhat more room for individual differences in dream contents to begin to reflect coherently individual differences in personal style ("personality": i.e., typical waking behaviors, interests, and attitudes). It is this self-revelatory aspect of dreaming that will, in turn, be subject to some consolidation in the immediately succeeding years of preadolescence. But it is important to remember that self-revelation (in the "personality" sense) may only be generally possible at ages in which imperatives of cognitive development are less than paramount influences in dream generation, and that at ages 9 to 11 there still seem to be at least some forms of dream representation in which differential cognitive aptitudes play leading roles.

CHAPTER 7 _____

Ages 11 to 13

Of the 16 children whose dreams were collected at ages 9–11, 14 were restudied two years later, at ages 11–13.[1] Joining the six boys previously studied were six boys studied for the first time at ages 11–13. Thus in late preadolescence our total study group was comprised of 20 children: eight girls and 12 boys. At the start of the study year, the typical (median) girl was aged 11 years, 8 months, and the typical boy was aged 12 years, 2 months. During the study year the typical girl was in sixth grade (last year of grade school) and the typical boy in seventh (first year of junior high school).

In comparison with veteran boy subjects, the new recruits at ages 11–13 were not significantly different in age, family occupational status, or I.Q.[2] The veteran and novice boys also demonstrated *no* significant differences in presleep adaptation (rating for anxiety–relaxation), in actual sleep behavior (sleep latency, REM latency, number of spontaneous awakenings, time awake on experimental awakenings), in REM report rate, in REM dream word count, in REM dream ratings, or in any of 163 applicable REM-dream content-analysis categories. These overwhelmingly negative findings suggest rapid adaptation of the novices and an absence of long-term study effects for the veterans. They also justify our pooling of data from the two groups in subsequently reported analyses of boys' (or children's) dreams at ages 11–13.

Methods of study generally were identical to those at ages 9–11. Major differences between the two study years were as follows:

1 In early Year 3 the laboratory moved to a new building, a move seemingly without great manifest impact on children's behavior, sleep, or dreams (see Chapter 2).

2 Children were asked, following electrode attachment on each laboratory night, to describe on a paper-and-pencil form significant recent events in their lives and to give an hour-by-hour accounting of their activity since

[1]Two boys, brothers, moved from Laramie at the end of Year 1.
[2]Their group did, however, include a wider range of intellectual competence than did the veteran group (see Table 2.3).

waking that morning. (A modified version of this form also was employed at ages 13−15).

3   We generally scheduled three, rather than two, subjects per night. (However, since they often were not all from the same age group, there was not much change in effective presleep social encounter, because younger children generally went to bed earlier than did older children).

4   There seem to have been a few adjustments in my interview technique and in the judges' use of scoring criteria in evaluating dreams (as discussed in Chapter 6).

In terms of cognitive stage analysis, in the absence of directly relevant data, it can only be presumed that the children were at least "concrete-operational" by ages 11−13. The possibility exists that, among the brighter and older children, there was some movement into the stage of formal-operational reasoning.

THE REPORTING OF DREAMS

The 11- to 13-year-olds reported dreams on 66% of their REM, on 31% of their NREM, and on 67% of their sleep-onset awakenings. Typical (median) *child* figures were: REM, 79% recall; NREM, 24% recall; sleep-onset, 67% recall. There was no significant change in report rate for any stage of sleep between ages 9−11 and 11−13. Pooled REM recall was identical (60.9%) for veteran and novice boys. Girls' REM recall (pooled: 75%) was marginally (p < .10, 2-tail) superior to that of boys, but the girls also tended, for their age, to be brighter than the boys (their median Year-3 I.Q. was 118, while that for the boys was only 106), and full-scale I.Q. was a correlate of REM report rate ($r = .44$, $p = .052$, 2-tail). The discrepancy between pooled REM recall and typical-child REM recall again indicates a distribution with many high-rate reporters and a few low-rate ones (see Chapter 6).

Also, once again NREM report rates were significantly inferior to both REM and sleep-onset report rates, which were not significantly different from one another. "Light"-NREM awakenings continued to be associated with reports more often (42%) than did "deep"-NREM awakenings (25%; p < .10, 2-tail), and the absolute figures here were almost identical to those at ages 9−11 (42% vs. 26%).

In general, late-night awakenings in both REM and NREM sleep were more likely to produce dream reports than were early-night awakenings (REM awakening 1, 58%; REM awakening 3, 74%; NREM awakening 1, 26%; NREM awakening 3, 42%). Only NREM ordinal-position effects (awakenings 1 and 2 vs. 3) were significant, however.

As at ages 9−11, it was competent, achievement-minded, assertive, and verbally imaginative children who reported dreams most often on REM awakenings. The similarity is not surprising, because for continuing subjects

REM recall was highly stable ($r = .87$) between ages 9–11 and 11–13. Once again, also, the positive cognitive correlates (WISC Information, Digit Span), in conjunction with associated behavioral-personality correlates, are more suggestive of mediation at the report level (brighter children generally try harder) than at the experience level. One gets a picture of the high-rate reporters as children who would put themselves out and try to excel at any task adults set for them—here, in the gathering together of dream experiences for reporting to an adult. Perhaps for this reason, a waking measure of "dream-recall frequency" was predictive of REM report rate. In the absence of *general* visuospatial or performance correlates, and in the presence of a well-defined pattern of effective socialization, it seems less likely than it did at ages 5–7 or 7–9 that the cognitive correlates of REM reporting reflect influences operative in the actual generation of dreams. As pointed out in Chapter 6, the significant WISC Block Design correlation with REM recall at ages 11–13 may not be *general* because, for our sample, it depended on the inclusion of two novice males with aberrantly immature Block Design scores.

But if the Block Design correlation is not informative about typical influences on ages 11–13 dream experiencing or reporting, it may be highly instructive concerning the role Block Design–assessed skills play in earlier stages of dream development, for, in studying Fred and Phil at ages 11–13, we were studying children who, based on their Block Design talent, belonged in our younger study group. Their Year-3 Block Design raw scores were, respectively, 6 and 19; the median score attained by their age-matched male peers was 31, and the median score attained by our 7- to 9-year-old boys also was 31. At ages 11–13 their age-matched male peers had a typical REM report rate of 71%; for the 7- to 9-year-old boys, the figure was 73%. Fred's REM report rate at age 12–13 was 33%; Phil's at age 11–12 was 27%. At age 11–13, Fred and Phil socially were late preadolescents, and they were doing seventh- or sixth-grade work in school. In Block Design skill, however, they "were" only early grade-schoolers.

In REM report rate, of course, they also "were" only early grade-schoolers, and the coincidence of these two forms of cognitive retardation is revealing, because in interpreting earlier Block Design correlations with REM report rate, we could not be certain that Block Design had any unique predictive significance. Perhaps it was just another indication of the fact that dream maturation follows general maturation. But in Fred and Phil we have, fortuitously, children who are generally mature but not Block Design mature, and their dream reporting (and experiencing?) follows the trend of their Block Design maturation rather than of their general maturation. This is a point to which we will return in further detail, and with further documentation, in Chapter 8, where Fred's and Phil's data make the same point but even more clearly.

Unsurprisingly, in view of its significant intercorrelation with REM report rate ($r = .66$), NREM report rate also was positively associated with various signs of social and intellectual competence. Once again cognitive correlates were largely "verbal." Our waking measure of "dream-recall frequency," that is, children's waking impressions of how often they dreamed, was significantly associated with NREM report rate in the laboratory and with sleep-onset report rate as well. Other sleep-onset correlates included now-familiar signs of social and cognitive competence: imagination, assertiveness, school achievement, and verbal cognitive ability. Sleep-onset report rate correlated significantly with REM ($r = .76$) and with NREM ($r = .47$) report rate.

THE CHANGING CONTENT OF REM DREAMS

Dream content comparisons across the time span in which our older-group children were studied promise to be uniquely valuable, because, unlike the cross-sectional contrasts between ages 7–9 and 9–11, they involve the same children and, unlike the longitudinal contrasts for the younger group, they cover a period in which neither recall rates nor word counts were changing. Here, for a relatively stable dreaming process in a constant population, one can ask how changes in particular contents of children's dreams seem to reflect their personal growth and social development.

Table 7.1 presents the dream content variables that were scored as showing significant decreases or increases between ages 9–11 and 11–13. Some of these changes—indeterminate-sex characters, unclassifiable settings, and self-mediated outcomes being higher in Year 1; approach-object interaction and visualization ratings being higher in Year 3—have been discussed in Chapters 4 and 6 as most likely being artifactual and will not be given further attention here. The other changes may be summarized as follows.

First, in characterization, children's dreams less often contained family members, particularly female family members, including the mother. The evidence is less clear-cut that a peer focus was replacing a family focus. Only the incidence of known female peers increased significantly, and that change was largely a function of a significant increase in their incidence in the girls' dreams. The dominantly female basis of these changes may reflect the fact that, at ages 9–11, girls dreamed relatively more often than boys of family members but relatively less often than boys of like-sex peers, but it also suggests that it is specifically the maternal-female value structure of the family that becomes less important to children of both sexes as they approach adolescence.

Second, in line with these family-distancing changes in dream characterization, children dreamed less often of their own homes ($p < .10$, 2-tail), but significantly more often of unfamiliar residential settings (cf. Chapter 8, n. 8).

Third, in the area of dream activities, there was an increase in the assignment of relatively subtle and "psychological" acts (seeing, sensing,

Table 7.1 **Dream Variables Showing a Significant Difference in Magnitude or Frequency of Occurrence Between Ages 9–11 and 11–13**

Significantly Higher at Ages 9–11	Significantly Higher at Ages 11–13
REM Reports	REM Reports
Characters	Characters
Mother	Known peer, female
Parent, either	Settings
Sibling, female	Home, unfamiliar
Parent-siblings, female	
Known, any indeterminate	Activities
Strangers, any indeterminate	Vision, other
	Any sensory, other
Settings	Verbal, other
Unclassifiable	Manual, dreamer
	Manual, either
States	Locomotor, dreamer
Sad, either	Locomotor, either
Feelings, any, other	Any motor, dreamer
Feelings, any, either	
	States
Outcomes	Approach social, either
Unfavorable, other mediated,	Approach object, dreamer
dreamer	Approach object, other
Favorable, self-mediated, dreamer	Approach object, either
Ratings	Outcomes
Hedonic tone	Favorable, other mediated, other
	Favorable, other mediated, either
NREM Reports	
Characters	Ratings
Strangers, any indeterminate	Visualization
	Sleep-Onset Reports
	States
	Approach object, dreamer

talking) to nonself-characters, but an increase in the assignment of more "physical" behaviors (manipulating, moving) to the self-character. Once again, the increase in self-ascriptions of motor behavior depended primarily on the girl dreamers,[3] and may have been artifactual. If, as I have suggested, the motor quality of girls' dreams was inhibited by ill-adaptation at ages 9–11, then the "increase" in this quality at ages 11–13 may be a recovery phenomenon specific to our experimental design rather than a true develop-

---

[3]These increases were significant only for the female subgroup: manual activity, dreamer and either; locomotor activity, either; any motor activity, either.

mental change. However, the increasing subtlety of other-characterization is consistent with ideas developed earlier concerning true developmental changes in self- vs. other-participation in children's dreams (children at ages 11–12 have effectively reintegrated others into dreams that retain genuine self-participation), and the increasingly verbal, as opposed to "physical," quality of interpersonal behavior in dreams reflects a long-run developmental trend seen throughout our two longitudinal series. As children's waking lives become increasingly symbolic, so too apparently do their dreamworlds.

Finally, children's dreams became increasingly pleasant at ages 11–13. Only at these ages were *both* boys' and girls' typical dreams scored as being more pleasant than unpleasant, because only at these ages were boys' typical dreams so scored. On a 1 = pleasant to 3 = unpleasant scale, the mean Hedonic Tone score for boys' dreams was 1.93, for girls' dreams, 1.77. (At all ages studied, girls' typical dreams were dominantly pleasant, and more pleasant than were boys' typical dreams.) Components of the longitudinal change from ages 9–11 to 11–13 were decreases in sad feelings, overall affect, and unfavorable outcomes for the dreamer at the hand of other dream characters, and increases in favorable outcomes and prosocial initiations.[4]

In one view of human development, late preadolescence is associated with an early integration of cognitive functions and with an early, presexual crystallization of personality structure (e.g., Kagan & Moss, 1962; Kohen-Raz, 1971). It is a period of organization and consolidation whose products will guide the child through the flux of adolescence toward a second and more mature structuring of the self, this time based on an acceptance of one's heterosexual feelings and impulses. Our dream data are largely consistent with the hypothesis of a preadolescent attainment of self-mastery and self-control. By late preadolescence children's dreams are, within the time span of our two observational series, as generally well organized and well controlled as they ever have been or ever will be. Family and home themes are decreasing, but the extrafamilial world is being explored with increasing confidence and competence. There is an effective integration of the self vis-à-vis others, and dream activities are increasingly verbal-symbolic in nature. Because of the parallel between preadolescent dream achievement and preadolescent character formation, one wonders whether, for dreams as for waking character, the preadolescent integration is an especially good predictor of the adult integration to follow.

---

[4]A methodological implication of these results is that laboratory dreams cannot be bland because subjects are unfamiliar with the laboratory setting and personnel, and hence "on guard" (Domhoff, 1969). Our 11- to 13-year-olds had already been studied for 17 nights over a two-year period and, by all evidence, had adapted very well to being in the laboratory. Yet their dreams after such adaptation were *less* emotional and unpleasant than before (cf. Foulkes, 1979b).

WHO REM-DREAMS WHAT, AND WHY

Two factors suggest that our waking–dreaming correlational data may be especially valuable at ages 11–13. First, as we have just seen, these ages seem to represent a period of crystallization in dream development, a period in which, therefore, it is particularly appropriate to ask how individual differences in the form of that crystallization are to be understood. Second, at these ages there are relatively many dream data (as compared, for instance, to ages 5–7) that seem to be little contaminated by adaptation effects or by the inclusion of newly studied subjects (as compared, for instance, to ages 9–11 or 7–9). However, as we shall see, the fact that some of the ways in which dreams are consolidated at ages 11–13 seem, naturally enough, to differ for boys and for girls will introduce some interpretive problems, for our correlations included children of both sexes.

Dream Length

Consistent with the idea that socialization-induced motivation may now be the most effective determinant of dream reporting, and with the significant correlation (r = .57) between REM report rate and REM word count, describers of longer REM dreams were, at ages 11–13, verbally facile, compliant, and socially pleasant children. At these ages the typical dream of both boys and girls within our observational series was as long as it ever would be, and equivalent in length to dreams we have collected and scored comparably from college students (Foulkes, Spear, & Symonds, 1966).

Characters

Cognitive factors played no consistent role, but personality and family-life variables did, in determining who still dreamed relatively often of nuclear family members in an era in which the incidence of such characters was decreasing. High-rate family dreamers were, as at ages 3–9, socially immature (here, irresponsible, mischievous, flighty, etc.). As at all other ages, high-rate family dreamers at ages 11–13 had parents with attitudes or traits that seem likely to have fomented intergenerational conflict (here, mothers were loving yet strict and punitive, while fathers were distant, punitive, and unsupportive).

The relative incidence of dreams containing known like-sex peers was at its zenith at ages 11–13, 24% for boys and 26% for girls. There was a strong and significant sex bias toward dreaming of known peers and other nonfamilial persons of one's own sex. Known persons included in dreams were highly likely to be peers, while that was not so for strangers, suggesting that strangers derive from a different set of concerns than those of contemporary peer life.

Because of the sex differences, correlates of dreaming of nonfamilial known males or females often merely mirrored boy–girl differences more generally. For known male characters, measures of children's peer orientation (e.g., time spent with peers) predicted peer dreaming, while children's adult orientation predicted adult dreaming. There was a tendency for boys to dream more often of male strangers and for girls to dream more often of female strangers, but these sex differences in character selection were not significant. Cognitive correlates of stranger dreaming were negligible, and parental correlates suggested (more strongly for the father than for the mother) that frequent dreaming of strangers did *not* imply unhappy home lives that "drove" children defensively to distort family figures or situations. The most consistent correlate of stranger dreaming, across both character and dreamer sex, was the Children's Personality Questionnaire (CPQ) Tender-Mindedness Scale. Judging from this finding, stranger dreamers were characterized by an anxiety-sensitive tendency to daydreaming and a tendency to internalize rather than to act out their conflicts. Overall, then, it seemed that stranger dreaming reflected children's cognitive "styles" rather more consistently than it did either cognitive aptitudes or intergenerational conflicts.

Dreaming of animals remained relatively infrequent, and was again more likely to occur for girls than for boys. Mothers of animal dreamers seemed relatively uninterested in their children's social adjustment, and the children themselves reported spending relatively much time alone and had a low need for social approval. Although the animal dreamers seemed good-natured, they were becoming less assertive. The overall pattern, combined with long self-reported latencies to sleep onset, suggests a proneness to daydreaming or fantasy.

Settings

Residential and recreational environments remained the dominant locales in which dream events "took place" at ages 11–13. Relatively frequent dreamers of the declining class of own-home settings had mothers who seemed to be both the control and social-emotional centers of their families. These mothers were strict but increasingly supportive as compared to the fathers, who were distant and uninterested in control. Thus home-environmental factors (and the mother generally constitutes more of that environment than does the father) may be a determinant of residual own-home dreaming at ages 11–13. On the other hand, as at most other ages, recreational settings seemed at ages 11–13 to reflect children's own hostility or competitiveness. High-rate dreamers of such settings, whose incidence was approximately the same for boys and girls, were hostile and obstructive, and preferred violent mass-media content. Beginning at ages 11–13, however, it no longer was the case that "outgoing" children dreamed relatively often of general "outdoor" settings; in fact, such settings were reported most often by children who were becoming more shy and less talkative in the laboratory.

What is perhaps the most interesting development in correlates of dream settings at ages 11–13, however, concerns the class of "vague or unclassifiable" settings. Freed from problems of insufficient interview probing and/or inadequate laboratory adaptation, it now was, as might more generally have been predicted, cognitively talented children who most often reported dreams with unusual or unclassifiable settings. The children also were conscientious and responsible, suggesting that the relative absence of well-defined settings in their reports was not merely a consequence of shoddy reporting.

Activities

At ages 11–13 sensory activity—generally, seeing—was ascribed to characters (almost as often to others now as to the self) in roughly three of every 10 dreams, and motor activity of various forms was ascribed to characters (almost as often to the self now as to others) in almost every dream. The ratio of dreams with verbal acts to dreams with locomotor acts reached a new developmental high (6:10 for girls, 7:10 for boys), and some motor activity was portrayed in REM dreams more often than at any other age at which we studied children's reports. Operating at this level of high overall representational capacity, children proved not to be highly differentiable in terms of who did and who did not dream highly general classes of dream activities. An index of antisocial aggression was related to the incidence of dreamer motor acts, while CPQ Tender-Mindedness predicted the incidence of motor acts for other dream characters. Paternal authoritarianism continued its positive association with dreamer motor activity, but no longer, as at ages 9–11, in the company of "tender-mindedness."

Dreamer sensory activity continued its association with waking mischievousness, but the sensory activity of other dream characters, which had increased significantly since ages 9–11, no longer was associated, as at ages 7–11, with waking assertiveness. Rather, sensory-other dreamers seemed increasingly differentiable from sensory-self dreamers. Specifically, they were intropunitive and were becoming increasingly dependent and anxious.

Once again, as at ages 9–11, differential cognitive abilities seemed to play some role in determining verbal vs. physical-movement representation in dreams. Children at ages 11–13 who were relatively high and improving relatively much in verbal intelligence most often dreamed of verbal acts, while children improving in visuospatial aptitude most often dreamed of locomotor activity, at a time when such activity was significantly increasing. Given the role Soviet theorists have ascribed to verbal activity in effective self-regulation (as described by Flavell, 1977), it is perhaps not surprising that high-rate verbal dreamers also showed such regulation. They were high

in "ego development" (Loevinger & Wessler, 1970), but low in mischievousness, restlessness, emotionality, and "childishness." Locomotor-other
dreamers, on the other hand, were seen as becoming *more* anxious and
mischievous. Locomotor-either (-self or -other) dreamers showed signs of
emotional dependency on others, but locomotor-self and locomotor-either
dreamers also were showing improvement in emotional stability. By and
large, the circle turned at ages 9–11 seems to have retained its position at
ages 11–13: Dreaming of gross locomotor activity is not, in or past middle
childhood, diagnostic of a healthy waking assertiveness.

States

Over one dream in five at ages 11–13 contained some mentalistic act,
generally one ascribed to the self-character. A pattern of positive cognitive
correlates, lost at ages 9–11, returned at ages 11–13. These correlates
consisted entirely of verbal-skill or general ability measures; performance
variables were not represented among them. Behaviorally, dreamers of
cognitive acts were stable, outgoing, and happy children with high levels of
aspiration.

Only a minority of dreams for children of either sex contained any feeling
content at all. Although happiness claims by girl dreamers, which I have
suggested were artifactually high at ages 9–11, did decline at ages 11–13,
the small but significant decline in feeling content in dreams at ages 11–13
seemed to rest at least as much on dysphoric as on euphoric affect. It was
"sad" feelings, in particular, that were significantly reduced. Overall, dream
happiness was more frequent than dream fear, mostly because that was so
for girls; dream happiness was about twice as frequent as dream anger.

Developmentally, for the first time, at ages 11–13 fear (generally
dreamer fear) in dreams had positive cognitive correlates. By criteria I have
been applying to the appearance of other forms of affect in children's
dreams, one would have to consider these fear reports to be the first
generally credible ones given by children. While intuitively the associated
ages seem rather late, this hypothesis should not be discarded out of hand,
for waking research (Shantz, 1975) suggests that development of symbolic
comprehension of negative emotion, a requisite (one imagines) for experiencing such emotion in dreams, also occurs surprisingly late in childhood. At any rate, it also was at ages 11–13 that reports of dreamer fear first
had an unequivocally interpretable set of correlates. These correlates
suggested socialized apprehension rather than primitive anxiety. Fear
dreamers came from higher social class backgrounds, had generally noncontrolling parents, and were themselves adult oriented, successful in school,
and emotionally controlled. It also is interesting that certain "cognitive"
correlates of dream fear and of intradream cognition were similar (e.g.,
WISC Vocabulary and Loevinger Ego-Level), suggesting that cognitive
development may play a similar role in the elaboration of feeling in dreams,

where one might not have guessed its role, as in the elaboration of mental acts in dreams, where its role is more obvious. However, personality patterns *were* somewhat different in these two cases, with there being a stronger flavor of socialization of emotional control for dream fear than for dream cognition.

As at ages 9–11, the relative incidence of anger dreams (now almost exclusively self-anger dreams) was correlated with Wechsler Information. The associated personality pattern, however, no longer was diffuse excitability but was more aggression-specific: anger-self dreamers were relatively hostile in the presleep period, while anger-either dreamers scored high on a measure of the tendency to project aggression to others. Fathers of high-rate anger dreamers seemed controlling, but not particularly abusive physically; their role may have been more as stimulus to, rather than as model of, aggression.

There were relatively few correlates of dream happiness at ages 11–13. Children with happy-feeling dreams were outgoing, did not seem to have particularly supportive parents, and increasingly sought emotional support in the laboratory. Perhaps because reports of all separate feeling classes now were credible—that is, the developmental timetable for inserting various kinds of feelings into dream scenarios now was fulfilled—there was for the first time at ages 11–13 a convincing pattern of positive cognitive correlates for the overall incidence of dream affect. Feeling dreamers also were mature and socially responsible; interestingly, they did not themselves seem to be particularly emotional. Appropriately elaborating dream narratives with affect probably involves the spillover or projection of one's own waking feelings less than it does the attainment of requisite cognitive skills and social understandings.

Motives and Outcomes

Overall, prosocial initiations outweighed antisocial ones by a ratio of two to one at ages 11–13. For specifically dreamer initiations, the ratio was closer to four to one. In their own personal receipt of dream outcomes, dreamers portrayed favorable outcomes about twice as often as unfavorable ones. But strong sex differences appeared in the social world of children's dreams, making these overall statements of effective dream regulation depend more on data from girls than from boys. For both sexes, however, prosocial initiation by the self was at its childhood zenith, and at no other age did boys dream of so many favorable outcomes.

Despite this flowering of generally placid social interaction, children's dreams continued to portray themes related to the body needs of hunger (in about one dream of five) and of sleep (in about one dream of 10). More frequent dreamers of both hunger-self and fatigue-self themes were judged socially insensitive, which suggests that such dream themes were continuous with a kind of waking egocentrism. Hunger dreamers showed signs of being unable or unwilling to transform self-stimuli (they were low in projection but high in intropunitiveness) and also seemed to be socially inhibited. In addition, self-fatigue dreamers continued to show signs of excitability or distractibility befitting their possible distraction during dreaming by their own body state.

No convincing pattern of child correlates emerged at ages 11–13 for prosocial behavior in dreams; perhaps our classification of prosocial behavior was too crude, or perhaps such behavior had become sufficiently commonplace or banal in children's waking lives to make their recourse to it in their dreams nondiscriminating. Consistent with its conventionality and social acceptability, self-initiation of prosocial behavior was favored by authoritarian parenting. Other-initiation of prosocial behavior (approximately equivalent in girls' and boys' dreams) was negatively associated with interests in competitive physical activities, which may be consistent with the tameness of the dream social acts in question. But these are hardly broad demonstrations of waking/dreaming continuity.

For whatever reason, attack behaviors, both more precisely defined by our scoring system and less frequently scored in children's dreams at ages 11–13, proved to have a more coherent pattern of correlates than did approach behaviors. Relatively frequent dreamers of self-initiated dream attacks were competitive, assertive children with a strong interest in fantasy violence and with some waking skill in weaving their own fantasies of aggression. They had fathers who were powerful, authoritarian, and punitive. For dreamers of attacks initiated by other dream characters (mostly boys), however, a rather different picture emerged. These children also were frequent consumers of media violence, but they were anxious and socially insecure, although seemingly self-satisfied. *Their* fathers, with whom they spent relatively much time, were supportive. Because most dream attacks were initiated by others, the correlates of the overall incidence of antisocial initiations were much like those of the incidence of other-initiated attacks.

Dreams in which characters received antisocial acts or other misfortunes varied substantially, and sometimes significantly, by the sex of the dreamer; boys had more such dreams. Thus some child-behavior correlates of the rate at which such outcomes were reported (e.g., preference for media violence) may simply be boy characteristics, rather than dysphoric-dream characteristics. Whatever the mediation, however, television addiction in general and violence addiction in particular were consistent correlates of dreaming "bad" dream outcomes. As at ages 9–11, it was children of authoritarian-controlling mothers who dreamed most often of their own ill fortune. Sleep disturbance (frequent spontaneous awakenings) predicted ill-fortune outcomes by both the self-character and other dream characters; cognitive skill, however, including skill at fantasy generation, was associated with other-receipts but not with self-receipts. Overall, ill fortune in dreams, by whomever it was received, was associated with waking dependence and anxiety, and with the centrality (but not with the negativity) of the father.

Boys dreamed significantly more of ill fortune than did girls, which explains the paternal influence rather better than it does the dependence and anxiety.

As for prosocial initiations, so too for favorable outcomes: Correlates were generally uninformative. However, as at ages 9–11, such outcomes were generated most often by children with some indication of superior narrative ability, and, overall, favorable-outcome dreamers were conscientious, socialized children with authoritarian mothers.

Global Ratings

As in the case of fear in dreams, so also, for overall REM-dream unpleasantness: There was suggestion of a correlation with socialized apprehension. In an era of general dream blandness, the most unpleasant dreams were reported by higher-social-class children who were compliant in a description task but not socially spontaneous. Sleep disturbance accompanied the pattern. Increases in dream pleasantness since ages 9–11 were associated with childlike spontaneity at school and with increasingly mischievous and resistant laboratory behavior. At ages 9–11 these immature children may well have been most influenced (in the direction of having uncharacteristically unpleasant dreams) by the novelty of the laboratory setting. They reported spending relatively much time alone, which also is consistent with this hypothesis.

In late preadolescence there were, for the first time, signs that children who were relatively capable of managing their own waking lives were assuming, or beginning to assume, that same role in their REM dreams. Increasingly individualistic and assertive children with a tendency toward violence were most active in their REM dreams. Self-reliance and emotional stability characterized children with increasing self-participation since ages 9–11.

Our fluctuating pattern of REM self-participation correlates in earlier childhood may, of course, simply reflect the unreliability of our single-year observations. There may, however, be a more methodologically interesting story behind this pattern. In early childhood cross-year comparisons are made difficult by shifts in the *kind* of self-participation children apparently are able to portray in their dreams, as well as by the fact that some children's claims of self-participation may not be veridical. Thereafter there may be periods in which there are representational hurdles to be passed on children's path toward adult forms of dream participation. In these periods cognitive maturation may be at least as important as social skills in determining self-participation in dreams. Only, perhaps, when all these other considerations are equal, as at ages 11–13, can one expect to find anything approximating "expected" social-life correlates of dream self-participation.

If this analysis is correct, it suggests the futility of cross-sectional research in which correlates of a dream characteristic are sought without knowledge of age- and stage-related fluctuations in the baseline appearance of that characteristic. It also suggests more generally how research on children proceeding in the absence of such knowledge can produce so many "nonreplicated" results with "similar" samples. Finally, it argues strongly for longitudinal study designs in which one knows, for children studied at any one point in time, where they have been, where they are now, and where they are headed.

Setting and character distortion ratings at ages 11–13 remained significantly intercorrelated ($r = .48$), and in neither case did dream distorters seem particularly unstable or socially maladjusted. Character distortion was at its childhood nadir. Against this background of general character familiarity—which suggests less need or challenge to elaborate strangers than at earlier ages—it was children inclined to internalize their feelings, particularly aggression, who were highest in character distortion. These children had positive self-concepts, however. Increases in REM character distortion—opposite to the group trend—from ages 9–11 to 11–13 were associated with internalization, social insensitivity, and frequent exposure to television. Children high in REM setting distortion were peer rather than parent oriented, older than their peers in our study, and zestful, if somewhat socially insensitive. Although not characterized by waking disturbance, they did show signs of sleep disruption. Children with increases in REM setting distortion—the group trend—were, again, older than their peers in our study and somewhat socially insensitive. The indwelling insensitivity of distorters suggests that dream distortion may depend on simple inattention to fine details of external reality (a hypothesis consistent with frequent exposure to television). At any rate, one would be hard pressed to make a stronger case from our data for the alternative hypothesis that dream distortion is a defensive response to interpersonal or intrapsychic conflict.

SEX DIFFERENCES

Significant sex differences were relatively most frequent in our REM-dream data at ages 11–13. This may have been because of the stability here of factors otherwise confounding cross-sex comparisons and/or because of genuine and increasingly wide sex differences in waking socialization. Whatever the reason or reasons, there were, absolutely, still relatively few variables that differentiated boys' and girls' dreams. Evidently the "program" that guides REM dreaming is relatively similar for both sexes, even at ages where their waking behavior is becoming increasingly divergent.

Nine variables significantly differentiated boys' and girls' REM reports at ages 11–13. Four of them (boys had more known male peers and persons, girls had more known female peers and persons) represented the culmination of a trend toward sex bias in the selection of known peers that began with the younger-group children at ages 7–9 (and the summary "persons" category is involved, because, as noted, most known nonfamilial persons in dreams were peers rather than adults). These differences reflect the increasing sex-typing of children's social interests and behavior during the first six to eight years of their formal education.

Also consistent with sex-typing were the following four differences. Boys had more social attacks by other dream characters (the major antisocial initiation category) and, as a consequence, more unfavorable outcomes: (1) both received and mediated by a nonself character; (2) received by any character, but mediated by a nonself character; and (3) overall. Because all of these differences reflected decreases since ages 9–11 for girls, rather than increases for boys, the effect seems to have been one of suppression of dream aggression by girls rather than of its intensification by boys. This pattern is consistent with the declining toleration, during late preadolescence and early adolescence, of tomboyish behavior; until then girls have been allowed rough-and-tumble activity rather more freely than boys have been permitted gentle-and-tender activity. It also is consistent with the increasing use of female characters in the girls' dreams.

The final category significantly discriminating boys' and girls' REM[5] dreams was sensory activity by the dreamer, that is, activity in which the dreamer, in the dream, sees or hears something. More such activity was scored for boys than for girls. Trend data (i.e., from ages 9–11 to 13–15) suggest that here too it is the girls' relatively *low* scores that deserve attention rather than the boys' high ones. As suggested in Chapter 5, sensory activity by the self-character must be one of the best indications of self-involvement in dreams; in this sense girls seem to have been less concretely involved in their dreams than were boys (and, although not significant, the Active Participation rating difference for the two sexes was consistent with this interpretation; the typical boy's scale mean was 2.34; the typical girl's, 2.08). This difference too may reflect sex-typing.

A marginally significant difference ($p < .10$, 2-tail) was that boys dreamed more often of male strangers than did girls. Once again, while girls introduced male and female strangers in approximately equal degree, boys clearly favored males as invented characters. Hall (1963) has reported similar findings with home-collected dreams and has interpreted them as an empirical confirmation of Freud's Oedipus complex. His reasoning is that: (1) strangers symbolize fearful aspects of one's waking environment, and (2) developmentally boys have more reason to fear their fathers than do girls. Therefore boys, whose early resentment of their fathers' competition for mothers' attention is heightened by oedipal rivalry, have more fear of adult males than do girls. But clearly there are equally plausible alternative explanations of the basic finding. Specifically from a developmental perspective, it may be that boys learn their sex-role identification by looking toward males and acting as they do, while girls learn theirs by looking toward males and becoming experienced in interacting with them. In a sense it is the boys'

[5]No variables differentiated boys' and girls' NREM or sleep-onset reports.

stranger imbalance that requires explanation, since the girls' 50:50 male to female ratio approximates social reality. The male child's special preoccupation with males is the problem. As Kohlberg (1966) has observed, the answer may be that "girls have the option of playing a feminine role in a man's world, whereas boys do not have the option of playing a masculine role in a feminine world. In other words the girl can have 'opposite sex' interests, and yet maintain her same-sex values more readily than the boy" (p. 121).

TELEVISION WATCHING AND REM DREAMS: A NATURALISTIC EXPERIMENT

While we shifted laboratory quarters early in the third year of our longitudinal studies, we conducted a study of the effects of television violence on the REM dreams of 40 10- to 12-year-old boys. None of our longitudinal dream-study subjects participated in this other experiment. The boys studied were told that the aim of the study was to determine whether a change in laboratory setting would influence the dreams of our regular (longitudinal) subjects. In line with this cover story, the 40 boys slept one night (for adaptation) in the old laboratory and two in the new one. On each night they were awakened to report REM dreams. Each bedroom in the new laboratory "happened" to contain a television receiver, on which, we told the boys, they could watch "whatever programs happened to be on" the university's closed-circuit channel during a presleep hour of waking EEG monitoring. In fact, we had programming under experimental control, and the boys saw, in counterbalanced order, a nonviolent episode and a violent episode of a "western" series on their two nights in the new laboratory.[6]

This extralongitudinal experiment left us with both unresolved questions and some physical artifacts that might be used in answering them. The major question in our minds was what the dream "effects" might be if children were allowed, *but not forced*, to watch television shows that were preselected either as violent or nonviolent. "Effects," of course, must be put in quotes, for in permitting children the choice as to whether they watch television or not, one loses the kind of control that permits causal attribution. It cannot be clear whether a certain television show, or the predisposition that leads children to watch it, causes the results observed in a self-selective exposure design. Nevertheless, we felt that the findings of a study with such a design might prove useful in evaluating the findings of enforced-viewing studies. In its favor was its more naturalistic experimental

---

[6]Results of this study are described in detail elsewhere (Foulkes, Belvedere, & Brubaker, 1971). As indicated in Chapter 2, however, they did not form a coherent pattern with results of earlier studies we had conducted on the dream effects of "one-shot" forced exposures to violent vs. nonviolent filmed stimuli. None of our three studies, however, found dream anxiety or hostility to be *increased* by a single exposure to a violent film stimulus.

situation—children generally are not forced to watch particular programs. In addition, enforced-viewing studies themselves had produced such inconclusive findings that it scarcely seemed worthwhile simply to repeat the paradigm one more time.

Our extralongitudinal experiment left us, courtesy of the Surgeon General's Scientific Advisory Committee on Television and Social Behavior, with the equipment necessary to implement a self-exposure television study. When our regular longitudinal subjects began sleeping in our new laboratory, they found that it contained television cameras, receivers, and monitors. They were informed that this equipment had been installed for a previous 40-boy study and would be used neither for their viewing nor for viewing them. In fact, as the children could verify, there were no programs on the university's closed-circuit system in the evening. While the children occasionally expressed the wish that there would be, by the end of the third study year the equipment pretty much had been accepted as a nonfunctional background feature of this particular laboratory environment.

Early in the fourth study year, however, we reactivated the television receivers for use in a self-selection television study with our older longitudinal subjects. That we let the children decide whether they would view the programming we provided was entirely consistent with our otherwise nonmanipulative, nondeceptive methods. It was, in fact, unclear to us what sort of plausible "cover story" we could have provided for telling the children that they *must* watch television.

In our "News Notes," a flyer irregularly circulated to families with children participating in our longitudinal project, we announced plans for our older children's fourth study year as follows:

> We'd like some better idea of how dreams draw on experiences before sleep. So on two nights this summer we'd like the children to arrive early—say 7:30 p.m.—and spend a longer presleep period here than they usually do. The children needn't go to bed any earlier than usual; we only plan to see more of them before they do.

Later on, in the "News Notes," there was a seemingly unrelated announcement: that, on a provisional basis,[7] we'd arranged to provide evening programming on our television receivers.

But the two announcements were, in fact, intimately related. During their first two nights of the fourth study year, older children arrived at 7:30, had their electrodes attached, and then were permitted a free period between 8:00 and 10:00 p.m. Among activities available for their amusement during these hours was a two-hour feed, via the university station, from Denver

---

[7]In fact, at the end of the study described here, the receivers were removed from subjects' bedrooms with the (truthful) explanation that we no longer had sufficient funds to permit us to tap into extracampus programming.

television. On one night that feed was of the most violent program(s) available on Denver channel(s); on the other, of the least violent program(s) available. Order of presentation was counterbalanced across subjects. If asked about what programs were to be shown on any given night, I said I didn't know: it was at the local station's discretion.

Seventeen of our 18 Year-4 older-group children participated in this study: Seven girls and 10 boys. It was indicated to the children that they need not watch television in the two-hour free period, and they were apprised of a wide range of alternative materials available to them: gerbils, board games, games of manual skill, playing cards, a design-etching apparatus, books and magazines, and so forth. Some of these materials had been present on earlier sessions, but some were acquired specifically for this project.

I was experimenter on these evenings, and beyond turning on one receiver and playing it at low volume (and, when subjects were not themselves watching television, occasionally glancing at it to indicate to the children that it still was operational), I did nothing else to deliberately encourage or discourage television viewing. Generally I acted as if I had other things to do, which I did: Surreptitiously I was keeping a record, in five-minute time blocks, of the quantity, quality, and social conditions of children's television viewing or of their other free-period behaviors.

Experimental nights were arranged in either Monday–Wednesday, or Tuesday–Thursday sequences. All subjects had been scheduled to run in pairs or trios, but, because of cancellations or missed appointments, four of the boys ended up being studied solo. Partners, when present, always were of the same sex. Some problems arose in preselecting, from *TV Guide*, suitably violent or suitably interesting nonviolent programming, and on two occasions unannounced substitutions appeared for scheduled programs. In general, however, the two television regimes were appropriately different from one another. For example, in the first week of the study the television "diet" available on violent nights was *Wild Wild West* and either *Gunsmoke* or *Mod Squad*, while on nonviolent nights it was either the comedy movie *If a Man Answers* or the programs *Love on a Rooftop, Trini Lopez Special*, and *Kraft Music Hall*.

At the conclusion of each night's free period, children were put to bed. They were told that, although I would be in constant attendance throughout the night, another man would be conducting their dream interviews. This nocturnal interviewer always was unaware of the presleep television-viewing condition. Four REM awakenings were scheduled each night for the collection of dream reports and were made 10 minutes after the onset of the child's second through fifth REM episodes of the night. Reports were reliably judged by a person with no knowledge of the children or the conditions of the study. Reliability was computed by comparing his judgments with those of a second judge for a subset of reports, and it was found to be comparable to that observed in normative-year dream scorings.

On the morning immediately following each experimental night, subjects were scheduled for a waking test session, ostensibly merely to "save them a trip" by combining regular waking test sessions with laboratory nights. During these sessions the nocturnal dream interviewer, still unaware of the presleep television-viewing condition, administered, in counterbalanced order, alternate halves of the Rosenzweig Picture-Frustration Study (Revised 1948 Adult Form). In this test cartoons are presented of various frustrating situations (e.g., being splashed by a passing auto), and respondents are to complete the verbal or mental reactions of the victim by filling in the "balloon" over that character's head. The test was reliably scored for extropunitiveness (blame others), intropunitiveness (blame self), and impunitiveness (deny blame or frustration).

A wide range of actual television viewing was observed for both the violent and the nonviolent program diets—0–116 minutes viewing for the violent diet and 1–119 minutes viewing for the nonviolent diet. But every child watched at least 10 minutes of one diet, and all subjects but one watched at least some of the program content from each diet. Boys, however, were the more indiscriminate viewers, and they watched significantly more (minutes of exposure) of the violent (but not the nonviolent) material than did the girls. But in intrasubject comparisons, neither girls nor boys attended more often to one program diet than to the other, and neither girls nor boys attended with greater qualitative intensity (a rating scale: absorbed, average, casual) to one television diet than to the other. Across subjects, however, the boys again were the more indiscriminate viewers, watching both violent and nonviolent programming with greater qualitative intensity than did the girls. This was related to the fact that, when equated for opportunity of joint viewing, the boys watched nonviolent programs alone more often than did the girls, for whom viewing was a more social act. Perhaps the most important difference observed in the presleep free period, however, was the difference between nights of high and low television viewing, whatever the program content. On nights of low viewing, children were verbal, mobile, and expressive. Nights of high viewing were nights of quiet, passivity, and emotional restraint.

Fifteen children (seven girls, eight boys) reported at least one dream after viewing each television diet.[8] Of many scoring-system variables tested, only two significantly discriminated the television diets: There was greater rated REM Character Distortion following the nonviolent programming and a higher relative incidence of dreamer verbal activity after the violent programming. On the basis of ages 11–13 normative data, the former difference seemed to be an enhancement of distortion after nonviolent programming rather than a reduction of distortion after violent programming.[9] The result

---

[8]Recall rates (pooled: for violence nights, 73%; for nonviolence nights, 68%) were comparable to report rates during the third study year, suggesting once again (see Chapter 2) that recall rates I elicited in normative study years generalized well to those obtained by other interviewers.
[9]Clearly there are advantages in performing manipulative studies on subjects for whom extensive prior baseline data are available.

seemed to rest upon a higher incidence of peer strangers after the nonviolent diet, and for girls to be related to actually having watched that diet. But it was not a simple function of differential television viewing per se, because it also was observed for boys who watched substantial portions of both diets. On the basis of adjacent normative data, the verbal-activity difference also seemed to be more a nonviolent effect (a reduction in verbalization) than a violent effect (an enhancement of verbalization). But this result seemed to depend in no orderly way on how long diets were actually attended to. More generally, in view of the number of variables tested, one has little confidence that there were, in fact, any diet "effects" at all.

Consistent with the results of earlier studies (Foulkes & Rechtschaffen, 1964; Foulkes, Pivik, Steadman, Spear, & Symonds, 1967; Foulkes, Belvedere, & Brubaker, 1971), there was no evidence that the violent television programs increased dysphoric affect or antisocial activity in REM dreams. Our results suggest that in one-night doses, the availability of only violent television programs, and whatever viewing they subsequently attract, is not reliably associated with more dream aggression, dysphoria, and passivity than is the availability only of nonviolent television programs, and whatever viewing they subsequently attract. But in view of observed differences in how long and how intensely children actually chose to watch the two television diets, it hardly is surprising that diet per se had so few effects.

Because of these differences in actual viewing behavior, we chose to make three additional tests. In the first two, we were able to show that: (1) when analysis was limited to six children who watched both diets for long and equivalently long periods of time, there still was no pattern of association between presleep exposure to violent content and dream dysphoria or aggression; and (2) nights of higher viewing, regardless of what was watched, were not associated with dreams with more violent or dysphoric content. Finally, awash in this sea of insignificant or unreliable results obtained when we focused on violence as an independent and/or dependent variable, there was one finding that was predicted, that makes sense theoretically, and that was strong statistically. Nights of high viewing, regardless of the programs viewed, were associated with dreams in which children themselves took a more passive role (typical subject's Active Participation rating was 2.00) more than were nights of low viewing, regardless of what was viewed (typical subject's Active Participation rating was 2.67; the difference was significant at $p < .002$, 2-tail). Just as the most obvious difference observed in the presleep period was the quieter, more passive behavior associated with television viewing, so too the strongest difference observed was the children's greater passivity in REM dreams collected after higher rates of television viewing.

Using adjacent normative data, it seemed that the dream difference depended both on enhanced self-participation following lesser television viewing and on diminished participation following greater television viewing. Our results suggest (but obviously do not by themselves prove) that there is continuity between television behavior and dream behavior, but the continuity is more at the level of how much television is watched and of the behaviors viewing itself entails than at the level of what is watched. This is precisely the sort of result likely to be missed in controlled experimental studies in which exposure is enforced to be constant, and only program content varies.

The Rosenzweig test scores from mornings following our experimental nights did not discriminate the violent vs. nonviolent program diets. However, significantly ($p < .01$, 2-tail) fewer self-blaming cartoon captions were observed following nights of children's higher viewing rate. That is, higher viewing rate the night before was associated with less internalization or assumption of responsibility the morning after. This effect was significant for boys alone, and for subjects with long and equivalently long viewing in both conditions. But it did not hold for girls alone, because three girls who extensively watched only the violent diet were the only children to show results in the opposite direction. For girls, but not for boys, the guilt-assuaging vs. guilt-reinforcing effects of media exposure may depend on the particular contents to which they have been exposed.

Our data afforded a relatively rare (but, as it turned out, unproductive) opportunity to investigate the "function" of dreams. We had observations of children's presleep behavior, of their postsleep behavior (the Rosenzweig scores), and of the dreams that occurred in between. We could ask whether, for instance, following exposure to the violent stimulus, the way in which dreams "dealt with" that stimulus predicted subjects' morning aggressivity or guilt. In particular, we were interested in two kinds of dream "elaboration" of the presleep violent stimulus: an "excitatory" elaboration (social-attack dreams) and an "inhibitory" elaboration (afraid dreams). We restricted our analysis to children who watched enough violent content to make the contrast meaningful. We found two nonoverlapping subgroups: four children with social-attack dreams and three children with afraid dreams after watching violent programs. But we were able to find no consistent relationship between the "dream elaboration" of media violence and a subject's tendency the next morning to be more or less extropunitive/intropunitive than after exposure to media nonviolence.

Overall, then, our results suggest little effect on conceptually related dream or waking variables of *ad libitum* exposure to violent vs. nonviolent television diets. However, degree of actual television watching, whatever the program content, was correlated negatively both with level of self-participation in subsequent REM dreams and with level of self-acceptance of responsibility in subsequent waking test performance. When, for whatever reason, our children decided to watch television relatively heavily, conceptually reasonable effects or correlates of the behavior engendered by this decision could be observed hours later in both their dreams and subsequent waking dispositions. Clearly, our study permits assessment of neither the causality nor the generality of these results. However, our results do raise interesting questions about the long-term effects of children's exposure to television as a medium and do suggest the usefulness of methodological variants of one-shot, manipulative experiments in addressing those questions.

DREAMING OUTSIDE REM SLEEP

Non-REM reports at ages 11–13 were, once again, contributed most often by children who had high rates of REM recall and who were cognitively relatively competent. Because of the relative stabilization of dream-report characteristics at ages 11–13, it may be appropriate here to examine non-REM content correlates in a more detailed and systematic way than we have before. Although, because of the smaller samples available for NREM and sleep-onset reports, we did not compute correlates for individual non-REM content-analysis categories, we did compute them for dream word-count and for four dream-rating variables. In the case of word count, NREM and sleep-onset reports both were significantly different—shorter— than REM reports, but neither report class differed systematically from REM reports in hedonic quality, relative degree of dreamer self-participation, setting distortion, or character distortion.

Longer NREM reports came from placid, self-assured children who were spending much and increasingly much time with peers rather than parents. Children with longer NREM reports also showed some signs of disturbed sleep, which is consistent with Zimmerman's (1970) observation that the frequency of NREM dreaming in adults is related to the experiencing of "lighter" NREM sleep. Longer sleep-onset reports came from relatively open and expressive children who spent relatively much time with peers rather than parents. Thus neither for ordinary NREM sleep nor for sleep onset does it seem to be the case that one dreams in proportion to one's need to work through conflicts or to deal with anxieties. Rather, psychological *health* seems to be positively correlated with non-REM dream extensity.

As in the case of REM dreams, so too for NREM dreams was there the suggestion that dream unpleasantness was correlated with waking apprehension. But the unpleasantness of sleep-onset dreaming was greater for emotionally stable children who were gifted at fantasy elaboration. The difference between REM/NREM on the one hand, and sleep onset on the other, is consistent with adult data (Foulkes, Spear, & Symonds, 1966), and with the involuntary vs. semivoluntary nature of thinking in sleep vs. sleep onset. In sleep apprehensive people involuntarily think of their apprehension, while in wakefulness and, therefore, at sleep onset, it can be emotional stability and imaginative facility that permit one to entertain relatively unpleasant thoughts, and emotional instability and imaginative poverty that forbid one to entertain them.

There was, however, agreement in ordinary NREM and sleep-onset correlates of dream self-participation ratings. Imaginative poverty coupled with a peer orientation (turning to peers rather than adults for advice, support, or companionship) predicted self-participation in both conditions. But in neither case was there a strong indication of a continuity with waking initiative taking (although later, at ages 13–15, it did seem that more outgoing and socially active children participated more strongly in both their NREM and sleep-onset dreams).

Dream distortion was the global dream dimension relatively most likely to show continuity across sleep stages at ages 11–13. REM Setting Distortion rating correlated .47 with NREM Setting Distortion and (significantly) .63 with sleep-onset Setting Distortion. REM Character Distortion correlated .35 with NREM, and .53 with sleep-onset, Character Distortion. For neither non-REM condition, however, was there much evidence that dream distortion was associated with waking conflict or anxiety. Sleep-onset setting distortion, similar to that in REM reports, was associated with social insensitivity, and NREM character distortion, similar to that in REM reports, was associated with internalization of feeling, particularly aggression. But NREM character distortion also was associated *negatively* with teacher ratings of anxiety, and sleep-onset character distortion was associated with emotional stability, conscientiousness and responsibility, self-esteem, and teacher ratings of seriousness of purpose and imaginativeness. Even more clearly than for REM mentation, in non-REM states dream distortion at ages 11–13 does not seem to be defensively motivated.

Table 7.2 reports differences observed at ages 11–13 between the content of reports collected in non-REM vs. in REM sleep. (No variable significantly differentiated NREM from sleep-onset reports.)

The cautions discussed in the last chapter also apply to the interpretation of sleep-stage dream differences at ages 11–13. Nevertheless, again we may draw some reasonable conclusions from the data at hand.

1 Non-REM reports do not seem to be *qualitatively* different from REM reports. No global rating dimension (including Visualization) discriminated REM reports from non-REM ones. Many individual content-analysis categories did so discriminate, but that fact may reflect the *quantitative* difference between children's REM and non-REM mentation. Their REM reports are longer and hence have a relatively greater opportunity to contain various contents. But, on balance, it does not seem that non-REM reports are so much unique forms of mentation as scaled-down versions of REM mentation.

2 In line with this conclusion, there continued to be no selectivity of REM vs. non-REM characters on the basis of their familiarity or unfamiliarity. Both unknown *and* known characters occurred more often in REM than in non-REM reports.

3 In qualification of the first conclusion, however, it does seem as if ordinary NREM reports are *beginning* to become discriminable from REM reports

Table 7.2 **Differences in Dream Reports as a Function of Stage of Sleep**

REM vs. NREM	REM vs. Sleep Onset
Higher incidence/score in REM	Higher incidence/score in REM
Word count	Word count
Characters	Characters
Father	Father
Known peer, female	Family, any female
Known, any female	Known, any male
Stranger, adult female	Stranger, adult female
Stranger, any female	Stranger, any indeterminate
Stranger, any indeterminate	Settings
Animals, any	Home, specifiable other
Settings	Home, unfamiliar
Conveyance	Commercial
Activities	Activities
Vision, other	Vision, other
Any sensory, other	Any sensory, other
Manual, either	Verbal, other
Locomotor, either	Locomotor, either
Any motor, dreamer	States
Any motor, other	Cognitive, other
Any motor, either	Thirst, dreamer
States	Thirst, other
Cognitive, either	Thirst, either
Angry, dreamer	Fatigue, other
Angry, either	Approach object, either
Any feelings, other	Attack social, other
Hunger, dreamer	Outcomes
Hunger, other	Unfavorable, unmediated,
Hunger, either	dreamer
Avoidance social, other	Unfavorable, unmediated, other
Avoidance social, either	Unfavorable, unmediated, either
Outcomes	Unfavorable, any, either
Favorable, other mediated, either	Favorable, other mediated, either
Favorable, any, either	Favorable, any, other
	Favorable, any, either
Higher incidence in NREM	
Settings	
Unclassifiable	

in ways that have been described in the adult literature and in ways in which sleep-onset reports are *not* so discriminable. Specifically: (*a*) the overall level of motor activity is significantly less in NREM than in REM reports; (*b*) dysphoric affect (anger) is less often observed in NREM than in REM reports; (*c*) a setting implying motion (conveyance) was scored significantly more often in REM than in NREM reports,[10] and another

---

[10]This replicates a finding made with the younger group at ages 7–9.

such setting (recreational) just narrowly missed ($p < .10$, 2-tail) being similarly differentiating; and (*d*) for the first time the scoring category referring to the lack of clarity of dream settings was scored relatively more often for NREM than for REM reports. These findings would have been predicted by adult studies (e.g., Foulkes, 1962) of REM–NREM report discriminability. In support of the first conclusion, however, we must reiterate that other expected lines of REM–NREM report differentiation were not found in the 11- to 13-year-olds' data (e.g., visualization of the dream, self-visualization in the dream, dream distortion).[11]

4 In general, the activities discriminating sleep-onset from REM reports were "subtle" ones (vision, sensation, verbalization) ascribed to other dream characters. Coupled with the fact that overall activity level did not discriminate sleep-onset from REM reports, it seems as if at ages 11–13 it may be claimed that reports of sleep-onset, more so than of NREM sleep, are merely insufficiently elaborated, rather than qualitatively different, compared to REM reports.

5 There continued to be signs of a selective attenuation of affective material at sleep onset, although they were weaker and somewhat different from those at ages 9–11. Specifically, at ages 11–13 there were more unfavorable outcomes in REM than in sleep-onset, but not than in NREM reports.

6 Body-state imagery (hunger, thirst, fatigue) was more frequently observed in REM than in non-REM reports, but it remains unclear whether the difference directly reflects the bodily activation of REM sleep or merely the fact that, in a more nonspecific way, REM reports were longer.

7 Away-from-home settings were more frequently observed in REM than in sleep-onset reports. Specifically, in REM there were relatively more reports with other persons' houses, unfamiliar houses, or downtown-commercial areas as settings than there were at sleep onset (but not than in NREM). Sleep-onset dreaming was less sensitive to the dreamer's current social situation (i.e., being away from home).

One begins, then, to see some possible first signs of NREM vs. REM branching at ages 11–13, with NREM reports inclining somewhat more toward the form they characteristically will assume at the adult level. In this regard one anticipates further evidence of that movement at ages 13–15, and, as we shall see in Chapter 8, there is such evidence.

However, at this point it may be appropriate to look backward and to ask why, at least up until the beginning of adolescence, children's REM and NREM reports are not more discriminable, on the model of adults' REM and

[11]That children's REM dreams were exceptionally well controlled at ages 11–13 may, of course, be partly responsible for residual indiscriminability of their REM and NREM reports; by adult standards of bizarreness, for instance, the children's REM reports may not be sufficiently "REM-like."

NREM reports.[12] In light of much data already discussed, it does not seem that it can be because children have simply "made up" their NREM dreams after having been awakened. It might, however, be possible that at first children can access only the most REM-like of their NREM mentation, while later they are able to access the more subtle forms of NREM mentation that permit marked REM−NREM discrimination for adults.

There are two objections to this argument, one empirical and one theoretical. Empirically, NREM recall rates did not improve significantly from ages 9−11 to 11−13, yet the conformance of NREM−REM discriminability to the adult model seemingly did so improve. The same reasoning applies with even greater force, as we shall see, to the contrast of ages 11−13 and 13−15. Theoretically, it must be asked how younger children, whose waking thought does not seem particularly subtle, could come to *generate* subtle but unmemorable NREM mentation on the adult model.

It seems to me more likely, therefore, that imaginal narratizing is, in fact, the most developmentally primitive form in which NREM mentation occurs. The REM data suggest that that form or program seems to become a general possibility with children's approach to concrete-operational reasoning, and it is with that approach that children first give evidence of producing reliable and moderately frequent reports of NREM mentation. It also seems to me likely that the very subtlety that permits NREM reports to be discriminable from REM ones at the adult level must rest on cognitive skills that appear late in their waking manifestation and in their application to mentation occurring during sleep. Narratizing during sleep seems to require relatively less skill; our brains all seem to be "wired" for it, and the maturation of this potentiality seems to be at such an early developmental level that, all over the world, persons of almost all ages think in narrative form during sleep. The supreme developmental achievement in sleep thinking seems to be *not narratizing*, or detaching one's thought from the peremptory narrative schemata that otherwise rule our fanciful sleeping (or waking) minds. Later in this chapter, and in the next, we will get a first view of what this final developmental achievement might be.[13]

STIMULUS INCORPORATIONS

By net-incorporation figures, ages 11−13 were associated with our second-best (after ages 9−11) rate of success in influencing dreams, but that rate was exceedingly modest. Experimental procedures were identical to those in

---

[12]In a preliminary note, Kales, Kales, Jacobson, Po, and Green (1968) also suggested the greater difficulty of discriminating children's than adults' NREM and REM reports.

[13]To call this achievement final may, of course, be premature. What is one to make of the claims of some Eastern mystics that they can think with waking clarity, or with an absence of discrete contents of mind, 24 hours a day?

other study years, and methods of judgment were identical to those for ages 5–7. (As described in Chapter 4, the ages 5–7 and 11–13 incorporation-night reports were judged together.)

There were 58 REM awakenings after stimulation, 42 of which (72%) produced dream reports, and 57 NREM awakenings after stimulation, 14 of which (25%) produced dream reports. Once again, stimulation did not consequentially alter recall rates in comparison to no stimulation. Nineteen of the 20 children had at least one poststimulation report.

The first judge, who was more conservative in guessing incorporations, produced net-incorporation estimates reasonably comparable to those obtained by the two judges employed for ages 9–11: 0% for cotton judgments, 7% for limb judgments, and 12% for water judgments, with an overall net-incorporation rate of 8%. The second judge, however, generated an overall incorporation rate of only 4% (–5% cotton, 20% limb, –9% water). Her willingness to go out on one produced better limb judgments, but a reduced rate of success overall. Both judges were correct slightly more often than chance (33%) in their overall assignment of reports to stimuli: Judge 1 was correct in five of 11 "certain" assignments (45%) and in six of 13 "uncertain" assignments (46%); Judge 2 was correct in six of 13 "certain" assignments (46%) and in only seven of 22 "uncertain" assignments (32%). Overall, Judge 1 was correct 46% of the time, and Judge 2, 37%. Forced-choice assignments to stimulation condition of report pairs matched by subject and stage of sleep, however, were below chance (50%) for both judges: 44% and 41%, respectively. In evaluating report pairs matched by subject and stimulus but discrepant for stage of sleep in terms of "clarity" of relationship to the stimulus, there was no consistent tendency to see REM reports as more stimulus influenced than NREM reports. Judge 1 said in seven of 12 pairs, and Judge 2 in six of 12 pairs, that the stimulus influence was more direct for REM reports.

Table 7.3 presents abstracts of those reports on which both judges were either certain or correct or both as to the associated stimulus. On the spot, I "missed" three of the seven jointly correct judge identifications, apparently because of my more precise knowledge of the limb-stimulation employed: Luke's arm, not his leg, was stimulated, and the same was true for Melinda; Donald was leg-stimulated, but dreamed of a manual activity. It is possible, of course, that the judges were correctly identifying a transformed stimulus effect. I also "saw" three instances of incorporation where the judges did not, also apparently because of my more precise knowledge of the limb-stimulation employed. The most convincing of these three cases was when I vigorously rocked Clint's knees, which were bent in an upright position as he lay under his blankets, sleeping on his back. On this NREM awakening, he reported saddling his horse, but it bucked, and the saddle fell on Clint, hurting his back and giving him a "weird" feeling in his belly. I thought that my rocking movement nicely fit a "bucking-bronco" theme. After the accident, Clint said he went to visit a local doctor (he, unlike most of the other children, called me "Doc"), but the doctor didn't have enough

Table 7.3 **Judges' Consensually Correct and Consensually Certain Incorporation Judgments: Ages 11–13**

	Judges Both "Certain"	One/Both Judge(s) Not "Certain"
Judges Are Consensually Right	*Luke:* Night 9, Awakening 2. Walking down the street, being followed by a "guy." He starts walking faster, and the guy does too (a limb-REM stimulation). **A** [a] *Dick:* Night 2, Awakening 3. In the school auditorium, at an assembly. Painting the bleachers. "And then a drop fell on the floor and they said, 'You better clean that up' " (a water-REM stimulation). **N**	*Jules:* Night 9, Awakening 2. Running around, looking for his school locker (a limb-REM stimulation). **N** *Melinda:* Night 2, Awakening 2. Bicycle riding (a limb-NREM stimulation). **M** *Clint:* Night 2, Awakening 3. In the kitchen, doing dishes (a water-REM stimulation). **N** *Dick:* Night 9, Awakening 2. A sequence of events at school. Then "we started running home" (a limb-REM stimulation). **M** *Donald:* Night 9, Awakening 2. Strangling a classmate, trying to get his lunch ticket back (a limb-REM stimulation). **M**
Judges Are Consensually Wrong	*Patty:* Night 2, Awakening 3. Writing her name on a paper (a water-REM stimulation, judged "limb"). **N** *Charmane:* Night 9, Awakening 1. Dancing the "funky chicken" (a cotton-NREM stimulation; judged "limb"). **M** *Emily:* Night 9, Awakening 1. Painting a brick wall (a cotton-NREM stimulation; judged "limb"). **N**	

Reports judged = 56
"Certain" and right = 4%

---

[a] **A** = awakened by stimulation; (**M** = moves during stimulation but does not awaken; **N** = no visible response to stimulation).

blankets. I also prejudged two other equivocal reports about which the judges understandably were undecided. For instance, I saw a face-washing REM report as cotton-puff related, while the judges noted the water element to which I, who had just cotton-stimulated the child's face, was less attentive.

Overall, then, as in most other years, the findings at ages 11–13 offer rare glimpses of what might be genuine instances of dreams being influenced by body stimulation during sleep. But one also sees that, with appropriate controls, the best estimate as to how often dreams were so influenced would have to be "very rarely." Evidently the children's minds during either REM or NREM sleep were relatively impervious to excitation or redirection by extrinsic stimuli. And at least in some of the consensually correct reports (e.g., Dick's), there is continuing indication that if stimuli *do* influence dreams, their role is subsidiary to the course of an already ongoing narrative.

EMILY'S DREAMS

At the start of her third year in our study, Emily was aged 12 years, 5 months. During this year she was a student in seventh grade, her first year of junior high school. She reported dreams on 12 of 14 REM awakenings (86% recall), on six of nine NREM awakenings (67% recall), and on all three sleep-onset awakenings (100% recall).

Her *REM reports* were these:

1-2   Someone was telling me a joke and they asked me to measure a foot so I put down the length of my foot, and they said it was wrong because a foot had to be 12 inches long. [Was it visual?] Yes. [What could you see?] I could see me and a room and a table and some chairs and another person. [Who was that person?] I don't know. . . . I think it was a girl . . . about my age. [What were you doing in the dream?] I was writing down what I thought was the answer to the thing. [And what was the other person doing?] Well, she was standing up and telling me what I was supposed to do. [Was the room familiar to you?] No. [Did you have any feelings in the dream?] No. [Did the "joke" strike you as humorous?] No.

2-1   There were these four people sitting around a table, and one of the people had some homemade butter and was putting it on something different. One person put it on bread, another person put it on oysters or something like that. They were all telling the other person how good the butter was. [Who were these four people?] I don't know . . . girls, I think . . . about my age. [Where were they?] Well, we were in this great big room and there wasn't anything else in the room but a table full of chairs and they were sitting at it. [Was it any place that you know?] No. [Were you in this?] No. [Did you have any feelings?] No.

2-3   My sister was playing with those little tiny dolls and she had a big dollhouse and it had all this little furniture in it and I had two, my hamster and a little tiny dog, and it was alive and I went and put it to bed in that house but I couldn't put it to bed because they were playing with it. [What was happening just before I woke you up?] They were starting to play in the house, they were. [Who were "they"?] (My sisters.) [Do you have a dollhouse like this or was this made-up?] M——— (one sister) has one like that. [Was this hers?] Yeah, I think so. [What about the hamster and the dog, do you have those?] Yeah, we have a dog, only it wasn't that little. [This was a very little dog?] . . . real tiny . . . I was holding the dog and the hamster. . . . I was moving around. My sisters were moving around the house, using their hands to move their dolls. [Was there anyone else in the dream?] My dog, the hamster, and the little dog. [Your real dog was in the dream, pretty much like he really is?] Yes. [Where did the dream seem to take place?] It was in the living room or something. It wasn't ours. [Did you have any feelings?] No.

3-2   I was dreaming there was this line of bookshelves and there was a boy and he was putting the books in them. He was doing them just any old way, he wasn't doing them right. . . . He was sitting on his knees and he was handling the books. . . . It was inside of a room. I don't know where the room was . . . like a private house. [The boy, was he somebody that you know?] He was made-up. . . . [Were you in the dream?] No. [Did you have any feelings in the dream?] No.

4-1   I was having a dream with a girl I have a class with, I have her in band. She was all dressed up and she had a lunch ticket in her hand, and she was standing on the sidewalk. It was sunny outside. She was telling me how much she hated the guy who used to go to her school. . . . I could see her, and the sidewalk, and a little bit of background. [Were you in this?] Yes . . . I was talking to her. [What did you say in the conversation?] I said, "What is that guy's last name?" [And did she tell you?] Yes. [Some name you really know?] No. [Could you recognize where the dream took place?] No. . . . There were trees in the background, but I didn't know where it was. [Did you have any feelings?] No.

4-3   We were in this car with a friend of mine and we, they were taking us home, and her mother was French, and she had a French accent, and she was talking to us, and something was in the street that was mine, and we stopped and this other girl got out to get it, and this other guy just drove off, and left her there, and she was standing out in the middle of the street. And we were just looking at each other in the car. [Did you know any of these people?] Yes . . . one of them was my friend that lives next door and one of them was a friend that goes to school with me. [The mother that had the French accent, is that somebody you know?] No. [The friend . . .] There was two of them, the one that got out to get the thing was just the girl who went to school with me. [And someone stayed in the car with you?] Yes. [Is that the one who had the mother who spoke French?] No, well, yeah, and then another girl stayed in there too. [The guy (who) drove away and left the girl there, who was that?] Her father was in the car too, and when she got out to get the thing, he just drove off. [What did you do in the dream?] I was just sitting in the car. . . . I told them that that was my thing that was out there in the street. [What was that thing?] . . . a choker. [Is this like the thing that I made a comment about last night that has the peace symbol on it?] Yes . . . [The same one?] . . . I couldn't tell. [Where did all this take place?] In a town, it looked kind of like Laramie, but there were different streets in it . . . a residential place. [I'm not quite sure (whether) the mother and father are people you really know.] They were made-up people. [Did you have any feelings?] . . . at the end of the dream I was, well, you know, kind of excited because . . . he left her standing out there in the street all alone. . . . We were all looking at each other and wondering. [Was it like you felt worried about the girl or angry toward the father, or didn't you feel those things?] Well, kind of angry toward the father.

5-1 There were a bunch of ladies and they were in a band, and they all wore long dresses instead of uniforms, and they marched to the street, and they were playing songs and stuff. [Could you tell who they were?] No. [Was there any audience?] No, there wasn't any audience. [Were you in this dream?] No, I don't think so. [Could you hear the music?] Yes . . . it was kind of fast music, and it was like a regular band would play. . . . [What kind of music was this instrumentally?] I remember the trombone. [You could see somebody playing the trombone?] Yes. [and moving this thing back and forth?] Yes. [Did you have any feelings?] I was kind of excited. [Can you tell me a little more about that, why you felt that way, what made you feel that way?] I was excited about the band going by with just the women in it, playing fast music.

6-2 I was sitting in a bed and somebody asked me to read something to them, it was on the page of a book, and I didn't have my glasses on, and I said, ''I can't read it, it's too far away.'' Then I got up out of bed and then you woke me up. [Who was it that asked you this?] Dean (who was a co-subject on this night). [What did he want you to read?] I don't know, I can't remember. [Where did this take place?] It wasn't . . . familiar. [Was this in a bedroom?] Yes. . . . It looked like the bedroom of a private house. [What was he doing in the dream?] He was just sitting in the bed, reading the book . . . just looking at the pictures. [Did you have any feelings that you can remember?] No . . . I wasn't too interested in reading to him.

7-2 I was on a television show, *Bewitched*, and they were having this party there. The mother told me to go have some snacks, or something like that. My little cousin was there, I guess she was doing something, but I didn't know what it was. [A real cousin?] A television cousin . . . she was Elizabeth Montgomery, because she plays her cousin in the show too. [When you say the mother, do you mean the Elizabeth Montgomery character (Samantha) or the older one?] Yeah, the Elizabeth Montgomery one. [You say you were on television. Do you mean that you were just with people who were on television, or did you think you were on a television stage?] I think I was just with people who are on television. [Did it look like the television house that they live in, or did it seem to be someplace different?] No, it was like the same place. [Was there anybody else in this besides you, and the cousin, and Elizabeth Montgomery?] Oh, there were people at the party . . . I don't know (who), they were girls, though. [Did you think that this was Elizabeth Montgomery, or did you think that this was Samantha?] I thought it was Samantha, I think. . . . I was standing and talking, I wasn't saying very much, because Samantha was talking to me most of the time. She said that I was supposed to go have some snacks or something like that. Then when her cousin came, she said, "Serina," and that's when I woke up. ["Serina"?] That is her cousin. [What were the other people doing?] Just standing around talking, you know, like in a theater party. [Did you have any feelings?] No.

7-3   I dreamed that I was talking to my father. He said that if you swallow something and then can't get it back out, then he said something, and I can't remember what it was. I said, yes you can, if you tie a piece of string to it, because there is this experiment in my science book, where a guy put food in his mouth, and waited until it went through his digestive system, and then he'd pull it back out. I had a piece of hair that I swallowed, or something like that, and I swallowed it and then just took it back out. [Was there anybody else in the dream?] My mother came in, in about the middle. [What did she do?] She was talking about some science classes, but I wasn't listening. [So the dream mostly had to do with you and your father?] Yes. [You swallowed this thing before your father started talking to you about it, or did you do it to illustrate a point that you were making to your father?] To illustrate it. [Where did all this take place?] In our kitchen. [Can you remember what your father said to you at the point before when you said you couldn't remember just what he said—do you remember what the . . . nature of what he was saying was?] He said something like, anyone (who) was determined could swallow anything, or something like that. [Have you ever talked with your parents about this particular science lesson?] I don't know, because it was last year that it was in my science book, and I don't remember if I told them or not. [Have you been thinking about it recently, or do you have any idea why you were dreaming about it now?] No. [Did you have any feelings?] No.

8-1   I was skiing at Medicine Bow (local ski area) with my dad, and there was a great big line or something, and my dad didn't want me to ski there, and I told him that he should go to Jackson (a ski area also in Wyoming, but some 400 miles away) or something, and that was the end. [Was that a serious suggestion to him, or were you just kind of joking?] It was serious. [What could you see?] I saw a bunch of trees, and then a great big, long, tall one, then it was a T-bar tow, and a bunch of people were on the tow. [Did this look like the way that Medicine Bow . . . really looks, or was it changed in any way?] I think that it was changed a little . . . the tows were closer together and they were like one right after another. . . . I just remember going up the tow. [Your dad, did he do that too?] Yes. [What were the other people in the dream doing?] They were skiing and going up the tow. [Did you have any feelings?] No.

8-3 I was walking with my friend, my friend was on a bike, and I was just walking, and I was looking at the flowers in these people's yards and then I drove, I mean I walked over to this place of dirt, there was this big pile of dirt, and my friend was going to show me something, but then I woke up. [Was this a real friend?] Real (girl) friend. [Did you recognize where this was taking place?] It was in Washington Park. It was kind of in the street and then we drove over to the park. She was on a bike, and I was . . . just walking beside her. . . . When I saw the flowers, I said, "Oh, look at the flowers." [Was there anybody else in the dream besides you and (your friend)?] Well, before we came over to her house, there was this one guy with this great big duffle bag, and he was sitting on it, and he was looking around the corner. [Was he your age, older, or younger?] I think that he was about a year or so younger. [Did you have any feelings?] No.

In line with the question raised earlier about whether the relative overall passivity of Emily's age 10−11 REM dreams represented an enduring "female" effect or whether it was a more transitory initial-testing or developmental effect, it is significant to note that her age 12−13 REM dreams generally contained more overall activity, and more self-participation, than did her earlier ones. Her age 12−13 REM dreams also generally were more complex from a narrative point of view, and they were less clearly tied to identifiable presleep or situational stimuli. Her "dream generator" apparently had been freed from restraints or inhibitions that seemingly affected it in Year 1, particularly early in that year. Each of her age 12−13 REM dreams has, moreover, at least one well-formulated but incongruous or implausible kernel dream element (given her waking life):

1-2 The double meaning of "foot."
2-1 Different things to put homemade butter on.
2-3 The doll-sized but live dog.
3-2 The boy's imprecision at book sorting.
4-1 The hated boy; his last name.

4-3   The French-speaking woman; the girl left behind; the "choker" in the street.
5-1   The all-female marching band; long dresses rather than uniforms.
6-2   "I can't read it, it's too far away."
7-2   Conversing with a "witch's" family; the double identity of Elizabeth Montgomery.
7-3   The "science" experiment; the multiple meanings of "swallow."
8-1   "Go to Jackson"; tows "one right after the other."
8-3   The pile of dirt; the guy's "great big duffle bag."

That is, each REM dream contains symbolic elaborations of Emily's ordinary reality that invite deeper interpretation. None of her age 12−13 REM dreams has, in this respect, the "superficiality" of some of her age 10−11 REM dreams (e.g., 1−2, 1−3, 2−1, 3−2, 7−2).

It cannot be clear, of course, whether the change in Emily's REM dream quality from Year 1 to Year 3 reflects true developmental growth or merely release from some inhibition that previously masked her mind's generative power. Nor can it be clear whether, if inhibition was involved in her age 10−11 laboratory dreams, it was situationally induced. But the growth of her dream generative performances from early Year 1 to Year 3 is unmistakable.

If overall activity level, or self-engagement in dream activity, is markedly enhanced in Emily's third-year REM dreams, there is a sense in which activity direction or activity nature increasingly serves the goals of specifically feminine developmental interests. Activities or self-involvements are not increasing randomly across activity classes (there is no physical aggression, for instance) or across setting contexts (except for the skiing of 8−1, which, in Wyoming, is practically prescribed for both sexes, there are no activities integrally related to outdoor settings). Most of Emily's dream scenarios have a rather more "mellow" ambience than do boys' dream scenarios sampled at a comparable age.

In terms of stereotypical Freudian notions of dream symbolism and of psychosexual development, one can see suggestions of images of feminine inadequacy (e.g., her wrong-sized foot in 1−2; her "tiny" dog in 2−3; her "something" lying in the street, which the father prevents her from retrieving in 4−3; the boy's sitting on a huge duffle bag in 8−3). But much more clear are signs of her comfort and pride in her femininity. Emily's dreamworlds are largely female populated, and these females generally contribute substantially to the "mellowness" of her dream scenarios. Males, young or old, tend not to do or "get" things correctly (3−2, 7−3); to be unlikable, unpredictable, and/or unreasonable (4−1, 4−3); and to make tiresome requests (6−2) or impatient comments (8−1). Generally both brother and father figures are portrayed rather unsympathetically. Two dreams with all-female casts, however, portray adult female competence in relatively striking ways. The female band in 5−1 rejects masculine band dress and excites Emily by being able to play fast (trombone) music as well as any other; Samantha in 7−2 entertains a group of young women and displays her versatility in manipulating her environment. It is suggestive that, in selecting a TV show for use in dream construction, Emily picked that one which, at the time, most strikingly portrayed the "magic" and potency of femininity against a background of male ordinariness (or, often, sheer incompetence). But the emphasis in these two dreams seems not to be so much in "putting down" males as in elaborating capable female models. Elsewhere, however, Emily tells her father "where to go" (8–1) and specifically refutes her father's suggestion that she cannot, at her own will, incorporate and then expel substances from her body (7–3). She has "science" on her side, and knows better.

The statistical data reviewed earlier suggested that it was at ages 11–13 that our children generally displayed the most competent management of their dream scenarios. The substantial increase in Emily's versatility in REM-dream elaboration in Year 3, the generally constructive nature of the plots or themes of her REM dreams, and her increasingly active role in her REM-dream scenarios, in conjunction with the continuingly good control she displays in managing dream affect and impulse expression, amply illustrate this competence. One index of the increase in her dream control from age 10–11 to age 12–13 can be seen in a contrast of her dreams 8–3 (Year 1) and 2–3 (Year 3). In both there is difficulty in putting lively creatures to bed in one's "sleeping house." In Year 1, however, the rowdy creatures are full-sized humans and the house is a full-sized human dwelling; by Year 3, on the other hand, the whole task is cast as a species of "doll play," and the would-be sleeper is a dog so tiny it can sleep in a doll's bed.

Emily's Year-3 *sleep-onset dreams* were as follows:

4-2 I think I can remember another (cf. 4–1, above) sidewalk. [Could you see it?] A driveway that went off the sidewalk . . . it kind of looked like our driveway in front of our house. [Were there any people in this?] No. [Were you in it?] No. [Did you have any feelings?] No. [Did this seem similar in any way to the sidewalk that you saw before (4–1) or was this quite different?] It was different . . . further away, and the sun wasn't shining on it or anything.

5-3 There was a bunch of people standing around and they were passing something around. I don't know what it was. I think it was something you wear, like a choker or bracelet or something. [Who were the people in this?] They were a bunch of girls my age. [Did you recognize them? Were they girls you really know?] No. [Where were they?] They were in a room and it was really small and they were all really close together. . . . I couldn't tell what kind of building it was. [Were you in it?] Yes. . . . I was looking at the things that they were passing around. I was passing them around too. We were just sort of standing around. [Did you have any feelings?] No.

6-1 I dreamed I was skiing . . . and I was taking little rubber things off my skis that held them together. [Where did this take place?] At a ski area, down right in front of a hill. It was like Medicine Bow (but) it was changed a little bit, the tow was on the other side. There were a lot of people standing around, but I didn't know who they were. [You said you were taking this binding or something off that connected the skis; were you doing anything else?] I was just fixing them, getting ready to go skiing. [Do you remember what the other people . . . were doing?] Just standing around or standing in line. [Did you have any feelings?] No.

Once again Emily's sleep-onset fantasies do not seem as elaborated as are most of her REM reports. One of the sleep-onset situations (4–2) seemed to be a partial perseveration of an image from the preceding dream, and another (6–1) simulates a familiar waking experience of a kind the subject finds enjoyable and presumably about which she might also have anticipatory fantasies in wakefulness. The most interesting and REM-like sleep-onset report is 5–3. This report does not seem to draw literally either on actual waking experience or on probable waking fantasies. The choker symbol, which is repeated from REM dream 4–3, dreamed a month and a half earlier, again appears in somewhat mysterious circumstances (in 4–3, the girl who got out of the car to retrieve Emily's choker was unaccountably left behind, as the father suddenly drove away; here the choker is the central symbol of an almost ritualistic celebration of girlish communion). Both by the nature of the symbol itself and by the contexts in which it appears, it is tempting to view it as representing, denotatively, femaleness and, connotatively, the constraints Emily imagines anatomy to impose on her as yet vaguely apprehended destiny (the father wants nothing to do with it; it is part of a specifically constricting world that only girls can experience in common). Report 5–3 suggests, if nothing else, that REM-like programs are beginning to become capable, at age 12–13, of organizing Emily's mentation at sleep onset as well.

Emily's Year-3 *NREM dreams* were as follows:

3-1   There was a great big balloon and it was shaped like a map, and a bunch of guys were playing with it . . . in front of the school. [Was this visual?] Yes. [What exactly could you see?] Well, there was a great big balloon, and a bunch of kids standing around, and some steps that went up to the school, and a sidewalk. [Could you recognize any of the people in the dream?] No . . . it was boys and girls my age. [Were you in the dream?] Yes. I was watching. [The other people . . . were they making any movement toward the balloon, were they doing anything with it, or were they . . . just sort of standing still?] Well, they had their hands on it and they were trying to bounce it, see. [Was it your school, or what?] Well, it wasn't familiar. [Did you have any feelings?] No.

3-3   Some rice, and the rice was cut in half, and it was strung together. [Could you picture it?] Yes. [What could you see besides the rice, anything else?] No, just that there was a background . . . it was outdoors or somewhere, I think there was a sidewalk, 'cause it was on the sidewalk. [This rice that was strung together, was this like rice that was still growing, or was this like you might get in a box?] It was rice like you might get in a box. [Did the idea seem to be that somebody had strung it together, or did it come that way naturally?] Well, it didn't happen naturally. [Did it look like a man-made kind of thing?] Yeah. [Were there any people in this dream?] There was somebody holding the rice, but I don't know who it was. . . . It was a boy . . . about my age. [Were you in the dream?] No. [Did you have any feelings?] No.

5-2   I dreamed that I had a leather jacket and it was daytime and I was walking down the street, and I was alone, and I wasn't doing anything. [You were wearing this jacket?] Yes. [Was this supposed to be yours?] Yes. [Do you really have a leather jacket like the one in the dream?] I have a vest, but it isn't a jacket. [Was this some particular street that you know?] It was kind of made-up . . . like downtown. [Did you have any feelings?] No.

6-3   I could see a picture of a shell, and it had a lining, a kind of lining in it that was an outside of a shell and then the real outside of the shell was like a coconut. . . . It was a little bigger than a coconut. [Were there any people in this?] No. [Do you have any idea where this was, or did it seem to just be off by itself with no setting?] It was just all by itself. [Were you in this?] No. [Did you have any feelings?] No.

9-1   I was painting a fence, or something, red and black, or something. It was kind of a brick wall, and it was red and black. . . . It kind of looked like the one on our neighbor's house. . . . It wasn't just the same. [Was anybody else in this besides you?] No. [Did you have any feelings?] No.

9-3   A piece of toast, and it had a whole strawberry on it, and you (one) smashed it up and made strawberry jelly out of it, for your toast. [Could you see anything besides toast and strawberries?] No. [No place?] No. [No people?] Well, I was in it, I was holding the toast. . . . I was going to smash (the strawberry) down. [Did you have any feelings?] No. [Can you think of any reason that you would have this going through your head? Have you ever thought anything like this or seen anything like this, when you were awake, that would make you think that this was the way you got jelly?] No.

It is not clear that Emily's age 12–13 NREM reports can be dismissed for their superficiality as readily as can her age 10–11 NREM ones (or as can her brother's age 8–9 NREM reports). The one report coming closest to meeting such a characterization at age 12–13 is 5–2: She walks down the street in a leather jacket (she has such a vest; perhaps she also would like a jacket?). But the narratives of 3–1 and 9–1 seem less plausibly related to (or explicable in terms of) either waking experience or presumptive waking fantasy than do any of her age 10–11 NREM narratives. (Balloons usually do not have the features of maps; brick walls generally are not suitable objects for painting.) And, rather uniquely in the series of NREM reports we have encountered thus far, there are NREM reports in Emily's third-year sample that have no real narrative quality but that focus on isolated images of relatively unusual inanimate objects (rice, cut in half and strung together [3−3]; a coconut with a shell inside [6−3]; a piece of toast with a smashable strawberry on top [9−3]). The previously presented report that most nearly matches these in image quality is Dean's NREM report 9−3 at age 8−9, in which a mouth seemingly was treated as an isolated object.

Interestingly, all four of these reports came from late-night NREM sleep, which tends to be relatively "light" (i.e., more cortically aroused). It also is of considerable interest that these isolated-object reports seem to emerge later developmentally than do narrative reports. One might have imagined that "lighter" NREM sleep would be better able to sustain narratives than would "deeper" (early-night) NREM sleep, and, especially, that it would be younger ages at which "pieces" of dream scenery would be experienced in isolation and older ages at which they would be fused together in synthetic dream narratives.

But, in fact, the data suggest that the generation of images of rather anomalous and isolated objects is the more advanced cognitive performance. Synthesis predates analysis (cf. Werner, 1948). Apparently the more primitive program for NREM mentation, as for REM mentation, is a narrative one. Life-span developmental data suggest that narrative programming, at least for relatively bright and reflective persons,[14] later can be overridden by analytic programs that probably emerge developmentally along with skills that Piaget would label "formal-operational."

But, at least for normals,[15] it seems to be *non*-REM sleep where the narrative imperative more easily can be derailed. Emily's age 12−13 NREM reports 3−3, 6−3, and 9−3 are prototypes of the kind of adult NREM report that makes REM/NREM discrimination relatively easy (e.g., Monroe, Rechtschaffen, Foulkes, & Jensen, 1965). Narrative NREM reports, on the other hand, presumably are more difficult to discriminate from REM reports. Since Emily's NREM recall did not improve appreciably from age 10−11 to 12−13 (56% to 67%), it cannot be that at age 12−13 she was better able simply to *recall* more fragmented NREM imagery. Rather it seems likely that she was better able to *generate* it, that is, better able to substitute a late-developing cognitive mode for the more primitive narrative one. This suggests that adult-level discrimination of NREM from REM reports may depend on the application to NREM mentation of cognitive skills that are largely, if not wholly, absent until late preadolescence or early adolescence.

Because most of Emily's NREM reports at age 12−13 seem less trivial or immediately explicable than her own earlier NREM reports, they present

---

[14]This characterization fits the subjects of almost all systematic research on NREM mentation.
[15]Dement (1955) observed isolated-image REM reports in a study of schizophrenic patients, but their REM narrative programming itself may have been defective rather than overridden.

correspondingly greater opportunity for the admittedly perilous exercise of deep interpretation. From Emily's first-year REM report 8−3, we learned about the danger of deflation for a girl's balloon, and from her first-year REM report 9−2, of somebody handling a "big orange" sphere. In her third-year NREM report 3−1, a bunch of "guys" have their hands on a topographic maplike balloon, and are trying to bounce it; the scene takes place "in front of the school," to which a sidewalk and some steps lead. A male peer in NREM report 3−3 holds a string of rice (a wedding symbol?), each piece of which has been split in half, in another sidewalk setting. In 6−3 there is a hard-shell representation of a container's double linings. In 9−3 a red fruit is about to be smashed into jelly. If these are, in fact, anatomical references,[16] then motives or programs such as those seemingly operative in the organization of REM mentation now also may be operative in the formation of NREM imagery.

In general, however, one would have to say that the stage on which these motives or programs are represented is somewhat more intrapersonal in NREM sleep and somewhat more interpersonal in REM sleep. In this sense the specific reference of Emily's isolated-object NREM images may have been to body parts, specifically sexual ones, which are of increasing interest with the approach of adolescence. Freud's (1905) theory of psychosexual development seems to imagine a part-to-whole synthesis of anatomical conceptualizations in the achievement of sexual identity. However, the younger children's dream data previously described offer little support for the hypothesis of discrete anatomical references (or "pregenital" psychosexual stages) in early childhood. The data now under review suggest that it may be only as adolescence approaches that componential anatomical concepts are, or even can be, entertained regarding one's sexual identity.

SUMMARY

It is in late preadolescence that REM dreaming seems to achieve its first grand synthesis. The rate of dream occurrence or, more likely, of dream accessibility to waking memory is stabilized at a near-adult level and has predictable cognitive correlates. Dream activities are increasingly subtle and diversified in form, and dream scenarios contain a rich balance of self and other action. Affectively dreams are particularly well controlled. The specific contents of children's dreams reflect increasingly well children's life situations: Dreams are less home and family centered and are more peer oriented; they reflect with heightened clarity the different paths of sex-role development pursued by boys and girls; and they show continuities with individual differences in children's waking cognitive styles, social skills, and character structures.

---

[16]For supporting data, see the discussion in Chapter 8 of Emily's early-adolescent dreams.

It is a now-familiar feature of cognitive development, however, that stages of consolidation and crystallization not only are integrations of previous achievements but also are platforms from which further growth proceeds. In the pursuit of such growth, it often is necessary to undo or redo what one already has learned to do so well, so that one eventually can do not only what currently is possible but also what currently is impossible. In this respect, at ages 11–13 there are some signs of beginning efforts at rethinking the very basic narrative form of dream construction. As we shall see, these few signs portend a succeeding stage of dream development in which new potentialities emerge and old ones no longer may be so easily accomplished.

CHAPTER 8

Ages 13 to 15

Eighteen of the 20 children studied at ages 11–13 also were studied two years later at ages 13–15.[1] Our "early-adolescent" study group consisted of seven girls (median age at the start of the study year: 13 years, 9 months) and 11 boys (median age at the start of the study year: 14 years, 2 months). During the study year four girls and three boys were in eighth grade and two girls and six boys were in ninth grade (the middle and final grades, respectively, of Laramie Junior High School), and one girl and two boys were in tenth grade (the first year of Laramie Senior High School).

Three of the seven girls had experienced menarche before the onset of their final study year, and Emily experienced it during that year. By other physical measures (high end-of-study weight to height ratios and decelerating rates of height-growth during Year 5 as compared to during Year 3), these four girls also were "adolescent," while only two of the seven girls still seemed relatively untouched by the physical changes of early adolescence. The typical boy studied also had "filled out," having an end-of-study body weight (in pounds) slightly more than twice his body height (in inches). Five of the 11 boys (including Fred) were experiencing accelerated growth (height increment in Year 5 vs. in Year 3), while the other six (including Phil) already were (by the same criterion) in a period of decelerated growth.

Thus both by social-environmental (school grade) and physical-maturational criteria, most of our 13- to 15-year-olds had become or were becoming "adolescent." Our interest in this chapter is to determine how dreams are affected by children's accession to this sociobiological stage.

Authors of sensibility would have us believe that puberty and adolescence are times of great personal upheaval and inner stress. Thus, in *Demian,* Hermann Hesse writes:

> Then came those years in which I was forced to recognize the existence of a drive within me that had to make itself small and hide from the world of light. The slowly awakening sense of my own sexuality overcame me, as it does every person, like an enemy and terrorist. . . . I lived in a world of dreams, drives, and desires of a chthonic nature, across which my conscious self

[1] A brother-sister pair moved from Laramie at the end of our third study year.

desperately built its fragile bridges, for the childhood world within me was falling apart. . . .

Everyone goes through this crisis. For the average person this is the point when the demands of his own life come into sharpest conflict with his environment, when the way forward has to be sought with the bitterest means at his command. Many people experience the dying and rebirth—which is our fate—only this once during their entire life. Their childhood becomes hollow and gradually collapses, everything they love abandons them and they suddenly feel surrounded by the loneliness and mortal cold of the universe. (1919, pp. 40–41)

Freud, of course, also would have to be numbered among those authors espousing a highly stressful interpretation of adolescence. In psychoanalytic theory adolescence not only introduces new complications into peer relationships, it also reawakens, especially in the male, heretofore repressed infantile and childish fantasies relating to body areas other than the genitals and to persons other than the ostensible objects of adolescent crushes.

As colorful as these accounts are, it is not clear that they are generally correct. What may be true for an articulate and imaginative minority or for an upper-class analysand does not, in fact, seem to apply very well to the typical adolescent. Most do not seem to experience symbolic deaths and rebirths in adolescence; their development is far more continuous and untroubled than that (e.g., Douvan & Adelson, 1966; Offer, 1969).

This is not to deny that there are characteristic changes associated with adolescence. Feelings and "moods" are increasingly important and are recognized more as personal creations than as obligatory correlates of external events. As such they are objects of heightened personal scrutiny. There seem to be genuine increases in restless energy, in the potential for energization of behavior, and in the moment-to-moment lability of behavior (Shaw, 1966; Martin, 1972). However, affective fluctuations for the typical adolescent seldom eventuate in debilitating levels of anxiety or depression (Offer, 1969).

In recent years there has been much controversy over the extent to which the stereotypic experiences and behaviors of adolescence in industrial or postindustrial societies are sociologically, as opposed to maturationally, determined. However that controversy ultimately may be resolved, it almost certainly is no coincidence that the years of greatest adolescent stress in American society seem to coincide with the junior high school years (Shaw, 1966; Offer, 1969). The junior high school is that link in the American public education system whose role is most poorly defined. It stands removed both from childhood proper and from even the fringes of maturity. It serves as something of an educational wasteland, and its most evident function is purely custodial. The attendant anomie must offer a powerful social reinforcement to whatever maturational patterns are associated with adolescent distress (Martin, 1972). By high school proper much of the symptomatology of adolescent distress has disappeared (Offer, 1969).

Also in recent years there has been increasing awareness of the role that cognitive maturation may play in mediating both the extraordinary (Demian-like) and the more characteristic changes children experience in early adolescence. Adolescence can be associated with the development of "formal-operational" reasoning, that is, with an increased capacity for abstract or "what-if" thinking and with the possibility of "losing" oneself in one's own thoughts. Children move, in effect, from being merely pragmatists and empirical scientists toward also being philosophers and theoretical scientists. These changes have considerable implication not merely for the child's experience of the world, but particularly perhaps for the child's experience of self. They surely play a major role in creating the seemingly heightened moodiness or affectivity of adolescence (Kohlberg & Gilligan, 1972). And to the degree that the theory of adolescence as a social invention is correct, the mediation of sociological influence at the individual level is almost certainly heavily dependent on the appearance of Piagetian forms of sophisticated adolescent reasoning in highly developed societies.

Thus in asking questions about what changes one might reasonably expect to find in the dreams of children passing into and through early adolescence one needs to be aware both of the minimal support research has accorded storm-and-stress theories of emotional development and of the probability that it is new forms of cognition that permit and/or determine many of the more characteristic changes associated with adolescent development.

Another trend in recent research findings should be borne in mind in predicting adolescent dream development: Early adolescence seems to be a somewhat more tense period of development for boys than for girls (Kohen-Raz, 1971).[2] This sex difference has been explained plausibly in both social and biological terms. The boy's prescribed line of sex-role learning in adolescence calls for a sharper break with his family and its maternal psychosocial center (Bardwick, 1971). Moreover, precocious heterosexual interests have not been so heavily proscribed in childhood and preadolescence for girls as for boys. Thus there has been a greater continuity in developmental expectations and reinforcements for girls than for boys in this important area of adolescent experience. Another reason why male development may be more stressful in early adolescence is the greater strength of basic motives against which boys are defending or with which they are trying to cope. This difference generally is acknowledged for impulses to act out hostile feelings to others (Maccoby & Jacklin, 1974). Research data (Douvan & Adelson, 1966; Bardwick, 1971; Sherman, 1971) are consistent with the hypothesis that the sex drive also is less peremptory for girls than for boys.

Finally, in predicting dream development in early adolescence, we need

---

[2]This argument is being advanced only for early adolescence. There are indications that middle and late adolescence bring special problems to girls, both in identity formation (Douvan & Adelson, 1966) and in controlling male sexuality (Bardwick, 1971).

to remember the steadily decreasing leeway children of both sexes are permitted for the display of behaviors thought of as appropriate to the opposite sex. Before adolescence vigorous activity is permitted girls; during adolescence, however, it becomes increasingly less acceptable, and girls in fact seem to assume more passive roles during adolescence (Douvan & Adelson, 1966). The modal sex types of adolescence—the vigorous, aggressive boy and the more sedate, passive girl—build on biological differences between the sexes that have been apparent since early childhood, but to these differences are added, with increased force in adolescence, differential parental and peer reinforcements for "sex-appropriate" and punishments for "sex-inappropriate" behavior. Kagan and Moss (1962) found that dominance, aggressiveness, and competitiveness were stable masculine traits, and that passivity and dependence were stable feminine traits, from the earliest years of childhood. Presumably it was parent and peer reinforcement systems that undermined the stabilization of passive behavior for boys and of dominance behavior for girls.

THE REPORTING OF DREAMS

Our 13- to 15-year-olds reported dreams on 67% of their REM awakenings, on 40% of their NREM awakenings, and on 67% of their sleep-onset awakenings. Except for NREM awakenings, these figures are nearly identical to those observed at ages 11−13 (the third-year NREM figure was 31%). The typical *child* had 73% REM recall, 39% NREM recall, and 67% sleep-onset recall. Once again, only the NREM change (third-year value: 24%) was marked. But overall there was no significant change in report rate for any of the sleep stages between ages 11−13 and 13−15. Our older group's rates of REM and of sleep-onset recall were, despite some shifts in the composition of our subject samples, remarkably consistent from year to year; only for regular NREM sleep was there any hint of growth in mentation generation and/or mentation reporting over the span of our study of this group.[3]

There were no significant (or even marginally significant) sex differences in recall rate for any stage of sleep, although the pooled REM difference was appreciable (girls, 83%; boys, 57%). The girls, as a group, were both smarter for their age than were the boys for theirs (see Chapter 7) and more highly motivated in the laboratory than were the boys (the girl mentioned in Chapter 6 as our main motivational problem in this study group dropped out of the study at the end of its third year). Another "artificial" depressant of the boys' low pooled rate of REM recall was the inclusion in our sample of

---

[3]In Chapters 5 and 6 I discussed some artifacts that might generate a pattern of report-rate constancy in longitudinally studied developmental periods in which one might expect some growth in actual mentation generation. The NREM data, however, suggest the possibility that our methods were, in fact, sensitive to such growth, where it was occurring.

Fred and Phil, the two boys mentioned in the last chapter as having had extraordinarily immature Block Design *and* REM-recall scores. Without these two boys, the typical boy had 73% REM recall (vs. 87% for the typical girl), and boys' pooled REM recall was 69%. Thus it does not seem likely from our data that there are either significant or large differences in dream occurrence or accessibility between boys and girls at ages 13−15.

Our early-adolescent subjects continued to discriminate sleep conditions by their rates of dream reporting in a fashion predictable from adult data. Specifically, they reported dreams at a significantly higher rate on REM and on sleep-onset awakenings than on NREM awakenings, while their sleep-onset and REM rates were not significantly different. Once again, also, "light"-NREM sleep generated reports at a higher rate (43%) than did "deep"-NREM sleep (31%), but this difference no longer attained marginal significance, as it had at ages 11−13. In relation to the comparable age 11−13 figures (42% and 25%, respectively), it is interesting to note that "deep"-NREM sleep seems to be the source of the overall enhancement in NREM report generation/recall.

Another continuity in our data lies in the relationship of time of night (awakening number) to report rates. Early-night (Awakening 1) REM recall was 63%, while late-night (Awakening 3) REM recall was 69%; early-night NREM recall was 41%, while late-night NREM recall was 48%. The only even marginally significant ($p < .10$, 2-tail) ordinal position effect, however, was for NREM recall to be higher on Awakening 3 than on Awakening 2 (30%). Interestingly, it was early-night NREM that was the major source of the overall enhancement of NREM report rates (41% at ages 13−15 vs. 26% at ages 11−13). Thus it was more "difficult" (early-night, deep-sleep) forms of NREM mentation whose generation and/or accessibility was enhanced in early adolescence.

As at earlier ages (except 3−5), REM, NREM, and sleep-onset report rates all were significantly intercorrelated (REM−NREM, $r = .81$; REM−sleep onset, $r = .77$; NREM−sleep onset, $r = .73$). Thus relatively prolific REM reporters also were relatively prolific reporters in other sleep stages as well. The stability of REM report rate across time for continuing older children was remarkable (from ages 11−13 to 13−15, $r = .89$; from ages 9−11 to 13−15, $r = .84$). Consistent with the hypothesis that ages 9−15 are associated with some growth in NREM, but not REM, dreaming/reporting, the long-term (ages 9−11 to 13−15) stability of NREM report rate was not significant ($r = .46$), although significant shorter-term constancy could be demonstrated (e.g., ages 11−13 to 13−15, $r = .77$).

Who were the children most often reporting dreams at ages 13−15? In the case of REM sleep, they were children from higher social-class backgrounds who had relatively democratic parents and whose own traits form a veritable litany of middle-class values (intelligence, social maturity, conscientiousness, emotional control, social pleasantness and sensitivity but an absence of hostility in relationships with others, high level of personal aspiration, imaginativeness, etc.). Overall, 64 variables (or 16% of all test-file variables) correlated significantly ($p < .05$, 2-tail, in a single test) with REM report rate. Both quantitatively (58 significant correlates, or 14.5% of all test-file variables) and qualitatively, findings on correlates of NREM recall were highly similar to those for REM recall. For the hypothesis that NREM reports are confabulations, there are a number of specific embarrassments: High-rate NREM recallers were good stimulus describers, had effective memory skills, were conscientious, and had particularly low scores on a psychometric scale of carelessness. Increases in NREM recall since ages 11–13 also had correlates indicative of intellectual ability and social responsibility. The middle-class background and cognitive-ability pattern also was observed for high-rate sleep-onset recallers but not the conscientiousness-responsibility pattern. (The self-control pattern that facilitates NREM and REM *reporting* might interfere with the *production* of memorable sleep-onset mentation [Foulkes, Spear, & Symonds, 1966]; among the correlates of *decreased* sleep-onset recall in early adolescence was precise associative control.)

Even more strongly than at ages 11–13, there was patterning in the correlates of REM dream recall at ages 13–15 more suggestive of report effects than of experience effects. Although cognitive variables were well represented among these correlates, the overall results may well reflect the fact that, from the perspective of middle-class values, good dream reporters were just general, all-around "good kids"—children who tried hard at all manner of tasks that responsible adults set for them. The specific presence among Wechsler correlates of performance variables, including Block Design, along with the absence among these same correlates of verbal-test raw scores, does suggest possible influence, only for *REM* sleep, at the level of dream construction as well. In the case of Block Design, however, the force of this suggestion as a *general* statement about dream construction in adolescence is mitigated by knowledge (see Chapter 6, n. 3) that the relationship depends on the inclusion of Fred and Phil, whose ages 13–15 Block Design scores were, as we shall see, decidedly pre-preadolescent. Nonetheless, because later we shall uncover data suggestive of new constructional possibilities and of new obstacles to effective dream construction in early-adolescent REM dreaming, the hypothesis of visuospatial determinants of actual dream experiencing cannot be discarded immediately in favor of the hypothesis of socialization influences on dream reporting. If there is any place where cognitive variables might be guessed actually to have facilitated dream *generation* for our older group, that place would have to be at ages 13–15.

BLOCK DESIGN TESTS AND REM DREAMING

Our most consistent Wechsler correlate of REM report rate was raw score on the Block Design subtest, which was significantly associated with REM report rates at ages 5–7, 7–9, 11–13, and 13–15. By contrast, the most consistent "verbal" subtest correlate of REM report rate, Information, attained significance in only two study years: ages 7−9 and 11−13. In the preceding chapter we saw some evidence that Block Design score might be something more than merely a leading indicator among a whole package of correlated maturational variables. Specifically, we saw that two boys, Fred and Phil, with relatively circumscribed deficits on Block Design−type tests at ages 11−13, also manifested very low rates of REM dream reporting at these same ages. Their data suggested that Block Design tests measure skills that are necessary conditions either of dreaming dreams in REM sleep or of remembering dreams dreamed there. Since Block Design performance (the child constructs color patterns with small blocks to match those appearing on a card before her or him) seems to make no great demands either on verbal skills or immediate memory, it would seem more likely that the effect is at the level of actual dream construction than at that of remembering or describing dreams. Thus Fred's and Phil's age 11−13[4] association of poor Block Design performance and poor REM-report performance may indicate the Block Design tests measure cognitive skills that are necessary conditions for actually having dreams in REM sleep.

Fred's and Phil's age 13−15 Block Design and REM-report performances largely replicated their age 11−13 performances on these same tasks. Fred scored 6, and Phil 13, on WISC Block Design. Seven[5] male peers who took this same test had scores ranging from 29 to 52 (median = 46). As noted in Chapter 7, the median score for 7- to 9-year-old boys was 31 (range 11−47). For boys at both age levels, Block Design strongly predicted REM recall (r = .84 at ages 7−9; r = .71 at ages 13−15). The age 13−15 correlation reflected the fact that Fred and Phil also had abysmally low REM report rates: 0% and 7%, respectively, for 15 awakenings each. Thus once again a severe retardation in Block Design performance was associated with a severe retardation in the reporting of REM dreams.[6]

But how specific was this association, and what evidence is there that it was at the level of dream construction rather than at that of dream remembering or dream telling? At ages 13−15, both Phil and Fred had full-scale I.Q.'s in a low−normal range (89 and 99, respectively). Among our 18 older children, they ranked 16th and 13th, respectively, in I.Q. They were not brilliant. But neither did they show any *general* intellectual impairment that, like their Block Design deficit, would place them alongside much younger children (and it should be remembered that their I.Q.'s *included* Block Design). The boys had general intellectual talent commensurate with their true age levels. Block Design omitted, Phil and Fred had Performance

---

[4]These were the first ages at which we studied these two boys.

[5]Two boys were administered the Wechsler Adult Intelligence Scale because of their ages.

[6]That Fred's and Phil's report rates actually declined since ages 11−13 may reflect one or more of the following: novelty effects (cf. Chapter 5) at ages 11−13; confabulations at ages 11−13 to appease an experimenter who clearly expected *some* dream reports; motivational decrement at ages 13−15.

I.Q.'s of 107 and 104, respectively. Thus they had no overall *nonverbal* or *visuospatial* deficit; apart from Block Design, they had performance abilities that also were commensurate with their true age levels. Phil and Fred had, on the Wechsler Digit-Span (memory) test, scale scores of 12 and 10, respectively, indicating above-average or average memory for their ages. Thus it seems somewhat unlikely that they had dreams but merely were unable to remember them as often as did their peers.

There *was* one other test on which Phil and Fred performed as poorly as they did on Block Design: the Embedded Figures Test (one must pick a sample pattern out of a larger figure in which it is hidden). There is much evidence (O'Gorman & Jamieson, 1979) suggesting that the information-processing requirements of embedded-figures and block-design tests are similar. Phil and Fred took, respectively, 149.6 and 163.3 seconds to disembed the average test figure; these were the longest mean solution times for their age group (the median solution time was 61.4 seconds, and the range for other children was 17.5–108.8 seconds).

How is the deficit Phil and Fred showed on these two tests to be understood? What skills did they lack that seem to enter into the ability to generate dreams during REM sleep? Following studies of patients with commissurotomies ("split brains"), several authors (Ornstein, 1972; Galin, 1974; Bakan, 1978) have proposed that dreaming is a right-hemi-sphere–dominant brain process. This hypothesis is consistent with an apparent preference of the right hemisphere for visual, as opposed to verbal, thinking. Various experimental data have been adduced in support of the hypothesis (e.g., Goldstein, Stoltzfus, & Gardocki, 1972; but cf. Antrobus, Ehrlichman, & Weiner, 1978). Following the hypothesis, it might be proposed that the skills assessed by block-design and embedded-figures tests that are critical to effective dream construction are right-hemisphere skills, and that, in their absence, dreams cannot occur or be remembered because of deficits in the visual mode of thinking that makes dreams possible or memorable.

Although at present it cannot safely be said precisely what sorts of skills *are* assessed by block-design and embedded-figures tests that are critical to dream recall/experiencing, there are ample grounds to reject the proposal that these skills are localized in the right hemisphere of the brain and that they are specifically visuospatial in nature:

1 Dream experiencing does not seem to depend on the right hemisphere. It can be eliminated with damage to the left (verbal) lobe (Foulkes, 1978c) and is retained in the left lobe surgically isolated from the right (Green-wood, Wilson, & Gazzaniga, 1977).

2 Subjects with specific visuospatial deficits that prevent dream visualiza-tion still experience and are able to report dreamlike stories during REM sleep (Kirtley, 1975; Kerr, Foulkes, & Jurkovic, 1978); that is, there is no evidence to suggest that failure to be able to visualize a dream story interferes with either the production or the recall of such a story.

3   Block-design tests seem to measure not only aptitude with visuospatial displays but also general analytic abilities that are highly correlated with "verbal" and "general" intelligence (Rose, Harris, Christian, & Nance, 1979; McGee, 1979) and that are probably left-hemisphere mediated (Bouma, 1980; Zaidel, 1980).

For these reasons I suggest that, although the data of Fred and Phil superficially seem compatible with a model stating that dreaming is right-hemisphere thinking, their real import almost certainly lies elsewhere. The right-hemisphere model itself is beset with empirical difficulties and rests on a confusion of the surface representations of most dreams, which are visual, with the underlying processes of their generation, which must involve integrative-narrative mechanisms of left-hemisphere localization and have a strongly verbal basis (Foulkes, 1978c).

Whatever their implication for mechanisms of adult dream generation, the cases of Fred and Phil offer considerable support for the developmental hypothesis advanced in Chapter 3 that REM periods are not necessarily dream periods and that young children's frequent failure to report dreams on REM awakenings often reflects failures of dream generation rather than of dream remembering or dream describing. There is little reason to believe that Fred and Phil simply were unable, as adolescents, to remember or describe their dreams. But as they had a specific cognitive defect mimicking much earlier stages of normal cognitive development, most often they did not report dreams. The most reasonable interpretation of this failure is that they, like much younger children, most often did not experience dreams. It cannot be REM sleep that guarantees dreaming; the necessary condition of dreaming must be the possession of representational abilities that permit one, against the background of the permissive cortical activation of REM sleep, symbolically to construct storylike narratives. Lacking these abilities, no matter what the ontogenetic or phylogenetic level, the organism does not dream.

CHANGES IN DREAM CONTENT AT ADOLESCENCE

Methods of study were as nearly identical as we could make them at ages 11–13 and 13–15, and children's typical rates of REM dream reporting and the typical length of their reports were stable across this period. In addition, children at both age levels either had had the experience of at least two prior years of adaptation to sleeping in the laboratory or gave evidence of having dreams that were in no way significantly different from those reported by children with such experience. On all counts, then, comparisons of dream content at ages 11–13 and 13–15 should offer us an artifact-free picture of how children's dreams typically are affected by the entry into adolescence.

Table 8.1 presents the relevant data and the result of content contrasts

Table 8.1 REM Dream Variables Showing a Significant Difference in Magnitude or Frequency of Occurrence Between Ages 11–13 (also 9–11) and 13–15

Dream Variables	Age at Which Magnitude/Incidence Was Higher	
	11–13 vs. 13–15	9–11 vs. 13–15
Characters		
Sibling, male	11–13	9–11
Sibling, female		9–11
Sibling, either	11–13	9–11
Parent-siblings, male	11–13	9–11
Family, male	11–13	
Known, any indeterminate		9–11
Settings		
Home, unfamiliar	11–13	
School, own		9–11
Commercial	13–15	
Unclassifiable	13–15	
Activities		
Manual, either	11–13	
Locomotor, dreamer	11–13	
Locomotor, other	11–13	
Locomotor, either	11–13	
Any motor, dreamer	11–13	
Any motor, other	11–13	
Any motor, either	11–13	
States		
Angry, other	13–15	
Hunger, dreamer	11–13	
Hunger, other	11–13	
Hunger, either	11–13	
Fatigue, dreamer	11–13	
Fatigue, either	11–13	
Approach social, dreamer	11–13	
Approach social, other	11–13	13–15
Approach social, either	11–13	
Approach object, dreamer		13–15
Approach object, other		13–15
Approach object, either		13–15
Avoidance social, other	11–13	
Outcomes		
Unfavorable, self-mediated, either		9–11
Unfavorable, any mediated, other		9–11
Favorable, other mediated, other	11–13	
Favorable, other mediated, either	11–13	
Favorable, any mediated, other	11–13	
Favorable, any mediated, either	11–13	
Ratings		
Character distortion	13–15	
Hedonic tone		9–11

between ages 9–11 and 13–15. As the table indicates, compared to the stabilized dreaming of late preadolescence, there were indeed some remarkable changes in REM dream content in early adolescence.

1   Adolescent dreams contained significantly fewer portrayals of "physical" activity by dream characters. Verbal acts, on the other hand, did not decrease significantly, and the ratio of verbal activity to locomotor activity was at its developmental maximum (about seven dreams with verbal acts for every 10 dreams with locomotor activity). But neither did verbal activity increase (in fact, it decreased nonsignificantly for boys), so the overall effect is not of equally active but more symbolic dreams but rather of *less activity in adolescent dreams.*

2   Specifically decreasing were acts of prosocial initiation and acts eventuating in favorable outcomes for dream characters—there was *less prosocial behavior in adolescent dreams.* Ascriptions of anger to nonself-characters, on the other hand, increased in adolescent dreams.

3   Also decreasing significantly in adolescent dreams were hunger and fatigue themes—*adolescent dreams less often contained body-state imagery,* particularly the forms of body-state imagery otherwise most prominent in children's dreams (i.e., hunger and sleep; manifestly sexual imagery remained highly infrequent—its relative incidence in boys' dreams was 1%, in girls' dreams, 3%).

4   In other respects as well, *adolescent dreams seemed less strongly to draw on highly familiar waking-life situations.* Family members appeared significantly less often than in late preadolescence, while character distortion increased significantly; the incidence of downtown-commercial settings increased significantly, as did that of vague or unclassifiable settings. In the cases of the decline in family representation and the increase in urban settings, one can, of course, point to the changing circumstances of waking adolescent social life, but there were no significant increases in peer portrayals or in the incidence of peer (school/recreational) settings. There were, however, increases both in unfamiliar characters and in vaguely portrayed or highly unusual settings.[7] Thus the overall effect seems to have been that children's dreams in adolescence portrayed both persons and places increasingly removed from those concretely experienced in their admittedly changing waking worlds.[8]

Having outlined the general dimensions of dream change in early adolescence, we still face the task of explaining why they changed as they

---

[7]There was a marginally ($p < .10$, 2-tail) significant increase in rated Setting Distortion at ages 13–15.

[8]In retrospect, the increase in unfamiliar home settings at ages 11–13 (Table 7.1) seems to have been something of a fluke; they decreased significantly at ages 13–15.

did. Recalling my introductory remarks about how we might have *expected* dreams to change in adolescence, we have possible two obvious lines of explanation. Psychodynamically it can be proposed that adolescents' dreams were motorically inhibited because of an increased need to inhibit action that no longer seemed so simple in its intent or consequences. Cognitively it can be hypothesized that adolescents' dreams no longer needed to be so literal or concrete in their surface representations. Offhand it would seem that a psychodynamic hypothesis might better encompass the first two lines of change noted above, and a cognitive hypothesis the latter two.

However, as will be elaborated when we look at which children in particular were dreaming most often of generally decreasing motor acts, it is not clear that the cognitive hypothesis need settle so cheaply as this seemingly plausible, offhand compromise suggests. Decreases in the visible activeness of REM dreams may have reflected altered representational possibilities in adolescent dreaming as much as did decreases in the dream's sensitivity to concurrently active body states or in its use of familiar characters and settings. As also has been suggested for waking alterations in experience concomitant with adolescence, many of the characteristic changes in dream experience at adolescence may have far less to do with adolescent impulsivity or sexuality than with the adolescent's acquisition of new ways of thinking about world and self.

At ages 11–13 it was noted that declines in family representation since ages 9–11 mainly involved female characters and dreamers. At ages 13–15 that situation was reversed. As Table 8.1 indicates, it was male family members, particularly brothers, who were in eclipse in adolescent dreams, and, for boys but not for girls, the following family-member classes declined significantly at adolescence: sibling, male; sibling, either; parent-sibling, male; parent-sibling, either; family, male; family, either.[9] At ages 13–15 the girls retained more attachment to family characters, particularly female ones, in their dreams than did boys; boys, on the other hand, shifted down from earlier levels of use of male family characters. At ages 11–13 they dreamed more than twice as often of male as of female family characters, but, by virtue of their decreasing employment of male family characters at ages 13–15, in early adolescence they showed no particular preference by family-member sex in their relatively infrequent use of family characters. Boys, but not girls, showed a significant decrease also in the use of any-home settings. Their diverging paths of sex-role development clearly left the boys and girls with different levels of residual interest in home and family.

Changes in activity in dreams, and in the affective and motivational properties of that activity, tended not to show marked differentiation by the

---

[9]However, 10 boys but only seven girls participated in the longitudinal comparisons (Fred had no REM dreams in his final study year).

sex of the dreamer.[10] Generally they reflected patterns that held equally well for boys and girls. There were two interesting exceptions to this generalization, however. For girls only, dreamer receptions of unfavorable outcomes mediated by others and other initiations of antisocial behavior increased significantly from ages 11–13 to 13–15. These changes may reflect the girls' realistic perceptions of increased male aggressiveness and of increased danger thereby to themselves. Changes of this sort, at any rate, would seem to demand psychosocial rather than cognitive interpretation.

Having looked at these various changes in dreaming at adolescence, one cannot help but be impressed with how faithfully many of them agree with prior expectation, whether psychosocial or cognitive, and with how, when children's life situations really do change, so too do their dreams. But there is a danger here, as there always is, in viewing statistically reliable differences as necessarily representing very large ones. In point of fact, *our normative data reveal no cataclysmic changes in children's dreams with the onset of adolescence and no substantial support for a storm-and-stress view of adolescence.* The overall pleasantness–unpleasantness of dreams has not changed significantly; the average girls' dream at ages 13–15 was slightly pleasant, while the average boys' dream was not unpleasant. Even during the "crisis" of adolescence, for both girls and boys prosocial motives occurred more often than antisocial ones, and the self-character was more likely to receive friendly than hostile acts from others. Particularly damaging to the hypothesis of adolescence as a highly disruptive period of life is the one overall dream-rating variable that discriminated children's dreams at ages 9–11 from those at ages 13–15: Dreams became *more* pleasant over this five-year span.[11]

That activity variables did not significantly differentiate children's dreams at ages 9–11 and 13–15 is explained by the fact that, in comparisons with both age levels, dreams at ages 11–13 were significantly higher on such variables. Thus *from the point of view of the concrete representation of physical acts and social interaction in dreams, late preadolescence is the era of childhood in which dreaming has reached a zenith.*

CORRELATES OF REM-DREAM CONTENT

Dream Length

Children at ages 13–15 who told *long* REM dreams had a number of the same characteristics as those who had *many* REM dreams, an unsurprising

---

[10]Thus the activity findings do not depend on girls' increasing waking "passivity."

[11]Separately, this change was significant for girl dreamers but not for boy dreamers. The sex-typing of aggressive behavior (desirable for boys, undesirable for girls) probably explains this difference, rather than the alternative hypothesis of greater adolescent disruption for boys than for girls.

finding since REM word counts and report rates were significantly related to one another ($r = .64$). Specifically, tellers of longer dreams came from higher social-class backgrounds, were socially pleasant and sensitive, and showed signs of effective application of their intelligence. It is of interest, however, from the perspective of the question of whether the cognitive correlates of REM *recall rates* were constructional or merely reportorial, that correlates of REM *word count* at ages 13—15 did not include any unequivocal measure of cognitive skill. Were the cognitive correlates of recall operative merely at the level of dream reporting, one would have expected such variables to have been even more prominent among correlates of report extensity; instead they were absent.

At ages 13—15 middle-class socialization clearly has something to do with who tells longer dreams, and the effect is not reducible to differences in cognitive ability. For those who tell more dreams, on the other hand, the apparent socialization effect may reflect an underlying relationship of cognitive talent, which only happens to be social-class—related, to dream construction. Putative constructional variables such as Block Design and Embedded Figures Test raw scores never were correlated significantly with REM word counts, but relatively often were correlated significantly with REM report rates. In general, at later ages in child development (e.g., 11—15), differences in reported dream length seem most likely to have reflected only motivational or attentional variables and not true differences in the amount of dream generated or experienced. At some earlier ages, say ages 7—9, where REM report rate was expanding significantly, it seems possible the word count differences might also have reflected dream-constructional differences as well as (or rather than) report-bias factors.[12]

Characters

As we have already seen, male family members appeared less frequently in boys' dreams at adolescence, although girls continued to dream of female family members relatively often. Consequently, the less frequently appearing male family members showed only slight differences in incidence between boys and girls, while female family members were dreamed of considerably more often by girls than by boys. Thus the main answer to the question of what kind of children continued to dream of mothers and sisters at adolescence is "girl children," and other personality or behavioral correlates of such dreaming no doubt were slanted toward characteristics either inherently or accidentally (in our sample) "feminine" in nature. This slant should not have been operative in correlations with the dreaming of fathers and brothers.

Dreamers of fathers and brothers showed indications of physical immaturity but of effective (e.g., flexibility, tolerance, achievement, self-control) or

---

[12]This possibility also may apply to ages 5—7.

of overly effective (e.g., defensiveness, low self-acceptance, increasing tenseness) middle-class socialization. Paternal characteristics were little involved in this pattern, but mothers of these dreamers had an authoritarian child-rearing ideology, although they seemed lax in their enforcement of it. Dreamers of mothers and sisters were energetic and imaginative but also were relatively immature physically. Their fathers were perceived as granting them less autonomy now than they had formerly. Overall, parents were dreamed of most often by imaginative children who were as yet little interested in opposite-sex peer relationships, and family members in general were dreamed of most often by physically immature children who reported spending little time with their peers.[13]

Thus there seem to be several new features in our data, at ages 13–15, on who dreams relatively most often of their own families.

1 The potential in parental attitudes or behaviors for generating intergenerational conflict remains but now, depending on the particular family-member dream class involved, seems more clearly focused on one parent or the other (specifically, on the parent of the opposite sex of the character class). In adolescence, evidently for the first time in childhood (cf. Chapter 4), children seemed to be making discriminations on the basis of the sex of the family members in question as to both whether and why they dreamed of them.

2 Also for the first time in adolescence, there were signs that high rates of dreaming of family members reflected "experiential" factors (lack of peer contact or interest, perhaps related to physical immaturity), rather than children's own dependency needs or demonstrable maladroitness in peer interaction. In this sense it might be said that the very "meaning" of family dreaming has changed at adolescence, markedly so, in fact, as compared to late preadolescence.

3 For the first time since ages 5–7, where I have hypothesized that it takes cognitive skill to represent even highly familiar family-member dream characters, cognitive correlates of family dreaming at ages 13–15 were universally positive in direction. This too is a sign that family dreaming in adolescence may have new meanings.

At ages 13–15 the nonfamilial known persons recruited for dream performances continued mostly to be peers rather than adults, and they continued to be recruited on a largely like-sex basis. But sex differences in the relative incidence of male and female known characters no longer were significant, as at ages 11–13. Reading this, one naturally assumes: Of

---

[13]Even at marginal significance, the most frequently appearing physical-maturation measure (weight/height ratio at the beginning of the study year) was not scored at higher values for boys than for girls, so it cannot reflect simply the sex of the dreamers involved in these various correlations.

course, in adolescence, children begin to show more interest in the opposite sex in their daily lives. But this does not seem to have been the case in their dreams. Statistically (but not significantly), the major difference in adolescents' dreams seems to have been a decreasing tendency for girls to dream of their female friends; there was no increase in dreaming of opposite-sex peers either for boys or for girls.

The persisting sex differences in the employment of male and female acquaintances led to strong sex-typing in their correlates. Dreamers of male acquaintances were "actors-out," for instance, showing indications of a lack of mature behavioral control, while dreamers of female acquaintances were intelligent, expressive children with effective regulation of their cognitive performances.

At ages 13–15 strangers continued to be adults more often than peers, and their distribution also showed some (nonsignificant) sex-typing, with boys dreaming more often than girls of male strangers, and girls more often than boys of female strangers. Cognitive correlates of male-stranger incidence were negative, while for female-stranger incidence they were positive. The most balanced category, across dreamer sex, in stranger incidence was the overall appearance of male strangers. High-rate dreamers of male strangers seemed to manifest a laconic, tough-guy stance, while high-rate dreamers of female strangers (largely, but not entirely, girls) were adult oriented, and increasingly so. It is as if, in the human characters they invented, the children selected emblems of their own current identities: macho-masculine, or socialized-feminine. Interestingly, typical cognitive/behavioral correlates did not hold well for specifically *adult* strangers, where, for instance, cognitive correlates were positive for the incidence of male characters. The age as well as the sex of the stranger invented may also serve as an emblem of one's current identity. In female stranger selection, those who invented peers were peer oriented, while those who invented adults were increasingly adult oriented.

Overall, then, in their elaboration of extrafamilial human characters at ages 13–15, children seemed to be following their own personal interests and "styles." In adolescence these interests and styles were increasingly sex-typed. More generally, past ages 9–11, children's character selection in their dreams seemed not to be responding to any strong cognitive imperatives; it was elective. Children *could* create any character; whom they *would* create reflected what their interests were.

Animal-character dreams at ages 13–15 were relatively infrequent, and again more likely for girls than for boys. Animal dreamers were introspective, and increasingly so, rather than behaviorally expressive. They did not seem overtly aggressive but had increasingly rich waking fantasies high in aggression, and increasingly so. The suggestion, as at ages 11–13, is of an orientation to fantasy.

Animal dreaming, then, is another argument against searching for universal meaning in children's dreams. For young children (i.e., ages 5–7) animals may represent an impulsive self, whereas for older children (i.e., ages 9 and on) such characters may reflect a retreat from human reality into nonhuman fantasy. What a dream feature signifies depends not only on who dreamed it but also on the stage of development at which it was dreamed.

Settings

For the first time at ages 13–15 significant sex differences were observed for dream settings. Consistent with the character data reviewed above, residential settings (any home, the dreamer's own home) occurred more often in girls' than in boys' dreams. As already noted, there was a significant increase in the occurrence of dreams with vague or unclassifiable settings: 15% of dreams were scored as having had such settings.

As for the elaboration of family characters, environmental inexperience also loomed as a determinant for the elaboration of home (any or own) settings. Frequent dreamers of home settings were effective fantasizers but social "loners." They had indulgent and protective fathers who increasingly were loathe to grant them autonomy. However, it seemed to be more an absence of effective peer relationships than the presence of dependency on parents or adults that was predictive of home dreaming. Frequent dreamers of their own homes specifically were judged uninterested in the opposite sex, and they were physically immature.

Recreational settings (i.e., play themes) continued their general association with competitiveness rather than with comradeship or creativity. Children who dreamed often of such settings at ages 13–15 were aggressive and described as leaders, although they did for the first time also score high on a creativity measure. The parental pattern was authoritarian-controlling. Insofar as our developmental findings on dreams of play cast light on the larger meanings of children's play and recreational behaviors, they suggest that these behaviors are part of the deadly serious "work" of childhood: the seeking of competitive advantage and identity through personal power.

Nonrecreational outdoor settings were not terribly frequent by adolescence (12% of dreams contained such settings), and, as at ages 11–13, their incidence no longer seemed to index dreamers' waking "outgoingness." In fact, children who most often reported such settings reported spending relatively little time with their friends as compared to with their parents. This is but another instance of the shifting meaning of dream features from early childhood to adolescence.

As at ages 11–13, there was clear evidence at ages 13–15 that dreaming of unusual or unarticulated settings reflected cognitive skill. The cognitive pattern at ages 13–15, where, of course, such settings increased significantly in their occurrence, was especially interesting. As we shall see illustrated in Emily's adolescent dreams, at least some of this increase is attributable to REM dreaming of isolated objects analytically detached from any larger setting or context, a feat that one might imagine to depend on skill in visuospatial analysis.[14] *All* cognitive correlates of the occurrence of unusual/unarticulated settings at ages 13–15 were measures of precisely this sort of skill: Block Design (increases), Embedded Figures Test (speed of solution, fewest times referring back to the illustration of the simple form embedded in the larger context), and a "Speed of Closure" measure. There was no evidence that dreaming of atypical or vague settings was related to anxiety or conflict, that is, that such dreaming was defensively motivated. Clearly here is at least one characteristic change in adolescent dreaming whose explanation is cognitive rather than psychosexual.

Activities

As we have seen, the likelihood that dreams would contain concrete portrayals of motor activity, particularly locomotor activity, decreased significantly at adolescence. Increases, however, were observed in the relative incidence of dreamer and overall visual activity in the dream:

	Ages 11–13		Ages 13–15	
Dream Activity	Girls(%)	Boys(%)	Girls(%)	Boys(%)
Vision, dreamer	17	28	27	34
Vision, either	28	34	34	40

These categories are important exceptions, then, to the decreasing eventfulness of adolescent dreams. From the inherent passivity of the events they describe, one would imagine waking passivity as a plausible correlate. However, as we have seen, from ages 7–13 it was aggressive and/or mischievous children who most often reported sensory activities for the dreamer character. At ages 13–15, however, plausibility took a small step toward reality: Dependent, self-controlled, and conventional, adult-oriented children dreamed most often of their passive, sensory participation in dreams. Correlates were not greatly dissimilar for the ascription of sensory activities to others (which was significantly correlated with self-participation at the sensory level: $r = .63$), nor, of course, for the overall incidence of sensory acts in dreams.

As suggested earlier, the motor-activity decrease in adolescence might reasonably be imagined to reflect children's increased need to defend against their own burgeoning impulses. Correlates of self-activity at ages 13–15 suggest an alternative, and cognitive, hypothesis: There are new difficulties in effectively representing self-action in dreams. In the face of these hypothetical difficulties, one would expect that it would be visuospatially talented, rather than impulsive or defensively impoverished, children who

[14]Emily ranked first among the girls, and third overall, in the relative incidence of "vague" or "unclassifiable" REM settings.

most often would dream of their own activity. That, in fact, was the case. Children high in Block Design performance (raw scores and increases) and in Torrance figural imaginativeness, but not particularly high in anxiety/ conflict measures, dreamed most often of their own motoric participation. Conversely, children who were least talented visuospatially were least able to dream of such participation.

Why might this be? I offer the following speculation. It seems to be only toward adolescence that children learn to step back mentally from self-other interactions and to think about such interactions as a third party might (Shantz, 1975). This ability presupposes a cognitive operation that has a strongly formal-operational flavor: disengagement from an ongoing situation. As transposed to dream experiencing, the development of this ability implies a new possibility, namely, double self-reference: "You" can watch "you" doing something as another person might. Unlike the situation I have proposed for early childhood, there really is a "you" out there, and, unlike the situation I have proposed for later childhood, there is another "you" watching that "you." In the imagistic medium of dreams, double self-reference must be a rather tricky matter. Only children particularly skilled in managing that medium, therefore, can pull it off; in essaying it, other children fail and end up with dreams relatively lacking in self-activity and in effective dream scenarios more generally. There may be "a watching you" (cf. the sensory-self category increases), but there is less to watch. This speculation, therefore, not only accounts for the correlates at hand but also for the longitudinal decreases in dream activity observed in early adolescence. If it is to be judged plausible, however, it must accord with correlates of self-locomotion at ages 13–15, for, of the various motor acts summarized in the category of current concern, self-locomotion poses representational difficulties in a way self-vocalization, for instance, does not, because it alone implies a full imaginal-spatial displacement of one of the "you"'s.

It was children relatively impoverished in figural inventiveness who, at ages 13–15, dreamed relatively most often of others' activities. Thus there seems to be no new difficulty in managing *others'* activity in dreams. And given the cognitive-correlate contrast of self and other activity, it is instructive that, psychosocially, dreamers of self- and other-initiated motor activities did not prove to be highly discriminable. High-rate motor-self dreamers were getting more cheerful and were energetic; high-rate motor-other dreamers were cheerful and were becoming more expressive. Overall, Torrance Figural Fluency (but also error-proneness in perceptual processing) predicted the rate at which dreams contained some motor activity.

When we focus on correlates of self-locomotion in early-adolescent dreams, we find, in fact, the sort of correlates that my speculation requires. Imagining self-displacement through dream space in early adolescence was correlated with Block Design (raw scores and increases), Torrance figural imaginativeness, and a measure of perceptual speed. Evidently, from the reduced level of self-locomotion dreams, portraying such movement no longer is so easy as it earlier was, and it is the most visuospatially talented children who achieve such portrayals most often. Once again the "expected" psychosocial correlates did not appear. I conclude from our correlational data that *decreases in dream activity at adolescence reflect the presence of new possibilities of cognitive self-representation and attendant difficulties in realizing these possibilities, rather than any psychosocially or psychosexually induced inhibition of action.*

Frequent dreamers of locomotor activity by nonself-dream characters were not particularly talented cognitively. Socially these children were wary, anxious, and unfriendly, although their everyday school demeanor apparently was conventionally pleasant. Anxiety and hostility also correlated significantly with the overall incidence of locomotor behavior in dreams.

Frequent dreamers of verbal activity, on the other hand, were, fittingly enough, emotionally expressive and talkative. They also seemed to be highly socialized (High School Personality Questionnaire: Intelligent, Apprehensive, Controlled), befitting the socialized medium in which they frequently portrayed dream interaction.

The positive figural correlates of *both* unarticulated-setting dreams and self-locomotion dreams in early adolescence are worthy of notice, because they suggest that general decreases in self-activity are not simple by-products of the concomitant increase in dreaming about isolated objects outside of a strong, self-involving narrative context. On that hypothesis, children dreaming frequently of contextless objects should have had different and/or superior cognitive skills than children retaining self-locomotion in their dreams at relatively high levels. Thus the more likely situation is that *the early adolescent's unfolding operations of formal and abstract reasoning simultaneously permit new possibilities of both narrative realization and detaching dreams from narrative constraints altogether.*

States

The portrayal of *symbolic activity* within the dream itself reached its developmental maximum at ages 13–15, appearing in roughly one of every four dreams. In the context of the simultaneous maximum for sensory activity, and of the significant declines in gross motor activity from ages 11–13 to 13–15, this finding indicates the increasingly mentalistic, and decreasingly physically active, nature of dreams in early adolescence. It was bright, well-socialized, higher social-class children who reported cognitive acts most often in their dreams at ages 13–15.[15] Most such acts were ascribed by children to themselves rather than to other dream characters.

---

[15]The children's parents seemed to be nonauthoritarian and nonpunitive, suggesting that intradream cognition is not defensively inhibited action so much as it is a freely chosen style of dream expression.

Not surprisingly, the most constant correlate of intradream symbolic activity from ages 7−9, the point where such activity first emerged as a significant and credible dream feature, through ages 13−15 was cognitive skill.

Higher social-class standing, cognitive skill (specifically, only visuospatial or figural skill), and a well-bred docility also predicted the incidence of *feelings* in dreams at ages 13−15. Children's own spontaneity, emotionality, and so forth were not related to the incidence of feeling in dream reports. The weakening influence of cognitive variables, however, and the appearance of social class in age 13−15 feeling correlates suggest the heightened possibility here (as vs. ages 11−13) of report bias: Possibly only children more sensitive to the role feelings play in their everyday lives bothered to report them in their dreams. However, it seems impossible to dissociate the possession of such sensitivity from the possession of symbolic capabilities that would have to enter into the generation of dream feelings in the first place. Overall, our data for separate feelings at different points in childhood and for feelings in general in preadolescence and early adolescence strongly suggest that endowing characters with emotions initially depends more on cognitive skill than on the sheer "possession" of such feelings in wakefulness. *Waking cognition, rather than waking affect, determines the earliest childhood manifestations of feelings in dreams. Even in the hypothetical emotional turmoil of adolescence, it is cognitive ability more than waking affectivity that determines the presence of feelings in dreams.*[16] Developmentally it seems that one's own feelings neither "cause" dreams nor play a major role in their elaboration. Rather, affect seems to be an ancillary means of qualifying a dream narrative (Foulkes, 1978c), and a means most readily available to cognitively competent and interpersonally sensitive children rather than to those whose behavior is highly impulsive or emotional. So much for the "primacy" of affect in dreaming.

However, when, as in adolescence, minimal levels of the representational competency and the social comprehension requisite to making dreams emotional have been attained, it does seem that then there is a tendency for children to put into their dreams particular emotions that they know well from their own personal experience. For instance, at ages 13−15 it was anxious children who most often were fearful in their dreams. Even here, however, social class and figural-representational skill also were positive correlates of dream fear. Likewise, the relative incidence of anger in dreams (twice as high for boys as for girls, and more likely for boys than for girls to be self-ascribed) was positively related to fantasy aggression and social dominance, as well as personal malaise, but it too was related positively to social class and representational skill. In this case there was not a direct association of the overt expression of waking and dreaming hostility, but the

---

[16]The overall incidence of affect in dreams actually declined slightly in adolescence.

waking pattern was broadly consistent with the dreaming one. More generally, our data on waking correlates of "negative" feelings suggest some subtlety in the ways in which waking–sleeping "continuity" can be achieved. At ages 11–13, for instance, it was hostile children who felt hostile in their dreams, but at ages 9–11 it was children whom one might imagine to be predisposed to anger (heedless, excitable ones), rather than ones who were overtly hostile, who dreamed most often of their own hostility. Likewise, at ages 13–15 it was anxious children who were anxious in their dreams, but at ages 11–13 it was children whom one might only imagine to be anxious (socialized in ways suggesting apprehension), rather than ones who were overtly anxious, who dreamed most often of their own anxiety.[17]

The rate at which happiness occurred in boys' dreams was halved between ages 11–13 and 13–15, while the girls' rate was constant. Consequently girls' dreams were over three times as likely as boys' to contain happiness, and, for the first time for either boys or girls anywhere in our normative data, boys experienced relatively more cases of a negative emotion (e.g., anger: 12%) than of happiness (6%). Note, however, the low absolute values in both cases: 70% of boys' dreams contained no emotion at all (vs. 60% for girls). The (mainly girl) dreamers of happiness at ages 13–15 were judged increasingly compliant and well behaved in school.

In one romantic view, childhood is coextensive with a primitive, untutored *joie de vivre.* As I have interpreted our data, however, it seems unlikely that there is much feeling at all, of any kind, in children's earliest, untutored nocturnal thoughts. By ages 7–9 happy feelings can accompany dreams, but this fact seems to depend on cognitive maturation, not on personal satisfaction. Thereafter, correlates of dream happiness suggest, as at ages 13–15, a continuity not so much with personal joy as with the assumption of conventional social roles in which one is supposed to manifest happiness. The sex differences observed from ages 9–15 are consistent with this picture. In dreams as in waking life, "happiness" seems not to be all that we might hope for it to be.

Motives and Outcomes

As noted earlier, hunger and fatigue themes decreased significantly at adolescence. So too at marginal significance ($p < .10$, 2-tail) did dreams of self-ascribed thirst. Overall, body-state dreaming was, within our observations, at its developmental nadir. Self-hunger themes were observed relatively most often for children who were achievement oriented, apprehensive, and increasingly inhibited socially at school. The girls in this group were sexually immature. Hunger dreaming more generally had comparable

[17]It is interesting that in each of these cases the expected behavioral correlate emerged at an age level immediately succeeding that at which I have hypothesized, on the basis of initial positive cognitive correlates, that children first learned to portray the emotion. Perhaps first you learn the general possibility, then to connect it with your own salient needs.

correlates, including tenseness and a lack of interest in the opposite sex. Social disinterest or incompetence clearly might be responsible for egocentric hunger dreams in adolescence, but there was no direct evidence supporting the hypothesis that cognitive immaturity underlies such egocentricity.

Unlike hunger dreaming, fatigue dreaming had significant cognitive correlates, but their direction was mixed. Socially, fatigue dreamers were seen as outgoing, friendly, and cheerful but, as at earlier ages, also as excitable-distractible (here for self-ascriptions) and socially insensitive (here for overall ascriptions).

In general, both classes of organic-motive dreaming seemed to follow a now-familiar course of shifting developmental meaning. At earlier stages of development the weaving of a dream about a body-state concern might merely reflect cognitive competence; later on, however, body-state dreams seemed more likely to reflect social inexperience or insensitivity and/or distractibility-excitability. However, we were unable to demonstrate that in early adolescence body-state dreaming unequivocally reflected cognitive incompetence, as might have been predicted by the hypothesis that children who are becoming formal-operational are less likely to have their thoughts driven by here-and-now considerations. This hypothesis better explains the longitudinal decreases than the correlates at ages 13–15 of body-state dreaming.[18]

Social-approach (but, interestingly enough, not object-approach) dreaming declined significantly at adolescence; naturally enough, given our scoring system, so too did favorable-outcome dreaming. Prosocial initiations by the *self* (the less frequent case) had one positive cognitive correlate (Torrance Figural Fluency) and were associated with waking spontaneity. Prosocial initiations by *others* (the more frequent case) also were correlated with the Torrance measure and with WISC Block Design increases, but negatively with sociability-extroversion (and with WISC Digit Span). Thus the developmentally more frequent form of prosocial dreaming, namely dreaming of others' social acts, seemed from ages 5–15 to reflect the dreamer's social concerns more than her or his social accomplishments. At ages 13–15 the overall incidence of prosocial interaction was, for instance, positively associated with introversion and waking disinterest in the opposite sex.

Attack themes at ages 13–15 were more equally distributed across sex lines than at ages 11–13: Boys showed a small decrease, and girls, a small increase. Self-initiations of attack behavior remained relatively rare and

---

[18]But this difficulty may reflect the breadth of definition of our body-state motive classes. Hunger, for instance, was scored not only for feelings of hunger and eating behavior but also for food objects, restaurant settings, and so forth. Thus, among our residual "hunger" dreams at ages 13–15, there may be dreams deserving that designation but also others that have been motivationally misclassified. Against a background of decreases in the first class, the dreams of the second class may have been more confounding at ages 13–15 than elsewhere.

were relatively equally apportioned by dreamer sex. A considerable change occurred between late preadolescence and early adolescence ($r = -.12$) in who dreamed of initiating attacks. Earlier self-initiated attacks were dreamed by assertive, competitive children. Later, in adolescence, they were dreamed by relatively depressed children who described their own behavior as withdrawn and who, on a psychological test, appeared increasingly tense and decreasingly assertive. Dreaming of other-initiated antisocial behavior, however, was stable over this same period ($r = .80$), and children at both age levels showed signs of anxiety. At ages 13–15 they also were relatively depressed, withdrawn, and lacking in energy or expressiveness.

As for the "negative" emotions discussed earlier, so too for the more frequently occurring "negative" acts considered here are there evidently different levels at which waking–sleeping "continuity" can be manifested. In early years, dream aggression seemed directly to reflect children's waking perceptions (ages 5–7) or behaviors (ages 7–9). But later on (ages 11–13 for other initiations, ages 13–15 for self-initiations), dreams of aggression seemed most often to be reported by children who were anxious and insecure, which also makes sense, but a different kind of sense. The developmental change is consistent with the increasingly complex cognitive mediation available in dream formation, and it reminds us that general hypotheses of relationships between waking and dreaming experience need to be qualified by an understanding of the stage of development of these mediational abilities.

Consistent with my hypothesis about new possibilities, and new difficulties, in self-representation at ages 13–15, it was not merely in activity initiations but also in activity receptions that cognitive visuospatial ability level predicted *self*-participation. Block Design and Torrance figural scores predicted the receipt of unfavorable acts by the self (in the absence of strongly patterned personality correlates), and the Torrance scores also predicted the receipt of favorable acts by the self (also in the absence of strong personality correlates). Another figural variable, an impulsivity (error) score from a perceptual-matching task, predicted self-receipt of both kinds of interaction.

For other than the self-receipt categories, cognitive correlates were scattered but were positive for favorable outcomes and negative for unfavorable ones. Differential personality patterns of these favorable- and unfavorable-outcome dreamers were consistent with this cognitive picture. Like prosocial-initiation dreamers, favorable-outcome dreamers were introverted; they seemed to be highly socialized children of the sort who apply themselves well in school, and they had conventionally pleasant waking fantasies. Physiologically (in the case of the girls) and psychologically, they were sexually immature. One continuity in favorable-outcome reporting from ages 9–11 on was that such reports came from children with some narrative or expressive talent, which might explain the "good" management of their dream scenarios. In contrast, children with high rates of other-received or any-received unfavorable outcomes had personality patterns consistent with a hypothesis of obstructed cognitive functioning. They were ideationally impoverished, doubting, defensive, anxious, withdrawn, emotionally constricted, and so forth. For the first time presleep unfriendliness and depression predicted dream malevolence.

In general, throughout childhood favorable outcomes seemed better to reflect social concern than social skill, and, as we have just seen, by adolescence they reflected in particular an introverted apprehension. But if we imagine that introversion or socialized apprehension provided the fuel for the children's pleasant dreams, we also must allow that narrative or imaginative fluency provided the means. By late preadolescence and early adolescence, emotional insecurity was associated with dreaming of unfavorable character outcomes; in adolescence that insecurity coalesced into a pattern of behavioral sullenness, with accompanying ideational impoverishment. Thus by adolescence one can see a certain kind of continuity between children's world view and their dreamworld configuration. The favorable-outcome dreamer is the inexperienced optimist; the unfavorable-outcome dreamer is the world-weary cynic. But this is a relatively subtle kind of cognitive-attitudinal similarity, not a simple behavioral one (e.g., "friendly people dream friendly dreams, hostile people dream hostile dreams").

Global Ratings

Not surprisingly, at ages 13–15 some of the traits of unfavorable-outcome dreamers (e.g., ideational impoverishment, presleep depression) also were associated with global ratings of dream unpleasantness. But others (anxiety, hostility) were not. Ratings of dream unpleasantness reflected not merely the presence of negative outcomes, motives, or feelings, but also their balance relative to positive outcomes, motives, and feelings. And, unlike any of those discrete observational dimensions, these ratings were significantly different for girls (lower) than for boys (higher). The typical girls' dream was on the pleasant side; the typical boys' dream occupied a neutral scale position. Thus relative dream unpleasantness was associated with psychological (Minnesota Multiphasic Personality Inventory) masculinity and with time spent with the father. It also was associated with interest, and increased interest, in the opposite sex, but with a self-absorbed and socially insensitive interpersonal style. Increases in dream unpleasantness since ages 11–13 were associated with clear signs of cognitive insufficiency and with entanglement in a less than supportive family environment. Waking apprehension, however, was *negatively* related to both absolute level of dream unpleasantness and increases in dream unpleasantness.

Thus at no age level did we find evidence that unpleasant REM dreaming (or less-than-pleasant REM dreaming) reflected children's waking anxiety or apprehension. Nor in general was there much evidence to suggest that such dreaming was engendered by unsatisfactory parent or peer relations. Unpleasant REM content often was associated with dream aggression, but we found little consistent evidence that unpleasantness dreamers were interpersonally aggressive. And yet, it will be recalled, dream unpleasantness—pleasantness was a stable child trait from ages 9—15. What *did* this trait reflect? More generally, why is it that some children seem to dream unpleasant dreams more often than others?

The most that might be said on the basis of our failure to find "expected" *behavioral* correlates of dream pleasantness—unpleasantness is that the hedonic tone of dreams must reflect mental attitudes or sets or, again, children's "world views." These world views must have some behavioral implications, but they may be more for the style than the discrete contents of children's actions. At ages 11—13, for example, pleasantness dreamers were spontaneous and unpleasantness dreamers were restrained, and that sort of open vs. constrained dimension also may be read into some of the correlates of pleasant vs. unpleasant dreams at ages 13—15. From the correlation of unpleasantness dreaming with "psychological" masculinity (at ages 7—9 and 13—15; directly pertinent variables were not in our test file in the intervening years), and from the fact that, throughout all six study years examined from ages 3 to 15, the typical boys' dream was less pleasant than the typical girls' dream, it appears that the world views associated with pleasantness vs. unpleasantness dreaming are related to sex roles. They may be part of what Bakan (1966) has called the communion-agency distinction (females are social and expressive, males are individualistic and repressive), a distinction that Trupin (1976) found to be reflected reliably in the girl vs. boy dreams of our study group at ages 11—13. Trupin's success, the failure of our correlational data directly to illuminate the meaning of hedonic-tone differences, and the argument advanced here converge on a methodological point of potentially great significance for further research on dreams: Dreams may better reflect (and be more highly correlatable with) global mental organizations than discrete behavioral traits. For our data the most important point may be that dream unpleasantness in adolescence is not so much an index of specifically adolescent upheaval as it is the logical extension of a mental organization that greatly predates adolescence.

I have proposed that the portrayal of the self becomes a more complicated process with children's accession to certain features of formal-operational reasoning. Consistent with that proposal, visuospatial measures presumptively related to dream construction, namely Block Design and Embedded Figures Test scores, predicted dreamer participation at ages 13—15. So too did dreamer age. The parental pattern was noncontrolling. At school the children themselves did not seem socially dominant, or even socially inclined, although they showed good social adaptation in the presleep period in the laboratory. Children high in active participation were low in dream unpleasantness ($r = -.70$), but the "world view" associated with dream self-participation was not unequivocally "feminine," nor was there a significant or marked sex difference for this rating variable. Increases in self-participation were significantly associated with Block Design proficiency and Embedded Figures Test speed-of-solution. It is interesting that, with the hypothesized appearance of a new *cognitive* hurdle in self-representation in dreams, the plausible *psychosocial* correlates of such participation observed at ages 11–13 (self-reliance, aggression) disappeared.

Once again the inventiveness or real-life distortion of settings and that of characters were significantly interrelated at ages 13–15 ($r = .54$). Both forms of distortion increased in adolescence, character distortion at full significance and setting distortion at marginal significance. Were these increases caused by children's heightened defensiveness against surging impulses? That is, is dream distortion defensively motivated? Our data say no. Setting distorters in adolescence showed no signs of personality dysfunction; they were peer oriented and increasingly interested in the opposite sex. They made few errors on the Embedded Figures Test. Increases in setting distortion also were associated with mental precision rather than imprecision; Torrance Figural Fluency, however, was a significant negative correlate. Behaviorally, children with increased setting distortion were relaxed rather than tense. Likewise, relaxed rather than tense children were high in character distortion, and increases in character distortion also were associated with an *absence* of anxiety.

Our data, then, seem to suggest that, in the "throes" of adolescence, an absence of anxiety permits dream inventiveness, rather than that the presence of anxiety necessitates dream distortion. For at least one form of setting (the vague or unclassifiable setting), we know that visuospatial representational skill also seems to be requisite to enhanced dream inventiveness. The data above suggest that mental precision, rather than uncontrolled associative fluidity, is another cognitive correlate of setting distortion. Setting distortion looks, then, to be more like a constructional success than a constructional failure. For character distortion, however, by early adolescence the role of cognitive variables seems to be minimal. But whatever the role cognitive maturation plays in mediating dream distortion in early adolescence, it seems clear that *adolescent increases in dream distortion do not index affective disruption or personal malaise. More generally, throughout childhood we found relatively little data to support, and relatively much data to refute, the hypothesis that dream distortion results from a motivated desire to evade unpleasant family/peer situations or from high levels of personal distress.*

Where, then, does distortion come from, and why is it such a hallmark of adult dream experience? Even in childhood distortion does not seem to be a reporting artifact. At the first point where our data permit us to speak unambiguously of the emergence of distorted settings and human characters (ages 5–7), it was brighter children and better waking stimulus reporters who made the most claims of dream distortion. Dream distortion at ages 5–7 seemed to emerge because it was possible, not because it was·demanded. Beyond those ages, however, individual differences in cognitive aptitude seemed to play less of a role in mediating dream distortion. And our data on intraindividual consistency fail to indicate even that dream distorting is a strongly stable personal trait.

Given the fact that, from early childhood (i.e., ages 5−7) on, children *can* create distorted dream representations, and the fact that to actually do so is not a highly stable trait, much less a trait with stable waking correlates, it seems most likely that whether a particular dream is highly distorted or not depends on the degree to which a distorted representation is appropriate to expressing a particular thought, feeling, or attitude and on the degree to which such a representation is consistent with an ongoing narrative sequence. These contingencies would not have to be predictable from the general kinds of memories or motives active in dream formation (as these can be discerned from waking observations), and they could be highly variable from dream occasion to dream occasion. Perhaps the better way to think of distortion, then, is not as a defensive motive but as an expressive means (Hall, 1966). In this respect, distortion is not *the* key to dream meaning, but rather a subsidiary problem of dream formation, one whose elucidation will follow more directly from studies of how thematic concerns are dealt with in dream formation (e.g., Foulkes, 1978c) than it will from research that focuses on distortion per se, as if it always were or meant the same thing.[19]

REM Ratios

As described in Chapter 5, for fifth-year dreams we calculated correlates of ratios at which content classes appeared relative to one another and of differences in rate of appearance of paired categories.

1 Correlates of the rate at which verbal acts occurred relative to gross locomotor acts in REM dreams were generally similar to those for verbal acts alone (e.g., intelligence, socialization, expressiveness), but, uniquely for the ratio, there was a positive association with expressional (linguistic) fluency. Interestingly, energy level and restlessness also predicted relatively *much*, rather than little, verbal activity in relation to gross locomotor activity. But so too did talkativeness.

2 Correlates of the rate at which sensory acts occurred relative to motor acts were, perhaps for reasons suggested in Chapter 5, largely uninterpretable.

3 Correlates of the rate at which cognitive acts occurred relative to motor acts were similar to those of the numerator of the ratio, and included numerous positive associations with cognitive-skill variables.

---

[19]This is not to say that, as individuation proceeds, there will not be some regularities observed in who distorts and who does not. Adult research (e.g., Foulkes & Rechtschaffen, 1964) suggests such regularities. But it can be questioned how much we stand to learn from them about how dreams in general are put together (Foulkes & Vogel, 1974).

4 Correlates of the difference in rate between external-world themes and body-state themes suggested that it was superficial sociability rather than social competence or cognitive mastery that predicted relatively much external-world dreaming.

5 Dreamers of male (vs. female) strangers had, as at ages 7−9, "tough-guy" characteristics (sullenness, disinterest in adult support, low psychological awareness). Interestingly, among girls alone it was the physiologically least mature children who had the most male as compared to female strangers. Or, to put it another way, postmenarcheal girls had relatively many *female* invented characters, suggesting that identity rather than heterosexuality was their more salient dream concern.

6 Correlates of the difference in rate between nonfamilial and familial known persons indicated that social experience outside the home was, unsurprisingly, a determinant of dreaming relatively often of extrafamilial acquaintances.

SEX DIFFERENCES IN REM DREAMS

At ages 13−15 our girls dreamed significantly more often than did our boys of three different classes of home setting: own home, unfamiliar home, and any home. For boys the relative incidence of residential settings had been halved since ages 11−13, while for girls it had increased slightly. Thus sex-role differentiation at adolescence in residential dreaming was achieved largely as a function of the reduced interest boys showed in residential settings.[20]

Only two other scoring-system categories significantly discriminated girls' and boys' REM dreams. There was more manual activity by nonself-characters in boys' dreams, and boys' dreams were rated significantly less pleasant than were girls'. The difference in dream pleasantness reflected continuing (but, taken individually, nonsignificant) sex differences in the dream incidence of antisocial interaction sequences, as well as the boys' greater incidence of negative dream emotion than of "happy" dream feelings. Since ages 11−13 the boys' dreams had become slightly less pleasant and the girls' slightly more so. It is interesting that, as judged by teacher ratings at school, boys had become less cheerful while girls had maintained a steady level of cheerfulness; this difference in waking-change scores between boys and girls also was statistically significant.

In line with my general comments on adolescence at the beginning of this chapter, it would be tempting to see the sex difference in dream pleasantness as reflecting the fact that early adolescence entails more distress for boys

---

[20]At marginal ($p < .10$, 2-tail) significance, boys' dreams also contained fewer nuclear family members (parents/siblings) than did girls' dreams.

than for girls. It is not clear, however, that this interpretation actually fits the data.

1 The typical boys' dream in early adolescence was not *un*pleasant; as already noted, it was hedonically neutral or balanced. And, as also has been noted, most boys' dreams in adolescence were experienced without any feelings whatsoever. Thus our finding is only that boys' dreams were less pleasant than girls' dreams, not that boys' dreams were generally unpleasant.

2 Since the difference in dream pleasantness at ages 13−15 is only a mild accentuation of a comparable (but nonsignificant) difference at ages 11−13, not much of it can be laid to specifically "adolescent" determinants.

3 This last observation suggests the possibility that the dream difference in adolescence reflects a positive developmental achievement, rather than any kind of developmental upset.

Specifically this difference probably indicates the increasingly divergent assumption by boys and girls of behaviors thought to be masculine and feminine. The process of sex-role acquisition, of course, greatly predates adolescence, but adolescence is the occasion for its solidification. The waking rating-change difference we observed may have been a token of such solidification, rather than of distress experienced by boys. The dream difference we observed may also have been such a token. The boys' "less pleasant" dreams actually may have been simply "more (stereotypically) masculine" dreams. That is, following sex-role norms, boys' dreams dealt more overtly with anger and hostility themes than did girls'. Our normative dream data suggest that this differentiation depends more on girls' suppression of aggression than on any newfound expression of it by boys.

The course of significant sex-role differentiation in children's dreams began at ages 7−9, with the differential use of like-sex vs. cross-sex peer acquaintances. This trend reached its zenith at ages 11−13. In adolescence there was no statistically significant difference in the use of male or of female peers in dreams, but, as already noted, this was *not* because girls were dreaming more often of boys or the boys more often of girls. Girls, in fact, were dreaming less often of girls but not more often of boys. And, as we also have seen, in early adolescence both boys and girls were dreaming less often of familiar persons in general, relative to unfamiliar persons.

A later-developing trend in sex-role differentiation in children's dreams began at ages 11−13, with indications that girls were beginning to eschew aggression themes, while boys were not. As we have seen, that trend persisted, in the form of a pleasantness−unpleasantness dream difference, into adolescence. And only in adolescence proper was another dimension of sex-role differentiation observed: Both in setting and characterization, girls remained "homebodies" in their dreams to a degree boys did not.

DREAMING OUTSIDE REM SLEEP

Non-REM vs. REM Dreaming

The only even minimal sign of growth in dream reporting/experiencing that we observed after ages 9–11 was the nonsignificant increase in NREM report rates in adolescence (pooled: 31% to 40%; median-subject value, 24% to 39%). If, as I have speculated, the most distinctively "NREM" types of experiences first become mentational possibilities with accession to formal-operational or abstract reasoning, then one might predict enhanced REM vs. NREM discriminability *along adult lines* in early adolescence. In fact, we believe we have some evidence of enhancement in such discriminability.

Table 8.2 indicates variables on which REM reports were significantly different from NREM (and sleep-onset) reports[21] at ages 13–15.

Once again REM reports were longer than NREM reports, contained more cognitive, feeling, and body-state content, and (as at ages 9–11 but not 11–13) had a higher relative incidence of specifically unfavorable outcomes for dream characters. However, in the few character and setting categories that significantly discriminated REM and NREM reports in early adolescence, there seems to be an indication that *distorted* elements are beginning to appear relatively more often in REM than in NREM reports. This pattern would conform to that found for adults (Foulkes, 1962; Rechtschaffen, Verdone, & Wheaton, 1963).

Perhaps an even more promising development, however, is the fact that for the first time visual acts by the dreamer were scored significantly more often in REM than in NREM mentation reports. For this same study group at ages 10–12, we previously had shown that this variable[22] was the only one reliably discriminating awakenings made at actual eye-movement bursts from those made during ocularly quiescent moments of REM sleep (see Chapter 2). The eye-movement-burst ("phasic REM") awakenings generally would be considered to be associated with the most distinctively REM-like of physiological processes, while the ocularly quiescent REM awakenings ("tonic REM") would be considered less REM-like and more NREM-like (Molinari & Foulkes, 1969). The present finding, then, suggests that in early adolescence our children were beginning to discriminate *REM-phasic* awakenings (all REM awakenings were made at an eye-movement burst) from *NREM-tonic* awakenings (REM bursts are absent in NREM sleep, of course, and the distribution of other REM-associated phasic events is very sporadic [Rechtschaffen, 1973]) in the same way that they previously had discriminated *REM-phasic* awakenings from *REM-tonic* ones. The results

---

[21]Two variables (dreamer verbal acts and anger for any dream character) were scored significantly more often in sleep-onset than in NREM reports. As will be discussed, these differences may reflect the enhanced "dreamlike" quality of sleep-onset, but not of NREM, mentation at adolescence.

[22]Along with several of its derivatives: vision, either; sensory, self; sensory, either.

Table 8.2   **Differences in Dream Reports as a Function of Stage of Sleep**

REM vs. NREM	REM vs. Sleep Onset
Higher incidence/score in REM	Higher incidence/score in REM
Word count	Characters
Characters	Father
Known adult, Male	Mother
Stranger adult, Male	Parent, either
Stranger adult, Female	Parent/sibling, Male
Settings	Parent/sibling, Female
School, unfamiliar	Parent/sibling, any
Activities	Animals, any
Vision, dreamer	Settings
Any sensory, dreamer	School, unfamiliar
Any sensory, either	Classifiable, other
Verbal, other	Activities
States	Vision, either
Cognitive, other	Hearing, either
Cognitive, either	Any sensory, either
Any feeling, either	States
Hunger, dreamer	Excited, either
Hunger, other	Hunger, dreamer
Outcomes	Fatigue, dreamer
Unfavorable, other mediated,	Fatigue, other
dreamer	Fatigue, either
Unfavorable, other mediated, other	
Unfavorable, other mediated, either	
Unfavorable, any mediated, other	

are consistent with the hypothesis that it is only its greater susceptibility to the intrusion of phasic activation that distinguishes REM sleep from NREM sleep, and thus that NREM mentation should be discriminable from REM-phasic mentation in ways similar to those in which REM-tonic mentation is so discriminable.

In our ages 10–12 study, as also in all of our normative-year REM–NREM comparisons, the visual-imaginal quality of mental activity itself did not discriminate phasic and tonic awakenings. *Both* REM and NREM reports were dominantly experienced as sensory imagery. Rather, in that second-year study, and in the adolescent data, it was whether, *within* a visual-imaginal experience, the self-character was seeing events that was the discriminating criterion. In early development an apparent hallmark of sleep mentation associated with the phasic activity of REM sleep is that one can "see" through the eyes of a self-character participating in dream events as opposed to merely "seeing" the events that constitute the dream. Conversely, an apparent hallmark of early-adolescent "tonic" mentation is that one can see dream events but not in the role of participant in those events. The association of this inability to see through your own eyes as a dream character with an absence of preawakening eye movement is consistent with early (but now controversial) adult evidence associating dreamer visualization within the dream with eye-movement activity (Roffwarg, Dement, Muzio, & Fisher, 1962; cf. Jacobs, Feldman, & Bender, 1972).

Thus there was at adolescence some evidence that NREM and REM mental activity were becoming increasingly discriminable in ways predictable from comparable research conducted with adults. As discussed in Chapter 7, it does not seem likely that earlier failures to demonstrate selective discriminability along adult lines derived from report biases or confabulation of NREM reporting. Rather it seems likely that the form of mentational possibility within NREM sleep itself changes with cognitive maturation. In this regard, even early-adolescent NREM mentation can only be a way station on the path toward adult NREM mentational competence. Still lacking among the children's NREM reports are the specifically verbal, "thoughtlike" reports obtained on a minority of NREM awakenings from adults: for example, "I was thinking of tax exemption" (Foulkes, 1962). Presumably such reports might accompany a still further increase in the reporting of NREM mental activity toward the early adult years.[23] Another problem in establishing fully adultlike REM–NREM discrimination in early adolescence is, as we shall see, the fact that "typical" NREM mentation (fragmentary object imagery occurring outside a narrative context) seems at this point in development to "spill over" into REM sleep, as if there were an imperative to employ this new mentational possibility as widely as possible before reining it in to its apparently most naturally supportive environment: NREM sleep.

In early adolescence sleep-onset and REM dream scenarios no longer differed in their relative incidences of "physical" acts or of social interaction (motives/outcomes). In these respects REM reports no longer could be described as being more "dramatic" than sleep-onset ones. Unlike the situation at ages 9–13, in early adolescence REM reports were not longer than sleep-onset reports. In part this decreased REM vs. sleep-onset differentiation seemed to reflect real increases in the dreamlike (lengthy, active, interactive) quality of sleep-onset dreaming, increases that would help to account for the fact that adults' sleep-onset reports are quite difficult to discriminate from their REM reports (Vogel, Barrowclough, & Giesler, 1972). In part, however, the decreased discriminability of REM and sleep-onset reports along "dreamlike" dimensions also must reflect the decrease in the dreamlike quality of REM mentation in adolescence, a decrease I would presume, from adult data, to be temporary.

---

[23]Pivik and I (1968) found that Wyoming college students had a pooled NREM recall of 65%. Part of the difference between that figure and our children's 40% pooled NREM recall may, of course, reflect an educational-intellectual difference, which itself enhances the likelihood of merely "thinking" during NREM sleep.

Yet a number of other dimensions did discriminate the sleep-onset and REM reports of early adolescents. In general agreement with results at earlier ages, sleep-onset reports were less likely than REM reports to include body-state themes or potentially disruptive affect (and the body-state deficit in sleep-onset reports no longer can be attributed, as was possible at ages 11–13, to differences in report length). These results are convincing in their generality: To fall asleep, one must lose the sense of one's own body and not experience excitement. Intradream sensory activity (but not specifically self-sensations) also occurred less often in sleep-onset than in REM reports. Evidently REM mentation, despite its capacity for the portrayal of a wide range of highly "active" events, also retains a capacity not shared by sleep-onset mentation for the portrayal within the dream of more "passive" or "subtle" acts such as sensation. REM dreams contained significantly more settings that were either distorted or vaguely defined than did sleep-onset dreams (most "classifiable other" settings were rooms, corridors, or buildings whose larger function—commercial, educational, residential, etc.—could not be identified). REM reports also contained more family and animal characters than did sleep-onset ones. In general there was a low incidence of family members in children's sleep-onset mentation, both absolutely and relative to the representation of peers. This may have been situational: Children were with peers, and not family, in the presleep period in the laboratory. The implication would be that sleep-onset reports are more sensitive to immediate social stimuli and REM reports more sensitive to persistent interpersonal concerns.

Longitudinal Changes

As we have seen (Table 7.1), there were no nonartifactual longitudinal changes in children's non-REM reports from ages 9–11 to 11–13. From ages 11–13 to 13–15 there were some non-REM changes that cannot be interpreted as procedural artifacts, but that generally were consistent with comparable REM changes. For instance, one index of NREM character distortion (indeterminate-sexed stranger) increased significantly from late preadolescence to early adolescence. Since this index did not increase significantly for REM reports (or for the younger group from third-year to fifth-year dreams), there can be no question of a general scoring change; rather it seems most likely that less well-characterized NREM scenarios are being generated and/or recalled. From ages 9–11 to 11–13 there was a significant trend toward enhanced ascription to nonself-characters in REM dreams of subtle, mentalistic acts. Likewise from ages 11–13 to 13–15 there was a significant increase in NREM other-ascribed visual acts.

Along with increased REM character distortion in adolescence, there also was increased sleep-onset character distortion. The overall rating variable increase attained marginal ($p < .10$, 2-tail) significance, as did an increase in relative incidence of male strangers. An increased incidence of female strangers was significant. Interestingly enough, it was significant for boys alone but not for girls alone. The ascription of sensory acts to dream characters *decreased* significantly in adolescent sleep-onset reports; in this sense, increasing subtlety and mentalism seem *not* to be a sleep-onset developmental trend.

From ages 9–11 to 13–15 both sleep-onset and NREM reports increased, at marginal significance, in length (word count). There were significant NREM increases in setting distortion and manual activity. Only for sleep-onset reports, however, were increases in report length accompanied by significant increases in interpersonal activity (e.g., verbal, either; approach social, other and either). Sleep-onset dreams seem to have become more dramatic in a narrative sense in later childhood, while NREM dreams were moving in a somewhat contrary direction of increasing mentalism. The NREM increase in setting distortion suggests an increase in the sort of diffusely articulated dreams that Emily began experiencing at ages 12 and 13, and refutes the hypothesis that children first recall only their most distorted NREM mentation. These differential sleep-onset vs. NREM changes are, of course, consistent with the longer-run trajectory of each mentational class; as assessed for adults, NREM reports are relatively "thoughtful" and undramatic, while sleep-onset reports are mini-dramas. If there is one sense in which both NREM and sleep-onset reports were changing together from late preadolescence to early adolescence, it seems to have been in decreasingly literal use of familiar persons/places, that is, in increased dream distortion. This path runs parallel to one being followed concurrently in the elaboration of REM mentation.

Sex Differences

Boys' and girls' early-adolescent non-REM dreams differed in several ways that their REM dreams did. For example, in their REM dreams boys had significantly more other-ascribed manual activity than did girls and a nonsignificant superiority to girls in the incidence of male strangers. In their NREM dreams boys had significantly more manual acts (other, either) and more male strangers than did girls. Likewise in their REM dreams boys generally had higher incidences of dysphoric affect and interaction (thus significantly less pleasant dreams) than did girls. In their sleep-onset dreams boys had significantly more anger (either), feeling (either), attack social (other, either), other-mediated unfavorable outcomes (other, either), and any-mediated unfavorable outcomes (other) than did girls. Thus both NREM and sleep-onset reports showed similar relationships to dreamer sex as did REM reports in early adolescence.

Correlates

As we have already seen, NREM and sleep-onset report-rate correlates at ages 13–15 were such that we can again assume children's non-REM reports to have been credible ones. But what kind of child told what kind of non-REM report? As I did for ages 11–13 (see Chapter 7), here again I will report on personal correlates of those few non-REM variables (word counts, global ratings) that entered into our correlational study.

In early adolescence positive Wechsler verbal correlates were added to the indication of psychological health that characterized preadolescent correlates of NREM report length. That these cognitive correlates were verbal is consistent with the more verbal or "thoughtlike" quality of adults' NREM mentation (Foulkes, 1962; Rechtschaffen, Verdone, & Wheaton, 1963). Longer sleep-onset reports came (as did longer REM reports) from early adolescents of higher social-class backgrounds. These children were verbally active and competent, socially dominant, and seen by their teachers as emotionally expressive. Thus, from the point at which we first reliably could assess it, dream extensity as well as frequency in non-REM sleep seemed *not* to index psychological disturbance. Even the possibly more "elective" non-REM dream did not seem to arise as a means of coping with waking conflicts.

For neither NREM nor sleep-onset reports was there evidence that waking dysphoria predicted dream unpleasantness (but sleep-onset dreamers with unpleasant dreams were judged by their teachers not to be kind or considerate). Adolescent physical maturation was positively associated with sleep-onset dream unpleasantness, which may explain the breakdown of the pattern observed in preadolescence, where the unpleasantness of sleep-onset dreaming was associated with psychological health. Unpleasant sleep-onset dreaming also was associated with the amount of time children reported spending alone, suggesting both social isolation/withdrawal and opportunity for rumination.

Increase in Block Design skill (which was associated with REM active participation) predicted NREM active participation at ages 13–15. But rather more strongly than for REM active participation, it was also outgoing children who played major roles in their non-REM dreams, and there were no correlates of absolute levels of visuospatial proficiency with non-REM self-participation. Evidently within the simpler confines of non-REM narratives, there is less scope for the evolution of more cognitively complex forms of self-representation to interfere with waking–sleeping continuity in self-expression.

There was no evidence that either NREM or sleep-onset distortion (setting, characterization) was associated with personal distress. In fact, sleep-onset character distortion was favored by emotional expressiveness and an absence of tension and depression. For non-REM as well as REM dreaming, then, there seems to be little reason to believe that distortion (or inventiveness or novelty) arises in response to anxiety that the dreamer wishes to evade or deny.

Conclusions

For early adolescence we have seen much evidence that non-REM dreaming conforms to the same principles that guide REM dreaming. In terms of its longitudinal development, its relationship to sex of the dreamer and to time of night or ordinal position of awakening, and its correlation with waking variables, non-REM dreaming is much like REM dreaming. And while ordinary NREM dreaming and sleep-onset dreaming each have some distinctive features, features that in adolescence give signs of blossoming toward their ultimate adult forms, it still cannot be held that our data on REM vs. non-REM report discrimination support the claim that either form of non-REM mentation is "qualitatively unique." In each sleep stage the typical form of mental experience seems to be a somewhat unrealistic dramatic scenario. When narrative length, which still discriminates NREM from REM reports, is controlled for, as in our scoring system's rating variables, there seem to be no differences in the general form of mentation reported from REM sleep, NREM sleep, and sleep onset.

That this fundamental similarity among the programs driving the three kinds of sleep mentation may be in the process of breaking down in the face of further advances in cognitive and social maturation is an interesting adolescent development, and one calling for more intensive research on subsequent stages of non-REM mentational elaboration. But it is an equally interesting fact that the three forms of mentation seem to share so many features (and this fact reminds us that, scrupulously interpreted, adult research also indicates much similarity in the form of mentation across different sleep stages). Once we have accepted the reality of non-REM mentation and the general credibility of non-REM reports (and our data from ages 5−7 on point unequivocally to such reality and such credibility), then it obviously becomes a major problem of both dream psychology and cognitive-developmental psychology to trace out the differential evolution of mental activity in different stages of sleep. In the years to come students of adult dreaming and of cognitive development must rise to the challenge of refining and enlarging our understanding of what now appears to be an orderly ontogenesis not only of REM dreaming but also of non-REM dreaming.

STIMULUS INCORPORATION

There was no reliable evidence at ages 13−15 that my manipulation of children during sleep caused dreams or influenced ongoing dreams. However, some findings did suggest a differential NREM vs. REM sensitivity to the manipulation, with *NREM* mentation being the more easily influenced form.

The experimental procedures and judging practices were identical to those employed with the 7- to 9-year-olds. (As described in Chapter 5, the age 7−9 and 13−15 incorporation-night reports were judged together.)

I made 51 awakenings in REM sleep following body manipulation, 40 of which (78%) were associated with dream reports, and 51 awakenings in

NREM sleep following body manipulation, 21 of which (41%) were associated with dream reports. Report rates were in general agreement with those obtained on nonstimulation trials. Sixteen of 18 children studied had at least one postmanipulation report (the exceptions were Fred and Phil).

The two judges' overall net-incorporation estimates were, respectively, 1% and −2%, and neither judge demonstrated appreciable success with any individual judgment class (cotton, limb, water). Judge 1 was successful in only two of her six free-choice "certain incorporation" judgments (33%). Judge 2 was correct in five of nine such cases (56%), but was inferior to Judge 1 in her free-choice "uncertain incorporation" judgments (19%, vs. 36%), leaving the two judges, overall, with "success" rates of 35% and 30% (vs. 33% chance). Forced-choice judgment results were similarly unpromising: 36% success for Judge 1, and 50% success for Judge 2 (vs. 50% chance). Judge 2 saw 62% of 21 NREM reports more clearly related to the stimulation than their paired REM reports, while the comparable figure for Judge 1 was 48%. Overall, for the first time these results pooled across both judges suggested incorporation slightly more often in NREM than in REM sleep.

Qualitative data presented in Table 8.3 offer mild support for the hypothesis of better NREM than REM incorporation. Of the six reports both judges correctly matched with preawakening stimulation, four were NREM, representing 19% of the NREM reports available for judgment, and two were REM, representing 5% of the REM reports available for judgment. My own (stimulus-knowledgeable) judgments were more conservative than those of the outside judges. Knowing that I had stimulated Dick's hand, rather than his leg, I did not identify the movie-director dream as an incorporation (thus four of my five "incorporation" cases were for NREM sleep). Once again the erroneous "certain" guesses shared by both judges nicely illustrate the problems introduced by the baseline appearance of stimulus-related elements and by the fact that being stimulated can be incorporated even where the precise form of stimulation is distorted.

Overall, then, our data suggested that REM reports may be less susceptible, and NREM reports more susceptible, to stimulus influence at adolescence than in earlier years (ages 9−13). However, generalizing across sleep stages, evidence for reliable stimulus effects was nil. And as we have seen, that same conclusion generally has applied throughout our childhood observations. Some of the reasons why our stimulus manipulations may have been (or merely seemed) so relatively unproductive have been presented in Chapter 3, along with my reevaluation of the adult research that generated expectations of greater success for these manipulations.

Now that we have seen the whole range of developmental data on stimulus incorporation, however, it may be worthwhile to reconsider what our dominantly negative incorporation results do and do not mean.

1 They cannot imply support of the hypothesis that our children's dream reports were false accounts of their preawakening mentation. We have

Table 8.3 Judges' Consensually Correct and Consensually Certain Incorporation Judgments: Ages 13–15

	Judges Both "Certain"	One/Both Judge(s) Not "Certain"
Judges Are Consensually Right	*Sven:* Night 9, Awakening 3. A boy sits in a chair. Someone puts water on his neck (a water-NREM stimulation). N [a]	*Cissy:* Night 2, Awakening 1. Choosing houses: one has dust around it, like "cotton" from cottonwood trees (a cotton-REM stimulation). **A** *Donald:* Night 2, Awakening 2. Sweeping a great big parking lot with a broom (a limb-NREM stimulation). **M** *Clint:* Night 2, Awakening 2. Running through forests while hunting (a limb-NREM stimulation). **A** *Clint:* Night 9, Awakening 3. A cattle drive along the Mississippi River. A flood forces an evacuation (a water-NREM stimulation). **M** *Dick:* Night 9, Awakening 2. A movie director walks to a projector (a limb-REM stimulation). **N**
Judges Are Consensually Wrong	*Emily:* Night 9, Awakening 3. Cotton balls with gold braid on them, sitting on a table (a water-NREM stimulation; judged "cotton"). **N** *Patty:* Night 2, Awakening 3. Waking a little girl by shaking her (a water-REM stimulation; judged "limb"). **N**	

Reports judged = 61
"Certain" and right = 2%

[a] N = no visible response to stimulation (A = awakened by stimulation; M = moves during stimulation but does not awaken).

amassed too much other evidence in refutation of the hypothesis for the stimulus-incorporation data to imply this.[24]

2   It does not seem likely that our predominantly negative results simply reflect insensitivity of our judging procedure. In Chapter 3 I indicated some potential problems in our methods of analysis, but it seems unlikely that they have had major impact on our results. The ambiguity attaching to limb-manipulation judgments (arm? leg?), for instance, could not have affected water-manipulation judgments, and yet, in general, the judges' water guesses were no better than their limb guesses. Our judging methods were conceptually appropriate. The particular judges employed always proved to be sensitive, reliable judges of other dream and test materials. The two judges employed in our first-year analyses produced results generally comparable to those found with a second pair of judges in third-year analyses. Our problems do not seem to have been with the particular methods, or the particular judges, we employed.

3   Our results do support a conservative interpretation of the adult literature claiming relatively high rates of stimulus incorporation. In particular, they demonstrate the need for methodological controls largely or wholly lacking in many of the more widely cited adult studies.

4   I suggest that our results may imply that children do, in fact, at least sometimes find it more difficult to incorporate extrinsic stimulation into their dreams than do adults. I further suggest that there is a sensible reason why this must be so: namely, that the "incorporation" of a stimulus into an already ongoing narrative demands certain kinds of cognitive skills (e.g., simultaneously juggling and intermixing separate ideational trains) that are less likely to be held by children than by adults.

5   Finally, I want to suggest that developmental studies of stimulus incorporation need to be conducted in the context of knowledge of the background mentational possibilities of a given sleep stage. Thus, given the episodic nature of children's preoperational REM and concrete-operational NREM mentation, and children's general difficulties in entertaining several lines of thought simultaneously, one might predict that children's preoperational REM and concrete-operational NREM incorporations would have a relatively direct quality. The child's mind would, in effect, have the choice: to be inner driven or to be externally driven (but not both). Because at these ages and stages continuously peremptory narrative programming is absent, there is the possibility of

---

[24]For example, children's reports: discriminated sleep stages as do adults' reports; had predictable relationships to tonic vs. phasic physiology; had waking cognitive correlates suggesting their credibility; both home and laboratory, differed in ways highly similar to those observed for adults' home and laboratory reports, and so forth. Nor, having read Emily's dreams, would we want to consider them less than genuine, although she never "successfully incorporated" an experimental stimulus.

experiencing "dreams" that are nothing more than slightly elaborated "interpretations" of the external stimulus. There is a real sense in which the stimulus probably has "caused" the dream. Our preoperational REM "incorporations" (e.g., Christopher [Chapter 3] and Linda [Chapter 4]) have this interpretive quality. But as we have seen, even this kind of mentalistic response to an external stimulus seems less likely than some kind of physical response; presumably even the interpretation of a disturbing extrinsic stimulus demands mental effort and skills generally lacking in early childhood.[25] Our earliest plausible NREM "incorporations" (e.g., Patrick [Chapter 6] and Clint [Chapter 7]) also have an interpretive rather than incorporative quality.

The immediately succeeding stage of REM programming would seem to involve more capability for ideational elaboration, whether an idea is internally or externally generated. Thus our REM "incorporations" at ages 9–13 generally do more than account for the stimulus; they either use it as a take-off point in elaborating a narrative (e.g., Patty [Chapter 6]) or truly incorporate it into an ongoing narrative (e.g., Dick [Chapter 7]). But one is led to imagine from children's apparently declining use of external stimuli in REM dreaming from ages 9 to 15 that the peremptory quality of internally generated REM ideation is increasing over this time span. Presumably only the further development of cognitive skill will permit this increasingly strong penchant for continuous inner programming to be overridden occasionally, as it apparently is for adults, in the service of attending to external stimuli.

The immediately succeeding stage of NREM programming, on the other hand, would seem to involve much less capability for sustained ideational elaboration (hence the fragmentary nature of typical adult NREM reports) and a much less peremptory quality for the inner-driven ideation that now is becoming rather more continuous in its distribution. Thus, relative to REM "incorporations," our adolescent NREM "incorporations" were rather more frequent but rather less elaborated. They were, in fact, still largely "interpretive." One might explain further developments in NREM "incorporation," that is, the less than adequately documented "inability" of adult NREM dreamers to incorporate extrinsic stimuli, in terms of a late developmental enhancement of the peremptory nature of memory-driven ideation in NREM sleep.

Little more can be said of this line of post-facto reasoning than that it is consistent with the observations we have made of stimulus effects in childhood. It cannot be clear that it has generality, or that it is "correct." The claim I would like to make for it is only that it has the *form* of the kind of interpretation that ultimately will prove necessary to explain stimulus effects during sleep. Specifically, it: (1) acknowledges that stimulus-incorporation

---

[25] And for children's earliest REM mentation, there is the additional problem that it seems to be driven by peremptory body-state stimuli, which it does "incorporate."

depends on cognitive skill; (2) charts a developmental course of stimulus-effect possibilities consistent with the course of waking cognitive development; (3) allows for later and less complete application of cognitive-skill potential to NREM than to REM sleep; and (4) acknowledges that new stages of nocturnal mentational development can be double-edged swords, both permitting incorporation (because of accession to skill) and interfering with incorporation (because of increased distraction from ongoing applications of that skill to autogenous sources of ideation).

It is useful to remind ourselves that the "incorporation" of external (or body) stimulation should not be regarded as some sort of expectable, automatic outcome whose absence makes us suspicious. Rather such incorporation must depend on relatively complex cognitive skills, with the efficiency of the incorporation increasing in proportion to the efficiency of the cognitive apparatus. It also may be useful in the context of our generally (but not exclusively) negative results with the stimulus-incorporation paradigm to remind ourselves that, if the stimulus effect depends on the baseline mentational state, then studies of stimulus effects must have considerable potential for revealing baseline properties of ongoing mentation during sleep. I would hope that our results will stimulate rather than deter further research on stimulus effects on children's dreams, for I still think the paradigm to be a promising one. I would suggest, however, two modifications in the methods we have pursued here: (1) stimuli should be verbal; and (2) if the intention is to use the paradigm to model how the mind transforms, at various ages and in various sleep stages, its own typically internal sources of ideation, then it will be more appropriate to study what dream differences the stimuli reliably are associated with than to merely look for "incorporations" (i.e., relatively untransformed traces) of those stimuli.

EMILY'S DREAMS

At the start of her final study year, Emily was aged 14 years, 5 months, and was in ninth grade. She experienced menarche one week before her second night of study during this year. During her final study year Emily reported dreams on 13 of 15 REM awakenings (87% recall), on six of nine NREM awakenings (67% recall), and on two of three sleep-onset awakenings (67% recall).

Her *REM reports* were as follows:

1-1   I was getting ready to take a gymnastics lesson, and it was about in the middle of the country somewhere. And there was just a mat on the ground, and everybody that was going to take the lesson was standing around on the mat. I can't remember very much about it. [About how many people were there waiting?] About eight or ten. . . . They were women. I think some of them were older and some of them were about my age. [Was there supposed to be a teacher or leader?] Yes, but he wasn't doing anything, or she wasn't. [It was a woman?] Yes. [Do you take gymnastics?] I don't take it, but I went to a clinic for gymnastics (a couple of months ago). [In the dream, what was your role?] I was just standing there for a while. And I think I was talking but I don't remember what I was saying. [Who were you talking to?] I don't know. [Did you have any feelings?] I think I was kind of worried or excited, 'cause I was waiting for it to start and I was worried that it wasn't going to start on time, or something.

1-2 Somebody was throwing candy at a parade. But there weren't any floats or anything in the parade. They were just throwing them into the street, and I went out and got it. [Was there anybody or anything marching in the street, or was it just that candy was being thrown out there?] Just the candy. . . . I didn't know where it was coming from really. [Who was in the dream?] Just me, I guess. I was alone. [Where was this?] It was just on a street in Laramie, I guess. [Did you have any feelings in the dream?] No, I don't think so.

1-3 I was dishing some water out of the well with a ladle. I was going to give it to my friend, only she didn't want it. [What friend was this?] J———, who lives next door to me. [Where did all this happen?] It looked like it was . . . I don't know where. It just didn't have a setting. [Was there anybody else in it besides you and J———?] Yeah, I think one more person was in it, but I don't know who he was. He was standing around the well. [It was a he?] Yes. [Your own age?] Older, about middle-aged, I think. [About like your parents?] Yes. [Did you have any feelings?] No.

2-1 I had some sort of disease or something on my tonsils. And we didn't know what it was. And I was looking at them in the mirror and I didn't see anything at all. [Was there anybody else in the dream besides you?] No. [Where was this happening?] I don't know, in some house somewhere or something. [Did you have any feelings?] I guess I was kind of worried about the disease.

2-3 I was playing a game or something and I don't remember what kind it was or anything. All I can remember is that we had to hide behind somebody's room, to hide something behind somebody's room. And I don't know what it was. And after that was over, we went on a bike ride. We all rode down the hill on our ten-speeds (bicycles). [Who was "we"; who was with you?] My (younger) sister M———. [So at the end you were riding ten-speeds down the hill. Tell me a little bit more about this part where you were hiding.] All I remember is that we had to get something hidden behind these rooms or something. [Where did that take place?] I think it was at our house. [Do you remember whose room it was?] No. . . . We were just kind of hiding something. [Something that you were carrying or what?] Yes. [Do you remember what it was?] No. [How do you mean when you say you were trying to hide it? What were you doing?] I don't know. Going to put it somewhere where somebody couldn't find it. [Do you know who it was that was supposed to be looking for it?] No. [Was your house just the way it really is, or was it changed?] I think it was a little different . . . just like a regular house, only the rooms were changed around a little different. I don't remember much what the house looked like. [You thought it was your house though?] Yes. [When you were riding bikes, where were you riding them?] Down the hill. [By your house?] Yes. [Did you have any feelings?] I don't think so. [There was no feeling involved with this trying to hide whatever it was?] Not that I can remember.

3-2   I was at school and I was cleaning out my locker. And I had to bring my mom's gloves home, because I had took them to school and forgot to bring them home. And I had just remembered that I had to bring them home, so I was trying to find them. And then I found them and I took them out, and left. [Is this like anything that's ever really happened . . . you taking your mother's gloves to school?] Yes . . . a couple of weeks ago, I had to ride my bike to school and I didn't have any gloves, so I took hers because it was really cold out. [Did you have to look in your locker and find them and take them home? Is the dream true to that?] I was supposed to look in my locker, but I didn't. [That's in real life?] Yes. [So what happened? Did you ever get the gloves back?] No. [So this is something you're still supposed to do, find the gloves and take them home?] Yes. [Did this look like your school, or was it different in any way?] The same. [Was anybody else in the dream besides you?] No. [And the whole dream took place just by your locker?] Yes. [Did you have any feelings in the dream?] No.

4-1   I had a dream that I had to do a dance in front of a whole bunch of people. And I had different socks, and I had great big holes in the bottom of my socks. And I didn't know it. [But the other people could see them?] Yes. [Where was all this supposed to be happening? Where was the dance?] It was on a stage, kind of . . . a made-up place. There were a whole bunch of people that were in the show that were watching. I think it was before an audience too, but I couldn't see the audience. [Did you recognize any of the people that were there?] No. They were men and women. [No kids your own age? Just older people?] Yes. [Did you have any feelings?] No. . . . I felt embarrassed after I found out. [How did you find out?] I looked and I saw them (the socks).

4-3   I had this green-tipped pen and it was one of the kinds you can switch the needles on. And you had all these different colors and everything. And I was trying to figure out how to do it. And I didn't know how to do it. . . . My next-door neighbor was with me, N——— C———. [She's about your age?] Yes. . . . She's a close friend. [What was she doing?] She was just looking at the pen. [And you were the one who was actually working it with your hands?] Yes. [Where did you and

N——— seem to be in the dream?] I don't know. [Was it indoors or outdoors, or couldn't you even tell that?] I couldn't tell. [Did you have any feelings?] No. [Did you feel any way about not being able to figure out the pen?] I wasn't finished with it. I was still working. I think I knew how to do it. . . . N——— asked me what it was and I told her it was a pen. And she said, "That doesn't make any sense," 'cause she didn't think it looked like a pen at all. [What did it look like? Did it look different in some way that would make what she said be sensible?] Oh, it looked like a great big piece of pipe . . . about eight inches long. [OK. Tell me again a little bit more about what you were trying to do with it.] I was trying to put one of the pen things out so I could write with it, 'cause they were all inside. [Did it look like the points were retracted, and you were trying to get one out?] Yes.

6-2   I dreamed we were on a bus that was going to (state basketball) tournament, no, coming back from tournament. And then we were talking about the people that lost money at the tournament. [What were the details of the discussion?] We just said somebody lost some money, and somebody said somebody else did. [This took place inside the bus?] Yes. [Did it look like the bus you really came back on?] Yes. [Who was in the bus?] A bunch of girls. I don't know who they were exactly. I think they were people I knew, they just weren't recognizable. [So was the situation more or less like the situation you really were in when you came back on the bus (from state tournament)?] Yes. [You really came back with the conversation of people losing money?] No. [Who, specifically, was doing the talking? Were you doing any, or what?] Yeah, I was doing some and so was other people. . . . [What did you say?] I said somebody lost some money but I can't remember who. [In the dream you said, "I can't remember who"?] Yes. [Did you have any feelings?] No. [The lost money . . . was that a small amount or quite a bit or what?] I think it was like a small amount. [When you say "lost," do you mean like dropped a wallet in the street or something like that, or lost through betting?] I don't know. They just lost it. I don't know how.

7-2   I had a dream that my mom was going to a sewing-club meeting. And it was at our house, and she was getting everybody some coffee. [Were you in the dream?] No. [Where was the dream at?] In our living room. I think it looked pretty much the way it really does. [Who was in the living room besides your mom?] A bunch of her friends. . . . [Do they really belong to a sewing club that she belongs to?] Yes. [So this is fairly realistic?] Yes. [She was pouring coffee for them?] Yes. She was walking around the room. They were drinking their coffee and talking. [Do you remember anything that was said?] No. [Have you been at home when your mom has had these meetings and seen something like this?] Yes . . . a few weeks ago, I think. [Did you have any feelings?] No, I don't think so. [Can you think of any reason why you would be thinking of this?] No. [Do you sew?] Yes. [When's the last time?] About two weeks ago . . . a pair of pants. [For you?] Yes.

7-3   I was dragging around a great big bow, made out of ribbon. [Like a hair bow?] Yes. . . . I was pulling it around on the floor. [When you say "great big," what physical dimensions do you mean?] About five feet long, and the ribbon was a half an inch wide. . . . I think it was indoors. [Could you say anything more about what kind of place it was in?] No. [Was there anybody else there?] No. [In the dream, did you have any idea why you were doing this?] No. [When you say "dragging," do you mean pulling it behind you?] Yes. [Did you have any feelings in this?] No, I don't think so. [Can you remember anything else? Did this just seem to be a small part of the dream, or the whole thing?] I think it was just the whole dream.

8-3   I went up to the mountains somewhere. And there was a town in the country and there's a really fat lady who worked in a store there. And she had a bunch of pet dogs and a bunch of pet mice. And she let them run all over the neighborhood, and then she'd just call them, and they'd all come back to her. [Did this look like any place you've ever really been?] No. [What about this lady, did she look like anybody that you really do know?] No. [Was there anybody else in the dream besides you and her?] I don't think so. [Do you remember any part of the dream that showed you going up there, or was it just starting there without you knowing how you got there?] It was just starting there. [Could you describe the store for me?] All I could see was the counter. It was wood, and there was a cash register on it . . . (a) kind of old-fashioned (store). [What were you doing?] I went around and petted all the dogs. [Did you do anything with (the mice)?] No. [What about this thing about her calling them?] I can't remember what she called them, but she called them something, and they just all ran up and gathered around her. . . . I think there were three big dogs and the rest were little dogs. They were all the same kind, only different colors. The mice were just all the same thing. [Did you have any feelings?] I don't think so. [Do you have any idea why you might have dreamed this dream, where this scene of the fat lady with the animal friends might come from?] No. [Can you tell me anything more about the lady?] She had glasses, and she didn't remind me of anybody I know.

9-2   Something about an Indian. I can't remember anything else. [Could you see him?] Yes. [What was he doing?] I don't know. Walking. [Walking where?] I couldn't see. He had on an Indian suit, though. [This was an adult male?] Yes. [Was the Indian inside or outside?] Outside. [Was there anybody else in the picture besides him?] No. [Were you there, wherever he was?] I don't think so. [Did you have any feelings?] No. I don't think so.

Emily's REM dreams help to put the significant increase in unclassifiable settings between preadolescence and adolescence in a broader context. A number of her adolescent REM dreams seem, in fact, to be approximations of the relatively contextless, discretely imaged objects that she began to report from NREM (but not REM) sleep in late preadolescence: for example, in 1−2, a piece of candy thrown onto the street;[26] in 1−3, a ladle coming out of a well; in 2−1, her own tonsils; in 3−2, a locker at school; in 4−1, socks with holes in the bottom; in 4−3, the retractible, pipelike pen; in 7−3, the giant ribbon bow. In general, these adolescent REM images had more of a narrative context than did the objects in her late-preadolescent NREM reports 3−3, 6−3, and 9−3, but not much more. The contrast with the generally strong narrative, interpersonal quality of her third-year (and first-year) REM dreams is striking. Emily's fifth-year dreams clearly show some at least transitory movement away from interpersonal themes portrayed in synthetic story-line fashion and toward object-centered themes portrayed in more analytic images without the benefit of much supporting interpersonal imagery. Formally, it is as if those "kernel" incongruous elements that in late preadolescence generally played only a supporting role in Emily's manifest REM imagery, had, at least during part of her final study year, become elevated to the focal role in such imagery.

I have suggested that Emily's NREM object images in late preadolescence might have carried sexual-anatomical meanings and might have been related thematically to her increased interest in anatomy's role in her maturational destiny. Emily's adolescent REM reports offer, I think, striking contextual support for the hypothesis that her anomalous dream objects are body parts, and that the focus on body parts reflects her larger concern with her sexual identity. Specifically, at age 14½, she still awaited menarche. On her last experimental night of such anticipation, she dreamed: of being in the company of older women and peers, waiting for a physical exercise to begin and "worried" that it wasn't going to start on time (1−1); of a piece of candy flying, from no known source, out into the street (1−2); and of seeing herself dishing water out of a well, while a man waited at the side of the well (1−3). On her first experimental night following menarche, she dreamed of having a "disease" and of looking inside her body to verify that she was all right (2−1), and of her and her sister having something to hide behind somebody's room so that somebody couldn't find it—the dream was set at her own house, but "the rooms were changed around a little different" (2−3). In 3−2 she was emptying her locker, so as to find a piece of her mother's apparel. In 4−1 she was embarrassed appearing before older people, because her socks had "great big holes" in them. In 4−3 she was inspecting a retractible pen, but it was difficult to figure out; it seems to have been more like a piece of pipe whose mechanisms were "all inside." At least some of this imagery is strikingly "Freudian." It was elicited from a person

---

[26]This would have been a familiar image to children in Laramie. Several times a year there were civic or university-related parades through the university/downtown area, and adults riding on floats often threw pieces of wrapped candy for the children watching the parade to retrieve.

who was totally untutored in Freudian theory, but at a most appropriate point in her life, at about the time of the most significant landmark she had yet experienced in her development as a woman.[27]

But it is not appropriate to think of this imagery as "regressive," for we found no evidence of such imagery in early childhood. Rather the imagery in question seems to have depended on Emily's later developmental accession to analytic reasoning, as manifested first in her preadolescent NREM reports and then in her adolescent REM reports. Emily's use of object symbolism for body parts (i.e., Freudian imagery) depended neither on early-childhood sexuality nor on "primary-process" thinking, but rather on her application of analytical-abstract reasoning to some newfound concerns of adolescence. If some of the lexical terms in Emily's adolescent dream language were sexual (or Freudian), the language itself was formal-operational (or Piagetian). This, of course, suggests the inappropriateness of generalizing adult-level dream symbolism back to children's dreams. That we can think in certain ways in sleep may depend more on our current cognitive status than on our psychosexual history.

Following her fourth Year-5 laboratory night, Emily's REM dreams began to recapture their more characteristic interpersonal-narrative format. But it was not as if her dreams no longer served interests of feminine development; rather those interests once again were being conceptualized in less self- and body-centered ways. In 6−2 she reworked memories of a trip back from the boys' state high-school basketball tournament so as to introduce the idea of girls losing their valuables. In 7−2 she scarcely changed her recollections of a recent gathering, in which her mother and other female adult models enacted a conventional sort of woman's role. Dream 7−3 reverted to the object-centered mode: She dragged a grossly oversized feminine-style hair bow behind her. But in 8−3 a "really fat" (pregnant?) lady offered a demonstration of how to keep your personal animals under voluntary, "old-fashioned" control; Emily "petted" the larger and more sympathetic of them; the fat woman simultaneously demonstrated how to get apparently affectionate beasts (males?) to gather around you, beasts of a sort perhaps also portrayed in the stereotyped male-savage image of the very fragmentary 9−2.

Emily's adolescent *sleep-onset dreams* were as follows:

4-2 They were singing "Silent Night." A bunch of people were singing "Silent Night." [Could you see them?] Not really. [It was more like just hearing?] Yes. [Did you have any idea who these people were supposed to be?] I think they were kids, but that's all I know . . . about my own age. [Did you have any idea where this was supposed to be

---

[27]Incidentally, the home-collected dream of one of our younger male subjects (Christopher) on the occasion (at age 11) of his first nocturnal emission was that "I threw up, but just water. I threw it up out of a tall building."

happening?] No. [Did you imagine yourself as part of this situation or weren't you in it?] I wasn't in it. [Did you have any feelings?] No. [Can you remember specifically the words they were saying, the point they were at in the song?] . . . they were singing "sleep in heavenly peace."

6-1 This guy who was pole vaulting. I don't know where it was or anything. [What could you see?] There was this guy and he was holding a pole and he was running down toward a thing, ready to vault. [Who was the guy?] I don't know. I think he was about 25 and he had pretty long hair. I didn't know what he looked like. [Was there anybody else in the dream?] No. I wasn't in it. [Have you watched anybody pole vaulting recently?] No. [Did you have any feelings?] No.

Again, sleep onset for Emily was associated with "dreamlets" or dream sketches rather than with fully elaborated dreams. The content of these adolescent dreamlets was, however, somewhat less banal than it was in her first-year sleep-onset reports. Report 4−2, dreamed a week before Christmas, had a message that was appropriate both seasonally and with respect to the sleep period from which it was retrieved. Sleep-onset report 6−1 presents an image with obvious psychosexual interpretive possibilities. It is interesting that this report's male symbolism was introduced the night on which her REM reports seemed to be shifting from their earlier preoccupation with feminine anatomy toward a more heterosexual/interpersonal view of sexuality (REM report 6−2 told of girls who lost their money at a boys' basketball tournament). It would seem from Emily's late-preadolescent and early-adolescent sleep-onset reports that her sleep-onset mentation had, since her first study year, become somewhat more susceptible to organization by significant feelings and interpersonal-motive dispositions. However, the nature of the sleep period in question seemed to impose a continuing constraint on the degree of elaboration these themes could receive at sleep onset. Thus, as our group statistical data also suggested, sleep-onset reports had become more dreamlike by adolescence, but not fully dreamlike on the REM model.

Emily's adolescent *NREM dreams* were as follows:

3-1 I was making some cookies or something, and I was using a certain pattern to make them with. [What do you mean by "pattern"?] Well, recipe. [Was there anybody else in this besides you?] No. [Where were you?] I was outside, and I was at the top of a hill and I was going down. [. . . Making cookies as you were going down the hill?] I wasn't doing it as I was going downhill, but I would make the cookies then I'd go down the hill. And I'd do some more on the cookies, and go down the hill again. [Making the cookies, where were you?] I'm not sure. I think I was on the hill. [What did you see?] I was outside and I was on a hill, and all the time I was going down the hill. And there was a table with cookies and cake and stuff on it. [You said you were making them according to a pattern or recipe. Was there like a book or a card or

something? Or why did you say that?] I think there was a card. [Did
you have any feelings?] No.

5-2 A package of green paper napkins. [You could see them?] Yes. [Where
were they?] I don't know. [Were there any people? Was there any
action?] No. [Just green napkins?] Yes. I was just looking at them. . . .
[Did you have any feelings?] No.

6-3 I was dreaming about a piece of pineapple. All I could see was a chunk
of pineapple and it had skin on it that looked like bark off a tree. [Could
you see anything besides the pineapple?] No. [Were there any people?]
No. [Were you in it?] No. [How big a piece was this?] About two
inches long. [Was this like a fresh pineapple or a canned one?] It was a
fresh one. [Did you have any feelings?] No.

7-1 We were, I was jumping back and forth across the beds. I could see a
room and a pair of beds in there, and a lady, watching us. [Who was
"us"? Who was doing the jumping?] I don't know. I can't remember.
[Do you know who the lady was?] No. [Where were you doing this?]
I'm not sure. . . . I think at home or something. [Do you have a room at
home where you have two beds like this?] Yes. My little sister's. . . .
[Did it look like that room?] Yes . . . the same general thing. [Did you
have any feelings?] No. [Any feeling that it was enjoyable?] No. [Do
you have any idea at all (about the) somebody else . . . doing this with
you?] I thought somebody else was doing it. I don't know who it was. I
think it was a girl. . . . I'm not really sure.

8-2 I was having a box of . . . [Pardon?] I was having a box. [What do you
mean, you were having a box? Where were you having it?] I was in a
box, a small box. [Would you describe it for me?] It was a small box,
the kind animals were in, and it had holes in the side. And the top was
open so you could get in or get out of it if you wanted to. [Where was
this?] I don't know. [Was anybody else in the dream?] No. [Did it seem
like you were in the box because you wanted to be there, or was it
against your will?] I think it was because I wanted to be there.[28]

9-3 Some cotton, with a bunch of gold braid around it . . . spread out on the
table. [Cotton like cotton cloth, that you would sew with, or cotton like
you use in make-up and things like that?] Like the second kind. [Cotton
like cotton balls?] Yes. [With gold braid around it?] Yes. [Were there
any people?] No. . . . I didn't think I was there. I just looked at it. [Did
you have any feelings?] No.

The remarkable shift noted in the formal quality of Emily's NREM
mentation between age 10–11 and age 12–13 was sustained, even extended,
in her adolescent NREM reports. Reports 5–2 (green napkins), 6–3

---

[28]This awakening interview was not tape-recorded. Immediately following each nocturnal
interview, I played back the tape to verify that the interview had been recorded. Where it had
not been, I then dictated my recollection of that interview. According to my notes, this account
can be considered an almost verbatim rendition of the original interview.

(pineapple), and 9−3 (cotton with gold braid) described contextless or almost contextless object images. There was no narrative quality to these reports at all. There was no interpersonal context for the objects, and no dreamer intentionality with respect to them. They were just "there." Once again these were relatively "late"-night NREM reports. Emily's most clearly narrative NREM reports were those from awakening position 1: making cookies, alternating with descending a hill (3−1) and jumping from bed to bed (7−1).[29] Report 8−2 was an intermediate case: It was largely object centered (the cagelike box with holes in the side and a lid permitting access and egress), but Emily did imagine her presence in the box.

Also once again, particularly now given the context of Emily's adolescent REM imagery, it is difficult not to assign anatomical significance to at least some of her adolescent NREM object imagery. The cyclicity of making cookies/running down/making cookies, and so forth (3−1), suggests the creative and degenerative phases of her own newly operative reproductive cycle. Female cyclicity also is suggested in the actions of 7−1. Napkins (5−2) also may plausibly be related to the same phenomenon; "green" is of uncertain denotative value, but it is consistent with her own REM imagery (in 4−3, the pen/pipe with the hidden mechanism had a green tip). The absorbent cotton of 9−3 and the animal-cagelike box with holes in the side of 8−2 are obvious candidates for inclusion in this same symbol class. The pineapple with an outer bark covering is somewhat more obscure, but it is reminiscent of Emily's third-year NREM report 6−3 in which an extra-hard fruity (coconut) layer was superimposed on an inner shell.

In fact, this is but one of several instances in Emily's total dream series in which recurrent "figures of speech" seem to have been employed. For instance, the similarity of her first-year dream 8−3 and her third-year dream 2−3 already has been noted. In both an attempt was made to put rowdy/lively creatures to sleep in a house, but the playfulness of others interfered with this intention; her third-year REM dream 4−3 and sleep-onset dream 5−3 both used "choker" as a central symbol. In these cases, as in the NREM recurrence just noted, it is the fact that related, plausible interpretive themes can be formulated for the paired dreams that suggests the "figure of speech" metaphor. It does not seem to be merely that an object class or situation is put to contextually different usage in otherwise unrelated dreams.

One of the objections to Freud's ideas about dream symbolism, most urbanely discussed by Hall (1953), is that it is not clear why the same referent object should have so many different symbols. In part, as Hall demonstrates, it may be that different connotations of the denoted referent are being entertained. But given Emily's apparent tendency to employ certain figures of speech in her dreams, it also seems possible that, within a

---

[29]Compare the stereotyped alternation/repetition style of her brother's NREM reports (Chapter 5, n. 25).

given person's dreamlife, particularly over a relatively brief span of her or his life, there may not exist such a fluid set of possibilities for dream symbolism. Rather one may be committed to employing a relatively limited set of current or habitual metaphors for any given referent object or situation. At least over such spans of time or development, each particular dreamer may speak an individualized dialect. The "language" of dream symbolism, if it is a language at all, can be infinitely creative only at the combinatorial level, not at the lexical one.

There are several important implications of this line of reasoning for conduct of dream research. It indicates that, as Hall (1966) and others have suggested, the most reasonable way to interpret (assign meaning to) individual dream images is through the examination of extended dream series from the same dreamer. But these suggestions often have focused on the utility of this approach for the piecemeal analysis of individual dreams. This approach may, however, open another, theoretically more exciting possibility: that one could formulate lexicons for individualized dream dialects and, in this way, begin more seriously to develop the empirical implications of the position that dreaming is a language (Foulkes, 1978c). If dreamers do speak different dialects, or even languages, then it makes little sense to approach these dialects or languages by attempting to obtain tiny samples of each. Clearly the anthropological linguist would prefer to settle down for a while in some one "linguistic culture" and become thoroughly familiar with the patterns of its surface expression. The linguist then would look for recurrent symbols, and for the contexts in which they were being employed, in an attempt to begin to formulate a systematic description (grammar) of that language. She or he then might want to look at a second, possibly related "linguistic culture" in the same vein, and so on. That the concrete symbolism of individual dreamers may not be infinitely creative—that it in fact may use a limited number of recurring objects or events—makes this approach seem feasible. The traditional group-sampling methods of experimental psychology may simply be *scientifically* inappropriate in any serious attempt at understanding dreams.

SUMMARY

In clinical psychiatry, the field in which the study of dreams has for so long been embedded, the term "adolescence" is likely to conjure up images of recrudescent sexuality, emotional turmoil, social disorientation, and failed identity. For academic cognitive psychology, the behavioral and experiential changes associated with adolescence are likely to be pictured less as primitive disruptions and more as broadened opportunities: One can abstract, one can analyze, one can reason as philosopher, scientist, and poet. It is a mark of the extent to which dreams have been misclassified in the scientific order of things that our empirical observations on dreaming in early adolescence have dovetailed so nicely with the cognitive scientists' portrait and so poorly with the psychodynamicists'. This is not to say that adolescents' dreams do not reflect their sexual maturation, sex-role development, and enhanced anatomical curiosity; they clearly do. But almost as compellingly as in much earlier dream development, when operational thinking and programmatic narratizing became forces on the dream scene, so too in adolescence many of the most important features of, and changes in, dream content seem to depend on cognitive maturation. At the same time, in the "deep" and involuntary ruminations of their dreams, early adolescents give us scant evidence of cataclysmic changes in what they think and feel about themselves and their worlds. Our data join with those of other researchers in characterizing adolescence as springboard, rather than watershed, and they argue strongly for cognitive-developmental analyses of dreams, not merely in early childhood, but well into the second decade of life.

PART 3

Two Summary Essays on Dream Development

CHAPTER 9

Dreams and the Growth of Mind

DREAMING AND COGNITION

The development of REM dreaming follows a course parallel to the better-documented and well-known stages of waking cognitive maturation. That is the major finding of our study. From the perspective that dreaming *is* a cognitive act (the reorganization of memories, generally in a narratized imaginal form), the finding is unexceptional. However, from the perspective of traditional dream psychology, which never has assimilated fully the implications of the fact that dreaming is cognition, our data constitute a valuable empirical demonstration of the centrality of this fact to the understanding of dreams.

In the case of children's dreams, we have shown that their content seems to be more a function of what children are able to portray symbolically than, as traditional dream theory would have had it, of what their anxieties, conflicts, fixations, and so forth force them to portray symbolically. Developmentally dreams reveal more about the unfolding of human representational abilities than they do—or can do—about the sources or meanings of children's waking behaviors. This is so because, until children are reasonably capable of reflecting on and symbolically elaborating on their own waking experiences and behaviors, they must remain incapable of dreaming effectively about these experiences and behaviors. Our data, as well as (waking) cognitive-developmental theory, suggest that effective nocturnal self-reflection and symbolic self-expression generally cannot occur until the consolidation of concrete-operational reasoning.

From the perspective of the discipline of cognitive psychology, or of cognitive science more generally, our data constitute a powerful demonstration of the obvious, but almost invariably overlooked, linkage of dreaming with other cognitive processes. They have illustrated that the growth of dreaming proceeds in an orderly manner that is both reminiscent of and temporally associated with the unfolding of other complex mental operations.[1] And yet one looks in vain in most texts of cognitive or cognitive-developmental psychology for acknowledgment of dreaming's status as an apt and potentially revealing cognitive subject matter. It seems to be the peculiar fate of dreaming that, as Freud (1900) quoted Anatole France, *"les savants ne sont pas curieux"* (p. 93). Why?

One can think of several reasons why dream study has escaped the serious attention of, and even has proven capable of mobilizing the antipathy of, cognitive scientists. Dreaming lies outside the research paradigms currently favored by cognitive psychologists; the study of dreaming must deal with motives (conation) as well as with cognition, and it is not well suited to the prevailing form of input–output analysis in which inputs are under strict experimental control. The sources of dream imagery often seem to be self-referential representations with strong motivational properties, and they most often only can be guessed at after the fact.

But to recognize that dreaming cannot be cast within the mold of today's favored information-processing paradigm is not to say that dreaming is not cognition. The exclusion indicates a limitation of the paradigm, not of the subject matter (Estes, 1978). Before "information processors" transformed the psychology of higher mental processes into "cognitive psychology," dreaming was, in fact, generally acknowledged as an integral subject matter of mentalistic psychology (e.g., Werner, 1948; Vinacke, 1952). It may be objected that this is precisely the point: that recent advances in cognitive science have stemmed from rigid adherence to newer and more rigorous observational paradigms and from the simultaneous sloughing off of subject matters or problems ill suited for study in these paradigms. The objection obviously has some substance. One cannot help but be impressed by recent achievements that have made cognitive psychology one of the most productive and promising areas in the behavioral sciences (Simon, 1980). Clearly the line must be held: Commitment to scientific rigor in model building must be retained if cognitive science is to continue its productivity and to fulfill its promise.

But where shall that line be drawn? Not, I would hope, so tightly as to exclude dreams and other pervasive if heretofore ill-studied forms of spontaneous fantasy. Dreaming, we now know, comprises a surprisingly large part of what we do with our minds, and the potential to narratize dreams is as surely wired into the human brain as is the potential to speak language. Dreaming must be a central focus of our attempts to understand the human mind and to trace mind's dependence on brain activity. It would be ironic if the information processors were now to draw their wagons in so

---

[1]It remains to be demonstrated, however, that cognitive "staging" reliably characterizes individual children's dream maturation and that it is reliably associated on an individual basis with shifts in waking cognitive development. Patricia Maykuth, a Ph.D. candidate at Emory University, now is examining our data to see if, in fact, they offer these kinds of support for a cognitive-stage model of dream development.

tightly as to exclude dreaming from the possibility of scientific study in precisely the same fashion as, for a substantial portion of this century, an arrogant behaviorism also excluded subject matters central to understanding human nature—subject matters including both dreaming and those topics now so much in favor in contemporary cognitive science.

It is *not* true that spontaneous fantasy cannot be studied following rigorously empirical methods. We can make meaningful observations of dream differences consequent to independently assessed differences in dreamers' knowledge bases and neuro-cognitive abilities. We can search for the story grammars that characterize dream narratives. We can perform computer simulations of dream generation. We can study reliably and systematically the associative contexts to which dream elements seem to be related and can attempt to establish the bases on which these elements have been recruited for dream representation and the transformation they have undergone in achieving such representation. In the dream's treatment of external stimuli, we have an experimental model for studying both stimulus selection and stimulus transformation in dream formation.

Nor is it true that, in using such observations to formulate, refine, modify, and discard models of dream processes, we would be deviating in any significant way from current methods in mainline cognitive science. All mind study is indirect, or inferential. From relevant observation we try to imagine how mind might best be conceptualized as operating in a given situation. Our model suggests further observations that either conform to it, refute it, or suggest necessary modifications of it. I do not see that this process need work out much differently in the modeling of dream generation than, for example, in the delineation of "semantic networks" or in the modeling of processes of language production. Surely it is not beyond human ingenuity to specify and to collect empirical observations relevant to the formulation of models of dreaming. And it should not place too great a strain on the goodwill of cognitive scientists to tolerate, abet, and participate in the formulation of such models, when they so clearly are relevant to many of their own daily interests (e.g., imagery, the organization of semantic and episodic knowledge, processing of external stimuli, narrative generation and comprehension, amnesia, etc.).

A second reason for cognitive psychology's oneirophobia probably derives from the unfortunate consequences of organized psychology's last attempt to cast dreams beyond the pale: the implicit assignation, during behaviorism's heyday, of dreams to psychoanalysis and other quasi-scientific or frankly unscientific systematizations of "clinical wisdom." Clinicians' continuing pretensions to deeper and superior forms of knowledge than mere scientists could understand or mere empiricists could study most likely have constituted a major stumbling block to the acceptance and study of dreams by cognitive scientists. If so, dream psychology has double impetus to cleanse its own house by renouncing dominant reliance on anecdotal clinical impressions and on hopelessly archaic clinical dream theories—not only because its own progress demands it, but also because it may help to encourage other cognitive scientists with their unique points of view and knowledge to join in the effort better to understand the dreaming mind.

But such collaboration should not be conducted along a one-way street, or at the cost of rejecting those features of dream psychology's heritage that realistically reflect properties of dream cognition that are less visible in the kinds of cognition studied or that historically simply have been ignored by other cognitive scientists. Classical dream theory is not *all* bunkum, and a rush to scientific respectability would be ill-advised were it to entail the disowning of substantial insights that have evolved in the clinical dream tradition. It is the cognitive psychologists who have ignored the role of meaningful self-reference in mental functioning (but cf. Bower & Gilligan, 1979) and who have striven so valiantly to separate mind from motive and feeling (but cf. Zajonc, 1980). These luxuries rarely have been permitted to students of dreams. It is the cognitive psychologists who need to be reminded of the value of naturalistic and descriptive analyses of typical cognitive performances as well as of contrived experimental analyses of maximal cognitive attainment (but cf. Neisser, 1976). For all its many flaws, dream study has a much better history of conceptualizing minds-within-persons and minds-within-bodies than minds as disembodied, depersonalized abstractions. It has strength precisely where cognitive science has weakness, just as cognitive science has strength precisely where dream study has weakness. These are ideal conditions for collaboration rather than for annexation.

My hope is that the data presented herein may lay some of the groundwork needed for such collaboration. Not only have our data indicated the dependence of dreaming on general cognitive development, they also have contributed to clearing away some of the clinical rubble that heretofore has impeded communication between cognitive science and dream psychology. An ancillary hope is methodological: that dream psychologists will see that the purgation requisite to progress in their field is better accomplished by comprehensive, long-term empirical research than by theoretical argument.[2]

---

[2]At least in the United States, there now is reason to doubt whether reward systems of academic research institutions or governmental grant agencies will continue to provide suitable institutional encouragement for this kind of basic research, with its "impractical" goals and its long delays between program initiation and program conclusion. An additional impediment is the increasing meddlesomeness and effrontery of various government-instigated research review committees. These committees serve little or no useful societal function, but they present clear peril, in my judgment, both to academic freedom and to the future of the scientific study of human behavior.

REPORTS AND EXPERIENCES

There may be one possibly fatal flaw in concluding that our data indicate that dreaming follows a developmental course dictated and constrained by that of general waking mental ability. That is that our data may refer only to dream reports, and not to dreams as children actually experience them. It is the perpetual bane of dream psychology that one can study only verbal reports of the experiences of primary interest, not those experiences themselves. Careful analysis of this problem (Rechtschaffen, 1967) has indicated that it constitutes no general impediment to meaningful research on dreams. However, I have often encountered the objection that our findings on early childhood dreaming must reflect report limitations rather than dream limitations. It is suggested that even very young children have vivid and richly imaginative dreams, but that they simply cannot (or will not) describe them very well to others. It is suggested, further, that what our longitudinal data on changes in dream experience actually indicate are changes only in how well children are able to remember and describe what is a relatively constant internal process. Thus, the argument concludes, it should be no surprise that we have found "dreams" to conform to principles of waking cognitive development, for what we in fact have studied is not "dreaming" at all, but only waking cognitive processes of memory and verbal description.

Because our data *do* consist of verbal reports of dreams rather than of dream experiences per se, this report-artifact interpretation of our data cannot be proven erroneous. It can, however, be demonstrated to be highly implausible.

For the report-artifact interpretation to be correct, it would be necessary to show that children's descriptions of constant and known stimuli presented to them in wakefulness improved over time in ways that paralleled their apparent growth in dream competence. Not surprisingly, we were able to collect data showing just that. Specifically, in the first and fifth years of our project, all children then in experimental service were administered a "Description Test" in which they were asked to describe projective-test (Thematic Apperception Test, Children's Apperception Test) picture cards (either when physically present or from memory). In both groups children reported significantly more wholistic stimulus interpretations, more large and small details of stimuli, and fewer elaborative elements not actually present in the stimulus cards at the time of their retest than at the time of their first test. Also, in a midstudy (Year 3) comparison, we were able to show that older-group children gave significantly longer and more detailed reports of a film stimulus (Ray, 1947) than did our younger-group children. These data are consistent with the report-artifact hypothesis and lend to it whatever degree of plausibility it has, but they are far from sufficient to confirm it.

To confirm the hypothesis one also would want to demonstrate that individual differences in dream reporting were related to individual differences in waking-stimulus reporting, and that those correlations existed to the exclusion of other correlations supportive of the counterhypothesis that dream-report differences reflect dream-experience differences. As my discussion in Chapters 3–8 already has indicated, these additional conditions generally were *not* met in our data. Specifically: (1) Description Test measures correlated significantly and positively with REM report rates only at ages 7–9 and at ages 13–15, and then only in the presence of simultaneous correlations of visuospatial or integrative representational/ constructional skills with REM report rates; (2) for younger-group children (for whom the report-artifact hypothesis is more relevant), Description Test measures did *not* predict increases in REM report rates, while visuospatial processing skills did do so; (3) while there was an indication that report skills or habits may have played some role in mediating individual differences in REM report length at ages 3–7, at ages 7–9, where there were significant increases both in REM report rate and in REM report length, it was Piagetian stage measures and Torrance figural-creativity measures, rather than measures of descriptive abilities, that predicted both REM report length and increased REM report length.

There are, in addition, other embarrassments within our description-testing data for the report-artifact hypothesis. These include: (1) although the older group had significantly better Description Test performances at ages 13–15 than at ages 9–11, they did not report REM dreams significantly more often nor at greater length at ages 13–15 than at ages 9–11; (2) our younger-group children at ages 7–9 had significantly *better* Description Test scores (more large details, fewer stimulus elaborations) than did our older-group children at ages 9–11, although their REM report rates were significantly *lower* than those of the 9- to 11-year-olds. Presumably both of these observations indicate that repeated exposure to the demands of our study may have facilitated performance in verbal description, but it is noteworthy that such facilitation was not accompanied by enhanced REM dream reporting.[3]

But the major problem with the hypothesis that young children are having fanciful and imaginative dreams that they are incapable of describing is a conceptual one. The problem is that the hypothesis does not explain how children could be capable of *generating* such dreams. The hypothesis's

---

[3]The Description Test and film-report tasks provided data germane to another report-artifact hypothesis that might be applied to young children's dream reports: the hypothesis that children make up dreams in the report situation rather than describe dreams they have experienced. Our 3- to 5-year-olds did not elaborate (confabulate) Description Test stimuli at all often. The same was true in Year-3 film reporting. In neuropsychological testing, Williams (1970) has noted that "Children are less inclined to confabulate when pressed for recall than are adults. They tend, instead, to remain mute" (p. 51). Flapan (1968) also found that children committed relatively few errors of confabulation in reporting stimuli. What was reported was accurate, even if it was, by adult standards, often incomplete.

implicit assumption seems to be that dreaming is a perceptual process, and that since children can see the waking world in ways perhaps not grossly dissimilar to our own, they also ought to be able to "see" their dreams much the way we "see" ours.

Dreaming, however, is no kind of "passive seeing," it is "active imagining." Neurally and cognitively, these are separate functions. Late-adventitiously blind persons may be able to imagine visually, even if they cannot see (Kirtley, 1975); persons with specific cognitive deficits may be able to see perfectly well, but be unable to dream visually (Kerr, Foulkes, & Jurkovic, 1978). Literally, of course, the conditions of sleep make it impossible for dreaming to be any kind of perception. Dreaming is a mental-imaginal process; it can be nothing else. In asking, then, what kinds of dreams young children (or animals) might have, we need to consider not what they can accomplish perceptually but how well they can think. It seems highly unlikely that at any point in cognitive development dreams could be generated that would be *more* complex, organized, or creative than one would guess from children's general level of waking cognitive maturity. It has been amply demonstrated that young children's conceptual organization—their thinking—is much more primitive than our own (Flavell, 1963). It makes no sense, then, to imagine that children function as conceptually sophisticated adults in their sleep (dreaming vivid, well-organized dreams), but revert to childish insufficiency only when they awaken (and fail to report or adequately to report those dreams). The report-artifact hypothesis now under consideration is absurd, because it provides no plausible explanation as to how young children could be able to create highly organized narrative dream imagery. It forgets who it must be who is making those vivid, imaginative, but later forgettable, dreams.

It is the contrary hypothesis that is plausible—the hypothesis that states that, hand in hand with increases in verbal reporting skill and in general intellectual ability, there also must be genuine increases in the complexity of actual dream generation. Our waking-test data indicate developmental increases not only in the ability to verbally describe waking-test stimuli but also in the sorts of imaginative and representational operations that must be involved in the actual generation of dreams. In my discussion of Block Design skill (see Chapter 8), I alluded to some of the representational or general-integrative operations that may be critical to dream generation (see also below). Here I would like to indicate something of the course of children's development of verbal-imaginative ability concomitant with their increased reporting of REM dreams and their reporting of more structurally complex REM dreams.

At ages 4 and 5, Linda had a 15% REM report rate, and her reports' average length was 25 words. At ages 8 and 9, she had a 53% REM report rate, and her reports' average length was 71 words. Let us now examine her responses at ages 4 and 8 to a test designed to determine children's ability to tell stories about a series of line-drawing figures (Pickford Projective

Pictures, Pickford, 1963). The same six stimuli were employed on each occasion:

Card 1   An adult male with his hands on a boy's neck or shoulders.

Card 8   A person has fallen down; another person (female) is pointing at her or him, laughing.

Card 9   A man wearing a hat is positioned between a woman wearing a hat and evidently going out of a door, and a child.

Card 12   An evidently contrite child stands by a doll whose head is severed from its body. A woman points her finger scoldingly at the child.

Card 79   Two human figures inspecting a four-legged buglike creature twice as long as they are tall and of almost equal height as they. It has four thin legs, hair or quills extending upright from the dorsal surface of its body, and a beaverlike tail.

Card 7   A figure sitting on a stool, in a thoughtlike pose, in the corner of an otherwise empty room.

Here are the stories Linda told at age 4 (S: Subject; I: Interviewer):

Card 1   S   He is holding the boy's neck. Who's talking?
           I   That's just someone down the hall.

Card 8   S   Hey, he's swimming in the water, isn't he? The fishes are going to bite him up. This guy is sticking his finger at him. Do you know what one of my mother's friends did? She threw her little girl in the creek to see if she could swim and she never got near the water again.

Card 9   S   He's trying to hold the little girl's hands. (My brother) always tells me to read stories and I do. They're going to church.

Card 12   S   She's sticking her finger at him.
           I   Is anything else happening?
           S   No.

Card 79   S   I'll take this monster one. That's a monster trying to bite them up. His mouth is shut, he can't.

Card 7   S   She's putting her hand on her cheek. She's fat. She's old like my grandma, but my great-gram died.

These stories indicate, correctly, I think, that the average 4-year-old is not highly imaginative and is, in fact, a quite unlikely source of complex nocturnal dream scenarios on anything like the model of adult dreams. As in our children's dream reports at ages 3–5, there is either a static scene or an extremely simple story line. The preoperational child's susceptibility to distraction, either by external stimuli or by intrusive personal history, is amply demonstrated.

Consider now the generative, creative properties of the stories Linda told four years later:

Card 1   One day my father was waiting for me to get out of school and I ran to him. And he looked at me and said, "Where did you get all those scrapes and cuts?" "Well, I was playing on the playground and I fell down really hard. And I had to stay after school at the nurse's. And that's why I was late and the nurse said I would have to go to the doctor's." And the boy's father took him to the doctor's and the doctor said that he would be OK. And he was OK and he didn't fall and hurt himself that way any more because he didn't run that fast on the playground.

Card 8   One morning my brother and I were running in a field and my brother tripped and fell in a mud puddle. And I went and told my mom and she came and said that he had to come home and take a bath and then it would be time for dinner. And after dinner he would have to go to bed and come and run in the field the next morning. And when he came to run in the field the next morning, he ran all the way around the field without falling in a mud puddle. And so he didn't have to take a bath and eat his dinner and come and run in the field the next morning. That time he could play after dinner instead of going to bed. And at 12 o'clock he had to go to bed and he came and ran in the field the next morning. And he went and weighed himself and he weighed 20 pounds and before he started running in the field he weighed 70 pounds, so he lost 50 pounds. And so he ran in the field every day from then on. He ran all the way around it and watched out for mud puddles and then he could play with the toys until 12 o'clock and go to bed and play in the field the next morning. That's all.

Card 9   One night my mother and father and I were going out to eat and my mother and father kept looking for the key. And they went outside to look in the car and it wasn't in the car. And they looked in their coat pocket and everywhere in the house and I kept trying to tell them that I had it and they still didn't listen. And they started to look somewhere and I told them that I had the key and I kept trying to tell them that. So we walked back to the car and we went in the car and that taught my mother and father to listen to me. And they listen to me now and they listen to my mother and father. And I listen to them. And so we listen to each other now and we find things faster.

Card 12   One morning I was playing with my toys when my mother wasn't there. And my brother came in and I accidentally knocked him down and my mother made me go to bed without my dinner and she told me to take a bath, even though I hated baths. And the next morning I had to sit in the corner until lunchtime and then I could eat my lunch and have as much fun as I wanted. And so I didn't knock my brother down or anything like that any more because I would have to go to bed without any dinner and stand in the corner and take a bath. So I never ever, ever, ever did it again and my mommy gave me a ring for not doing it again. And I never lost the ring and I still have it now, even though I am as old as I am. And I gave the ring back to my mother so she could give it to somebody else. And she gave it to my brother and my brother had it and he had it until the age that I had it and then after he got the age that I was when I gave it back to my mother, he gave it back to his mother too. And she gave it . . . and she kept it then and saved it and saved it and saved it and then when I was 101 and my brother was 99, she showed us the ring and showed us that she still had the ring and gave it back to us.

Card 79   One morning my mother and my father went out into the woods and they saw a giant porcupine. And the giant porcupine was just us because we were playing a trick on my mother and father. And they started running for the house and we went there and we came in through the bedroom window and my mama hadn't looked there yet and she came up and looked and we were there. And she didn't even know that it was us. And they never went out in the woods again. And they decided to go on the sidewalk for walks the next time instead of in the woods because they didn't want to see a giant porcupine again.

Card 7   One day my mother was sitting in a corner at 6:30 waiting for my father to come home and he never got home and never got home and it was finally 4 o'clock the next day. And he still wasn't there. And then she waited and waited and waited and waited and the next day at 10 o'clock at night he wasn't home yet and she forgot that he went to Thailand. And she waited and waited until the next day at 4 o'clock in the morning and he wasn't home yet. And he wasn't home for 15 weeks. And that day he got home and she ran to the door to see who was there and it was her husband. And she said, "Where were you? I waited for 15 whole weeks and you never got home." And he said, "Don't you remember? I told you that morning that I was going to Thailand." "Well, maybe you didn't tell me but you told your son and your daughter because they kept trying to tell me where you were." "But you didn't listen." "But I didn't listen because I knew they couldn't know where you were. So I think you should have told me you were going to Thailand. I've been waiting in this corner since the day you left." "Well, I guess you were just asleep when it was time for me to leave." "Well, I think you should have told me you were leaving before." "I didn't think about it. That's why I didn't tell you." "Well, good night!"

These stories nicely illustrate the kind of creative (but still reasonably literal and concrete) narratizing that also was evident in Linda's final-year REM dream reports. In place of static, stimulus-bound descriptions, there now are thematically complex stories with an overall point of view, or "moral." In view of the contrast with her waking stories at age 4, is it really plausible to hypothesize that Linda's nocturnal dream generation was a constant factor from ages 4 to 8, but that she merely reported her dreams better at the later age? I think not. Clearly one needs to attend not only to the growth of intellectual operations that register and report events such as dreams, but also to that of imaginative-constructive operations that are capable of generating dreamlike narratives. It seems unlikely that, at *any* point in human cognitive development, the former operations could be greatly outstripped by the latter, active ones. Children's report capabilities always must be roughly proportional to their generative ones. The fallacy in using our Description Test–type results to explain our data is that the test holds, and the explanation assumes, creative factors to be constant. But that surely is neither how it is nor how it could be. I conclude that most of our "dream-developmental" data *do* refer to genuine changes in the occurrence and nature of dream experiences in childhood, rather than merely reflecting increased accuracy or probity in the reporting of such experiences.

DREAM DEVELOPMENT: ANSWERS AND QUESTIONS

Our data suggest the following course of development for the dream process. The *preoperational* child (ages 2–5) is capable of rudimentary dream activity during REM sleep, but such activity may accompany only a minority of moments of a minority of REM episodes. When "dreaming" does occur, it consists of static imagery portraying events isolated from any larger narrative context. Also lacking are affective accompaniment of dream imagery, portrayal of an active self-character, and portrayal more generally of any social interaction. The content of dream imagery is more susceptible to influence by dreamer body states (fatigue, hunger, thirst) than it is responsive to symbolic representation of the child's daily social life. Animal characters are fairly common and probably often stand for the self, which is incapable of achieving any more literal representation because of children's deficiencies in self-knowledge and self-reflection.

Children in *transition to operational* thinking (ages 5–7) are beginning to experience dreams with sequential, narrative properties. Thus their dream reports are longer than before and contain kinematic imagery and simple story lines. But dreaming still continues to characterize only a minority of moments of REM sleep. Absolutely, the body state of sleep or fatigue is a declining influence on dream imagery. Dreams now portray social interaction and physical activities, but continuing deficiencies in self-representation mean that these activities are largely executed by and directed toward nonself-characters or entities. It continues to be difficult or impossible to generate feeling accompaniments during the act of dreaming itself (although children are, of course, capable of responding to their waking remembrances of dreams with apprehension, amusement, etc.). Whereas the preoperational child had some difficulty conjuring up definite settings for dream events, the transitional child generally can supply such a setting. In the absence of effective self-representation, animals continue to be frequent dream characters, but family members also are portrayed relatively often. Unfamiliar human characters, absent in preoperational dreaming, make their first appearance, but such characters probably are constructional failures, that is, unsuccessful attempts to image familiar persons, rather than successful attempts to invent genuinely novel dream characters.

The *early concrete-operational* child (ages 7–9) shows significant quantitative and qualitative enhancement in dream experiencing. For the first time probably both a majority of REM episodes and a not insubstantial minority of NREM episodes are accompanied by dreamlike narratives. The REM narratives show continuing increases in sequential organization, and, for the first time, they have an "edited" quality rather than that of a "single camera left running." Dreams now contain a self-character, through whose "eyes" dream events can be apprehended and who seems capable of participation in a wide variety of dream activities and interactions. The self-character is not yet at parity with nonself-characters in dream participation but, for the first time, seems reliably to be capable of thinking thoughts and feeling feelings within the dream itself. The most reliably occurring feelings in children's dreams are happy or pleasant ones, and it is specifically prosocial interaction that has increased significantly since the transitional period. Concomitant with the rise in genuine self-participation in dream narratives, the frequency of animal characters is diminishing. The range of familiar human characterization expands beyond family members. Growth in dream competence proceeds along somewhat different paths for different children; there can be simultaneous increases in dream occurrence and dream length, or increases in only one or the other of these variables.

In the period of *consolidation of concrete operationalism* (ages 9–13), however, frequent dreamers also are dreamers of relatively long dreams. There is an increasing ability to generate dreamlike narratives during REM sleep. Self-participation in such narratives increases to a point where self and nonself dream activities are at relative parity. The portrayal of concrete physical acts and of social interaction in dreams reaches its child-developmental zenith in late preadolescence. An increasingly diversified affective accompaniment of dream narratives becomes possible, including such "negative" affect as fear and anger, but most dreams remain without affect. When affect is present, it tends to be neither unpleasant nor disruptive. The range of human characterization now expands to include deliberate portrayals of unfamiliar or "purely invented" persons. In this era of relative dream stabilization, increasing opportunity is afforded to "personality" variables in the determination of particular dream features, and dreams begin to become more sensibly self-revelatory than at earlier ages.

Finally, in the *transition to formal operationalism* (ages 13–15), opportunities for new forms of dream representation seem to emerge and to force some reorganization of previous developmental achievements. A new "analytic" mode of REM dream experiencing seems to permit occasional detachment of REM dream imagery from a strong narrative context, as indexed by dreams in which, as it were, a zoom lens zeroes in on discrete object representations. Simultaneously there seem to be new possibilities of self-representation, possibly including double self-reference. In consequence of these several new possibilities, compared to the preceding stage of development dreams are less likely to portray physical activity or prosocial interaction. Dream content is, in several senses, more abstract. The portrayal of body-state imagery is at its child-developmental nadir; both settings and characters draw with decreasing literalness on the child's waking experience; and the portrayal of purely thoughtlike activity in dreams is at its child-developmental zenith. None of the changes observed in dreaming during this late-transitional period seem to be related to psychosocial distress attendant to entry into adolescence. On the other hand, they *are* related rather clearly to cognitive attainment. NREM dreaming that, during the concrete-operational period, conformed fairly closely to the concomitant REM narrative format, gives some indication of moving away from that program and toward some of its own more distinctively adult qualities. However, movement to adult NREM competency is, as yet, far from complete.[4]

[4]In a systematic study of children's waking creation of and response to stories, Applebee (1978) has demonstrated a number of parallels to our findings on the development of dream (-report) narratives. Children's self-constructed stories begin as syncretistic wholes, next develop a sequential form, then become genuine narratives, and finally integrate separate narratives into still more complex structures. The content of children's first stories begins from a center in their own personal experience and only later broadens to include less "realistic" activities and elements. In the preoperational period stories elicit global affective evaluations ("It was nice"), but these judgments are not integrated with particular story features. Stories presented to early adolescents are analyzed into structural elements, and the children consider other possible arrangements of these elements. By later adolescence this analytic attitude is less salient, and a global consideration of story theme or point of view is more prominent.

That our data suggest this developmental progression and that the progression is sensibly related to the course of children's waking cognitive growth do not, of course, prove that it is a true description of early dream development. The first question raised by our data is the degree to which they can be replicated in independent studies. Only future research, research that presumably now can be better focused than our own study was, can answer this question. It is our hope that both dream researchers and developmental psychologists will rise to the many pertinent challenges posed by our data and interpretations.

A second question raised by our data has to do with the course of dream development *past* early adolescence. Our data stop at a point at which nocturnal cognition during neither REM nor NREM sleep seemed to be stabilized in a form approximating its typical adult status (as suggested by numerous research studies with young adults). Specifically, our older group's last-year REM reports still seemed to be under the influence of transitory perturbations attendant to the children's movement into increasingly abstract or formal-operational modalities of cognition, and neither in frequency nor in quality did this group's last-year NREM reports begin to approximate typical young-adult NREM reports (although there were some signs of movement in that direction). What our early-adolescent data, in fact, suggest is that it should by no means be imagined that the influence of general cognitive maturation on the form and content of dreaming is limited to early childhood; rather it seems that such influence must extend well into the heart of adolescence.

Obviously further study of the late-developmental course of that influence is required, for both REM and NREM sleep. When, and how, do REM dreams get back on a strongly narrative track? Even at the adult level, how are persisting individual differences in absolute cognitive attainment (e.g., formal-operational vs. high-level concrete-operational skill) related to the way in which REM dreams are experienced and to the kinds of representational possibilities they can encompass? When, and how, and for whom (in terms of associated cognitive-skill measures) does purely "thoughtlike" representation become a general possibility in NREM sleep? In addition, of course, there is need to implement a full life-span developmental approach, and to ask how dreams change with waking cognitive changes associated with the aging process. Are dreams of the aged characteristically different from those of mature adults not because of psychosocial status so much as because of cognitive status? Our child data certainly raise that possibility.

A third question, as tantalizing as it may be fundamentally unanswerable, lies at the earliest boundary of our data. When, and how, do dreams begin? My assumption has been that REM periods are "empty" of dream content until it can be demonstrated that children have accessed the symbolism of imagery and language, that is, until Piaget's preoperational period, and that they often remain empty even thereafter.[5] But this assumption may be more satisfying methodologically—it is better not to guess that dreams occur or what they are like when we have no direct evidence on either point—than correct substantively. And even if the assumption is correct, it may not date children's accession to dreaming with any precision, since conventional age assignments corresponding to movement through Piagetian stages may be quite wide of the mark; the tests generating these assignments may index underlying cognitive capacity only in highly imperfect ways.

But could there not be dreaming before Piaget's preoperational period? Overt behaviors during sleep (e.g., smiling, fussing) lead many parents to believe that dreaming must begin in early infancy. However, overt acts (e.g., walking, talking) are not reliable indices of dream activity in adult humans, where they seem to reflect most often disinhibited and/or dissociated motor-system activity rather than any kind of active cognitive processing. Furthermore, the acceptance of motor acts as sufficient evidence of dream activity would entail ascribing dreaming to a wide range of organisms (e.g., baby chipmunks) for whom the possibility of dream experiencing seems most problematic.

What exactly could one mean in asking about infant "dreaming"? Just as the concept of "sleep" breaks down when it is pushed back too far ontogenetically, so too the concept of "dream" must lose most or all of its meaning as applied to very early human development. Ordinarily the term implies a story running through one's mind that one apprehends as if its events actually were transpiring in the outside world. But in this sense even preoperational children's REM reports are not fully indicative of "dreaming"—for there is little or no "story" to them. It is quite difficult to imagine that infants could narratize during sleep, or if they can, why they give no indication of comparable intellectual synthesis in the waking state.

But, the objection will be made, "This is all semantics. You define dreams so that infants may not be able to have them. But what I'm interested in is what goes through an infant's mind in REM sleep. I don't care whether you call it a dream or whatever else. Surely infants have consciousness during REM sleep. What is it like? What is it of?" Just now such questions do not suggest any means by which they can be answered definitively, but there is no way in which intellectually curious people can be kept from asking them, and I see no harm in trying to think about them in reasonably well-disciplined ways.

The problem of consciousness remains one of the great puzzles of cognitive science and of psychobiology. There is no reason to believe that here we will be able to resolve it in ways that far more learned persons in far more learned discussions have not been able to do. However, several

---

[5]My assumption has been summarized in a piece of doggerel (where REMP = REM period):
  Empty REMPty sat in bed,
  Empty REMPty scratched his head,
  But all his resources and acumen
  Could not retrieve a dream just then.

remarks may help to put the problem of consciousness in an appropriate context for reflecting about the nocturnal mental life of the infant and even of our hypothetical, preoperational "Empty REMPty."

When we think or talk about consciousness, generally we mean something more than the kind of awareness indexed by behavioral responsiveness to exogenous stimulation. That the earthworm changes its course as we poke at it with a stick is not sufficient to index the kind of consciousness about which we are curious. Our kind of consciousness connotes something more than sheer environmental sensitivity. But what is that "something more"? It seems to involve multiple levels of cognitive processing, with some awareness of or attention to our own internal processing (metaprocessing), and a consequential splitting of our own internal self-reference: I see something, but *I* am aware that *I* am seeing it; *I* am aware of several lines of thought running through *my* mind.

It is one of the peculiarities of *experiencing* dreams, as Rechtschaffen (1978) has observed, that self-consciousness, in this sense, is largely absent. In our dreams we observe or act or feel, but without reflecting on what it is that we are doing. That is, perhaps, why our dreams seem so "real" to us.

But it seems to me that *creating* dreams must presuppose the attainment of some measure of self-consciousness and of divided self-reference. The dream self, whether passive observer or active participant, is an inherently dissociated system of self-reference. More generally, the experiencing during sleep of *any* self-referential cognition must depend on self-consciousness, which, in turn, depends on the interiorization of word speaking, visual displays, or gestures as systems of internal reference. As, from different perspectives, both Jaynes (1976) and Piaget (1974) have argued, consciousness in our sense is a symbolic construction. And, no more than waking reflection or nocturnal dreaming, is it something that simply "comes with" our nervous system. It is something that, with appropriate experience and neural maturation, we learn to do with our nervous system.

We learn, the evidence suggests, slowly. And even as adults we display our learning, the evidence suggests, only imperfectly. As both Jaynes (1976) and Rechtschaffen (1975) have pointed out, there are many moments of our adult experience when we function little more than as automata, when we do not evidence "self-consciousness," when the current contents of our alleged "stream of consciousness" (James, 1892) are, in fact, nil. From these perspectives it would not be surprising, then, were infants not to dream and were humans with some capacity for self-consciousness and self-reference not always to take advantage of occasions of cortical activation (e.g., REM sleep) to deploy these capacities.

Clearly, we sometimes forget our dreams. Equally clearly, children must do that too, probably even more often than we do. But I would not deduce from these facts that the "true" incidence of REM dreaming at ages 4 or 8 or even 40 must be 100%. In the case of the 4-year-old, I would not imagine it to be anywhere near 100%. Nor can I imagine any kind of dream or "conscious experience" occurring during either the sleeping or the waking life of the preoperational infant.

Contrary to the romantic suppositions of some theorists, then, I see little reason to believe that preoperational children lead a rich and imaginative fantasy life. That children can play imaginatively with toys or other external props does not imply that their behavior is an externalization of such a fantasy life. Certainly *our* observations, on the most temporally extensive, obligatory, and imaginative form of fantasy more generally experienced by human beings, are not supportive of the idea that young children experience an autonomous stream of imaginative thought that only slowly is harnessed to and/or suppressed by the exigencies of everyday reality. Dreaming, no less than waking reality-oriented thinking, is something we learn to do, and learn only slowly; it is not something that children (or adults) are just "naturally" good at.

If, then, dreaming is a "window" on the fantasy life of children, one must now conclude, even with due respect for the fact that the window is somewhat clouded by children's difficulty in remembering and describing dreams, that there is in fact nothing terribly fantastic or startling to be seen through it. But here again other researchers will need to step up to that window, perhaps with more elaborate and imaginative research strategies than we have been able to follow, before any definitive conclusions can be reached.

DREAMING AS A SKILLED MENTAL ACT

If our observation that dream ontogeny follows a course similar to the ontogeny of the waking mind is an unremarkable one, our findings on the particular kinds of cognitive skills that may be involved in developing dream competence are less obvious and more provocative. Briefly, our correlational data at ages 5–9, and our observation of simultaneous waking and dream cognition defects in two adolescent boys (discussed in Chapter 8), suggested that skills assessed in performance on block-design and embedded-figure tests are necessary conditions[6] of experiencing dreams during REM sleep. These findings are among those most requiring cross-validation by others, and the observations with Phil and Fred serve to remind us how much one may be able to learn about ordinary dreaming from the investigation of extraordinary cases.

As discussed in Chapter 8, we do not take our observations as supporting either a right-hemisphere neural model of dream generation (e.g., Bakan, 1978) or the hypothesis that the achievement of visual-imaginal realizations is a critical feature of the normal dream process. The latter hypothesis is contradicted by the presence of dreamlike narrative experience in the

---

[6]But perhaps not sufficient conditions (cf. Chapter 6).

congenitally blind (Kirtley, 1975) and in those sighted persons with visuospatial cognitive defects that interfere with dream imaging (Kerr, Foulkes, & Jurkovic, 1978). The right hemisphere model is contradicted by the preservation of dream reporting in commissurotomized patients (Greenwood, Wilson, & Gazzaniga, 1977) and by the apparent cessation of dream experience in patients with profound disturbance of left-hemispheric-mediated overt and "inner" speech (Foulkes, 1978c). The neurocognitive mediation of dreaming evidently is a more complex matter than envisioned by most dual-brain, dual-mind theorists. In particular, these theorists have failed to consider that dreaming is a complex and integrative process whose several components probably have quite disparate neural bases. Researchers no longer look for a "thinking" center or a "thinking" lobe in the brain, and it is no doubt equally archaic to conceptualize the mediation of dreaming in so simple a manner.

We would interpret the block-design and embedded-figure performances related to dream-report rates as reflecting integrative processes that are probably neither right-hemispheric in their mediation nor specifically visuospatial in their application. We do this because of both internal evidence (Phil and Fred were not particularly deficient in visuospatial abilities assessed by other tests) and two forms of external evidence. First, it is clear that block-design and embedded-figure tests make "analytic" and "integrative" demands on respondents, and there is evidence that compliance with these demands is mediated by the left hemisphere (Bouma, 1980; Zaidel, 1980). Second, we have been able to make dream observations suggesting that, while specifically visual dream realizations may depend on an intact right hemisphere, the dreaming of memorable dream narratives does not, but can proceed unimpeded regardless of substantial right-hemisphere damage and of substantial visuospatial cognitive impairment (Kerr & Foulkes, in press). Specifically we found that a 44-year-old man with considerable right-hemisphere lesioning reported well-narratized dreams that were, as he put it, like "a radio drama or tape with an occasional picture."

Both this man, with his considerable but not total deficit in dream visualization, and an earlier adult we studied, with a total deficit in dream visualization (attendant to the "space-form" blindness of Turner's syndrome; Kerr, Foulkes, & Jurkovic, 1978), performed adequately on block-design tests. And they both dreamed memorable, if generally or totally nonvisual, dreams. Their common cognitive deficit in wakefulness was an inability to rotate mental images through imagined space, an inability indexed not in block-design or embedded-figure tests but in tests such as the Thurstone Space Test (where you must determine if test figures presented at different angles of rotation are identical to a standard figure). Both subjects simply were unable to perform the sort of "mental rotation" required to solve problems on these tests. Hence our data indicate that block-design or embedded-figure visuospatial analysis is unrelated to dream visualization, which depends instead on the ability to perform mental rotations of images.

Furthermore, the man's case suggests that the ability to perform mental rotations—and, therefore, dream visualization—may depend on intact right-hemisphere functioning, although dreaming in a larger sense does not. The findings of Greenwood, Wilson, and Gazzaniga (1977) seem to contradict this assertion—for their "complete" commissurotomy patient, "J.H.," is claimed to have dreamed visually. But I do not find this claim compelling, for visualization was assumed from the content of J.H.'s dreams (he dreamed of watching television, for instance) rather than directly probed. When we directly probed our Turner's-syndrome subject about a similar television-watching dream, she claimed that, contrary to one's casual assumption, it was not experienced in visual imagery. Obviously more research and more cognitively sophisticated research will be required to resolve this issue.

It is apparent that neuropsychological research starting from demonstrated cognitive deficits and/or demonstrated neural lesioning may have a great deal to tell us of the neural and cognitive systems involved in dreaming and in dreaming particular kinds of dreams. In taking advantage of these kinds of research data, dream psychology will be one step ahead of waking cognitive psychology, which rarely has interfaced with neuroscience data or methodology. But to be fully productive, a neuropsychology of dreaming must begin by being as well informed of the complexities of dreaming and of the dream research literature as it is of the particular resources and skills of neuropsychology more generally.

Returning to our findings linking block-design and embedded-figures abilities to dream competence, we well may ask, "Why these abilities?" Conceptually, what role might they be expected to play in dream formation? A plausible answer is suggested by observations of waking cognition and language as children become preoperational (Foss & Hakes, 1978). Children's reasoning and their use of language both suggest a shift from dealing with environmental objects and events as undifferentiated units to conceptualizing them as collections of features or discrete properties. The *analysis* of perceptual inputs must be critical to such a shift, and it is this ability on which skilled block-design and embedded-figures performances must depend.

Even in early childhood, our observations suggest, it is in the nature of dreaming that it is *a creative recombination of memories and knowledge.* Dreaming is *not* a simple "replay" of undifferentiated global units from our past experience. In this sense dreaming inherently involves the dissociation of features from representations of objects and events and their assignment to representations of other objects and events. It must presuppose both the sort of representation by features that analytic skills make possible and the ability to operate analytically on these representations.

CHAPTER 10

Dreams and the
Growth of Self

Although our waking test program originally was conceived with more of a psychosocial than a cognitive focus, it turned out that it was the less numerous waking-cognitive variables that generated the more coherently patterned correlations with dream variables. But our data are by no means silent on the relationship between dream development and "personality" development.

DREAMS AND THE REGULATION OF DRIVE-STATES

In Freud's (1900, 1917, 1933) account of dreaming, it is a primitive kind of thinking ("primary-process" thinking) in which instinctual wishes are represented as being at least partially fulfilled. The form of this representation is thought objectified as experience, that is, a hallucination. Following the publication of *The Interpretation of Dreams* (1900), Freud's interests turned increasingly away from the basic scientific problems addressed in that book and toward his clinical work, in which he stressed the primacy of an infantile ("pregenital") sexuality in the formation of pathological symptoms. As a "normal" form of pathological symptom, dreaming also became seen as a medium in which infantile sexual (or hostile) impulses invariably were operative. This stress was strongly prefigured in theoretical sections (e.g., Chapter 7) of *The Interpretation of Dreams,* but it did not play a substantial role in the operative level at which Freud interpreted individual dreams or illustrated his ideas about the mental processes by which they were formed,[1] and in this book Freud still allowed that, particularly in childhood, nonsexual wishes might be the basis of dream formation.

Later on, however, Freud's early qualifications or hesitations about tying dreaming to infantile sexual impulses gave way, even for children's dreams, to an enlarged sense of the significance—contemporary as well as

[1]E.g., in Chapter 6 of *The Interpretation of Dreams.*

retrospective—of infants' and children's sexual instincts. By 1925 (Freud, 1900, p. 127 n.), Freud was inclined to see something more than simple everyday wishes (e.g., wanting to make up for meals or trips denied to them in wakefulness) in children's earliest dreams. In his famous "Wolf Man" case study (1918), he interpreted a 4-year-old's birthday dream in terms of the dreamer's supposed wish to be seduced by his father, and he alleged that this wish had had a substantial developmental history spanning back to before the Wolf Man's second birthday.

Thus "primary-process" thinking, in which instinctual wishes demand hallucinatory gratification apart from any consideration of logic or reality, increasingly became primary not merely in its role in adult symptom formation but also in terms of its supposed developmental status. The idea that logical or reality-oriented thought ("secondary-process" thinking) develops only grudgingly in response to the adaptive failures of primary-process thinking always has been a difficult one for disciplined observers of children to accept, whether they be developmental psychologists or simply parents. And yet in that absence of reality testing that has been a general condition of much clinical practice and dream theorizing, this idea has retained a pertinacious hold on the minds of many persons with clinical backgrounds, with a resultant chasm between their understandings of child development and those emerging in recent years within the behavioral sciences. Responsible clinical theorists (e.g., Holt, 1967) have attempted to bridge the chasm with the recognition that both reality-directed *and* autistic thought must be developmental emergents of the infant's earliest efforts at behavioral adaptation, but such theorists generally have received more approving responses from behavioral scientists sympathetic to the aims of psychoanalysis than from workaday clinicians.

We think that our data on children's dreams provide a substantial empirical basis on which to reject the classical psychoanalytic account of the ontogeny of thought and a means by which empirical observers of dreaming can reconcile their work with that of other developmental sciences. *Dreaming—presumably that form of thinking most susceptible to primary-process organization—does not conform to the primary-process model in early childhood.* In preschoolers' dreams one does not, in general, see either everyday wishes being fulfilled or intimations of the sorts of impulsivity, anatomical fixations, or affectivity stressed in Freud's theory of instinctual development. Nor at any age level do our data on children's dreams offer any appreciable empirical support for the hypotheses that either dreaming or dream distortion arises in response to demands to cope with otherwise uncontrolled impulses or with bothersome feelings, fantasies, or fixations. That children's dreams occur, and that the dreams manifest increasing talent in elaborating novel or unexpected imagery, seems rather to be a natural and inevitable concomitant of children's waking cognitive maturation.

Thus we found no evidence that the emergence of dream experiencing is associated with anxiety or impulsivity. We observed at ages 3−5 that REM character distortion was not predicted by waking anxiety, but by the *absence* of anxiety, and we found at ages 5−7 that REM distortion had substantial positive cognitive correlates. Increases in REM distortion from ages 3−5 to 5−7 also had positive cognitive correlates. At ages 7−9 increased REM dream extensity and baseline non-REM dream extensity had significant *negative* correlations with anxiety, and increased dream unpleasantness also was associated with *low* anxiety. REM dream unpleasantness, more generally, *never* was associated with waking anxiety. As we have seen, the emergence of feelings in dreams seemed to depend more on cognitive maturation and skill than on salient experience of feelings in the waking state. And even in early adolescence, increases in dream distortion were associated with an *absence* of tension or anxiety. From this picture one is inclined to see dreaming—REM and non-REM—as a cognitive medium in which, as in other forms of thinking, anxiety is more a hindrance to the unfolding and flowering of self-expression than the stimulus that drives it.

Our data cannot, of course, refute the possibility that there does in some sense exist a world of infantile drive-states and affective tendencies corresponding to the classical psychoanalytic model. There may be observational contexts in which it proves necessary, in the orderly explanation of behavior, to postulate such a world. But our data *do* refute the hypotheses that dreaming is the "royal road" to the discovery of this world and that dreaming is the quintessential product of such a world. *Dreaming is not an observational context in which, in explaining the orderly development of human experience, it proves necessary to postulate an underworld of infantile impulsivity. The explanatory requirements of the area of dream ontogeny are qualitatively no more complex than, and probably substantively little different from, those of the development of cognition more generally.*

Our data cast serious doubt on hypotheses of dream function that stress that *dream experiencing,* however it is instigated, serves an essential role in the regulation of drive-states. It may or may not prove to be the case that *REM sleep,* as a physiological process, serves such a function (Vogel, 1975). But even were this latter hypothesis correct, its implications for the functions of dream experiencing remain moot. In lower mammalian organisms REM sleep would most likely accomplish whatever functions it has in the absence of concomitant dream experience. The symbolic processes permitting, and guiding, dream formation would be absent. Even in human ontogeny, until the concrete-operational stage has been reached, it is difficult to imagine that the cognitive processing during sleep that we call dreaming has the requisite power or scope to achieve any function such as effective drive regulation. While there may be REM-sleep processes subserving such regulation, once again, it is difficult to conceive how the experiencing of dreams could be one of them.

Any *developmental* analysis of the function of dreaming must start with the fact that the ontogeny of dream experiencing is keyed to cognitive or symbolic development more generally, rather than to waking affective or motivational states or contingencies. Presumably the *functions* of dreaming, if any, will be sought more plausibly in observations of how the contents and processes of dreaming relate to cognitive-symbolic processing more generally than in observations of the ontogeny, phylogeny, or neurophysiology of REM sleep.

DREAMS AS INDICES OF WAKING BEHAVIOR

Other clinical-psychiatric theories than Freud's have proposed other sorts of relationships to waking variables and other sorts of functions for dream experiencing. For instance, two of Freud's early associates, Adler and Jung, proposed dream theories at opposite ends of a continuum of possible direct relationships between dream experience and waking behavior. For Adler (1931) dreams were essentially continuous with one's waking behavior, with the "style of life" one develops in coping with the world.[2] For Jung (1948) dreams served a compensatory function, bringing to the surface aspects of the total self that do *not* find expression in waking life.[3] Cast in somewhat simplified terms, then, Adler would predict that a shy man would exhibit shyness or diffidence in his dreams, while Jung would expect the same person to exhibit a hearty extroversion and social interest in his dreams. Because, despite their authors' own qualifications and hedges in the face of contradictory evidence, these theories seem to make clear-cut predictions about relationships of dreams to readily observed waking variables, the continuity vs. complementarity hypotheses have figured prominently in empirical research on dream correlates. Research findings generally, but not invariably, have favored the more plausible theory of waking–dreaming continuity (Foulkes, 1970), but they leave one with the feeling that much dream variability is still left unaccounted for in dream correlations with overt waking behavior.

Our data on behavioral correlates of children's dreams do much to reinforce that feeling. While we were able on occasion to demonstrate plausible continuities of waking behavior and dream content, and considerably less often observed complementary waking–dreaming relationships, no convincing *general* pattern of continuity emerged in our correlational data. At least at earlier age levels, the failure to demonstrate substantial continuity might be attributed to methodological difficulties, possibly including faulty dream reporting, unreliable waking measures, and children's lack of actual consistency in overt behavior. An additional problem would be the

---

[2]In fact, the theory is somewhat more complex than this, because Adler also believed that dreams can be self-deceptive.
[3]Once again the theory is more complex than this, in that attempts are made to subsume cases where compensation seems not to have occurred.

fact that until ages 7−9, it was not clear that there was much reliable self-participation in the children's dreams. Before those ages one could point to potential continuities—for example, impulsive children having relatively many animal characters—but these continuities were, perforce, less direct than those specified by any precise form of the dreaming−waking continuity hypothesis.

At ages 7−9 some stylistic similarities could be noted between children's waking social behavior and the kinds of social behavior they initiated in their dreams, and at ages 11−13, for the first time, it was assertive children who participated most actively in their own dreams. At ages 9−11 it was socially shrewd children, and at ages 11−13 competitive and assertive children, who were most hostile in their own dreams. For overt dream actions (e.g., seeing, talking, moving), some correlations were observed during childhood that also were consistent with a form of the continuity hypothesis, but the overall pattern was not compelling. Factors contributing to the inconsistency may have included cognitive-representational difficulties and the changing meaning of different acts at different ages (as physical interaction is superseded by verbal interaction in the waking state). We did, of course, observe a continuity of presleep passivity into children's dreams in our television study (see Chapter 7; cf. Hauri, 1966), and there is a sense in which the longitudinal changes we observed in children's dreams from preadolescence to early adolescence (e.g., less physical activity and less social interaction: a more indwelling quality?) might be considered indicative of waking−dreaming continuity.

But in early adolescence itself, active participation by children in their own dreams no longer was related to their waking social dominance, but was instead correlated with their visuospatial skill, suggesting that representational-skill factors were masking the expected dreaming−waking continuity. And although correlates of overt dream acts showed some continuity (e.g., talkative adolescents had relatively talk-filled dreams), correlates of dream social interactions showed more complementarity than continuity (e.g., prosocial interaction in the dream was associated with waking introversion, and self-initiated antisocial interaction in the dream was associated with depression and social withdrawal). One clearly can propose *mediated*-continuity hypotheses to explain the latter sort of findings. For instance, introverted children don't have, but crave, social contact; withdrawn and depressed children don't aggress against, but feel like blaming, other children. But once again, this no longer is so simple or unequivocal a form of continuity as is specified by the hypothesis that we dream what we do.

One way of looking at the whole body of our data on correlations between children's waking behavior and their dream content is not that they demonstrate support for the continuity hypothesis at a modest level commensurate with the various methodological difficulties encountered along the way, but rather that these difficulties in fact demonstrate a substantial flaw in the hypothesis itself. That flaw probably is peculiarly susceptible to revealing itself in studies with children.

At the adult level, where some waking–dreaming continuity has been demonstrated in various studies, the continuity hypothesis appears deceptively simple: If we do it in our waking lives, we do it in our dreams. But it cannot be that simple. It is not our actions *as such* that influence, or that can influence, our dreams. Dreams are symbolic elaborations of our memories and knowledge, and for the dream to portray who we are or what we do, we must be knowledgeable of ourselves and our actions, and able to recreate this knowledge imaginally. At a minimum, then, continuity between dreaming and acting depends on substantial cognitive mediation. While investigators have taken that mediational apparatus for granted in research with adults, our data indicate that this is a luxury one is not permitted in research with children.

Thinking of our preoperational and transitional-to-operational children, by what right does one expect that a child who is active and impulsive in wakefulness also will so represent herself or himself in dreaming? Does the child (and not merely the adult observer) see herself or himself in this way or indeed in any consistent way? Could the child symbolically recreate those behavioral properties assigned to her or him by others? It is precisely these kinds of questions, not about the child's overt "behavior" but about her or his self-knowledge and constructive imaging, that form the only plausible basis for guessing at children's dream self-reflections. It is not sufficient for waking–dreaming continuity that the child act in some consistent way; the child also must know that fact and be able to reproduce it imaginally. Our data suggest that these necessary conditions for demonstrating waking–dreaming continuity are, in fact, generally absent in early childhood and that their later course of development is a gradual one, subject to perturbations introduced by shifts in general cognitive maturation.

Thinking of the continuity hypothesis in terms of cognitive mediation, then, one would expect waking–dreaming "behavioral" parallels to be readily demonstrable only when children have developed a relatively stabilized and consensually accurate concept of what they are like and also when they are able to portray this knowledge imaginally. Our data suggest preadolescence as the first time when these conditions *generally* are met.

Late preadolescence, our data suggest, may also be the *last* point in childhood where continuity is as simple to conceptualize as the preceding argument has implied. In the second decade of life children's self-knowledge and self-conceptions begin to focus on thoughts and feelings, as well as on actions and social reputations. At this level significant discrepancies may begin to exist between the self others see and the self one knows personally. Interrelated but multiple self-representational systems also can develop: for example, "I know I'm shy and that others think of me as stand-offish, but I really want to have people like me."

From the perspective that dreams operate on self-representations, rather than on self-behavior as others see it, it thus becomes evident why, both in adolescence (our data) and in later life (earlier research), demonstrations of the continuity of dream portrayals with overt waking behavior carry so little conviction as telling us the better part of the story of why we dream what we do. Pitched behaviorally—at the level where we correlate behavior ratings of the dreamer by others with dream variables—the continuity hypothesis is cognitively deficient. It fails to recognize what a dream is or what its sources must be. Pitched even at the level of the simple self-report rating (on a scale from 1 to 5: How shy do you feel? How cheerful or depressed do you feel? etc.), the operations for accessing the dreamer's self-knowledge base are woefully inadequate in relation to the self-knowledge base available to the dreamer while dreaming the dream. These are the reasons why conventional continuity hypotheses with the conventional operational translations they have received only can be very crude orientations to problems that then must be conceptualized and studied in ways that do better justice to the complexity of the dream-generation process. From a purely scientific standpoint there are very definite limits to what we can learn about dreaming from studying overt-behavioral correlates of dream-report characteristics. Our task now must be to find equally objective means for studying the self- (and other-) *representational* sources of dream imagery (Foulkes, 1978c).

THE ENVIRONMENTAL SENSITIVITY OF DREAMS

The identification of dreaming with perception has, as noted earlier (e.g., Chapter 3), come to influence many popular expectations about the on- togeny (and phylogeny) of dreaming. Often it is imagined that organisms dream in proportion to their ability to see (or, more generally, to sense), and that the content of dreams bears some reasonably direct relationship to the content of one's waking perception. We dream as, and what, we perceive— insofar as radical behaviorism has attempted to develop any coherent account of dreaming, this seems to be it. For Skinner (1963) dreaming is simply the behavior of seeing. Such behavior is acquired in the context of stimulation from the outside world, but later it can occur in the absence of such stimulation. No plausible account of the "other variables" that might explain the particular form under which control is exercised over "seeing" during sleep ever has been given, but the assumption is made that we need to look to the development of waking perception in order to understand the development of such behaviors as dreaming.

Yet even at the adult level, this assumption seems to be belied by certain facts. How is it that certain persons (e.g., Kerr, Foulkes, & Jurkovic, 1978) with a reasonably standard history of waking perceptual development are unable to "see" in their dreams? Why should it be one's perceptual behavior at ages 5–7, a period that seems to constitute a critical period in the development of symbolic but not perceptual behavior, that determines whether acquired blindness results in continued dream "seeing" (Kirtley, 1975)? There is good reason to believe that the reason why a comprehensive Skinnerian account of dreaming never has been mounted is that, in the face of dealing with these and other treacherous questions, that account would have to become as "cognitive" and complex as those mentalistic theories for which behaviorism promotes itself as the simpler, more physicalistic alternative.

Certainly our data on the ontogeny of dreaming offer scant comfort for those who want to continue to think of dreaming as a perceptual act whose form is determined by concomitant waking perceptual attainments. It seems to be how children are able to think, rather than how or what they are able to sense or see, that determines the form and substance of their dreams. To take but one major example, preschoolers can *see* motion—motion is, in fact, one of the most interesting and salient perceptual properties of their environment—but they do not seem to *dream* motion until they achieve a stage of cognitive development permitting the requisite symbolic operations.

Because perception is the basis of our knowledge of the world, and of ourselves, clearly there are necessary connections between what we perceive and what we dream. Our data on the properties of parents whose children dream relatively often of family members and of their own homes can be read as indicating that salient waking-life perceptions or experiences often become salient dreamlife experiences. Social (i.e., social-perceptual) inexperience also seems to contribute to some children's later failures to expand their dream portrayals beyond the confines of such familiar and significant waking situations, just as enhanced social experience outside the home must play a role in children's generally reduced dreaming of family members in preadolescence and adolescence.

But waking perceptual experience cannot be a sufficient condition for guaranteeing "comparable" dream experience. Early in development children may lack the symbolic-representational skill to represent certain kinds of waking experience in their dreams. Later on, when the requisite representational skill *is* present, whole areas of waking perceptual experience (e.g., academic work at school) seem to be largely absent in children's dreams despite the many hours of such experience children regularly log in their schedule of daily activity. Here one has to presume that it is *the organization of experience as knowledge* that determines the dream, not perceptual experience itself. Once again one returns to the fact that the dream operates on our *knowledge,* and not directly on what we either *see or do.* The two necessarily are related, but they are far from identical.

There is good reason to believe both that, over time, children's knowledge becomes organized in an increasingly diversified self-referential way and that it is experience so classified that plays a major role in dream formation. In various contexts I have discussed features of older children's dreams as being emblematic of how the children see themselves vis-à-vis their social world. What this implies is that children's world knowledge is organized around a self-world focus, and that aspects of dream content often seem to be dictated by their centrality to this focus. Thus if whole areas of waking experience (e.g., academic work at school) are seen as largely irrelevant to who the child is or what he or she wants to become, then seldom will they be dreamed about.

Strong implications for sex differences in dream content are generated by this way of thinking about children's knowledge bases and about the dreams that operate on them. From an early age boys and girls are treated differently, and we as adults think of them differently. But it is not at this level of our environmental input to children that we should think about sex differences in children's dreams. Rather we need to think about what, in the children's own minds, it means to be a boy or a girl. In our expectation of massive sex differences between boys' and girls' dreams, we are bringing to bear on the problem a sophisticated, differential male–female typology that may largely be lacking in the children's organization of their own experience.

If one turns the problem around and asks what can we learn from children's dreams about their conceptions of what it means to be male or female, the answer seems to be that maleness–femaleness is only a gradually evolving and differentiating focus of self-reference. For early school-aged children it may mean little more than that, for example, you are the kind of person who associates with girls less than with boys. Later on it may also imply a certain style of relating to others, say (in our terms) "agentically" or "communally" (Trupin, 1976), and a certain kind of evaluation of the importance of home and family to your sense of personal identity. Derived in this fashion, the early-adolescent self-concept does not have a strong component of direct cross-sex attraction. It is not a circulating hormone but knowledge that guides the selection of dream imagery, and there seems to be no unmediated process whereby the former invariably alters the latter.

Thus children's dreams remind us of something we should have known anyway: that the dream, as the product of our *knowledge* of self and world, cannot directly reflect what we see or what we do or the state of our bodies; it can reflect only what we know, or think we know, of such things, and it will reflect waking experience only to the extent we have organized that experience as being central to our notion of who and what we are.

DREAMS AND SELF-AWARENESS

Dreaming is knowledge based. It is a cognitive process by which our knowledge is operated on so that imaginal narratives, generally self-referential ones, are produced. The only way by which waking feelings, behaviors, or perceptions can influence dreaming is by their representation as knowledge, generally as knowledge that is "self-knowledge." It is for this reason that external attempts to drive the dreaming process (presleep manipulations, stimuli applied during sleep itself) generally are so unproductive; the "sensory fact" most likely is not processed as being relevant knowledge (and it is only where it can be so processed that we see dream "effects" or "incorporations"). In linking dreaming to self-knowledge, both folklore and clinical dream theories have almost caught the heart of the matter.

I say "almost" because most self-knowledge theorists have dwelt more on the "self" than on "knowledge," and because "self" often has been interpreted in ways that lead away from cognitive self-representation and from the central fact that dreaming, as a symbolic process, can operate only on *knowledge*. A striking exception has been Calvin Hall (e.g., 1953, 1966), who consistently has portrayed dreams as cognitive-symbolic processes capable of revealing how we *think* about ourselves in relation to significant others and to the world about us. The data of this book offer, I believe, a striking affirmation of Hall's thesis, and indicate the considerable potential of dream study for telling us how self-knowledge—how the very sense of selfhood itself—develops. In children's dreams we find convenient objectifications—"projections," in Hall's terminology—of what and how children think of themselves.

In children's dreams there are vast, and as yet relatively untouched, stores of information about how we humans come to think of ourselves as we do. The very imperfections of young children's dreams in telling us what children *do* are but portentous signs of what they have to tell us about what children *think*. It is not just "dreams" that are developing throughout childhood: It is the "self" as well. If there is a core of human personality, it lies in our ideas about who we are. These ideas—the "self"—whether we consciously entertain them in wakefulness or not, are the key component of the programmatic regulation we exercise over our behavior. They, like any other symbolic system, can only be the product of a considerable process of developmental elaboration. Children's dreams afford a unique window through which to view that process and are essential subject matter for any serious scientific account of our development as human beings.

References

Adler, A. *What life should mean to you.* New York: Capricorn, 1958 (orig. 1931).

Agnew, H. W., Webb, W. B., & Williams, R. L. The first-night effect: An EEG study of sleep. *Psychophysiology,* 1966, **2**, 263–266.

Amen, E. W. Individual differences in apperceptive reaction: A study of the responses of preschool children to pictures. *Genetic Psychology Monographs,* 1941, **23**, 319–385.

Antrobus, J. S. Dreaming for cognition. In A. M. Arkin, J. S. Antrobus, & S. J. Ellman (Eds.), *The mind in sleep: Psychology and psychophysiology.* Hillsdale, N.J.: Lawrence Erlbaum Associates, 1978, pp. 569–581.

Antrobus, J. S., Ehrlichman, H., & Weiner, M. EEG asymmetry during REM and NREM: Failure to replicate. *Sleep Research,* 1978, **7**, 24. (abstract)

Antrobus, J. S., Fein, G., Jordan, L., Ellman, S. J., & Arkin, A. M. Measurement and design in research on sleep reports. In A. M. Arkin, J. S. Antrobus, & S. J. Ellman (Eds.), *The mind in sleep: Psychology and psychophysiology.* Hillsdale, N.J.: Lawrence Erlbaum Associates, 1978, pp. 19–55.

Applebee, A. N. *The child's concept of story: Ages two to seventeen.* Chicago: University of Chicago Press, 1978.

Arkin, A. M., Antrobus, J. S., & Ellman, S. J. (Eds.). *The mind in sleep: Psychology and psychophysiology.* Hillsdale, N.J.: Lawrence Erlbaum Associates, 1978.

Aserinsky, E., & Kleitman, N. Regularly occurring periods of eye motility, and concomitant phenomena, during sleep. *Science,* 1953, **118**, 273–274.

Bakan, D. *The duality of human existence.* Chicago: Rand McNally, 1966.

Bakan, P. Dreaming, REM sleep and the right hemisphere: A theoretical integration. *Journal of Altered States of Consciousness,* 1978, **3**, 285–307.

Bardwick, J. M. *Psychology of women: A study in biocultural conflicts.* New York: Harper & Row, 1971.

Bellak, L., & Adelman, C. The Children's Apperception Test (CAT). In A. I. Rabin & M. R. Haworth (Eds.), *Projective techniques with children.* New York: Grune & Stratton, 1960, pp. 62–94.

Bergan, A., McManis, D. L., & Melchert, P. A. Effects of social and token reinforcement on WISC Block Design performance. *Perceptual and Motor Skills,* 1971, **32**, 871–880.

Berger, R. J. Experimental modification of dream content by meaningful verbal stimuli. *British Journal of Psychiatry,* 1963, **109**, 722–740.

Bouma, A. Hemispheric differences in the detection of embedded figures. *The INS Bulletin,* March 1980, 13–14. (abstract)

Bower, G. H., & Gilligan, S. G. Remembering information related to one's self. *Journal of Research in Personality,* 1979, **13**, 420–432.

Breger, L. Children's dreams and personality development. In J. Fisher & L. Breger (Eds.),

The meaning of dreams: Recent insights from the laboratory. Sacramento: Dept. Mental Hygiene, State of California, 1969, pp. 64–100.

Bridges, K. M. B. Emotional development in early infancy. *Child Development,* 1932, **3,** 324–341.

Bronfenbrenner, U. Toward a theoretical model for the analysis of parent-child relationships in a social context. In J. C. Glidewell (Ed.), *Parental attitudes and child behavior.* Springfield, Ill.: Charles C Thomas, 1961, pp. 90–109.

Broughton, R. J. Sleep disorders: Disorders of arousal? *Science,* 1968, **159,** 1070–1078.

Brown, D. G. Sex-role preference in young children. *Psychological Monographs,* 1956, **70**(14, serial no. 421).

Bruner, J. S. On cognitive growth: I, II. In J. S. Bruner, R. R. Olver, & P. M. Greenfield (Eds.), *Studies in cognitive growth.* New York: Wiley, 1966, pp. 1–67.

Cartwright, R., & Ratzel, R. Effects of dream loss on waking behaviors. *Archives of General Psychiatry,* 1972, **27,** 277–280.

Castenada, A., McCandless, B. R., & Palermo, D. C. The children's form of the Manifest Anxiety Scale. *Child Development,* 1956, **27,** 317–326.

Cattell, R. B., & Cattell, M. D. L. *Handbook for the Jr.-Sr. High School Personality Questionnaire.* Champaign, Ill.: Institute for Personality and Ability Testing, 1969.

Coan, R. W., & Cattell, R. B. *Guidebook for the Early School Personality Questionnaire.* Champaign, Ill.: Institute for Personality and Ability Testing, 1966.

Cohen, D. B. *Sleep and dreaming: Origins, nature and functions.* Oxford, England: Pergamon Press, 1979.

Coleman, J. S., Campbell, E. Q., Hobson, C. J., McPartland, J., Mood, A. M., Weinfeld, F. D., & York, R. L. *Equality of educational opportunity.* Washington, D.C.: U. S. Government Printing Office, 1966.

Cowan, P. A. *Piaget with feeling: Cognitive, social, and emotional dimensions.* New York: Holt, Rinehart & Winston, 1978.

Crandall, V. C., Crandall, V. J., & Katkovsky, W. A children's social desirability questionnaire. *Journal of Consulting Psychology,* 1965, **29,** 27–36.

Delys, P., & Stephens, M. W. A locus of control (IE) measure for preschool-age children: Model, method, and validity. Presentation to Midwestern Psychological Association, Detroit, 1971.

Dement, W. Dream recall and eye movements during sleep in schizophrenics and normals. *Journal of Nervous and Mental Disease,* 1955, **122,** 263–269.

Dement, W. Perception during sleep. In P. Hoch & J. Zubin (Eds.), *Psychopathology of perception.* New York: Grune & Stratton, 1965, pp. 247–270.

Dement, W., & Wolpert, E. A. The relation of eye movements, body motility, and external stimuli to dream content. *Journal of Experimental Psychology,* 1958, **44,** 543–555.

Domhoff, B. Home dreams and laboratory dreams: Home dreams are better. In M. Kramer (Ed.), *Dream psychology and the new biology of dreaming.* Springfield, Ill.: Charles C Thomas, 1969, pp. 199–217.

Douvan, E., & Adelson, J. *The adolescent experience.* New York: Wiley, 1966.

Elkan, B. M. Developmental differences in the manifest content of children's reported dreams. Ph.D. dissertation, Columbia University, 1969.

Eme, R. F. Sex differences in childhood psychopathology: A review. *Psychological Bulletin,* 1979, **86,** 574–595.

Emmerich, W. Parental identification in young children. *Genetic Psychology Monographs,* 1959, **60,** 257–308.

Erikson, E. H. *Childhood and society* (2nd ed.). New York: Norton, 1963.

Estes, W. K. The information-processing approach to cognition: A confluence of metaphors and methods. In W. K. Estes (Ed.), *Handbook of learning and cognitive processes* (Vol. 5): *Human information processing.* Hillsdale, N.J.: Lawrence Erlbaum Associates, 1978, pp. 1–18.

Flapan, D. *Children's understanding of social interaction.* New York: Teacher's College Press, 1968.

Flavell, J. H. *The developmental psychology of Jean Piaget.* Princeton, N.J.: Van Nostrand, 1963.

Flavell, J. H. *The development of role-taking and communication skills in children.* New York: Wiley, 1968.

Flavell, J. H. *Cognitive development.* Englewood Cliffs, N.J.: Prentice-Hall, 1977.

Ford, L. H., & Rubin, B. M. A social desirability questionnaire for young children. *Journal of Consulting and Clinical Psychology,* 1970, **35,** 195–204.

Foss, D. J., & Hakes, D. T. *Psycholinguistics: An introduction to the psychology of language.* Englewood Cliffs, N.J.: Prentice-Hall, 1978.

Foulkes, D. Dream reports from different stages of sleep. *Journal of Abnormal and Social Psychology,* 1962, **65,** 14–25.

Foulkes, D. *The psychology of sleep.* New York: Scribner's, 1966.

Foulkes, D. Dreams of the male child: Four case studies. *Journal of Child Psychology and Psychiatry,* 1967, **8,** 81–98. (a)

Foulkes, D. Nonrapid eye movement mentation. *Experimental Neurology,* 1967, Suppl. 4, 28–38. (b)

Foulkes, D. Personality and dreams. In E. Hartmann (Ed.), *Sleep and dreaming.* Boston: Little, Brown, 1970, pp. 147–153.

Foulkes, D. Longitudinal studies of dreams in children. *Science and Psychoanalysis,* 1971, **19,** 48–71.

Foulkes, D. Children's dreams: Age changes and sex differences. *Waking and Sleeping,* 1977, **1,** 171–174.

Foulkes, D. Dreams of innocence. *Psychology Today,* 1978, **12**(7), 78–88. (a)

Foulkes, D. Dreaming as language and cognition. *Scientia,* 1978, **113,** 481–499. (b)

Foulkes, D. *A grammar of dreams.* New York: Basic Books, 1978. (c)

Foulkes, D. Effects of ad-libitum presleep exposure to violent vs. nonviolent television programming on older children's REM-dream reports. *The G.D.H.R. Bulletin of Current Research* (Atlanta), 1979, **5,** 15. (abstract) (a)

Foulkes, D. Home and laboratory dreams: Four empirical studies and a conceptual reevaluation. *Sleep,* 1979, **2,** 233–251. (b)

Foulkes, D. Bedside vs. intercom interview strategies in collecting children's laboratory dreams. *The G.D.H.R. Bulletin of Current Research* (Atlanta), 1979, **5,** 57. (abstract) (c)

Foulkes, D. Children's dreams. In B. B. Wolman (Ed.), *Handbook of dreams: Research, theories and applications.* New York: Van Nostrand Reinhold, 1979, pp. 131–167. (d)

Foulkes, D., Belvedere, E., & Brubaker, T. Televised violence and dream content. In G. A. Comstock, E. A. Rubinstein, & J. P. Murray (Eds.), *Television and social behavior* (Vol. 5): *Television's effects: Further explorations.* Washington, D.C.: U. S. Government Printing Office, 1971, pp. 59–119.

Foulkes, D., & Kerr, N. H. Cognitive factors in REM dreaming. *The INS Bulletin,* December, 1979, 9. (abstract)

Foulkes, D., Larson, J. D., Swanson, E. M., & Rardin, M. W. Two studies of childhood dreaming. *American Journal of Orthopsychiatry,* 1969, **39,** 627–643.

Foulkes, D., Petrik, J., & Scott, E. A. Analysis of children's dreams at ages 7–8 and 13–14: Normative data. *Sleep Research,* 1978, **7,** 175. (abstract)

Foulkes, D., Pivik, T., Steadman, H. E., Spear, P. S., & Symonds, J. D. Dreams of the male child: An EEG study. *Journal of Abnormal Psychology,* 1967, **72,** 457–467.

Foulkes, D., & Rechtschaffen, A. Presleep determinants of dream content: Effect of two films. *Perceptual and Motor Skills,* 1964, **19,** 983–1005.

Foulkes, D., Scott, E. A., & Pope, R. The tonic-phasic strategy in sleep-mentation research: Correlates of theta bursts at sleep onset and during non-REM sleep. *Ricerche di Psicologia,* 1980, **4,** 121–132.

Foulkes, D., & Shepherd, J. A scoring system for children's dreams. *Psychophysiology,* 1970, **7,** 335. (abstract)

Foulkes, D., & Shepherd, J. Effects of heightened arousal and suggestion on the dream reporting of preschool Ss. *Sleep Research,* 1972, **1,** 110. (abstract)

Foulkes, D., Shepherd, J., Larson, J. D., Belvedere, E., & Frost, S. Effects of awakenings in phasic vs. tonic stage REM on children's dream reports. *Sleep Research,* 1972, **1,** 104. (abstract)

Foulkes, D., Shepherd, J., & Scott, E. A. Analysis of children's dreams at ages 5–6 and 11–12: Normative data. *Sleep Research,* 1974, **3,** 117. (abstract)

Foulkes, D., Spear, P. S., & Symonds, J. D. Individual differences in mental activity at sleep onset. *Journal of Abnormal Psychology,* 1966, **71,** 280–286.

Foulkes, D., & Vogel, G. Mental activity at sleep onset. *Journal of Abnormal Psychology,* 1965, **70,** 231–243.

Foulkes, D., & Vogel, G. The current status of laboratory dream research. *Psychiatric Annals,* 1974, **4**(7), 7–27.

French, J. W., Ekstrom, R. B., & Price, L. A. *Manual for kit of reference tests for cognitive factors* (rev. ed.). Princeton, N.J.: Educational Testing Service, 1963.

Freud, S. *The interpretation of dreams.* New York: Basic Books, 1955 (orig., 1900).

Freud, S. Three essays on the theory of sexuality. In J. Strachey (Ed.), *The standard edition of the complete psychological works of Sigmund Freud* (Vol. 7). London: Hogarth Press, 1953 (orig. 1905), pp. 123–245.

Freud, S. Introductory lectures on psycho-analysis. In J. Strachey (Ed.), *The standard edition of the complete psychological works of Sigmund Freud* (Vol. 15–16). London: Hogarth Press, 1961–63 (orig. 1917).

Freud, S. From the history of an infantile neurosis. In J. Strachey (Ed.), *The standard edition of the complete psychological works of Sigmund Freud* (Vol. 17). London: Hogarth Press, 1955 (orig. 1918), pp. 7–122.

Freud, S. New introductory lectures on psycho-analysis. In J. Strachey (Ed.), *The standard edition of the complete psychological works of Sigmund Freud* (Vol. 22). London: Hogarth Press, 1964 (orig. 1933), pp. 1–182.

Galin, D. Implications for psychiatry of left and right cerebral specialization: A neurophysiological context for unconscious processes. *Archives of General Psychiatry,* 1974, **31,** 572–583.

Goldstein, L., Stoltzfus, N. W., & Gardocki, J. F. Changes in interhemispheric amplitude relationships in the EEG during sleep. *Physiology and Behavior,* 1972, **8,** 811–815.

Gough, H. G., & Heilbrun, A. B. *The Adjective Check List manual.* Palo Alto, Calif.: Consulting Psychologists Press, 1965.

Green, R. *Sexual identity conflict in children and adults.* New York: Basic Books, 1974.

Greenberg, B. S., & Gordon, T. F. Perceptions of violence in television programs: Critics and the public. In G. A. Comstock & E. A. Rubinstein (Eds.), *Television and social behavior* (Vol. 1): *Media content and control.* Washington, D.C.: U.S. Government Printing Office, 1971, pp. 244–258.

Greenwood, P., Wilson, D. H., & Gazzaniga, M. S. Dream report following commissurotomy. *Cortex,* 1977, **13,** 311–316.

Gruber, H. E., & Vonèche, J. J. *The essential Piaget.* New York: Basic Books, 1977.

Hall, C. S. A cognitive theory of dreams. *Journal of General Psychology,* 1953, **49,** 273–282.

Hall, C. S. Strangers in dreams: An empirical confirmation of the Oedipus complex. *Journal of Personality,* 1963, **31,** 336–345.

Hall, C. S. *The meaning of dreams* (new ed.). New York: McGraw-Hill, 1966.

Hall, C. S., & Nordby, V. J. *The individual and his dreams.* New York: New American Library, 1972.

Hauri, P. Effects of evening activity on subsequent sleep and dreams. Ph.D. dissertation, University of Chicago, 1966.

Hesse, H. *Demian.* New York: Bantam Books, 1966 (orig. 1919).

Hobson, J. A., & McCarley, R. W. The brain as a dream state generator: An activation-synthesis hypothesis of the dream process. *American Journal of Psychiatry,* 1977, **134,** 1335–1348.

Holt, R. R. The development of the primary process: A structural view. *Psychological Issues,* 1967, **5**(2–3), 345–383.

Huttenlocher, J., & Presson, C. C. Mental rotation and the perspective problem. *Cognitive Psychology,* 1973, **4,** 277–299.

Jacobs, L., Feldman, M., & Bender, M. B. Are the eye movements of dreaming sleep related to the visual images of dreams? *Psychophysiology,* 1972, **9,** 393–401.

James, W. *Psychology (briefer course).* New York: Holt, 1892.

Jaynes, J. *The origin of consciousness in the breakdown of the bicameral mind.* Boston: Houghton Mifflin, 1976.

Johnson, O. G., & Bommarito, J. W. *Tests and measurements in child development: A handbook.* San Francisco: Jossey-Bass, 1971.

Jung, C. G. General aspects of dream psychology. In *Dreams.* Princeton, N.J.: Princeton University Press, 1974 (orig. 1948), pp. 23–66.

Kagan, J., & Lemkin, J. The child's differential perception of parental attributes. *Journal of Abnormal and Social Psychology,* 1960, **61,** 440–447.

Kagan, J., & Moss, H. A. *Birth to maturity: A study in psychological development.* New York: Wiley, 1962.

Kagan, J., Rosman, B. L., Day, D., Albert, J., & Phillips, W. Information processing in the child. *Psychological Monographs,* 1964, **78**(1, serial no. 578).

Kahn, R. L., & Cannell, C. F. *The dynamics of interviewing.* New York: Wiley, 1957.

Kales, J. D., Kales, A., Jacobson, A., Po, J., & Green, J. Baseline sleep and recall studies in children. *Psychophysiology,* 1968, **4,** 391. (abstract)

Kerr, N. H., Corbitt, R., & Jurkovic, G. J. Mental rotation: Is it stage-related? *Journal of Mental Imagery,* 1980, **4,** 49–56.

Kerr, N. H., & Foulkes, D. Right-hemispheric mediation of dream visualization: A case study. *Cortex* (in press).

Kerr, N. H., Foulkes, D., & Jurkovic, G. J. Reported absence of visual dream imagery in a normally sighted subject with Turner's syndrome. *Journal of Mental Imagery,* 1978, **2,** 247–264.

Kimmins, C. W. *Children's dreams: An unexplored land.* London: Allen & Unwin, 1937.

Kirtley, D. D. *The psychology of blindness.* Chicago: Nelson-Hall, 1975.

Kohen-Raz, R. *The child from 9 to 13: Psychology and psychopathology.* Chicago: Aldine-Atherton, 1971.

Kohlberg, L. A cognitive-developmental analysis of children's sex-role concepts and attitudes. In E. Maccoby (Ed.), *The development of sex differences.* Stanford, Calif.: Stanford University Press, 1966, pp. 82–173.

Kohlberg, L., & Gilligan, C. The adolescent as philosopher: The discovery of the self in a post-conventional world. In J. Kagan & R. Coles (Eds.), *12 to 16: Early adolescence.* New York: Norton, 1972, pp. 144–179.

Kohn, M. L. *Class and conformity: A study in values.* Homewood, Ill.: Dorsey Press, 1969.

Larson, J. D., & Foulkes, D. Electromyogram suppression during sleep, dream recall, and orientation time. *Psychophysiology,* 1969, **5**, 548–555.

Laurendeau, M., & Pinard, A. *Causal thinking in the child.* New York: International Universities Press, 1962.

Lehmann, D., & Skrandies, W. Reference-free identification of components of checkerboard-evoked multichannel potential fields. *Electroencephalography and Clinical Neurophysiology,* 1980, **48**, 609–621.

Levinson, D., & Huffman, P. Traditional family ideology and its relation to personality. *Journal of Personality,* 1955, **23**, 251–273.

Loevinger, J., & Wessler, R. *Measuring ego development: Construction and use of a sentence completion test.* San Francisco: Jossey-Bass, 1970.

Maccoby, E. E. Sex differentiation during childhood development. Presentation to the American Psychological Association, Chicago, 1975.

Maccoby, E. E., & Jacklin, C. N. *The psychology of sex differences.* Stanford, Calif.: Stanford University Press, 1974.

McGee, M. G. Human spatial abilities: Psychometric studies and environmental, genetic, hormonal, and neurological influences. *Psychological Bulletin,* 1979, **86**, 889–918.

Marshall, H. R. Relations between home experiences and children's use of language in play interactions with peers. *Psychological Monographs,* 1961, **75**(5, serial no. 509).

Martin, E. C. Reflections on the early adolescent in school. In J. Kagan & R. Coles (Eds.), *12 to 16: Early adolescence.* New York: Norton, 1972, pp. 180–196.

Mathis, H. *Environmental Participation Index manual.* Washington, D.C.: Psychometric Studies, 1967.

Megargee, E. I. *The California Psychological Inventory handbook.* San Francisco: Jossey-Bass, 1972.

Mitchell, J. On Freud and the distinction between the sexes. In J. Strouse (Ed.), *Women and analysis: Dialogues on psychoanalytic views of femininity.* New York: Grossman, 1974, pp. 27–36.

Molinari, S., & Foulkes, D. Tonic and phasic events during sleep: Psychological correlates and implications. *Perceptual and Motor Skills,* 1969, **29**, 343–368.

Money, J., & Ehrhardt, A. A. *Man and woman, boy and girl: The differentiation and dimorphism of gender identity from conception to maturity.* Baltimore: Johns Hopkins University Press, 1972.

Monroe, L. J., Rechtschaffen, A., Foulkes, D., & Jensen, J. The discriminability of REM and NREM reports. *Journal of Personality and Social Psychology,* 1965, **2**, 456–460.

Morris, D. *The naked ape.* New York: Dell, 1969 (orig. 1967).

Neisser, U. *Cognition and reality: Principles and implications of cognitive psychology.* San Francisco: W. H. Freeman, 1976.

Nelson, K. Structure and strategy in learning to talk. *Monographs of the Society for Research in Child Development,* 1973, **38** (serial no. 149).

Offer, D. *The psychological world of the teen-ager: A study of adolescent boys.* New York: Basic Books, 1969.

O'Gorman, J. G., & Jamieson, R. D. Letter to the editor. *Psychophysiology,* 1979, **16**, 596.

Ornitz, E. M., Ritvo, E. R., Carr, E. M., Panman, L. M., & Walter, R. D. The variability of the auditory averaged evoked response during sleep and dreaming in children and adults. *Electroencephalography and Clinical Neurophysiology,* 1967, **22**, 514–524.

Ornstein, R. *The psychology of consciousness.* San Francisco: W. H. Freeman, 1972.

Person, E. Some new observations on the origins of femininity. In J. Strouse (Ed.), *Women and analysis: Dialogues on psychoanalytic views of femininity.* New York: Grossman, 1974, pp. 250–261.

Piaget, J. *The grasp of consciousness: Action and concept in the young child.* Cambridge, Mass.: Harvard University Press, 1976 (orig. 1974).

Piaget, J., & Inhelder, B. *Mental imagery in the child.* New York: Basic Books, 1971 (orig. 1966).

Pickford, R. W. *Pickford projective pictures.* London: Tavistock, 1963.

Pitcher, E. G., & Prelinger, E. *Children tell stories: An analysis of fantasy.* New York: International Universities Press, 1963.

Pivik, T., & Foulkes, D. "Dream deprivation": Effects on dream content. *Science,* 1966, **153,** 1282–1284.

Pivik, T., & Foulkes, D. NREM mentation: Relation to personality, orientation time, and time of night. *Journal of Consulting and Clinical Psychology,* 1968, **32,** 144–151.

Porter, R. B., & Cattell, R. B. *Interim manual for the Children's Personality Questionnaire.* Champaign, Ill.: Institute for Personality and Ability Testing, 1963.

Rabson, A. *Rating manual for the Fels nursery school and day camp behavior variables.* Yellow Springs, Ohio: Fels Institute, 1966.

Ray, W. S. The fidelity of report experiment: Directions to the student. *Journal of Psychology,* 1947, **24,** 297–312.

Rechtschaffen, A. Dream reports and dream experiences. *Experimental Neurology,* 1967, Suppl. 4, 4–15.

Rechtschaffen, A. The psychophysiology of mental activity during sleep. In F. J. McGuigan & R. A. Schoonover (Eds.), *The psychophysiology of thinking.* New York: Academic Press, 1973, pp. 153–205.

Rechtschaffen, A. Scientific method in the study of altered states of consciousness with illustrations from sleep and dream research. In *Altered states of consciousness: Current views and research problems.* Washington, D.C.: Drug Abuse Council, 1975, pp. 135–191.

Rechtschaffen, A. The single-mindedness and isolation of dreams. *Sleep,* 1978, **1,** 97–109.

Rechtschaffen, A., & Verdone, P. Amount of dreaming: Effect of incentive, adaptation to laboratory, and individual differences. *Perceptual and Motor Skills,* 1964, **19,** 947–958.

Rechtschaffen, A., Verdone, P., & Wheaton, J. Reports of mental activity during sleep. *Canadian Psychiatric Association Journal,* 1963, **8,** 409–414.

Rodgers, D. A. Estimation of MMPI profiles from CPI data. *Journal of Consulting Psychology,* 1966, **30,** 89.

Roethlisberger, F. J., & Dickson, W. J. *Management and the worker.* Cambridge, Mass.: Harvard University Press, 1939.

Roffwarg, H. P., Dement, W. C., Muzio, J. N., & Fisher, C. Dream imagery: Relationship to rapid eye movements of sleep. *Archives of General Psychiatry,* 1962, **7,** 235–258.

Rose, R. J., Harris, E. L., Christian, J. C., & Nance, W. E. Genetic variance in nonverbal intelligence: Data from kinships of identical twins. *Science,* 1979, **205,** 1153–1155.

Rosenberg, M. *Society and the adolescent self-image.* Princeton, N.J.: Princeton University Press, 1965.

Rosenzweig, S., Fleming, E. E., & Clarke, H. J. Revised scoring manual for the Rosenzweig Picture-Frustration Study. *Journal of Psychology,* 1947, **24,** 165–208.

Sastre, J. P., & Jouvet, M. Le comportement onirique du chat. *Physiology and Behavior,* 1979, **22,** 979–989.

Schachter, S. S., & Singer, J. E. Cognitive, social, and physiological determinants of emotional state. *Psychological Review,* 1962, **69,** 379–399.

Schaefer, E. S., & Bell, R. Q. Development of a parental attitude research instrument. *Child Development,* 1958, **29,** 339–361.

Schwartz, D. G., Weinstein, L. N., & Arkin, A. M. Qualitative aspects of sleep mentation. In A. M. Arkin, J. S. Antrobus, & S. J. Ellman (Eds.), *The mind in sleep: Psychology and psychophysiology.* Hillsdale, N.J.: Lawrence Erlbaum Associates, 1978, pp. 143–241.

Shantz, C. U. *The development of social cognition.* Chicago: University of Chicago Press, 1975.

Shaw, C. R. *The psychiatric disorders of childhood.* New York: Appleton-Century-Crofts, 1966.

Sherman, J. A. *On the psychology of women: A survey of empirical studies.* Springfield, Ill.: Charles C Thomas, 1971.

Simon, H. The behavioral and social sciences. *Science,* 1980, **209,** 72–78.

Skinner, B. F. Behaviorism at fifty. *Science,* 1963, **140,** 951–958.

Snyder, F. The phenomenology of dreaming. In L. Madow & L. H. Snow (Eds.), *The psychodynamic implications of the physiological studies on dreams.* Springfield, Ill.: Charles C Thomas, 1970, pp. 124–151.

Stoller, R. J. Facts and fancies: An examination of Freud's concept of bisexuality. In J. Strouse (Ed.), *Women and analysis: Dialogues on psychoanalytic views of femininity.* New York: Grossman, 1974 (orig. 1973), pp. 343–364.

Symonds, P. M. *Adolescent fantasy: An investigation of the picture-story method of personality study.* New York: Columbia University Press, 1949.

Torrance, E. P. *Torrance Tests of Creative Thinking.* Princeton, N.J.: Personnel Press, 1966.

Trupin, E. W. Correlates of ego-level and agency-communion in stage REM dreams of 11-13 year old children. *Journal of Child Psychology and Psychiatry,* 1976, **17,** 169–180.

Vandenberg, S. G., & Kuse, A. R. Spatial ability: A critical review of the sex-linked major gene hypothesis. In M. A. Wittig & A. C. Petersen (Eds.), *Sex-related differences in cognitive functioning: Developmental issues.* New York: Academic Press, 1979, pp. 67–95.

Vinacke, W. E. *The psychology of thinking.* New York: McGraw-Hill, 1952.

Vogel, G. W. A review of REM sleep deprivation. *Archives of General Psychiatry,* 1975, **32,** 749–761.

Vogel, G. W. Sleep-onset mentation. In A. M. Arkin, J. S. Antrobus, & S. J. Ellman (Eds.), *The mind in sleep: Psychology and psychophysiology.* Hillsdale, N.J.: Lawrence Erlbaum Associates, 1978, pp. 97–108.

Vogel, G. W., Barrowclough, B., & Giesler, D. D. Limited discriminability of REM and sleep onset reports and its psychiatric implications. *Archives of General Psychiatry,* 1972, **26,** 449–455.

Warner, W. L., Meeker, M., & Eells, K. *Social class in America.* New York: Harper & Row, 1960.

Weisz, R., & Foulkes, D. Home and laboratory dreams collected under uniform sampling conditions. *Psychophysiology,* 1970, **6,** 588–596.

Werner, H. *Comparative psychology of mental development.* Chicago: Follett, 1948.

Williams, M. *Brain damage and the mind.* Baltimore: Penguin, 1970.

Williams, R. L., Karacan, I., & Hursch, C. J. *Electroencephalography (EEG) of human sleep: Clinical applications.* New York: Wiley, 1974.

Winget, C., & Kramer, M. *The dimensions of dream content.* Gainesville: University of Florida Press, 1979.

Witkin, H. A., Oltman, P. K., Raskin, E., & Karp, S. A. *A manual for the Embedded Figures Tests.* Palo Alto, Calif.: Consulting Psychologists Press, 1971.

Yarrow, M. R., Campbell, J. D., & Burton, R. V. Recollections of childhood: A study of the retrospective method. *Monographs of the Society for Research in Child Development,* 1970, **35**(serial no. 138).

Zaidel, E. The split and half brains as models of congenital language disability. In C. L. Ludlow & M. E. Doran-Quine (Eds.), *The neurological bases of language disorders in children: Methods and directions for research*. Washington, D.C.: U.S. Government Printing Office (NINCDS monograph no. 22), 1980, pp. 55–86.

Zajonc, R. B. Feeling and thinking: Preferences need no inferences. *American Psychologist,* 1980, **35**, 151–175.

Zimmerman, W. B. Sleep mentation and auditory awakening thresholds. *Psychophysiology,* 1970, **6**, 540–549.

Appendixes

Appendix A

Reliability of the Dream Analysis

We here report interobserver reliability data from the application of our scoring system (Foulkes & Shepherd, 1970) to the children's normative-year dreams. Table A.1 presents the reliability of the content analysis. Where *a* stands for the number of dreams in which both judges scored an attribute as present, *b* equals the number of dreams in which an attribute was scored positively by the primary judge but as absent by the secondary judge, and *c* equals the number of dreams in which an attribute was scored positively by the secondary judge but as absent by the primary judge, reliability for that attribute is computed by the formula: $2a/(2a + b + c)$. This measure indicates the percentage of concordant positive scorings of any attribute by the two judges (Yarrow, Campbell, & Burton, 1970). Unlike a simple percentage of "scoring agreement," this method is insusceptible to spurious inflation by the relative rarity of the attribute. To give an idea of the report *n*'s, value *a* also is reported for each attribute in each year in which the primary judge scored it at least four times. In Year 1, 267 reports were judged independently by the two judges (24 more reports were scored consensually and served as standards for the remainder of the analysis); in Years 3 and 5, the numbers of reports scored independently by the two judges were, respectively, 376 and 484. In general, content-analysis reliabilities were satisfactory, especially for frequently scored and conceptually significant variables.

Table A.2 presents the data on interrater agreement in assigning global ratings to individual dream reports. Exact agreement was the rule, and for the 3-point scales (i.e., scales other than visualization), it was quite rare for the raters to assign different scale end points to the same dream. Only "dreamlike" (narrative and/or visualized) reports were scored for participation and distortion.

Table A.3 presents information on judges' agreement in counting the amount of substantive material in children's nocturnal reports. In computing "net" deviations between the judges, equal deviations of unlike sign for individual dreams were considered to cancel one another out; in computing "absolute" deviations, they were summed. In Year 3 there was a generally constant direction of difference between the two judges, the secondary judge counting more words in 259 dreams and the primary judge doing so in 90 dreams. By Year 5 the secondary judge no longer consistently "overcounted" the number of words in the children's dreams in comparison to the primary judge's word counts.

Table A.1 **Reliability of the Content Analysis**

	Year 1		Year 3		Year 5	
Category	Joint Positive	Reliability (%)	Joint Positive	Reliability (%)	Joint Positive	Reliability (%)
Characters						
Family						
Parental, M	31	97	33	100	40	99
Parental, F	40	98	43	98	58	98
Parental, either/both	54	99	54	98	66	98
Sibling, M	33	96	51	100	57	98
Sibling, F	35	100	27	98	30	100
Sibling, either/both	50	100	63	100	80	99
Parent/sibling, M	50	99	70	100	79	99
Parent/sibling, F	54	100	53	98	70	99
Parent/sibling, either/both	78	99	88	99	107	98
Grandparent, M	4	100	6	100	—	—
Grandparent, F	5	100	—	—	4	100
Grandparent, either/both	6	100	6	100	5	100
Uncle	4	100	—	—	8	100
Aunt	4	100	—	—	7	93
Aunt/uncle, either/both	4	100	—	—	9	95
Cousin, M	—	—	6	100	8	94
Cousin, F	—	—	—	—	6	86
Cousin, either/both	4	89	8	100	12	96
Any family, M	53	99	78	100	85	99
Any family, F	55	99	57	98	78	98
Any family, either/both	80	99	98	99	117	99

Table A.1 (continued)

Category	Year 1 Joint Positive	Year 1 Reliability (%)	Year 3 Joint Positive	Year 3 Reliability (%)	Year 5 Joint Positive	Year 5 Reliability (%)
Known						
Younger, M	—	—	7	93	—	—
Age-mates, M	19	86	45	95	53	88
Age-mates, F	13	84	41	92	42	88
Age-mates, I[a]	8	73	—	—	—	—
Older children, M	—	—	6	86	6	92
Adult, M	18	95	18	86	23	82
Adult, F	8	84	7	82	12	89
Adult, I	3	67	—	—	—	—
Any known, M	40	93	72	95	95	97
Any known, F	27	93	49	94	61	95
Any known, I	12	75	1	29	4	73
Strangers						
Younger, M	—	—	9	100	10	100
Younger, F	—	—	4	89	10	95
Age-mates, M	4	100	19	88	20	78
Age-mates, F	5	83	16	97	14	93
Age-mates, I	—	—	—	—	—	—
Older children, M	—	—	16	100	13	100
Older children, F	—	—	7	100	9	100
Adult, M	23	79	26	74	67	88
Adult, F	11	85	12	65	21	75
Aged/older, M	—	—	—	—	5	71
Aged/older, F	—	—	—	—	6	100

Any stranger, M	43	91	106	94	158	95
Any stranger, F	25	96	54	96	80	92
Any stranger, I	39	75	15	60	42	66
Celebrities, M	—	—	—	—	5	83
Groups	11	61	39	86	48	81
Supernatural	—	—	—	—	4	62
Animals						
Any, animal	39	99	61	96	65	98
Pets	11	96	23	90	19	90
Barnyard	17	100	19	88	19	93
Indigenous	11	88	10	80	17	87
Exotic	5	100	4	80	10	87
Dolls, etc.	6	100	—	—	4	67
Settings						
Conveyance	19	86	34	83	49	92
Home, any	60	94	82	82	105	91
Home, own	42	94	43	86	58	92
Home, other	9	82	10	74	15	73
Home, unfamiliar	6	63	29	76	31	78
School, any	27	98	31	91	40	91
School, own	19	95	26	95	26	88
School, other	—	—	2	67	2	67
School, unfamiliar	5	91	2	57	11	96
Recreational	60	93	98	84	153	92
Commercial	18	90	26	80	49	88
Other outdoors	28	86	34	69	50	75
Sleep lab	18	90	18	95	18	88
Unclassifiable	52	90	23	71	49	76
Classifiable, other	3	55	17	65	23	82

Table A.1 (continued)

	Year 1		Year 3		Year 5	
Category	Joint Positive	Reliability (%)	Joint Positive	Reliability (%)	Joint Positive	Reliability (%)
Activities						
Sensory						
Vision, dreamer	34	80	69	90	102	95
Vision, other	21	89	50	91	74	92
Vision, either	43	81	94	92	137	94
Hearing, dreamer	9	82	14	76	16	94
Hearing, other	—	—	—	—	9	90
Hearing, either	9	78	15	77	22	94
Skin senses, dreamer	—	—	5	83	—	—
Skin senses, either	—	—	5	83	—	—
Any sensory, dreamer	42	82	85	89	111	95
Any sensory, other	22	86	54	92	80	93
Any sensory, either	52	83	111	91	150	95
Motor						
Verbal, dreamer	25	94	70	95	77	94
Verbal, other	43	96	115	97	150	95
Verbal, either	52	97	130	97	169	97
Manual, dreamer	61	93	109	88	138	89
Manual, other	84	96	145	88	186	91
Manual, either	105	97	202	93	239	92
Locomotor, dreamer	80	96	164	95	178	94
Locomotor, other	99	95	197	93	244	96
Locomotor, either	120	96	244	96	291	96
Expressive fine, dreamer	—	—	4	80	—	—

Expressive fine, other	6	86	10	87	13	93
Expressive fine, either	6	86	11	85	14	90
Any motor, dreamer	114	98	221	96	257	96
Any motor, other	147	96	283	97	343	97
Any motor, either	179	97	329	99	406	99
Bodily, dreamer	—	—	—	—	2	57
Bodily, other	—	—	—	—	0	0
Bodily, either	—	—	—	—	2	36
States						
Cognitive, dreamer	14	78	39	73	50	79
Cognitive, other	7	82	13	74	26	80
Cognitive, either	20	78	48	75	67	82
Feelings						
Afraid, dreamer	14	100	28	97	43	97
Afraid, other	—	—	6	92	3	75
Afraid, either	14	97	31	97	43	96
Angry, dreamer	10	100	14	97	28	100
Angry, other	5	71	4	100	13	100
Angry, either	13	93	18	97	35	100
Sad, dreamer	14	97	10	100	11	92
Sad, other	4	89	—	—	3	75
Sad, either	17	97	10	91	13	90
Happy, dreamer	39	99	59	95	63	95
Happy, other	6	100	5	56	7	64
Happy, either	40	99	61	94	67	93
Excited, dreamer	10	91	15	77	15	81
Excited, either	10	91	15	75	16	80
Any feelings, dreamer	75	99	124	97	149	96
Any feelings, other	16	89	16	68	30	88
Any feelings, either	80	99	129	97	162	96

Table A.1 (continued)

Category	Year 1		Year 3		Year 5	
	Joint Positive	Reliability (%)	Joint Positive	Reliability (%)	Joint Positive	Reliability (%)
Motives						
Hunger, dreamer	11	85	33	89	30	86
Hunger, other	19	86	46	88	39	90
Hunger, either	25	89	58	89	50	92
Thirst, dreamer	—	—	8	84	7	82
Thirst, other	4	80	11	92	12	92
Thirst, either	7	93	15	91	16	94
Sex, dreamer	—	—	—	—	5	100
Sex, other	—	—	—	—	9	95
Sex, either	—	—	—	—	9	95
Fatigue, dreamer	27	92	26	81	34	88
Fatigue, other	12	92	17	77	37	87
Fatigue, either	35	92	33	86	46	88
Approach social, dreamer	36	80	77	83	97	83
Approach social, other	42	83	97	77	159	85
Approach social, either	52	85	111	80	174	86
Approach object, dreamer	17	64	70	75	141	86
Approach object, other	23	73	89	79	154	88
Approach object, either	27	64	127	81	218	90
Avoidance social, dreamer	—	—	4	67	3	75
Avoidance social, other	5	63	6	71	5	77
Avoidance social, either	7	67	8	70	7	78
Avoidance object, dreamer	—	—	—	—	4	62
Avoidance object, other	5	83	—	—	4	53
Avoidance object, either	7	88	1	29	8	59

Attack social, dreamer	14	82	14	60	35	83
Attack social, other	42	89	60	82	96	91
Attack social, either	44	91	66	82	101	91
Attack object, dreamer	6	86	1	33	2	50
Attack object, other	9	78	4	38	8	57
Attack object, either	13	81	6	46	10	61
Outcomes						
Unfavorable						
Other mediated, dreamer	12	65	20	67	47	87
Other mediated, other	39	84	58	82	86	91
Other mediated, either	45	87	69	82	104	91
Self-mediated, dreamer	7	70	3	46	6	50
Self-mediated, other	8	64	6	80	11	59
Self-mediated, either	13	68	9	69	17	59
Unmediated, dreamer	7	70	7	58	9	51
Unmediated, other	13	67	7	54	16	71
Unmediated, either	16	70	11	55	20	61
Any unfavorable, dreamer	27	75	32	69	66	84
Any unfavorable, other	57	86	74	85	114	92
Any unfavorable, either	74	90	95	85	146	92
Favorable						
Other mediated, dreamer	24	74	66	79	97	85
Other mediated, other	44	79	99	80	149	86
Other mediated, either	48	81	106	80	160	87
Self-mediated, dreamer	7	74	—	—	6	67
Self-mediated, other	7	78	—	—	11	79
Self-mediated, either	12	75	4	73	13	76
Any favorable, dreamer	32	78	67	78	103	85
Any favorable, other	49	82	101	80	158	86
Any favorable, either	59	88	109	80	171	87

[a] I = indeterminate sex.

Table A.2 **Reliability of the Global Ratings**

Rating Scale	Year	Number of Dreams Scored	Exact Agreement (%)	Agreement (%) ±1 Scale Point
Hedonic tone	Year 1	267	91	99
Hedonic tone	Year 3	376	80	97
Hedonic tone	Year 5	484	88	99
Active participation	Year 1	254	85	98
Active participation	Year 3	365	87	99
Active participation	Year 5	474	92	100
Setting distortion	Year 1	254	93	99
Setting distortion	Year 3	365	93	98
Setting distortion	Year 5	474	92	98
Character distortion	Year 1	254	95	99
Character distortion	Year 3	365	93	99
Character distortion	Year 5	474	94	98
Visualization	Year 1	267	99.6	—
Visualization	Year 3	376	99.7	—
Visualization	Year 5	484	99	—

Table A.3 **Agreement in Judges' Word Counts**

Word Count Variable	Year 1	Year 3	Year 5
Words counted by primary judge, all reports	17,418	33,093	44,362
Between primary and secondary judge			
Net discrepancy in total words counted	292	3,219	2,039
Net discrepancy in per-dream word count	1.1	8.6	4.2
Absolute discrepancy in total words counted	1,818	4,891	3,703
Absolute discrepancy in per-dream word count	6.8	13.0	7.7

Appendix B

Normative Dream Findings

This appendix presents some summary statistics for the primary judge's coding of the children's dreams from Years 1, 3, and 5 of each of our longitudinal studies. The data are tabulated separately by stage of sleep and by subject sex within each study year. In Table B.1 "young" children were ages 3–5 and "older" children, ages 9–11; in Table B.2 "young" children were ages 5–7 and "older" children, ages 11–13; in Table B.3 "young" children were ages 7–9 and "older" children, ages 13–15. Each entry in the appendixes, be it median, mean, or proportion, summarizes the *pool* of reports in its stage, age, and sex category; that is, it describes the typical *report* in that pool, rather than the typical *child* who contributed some report to it.

All statistical analyses of normative dream data reported in the text (longitudinal changes in dream content, sex differences in dream content, differences in dream content from different stages of sleep, nondream correlates of dream content) were performed on scorings of the judge whose data are summarized in this appendix.

Table B.1 **Results of Analysis of Children's Dream Reports: Year 1, Judge 1**

	Awakening Category											
	REM Sleep				NREM Sleep				Sleep Onset			
Series Number:	100	200	300	400	100	200	300	400	100	200	300	400
Age:	Young	Young	Older	Older	Young	Young	Older	Older	Young	Young	Older	Older
Sex:	F	M	F	M	F	M	F	M	F	M	F	M
Awakenings, *n*:	97	101	117	114	58	61	71	67	20	20	23	23
Awakenings with recall, *n*:	20	33	84	68	5	2	28	16	1	6	15	13
Word count												
Median	14	13	75.5	60.5	13	16.5	48	58.5	89	9	48	45
Minimum	3	2	8	10	8	12	11	14	—	1	24	8
Maximum	47	50	443	249	35	21	130	303	—	34	144	183
% ≥ 100 words	0	0	30	31	0	0	4	13	0	0	13	15
Ratings (means)												
(1) Hedonic tone	1.90	2.00	1.99	2.10	1.80	2.00	1.75	2.13	3.00	2.00	1.93	2.15
(2) Active participation	1.60	2.06	2.07	2.18	1.60	2.00	1.96	2.07	2.00	1.80	2.15	2.20
(3) Setting distortion	2.10	2.44	2.02	2.11	1.00	1.50	1.89	2.13	1.00	1.60	1.92	2.20
(4) Character distortion	2.15	2.25	2.00	2.15	1.80	—	1.96	2.23	2.00	2.00	2.25	2.13
(5) Visualization	.95	.97	.92	.87	1.00	1.00	.71	.88	1.00	.83	.87	.69
Content analysis (proportion)												
Characters												
Family												
Parent M	.00	.09	.21	.13	.00	.00	.11	.00	.00	.17	.13	.00
Parent F	.00	.09	.23	.15	.00	.00	.18	.13	1.00	.50	.07	.00
Sibling M/F	.15	.00	.26	.21	.00	.00	.25	.25	.00	.00	.13	.08
Family M/F	.15	.18	.38	.31	.00	.00	.32	.31	1.00	.50	.13	.08

Known persons												
Peer M	.10	.00	.06	.15	.00	.00	.04	.00	.00	.00	.07	.15
Peer F	.10	.00	.10	.00	.00	.00	.11	.00	.00	.00	.13	.00
Adult M	.05	.03	.05	.10	.00	.00	.04	.19	.00	.17	.00	.15
Adult F	.00	.03	.06	.03	.00	.00	.04	.00	.00	.00	.07	.00
Any M	.20	.03	.12	.25	.20	.00	.07	.25	.00	.17	.07	.23
Any F	.15	.03	.19	.07	.00	.00	.11	.00	.00	.00	.13	.00
Strangers												
Peer M	.00	.00	.00	.04	.00	.00	.00	.06	.00	.00	.00	.00
Peer F	.00	.00	.02	.01	.00	.00	.00	.00	.00	.00	.00	.00
Adult M	.00	.00	.17	.15	.00	.00	.00	.00	.00	.00	.13	.00
Adult F	.00	.00	.08	.04	.00	.00	.04	.00	.00	.00	.07	.00
Any M	.00	.03	.21	.31	.00	.00	.00	.25	.00	.00	.13	.15
Any F	.00	.03	.13	.15	.00	.00	.07	.00	.00	.00	.13	.08
Groups	.00	.03	.08	.10	.00	.00	.07	.06	.00	.00	.13	.00
Supernatural	.05	.00	.02	.01	.00	.50	.00	.00	.00	.00	.00	.00
Animals, any	.45	.33	.14	.04	.20	.00	.18	.13	1.00	.33	.27	.00
Pet	.00	.15	.05	.01	.20	.50	.11	.00	.00	.00	.07	.00
Barnyard	.25	.12	.04	.01	.00	.00	.07	.00	1.00	.17	.20	.00
Indigenous	.25	.12	.06	.00	.20	.00	.04	.13	.00	.00	.00	.00
Exotic	.00	.03	.04	.01	.00	.00	.00	.00	.00	.17	.00	.00
Dolls	.10	.00	.01	.01	.40	.00	.00	.00	.00	.00	.00	.00
Settings												
Conveyance	.05	.06	.14	.10	.00	.00	.07	.13	.00	.00	.00	.00
Home, any	.25	.18	.32	.26	.40	.50	.14	.19	1.00	.17	.07	.08
Home, own	.15	.12	.24	.18	.40	.50	.11	.19	.00	.17	.07	.00
School, any	.05	.00	.11	.07	.00	.00	.18	.06	.00	.00	.40	.00
School, own	.00	.00	.08	.07	.00	.00	.18	.00	.00	.00	.27	.00
Recreational	.10	.03	.26	.31	.00	.00	.21	.31	.00	.00	.40	.31
Commercial	.00	.09	.11	.06	.20	.00	.11	.00	.00	.17	.07	.00

Table B.1 (continued)

	Awakening Category											
	REM Sleep				NREM Sleep				Sleep Onset			
Series Number:	100	200	300	400	100	200	300	400	100	200	300	400
Age:	Young	Young	Older	Older	Young	Young	Older	Older	Young	Young	Older	Older
Sex:	F	M	F	M	F	M	F	M	F	M	F	M
Other outdoors	.15	.24	.17	.13	.00	.50	.04	.13	.00	.17	.00	.00
Sleep lab	.15	.09	.05	.04	.40	.50	.00	.13	.00	.17	.00	.23
Vague	.35	.30	.11	.25	.00	.00	.29	.19	.00	.33	.07	.38
Activities												
Sensory												
Vision, dreamer	.15	.09	.19	.25	.00	.00	.14	.06	1.00	.17	.20	.15
Vision, other	.00	.00	.10	.09	.00	.00	.11	.19	.00	.17	.13	.00
Vision, either	.15	.09	.24	.26	.00	.00	.18	.19	1.00	.17	.27	.15
Hearing, dreamer	.00	.03	.05	.07	.00	.00	.07	.00	.00	.00	.07	.00
Hearing, other	.00	.00	.01	.00	.00	.00	.04	.00	.00	.00	.00	.00
Hearing, either	.00	.03	.06	.07	.00	.00	.07	.00	.00	.00	.07	.00
Motor												
Verbal, dreamer	.00	.03	.13	.16	.00	.00	.04	.19	.00	.00	.07	.08
Verbal, other	.00	.03	.27	.25	.00	.00	.07	.19	1.00	.00	.13	.00
Verbal, either	.00	.03	.31	.28	.00	.00	.07	.19	1.00	.00	.13	.08
Manual, dreamer	.10	.09	.31	.31	.00	.00	.18	.31	.00	.33	.20	.23
Manual, other	.30	.09	.42	.44	.00	.00	.21	.25	.00	.17	.20	.31
Manual, either	.30	.15	.51	.53	.00	.00	.25	.38	.00	.50	.33	.46
Locomotor, dreamer	.05	.03	.37	.49	.20	.00	.29	.63	.00	.00	.20	.46
Locomotor, other	.20	.24	.46	.56	.20	.00	.39	.56	.00	.00	.33	.46
Locomotor, either	.25	.27	.52	.68	.20	.00	.39	.69	.00	.00	.33	.77

	1	2	3	4	5	6	7	8	9	10	11	12	13
Any, dreamer	.46	.40	.33	.00	.69	.43	.00	.20	.00	.63	.52	.15	.10
Any, other	.46	.40	.17	.00	.63	.54	.00	.20	.00	.78	.73	.36	.50
Any, either	.77	.53	.50	.00	.75	.61	.00	.20	.00	.90	.82	.42	.50
States													
Cognitive													
Cognitive, dreamer	.00	.07	.00	.00	.19	.07	.00	.00	.00	.07	.12	.00	.00
Cognitive, other	.00	.07	.00	.00	.13	.04	.00	.00	.00	.06	.08	.00	.00
Cognitive, either	.00	.07	.00	.00	.19	.07	.00	.00	.00	.12	.17	.00	.00
Affective													
Afraid, dreamer	.08	.00	.00	.00	.06	.00	.00	.00	.00	.07	.11	.00	.00
Afraid, other	.00	.00	.00	.00	.00	.00	.00	.00	.00	.00	.04	.00	.00
Afraid, either	.08	.00	.00	.00	.06	.00	.00	.00	.00	.07	.11	.00	.00
Angry, dreamer	.08	.00	.00	.00	.06	.00	.00	.00	.00	.09	.02	.00	.00
Angry, other	.00	.07	.00	.00	.00	.00	.00	.00	.00	.03	.08	.00	.00
Angry, either	.08	.07	.00	.00	.06	.00	.00	.00	.00	.09	.08	.00	.00
Sad, dreamer	.00	.07	.00	.00	.00	.07	.00	.00	.00	.04	.10	.03	.00
Sad, other	.00	.07	.00	.00	.00	.00	.00	.00	.00	.03	.02	.00	.00
Sad, either	.00	.07	.00	.00	.06	.07	.00	.00	.00	.06	.12	.03	.00
Happy, dreamer	.00	.27	.00	.00	.00	.21	.00	.00	.00	.10	.29	.06	.10
Happy, other	.00	.07	.00	.00	.00	.04	.00	.00	.00	.01	.05	.00	.00
Happy, either	.00	.27	.00	.00	.00	.21	.00	.00	.00	.12	.29	.06	.10
Any, dreamer	.15	.33	.00	.00	.19	.36	.00	.00	.00	.34	.48	.06	.10
Any, other	.00	.13	.00	.00	.00	.04	.00	.00	.00	.07	.18	.00	.00
Any, either	.15	.40	.00	.00	.19	.36	.00	.00	.00	.37	.50	.06	.10
Motivational-organic													
Hunger, dreamer	.00	.07	.17	.00	.00	.00	.00	.00	.00	.07	.11	.00	.05
Hunger, other	.00	.00	.00	.00	.06	.00	.00	.00	.00	.12	.15	.03	.20
Hunger, either	.00	.07	.17	.00	.06	.00	.00	.00	.00	.13	.19	.06	.20
Thirst, dreamer	.00	.00	.00	.00	.06	.00	.00	.00	.00	.00	.02	.03	.00
Thirst, other	.00	.00	.00	.00	.00	.00	.00	.00	.00	.03	.02	.03	.05

Table B.1 (continued)

	Awakening Category											
	REM Sleep				NREM Sleep				Sleep Onset			
Series Number:	100	200	300	400	100	200	300	400	100	200	300	400
Age:	Young	Young	Older	Older	Young	Young	Older	Older	Young	Young	Older	Older
Sex:	F	M	F	M	F	M	F	M	F	M	F	M
Thirst, either	.05	.06	.04	.03	.00	.00	.00	.06	.00	.00	.00	.00
Fatigue, dreamer	.20	.27	.05	.07	.20	.50	.04	.13	.00	.17	.00	.15
Fatigue, other	.05	.00	.06	.03	.60	.00	.00	.00	1.00	.00	.00	.08
Fatigue, either	.20	.27	.10	.10	.60	.50	.04	.13	1.00	.17	.00	.15
Motivational-socialized												
Approach social, dreamer	.10	.03	.25	.24	.20	.00	.21	.19	.00	.00	.00	.08
Approach social, other	.00	.00	.31	.29	.20	.00	.25	.19	.00	.00	.13	.15
Approach social, either	.10	.03	.38	.31	.20	.00	.29	.25	.00	.00	.13	.15
Approach object, dreamer	.05	.06	.08	.15	.00	.00	.04	.19	.00	.17	.00	.00
Approach object, other	.00	.00	.12	.21	.00	.00	.04	.13	.00	.00	.13	.08
Approach object, either	.05	.06	.13	.25	.00	.00	.04	.25	.00	.17	.13	.08
Avoidance social, dreamer	.00	.00	.04	.01	.00	.00	.00	.00	.00	.00	.00	.00
Avoidance social, other	.00	.00	.04	.03	.00	.00	.04	.13	.00	.00	.13	.00
Avoidance social, either	.00	.00	.06	.04	.00	.00	.04	.13	.00	.00	.13	.00
Avoidance object, dreamer	.00	.00	.02	.01	.00	.00	.00	.00	.00	.00	.00	.00
Avoidance object, other	.00	.03	.05	.03	.00	.00	.00	.00	.00	.00	.00	.00
Avoidance object, either	.00	.03	.06	.03	.00	.00	.00	.00	.00	.00	.00	.00
Attack social, dreamer	.00	.00	.08	.09	.00	.00	.04	.06	.00	.00	.00	.00
Attack social, other	.00	.06	.23	.26	.00	.00	.07	.13	.00	.00	.20	.00
Attack social, either	.00	.06	.24	.26	.00	.00	.07	.13	.00	.00	.20	.00
Attack object, dreamer	.00	.00	.05	.01	.00	.00	.00	.06	.00	.00	.07	.00

Attack object, other	.00	.03	.08	.03	.00	.00	.00	.00	.00	.00	.07	.08
Attack object, either	.00	.03	.11	.04	.00	.00	.00	.06	.00	.00	.07	.08

Outcomes

Unfavorable

Other mediated, dreamer	.00	.00	.14	.09	.00	.00	.00	.06	.00	.00	.00	.00
Other mediated, other	.00	.06	.25	.31	.00	.00	.11	.06	.00	.00	.27	.08
Other mediated, either	.00	.06	.27	.31	.00	.00	.11	.13	.00	.00	.27	.08
Self-mediated, dreamer	.00	.00	.06	.03	.00	.00	.00	.06	.00	.00	.00	.15
Self-mediated, other	.00	.00	.07	.09	.00	.00	.00	.06	.00	.00	.00	.00
Self-mediated, either	.00	.00	.11	.09	.00	.00	.00	.13	.00	.00	.00	.15
Unmediated, dreamer	.05	.00	.05	.04	.00	.00	.00	.06	.00	.00	.07	.00
Unmediated, other	.05	.00	.08	.07	.00	.00	.00	.06	1.00	.00	.07	.00
Unmediated, either	.10	.00	.08	.09	.00	.00	.00	.06	1.00	.00	.07	.00
Any, dreamer	.05	.00	.23	.16	.00	.00	.00	.19	.00	.00	.07	.15
Any, other	.05	.06	.36	.43	.00	.00	.11	.19	1.00	.00	.27	.08
Any, either	.10	.06	.42	.44	.00	.00	.11	.31	1.00	.00	.27	.23

Favorable

Other mediated, dreamer	.00	.00	.21	.16	.20	.00	.14	.13	.00	.00	.07	.08
Other mediated, other	.10	.03	.33	.28	.20	.00	.25	.13	.00	.00	.07	.15
Other mediated, either	.10	.03	.35	.29	.20	.00	.25	.13	.00	.00	.13	.15
Self-mediated, dreamer	.00	.00	.10	.03	.00	.00	.00	.06	.00	.00	.00	.00
Self-mediated, other	.00	.00	.06	.07	.00	.00	.00	.00	.00	.00	.00	.00
Self-mediated, either	.00	.00	.12	.09	.00	.00	.00	.06	.00	.00	.00	.00
Unmediated, dreamer	.00	.00	.00	.00	.00	.00	.00	.00	.00	.00	.00	.00
Unmediated, other	.00	.00	.01	.00	.00	.00	.00	.00	.00	.00	.00	.00
Unmediated, either	.00	.00	.01	.00	.00	.00	.00	.00	.00	.00	.00	.00
Any, dreamer	.00	.00	.27	.19	.20	.00	.14	.19	.00	.00	.07	.08
Any, other	.10	.03	.36	.31	.20	.00	.25	.13	.00	.00	.07	.15
Any, either	.10	.03	.42	.32	.20	.00	.25	.19	.00	.00	.13	.15

Table B.2 **Results of Analysis of Children's Dream Reports: Year 3, Judge 1**

	Awakening Category											
	REM Sleep				NREM Sleep				Sleep Onset			
Series Number:	100	200	300	400	100	200	300	400	100	200	300	400
Age:	Young	Young	Older	Older	Young	Young	Older	Older	Young	Young	Older	Older
Sex:	F	M	F	M	F	M	F	M	F	M	F	M
Awakenings, *n*:	101	103	118	174	62	62	71	106	21	21	24	36
Awakenings with recall, *n*:	25	39	88	106	4	6	26	29	4	9	19	21
Word count												
Median	50	25	83	103	36	11.5	58.5	89	47.5	46	59	78
Minimum	9	9	11	12	16	1	7	7	21	17	15	18
Maximum	168	149	268	668	101	84	198	258	87	129	119	215
% ≥ 100 words	8	3	43	53	25	0	12	41	0	11	11	38
Ratings (means)												
(1) Hedonic tone	1.60	2.10	1.77	1.93	2.25	2.33	1.73	2.07	1.75	2.44	1.84	1.71
(2) Active participation	1.76	1.51	2.13	2.24	2.25	1.60	2.31	2.16	2.00	1.67	2.19	2.10
(3) Setting distortion	2.12	2.18	2.09	2.23	2.00	2.60	2.15	2.40	2.00	2.11	2.13	2.10
(4) Character distortion	2.00	2.42	1.94	1.99	2.33	3.00	1.59	2.18	1.67	2.56	2.17	2.06
(5) Visualization	.88	.97	.99	.96	1.00	.67	1.00	.83	.50	1.00	.79	.95
Content analysis (proportion)												
Characters												
Family												
Parent M	.24	.08	.10	.12	.25	.00	.00	.00	.00	.00	.00	.05
Parent F	.20	.10	.12	.10	.25	.00	.19	.03	.25	.22	.05	.05
Sibling M	.36	.00	.12	.15	.00	.00	.19	.10	.00	.33	.05	.14
Sibling F	.12	.05	.14	.04	.25	.00	.12	.00	.25	.11	.05	.00
Any M/F	.40	.18	.31	.26	.50	.00	.35	.10	.25	.33	.11	.29

Known persons												
Peer M	.04	.10	.03	.24	.00	.00	.04	.14	.50	.11	.11	.19
Peer F	.12	.03	.26	.08	.00	.00	.15	.00	.50	.11	.16	.00
Adult M	.04	.03	.07	.06	.00	.00	.04	.21	.00	.00	.05	.00
Adult F	.04	.00	.06	.01	.00	.00	.00	.00	.00	.00	.16	.00
Any M	.16	.15	.16	.30	.00	.00	.08	.31	.50	.11	.11	.24
Any F	.16	.03	.31	.09	.00	.00	.19	.00	.50	.11	.21	.00
Strangers												
Peer M	.04	.03	.03	.08	.00	.00	.12	.10	.00	.00	.00	.14
Peer F	.04	.00	.10	.03	.00	.00	.08	.00	.00	.00	.11	.00
Adult M	.04	.08	.09	.11	.25	.17	.00	.10	.00	.00	.05	.10
Adult F	.04	.03	.07	.06	.00	.00	.00	.00	.00	.00	.11	.00
Any M	.24	.36	.24	.38	.25	.50	.19	.34	.00	.33	.16	.38
Any F	.20	.10	.22	.17	.00	.00	.12	.03	.25	.11	.16	.05
Groups	.12	.03	.12	.17	.00	.00	.08	.21	.00	.00	.16	.14
Supernatural	.00	.00	.00	.00	.00	.00	.00	.00	.00	.00	.00	.00
Animals, any	.20	.46	.17	.09	.50	.33	.08	.07	.00	.67	.00	.19
Pet	.12	.21	.06	.05	.00	.17	.08	.00	.00	.33	.00	.05
Barnyard	.00	.08	.08	.03	.25	.17	.00	.07	.00	.22	.00	.10
Indigenous	.04	.23	.00	.03	.00	.00	.00	.00	.00	.00	.00	.05
Exotic	.04	.03	.03	.00	.25	.00	.00	.00	.00	.11	.00	.00
Dolls	.00	.00	.01	.02	.00	.00	.00	.00	.00	.00	.00	.00
Settings												
Conveyance	.20	.08	.10	.20	.00	.00	.00	.03	.00	.33	.00	.10
Home, any	.44	.21	.31	.25	.50	.33	.27	.17	.25	.67	.21	.19
Home, own	.24	.13	.16	.09	.25	.17	.08	.10	.25	.22	.16	.19
School, any	.04	.05	.07	.15	.00	.00	.08	.07	.25	.11	.16	.10
School, own	.04	.00	.05	.13	.00	.00	.08	.07	.25	.11	.11	.05
Recreational	.32	.28	.30	.33	.00	.00	.27	.14	.00	.22	.21	.38
Commercial	.00	.08	.10	.10	.00	.00	.08	.14	.00	.00	.00	.05

Table B.2 (continued)

		Awakening Category										
	REM Sleep				NREM Sleep				Sleep Onset			
Series Number:	100	200	300	400	100	200	300	400	100	200	300	400
Age:	Young	Young	Older	Older	Young	Young	Older	Older	Young	Young	Older	Older
Sex:	F	M	F	M	F	M	F	M	F	M	F	M
Other outdoors	.12	.21	.11	.14	.50	.17	.12	.10	.00	.11	.16	.05
Sleep lab	.08	.05	.08	.03	.00	.17	.00	.07	.00	.00	.00	.10
Vague	.00	.03	.08	.06	.00	.33	.15	.14	.50	.00	.11	.10
Activities												
Sensory												
Vision, dreamer	.24	.13	.17	.28	.25	.00	.15	.17	.00	.00	.26	.14
Vision, other	.24	.13	.20	.16	.25	.00	.08	.03	.00	.22	.05	.05
Vision, either	.32	.21	.28	.34	.25	.00	.23	.17	.00	.22	.26	.14
Hearing, dreamer	.04	.00	.01	.07	.00	.17	.04	.07	.00	.00	.11	.14
Hearing, other	.00	.00	.00	.01	.00	.00	.00	.03	.00	.00	.00	.05
Hearing, either	.04	.00	.01	.07	.00	.17	.04	.07	.00	.00	.11	.19
Motor												
Verbal, dreamer	.08	.03	.25	.32	.00	.00	.08	.17	.00	.00	.05	.38
Verbal, other	.24	.10	.39	.47	.00	.00	.15	.31	.25	.11	.16	.38
Verbal, either	.28	.10	.45	.53	.00	.00	.15	.34	.25	.11	.16	.48
Manual, dreamer	.20	.21	.48	.38	.50	.17	.19	.28	.50	.00	.37	.33
Manual, other	.52	.59	.49	.43	.50	.50	.27	.34	.50	.56	.37	.33
Manual, either	.64	.64	.69	.57	1.00	.67	.38	.45	.50	.56	.53	.43
Locomotor, dreamer	.32	.18	.58	.58	.50	.33	.35	.45	.25	.44	.32	.43
Locomotor, other	.56	.59	.58	.66	.50	.50	.38	.45	.25	.67	.42	.48
Locomotor, either	.64	.62	.75	.76	.50	.50	.50	.55	.50	.89	.53	.57

States												
Any, dreamer	.44	.33	.75	.74	.75	.33	.50	.59	.50	.44	.42	.62
Any, other	.92	.85	.81	.81	.75	.83	.50	.59	.50	1.00	.63	.71
Any, either	.92	.87	.97	.92	1.00	.83	.73	.72	.50	1.00	.79	.86
Cognitive												
Cognitive, dreamer	.04	.08	.20	.17	.00	.00	.08	.21	.25	.11	.21	.14
Cognitive, other	.00	.00	.07	.04	.00	.00	.08	.00	.25	.22	.00	.00
Cognitive, either	.04	.08	.24	.19	.00	.00	.12	.21	.50	.33	.21	.14
Affective												
Afraid, dreamer	.04	.00	.08	.11	.00	.00	.04	.14	.00	.11	.05	.10
Afraid, other	.04	.00	.02	.01	.25	.00	.00	.03	.00	.00	.00	.00
Afraid, either	.08	.00	.09	.11	.25	.00	.04	.14	.00	.11	.05	.10
Angry, dreamer	.00	.00	.06	.08	.00	.00	.00	.00	.00	.00	.00	.05
Angry, other	.00	.00	.01	.01	.00	.00	.00	.03	.25	.00	.00	.00
Angry, either	.00	.03	.07	.08	.00	.17	.00	.03	.25	.11	.05	.05
Sad, dreamer	.00	.00	.03	.01	.00	.00	.04	.03	.00	.00	.00	.00
Sad, other	.00	.00	.01	.01	.00	.00	.00	.00	.00	.00	.05	.00
Sad, either	.00	.03	.05	.02	.00	.17	.04	.03	.00	.11	.05	.00
Happy, dreamer	.36	.10	.19	.12	.00	.00	.19	.10	.75	.00	.21	.24
Happy, other	.00	.03	.05	.03	.00	.00	.04	.00	.00	.00	.11	.05
Happy, either	.36	.13	.20	.13	.00	.00	.19	.10	.75	.00	.26	.24
Excited, dreamer	.00	.03	.07	.05	.00	.00	.04	.07	.00	.00	.11	.14
Excited, other	.00	.00	.00	.02	.00	.00	.00	.00	.00	.00	.00	.05
Excited, either	.00	.03	.07	.06	.00	.00	.04	.07	.00	.00	.11	.14
Any, dreamer	.40	.18	.40	.35	.00	.17	.31	.28	.75	.22	.37	.43
Any, other	.04	.03	.09	.08	.25	.00	.04	.07	.25	.00	.11	.05
Any, either	.40	.21	.42	.37	.25	.17	.31	.28	.75	.22	.42	.43
Motivational-organic												
Hunger, dreamer	.00	.00	.15	.14	.00	.00	.08	.00	.00	.00	.11	.10
Hunger, other	.16	.18	.20	.10	.00	.17	.04	.03	.00	.00	.11	.10

Table B.2 (continued)

	Awakening Category											
	REM Sleep				NREM Sleep				Sleep Onset			
Series Number:	100	200	300	400	100	200	300	400	100	200	300	400
Age:	Young	Young	Older	Older	Young	Young	Older	Older	Young	Young	Older	Older
Sex:	F	M	F	M	F	M	F	M	F	M	F	M
Hunger, either	.16	.18	.23	.19	.00	.17	.12	.03	.00	.00	.16	.10
Thirst, dreamer	.04	.00	.05	.05	.00	.00	.04	.00	.00	.00	.00	.00
Thirst, other	.04	.03	.03	.04	.25	.00	.04	.00	.00	.11	.00	.00
Thirst, either	.04	.03	.06	.07	.25	.00	.04	.00	.00	.11	.00	.00
Sex, dreamer	.00	.00	.00	.01	.00	.00	.00	.00	.00	.00	.00	.00
Sex, other	.04	.03	.00	.01	.00	.00	.00	.00	.00	.00	.00	.00
Sex, either	.04	.03	.00	.01	.00	.00	.00	.00	.00	.11	.00	.00
Fatigue, dreamer	.04	.13	.10	.09	.00	.00	.08	.10	.25	.11	.00	.10
Fatigue, other	.08	.15	.08	.03	.00	.00	.04	.03	.25	.11	.00	.00
Fatigue, either	.08	.18	.12	.09	.00	.00	.08	.10	.25	.11	.00	.10
Motivational-socialized												
Approach social, dreamer	.20	.10	.40	.33	.25	.00	.12	.17	.00	.00	.11	.33
Approach social, other	.56	.21	.45	.41	.25	.00	.35	.28	.25	.22	.21	.33
Approach social, either	.56	.21	.50	.47	.25	.00	.35	.28	.25	.22	.21	.33
Approach object, dreamer	.24	.10	.27	.34	.00	.00	.19	.31	.25	.00	.32	.24
Approach object, other	.32	.33	.41	.37	.25	.33	.31	.24	.00	.11	.26	.14
Approach object, either	.44	.36	.53	.52	.25	.33	.38	.45	.25	.11	.37	.29
Avoidance social, dreamer	.04	.00	.00	.05	.00	.00	.00	.00	.00	.00	.00	.05
Avoidance social, other	.04	.00	.02	.06	.00	.00	.00	.00	.00	.11	.00	.05
Avoidance social, either	.04	.00	.02	.08	.00	.00	.00	.00	.00	.11	.00	.05
Avoidance object, dreamer	.00	.00	.01	.02	.00	.00	.00	.00	.00	.00	.00	.00

Avoidance object, other	.00	.00	.01	.02	.00	.00	.00	.00	.00	.00	.00	.00	.00
Avoidance object, either	.00	.00	.02	.03	.00	.00	.00	.00	.00	.00	.00	.00	.00
Attack social, dreamer	.00	.03	.08	.12	.00	.00	.04	.07	.00	.00	.00	.05	.05
Attack social, other	.28	.23	.12	.32	.25	.00	.04	.24	.25	.22	.05	.05	.10
Attack social, either	.28	.26	.17	.33	.25	.00	.08	.24	.25	.22	.05	.05	.14
Attack object, dreamer	.00	.00	.01	.01	.00	.17	.04	.03	.00	.00	.00	.00	.00
Attack object, other	.00	.08	.02	.05	.00	.17	.00	.03	.00	.11	.00	.00	.05
Attack object, either	.00	.08	.02	.06	.00	.17	.04	.07	.00	.11	.00	.00	.05
Outcomes													
Unfavorable													
Other mediated, dreamer	.12	.05	.03	.13	.00	.00	.00	.17	.25	.00	.00	.05	.05
Other mediated, other	.20	.23	.16	.31	.25	.00	.08	.17	.00	.33	.33	.05	.19
Other mediated, either	.28	.26	.17	.35	.25	.00	.08	.24	.25	.33	.33	.05	.19
Self-mediated, dreamer	.04	.00	.02	.03	.00	.17	.04	.00	.00	.11	.11	.00	.00
Self-mediated, other	.00	.00	.03	.00	.00	.17	.00	.00	.00	.11	.11	.05	.00
Self-mediated, either	.04	.00	.05	.03	.00	.17	.04	.03	.00	.11	.11	.05	.00
Unmediated, dreamer	.00	.00	.05	.07	.00	.00	.00	.03	.00	.00	.00	.00	.00
Unmediated, other	.00	.05	.02	.05	.00	.00	.00	.03	.00	.11	.11	.00	.00
Unmediated, either	.00	.08	.05	.08	.00	.00	.04	.07	.00	.11	.11	.00	.00
Any, dreamer	.16	.05	.10	.21	.00	.00	.08	.21	.25	.00	.05	.05	.05
Any, other	.20	.28	.22	.34	.25	.17	.08	.21	.00	.56	.00	.11	.19
Any, either	.32	.33	.26	.42	.25	.17	.15	.31	.25	.56	.25	.11	.19
Favorable													
Other mediated, dreamer	.20	.10	.34	.28	.25	.00	.15	.17	.25	.00	.11	.11	.33
Other mediated, other	.44	.15	.47	.42	.25	.00	.23	.21	.00	.11	.16	.16	.33
Other mediated, either	.48	.18	.49	.44	.25	.00	.27	.21	.25	.11	.16	.16	.33
Self-mediated, dreamer	.00	.00	.00	.00	.00	.00	.00	.03	.25	.00	.00	.00	.00
Self-mediated, other	.00	.00	.00	.02	.00	.00	.00	.00	.00	.00	.00	.00	.00
Self-mediated either	.00	.00	.00	.02	.00	.00	.00	.03	.25	.00	.00	.00	.00

Table B.2 (continued)

Series Number:	REM Sleep					NREM Sleep						Sleep Onset					
	100	200	300	400		100	200	300	400			100	200	300	400		
Age:	Young	Young	Older	Older		Young	Young	Older	Older			Young	Young	Older	Older		
Sex:	F	M	F	M		F	M	F	M			F	M	F	M		
Unmediated, dreamer	.00	.00	.00	.00		.00	.00	.00	.00			.00	.00	.00	.00		
Unmediated, other	.00	.00	.00	.00		.00	.00	.00	.00			.00	.00	.00	.00		
Unmediated, either	.00	.00	.00	.00		.00	.00	.00	.00			.00	.00	.00	.00		
Any, dreamer	.20	.10	.34	.28		.25	.00	.15	.21			.25	.00	.11	.33		
Any, other	.44	.15	.47	.43		.25	.00	.23	.21			.00	.11	.16	.33		
Any, either	.48	.18	.49	.45		.25	.00	.27	.24			.25	.11	.16	.33		

Awakening Category

340

Table B.3 **Results of Analysis of Children's Dream Reports: Year 5, Judge 1**

	Awakening Category											
	REM Sleep				NREM Sleep				Sleep Onset			
Series Number:	100	200	300	400	100	200	300	400	100	200	300	400
Age:	Young	Young	Older	Older	Young	Young	Older	Older	Young	Young	Older	Older
Sex:	F	M	F	M	F	M	F	M	F	M	F	M
Awakenings, n:	203	104	104	164	125	63	63	99	40	21	21	33
Awakenings with recall, n:	89	57	86	93	21	19	28	36	10	9	14	22
Word count												
Median	70	48	76.5	96	58	42	63.5	99	88	58	61	100
Minimum	13	3	10	9	14	14	19	34	45	36	26	19
Maximum	337	201	350	506	219	135	163	436	135	150	181	239
% ≥ 100 words	27	22.8	39.5	46.2	23.8	10.5	7.1	50	40	33.3	14.3	50
Ratings (means)												
(1) Hedonic tone	1.91	2.07	1.72	2.00	2.05	1.79	1.75	2.03	1.70	2.11	1.79	2.14
(2) Active participation	1.76	1.77	2.22	2.13	1.86	1.84	2.22	2.14	1.70	2.13	2.00	1.95
(3) Setting distortion	2.09	2.25	2.21	2.34	2.38	2.21	2.52	2.37	2.30	2.13	2.14	2.19
(4) Character distortion	2.12	2.15	2.18	2.25	2.22	2.00	2.14	2.31	2.50	2.00	2.50	2.17
(5) Visualization	.98	1.00	.99	.95	.95	.95	.93	.92	1.00	.89	.93	.91
Content analysis (proportion)												
Characters												
Family												
Parent M	.09	.09	.09	.08	.05	.26	.07	.08	.10	.00	.00	.00
Parent F	.11	.18	.16	.10	.14	.26	.07	.08	.30	.00	.00	.05
Sibling M	.27	.11	.05	.06	.19	.11	.11	.11	.40	.00	.00	.05
Sibling F	.04	.09	.12	.02	.00	.26	.07	.00	.00	.00	.07	.05

Table B.3 (continued)

	Awakening Category											
	REM Sleep				NREM Sleep				Sleep Onset			
Series Number:	100	200	300	400	100	200	300	400	100	200	300	400
Age:	Young	Young	Older	Older	Young	Young	Older	Older	Young	Young	Older	Older
Sex:	F	M	F	M	F	M	F	M	F	M	F	M
Any M	.31	.16	.13	.14	.19	.32	.14	.14	.40	.00	.07	.05
Any F	.17	.21	.26	.11	.14	.32	.07	.11	.30	.00	.07	.09
Known persons												
Peer M	.09	.18	.03	.22	.00	.11	.07	.25	.00	.33	.07	.36
Peer F	.18	.07	.14	.06	.10	.05	.07	.08	.00	.00	.07	.14
Adult M	.04	.12	.06	.08	.10	.05	.00	.03	.10	.00	.00	.05
Adult F	.02	.04	.05	.01	.05	.00	.00	.08	.00	.00	.00	.00
Any M	.18	.25	.10	.30	.14	.16	.11	.25	.10	.33	.07	.36
Any F	.19	.09	.19	.09	.19	.11	.07	.14	.00	.00	.07	.14
Strangers												
Peer M	.04	.05	.05	.11	.00	.11	.04	.08	.00	.00	.00	.09
Peer F	.03	.02	.06	.02	.00	.00	.04	.03	.10	.00	.00	.09
Adult M	.26	.19	.12	.18	.14	.11	.00	.11	.40	.00	.14	.14
Adult F	.13	.00	.07	.03	.14	.00	.00	.00	.30	.00	.07	.14
Any M	.43	.35	.29	.40	.29	.32	.04	.36	.60	.11	.36	.45
Any F	.31	.04	.23	.13	.19	.11	.11	.03	.60	.00	.29	.32
Groups	.08	.16	.10	.14	.10	.16	.07	.14	.20	.00	.14	.09
Supernatural	.01	.05	.00	.01	.05	.00	.00	.00	.10	.00	.00	.00
Animals, any	.25	.19	.12	.06	.19	.21	.04	.08	.30	.22	.14	.00
Pet	.11	.05	.05	.01	.00	.05	.04	.00	.00	.11	.00	.00
Barnyard	.01	.05	.06	.04	.00	.11	.04	.08	.10	.00	.00	.00

	1	2	3	4	5	6	7	8	9	10	11	12
Indigenous	.08	.05	.02	.01	.14	.05	.00	.00	.10	.11	.00	.00
Exotic	.07	.07	.00	.00	.10	.00	.00	.00	.10	.00	.00	.00
Dolls	.02	.05	.00	.00	.00	.00	.00	.00	.00	.00	.14	.00
Settings												
Conveyance	.10	.14	.08	.12	.05	.11	.11	.08	.10	.00	.14	.23
Home, any	.31	.26	.33	.13	.24	.32	.14	.11	.10	.44	.14	.23
Home, own	.11	.21	.21	.08	.10	.21	.07	.06	.00	.11	.07	.14
School, any	.09	.02	.10	.11	.05	.11	.07	.08	.00	.22	.14	.23
School, own	.03	.02	.05	.06	.05	.11	.04	.08	.00	.22	.14	.23
Recreational	.38	.40	.24	.35	.43	.21	.25	.28	.70	.11	.29	.27
Commercial	.09	.12	.13	.16	.05	.16	.11	.08	.10	.11	.14	.05
Other outdoors	.17	.19	.12	.12	.10	.16	.11	.17	.10	.22	.14	.09
Sleep lab	.04	.09	.03	.03	.10	.05	.00	.06	.00	.00	.00	.00
Vague	.07	.07	.15	.14	.14	.05	.21	.14	.10	.00	.14	.27
Activities												
Sensory												
Vision, dreamer	.17	.14	.27	.34	.24	.26	.11	.17	.30	.00	.07	.27
Vision, other	.22	.12	.16	.17	.05	.16	.14	.11	.20	.11	.00	.14
Vision, either	.33	.21	.34	.40	.24	.26	.21	.22	.30	.11	.07	.27
Hearing, dreamer	.02	.00	.02	.06	.00	.05	.00	.11	.00	.00	.00	.05
Hearing, other	.03	.00	.02	.03	.05	.05	.00	.03	.00	.00	.00	.00
Hearing, either	.06	.00	.05	.08	.05	.05	.00	.14	.00	.00	.00	.05
Motor												
Verbal, dreamer	.11	.07	.22	.23	.10	.05	.11	.17	.10	.22	.21	.32
Verbal, other	.29	.21	.42	.39	.19	.26	.18	.39	.30	.11	.29	.50
Verbal, either	.34	.21	.45	.41	.24	.26	.25	.39	.30	.22	.36	.50
Manual, dreamer	.30	.35	.35	.34	.29	.37	.25	.39	.20	.44	.21	.41
Manual, other	.62	.49	.26	.44	.57	.53	.11	.53	.60	.22	.36	.50
Manual, either	.67	.63	.47	.54	.62	.58	.25	.61	.60	.56	.43	.59
Locomotor, dreamer	.27	.39	.43	.44	.33	.26	.36	.47	.40	.44	.36	.36

Table B.3 (continued)

	Awakening Category											
	REM Sleep				NREM Sleep				Sleep Onset			
Series Number:	100	200	300	400	100	200	300	400	100	200	300	400
Age:	Young	Young	Older	Older	Young	Young	Older	Older	Young	Young	Older	Older
Sex:	F	M	F	M	F	M	F	M	F	M	F	M
Locomotor, other	.62	.67	.44	.49	.62	.58	.18	.44	.90	.44	.43	.50
Locomotor, either	.65	.74	.62	.61	.67	.58	.46	.56	.90	.56	.50	.55
Any, dreamer	.46	.49	.65	.60	.43	.58	.50	.56	.50	.67	.57	.64
Any, other	.83	.81	.66	.74	.81	.79	.39	.67	1.00	.44	.79	.82
Any, either	.89	.88	.86	.86	.86	.84	.68	.78	1.00	.78	.86	.86
States												
Cognitive												
Cognitive, dreamer	.06	.05	.26	.15	.14	.05	.14	.22	.00	.11	.07	.23
Cognitive, other	.09	.02	.12	.06	.00	.00	.00	.03	.00	.00	.00	.05
Cognitive, either	.12	.05	.29	.22	.14	.05	.14	.22	.00	.11	.07	.23
Affective												
Afraid, dreamer	.07	.12	.08	.09	.05	.11	.04	.11	.20	.33	.14	.09
Afraid, other	.01	.00	.00	.01	.00	.00	.00	.03	.10	.00	.00	.00
Afraid, either	.07	.12	.08	.09	.05	.11	.04	.11	.20	.33	.14	.09
Angry, dreamer	.03	.04	.03	.09	.00	.05	.04	.06	.00	.11	.00	.32
Angry, other	.01	.00	.05	.04	.00	.00	.04	.03	.00	.00	.00	.09
Angry, either	.04	.07	.06	.12	.05	.05	.04	.06	.00	.11	.00	.36
Sad, dreamer	.04	.00	.02	.00	.05	.00	.04	.03	.00	.00	.00	.00
Sad, other	.00	.07	.02	.01	.05	.00	.00	.03	.00	.00	.00	.00
Sad, either	.04	.07	.03	.01	.10	.00	.00	.03	.00	.00	.00	.00
Happy, dreamer	.12	.18	.20	.06	.14	.16	.18	.08	.20	.22	.14	.14

344

Happy, other	.00	.02	.03	.00	.05	.05	.00	.03	.00	.00	.07	.00
Happy, either	.12	.19	.21	.06	.14	.16	.18	.11	.20	.22	.14	.14
Excited, dreamer	.07	.02	.07	.03	.10	.00	.07	.00	.00	.00	.00	.00
Excited, other	.00	.00	.01	.00	.00	.00	.04	.00	.00	.00	.00	.00
Excited, either	.07	.02	.08	.03	.10	.00	.11	.00	.00	.00	.00	.00
Any, dreamer	.29	.39	.37	.26	.33	.26	.25	.22	.40	.56	.29	.55
Any, other	.02	.02	.12	.06	.10	.05	.07	.11	.10	.00	.07	.14
Any, either	.30	.40	.40	.30	.38	.26	.29	.25	.40	.56	.29	.59
Motivational-organic												
Hunger, dreamer	.11	.07	.07	.11	.10	.11	.04	.06	.00	.00	.00	.05
Hunger, other	.12	.12	.08	.10	.14	.16	.00	.03	.20	.00	.07	.05
Hunger, either	.16	.14	.10	.12	.14	.16	.07	.06	.20	.00	.07	.09
Thirst, dreamer	.02	.02	.02	.00	.10	.00	.00	.03	.00	.00	.00	.05
Thirst, other	.07	.05	.01	.01	.10	.00	.00	.03	.00	.00	.00	.00
Thirst, either	.07	.05	.03	.01	.14	.00	.00	.03	.00	.00	.00	.05
Sex, dreamer	.01	.00	.01	.00	.00	.05	.00	.00	.00	.00	.07	.05
Sex, other	.02	.00	.03	.01	.00	.05	.00	.00	.00	.00	.07	.05
Sex, either	.02	.00	.03	.01	.00	.05	.00	.00	.00	.00	.07	.05
Fatigue, dreamer	.09	.09	.08	.06	.10	.21	.07	.06	.00	.11	.00	.00
Fatigue, other	.13	.14	.06	.08	.10	.16	.07	.03	.10	.00	.00	.00
Fatigue, either	.15	.16	.08	.10	.10	.26	.07	.06	.10	.11	.00	.00
Motivational-socialized												
Approach social, dreamer	.26	.18	.24	.25	.19	.26	.11	.19	.20	.22	.21	.23
Approach social, other	.42	.33	.37	.37	.33	.42	.29	.25	.30	.33	.43	.36
Approach social, either	.46	.35	.43	.38	.33	.42	.32	.28	.40	.33	.43	.36
Approach object, dreamer	.33	.37	.40	.39	.38	.26	.21	.25	.40	.33	.29	.36
Approach object, other	.48	.47	.29	.31	.43	.26	.14	.31	.50	.11	.36	.41
Approach object, either	.53	.60	.53	.48	.67	.32	.29	.42	.60	.44	.50	.45
Avoidance social, dreamer	.00	.00	.00	.03	.00	.00	.00	.00	.00	.11	.00	.00
Avoidance social, other	.02	.02	.00	.03	.00	.00	.00	.00	.00	.00	.00	.00

Table B.3 (continued)

	Awakening Category											
	REM Sleep				NREM Sleep				Sleep Onset			
Series Number:	100	200	300	400	100	200	300	400	100	200	300	400
Age:	Young	Young	Older	Older	Young	Young	Older	Older	Young	Young	Older	Older
Sex:	F	M	F	M	F	M	F	M	F	M	F	M
Avoidance social, either	.02	.02	.00	.05	.00	.00	.00	.00	.00	.11	.00	.00
Avoidance object, dreamer	.01	.00	.03	.01	.00	.00	.04	.00	.00	.00	.00	.05
Avoidance object, other	.03	.02	.05	.00	.00	.00	.00	.03	.00	.00	.00	.05
Avoidance object, either	.04	.02	.07	.01	.00	.00	.04	.03	.00	.00	.00	.09
Attack social, dreamer	.09	.04	.10	.12	.00	.00	.00	.11	.10	.22	.00	.27
Attack social, other	.26	.21	.19	.26	.14	.32	.04	.17	.10	.33	.00	.36
Attack social, either	.27	.23	.20	.28	.14	.32	.04	.19	.10	.33	.00	.41
Attack object, dreamer	.01	.02	.00	.01	.00	.00	.00	.00	.00	.11	.00	.00
Attack object, other	.03	.04	.02	.05	.10	.00	.00	.03	.00	.00	.07	.00
Attack object, either	.03	.05	.02	.05	.10	.00	.00	.03	.00	.11	.07	.00
Outcomes												
Unfavorable												
Other mediated, dreamer	.08	.12	.13	.15	.10	.21	.00	.06	.10	.22	.00	.23
Other mediated, other	.26	.18	.15	.24	.14	.16	.04	.17	.10	.22	.00	.41
Other mediated, either	.28	.26	.20	.29	.19	.32	.04	.17	.10	.33	.00	.41
Self-mediated, dreamer	.01	.05	.00	.02	.00	.00	.00	.03	.00	.11	.00	.00
Self-mediated, other	.03	.02	.01	.04	.10	.00	.00	.08	.10	.00	.07	.00
Self-mediated, either	.04	.07	.01	.05	.10	.00	.00	.08	.10	.11	.07	.00
Unmediated, dreamer	.03	.09	.05	.02	.05	.05	.07	.06	.10	.00	.07	.05
Unmediated, other	.09	.05	.02	.05	.10	.00	.04	.06	.10	.11	.00	.05
Unmediated, either	.11	.11	.06	.06	.14	.05	.07	.08	.20	.11	.07	.05

Any, dreamer	.12	.23	.16	.18	.14	.21	.07	.14	.20	.33	.07	.27
Any, other	.34	.25	.17	.30	.33	.16	.07	.25	.30	.33	.07	.45
Any, either	.39	.40	.24	.37	.43	.32	.11	.28	.40	.56	.14	.45
Favorable												
Other mediated, dreamer	.26	.16	.19	.30	.14	.26	.11	.22	.10	.22	.29	.23
Other mediated, other	.44	.28	.37	.30	.24	.37	.25	.28	.30	.22	.29	.36
Other mediated, either	.44	.30	.40	.34	.24	.37	.32	.31	.30	.33	.36	.36
Self-mediated, dreamer	.02	.04	.03	.00	.00	.00	.00	.00	.20	.00	.00	.00
Self-mediated, other	.04	.05	.02	.01	.05	.00	.00	.00	.20	.00	.00	.00
Self-mediated, either	.06	.07	.03	.01	.05	.00	.00	.00	.30	.00	.00	.00
Unmediated, dreamer	.00	.02	.00	.00	.00	.00	.00	.00	.00	.00	.00	.00
Unmediated, other	.00	.02	.00	.00	.00	.00	.00	.00	.00	.00	.00	.00
Unmediated, either	.00	.02	.00	.00	.00	.00	.00	.00	.00	.00	.00	.00
Any, dreamer	.28	.18	.21	.30	.14	.26	.11	.22	.30	.22	.29	.23
Any, other	.46	.33	.38	.31	.24	.37	.25	.28	.50	.22	.29	.36
Any, either	.47	.35	.42	.35	.24	.37	.32	.31	.60	.33	.36	.36

Appendix C _____

Extra-Dream Variables and Their Correlation with Dream Variables

This appendix contains a list and explanation of the nondream variables we studied and a tabulation of those correlation coefficients between nondream and dream variables that would have attained "significance at $p \le .05$, 2-tailed test" in individual statistical tests. Not all nondream variables were available for contrast with dream data in each study year or for each group of children studied in any particular study year. Table 2.2 indicates the scope of the test file at any given age level, and this appendix will indicate the dream variables available for study at each age level.

Table C.1 lists the nondream variables. The first column in this table gives the code number by which a variable's correlations with dream variables is identified in Table C.2. Variables are listed by group: "family-life" variables, 1–158; "cognitive" variables, 159–233; "personality" variables, 234–396; "sleep" variables, 397–426; "behavioral/observational" variables, 427–563; "physical maturation" variables, 564–598; and "nursery-school" variables, 599–657. We recognize that this classification system is less than perfect and that our assignment of particular variables to these categories occasionally does not do them full justice. Nevertheless, it provides the reader some basis for determining the kinds of variables associated with dream variables in Table C.2 without having constantly to refer back to Table C.1, and it is an economical alternative to spelling out all variables in Table C.2. Also for economy's sake, entries in the Scoring/Interpretation column of Table C.1 are not given unless they convey new information. For blank entries in this column, the last substantive entry in the column is to be understood as still applying to the variable in question. Parenthetical entries in this column add new information without diminishing the force of the previous, nonparenthetical entry.

In Table C.2 correlation coefficients (Pearson r) are given without decimals. An absence of correlations for a given dream variable at a given age level *always* indicates that that dream variable was not entered into correlation with nondream variables, rather than that no "significant" correlates were observed for that variable. Unless otherwise designated, all dream variables are *REM*-dream variables. Where two coefficients appear for any numbered variable in any given year, they reflect a dream correlation with test scores from two separate test administrations or from two separate judges of the test variable. At ages 7–9 and 11–13, the "*i*" following variables 184–187 indicates that the correlation is from a test administered at *i*ntake to new subjects only (*n*'s = 7 and 6, respectively).

Table C.1 Extra-dream Variables

Number	Variable	Instrument	Scoring/Interpretation
Family-Life Variables			
1	Social class	Revised occupation scale of Warner, Meeker, & Eells (1960), applied to family's primary wage- or salary-earner	Consensus of two judges; high scores indicate *low* social class
2	Encourages verbalization: mother	Adaptation of Schaefer and Bell's (1958) Parent Attitude Research Instrument (PARI)	Objective: attitude scale
3	Encourages verbalization: father	PARI	
4	Fosters dependency: mother	PARI	
5	Fosters dependency: father	PARI	
6	Seclusion of mother: mother	PARI	
7	Seclusion of mother: father	PARI	
8	Breaking child's will: mother	PARI	
9	Breaking child's will: father	PARI	
10	Martyrdom of parent: mother	PARI	
11	Martyrdom of parent: father	PARI	
12	Fear of harming baby: mother	PARI	
13	Marital conflict: mother	PARI	
14	Marital conflict: father	PARI	
15	Strictness: mother	PARI	
16	Strictness: father	PARI	
17	Irritability: mother	PARI	
18	Irritability: father	PARI	
19	Excludes outside influence: mother	PARI	
20	Excludes outside influence: father	PARI	

21	Deification of parent: mother	PARI
22	Deification of parent: father	PARI
23	Suppresses aggression: mother	PARI
24	Suppresses aggression: father	PARI
25	Rejection of homemaking: mother	PARI
26	Equalitarianism: mother	PARI
27	Equalitarianism: father	PARI
28	Approval of activity: mother	PARI
29	Approval of activity: father	PARI
30	Avoids communication: mother	PARI
31	Avoids communication: father	PARI
32	Inconsiderateness of husband: mother	PARI
33	Suppresses sex: mother	PARI
34	Suppresses sex: father	PARI
35	Ascendancy of mother: mother	PARI
36	Ascendancy of mother: father	PARI
37	Intrusiveness: mother	PARI
38	Intrusiveness: father	PARI
39	Comradeship: mother	PARI
40	Comradeship: father	PARI
41	Accelerates development: mother	PARI
42	Accelerates development: father	PARI
43	Dependency of mother: mother	PARI
44	Nonpunishing: mother	PARI
45	Nonpunishing: father	PARI
46	Avoids tenderness: mother	PARI
47	Avoids tenderness: father	PARI
48	Grants autonomy: mother	PARI
49	Grants autonomy: father	PARI
50	Expresses love: mother	PARI

Table C.1 **(continued)**

Number	Variable	Instrument	Scoring/Interpretation
51	Expresses love: father	PARI	Objective: attitude scale
52	Harsh punishment: mother	PARI	
53	Harsh punishment: father	PARI	
54	Traditional family ideology: mother	Measure of authoritarian family ideology (Levinson & Huffman, 1955)	
55	Traditional family ideology: father	As above	Objective: checklist
56	Social control: mother	Child-rearing value index (CRVI) (after Kohn, 1969)	
57	Social control: father	CRVI	
58	Personal development: mother	CRVI	
59	Personal development: father	CRVI	
60	Social adjustment: mother	CRVI	
61	Social adjustment: father	CRVI	
62	Maternal power index (vis-à-vis father)	"Cornell Parent Description (CPD) Device," a research instrument obtained from Urie Bronfenbrenner and his associates at Cornell University: children's descriptions	Objective: rating scales
63	Time child spends with parents together	CPD	
64	Time child spends with mother alone	CPD	
65	Time child spends with father alone	CPD	
66	Time child spends with peers	CPD	
67	Time child spends alone	CPD	
68	Time child spends with siblings	CPD	
69	Ratio: 63 to higher of 64/65	CPD	
70	Ratio: 65/64	CPD	
71	Ratio: 66 to higher of 64/65	CPD	

72	Ratio: 67/66	CPD
73	Ratio: 68/66	CPD
74	Rating: mother's nurturance	CPD
75	Rating: father's nurturance	CPD
76	Rating: mother's instrumental companionship	CPD
77	Rating: father's instrumental companionship	CPD
78	Rating: mother's principled discipline	CPD
79	Rating: father's principled discipline	CPD
80	Rating: mother's praise	CPD
81	Rating: father's praise	CPD
82	Mother's support (sum: 74,76,78,80)	CPD
83	Father's support (sum: 75,77,79,81)	CPD
84	Rating: mother's physical punishment	CPD
85	Rating: father's physical punishment	CPD
86	Rating: mother's deprivation punishment	CPD
87	Rating: father's deprivation punishment	CPD
88	Rating: mother's verbal retribution	CPD
89	Rating: father's verbal retribution	CPD
90	Mother's punishment (sum: 84,86,88)	CPD
91	Father's punishment (sum: 85,87,89)	CPD
92	Rating: mother's achievement demands	CPD
93	Rating: father's achievement demands	CPD
94	Rating: predictability of mother's standards	CPD
95	Rating: predictability of father's standards	CPD
96	Rating: mother's strictness	CPD
97	Rating: father's strictness	CPD
98	Mother's control (sum: 92,94,96)	CPD
99	Father's control (sum: 93,95,97)	CPD
100	Rating: rejection by mother	CPD
101	Rating: rejection by father	CPD

Table C.1 (continued)

Number	Variable	Instrument	Scoring/Interpretation
102	Rating: indulgence by mother	CPD	
103	Rating: indulgence by father	CPD	
104	Rating: autonomy granting, mother	CPD	
105	Rating: autonomy granting, father	CPD	
106	Rating: protectiveness of mother	CPD	
107	Rating: protectiveness of father	CPD	
108	Difference: 82 minus 83	CPD	(High scores: mother more supportive)
109	Difference: 90 minus 91	CPD	(High scores: mother more punitive)
110	Difference: 98 minus 99	CPD	(High scores: mother more controlling)
111	Longitudinal change: variable 82	CPD	Comparison with immediately prior longitudinal year: high scores are *decreases* in variable
112	Longitudinal change: variable 83	CPD	
113	Longitudinal change: variable 90	CPD	
114	Longitudinal change: variable 91	CPD	
115	Longitudinal change: variable 98	CPD	
116	Longitudinal change: variable 99	CPD	
117	Longitudinal change: variable 100	CPD	
118	Longitudinal change: variable 101	CPD	
119	Longitudinal change: variable 104	CPD	
120	Longitudinal change: variable 105	CPD	
121	Longitudinal change: variable 106	CPD	
122	Longitudinal change: variable 107	CPD	
123	Longitudinal change: variable 108	CPD	
124	Longitudinal change: variable 109	CPD	

No.	Variable	Measure	Notes
125	Longitudinal change: variable 110	CPD	
126	Longitudinal change: variable 62	CPD	
127	Longitudinal change: variable 69	CPD	
128	Longitudinal change: variable 70	CPD	
129	Longitudinal change: variable 71	CPD	
130	Longitudinal change: variable 72	CPD	
131	Longitudinal change: variable 73	CPD	
132	Mother's nurturance	Emmerich Parental Identification Interview (EPII, Emmerich, 1959)	By test administrator, naive as to dream data
133	Father's nurturance	EPII	
134	Own nurturance	EPII	
135	Identification with mother	EPII	
136	Identification with father	EPII	
137	Mother-child difference	EPII	(High scores: child less nurturant than mother)
138	Father-child difference	EPII	(High scores: child less nurturant than father)
139	Mother/father self-similarity	EPII	(High scores: child acts more like mother than father)
140	Conflict over father role	EPII	
141	Conflict over mother role	EPII	
142	Masculinity: IT Test	IT Test of Sex-Role Preference (Brown, 1956): total score	
143	Child figure-preference: IT Test	IT: Score of final section of test	Objective: verbal preferences
144	Possessions	Environmental Participation Index (EPI, Mathis, 1967): material artifacts in child's home (number)	Objective: checklist
145	Activities	EPI: enriching experiences (number)	
146	Sum: possessions and activities	EPI	

Table C.1 **(continued)**

Number	Variable	Instrument	Scoring/Interpretation
147	Maternal punitiveness: indirect	Kagan-Lemkin (1960) interview regarding child's indirect (doll play) and direct perception of parents	Objective: forced-choice responses (high scores indicate mother is high in trait *relative* to father)
148	Maternal punitiveness: direct	Kagan-Lemkin	
149	Maternal punitiveness: sum	Kagan-Lemkin	
150	Maternal competence: indirect	Kagan-Lemkin	
151	Maternal competence: direct	Kagan-Lemkin	
152	Maternal competence: total	Kagan-Lemkin	
153	Maternal nurturance: indirect	Kagan-Lemkin	
154	Maternal nurturance: direct	Kagan-Lemkin	
155	Maternal nurturance: total	Kagan-Lemkin	
156	Maternal identification: indirect	Kagan-Lemkin	(High score is supposed to indicate that child wants to grow up to be like mother, rather than father)
157	Maternal identification: direct	Kagan-Lemkin	
158	Maternal identification: total	Kagan-Lemkin	
Cognitive Skill/Style Variables			
159	Full-scale I.Q.	Wechsler tests: age appropriate WPPSI (Preschool and Primary Scale of Intelligence), WISC (Intelligence Scale for Children), or WAIS (Adult Intelligence Scale)	By trained test administrators, naive as to dream data
160	Verbal I.Q.	Wechsler tests	
161	Performance I.Q.	Wechsler tests	

162	Information: raw score	WPPSI
163	Vocabulary: raw score	WPPSI
164	Comprehension: raw score	WPPSI
165	Sentences: raw score	WPPSI (Year-1 administration only)
166	Block design: raw score	WPPSI
167	Geometric design: raw score	WPPSI
168	Information: raw score	WISC
169	Vocabulary: raw score	WISC
170	Comprehension: raw score	WISC
171	Digit span: raw score	WISC
172	Block design: raw score	WISC
173	Object assembly: raw score	WISC
174	Longitudinal change: variable 159	Wechsler tests	Comparisons with immediately preceding longitudinal year; on WPPSI, WPPSI to WISC, or on WISC (high change scores are quotient *decreases*)
175	Longitudinal change: variable 160	Wechsler tests	
176	Longitudinal change: variable 161	Wechsler tests	
177	Longitudinal change: variable 162/168	WPPSI or WISC	(Scores are gains; decrements entered as zero change)
178	Longitudinal change: variable 163/169	WPPSI or WISC	
179	Longitudinal change: variable 164/170	WPPSI or WISC	
180	Longitudinal change: variable 166/172	WPPSI or WISC	
181	Longitudinal change: variable 167	WPPSI	
182	Longitudinal change: variable 171	WISC	
183	Longitudinal change: variable 173	WISC	

Table C.1 **(continued)**

Number	Variable	Instrument	Scoring/Interpretation
184	Major and minor details noted: sum	Description Test: our own test, in which children described projective-test cards under stimulus-present and stimulus-absent conditions	Scored by pairs of judges: in different years interjudge agreement ranged from 92–97.5% (major details), 83–89% (minor details), and 88–96% (whole or integrative responses)
185	Major and minor details noted: stimulus-present condition	Description Test	
186	Major and minor details noted: memory condition	Description Test	
187	Whole responses: both conditions	Description Test	
188	Longitudinal change: variable 184	Description Test	Comparisons with immediately preceding longitudinal score; scores are gains; decrements entered as zero change
189	Longitudinal change: variable 185	Description Test	
190	Longitudinal change: variable 186	Description Test	
191	Longitudinal change: variable 187	Description Test	(Year 5 only: vs. Year 2 [younger Ss] or screening interview [older Ss])
192	Concept of dream	Laurendeau and Pinard's (1962) "Dream" subtest	Scored by pairs of judges: in different years interjudge agreements on subject classification ranged from 76–86%
193	Concept of life	Laurendeau and Pinard's (1962) "Life" subtest	Scored by pairs of judges: in different years interjudge agreements on subject classification ranged from 81–86%

No.	Variable	Instrument	Notes
194	Concept of night	Laurendeau and Pinard's (1962) "Night" subtest	Scored by pairs of judges: in different years interjudge agreements on subject classification ranged from 79–90%
195	Composite Laurendeau-Pinard	Stage assignments pooled from preceding 3 instruments	Scale from 0 to 9
196	Longitudinal change: variable 192	Laurendeau-Pinard	Comparisons with immediately preceding longitudinal year; scores are gains; decrements entered as zero change
197	Longitudinal change: variable 193	Laurendeau-Pinard	
198	Longitudinal change: variable 194	Laurendeau-Pinard	
199	Longitudinal change: variable 195	Laurendeau-Pinard	
200	Latency to first response	Matching Familiar Figures (MFF) Test (Kagan et al., 1964)	Median time, in seconds
201	Errors	MFF	Mean number per item
202	Items correct	MFF	Number of correct *first* responses
203	Embedded figures: CEFT	Children's Embedded Figures Test (Witkin et al., 1971)	Number correct
204	Mean solution time	Embedded Figures Test (EFT; Witkin et al., 1971)	Seconds per item
205	Number of items with errors	EFT	Self-explanatory
206	Number of times child refers back to simple form	EFT	The simple form is the one to be disembedded from more complex test figures.
207	Fa-1 associational fluency	Kit of Reference Tests for Cognitive Factors (KIT, French, Ekstrom, & Price, 1963)	Objective (producing synonyms)
208	Fi-2 ideational fluency	KIT	(quantitative production)
209	Fe-3 expressional fluency	KIT	(composing connected discourse)

Table C.1 **(continued)**

Number	Variable	Instrument	Scoring/Interpretation
210	Cs-1 speed of closure	KIT	(perceptual unification)
211	P-3 perceptual speed	KIT	(matching figures)
212	Ma-3 rote memory	KIT	(for names)
213	Ms-2 memory span	KIT	(visual digit span)
214	Associative control	KIT	(from Fa-1: proportion of associative responses which were synonymous)
215	Impulsivity	KIT	(errors on P-3)
216	Performance decrement	KIT	(from P-3: part-1 score minus part-2 score plus constant)
217	Memory maximum	KIT	(score on better half of Ma-3)
218	Memory minimum	KIT	(score on worse half of Ma-3)
219	Memory performance variation	KIT	(absolute difference of variables 217 and 218)
220	Internal locus of control	Stephens-Delys Reinforcement Contingency Interview (Delys & Stephens, 1971)	Blind judge, following authors' criteria
221	Fate orientation	Three items Coleman et al. (1966) found to predict poor academic achievement	Objective
222	Word count: spontaneous recall	Fidelity of report (Ray, 1947; examination of spontaneous and elicited recall of a film stimulus)	Reconciled judgment of 2 judges, trained and reliable in dream word counts
223	Item identification: spontaneous recall	Fidelity of report: number of 14 major details contained in report	2 judges: 75% exact agreement and 96% agreement ± 1 item
224	Elicited recall: accuracy	Fidelity of report: percent of items answered correctly	Objective

225	Verbal fluency	Torrance (1966) Tests of Creative Thinking (TCT)	2 judges; sample r for S classification: .96
226	Verbal flexibility	TCT	2 judges; sample r for S classification: .97
227	Verbal originality	TCT	2 judges; sample r for S classification: .91
228	Ratio of variables 227/225	TCT	Originality/fluency
229	Figural fluency	TCT	2 judges; sample r for S classification: .99
230	Figural flexibility	TCT	2 judges; sample r for S classification: .93
231	Figural originality	TCT	2 judges; sample r for S classification: .73
232	Ratio of variables 231/229	TCT	Originality/fluency
233	Figural elaboration	TCT	2 judges; sample r for S classification: .99

Personality-Test Variables: "Projective" Measures

234	Word count	Stories told to 3 different sets of cards in the Pickford Projective Pictures Series (Pickford, 1963)	2 judges; S-classification r = .97–.996 for different stimulus sets
235	Imagination	Pickford	2 judges; S-classification r = .88–.96 for different stimulus sets
236	Verbal aggression	Pickford	2 judges; S-classification r = .59–.92 for different stimulus sets
237	Physical aggression	Pickford	2 judges; S-classification r = .72–.86 for different stimulus sets

Table C.1 (continued)

Number	Variable	Instrument	Scoring/Interpretation
238	Pleasant hedonic tone	Pickford	2 judges: S-classification $r =$ .79–.89 for different stimulus sets
239	Spatial/temporal extensity of narrative	Pickford	2 judges: S-classification $r =$ .86–.96 for different stimulus sets
240	Longitudinal change: variable 234	Pickford	Year 2 vs. Year 1; Year 5, separately vs. Years 1 and 2; higher scores are increases
241	Longitudinal change: variable 235	Pickford	
242	Longitudinal change: variable 238	Pickford	
243	Longitudinal change: variable 239	Pickford	
244	Longitudinal change: variable 236	Pickford	
245	Longitudinal change: variable 237	Pickford	
246	Word count	Stories told to sets A and B of the Symonds (1949) Picture-Story Test	2 judges: S-classification $r =$ .993, .996
247	Imagination	Symonds	2 judges: S-classification $r =$ .68, .69
248	Verbal aggression	Symonds	2 judges: S-classification $r =$ .65, .74
249	Physical aggression	Symonds	2 judges: S-classification $r =$ .91, .87
250	Pleasant hedonic tone	Symonds	2 judges: S-classification $r =$ .68, .81
251	Spatial/temporal extensity of narrative	Symonds	2 judges: S-classification $r =$ .91, .84
252	Longitudinal change: variable 246	Symonds	Higher scores are increases
253	Longitudinal change: variable 247	Symonds	
254	Longitudinal change: variable 248	Symonds	
255	Longitudinal change: variable 249	Symonds	
256	Longitudinal change: variable 250	Symonds	
257	Longitudinal change: variable 251	Symonds	

258	Number of responses	Rorschach Test	Experienced, dream-blind scorer
259	W%	Rorschach Test	(wholistic/integrative interpretations)
260	D%	Rorschach Test	(large-detail interpretations)
261	Dd%	Rorschach Test	(unusual-detail interpretations)
262	F+%	Rorschach Test	(good-form interpretations)
263	A%	Rorschach Test	(animal-content interpretations)
264	H%	Rorschach Test	(human-figure interpretations)
265	Total movement %	Rorschach Test	(animate *and* object movement)
266	Extropunitiveness	Rosenzweig Picture-Frustration Test, scored following Rosenzweig, Fleming, & Clarke (1947)	2 judges: S-classification $r = .93, .92$
267	Intropunitiveness	Rosenzweig	2 judges: S-classification $r = .85, .88$
268	Impunitiveness	Rosenzweig	2 judges: S-classification $r = .75, .83$
269	Ratio of variables 266/267	Rosenzweig	Externalizing of blame
270	Ratio of variables 268/(266 & 267)	Rosenzweig	Denial of frustration or blame
271	Ego level	Loevinger Sentence-Completion Tests (Loevinger & Wessler, 1970)	See Trupin, 1976
272	Longitudinal change: variable 271	Loevinger	Raw increment in total protocol rating

Personality-Test Variables: "Objective" Measures

273	A. Outgoing	Early School Personality Questionnaire (ESPQ, Coan & Cattell, 1966)	Objective
274	B. Intelligent	ESPQ	
275	C. Stable	ESPQ	
276	D. Excitable	ESPQ	
277	E. Assertive	ESPQ	
278	F. Happy-go-lucky	ESPQ	
279	G. Conscientious	ESPQ	

Table C.1 (continued)

Number	Variable	Instrument	Scoring/Interpretation
280	H. Venturesome	ESPQ	
281	I. Tender-minded	ESPQ	
282	J. Doubting	ESPQ	
283	N. Shrewd	ESPQ	
284	O. Apprehensive	ESPQ	
285	Q4. Tense	ESPQ	
286	A. Outgoing	Children's Personality Questionnaire (CPQ, Porter & Cattell, 1963)	Objective
287	B. Intelligent	CPQ	
288	C. Stable	CPQ	
289	D. Excitable	CPQ	
290	E. Assertive	CPQ	
291	F. Happy-go-lucky	CPQ	
292	G. Conscientious	CPQ	
293	H. Venturesome	CPQ	
294	I. Tender-minded	CPQ	
295	J. Doubting	CPQ	
296	N. Shrewd	CPQ	
297	O. Apprehensive	CPQ	
298	Q4. Tense	CPQ	
299	Q3. Controlled	CPQ	
300	A. Outgoing	High School Personality Questionnaire (HSPQ, Cattell & Cattell, 1969)	Objective
301	B. Intelligent	HSPQ	
302	C. Stable	HSPQ	
303	D. Excitable	HSPQ	
304	E. Assertive	HSPQ	

305	F. Happy-go-lucky	HSPQ
306	G. Conscientious	HSPQ
307	H. Venturesome	HSPQ
308	I. Tender-minded	HSPQ
309	J. Doubting	HSPQ
310	O. Apprehensive	HSPQ
311	Q4. Tense	HSPQ
312	Q3. Controlled	HSPQ
313	Q2. Self-sufficient	HSPQ
314	Longitudinal change: variable 286	CPQ
315	Longitudinal change: variable 287	CPQ
316	Longitudinal change: variable 288	CPQ
317	Longitudinal change: variable 289	CPQ
318	Longitudinal change: variable 290	CPQ
319	Longitudinal change: variable 291	CPQ
320	Longitudinal change: variable 292	CPQ
321	Longitudinal change: variable 293	CPQ
322	Longitudinal change: variable 294	CPQ
323	Longitudinal change: variable 295	CPQ
324	Longitudinal change: variable 296	CPQ
325	Longitudinal change: variable 297	CPQ
326	Longitudinal change: variable 298	CPQ
327	Longitudinal change: variable 299	CPQ
328	Lability	CPQ
329	Longitudinal change: variables 286,300	CPQ, HSPQ
330	Longitudinal change: variables 287,301	CPQ, HSPQ

Year 3: higher scores are *decreases* in variable

Sum of absolute differences between scale scores at test and retest

Year 5: higher scores are *increases* in variable

Table C.1 (continued)

Number	Variable	Instrument	Scoring/Interpretation
331	Longitudinal change: variables 288,302	CPQ, HSPQ	
332	Longitudinal change: variables 289,303	CPQ, HSPQ	
333	Longitudinal change: variables 290,304	CPQ, HSPQ	
334	Longitudinal change: variables 291,305	CPQ, HSPQ	
335	Longitudinal change: variables 292,306	CPQ, HSPQ	
336	Longitudinal change: variables 293,307	CPQ, HSPQ	
337	Longitudinal change: variables 294,308	CPQ, HSPQ	
338	Longitudinal change: variables 295,309	CPQ, HSPQ	
339	Longitudinal change: variables 297,310	CPQ, HSPQ	
340	Longitudinal change: variables 299,312	CPQ, HSPQ	
341	Longitudinal change: variables 298,311	CPQ, HSPQ	
342	Dominance	California Psychological Inventory (CPI, see Megargee, 1972)	Objective
343	Capacity for status	CPI	
344	Sociability	CPI	
345	Social presence	CPI	
346	Self-acceptance	CPI	
347	Sense of well-being	CPI	
348	Responsibility	CPI	
349	Socialization	CPI	
350	Self-control	CPI	
351	Tolerance	CPI	
352	Good impression	CPI	(validity scale; dissimulation)
353	Communality	CPI	(validity scale; common responses)
354	Achievement via conformance	CPI	
355	Achievement via independence	CPI	
356	Intellectual efficiency	CPI	

357	Psychological-mindedness	CPI	
358	Flexibility	CPI	
359	Femininity	CPI	
360	L (lie)	Minnesota Multiphasic Personality Inventory (MMPI) scale score, estimated from CPI responses (Rodgers, 1966)	Objective
361	F (carelessness)	Estimated MMPI	
362	K (defensiveness)	Estimated MMPI	
363	Hs (hypochondriasis)	Estimated MMPI with CPI-based K correction	
364	D (depression)	Estimated MMPI	
365	Hy (hysteria)	Estimated MMPI	
366	Pd (psychopathic deviancy)	Estimated MMPI with CPI-based K correction	
367	Mf (feminine interest pattern)	Estimated MMPI	
368	Pa (paranoia)	Estimated MMPI	
369	Pt (psychasthenia)	Estimated MMPI with CPI-based K correction	
370	Sc (schizophrenia)	Estimated MMPI with CPI-based K correction	
371	Ma (mania)	Estimated MMPI with CPI-based K correction	
372	Si (social introversion)	Estimated MMPI	
373	Social desirability	Young Children's Social Desirability Scale (Ford & Rubin, 1970)	Objective
374	Manifest anxiety	Children's Manifest Anxiety Scale (CMAS, Castenada, McCandless, & Palermo, 1956)	Objective
375	Lie	CMAS	(validity scale: dissimulation)

Table C.1 (continued)

Number	Variable	Instrument	Scoring/Interpretation
376	Self-esteem	Scale of Rosenberg (1965)	High scores indicate *low* self-esteem
377	Traditional male appropriateness of vocational preference	Our own Vocational Preference Questionnaire (VPQ), modeled on questions of Douvan & Adelson (1966)	5-point scale
378	Social status of vocational preference	VPQ	By criteria of Warner, Meeker, & Eells (1960)
379	Definiteness of vocational plans	VPQ	3-point scale
380	Rule internalization	Adapted from Douvan and Adelson (1966)	7-point scale
381	Social desirability	Crandall Social Desirability Scale (Crandall, Crandall, & Katkovsky, 1965)	Objective
382	Self-concept: physical ability	Pauline Sears's test of self-concept (see Johnson & Bommarito, 1971)	Objective: high scores are favorable self-evaluations
383	Self-concept: attractiveness	As above	
384	Self-concept: convergent mental operations	As above	
385	Self-concept: social relations	As above	
386	Self-concept: social virtues	As above	
387	Self-concept: divergent mental operations	As above	
388	Self-concept: work habits	As above	
389	Self-concept: happy qualities	As above	
390	Self-concept: school subjects	As above	
391	Total self-concept	As above	
392	Aggression anxiety	Aggression scales of Robert Sears (see Johnson & Bommarito, 1971)	Objective
393	Projected aggression	As above	
394	Self-aggression	As above	

395	Prosocial aggression	As above		
396	Antisocial aggression	As above		

Physiological (Sleep) Variables

397	Latency to sleep onset	Experimenter's scoring of sleep patterns on dream-retrieval nights during normative year of dream study	Median, in minutes	
398	Sleep latency to REM onset	As above	Median, per night	
399	Number of spontaneous awakenings	As above	Median, per night	
400	Duration of spontaneous awakenings	As above	Median, in minutes, per arousal	
401	Longitudinal change: variable 397	As above	High scores are *decreases* in variable	
402	Longitudinal change: variable 398	As above		
403	Longitudinal change: variable 399	As above		
404	Longitudinal change: variable 400	As above		
405	Total lab time (to achieve 402.4 minutes sleep): night 1	Outside judges' scoring of 2 consecutive nights of uninterrupted sleep during Year 4. (Younger and older children's sleep patterns were, by the judges' scoring, practically identical: e.g., phasic REM, young 17.5, old 18; REM %, young 23.6, old 23.9; REM latency, young 87.2, old 87.7; waking/movement time, young 4.3, old 4.2. All of these figures are 2-night, median-subject values.)		Interjudge reliability calculated on a sample of 14 nights for all variables: for lab time, $r = .78$; for NREM time, $r = .84$; for REM time, $r = .81$; for sleep-onset latency, $r = .99$; for REM latency, $r = .48$; for REM %, $r = .82$; for waking/movement time, $r = .81$; for phasic REM, $r = .99$. Tonic variables were scored through the first 402.4 minutes of sleep; phasic REM was scored for the first 10.08 minutes of the first REM period of such duration.
406	Total lab time: night 2	As above		

Table C.1 **(continued)**

Number	Variable	Instrument	Scoring/Interpretation
407	Total lab time: night 1/2 median	As above	
408	NREM time: night 1	As above	
409	NREM time: night 2	As above	
410	REM time: night 1	As above	
411	REM time: night 2	As above	
412	Sleep-onset latency: night 1	As above	
413	Sleep-onset latency: night 2	As above	
414	Sleep-onset latency: night 1/2 median	As above	
415	Sleep latency to REM onset: night 1	As above	
416	Sleep latency to REM onset: night 2	As above	
417	Sleep latency to REM onset: night 1/2 median	As above	
418	REM %: night 1	As above	
419	REM %: night 2	As above	
420	REM %: night 1/2 median	As above	
421	Waking/movement time: night 1	As above	
422	Waking/movement time: night 2	As above	
423	Waking/movement time: night 1/2 median	As above	
424	Phasic REM %: night 1	As above	Number of 2.5-second intervals with at least one REM burst
425	Phasic REM %: night 2	As above	
426	Phasic REM %: night 1/2 median	As above	

Behavioral/Observational Variables

Number	Variable	Instrument	Scoring/Interpretation
427	Anxious, tense	Presleep Behavior Rating Scales (PBRS), completed by experimenter	5-point scales, summed over 9 nights

428	Shy, withdrawn	PBRS	
429	Mischievous	PBRS	
430	Resistant	PBRS	
431	Emotionally expressive	PBRS	
432	Restless, labile, spontaneous	PBRS	
433	Affection/support seeking	PBRS	
434	Talkative	PBRS	
435	Hostile	PBRS	
436	Depressed, gloomy	PBRS	
437	Longitudinal change: variable 427	PBRS	High scores are *decreases* in variable
438	Longitudinal change: variable 428	PBRS	
439	Longitudinal change: variable 429	PBRS	
440	Longitudinal change: variable 430	PBRS	
441	Longitudinal change: variable 431	PBRS	
442	Longitudinal change: variable 432	PBRS	
443	Longitudinal change: variable 433	PBRS	
444	Longitudinal change: variable 434	PBRS	
445	Longitudinal change: variable 435	PBRS	
446	Longitudinal change: variable 436	PBRS	
447	Responsible	PBRS	Cornell Teacher Rating Scales (CTRS, after Bronfenbrenner, 1961)
448	Dominant	CTRS	4-point scales, median of ratings available
449	Interested in opposite sex	CTRS	
450	Sensitive	CTRS	
451	Flighty	CTRS	
452	Accepted	CTRS	
453	Resistant	CTRS	
454	Emotionally expressive	CTRS	
455	High level of aspiration	CTRS	
456	Leader	CTRS	

Table C.1 **(continued)**

Number	Variable	Instrument	Scoring/Interpretation
457	Spontaneous	CTRS	High scores are increases in variable
458	Childish	CTRS	
459	Mischievous	CTRS	
460	Artistic, imaginative	CTRS	
461	Adult oriented	CTRS	
462	Competitive	CTRS	
463	Shy, withdrawn	CTRS	
464	Cheerful	CTRS	
465	Hostile, aggressive	CTRS	
466	Kind, considerate	CTRS	
467	Daring	CTRS	
468	Anxious, tense	CTRS	
469	Year 3 vs. 5 change in variable 447	CTRS	
470	Year 3 vs. 5 change in variable 448	CTRS	
471	Year 3 vs. 5 change in variable 449	CTRS	
472	Year 3 vs. 5 change in variable 450	CTRS	
473	Year 3 vs. 5 change in variable 451	CTRS	
474	Year 3 vs. 5 change in variable 452	CTRS	
475	Year 3 vs. 5 change in variable 453	CTRS	
476	Year 3 vs. 5 change in variable 454	CTRS	
477	Year 3 vs. 5 change in variable 455	CTRS	
478	Year 3 vs. 5 change in variable 456	CTRS	
479	Year 3 vs. 5 change in variable 457	CTRS	
480	Year 3 vs. 5 change in variable 458	CTRS	
481	Year 3 vs. 5 change in variable 459	CTRS	
482	Year 3 vs. 5 change in variable 460	CTRS	
483	Year 3 vs. 5 change in variable 461	CTRS	

484	Year 3 vs. 5 change in variable 462	CTRS
485	Year 3 vs. 5 change in variable 463	CTRS
486	Year 3 vs. 5 change in variable 464	CTRS
487	Year 3 vs. 5 change in variable 465	CTRS
488	Year 3 vs. 5 change in variable 466	CTRS
489	Year 3 vs. 5 change in variable 467	CTRS
490	Year 3 vs. 5 change in variable 468	CTRS
491	Unprovoked physical aggression to same-sex peers	Fels Nursery-School Rating Scales (Rabson, 1966), completed by regular classroom teacher	3-point scales
492	Unprovoked verbal aggression to same-sex peers	Fels
493	Retaliation to aggression from peers	Fels
494	Instrumental help seeking from adults	Fels
495	Affection and emotional support seeking from adults	Fels
496	Recognition seeking for achievement from adults	Fels
497	Effort on mastery of fine motor skills	Fels
498	Effort on mastery of gross motor skills	Fels
499	Effort on mastery in intellectual activities	Fels
500	Associative play	Fels
501	Restless activity	Fels
502	Loquaciousness	Fels
503	Dominance of same-sex peers	Fels
504	Conformity to adult demands	Fels
505	Imitation of peers	Fels
506	Body coordination	Fels
507	Quality of language	Fels
508	Amount of masculinity	Fels

Table C.1 (continued)

Number	Variable	Instrument	Scoring/Interpretation
509	Reported home sleep time	Sleep Habits Questionnaire (SHQ, Foulkes, Belvedere, & Brubaker, 1971), completed by children themselves	In hours and decimal fractions (median response: 9.65 hours)
510	Reported home sleep-onset latency	SHQ	In minutes (median response: 15 minutes)
511	Reported home spontaneous-arousal incidence	SHQ	4-point scale (median response: "once in a while")
512	Reported home sleep depth	SHQ	2-point scale (median response: "light" sleep)
513	Reported home dream recall rate	SHQ	6-point scale (median response: 2–3 times weekly)
514	Reported home nightmare incidence	SHQ	(median response: once a year)
515	Reported home sleepwalking incidence	SHQ	(median response: never)
516	Reported home enuresis incidence	SHQ	(median response: never)
517	TV viewing rate	Media Preference Questionnaire (MPQ; Foulkes, Belvedere, & Brubaker, 1971)	Number of programs regularly watched
518	Violent-TV viewing rate	MPQ	Number of regularly watched programs on list of Greenberg & Gordon (1971)
519	Violence favoring	MPQ	Index based on comparing child's 3 favorite programs to Greenberg & Gordon's (1971) list
520	Movie viewing rate	MPQ	Composite index based on reported TV and theater viewing behavior
521	Nonviolent movie interests	MPQ	Composite index
522	Violent movie interests	MPQ	

No.	Variable	Instrument	Scoring
523	Reading interests index	MPQ	5-point scale
524	Popular music interests index	MPQ	Number mentioned
525	Outdoor activities index	MPQ	Number mentioned
526	Church attendance	MPQ	Sum of variables 521 and 522
527	Club affiliations	MPQ	Variable 522 minus variable 521 plus a constant
528	Sports interests	MPQ	
529	Movie interests	MPQ	
530	Violent movie preference	MPQ	
531	Self-reported school grades	MPQ	8-point scale
532	(same as variable 377)	MPQ	(same as variable 377)
533	(same as variable 378)	MPQ	(same as variable 378)
534	(same as variable 379)	MPQ	(same as variable 379)
535	Self-rated outgoingness	66-item modification of the Gough Adjective Check List (ACL, Gough & Heilbrun, 1965), completed by children and experimenter for presleep mood of older children in Year 5	6-item bipolar checklist: 9-night sum
536	Self-rated outgoingness: variability	ACL	High nightly score minus low nightly score
537	Self-rated energy level	ACL	8-item bipolar checklist: 9-night sum
538	Self-rated energy level: variability	ACL	As for variable 536
539	Self-rated friendliness	ACL	10-item bipolar checklist: 9-night sum
540	Self-rated friendliness: variability	ACL	As for variable 536
541	Self-rated euphoria	ACL	10-item bipolar checklist: 9-night sum
542	Self-rated euphoria: variability	ACL	As for variable 536

Table C.1 (continued)

Number	Variable	Instrument	Scoring/Interpretation
543	Self-rated arousal	ACL	8-item bipolar checklist: 9-night sum
544	Self-rated arousal: variability	ACL	As for variable 536
545	Self-rated organization	ACL	10-item bipolar checklist: 9-night sum
546	Self-rated organization: variability	ACL	As for variable 536
547	Self-rated restraint	ACL	14-item bipolar checklist: 9-night sum
548	Self-rated restraint: variability	ACL	As for variable 536
549	E-rated outgoingness (E = Experimenter)	ACL	As for variable 535
550	E-rated outgoingness: variability	ACL	As for variable 536
551	E-rated energy level	ACL	As for variable 537
552	E-rated energy level: variability	ACL	As for variable 536
553	E-rated friendliness	ACL	As for variable 539
554	E-rated friendliness: variability	ACL	As for variable 536
555	E-rated euphoria	ACL	As for variable 541
556	E-rated euphoria: variability	ACL	As for variable 536
557	E-rated arousal	ACL	As for variable 543
558	E-rated arousal: variability	ACL	As for variable 536
559	E-rated organization	ACL	As for variable 545
560	E-rated organization: variability	ACL	As for variable 536
561	E-rated restraint	ACL	As for variable 547
562	E-rated restraint: variability	ACL	As for variable 536
563	E-rated lability	ACL	Total number of different items ever checked for a child

Physical Maturation Variables

564	Body weight: Year 2	All height and weight measurements were taken on standardized instruments following standardized procedures	Younger Ss
565	Body weight: Year 4	As above	
566	Body height: Year 4	As above	
567	Weight/height ratio: Year 4	As above	
568	Body weight: Year 5	As above	
569	Body height: Year 5	As above	
570	Weight/height ratio: Year 5	As above	
571	Percent height increase: Year 4 to 5	As above	
572	Percent weight increase: Year 4 to 5	As above	
573	Percent weight increase: Year 2 to 5	As above	
574	Weight/height ratio increase: Year 4 to 5	As above	
575	Body weight	As above	Older Ss: end of Year 1
576	Body height	As above	
577	Weight/height ratio	As above	
578	Body weight	As above	Older Ss: mid-Year 3
579	Body height	As above	
580	Weight/height ratio	As above	
581	Percent weight increase	As above	Older Ss: start to end of Year 3
582	Percent height increase	As above	
583	Body weight	As above	Older Ss: start of Year 5
584	Body height	As above	
585	Weight/height ratio	As above	
586	Body weight	As above	Older Ss: end of Year 5
587	Body height	As above	
588	Weight/height ratio	As above	
589	Percent weight increase	As above	Older Ss: start to end of Year 5

Table C.1 **(continued)**

Number	Variable	Instrument	Scoring/Interpretation
590	Percent height increase	As above	Older Ss: Year 3 to end of Year 5
591	Percent weight increase	As above	
592	Percent height increase	As above	
593	Weight/height ratio increase	As above	Older Ss: start to end of Year 5
594	Weight/height ratio increase	As above	Older Ss: Year 3 to end of Year 5
595	Height acceleration	As above	Older Ss: variable 590 minus variable 582 plus constant
596	Age, in months	Screening interview	As of June 1, 1968 (start of Year 1)
597	Nap frequency	Napping questionnaire	6-point scale
598	Time since menarche	Menstrual questionnaire (Year 4); Recent activities form (Year 5)	As of May 31, 1973 (end of Year 5)

Nursery-School Variables

| 599 | Initiation to peers | Time-sampled behavior (TSB) observations, with categories adopted from Marshall (1961). For initiation measures, there were 140 15-second observation occasions per child per year, and measures indicate the percentage of those occasions for which an activity class was scored. Reception measures were prorated to the number of possible occasions on which a child could have received the activity. In Year 3 two scores were entered into correlation with dream | Year 3 reliability of S classification, $r = .86$ |

		data for each TSB variable, one for each observer	
600	Initiation to adults	TSB	Year 3 reliability of S classification, $r = .95$
601	Association with peers	TSB	Year 3 reliability of S classification, $r = .91$
602	Association with adults	TSB	Year 3 reliability of S classification, $r = .93$
603	Pretend behavior	TSB	Year 3 reliability of S classification, $r = .90$
604	Hostile to peer	TSB	Year 3 reliability of S classification, $r = .78$
605	Hostile to object	TSB	Year 3 reliability of S classification, $r = .93$
606	Hostile	TSB	Variable 604 plus variable 605
607	Receipt of peer initiation	TSB	Year 3 reliability of S classification, $r = .47$
608	Receipt of peer association	TSB	Year 3 reliability of S classification, $r = .97$
609	Receipt of hostile peer initiation	TSB	Year 3 reliability of S classification, $r = .76$
610	Hostility to peers/initiation to peers	TSB	Ratio
611	Hostility received/initiation received	TSB	
612	Initiation to adults/initiation to peers	TSB	
613	Association with adults/association with peers	TSB	
614	Initiation to peers/initiation from peers	TSB	
615	Initiation to peers/association with peers	TSB	
616	Longitudinal change: variable 599	TSB	Year 2 vs. Year 3; high scores are increases in the variable
617	Longitudinal change: variable 601	TSB	

379

Table C.1 (continued)

Number	Variable	Instrument	Scoring/Interpretation
618	Longitudinal change: variable 603	TSB	
619	Longitudinal change: variable 606	TSB	
620	Longitudinal change: variable 610	TSB	
621	Longitudinal change: variable 611	TSB	
622	Longitudinal change: variable 612	TSB	
623	Longitudinal change: variable 613	TSB	
624	Longitudinal change: variable 614	TSB	
625	Longitudinal change: variable 615	TSB	
626	Physical aggression	Fels Nursery-School Rating Scales (Rabson, 1966): overall summer-session rating, in a forced-choice distribution. Because Year-3 reliabilities were markedly inferior to those in Years 1 and 2, both Year-3 judges' ratings were entered separately into correlation with Year-3 dream data, while one summed score was used in Years 1 and 2	Median inter-rater $r = .875$
627	Verbal aggression	Fels	Median inter-rater $r = .75$
628	Retaliation to aggression	Fels	Median inter-rater $r = .625$
629	Instrumental help seeking	Fels	Median inter-rater $r = .625$
630	Emotional support seeking	Fels	Median inter-rater $r = .625$
631	Associative play	Fels	Median inter-rater $r = .75$
632	Restless activity	Fels	Median inter-rater $r = .625$
633	Loquaciousness	Fels	Median inter-rater $r = .625$
634	Dominance	Fels	Median inter-rater $r = .75$
635	Conformity to adults	Fels	Median inter-rater $r = .75$

636	Imitation	Fels	Median inter-rater $r = .625$
637	Language quality	Fels	Median inter-rater $r = .625$
638	Masculinity	Fels	Median inter-rater $r = .75$
639	Body coordination	Fels	Not scored in Year 1; inter-rater r for Years 2 and 3 were .75 and .00
640	Longitudinal change: variable 626	Fels	Year 2 vs. Year 3; high scores are increases in the variable
641	Longitudinal change: variable 627	Fels	
642	Longitudinal change: variable 628	Fels	
643	Longitudinal change: variable 629	Fels	
644	Longitudinal change: variable 630	Fels	
645	Longitudinal change: variable 631	Fels	
646	Longitudinal change: variable 632	Fels	
647	Longitudinal change: variable 633	Fels	
648	Longitudinal change: variable 634	Fels	
649	Longitudinal change: variable 635	Fels	
650	Longitudinal change: variable 636	Fels	
651	Longitudinal change: variable 637	Fels	
652	Longitudinal change: variable 638	Fels	
653	Longitudinal change: variable 639	Fels	
654	Number of choices received	Sociometric test: each child pointed to pictures of 3 children with whom she/he would like to be scheduled the following year	"Choice status"
655	Number of like-sex choices made	Sociometric test	Out of 3 possible
656	Longitudinal change: variable 654	Sociometric test	Increases, Year 2 to 3
657	Longitudinal change: variable 655	Sociometric test	

Table C.2 Nondream Correlates of Dream Variables

Dream Variable	Ages 3–5		Ages 5–7		Ages 7–9		Ages 9–11		Ages 11–13		Ages 13–15	
	Correlate	r	Correlate	r	Correlate	r	Correlate	r	Correlate	r	Correlate	r
REM recall	10	57	1	-72	25	-56	2	52	5	-80	1	-59
	59	62	5	-54	27	-54	9	71	7	-60	4	-48
	61	-72	6	-68	46	-47	48	58	15	48	5	-74
	397	71	7	-55	168	48	59	64	20	-56	7	-56
	428	-56	16	-58	172	56	102	-55	27	-53	19	-57
	429	59	35	-59	184	53	159	55	34	-68	20	-64
	431	72	42	-62	185	55	160	51	42	-58	21	-55
	434	71	44	-54	203	67	235	52	49	61	22	-53
	604	73	53	-57	447	52	287	63	51	-52	24	63
	606	64	54	-57	453	-52	290	55	105	55	26	-66
	609	69	55	-62	491	-60	294	-52	168	51	27	-52
	610	58	58	57	505	-55	376	-57	171	46	34	-52
	629	58	166	63	573	-56	377	65	172	48	42	-59
	630	62	201	-69					187i	-82	46	-66
			202	54					247	73	56	-58
			610	-58					248	55	58	54
			640	-61					251	76	66	-47
			641	-77					271	52	102	-53
			648	-65					287	53	124	-58
									290	50	159	56
									397	-45	160	51
									409	-52	161	51
									411	55	172	66
									419	55	173	62
									420	56	184	57

185	67
204	−61
208	54
218	63
219	−58
233	52
246	55
250	50
254	−59
259	49
260	−49
271	55
301	65
306	50
308	50
310	64
312	64
339	59
367	73
431	51
434	49
435	−52
436	−55
438	55
441	−69
442	−54
444	−50
446	59
449	−57
450	51

442	−58
513	65
520	−47
524	47
528	−48
531	61

Table C.2 (continued)

Dream Variable	Ages 3–5		Ages 5–7		Ages 7–9		Ages 9–11		Ages 11–13		Ages 13–15	
	Correlate	r	Correlate	r	Correlate	r	Correlate	r	Correlate	r	Correlate	r
											455	49
											460	61
											471	−59
											472	52
											486	48
											539	−52
											547	−49
											551	73
											553	54
Longitudinal *decrease* in REM recall			3	−60	9	−61			9	73	14	59
			5	60	16	−54			37	−64	24	−63
			6	58	200	63			42	−74	26	70
			8	66	201	−55			57	−74	30	−52
			54	67	408	61			59	90	102	63
			55	67	410	−66			67	−65	103	64
			203	−70	417	58			72	−72	185	−53
			441	63	418	−71			109	61	204	47
			505	−56	420	−58			298	54	205	58
			628	59	433	54			396	−68	206	55
			629	66	435	−74			405	57	211	−49
			630	61	461	−64			412	59	301	−58
									417	53	306	−54
									424	−57	308	−54
									443	70	310	−71

NREM recall

13	−57	15	−68	13	48	13	52	451	−54	312	−56
27	−64	16	−62	36	49	14	76	520	−61	336	47
28	56	42	−61	46	−44	38	−63	522	−60	339	−53
40	−59	159	54	168	51	49	66			348	−49
		160	61	264	45	57	−76			367	−51
		162	61	265	49	61	61	15	50	441	51
		166	62	273	−44	96	−53	39	47	442	59
		174	−64	432	−47	159	61	127	65	449	52
		176	−62			160	73	159	45	472	−50
		203	63			170	56	168	53	478	51
		618	−59			375	−56	169	47	553	−58
		641	−65			376	−60	171	53	1	−57
						377	58	176	−57	7	−75
								271	53	26	−65
								290	74	34	−52
								449	46	46	−54
								455	53	56	−57
								513	51	66	−48
										68	−70
										73	−48
										87	−53
										89	−61
										91	−58
										114	50
										124	−78
										159	63
										160	70
										168	74
										169	63
										170	55

Table C.2 (continued)

Dream Variable	Ages 3–5		Ages 5–7		Ages 7–9		Ages 9–11		Ages 11–13		Ages 13–15	
	Correlate	r	Correlate	r	Correlate	r	Correlate	r	Correlate	r	Correlate	r
											172	54
											173	67
											184	53
											185	65
											204	−50
											209	48
											212	55
											218	67
											250	49
											271	61
											301	67
											306	47
											330	47
											333	−55
											339	53
											342	54
											343	64
											348	48
											351	62
											354	63
											355	60
											356	71
											357	48
											361	−51
											367	64

Longitudinal *decrease* in NREM recall

15	66	36	−58	30	80	404	−58
16	78	238	−63	37	−59	439	−48
29	71	265	−59	47	83	440	−58
39	−55	436	−55	127	−59	441	−56
192	−70			289	60	446	47
196	−55			294	−54	450	55
415	53			395	−72	453	−48
429	58			436	−56	455	53
430	55					460	55
596	−60					472	49
603	−67					551	57
603	−64					553	61
612	60					556	48
612	60					557	47
613	59						
						1	58
						13	48
						24	−53
						26	59
						30	−49
						56	61
						124	49
						178	−63
						185	−54
						211	−47
						225	−52
						226	−55
						228	−49
						301	−61
						306	−59

Table C.2 (continued)

Dream Variable	Ages 3–5 Correlate	r	Ages 5–7 Correlate	r	Ages 7–9 Correlate	r	Ages 9–11 Correlate	r	Ages 11–13 Correlate	r	Ages 13–15 Correlate	r
	10	65	613	60							310	−70
	59	63	614	−55							312	−51
	61	−74	618	−62							339	−74
			622	60							348	−47
											354	−47
											356	−48
											449	74
											476	−56
											546	−57
											557	−47
											583	50
											585	59
											588	55
Sleep-onset recall			6	−55	25	−70	17	−62	49	65	1	−66
			16	−80	32	−50	31	−61	85	−61	7	−70
			35	−66	46	−55	34	−63	160	47	9	−60
			37	−55	52	−45	42	−62	168	51	14	−56
			42	−78	156	−54	45	−67	169	50	19	−52
			59	54	158	−54	49	74	171	53	23	59
			60	−59	168	54	50	53	247	68	26	−56
			160	54	172	52	160	56	248	59	46	−50
			166	64	194	47	376	−55	251	65	56	−49
			201	−55	203	54	377	82	287	62	68	−56
			493	59	228	58	459	−54	319	55	168	51
			641	−68	273	−46			410	45	169	67

411	45	172	63
418	45	178	51
419	46	184	62
420	52	185	59
430	−47	188	62
456	53	211	56
513	56	219	−51
516	−49	233	52
522	−47	257	−64
524	62	301	52
531	50	339	64
		343	54
		356	49
		367	48
		398	52
		454	57
		460	47
		536	52
		557	52

34	−74	3	53
43	71	9	67
50	63	23	−48
76	−58	49	57
94	−65	103	48
105	−82	109	50
115	70	112	−68
183	54	176	−51
286	−63	183	52
317	55	214	47

285	46
424	61
426	54
596	44

16	−71
29	−59
42	−59
147	−64
155	54
175	58
258	65
259	−62
261	66
265	−82

6	64
8	68
14	−58
16	75
29	59
34	55
35	75
37	70
42	64
54	60

Longitudinal *decrease*
in sleep-onset recall

Table C.2 (continued)

Dream Variable	Ages 3–5 Correlate	r	Ages 5–7 Correlate	r	Ages 7–9 Correlate	r	Ages 9–11 Correlate	r	Ages 11–13 Correlate	r	Ages 13–15 Correlate	r
			166	−58	274	−77			437	57	261	−54
			429	62	399	−72			445	66	309	−63
			430	57	424	−57			446	59	336	55
			616	58					454	−64	338	−62
			619	−61					456	−62	341	−51
			633	69					463	62	345	62
			636	64							352	−61
			654	60							364	−47
											408	−60
											410	72
											418	72
											420	52
											440	−47
											485	69
											536	−71
											542	50
											546	−47
											552	−64
REM word count	5	−65	222	59	16	53	30	61	7	−52	1	−61
	33	−69	637	69	29	54	47	61	26	−59	7	−72
	56	−70			42	50	235	52	30	61	26	−74
	185	53			52	−52	237	56	62	−55	30	51
	400	59			154	−59	435	−56	64	−72	56	−62
	612	−58			198	74			69	64	60	56
					199	70			70	54	75	49

71	58	89	−54
160	47	180	53
168	57	185	57
169	54	250	56
177	77	301	63
246	62	330	49
247	54	333	−59
251	56	339	51
271	48	351	58
287	45	355	54
409	−45	356	53
411	45	362	51
419	46	367	50
430	−50	368	50
442	−63	433	60
452	45	434	50
464	44	440	−50
514	77	443	−54
581	−51	450	50
		454	53
		464	52
		472	59
		477	−49
		489	53

47	−88	32	−59
77	75	76	49
83	69	304	−56
84	−62	308	49
108	−84	344	−63

231	81
232	81
233	69
237	59
243	58
245	61
506	−62

52	−70
154	−62
199	63
231	72
232	75

403	−61
430	59
624	63
637	73
637	62

Longitudinal increase
in REM word count

Table C.2 (continued)

Dream Variable	Ages 3–5 Correlate	r	Ages 5–7 Correlate	r	Ages 7–9 Correlate	r	Ages 9–11 Correlate	r	Ages 11–13 Correlate	r	Ages 13–15 Correlate	r
					237	73			123	82	345	−59
					245	70			127	58	346	−65
					262	−62			128	−70	359	57
					468	−68			223	54	364	62
									394	−61	459	−48
									400	−63	545	−49
									404	65		
									406	−80		
									407	−55		
									413	−83		
									414	−64		
									429	−67		
									430	−66		
									431	−58		
									432	−71		
									433	−55		
									436	73		
									446	58		
									452	69		
									453	−64		
									459	−54		
									468	−60		
									510	−66		
NREM word count					237	77	109	59	4	51	10	59
					242	65	291	−58	10	48	26	−74

245	88			21	51	30	72
281	61			24	-62	47	60
283	-57			43	53	122	54
404	72			71	69	160	51
405	84			114	79	169	72
407	77			121	71	170	59
421	88	576	60	122	82	228	55
423	88			129	-74	252	-67
445	-66			297	-52	334	53
468	-69			325	69	342	56
503	67			408	47	343	63
				417	-53	351	52
				421	47	413	52
				515	52	434	52
						454	61
						474	-53
						484	-57
						587	68

20	56			69	55	1	-51
28	60			71	55	7	-64
36	68			87	52	10	56
45	-56			107	54	26	-68
184	61	30	66	175	65	30	62
186	59	41	-64	178	-61	35	52
196	72	47	89	295	-52	84	-56
283	-60	70	59	428	-60	104	57
416	-71	109	71	434	54	169	53
422	79	237	62	439	-61	342	54
440	-75	427	-59	441	69	343	53
449	68			521	-52	362	68

Sleep-onset word count

Table C.2 (continued)

Dream Variable	Ages 3–5 Correlate	r	Ages 5–7 Correlate	r	Ages 7–9 Correlate	r	Ages 9–11 Correlate	r	Ages 11–13 Correlate	r	Ages 13–15 Correlate	r
	30	67	27	−65	451	−80			524	51	364	50
	36	63	28	63	453	−78					409	−52
	59	68	40	−72	460	74					411	53
	140	64	57	67	464	71					419	53
	397	60	159	65	468	−78					433	51
	601	−61	161	81							434	59
	615	74	403	−68							454	64
			408	−75							472	53
			600	62							561	50
			602	81								
			602	66								
			609	73								
			612	89								
			612	75								
			613	86								
			613	77								
Parent, male					17	46	35	51	39	52	28	51
					28	51	45	−61	65	48	54	61
					32	51	50	52	107	−57	56	−55
					39	−49	234	54	110	−48	60	51
					52	45	235	55	125	62	88	−50
					171	48	239	50	177	54	89	−49
					196	67	289	58	427	46	90	−53
					234	−46	377	55	442	−61	180	71
					234	−48					185	57
					235	−58					219	−50
					235	−53					351	53
					239	−54					355	49
					239	−45					362	48
					245	−61					404	−54
					401	51					464	48
					403	48					472	57

Parent, female

												555	−50
30	71	621	70	27	−66	404	63	8	61	84	53	7	−62
36	70	622	90	28	62	427	55	15	52	123	−62	88	−63
38	54	623	86	40	−78	435	45	45	−65	130	69	90	−58
54	54			57	68	572	−58	50	51	175	66	120	62
140	68			159	61	574	−65	234	61	180	61	178	55
601	−61			161	72	5	−46	377	59	249	57	185	48
615	69			167	61	6	−48			394	48	209	57
				188	−58	13	52			398	50	225	52
				403	−67	17	48			400	61	227	48
				408	−64	19	−47			402	−59	231	54
				602	69	54	−53			429	53	265	62
				609	65	55	−51			430	48	397	−49
				612	79	171	51			451	49	484	54
				612	68	192	48			453	55	489	55
				613	76	203	83					537	64
				613	67	229	−57					538	57
				621	71	245	−57					543	55
				622	79	263	−56					546	55
				623	79	264	52						
						626	−63						
						628	−58						

Parent, either

30	70	27	−66	17	49	8	53	39	45	56	−51
36	68	28	68	18	49	17	−50	63	46	59	−58
59	60	40	−80	19	−52	28	53	107	−55	88	−64
140	67	57	71	54	−52	35	56	130	63	90	−60
601	−62	159	64	171	52	45	−70	249	58	120	60
615	72	161	78	203	65	50	55	400	50	178	64

Table C.2 (continued)

Dream Variable	Ages 3–5 Correlate	r	Ages 5–7 Correlate	r	Ages 7–9 Correlate	r	Ages 9–11 Correlate	r	Ages 11–13 Correlate	r	Ages 13–15 Correlate	r
			167	61	245	−57	54	56	402	−57	185	56
			403	−68	263	−52	234	57			209	61
			408	−72	264	46	235	54			265	63
			602	71	574	−63	377	72			397	−54
			609	65	626	−60					449	−50
			612	83							460	51
			612	65							537	51
			613	77							538	49
			613	67							546	49
			621	66								
			622	83								
			623	79								
Parent/sibling, male	4	82	27	−69	32	71	18	−62	11	65	54	51
	5	63	40	−66	48	−46	55	62	15	45	88	−63
	19	59	57	70	154	57	172	−52	84	62	92	−48
	20	77	159	69	155	57	222	−56	85	60	341	49
	33	69	161	84	156	71	454	−63	90	53	346	−50
	41	67	403	−60	157	66			91	49	350	49
	46	61	408	−71	158	72			101	51	358	50
	56	61	499	64	170	−50			175	72	424	53
	239	68	600	66	184	50			178	−64	583	−49
	427	58	602	85	186	52			180	62	585	−53
	430	68	602	69	196	65			249	79		
	433	53	609	73	373	−62			250	−54		
	600	79	612	93	398	62			392	−49		

Parent/sibling, female

ID	Coef.		ID	Coef.		ID	Coef.		ID	Coef.		ID	Coef.
602	78		30	64		612	75		13	−60		415	58
613	63		36	70		613	90		27	−66		454	51
637	−60		38	58		613	80		28	67		491	−60
			54	54		621	67		40	−69		492	−69
			140	59		622	93		57	68		493	−59
			601	−64		623	87		159	65		508	−77
			615	60					161	76			
									403	−66			
									408	−73			
									602	79			
									602	62			
									609	76			
									609	64			
									612	88			
									612	71			
									613	84			
									613	74			
									621	73			
									622	88			
									623	85			

ID	Coef.		ID	Coef.		ID	Coef.		ID	Coef.		ID	Coef.
13	48		15	60		400	60		11	60		7	−59
17	46		31	−67		429	46		13	46		88	−62
18	67		34	−65		447	−59		39	46		90	−50
52	54		39	54		451	60		45	−52		120	59
56	−45		45	−85		453	66		50	45		231	52
171	54		49	62		465	47		123	−67		250	52
242	60		50	58		466	−55		130	57		265	50
244	−55		54	52		511	48		180	62		312	50
263	−69		234	51					394	50		332	53
264	56		377	69					400	59		484	68
417	−60								402	−56		486	61
									429	45		489	54
												537	69
												538	49
												543	57
												557	55
												585	−54
												588	−56

Parent/sibling, either/both

ID	Coef.		ID	Coef.		ID	Coef.		ID	Coef.		ID	Coef.
4	82		27	−68		32	62		45	−75		11	71
5	66		28	58		48	−47		49	63		15	46

ID	Coef.
66	−51
88	−62

Table C.2 (continued)

Dream Variable	Ages 3–5		Ages 5–7		Ages 7–9		Ages 9–11		Ages 11–13		Ages 13–15	
	Correlate	r	Correlate	r	Correlate	r	Correlate	r	Correlate	r	Correlate	r
	9	54	40	−70	60	50	54	58	47	57	105	−50
	19	60	57	72	156	71	377	69	50	48	120	67
	20	75	159	69	157	63			78	−46	179	65
	21	54	161	82	158	70			79	−53	265	53
	22	57	167	62	170	−54			84	54	312	54
	33	77	189	−58	200	−67			85	53	344	54
	36	59	403	−60	229	−56			101	49	484	53
	38	67	408	−68	236	51			123	−73	486	65
	41	62	602	78	242	63			175	63	537	61
	56	61	602	61	263	−60			178	−60	543	57
	237	55	609	73	373	−64			180	61	557	57
	239	55	609	61	406	−61			249	67	583	−56
	427	67	612	89	491	−64			400	63	585	−62
	430	76	612	67	492	−62			406	48	586	−56
	432	59	613	83	508	−64			413	46	588	−63
	433	57	613	72					429	45		
	600	72	621	68					447	−51		
	602	74	622	89					451	57		
	612	57	623	83					453	58		
	613	74							466	−49		
	615	58							512	−49		
	637	−68										
	638	−56										
Known peer, male	2	−72	19	−65	2	45	4	74	4	73	10	65
	26	−64	25	−60	7	57	18	−79	5	67	23	65

398

-73	49	58	10	50	39	47	16	91	176	-63	48
58	178	46	19	50	43	51	22	-60	199	56	60
58	189	72	20	-56	161	52	29	59	234	87	141
57	215	60	21	58	377	65	34	71	235	-63	162
64	363	55	22	-52	432	64	37	84	239	-57	184
54	365	59	33	-59	454	-57	174	71	241	-59	185
52	437	57	34	-54	459	46	187	86	243	61	600
60	448	49	35	-80	462	62	191	78	424	59	612
62	457	53	38	51	463	73	198	74	426	63	654
-48	466	58	42			70	199	-59	439	-73	655
-59	478	60	43			62	230	-70	646		
51	536	62	46			92	231				
51	587	64	51			91	232				
56	593	50	58			71	233				
59	594	-55	62			66	237				
		46	65			63	245				
		49	66			59	424				
		61	70			52	464				
		-47	72			68	565				
		66	124			71	567				
		-46	173								
		-57	441								
		68	517								
		87	519								

Known peer, female

-48	1	-53	12	71	2	48	42	68	23	-54	8
59	48	69	24	73	3	57	151	63	42	68	235
57	61	-53	44	64	13	59	156	66	46	-58	638
49	81	-49	85	69	39	54	234	-69	160	-66	655
-50	115	-61	87	-68	45	46	234	-76	194		
55	161	-63	91	-68	57	58	235	-80	195		

Table C.2 (continued)

Dream Variable	Ages 3–5 Correlate	r	Ages 5–7 Correlate	r	Ages 7–9 Correlate	r	Ages 9–11 Correlate	r	Ages 11–13 Correlate	r	Ages 13–15 Correlate	r
			641	68	235	50	96	−58	93	−63	172	59
			642	70	239	68	234	71	115	−64	176	−61
			648	61	239	54	398	−53	183	−55	207	50
					240	58	456	50	246	54	211	53
					240	64			248	56	218	49
					241	59			251	60	225	50
					241	56			287	61	227	51
					243	78			291	−46	229	49
					243	66			393	−50	233	53
					276	44			396	−47	250	82
					465	−65			397	−67	368	54
					498	−61			408	−49	425	56
					506	−66			410	51	454	50
					572	59			418	51	470	−59
					574	63			420	51		
									437	−55		
									525	−60		
Known adult, male	3	−72	22	61	60	51	81	−61	47	55	87	−50
	6	63	189	−62	231	77			270	52	94	−49
	7	65	235	62	232	89			286	−59	95	−53
	8	53	239	65	233	60			395	−48	114	52
	25	54	241	62	236	51			435	−53	177	61
	31	70	243	66	238	−44			461	53	189	−59
	44	54	425	68	242	−57			462	−52	191	61
	49	−61	426	65	399	53			463	53	232	50

Known adult, female

No.	V	No.	V	No.	V	No.	V	No.	V	No.	V	No.	V	No.	V	No.	V	No.	V	No.	V
397	52	3	55	467	−44	12	−53	6	52	424	64	5	57	607	75	236	68	60	54	16	−57
401	−57	39	63	523	−48	24	59	7	89	428	48	50	47	646	−65	238	−66			60	−65
415	50	49	54	525	−53	95	49	12	−52	433	−47	187	57			400	67			138	−66
427	−60	69	−52			175	−59	27	60	434	−48	198	68			404	76			397	73
428	−57	77	49			178	71	50	−60	435	45	199	57			412	66			604	80
431	61	87	−49			179	73	236	57	565	63	230	63			437	−68			606	69
435	−59	89	−49			224	−60			567	65	234	46							609	79
436	−58	91	−50			249	−66					234	50							609	55
446	58	173	53			250	65					235	45							610	74
475	51	212	76			287	45					235	45							611	69
539	−59	217	75			291	−64					239	45								
549	59	218	73			319	55					283	52								
554	49	249	−57			393	−50					424	62								
		250	70			397	−59					426	65								
		313	−50			403	63					459	56								
		347	50			429	−54														
		361	−54			430	−49														

Table C.2 (continued)

Dream Variable	Ages 3–5		Ages 5–7		Ages 7–9		Ages 9–11		Ages 11–13		Ages 13–15	
	Correlate	r	Correlate	r	Correlate	r	Correlate	r	Correlate	r	Correlate	r
									437	−56	367	59
									459	−52	400	52
									520	−47	404	−64
									522	−52	451	−53
											453	−52
											487	52
											490	52
											540	−52
											541	64
											553	50
Known any, male	48	−56	10	−63	39	48	9	−67	4	60	10	62
	58	−53	25	−69	45	−48	456	−56	10	57	14	−58
	60	81	26	−63	172	46	463	60	21	56	23	51
	141	60	44	−62	198	70			33	53	26	−49
	162	−61	46	−65	199	73			35	51	30	52
	164	−60	61	60	231	81			43	59	49	−64
	184	−63	174	65	232	83			46	55	175	−56
	185	−66	176	82	233	74			51	58	178	54
	596	−54	239	73	237	47			66	49	251	−50
	654	75	243	75	262	−48			70	48	300	51
			630	−62	453	−50			180	54	343	48
					468	−54			395	−55	428	−49
					506	−56			517	59	434	51
					565	59			519	76	435	−52
					567	60					447	−53

Known any, female

Item	Loading	Item	Loading	Item	Loading	Item	Loading	Item	Loading	Item	Loading	Item	Loading	Item	Loading
6	−57	2	−59	574	58	41	55	7	72	24	67	7	−49	448	56
235	66	42	66			151	55	12	−60	44	−48	26	−52	451	55
638	−59	160	−82			185i	−80	13	57	49	53	36	54	453	55
655	−65	164	−61			198	65	27	63	58	47	48	49	457	63
		194	−76			199	58	40	63	85	−50	61	56	458	54
		195	−73			234	56	96	−52	87	−54	161	58	459	55
		435	−61			234	53	455	53	91	−53	172	56	466	−54
		493	−71			235	62			93	−62	173	53	478	−56
		641	68			235	56			103	−52	176	−63	536	49
		642	68			239	72			115	−60	212	51	549	52
		647	61			239	58			183	−56	218	54	587	55
		648	61			240	59			248	57	233	56	594	54
		652	78			241	62			251	63	250	86		
						243	76			287	66	301	50		
						243	60			393	−53	425	59		
						465	−62			396	−47	454	53		
						498	−60			397	−65	470	−59		
						506	−67			408	−52	489	49		

403

Table C.2 (continued)

Dream Variable	Ages 3–5		Ages 5–7		Ages 7–9		Ages 9–11		Ages 11–13		Ages 13–15	
	Correlate	r	Correlate	r	Correlate	r	Correlate	r	Correlate	r	Correlate	r
					574	63						
Stranger peer, male												
			5	−61	13	−58	26	−67	410	55	67	52
			55	−72	32	−47	30	63	418	54	128	50
			178	64	233	62	56	−50	420	56	206	57
			236	67	275	−44	60	61	437	−56	213	−57
			237	61	280	−46	68	−54	511	−47	215	63
			400	58	417	−60	73	−51	525	−62	217	−49
			404	78	424	59	103	−54	10	61	258	77
			437	−73	449	57	448	−50	64	−54	261	58
			445	−58	457	−55			70	48	308	−58
			633	−62	505	−62			71	62	337	−53
			634	−62					107	48	348	−50
			635	62					318	53	399	59
			635	61					321	−57	437	49
			638	−62					440	−69	453	48
									448	48	457	67
									459	52	459	52
											461	−56
											466	−61
											560	−55

Stranger peer, female

236	68	2	45	25	-54	13	48	586	59
238	-66	17	-55	52	-62	20	-63	588	55
400	67	184i	89	57	-66	22	-64	29	56
404	76	185	46	85	-67	42	-68	46	-51
412	66	185i	83	91	-59	44	-49	49	55
437	-68	186i	83	109	55	88	47	88	-63
		196	60	160	64	294	51	103	63
		263	46	169	54	392	63	131	57
		280	-58	186	-62	393	-52	161	50
		283	-48	237	51	401	79	173	62
		409	64	294	-69	520	-51	209	58
		411	-64	380	60	522	-58	313	-50
		419	-64			526	49	336	51
		449	81			532	-53	400	54
		457	-53					537	50
								538	62
								558	71

Stranger adult, male

19	61	10	-47	40	-68	79	50	18	-73
52	61	41	-47	58	50	266	-50	77	-51
222	62	159	-57	68	-74	267	50	79	-61
443	-60	160	-59	73	-72	269	-62	92	-61
495	73	174	55	75	61	290	-49	106	-54
502	63	187	-53	185	51	294	56	110	-58
505	-63	191	-68	458	-58	386	72	180	75
599	65	201	64			388	63	219	-65
603	63	227	-63			391	52	229	60
603	69	277	-48			399	50	230	52
614	74	280	-49			404	63	231	51
624	67	283	-45			427	53	300	-63
654	63	427	66			428	50	368	52

Table C.2 (continued)

Dream Variable	Ages 3–5		Ages 5–7		Ages 7–9		Ages 9–11		Ages 11–13		Ages 13–15	
	Correlate	r	Correlate	r	Correlate	r	Correlate	r	Correlate	r	Correlate	r
					428	48			431	−48	424	58
					436	49			436	48	449	−55
					442	−59			449	−48	477	49
					444	−60			450	−47		
					462	−52			454	−61		
					467	−54			462	−47		
					565	−68			521	61		
					566	−74			524	−49		
					567	−58			526	51		
					568	−46			529	50		
					570	−47						
Stranger adult, female			22	61	157	64	109	74	20	−54	111	−54
			189	−62	184i	81	159	56	22	−61	113	63
			235	62	186i	80	160	68	33	−49	308	50
			239	65	245	−66	170	50	34	−63	337	56
			241	62	278	−46	186	−82	42	−74	397	58
			243	66	280	−66	237	50	107	−49	401	−75
			425	68	283	−51			247	60	425	50
			426	65	404	71			294	51	476	−59
			607	75	412	64			392	55	483	62
			646	−65	427	54			405	47		
					436	58			442	−55		
					449	54			462	−44		
					459	−57						
					467	−64						

Stranger any, male

No.	r	No.	r	No.	r	No.	r	No.	r	No.	r
16	-57	52	77	494	66	26	-52	2	48	4	56
60	-65	175	-64	505	65	56	-56	23	45	5	80
138	-66	184	70	10	-56	60	55	62	-50	20	82
397	73	186	65	159	-49	68	-70	63	53	21	57
604	80	402	68	191	-60	73	-69	65	51	22	60
606	69			195	-45	75	61	70	63	24	-54
609	79			201	64	87	-54	81	50	42	59
609	55			227	-58	102	-50	83	50	46	59
610	74			228	-60	170	54	144	62	51	60
611	69			230	-62	377	58	182	67	59	-56
				280	-65			294	58	62	-51
				438	71			321	-54	87	53
				442	-72			322	-57	106	-58
				444	-76			383	53	114	-73
				462	-50			384	54	171	-67
				467	-53			385	62	182	-57
								387	53	204	76
								388	62	232	-53
								389	49	259	-68
								390	50	260	66
								391	59	263	56
								399	72	357	-74
								427	51	367	-52
								431	-45	409	55
								437	-53	411	-57
								440	-56	419	-57
								442	-54	433	-56
								517	52	435	62

Table C.2 (continued)

Dream Variable	Ages 3–5		Ages 5–7		Ages 7–9		Ages 9–11		Ages 11–13		Ages 13–15	
	Correlate	r	Correlate	r	Correlate	r	Correlate	r	Correlate	r	Correlate	r
									526	49	436	50
											446	-50
											475	-52
											487	-48
											551	-67
											553	-65
Stranger any, female	16	-57	17	61	10	-45	25	-58	20	-60	46	-52
	60	-65	402	71	60	-46	85	-63	22	-56	49	60
	138	-66	404	61	157	58	91	-56	42	-68	161	54
	397	73	632	-78	185	46	160	63	57	-63	173	66
	604	80			229	-62	169	55	59	71	176	-50
	606	69			241	-59	170	62	294	48	207	49
	609	79			244	-55	237	51	319	53	212	61
	609	55			245	-74	294	-58	392	57	217	56
	610	74			277	-44			401	59	218	62
	611	69			278	-46			522	-49	250	50
					280	-75					259	63
					284	51					260	-60
					404	68					400	64
					412	63					461	49
					433	50					483	50
					467	-65					539	-54
					494	60					558	62
					505	63					592	-57
Animals, any	1	-56	3	-69	34	-46	30	52	17	47	111	-55

Table C.2 (continued)

Dream Variable	Ages 3–5		Ages 5–7		Ages 7–9		Ages 9–11		Ages 11–13		Ages 13–15	
	Correlate	r	Correlate	r	Correlate	r	Correlate	r	Correlate	r	Correlate	r
Home, any	13	59	1	−64	45	−58	4	52	13	52	21	−50
	24	59	39	−71	152	63	12	−55	29	−60	66	−52
	629	58	224	−84	176	64	161	−62	44	−67	67	50
			415	80	189	63	168	−52	57	−69	103	56
			417	70	201	56	169	−60	59	54	107	49
			564	−58	236	56	172	−50	107	−51	120	63
			599	−66	237	65	173	−57	121	59	246	49
			601	−77	239	45	184	59	266	−68	247	61
			601	−71	242	−59	185	67	421	45	251	74
			603	−74	244	60	224	−62	423	45	329	−52
			603	−72	245	78	288	−61			334	−69
			604	−61	274	46	295	59			359	50
			606	−65	279	−52	466	57			397	−57
			608	−62	404	−62					408	−69
			608	−72	495	−67					410	60
			609	62	502	−56					418	60
			611	60							420	58
			612	75							421	−60
			618	−62							423	−62
			621	71							460	53
			630	81							486	65
			631	−77							490	−50
			638	−72							538	49
			651	80							542	62
											543	70

Home, own

48	−56	13	−68	3	54	6	54	15	46	29	58
57	−56	28	66	25	−45	12	−54	20	−55	57	56
193	75	39	−61	47	−50	161	−56	38	−66	65	−59
626	−75	161	69	273	−52	169	−52	44	−55	66	−61
627	−75	224	−61	275	−49	172	−51	47	61	67	64
632	−64	403	−62	279	−48	290	−50	51	−55	104	−51
633	−64	408	−67	285	62	465	−56	57	−54	105	−59
634	−75	415	65	397	−45	466	54	108	61	107	57
635	62	430	64	398	50	596	−57	115	−61	247	60
638	−63	434	59	402	−68			123	−66	251	72
		602	76	404	−59			180	68	305	−62
		602	62					186i	−93	329	−60
		603	−66					251	55	334	−76
		608	−61					436	−47	408	−64
		609	79					525	−48	410	60
		609	64							418	60
		612	85							420	50
		612	76							421	−53
		613	82							423	−55
		613	74							449	−50
		621	74							460	55
		622	84							486	67
		623	75							543	51
		651	65							583	−50
										585	−49
										586	−56
										588	−50

Recreational

3	−77	23	66	29	47	37	−50	31	57	4	60
7	53	44	−62	42	54	42	−62	64	47	5	75
9	54	193	−69	61	56	81	−56	76	51	20	67
31	63	195	−64	170	−54	184	−51	78	56	21	57

Table C.2 (continued)

Dream Variable	Ages 3–5 Correlate	r	Ages 5–7 Correlate	r	Ages 7–9 Correlate	r	Ages 9–11 Correlate	r	Ages 11–13 Correlate	r	Ages 13–15 Correlate	r
	49	−54	197	−60	263	−47	293	−55	80	52	24	−58
	611	57	242	63	425	−64	375	−63	82	58	33	52
			398	−75	444	56			111	−57	35	58
			430	−68	445	−58			112	−62	46	67
			434	−68	572	82			295	49	97	54
			495	−66	574	65			409	46	114	−56
			496	−84					410	−46	228	57
			606	60					411	−45	365	58
			610	75					418	−46	367	−57
			610	70					419	−46	403	57
			624	−66					420	−53	435	50
			629	−72					465	46	436	51
			644	66					518	50	446	−50
									519	52	456	55
									529	50	468	−49
									533	65	543	51
									582	53	551	−53
Outdoors	10	56	19	60	169	−48	9	76	30	55	29	−58
	12	59	174	−72	184i	−86	37	−54	184i	81	57	−73
	17	−64	175	−77	185i	−78	47	72	185i	86	59	67
	238	56	435	59	186i	−82	88	52	246	67	71	−50
	604	64	443	−70	196	60	93	67	383	47	78	49
	610	83	505	−76	235	−46	109	66	438	−57	312	54
			599	62	235	−47	186	−53	444	54	441	−66
			603	67	236	−62	397	68			442	−50

5	56	603	64	237	−55	399	−51					446	52		
23	−60	614	74	239	−47	428	−56					478	−69		
33	53	618	70	240	−62	429	55					543	−50		
56	67	624	62	241	−70	430	50					553	48		
162	−59			241	−69	431	69								
427	72			243	−65	432	52								
433	60			243	−62	433	54								
435	70			244	−64	436	−54								
436	69			245	−81	575	60								
602	58			273	46	577	62								
				404	76										
				412	70										
				466	53										
				494	62										
				566	−59										
				569	−49										
				572	−71										

4	66	13	−69	8	−52	20	−52	20	−71
30	72	35	−47	9	−60	22	−73	22	−60
33	78	57	61	15	−66	34	−54	113	69
36	75	184i	78	49	−62	42	−64	180	68
38	58	186i	78	52	−50	53	−54	204	−66
54	58	238	−58	103	−59	59	58	206	−48
186	64	263	51	222	58	69	50	210	48
188	64	264	−46	298	−60	124	−74	335	55
190	83	422	62			160	51	397	52
240	70	425	68			169	47	401	−68
409	68	427	57			271	45	417	48
411	−68	449	66			292	53	475	54
419	−67	505	−59			319	67	488	−54

Unclassifiable

413

Table C.2 (continued)

Dream Variable	Ages 3–5 Correlate	r	Ages 5–7 Correlate	r	Ages 7–9 Correlate	r	Ages 9–11 Correlate	r	Ages 11–13 Correlate	r	Ages 13–15 Correlate	r
			431	69					320	-62		
			432	83					387	62		
			434	64					388	54		
			617	69					390	62		
			625	-70					392	72		
			644	-67					405	47		
									429	-44		
									451	-46		
									453	-49		
									458	-55		
									466	46		
									514	58		
									531	56		
									533	-60		
Sensory, dreamer	29	-71	19	58	18	52	8	-52	2	49	26	-54
	36	-53	495	64	56	-56	17	51	4	64	39	51
	42	-54	505	-68	159	45	28	-50	5	57	68	-50
	429	-54	614	62	160	46	41	-53	21	58	73	-61
	431	-63	624	73	175	-72	64	-54	46	52	75	49
	432	-64	637	60	199	56	93	-64	58	-54	84	-50
	610	71			237	45	102	-58	62	-53	86	-49
					241	65	110	61	64	-58	87	-62
					243	59	294	-55	70	73	89	-63
					243	57	459	52	459	45	90	-56
					398	-54	465	54			91	-56

Table C.2 (continued)

Dream Variable	Ages 3–5 Correlate	r	Ages 5–7 Correlate	r	Ages 7–9 Correlate	r	Ages 9–11 Correlate	r	Ages 11–13 Correlate	r	Ages 13–15 Correlate	r
			606	−64					522	−58	477	−54
			608	−74					529	−53	487	54
			608	−64					578	−52	539	−50
			609	63					579	−51	551	50
			609	74					580	−46	553	54
			611	70								
			611	73								
			612	82								
			613	68								
			613	68								
			621	86								
			623	64								
			630	80								
			631	−73								
			638	−69								
			651	74								
Sensory, either	15	−62	45	64	46	44	8	−57	2	50	7	−55
	29	−63	195	58	148	70	28	−53	4	52	26	−64
	431	−60	430	59	149	60	41	−57	22	49	68	−52
	432	−61	505	−71	151	60	47	64	46	49	73	−56
	604	58	624	65	241	60	54	−51	62	−56	75	50
	610	82	629	66	243	59	64	−52	64	−72	87	−64
			630	71	243	56	70	51	70	74	89	−62
			637	61	245	69	93	−54	71	49	90	−49
			637	64	398	−57	102	−63	410	48	91	−57

Verbal, dreamer

30	71							110	63	418	47	114	65
36	70							290	52	420	50	124	-56
38	54							294	-65			218	48
54	54							375	-54			259	65
140	68							465	57			260	-61
601	-61											333	-48
615	69											337	56
		656	-68									351	55
				417	-57							355	53
												433	63
												434	56
												439	-52
												440	-56
												441	-50
												442	-55
												461	57
												475	53
												477	-67
												539	-51
												551	54
												553	54
												563	52
		13	-68	25	-52	4	55	23	55	23	47	6	-55
		16	59	46	-46	18	-76	26	-76	26	-55	7	-76
		28	58	235	49	94	-57	62	-57	62	-54	26	-51
		224	-67	236	59	96	-51	64	-51	64	-57	76	-50
		430	59	239	48	98	-58	109	-58	109	-51	106	-48
		596	-58	243	59	99	-54	177	-54	177	72	129	51
		603	-70	275	-55	161	-52	248	-52	248	54	253	-72
		603	-64	285	44	172	-56	251	-56	251	57	301	55

Table C.2 **(continued)**

Dream Variable	Ages 3–5 Correlate	r	Ages 5–7 Correlate	r	Ages 7–9 Correlate	r	Ages 9–11 Correlate	r	Ages 11–13 Correlate	r	Ages 13–15 Correlate	r
			612	65	498	-57	173	-57	394	-61	330	54
			622	61	500	-70			430	-45	339	68
			651	62					431	-44	421	55
									513	55	431	50
									578	-53	434	54
									580	-54	436	-56
											446	56
											489	73
Verbal, other	30	71	39	-61	52	-48	48	59	2	46	1	-51
	36	70	40	-67	194	48	56	-60	30	-48	26	-74
	38	54	403	-66	198	66	60	62	62	-49	30	51
	54	54	415	58	227	62	91	-54	64	-49	56	-53
	140	68	508	-61	228	77	102	-58	69	56	176	-50
	601	-61	599	-64	230	66	160	61	168	59	185	55
	615	69	603	-71	241	60	170	51	169	46	250	65
			603	-72	285	56	294	-70	177	57	301	63
			604	-66	450	55	376	-57	291	-50	310	52
			606	-68	498	-63	377	57	392	51	312	51
			612	75			432	-51	429	-49	367	55
			613	61					430	-46	368	52
			614	-65					431	-51	434	56
			615	-68					458	-57	454	60
			621	69					515	-51	472	51
			651	73							489	50
											539	-51

Verbal, either

30	71	28	61	25	−46	60	52	2	44	547	−52
36	70	39	−65	30	−49	85	−64	62	−54	551	49
38	54	40	−69	52	−52	89	−56	64	−46	26	−71
54	54	161	64	185i	76	91	−67	69	48	56	−51
140	68	403	−70	194	53	96	−55	168	63	180	57
601	−61	408	−62	198	62	102	−54	177	69	250	56
615	69	415	58	227	64	160	57	248	58	301	66
		508	−61	228	73	294	−69	271	47	310	55
		602	67	230	67			429	−52	312	51
		603	−68	241	66			430	−53	330	50
		603	−65	285	51			431	−54	339	58
		604	−61	450	60			432	−47	367	56
		606	−63	498	−65			458	−51	368	52
		609	61					513	47	434	56
		612	81					515	−53	441	−51
		612	75							454	51
		613	75							489	58
		613	73							547	−50
		614	−60							551	50
		615	−61								
		621	71								
		622	74								
		623	71								
		651	71								

Locomotor, dreamer

3	−77	236	73	13	58	12	−56	55	52	46	−59
6	64	237	71	24	51	23	−50	130	59	172	70
7	65	238	−73	28	−57	46	57	183	55	180	61
11	61	400	80	148	61	55	62	184i	96	187	55

Table C.2 (continued)

Dream Variable	Ages 3-5 Correlate	r	Ages 5-7 Correlate	r	Ages 7-9 Correlate	r	Ages 9-11 Correlate	r	Ages 11-13 Correlate	r	Ages 13-15 Correlate	r
	25	67	405	70	149	58	64	-58	185i	92	189	59
	31	86	407	62	194	-47	169	-62	316	-56	211	65
	44	59	421	69	258	-51	222	-72			219	-49
	49	-76	422	63	259	54	238	-50			229	82
	603	69	423	71	261	-50	377	55			230	67
	603	60	617	-64	264	53	466	56			231	68
	604	58	655	-68	401	-58					339	48
	611	56			571	64					404	-51
	654	71									546	60
Locomotor, other	10	56	1	71	17	57	22	-79	48	-75	2	53
	12	57	13	60	42	49	30	57	62	-49	4	49
	17	-72	31	65	60	53	37	-53	63	66	5	64
	238	58	49	-58	194	-50	42	-72	70	63	20	59
	610	75	224	71	258	-51	66	60	115	-64	21	64
			502	62	401	-77	73	-54	116	-69	24	-55
			564	70	449	-50	234	50	180	59	35	75
			599	61			235	55	182	62	46	55
			599	73			239	69	183	-57	51	64
			601	62			293	-64	251	53	60	51
			603	67			457	-52	294	51	62	-57
			603	61					437	-67	93	54
			604	72					439	-55	97	48
			614	62					516	-57	99	49
			615	62					526	48	106	-65
			626	68					528	-49	114	-53

Locomotor, either

10 64	627 76	1 63	13 51	66 79	14 −60	177 −52
12 58	629 −74	18 58	17 53	71 51	31 55	263 58
17 −57	630 −69	25 58	28 −50	73 −51	49 −70	357 −55
604 60	631 70	224 69	60 52	89 65	316 −56	362 50
610 66	632 61	502 61	258 −50	101 55	383 53	368 53
611 61	633 64	564 67	259 49	107 57	405 −53	403 65
	634 67	603 61	401 −63	239 51	412 −45	427 50
	638 64	627 71	409 −62	293 −51	417 −46	435 55
	646 −66	629 −64	411 64	400 60	433 46	466 50
		634 62	419 61		461 46	471 60
		646 −62	449 −52			476 61
						555 −57
						2 54
						14 55
						20 56
						31 −65
						35 54
						45 −64
						60 55
						62 −58
						106 −59
						114 −52
						179 −51
						182 −48
						211 51
						229 59
						230 56
						232 −51
						368 52
						403 65

Table C.2 (continued)

Dream Variable	Ages 3–5		Ages 5–7		Ages 7–9		Ages 9–11		Ages 11–13		Ages 13–15	
	Correlate	r	Correlate	r	Correlate	r	Correlate	r	Correlate	r	Correlate	r
Any motor, dreamer	25	65	3	−65	13	53	12	−55	55	68	427	50
	49	−64	7	58	28	−47	23	−55	92	−46	435	57
	235	60	11	81	48	−49	46	52	316	−53	447	59
	603	57	23	−59	242	60	55	73	396	49	451	−54
	609	71	31	63	401	−58	64	−52	513	49	458	−50
	611	82	41	67	571	70	159	−53			471	58
	626	56	44	59	572	59	161	−53			472	52
	627	56	49	−63			169	−70			476	53
	629	56	222	58			172	−54			480	−59
			400	59			222	−68			555	−50
			421	61			294	54			5	−56
			423	60			466	50			7	−53
			443	−67							19	−50
			496	68							27	−54
			502	73							34	−61
											46	−64
											172	66
											180	55
											229	73
											230	54
											231	58
											257	−61
											333	−53
											362	59
											404	−54

Any motor, other

id	val		id	val		id	val		id	val		id	val		id	val		id	val		id	val
1	−60		503	69		36	−72		17	46		22	−62		29	−55		2	65		446	50
10	56		617	−71		59	−60		28	−51		34	−67		57	−53		24	−60		551	53
17	−64		626	64		163	−74		276	54		42	−76		62	−48		31	−56			
27	−59		631	64		240	−69		401	−69		50	53		63	64		35	63			
611	58		637	74		442	−65		462	−58		66	54		65	46		48	53			
655	56		647	−60		444	−60		465	−69		73	−64		69	46		60	57			
						622	82		506	−66		103	−56		70	58		62	−48			
						632	62					376	−55		182	54		65	59			
											377	64		183	−78		70	54			
											432	−50		251	56		75	48			
														294	50		107	−49			
														437	−61		113	−54			
														516	−61		232	−49			
														526	71		397	−50			
																	403	62			
																	454	76			
																	464	56			
																	476	58			
																	536	55			

Any motor, either

id	val		id	val		id	val		id	val		id	val		id	val
1	−57		240	−75		13	48		9	64		63	54		2	58
10	61		406	−61		28	−53		59	65		116	−69		31	−58
17	−66		409	−82		232	56		64	−56		296	−54		45	−61
27	−57		410	61		276	63		66	68		298	−65		60	60
611	65		411	81		397	−59		71	61		316	−56		71	−48

Table C.2 (continued)

Dream Variable	Ages 3–5		Ages 5–7		Ages 7–9		Ages 9–11		Ages 11–13		Ages 13–15	
	Correlate	r	Correlate	r	Correlate	r	Correlate	r	Correlate	r	Correlate	r
	655	56	414	−58	462	−51	73	−73	327	54	106	−49
			419	80	465	−71	108	−57	405	−65	113	−71
			420	70					407	−48	184	48
			622	64					412	−57	186	57
									421	−46	215	50
									427	49	229	53
									516	−53	257	−58
									526	51	313	−55
									532	60	335	−49
											356	54
											397	−67
											401	69
											454	64
											464	59
											476	54
											557	60
Cognition, dreamer			11	58	37	57	10	59	3	52	1	−57
			52	59	159	45	24	−62	7	−68	6	−48
			222	66	161	53	33	58	15	52	7	−60
			443	−59	174	−64	38	−70	28	55	19	−49
			495	75	187	54			31	−53	20	−62
			502	60	191	60			54	50	22	−81
			505	−60	198	70			64	−47	34	−60
			599	64	230	56			69	50	38	−62
			603	64	231	79			159	47	42	−66

Index	Value		Index	Value
43	−54		169	48
52	−58		170	46
53	−63		271	63
55	−65		289	−49
69	−57		290	55
83	49		403	57
84	−50		430	−47
85	−52		455	60
87	−58		463	−45
89	−60		464	50
91	−62		465	−67
108	−49		526	−56
127	60		533	−65
159	59		581	−62
160	56		582	−65
161	53			
170	60			
172	56			
205	−49			
207	49			
212	66			
217	62			
218	67			
250	77			
271	60			
301	63			
306	50			
348	49			
353	51			
354	51			

Index	Value
232	75
233	57
237	55
506	−67
565	67
567	70
568	50
570	53
574	61

Index	Value
614	69
624	66
654	67

Table C.2 (continued)

Dream Variable	Ages 3–5		Ages 5–7		Ages 7–9		Ages 9–11		Ages 11–13		Ages 13–15	
	Correlate	r	Correlate	r	Correlate	r	Correlate	r	Correlate	r	Correlate	r
Cognition, either			11	58	22	47	10	50	7	−74	367	64
			52	59	37	55	33	63	15	51	433	58
			222	66	52	−50	38	−82	28	54	443	−66
			443	−59	174	−64	61	61	31	−52	453	−51
			495	75	187	62			34	−58	459	−51
			502	60	191	60			39	51	464	54
			505	−60	198	70			49	54	469	−52
			599	64	230	56			54	49	477	−52
			603	64	231	79			64	−52	487	63
			614	69	232	75			66	−46	488	−55
			624	66	233	57			69	54	489	54
			654	67	234	45			159	46	490	56
											540	−62
											1	−66
											2	50
											7	−73
											19	−55
											22	−75
											34	−72
											42	−65
											69	−60
											84	−52
											87	−53
											89	−55
											91	−54

124	−52	160	46
127	62	169	45
159	61	170	49
160	55	271	66
161	56	289	−45
172	62	290	48
173	57	403	66
204	−49	411	47
205	−51	419	47
212	54	430	−51
218	58	453	−49
249	−50	455	61
250	66	464	53
259	50	465	−69
260	−50	466	49
271	58	514	49
301	57	520	−48
306	50	533	−59
312	50	581	−68
333	−61	582	−67
354	51		
367	57		
433	59		
443	−67		
451	−48		
453	−57		
459	−54		
464	64		
469	−53		
487	67		

237	50
506	−67
565	67
567	70
568	61
570	62
574	61

Table C.2 (continued)

Dream Variable	Ages 3–5 Correlate	r	Ages 5–7 Correlate	r	Ages 7–9 Correlate	r	Ages 9–11 Correlate	r	Ages 11–13 Correlate	r	Ages 13–15 Correlate	r
Afraid, dreamer											489	53
											490	56
											540	−57
											551	48
			3	−75	14	−46	35	52	1	−52	1	−50
			6	71	26	−46	377	58	9	−65	2	51
			7	68	44	−59	466	65	14	−52	19	−56
			31	69	46	−44			41	−53	32	−60
			44	75	56	46			45	80	34	−61
			49	−67	228	64			55	−53	172	60
			166	−79	265	61			61	−57	180	52
			402	−58	275	−51			68	−48	229	75
			405	67	279	−50			69	70	230	78
			407	61	285	63			78	47	231	69
			421	74	400	48			84	−49	249	−55
			422	81	402	−56			117	−64	333	−80
			423	77					144	60	341	64
			502	67					146	54	425	51
			600	68					159	49	427	61
			655	−81					160	50	429	−72
			657	−73					169	49	430	−62
									271	72	432	−53
									287	49	472	52
									315	−72	546	50
									384	51	555	−59

Afraid, either

Item	Val	Item	Val	Item	Val	Item	Val	Item	Val	Item	Val	Item	Val
3	−81	14	−46	35	52	1	−56	387	65	1	−50	561	60
6	71	26	−46	377	58	7	−55	390	62	2	51	591	64
7	66	44	−59	466	65	9	−65	409	−50	19	−56	594	61
31	66	46	−44			11	−53	411	50	32	−60		
41	68	56	46			14	−56	419	50	34	−61		
44	77	228	64			41	−51	429	−46	172	60		
49	−65	265	61			45	77	430	−48	180	52		
166	−82	275	−51			55	−53	435	−56	229	75		
400	58	279	−50			61	−59	441	−61	230	78		
402	−60	285	63			68	−48	461	45	231	69		
405	80	400	48			69	74	512	47	249	−55		
407	71	402	−56			84	−52	514	54	333	−80		
421	88					144	65	523	56	341	64		
422	81					146	56	581	−59	425	51		
423	90					159	49			427	61		
498	−69					160	51			429	−72		

Table C.2 (continued)

Dream Variable	Ages 3–5 Correlate	r	Ages 5–7 Correlate	r	Ages 7–9 Correlate	r	Ages 9–11 Correlate	r	Ages 11–13 Correlate	r	Ages 13–15 Correlate	r
			502	63					169	47	430	-62
			504	-64					271	76	432	-53
			600	82					287	51	472	52
			600	70					315	-62	546	50
			602	61					384	54	555	-59
			655	-81					387	72	561	60
			657	-73					388	51	591	64
									390	69	594	61
									391	51		
									397	-45		
									409	-53		
									411	53		
									419	53		
									429	-50		
									430	-51		
									435	-55		
									441	-59		
									461	51		
									514	60		
									523	50		
									531	49		
									581	-62		
Angry, dreamer					2	-56	12	50	2	60	1	-61
					18	-47	17	-52	55	56	9	-58
					26	-58	20	70	62	-46	19	-70

48	−55	44	72	68	46	23	67
150	62	53	70	110	−51	70	55
170	−58	67	−53	125	75	248	60
171	−50	84	−60	168	47	254	58
275	−49	106	−55	184i	85	347	−70
279	−50	168	65	317	57	361	57
285	47	237	−50	400	49	439	49
398	49	295	−54	435	50	440	51
402	−68			444	−59	441	48
				512	−72	444	53
				579	−54	448	48
						535	−49
						546	53
						548	74
						554	−50

2	−59	17	−52	2	61	1	−71
26	−56	34	−60	62	−46	19	−69
48	−52	35	56	93	51	23	76
150	58	44	51	97	49	70	62
170	−55	74	−56	99	49	81	50
171	−48	106	−54	110	−50	122	54
279	−45	168	67	125	69	211	49
285	46	289	54	168	53	225	57
398	46	291	52	393	53	227	58
402	−62	449	55	400	60	248	54
				444	−56	336	−64
				512	−68	347	−73
				579	48	361	57
						370	62
						448	50

Angry, either

Table C.2 (continued)

Dream Variable	Ages 3–5 Correlate	r	Ages 5–7 Correlate	r	Ages 7–9 Correlate	r	Ages 9–11 Correlate	r	Ages 11–13 Correlate	r	Ages 13–15 Correlate	r
Happy, dreamer	6	−63	415	71	9	53	6	52	42	56	476	53
	8	−73	446	71	25	−52	7	70	50	−52	536	50
	10	−59	503	−61	43	−48	12	−52	185i	88	546	61
	13	66	599	−61	159	60	52	50	286	54	548	64
	18	61	601	−61	160	53	76	−52	315	−56	554	−50
	28	−63	603	−73	161	52	170	−58	443	−53	21	−48
	160	−56	603	−75	168	53	185	52			28	49
	165	61	604	−67	170	50	222	−63			30	−54
	185	54	606	−63	172	46	224	−61			88	−52
	193	76	608	−62	197	69	452	53			107	49
	596	69	608	−61	233	61	455	56			120	53
			612	63	264	49					131	50
			614	−61	265	71					397	−55
			618	−64	408	−63					404	−68
			626	−63	410	60					473	−49
			629	62	416	−58					480	−64
			631	−69	418	57						
			638	−63	419	56						
			651	77	420	61						
Happy, either	6	−63	1	−58	9	49	6	53	42	54	28	51

Table C.2 (continued)

Dream Variable	Ages 3–5 Correlate	r	Ages 5–7 Correlate	r	Ages 7–9 Correlate	r	Ages 9–11 Correlate	r	Ages 11–13 Correlate	r	Ages 13–15 Correlate	r
	165	61	405	58	279	–51	458	–51	271	47	230	57
	185	54	407	58	285	52	460	53	286	45	249	–48
	193	76	421	68			466	59	287	58	341	64
	596	69	422	69					315	–78	397	–62
			423	71					326	62	404	–53
			434	62					430	–46	429	–61
			439	–62					441	–70	430	–54
			498	–69					443	–76	480	–61
			506	–62					444	–64	485	–52
			600	66					523	47	561	50
			618	–71					534	52		
Any feelings, either	6	–63	16	62	25	–47	6	61	28	47	1	–57
	8	–73	29	60	197	64	108	–54	62	–55	21	–50
	10	–59	60	58	259	47	170	–53	63	57	32	–63
	13	66	166	–72	260	–54	184	64	69	57	46	–50
	18	61	175	63	264	46	185	65	126	55	66	–48
	28	–63	235	61	265	80	224	–61	144	51	72	52
	160	–56	241	61	273	–48	460	53	160	51	120	50
	165	61	405	59	279	–47	466	55	168	52	229	51
	185	54	407	61	285	50			179	61	230	56
	193	76	421	68	419	56			271	56	333	–49
	596	69	422	70	420	55			287	59	341	59
			423	71	631	–56			292	46	397	–65
			434	66					298	–45	404	–56
			439	–62					315	–68	429	–60

−57	430	57	326					−70	498			
−60	480	51	387					−64	506			
−49	485	49	390					67	600			
		56	403					−72	618			
		−48	430									
		−67	441									
		−75	443							−60	100	
		−69	444							54		
		57	534									
		−45	581									
−54	26	54	24	−63	7	52	26				15	
62	30	−58	26	57	15	−58	49				235	
50	301	−49	92	66	28	56	57				436	
56	310	−47	106	−72	45	−49	59					
49	330	68	121	74	54	−60	150					
48	355	−56	393	54	377	49	184					
48	358	−48	450			47	186					
58	399	−46	467			59	231					
−75	402	−49	528			71	232					
−64	403					52	237					
−58	417					61	421					
−58	441					56	423					
−51	444					60	444					
−62	471					51	455					
−49	474					59	460					
−58	478					68	565					
−58	483					74	567					
−86	598					59	574					

Hunger, dreamer

−58	483					74	567					
59	128	50	8	63	15	−46	3	−80	18	75	235	
56	129	−57	106	−55	17	46	26	−65	41	56	630	

Hunger, either

435

Table C.2 (continued)

Dream Variable	Ages 3–5		Ages 5–7		Ages 7–9		Ages 9–11		Ages 11–13		Ages 13–15	
	Correlate	r	Correlate	r	Correlate	r	Correlate	r	Correlate	r	Correlate	r
			179	72	41	45	27	−72	107	−59	301	48
			416	67	150	−74	45	−62	121	61	310	67
			417	70	152	−73	49	65	266	−56	311	53
			446	63	200	67	53	70	267	54	360	−50
			497	−64	237	47	377	57	269	−58	398	61
			626	−65	245	62			292	49	399	60
			627	−65	258	48			377	−52	402	−75
			628	−65	402	62			393	−47	403	−70
			631	−65	423	57			408	−46	417	−55
			635	64					427	53	449	−52
			639	−69					431	−48	471	−50
			646	65					578	−49	474	−51
									580	−47	483	−48
Fatigue, dreamer	15	67	25	−65	3	47	287	−55	35	−49	7	−56
	32	−57	32	−71	172	48	289	60	39	52	14	−55
	44	−56	43	−75	234	52			44	−48	81	−51
	142	64	50	69	234	45			114	68	83	−51
	166	61	176	−76	240	81			117	65	117	−67
	186	61	180	−83	240	72			121	74	125	56
	193	63	235	68	259	48			122	60	177	55
	236	63	239	90	260	−47			126	−63	179	81
	433	−55	241	68	285	59			328	53	182	51
	605	75	243	92	404	−56			404	70	228	−50
			424	81	407	−56			416	−50	230	−60
			425	73	412	−64			450	−45	232	48

15	67	2	60	426	85	414	−56	27	−55	47		68	13	45	523	−62	365	−64	9	−58
32	−57	32	−67	439	−64	498	−58	159	54	51		−65	35	−52		416	−53	14	−69
44	−56	43	−83	607	70	503	−61	161	52	289		70	39	54		417	−50	117	−62
142	64	50	62					172	54				44	−55		424	50	119	57
166	61	54	−63					203	65				114	60		428	−48	125	57
186	61	180	−84					240	74				117	58		430	54	130	57
193	63	220	−59					240	59				121	68		431	62	179	74
236	63	239	69					276	49				126	−58		432	61	216	−50
433	−55	243	71					285	63				517	−50		434	49	230	−52
605	75	424	59					397	−45				518	−49		435	−50	232	50
		425	84					412	−69				523	−55		436	−65	365	−50
		426	75					461	52							446	54	416	−51
								491	−56							482	56	450	−50
																486	55		
																539	−55		
																554	54		
																555	49		

Fatigue, either

Table C.2 (continued)

Dream Variable	Ages 3–5 Correlate	r	Ages 5–7 Correlate	r	Ages 7–9 Correlate	r	Ages 9–11 Correlate	r	Ages 11–13 Correlate	r	Ages 13–15 Correlate	r
Approach social, dreamer	7	-55	3	58	48	-65	377	69	38	58	474	52
	38	-54	6	-61	170	-45	466	58	52	46	539	-51
	50	-58	8	-68	242	71			54	53	86	-56
	160	-55	10	-78	401	-57			55	60	88	-48
	400	71	12	-65	437	-58			62	-60	97	-49
	427	-54	19	-64	445	-63			70	51	111	50
	435	-64	44	-61	465	-51			408	-45	128	53
	628	-58	54	-81	506	-72			410	45	229	62
	637	-64	61	60	573	60			415	-56	253	-59
	655	-73	618	-63					417	-55	258	48
									418	45	330	51
									443	-60	399	53
									516	-59	404	-56
											417	-54
											457	53
Approach social, other			3	64	47	-55	30	50	30	55	26	-49
			7	-61	48	-58	35	55	64	-53	171	-54
			10	-64	242	64	39	50	115	-62	180	58
			20	-65	275	-50	234	63	127	-57	229	59
			26	-59	279	-47	235	51	180	53	344	-55
			44	-70	284	48	377	60	222	-60	346	-49
			61	62	398	50	466	51	409	-45	372	61
			160	-75	450	53			419	44	397	-50
			175	63	494	57			420	49	442	-52
			184	-66					521	-52		

Approach social, either

7 −55	186 −58	3 64	47 −49	35	53	528 −69	62 −48	171 −52
38 −54	188 −60	7 −61	48 −57	234	63	529 −57	64 −49	180 59
50 −58	194 −74	10 −64	60 46	235	51		222 −58	229 56
160 −55	195 −67	20 −65	184i 76	239	51		516 −52	344 −58
400 71	199 −67	26 −59	242 67	377	58		528 −72	346 −48
427 −54	493 −70	44 −70	437 −64	466	54			372 63
435 −64	508 −63	61 62	445 −61					397 −54
628 −58	599 −66	160 −75	465 −50					442 −54
637 −64	614 −63	175 63	506 −72					449 −51
655 −73	615 −72	184 −66	573 60					
	628 −74	186 −58						
	644 71	188 −60						
	652 72	194 −74						
	657 67	195 −67						
		199 −67						
		493 −70						

Table C.2 (continued)

Dream Variable	Ages 3–5 Correlate	r	Ages 5–7 Correlate	r	Ages 7–9 Correlate	r	Ages 9–11 Correlate	r	Ages 11–13 Correlate	r	Ages 13–15 Correlate	r
			508	−63								
			599	−66								
			614	−63								
			615	−72								
			628	−74								
			644	71								
			652	72								
			657	67								
Attack social, dreamer			60	−66	8	48	24	−61	10	51	19	−59
			200	82	31	52	26	50	12	48	23	54
			201	−65	35	61	29	69	53	68	81	54
			202	60	37	50	168	57	55	61	215	59
			397	71	42	62	296	60	60	54	333	−54
			417	60	47	55			62	−60	341	48
			491	70	49	−52			65	48	347	−53
			492	65	56	−45			74	−53	363	54
			493	65	148	75			103	−65	364	53
			501	65	149	65			114	−61	437	50
			609	70	491	59			168	62	483	−53
			611	67	565	73			176	−60	535	−51
			611	82	566	61			177	56	591	50
					567	70			184i	93	594	57
					568	77			185i	92		
					569	64			248	55		
					570	74			251	54		

Attack social, other

16	−57	162	−63	572	70	42	59	68	−62	290	45	2	51
60	−65	220	−64	574	82	154	−56	73	−72	314	54	4	57
138	−66	236	78			245	63	76	−51	441	−58	5	80
397	73	237	62			506	−62	77	−63	452	51	21	54
604	80	238	−69			568	48	102	−66	462	54	35	59
606	69	242	−62			570	50			512	−54	46	65
609	79	400	66			572	64			518	49	63	63
609	55	407	58			574	74			532	56	64	50
610	74	422	60							23	48	65	66
611	69	506	−72							62	−47	80	64
		655	−71							63	54	82	50
										65	55	97	50
										70	47	114	−60
										78	48	208	−52
										81	54	362	49
										83	50	365	56
										177	68	403	60
										182	58	427	52
										294	48	431	−50
										383	54	435	55
										384	57	436	59
										385	53	446	−49
										387	50		
										388	48		
										391	53		
										399	56		
										427	47		
										442	−60		
										517	68		
										518	74		

Table C.2 (continued)

Dream Variable	Ages 3-5 Correlate	r	Ages 5-7 Correlate	r	Ages 7-9 Correlate	r	Ages 9-11 Correlate	r	Ages 11-13 Correlate	r	Ages 13-15 Correlate	r
									529	53	471	60
									534	62	476	55
											488	49
											547	49
											551	-48
											555	-50
											558	-56
Attack social, either	16	-57	162	-64	42	65	68	-60	23	55	2	51
	60	-65	220	-64	155	-62	73	-70	60	48	4	63
	138	-66	236	75	198	56	76	-52	62	-53	5	78
	397	73	237	62	231	59	77	-60	63	56	21	54
	604	80	238	-69	245	65	102	-68	65	63	35	54
	606	69	242	-64	491	58			70	51	46	66
	609	79	400	64	506	-64			77	51	58	-51
	609	55	407	59	568	50			81	51	63	69
	610	74	422	59	570	51			83	51	64	53
	611	69	506	-72	572	64			168	51	65	68
			655	-74	574	75			177	74	71	-49
									182	56	74	51
									222	56	80	65
									223	60	82	53
									246	55	97	50
									292	46	114	-58
									383	61	186	50
									384	68	187	-50

385	62	208	−51													
387	52	365	54													
388	51	403	56													
390	48	435	53													
391	61	436	55													
399	54	471	54													
427	50	476	53													
431	−52	488	55													
432	−50	558	−53													
442	−64															
510	−53															
517	62															
518	66															
521	49															
527	48															
529	51															
532	51															
534	58															

4	49	19	−57	54	8	
10	54	23	51	52	28	
21	45	48	49	−68	31	
43	48	172	77	−66	34	
54	49	189	65	56	35	
63	48	215	58	68	39	
93	52	229	69	66	41	
116	−63	230	69	−86	45	
125	65	231	50	57	54	
184i	82	257	−68	−53	292	
325	63	333	−64	61	377	

42	71	166	−64	39	−55			
148	57	236	81	48	−54			
245	63	237	63	193	68			
417	−57	238	−75	400	85			
419	57	400	82	602	59			
502	−57	405	67	655	−66			
		407	65					
		421	61					
		422	65					
		423	64					

Unfavorable outcome,
any, dreamer

Table C.2 (continued)

Dream Variable	Ages 3–5 Correlate	r	Ages 5–7 Correlate	r	Ages 7–9 Correlate	r	Ages 9–11 Correlate	r	Ages 11–13 Correlate	r	Ages 13–15 Correlate	r
Unfavorable outcome, any, other							466	56	399	46	401	51
									442	-59	437	53
									517	69	594	57
									518	75		
	12	-65	9	-59	3	-54	38	-71	3	-62	4	56
	15	-63	53	-62	25	55	73	-51	10	54	5	72
	132	-56	406	65	61	51	102	-59	23	63	35	49
	133	-61	410	-65	148	57			62	-58	46	57
	235	94	413	73	174	-57			63	51	63	59
	609	55	414	66	184i	-76			65	54	65	53
	611	69	418	-66	186i	-86			70	56	80	52
			420	-61	226	60			144	57	109	-56
			425	65	227	60			168	44	114	-62
			604	-66	231	71			177	59	171	-56
			606	-63	232	65			185i	87	208	-61
			610	-68	238	55			251	57	309	49
					261	56			383	60	362	55
					273	47			399	46	365	53
					500	60			441	-59	403	61
					506	-74			442	-65	427	56
					565	56			519	47	428	49
					567	64			523	51	431	-58
									532	60	435	58
											436	66

Unfavorable outcome, any, either

6	−59	162	−64	17	48			60	46	438	−55
132	−57	235	64	57	−54	38	−69	62	−61	446	−58
133	−55	236	84	61	58	48	53	63	63	471	69
143	−55	238	−74	148	60	66	53	65	58	476	58
235	66	241	64	154	−74	102	−54	70	64	488	52
638	−58	242	−64	155	−68			81	57	539	50
655	−64	400	66	184i	−92			93	49	547	53
		407	58	186i	−97			95	57	551	−56
		422	58	198	66			99	56	555	−56
		506	−71	231	69			144	57	558	−49
		610	−63	232	71			177	67	2	49
				233	68			185i	85	4	56
				238	48			294	45	5	70
				401	−63			383	61	20	54
				449	−60			391	47	46	49
				506	−57			399	55	60	54
								427	46	63	56
								442	−69	65	54
								516	−49	80	51
										109	−54
										114	−57
										171	−50
										208	−58
										215	52
										257	−59
										309	50
										362	54
										403	65
										427	57

Table C.2 (continued)

Dream Variable	Ages 3–5		Ages 5–7		Ages 7–9		Ages 9–11		Ages 11–13		Ages 13–15	
	Correlate	r	Correlate	r	Correlate	r	Correlate	r	Correlate	r	Correlate	r
									517	50	428	53
									518	59	431	−58
									534	51	435	58
											436	64
											446	−50
											471	61
											476	61
											488	49
											547	55
											551	−48
											555	−54
											557	51
Favorable outcome, any, dreamer			5	−65	48	−62	8	64	64	−55	86	−49
			6	−59	242	70	35	55	88	47	90	−51
			10	−67	275	−47	39	62	222	−54	128	55
			17	67	284	51	45	−69	410	45	171	−49
			19	−74	494	63	234	66	417	−54	178	62
			54	−58			377	58	418	44	215	49
			199	−58					528	−61	229	80
			646	−62					578	−45	230	61
											231	59
											257	−66
											457	50

446

Favorable outcome, any, other

7	−55	7	−58	48	−57	35	59	62	−57	24	72
38	−54	20	−61	184i	79	45	−62	63	63	26	−50
50	−58	44	−61	186i	91	234	63	64	−47	209	51
160	−55	160	−64	242	70	377	59	69	51	301	61
400	71	184	−75	275	−52			70	57	310	56
427	−54	185	−67	284	46			251	54	330	50
435	−64	186	−63	398	45			397	−44	338	−54
628	−58	189	−59	433	45			415	−50	397	−56
637	−64	194	−72	437	−61			417	−57	399	51
655	−73	195	−70	450	50			437	−58	417	−51
		242	58	494	56			439	−55	442	−55
		499	69	506	−65			516	−81	449	−63
		500	−66	573	59					486	49
		628	−63							598	−76
		641	61								
		642	71								
		644	71								
		652	73								

Favorable outcome, any, either

7	−55	3	60	48	−55	35	62	54	46	24	67
38	−54	7	−62	184i	76	45	−63	62	−56	26	−50
50	−58	20	−64	186i	88	50	50	63	62	209	49
160	−55	44	−66	242	72	234	61	64	−47	229	62
400	71	160	−71	275	−52	377	63	69	49	250	50
427	−54	184	−71	284	47			70	52	301	58
435	−64	185	−63	437	−60			185i	86	310	48
628	−58	186	−61	450	51			187i	−83	330	55
637	−64	188	−65	494	56			251	53	372	48
655	−73	189	−64	506	−62			292	46	397	−60

Table C.2 (continued)

Dream Variable	Ages 3–5		Ages 5–7		Ages 7–9		Ages 9–11		Ages 11–13		Ages 13–15	
	Correlate	r	Correlate	r	Correlate	r	Correlate	r	Correlate	r	Correlate	r
			194	−76					417	−55	399	54
			195	−73					437	−57	449	−65
			199	−66					439	−54	598	−77
			499	63					516	−81		
			500	−62					578	−45		
			508	−61								
			615	−61								
			628	−69								
			641	62								
			642	66								
			644	71								
			652	70								
Hedonic tone (REM)	13	−57	3	−58	4	47	6	−52	1	−48	4	64
	160	57	7	64	39	46	7	−69	7	−52	5	62
	193	−78	21	64	48	48	12	68	19	−44	21	61
	236	−78	44	64	157	−62	34	−63	44	51	24	−70
	238	54	164	61	184i	−82	38	−67	222	61	35	51
	400	−54	184	62	186i	−93	48	60	399	50	46	63
	605	−57	185	59	242	−65	50	57	416	45	58	−55
			189	58	245	69	170	53	417	58	65	61
			236	61	404	−68	221	−68	457	−49	97	50
			237	63	405	−62	223	56			208	−64
			238	−71	421	−55	224	55			263	49
			242	−70	433	−53					309	51
			400	61	450	−56					310	−51

Longitudinal *decrease* in hedonic tone (REM)

407	58	459	53			365	51		
422	74	494	−70			367	−62		
491	63	502	−70			403	65		
499	−73	508	63			436	48		
500	61					438	−54		
610	−61					446	−49		
610	−61					449	54		
627	64					471	56		
628	68					476	49		
644	−64					558	−51		
655	−65								

13	−58	23	−58	6	−58	4	−74		
21	−58	44	58	18	68	5	−64		
184	−69	176	−58	33	62	6	−60		
185	−66	236	−64	38	−70	21	−61		
236	−72	241	−61	67	61	24	69		
237	−67	242	83	76	56	37	−66		
238	78	244	−76	94	56	41	−62		
242	58	245	−73	104	73	46	−75		
400	−67	400	78	382	65	58	75		
422	−60	405	62	439	−62	63	−59		
446	66	407	65	440	−60	64	−61		
499	71	422	64	451	58	65	−68		
500	−76	423	60	457	64	68	−49		
		427	68	458	58	85	−59		
		437	−69	515	63	87	−49		
		447	63			91	−55		
		454	64			161	52		
		494	61			172	64		

449

Table C.2 (continued)

Dream Variable	Ages 3–5		Ages 5–7		Ages 7–9		Ages 9–11		Ages 11–13		Ages 13–15	
	Correlate	r	Correlate	r	Correlate	r	Correlate	r	Correlate	r	Correlate	r
					502	72					187	59
											204	−63
											209	55
											218	50
											219	−49
											256	60
											260	−53
											263	−67
											301	54
											310	60
											339	57
											367	49
											409	−48
											411	51
											419	50
											440	−55
											449	−72
											488	−63
											551	55
Hedonic tone (NREM)					41	61	15	−63	5	61	114	70
					48	64	44	66	20	59	174	−71
					50	62	55	78	122	−67	175	−59
					60	−62	57	71	129	71	189	−62
					150	−67	61	−71	131	−61	216	69
					184i	−99	379	59	180	−66	258	−52

					185i	−96	431	−59	297	58	259	55
					186i	−96			515	−65	261	−62
					194	−72			528	50	337	67
									529	52	397	59
											401	−54
											415	67
											461	75
											480	64
Hedonic tone (sleep-onset)					10	58	11	−75	29	−61	3	−55
					15	58	27	−75	36	−55	44	55
					21	62	38	94	38	−66	46	−54
					156	−69	61	−77	39	56	67	65
					229	67	67	−67	51	−70	114	61
					397	69	106	−63	52	−52	174	−50
					400	−86			63	74	260	−52
					412	73			76	68	340	57
					414	71			78	51	415	59
					457	66			80	52	466	−55
					492	78			82	65	589	66
					573	−72			178	−71	592	55
									251	69	593	60
									288	67		
									316	−70		
									381	56		
									533	62		
									534	59		
Active participation (REM)	13	57	11	62	27	−50	22	69	20	69	4	−54
	164	73	33	−68	60	46	42	76	22	54	5	−79
	166	73	40	−58	159	49	48	−61	41	47	20	−62
	167	59	222	60	160	46	52	51	43	50	21	−58

Table C.2 (continued)

Dream Variable	Ages 3–5		Ages 5–7		Ages 7–9		Ages 9–11		Ages 11–13		Ages 13–15	
	Correlate	r	Correlate	r	Correlate	r	Correlate	r	Correlate	r	Correlate	r
	184	66	238	−66	203	69	56	50	45	−53	35	−58
	186	75	400	68	259	49	67	54	55	53	46	−78
	195	55	617	−83	409	−62	72	51	92	−55	51	−61
	234	68	637	79	411	63	169	−63	144	−65	57	−54
	429	−56	647	−63	414	−58	170	−69	182	−61	85	−63
	430	−63			419	59	221	76	183	71	87	−55
	433	−59			453	−51	222	−67	186i	84	91	−51
	596	82			460	51	237	−55	294	−49	97	−64
	597	−65			571	71	238	−51	319	−62	114	52
	601	56					287	−67	322	72	172	59
	602	−62					376	64	396	49	187	59
	605	58							437	60	204	−60
	608	61							522	49	253	−69
	612	−72							526	−59	255	−59
	612	−61									256	58
	613	−61									331	50
	627	58									365	−54
	628	78									428	−53
	629	−75									431	54
	630	−57									433	51
	631	73									435	−63
	655	61									436	−62
											438	63
											441	−52
											446	71

Longitudinal *decrease* in active participation (REM)

163	62					7	68
224	77					101	62
402	59					183	-54
415	-64	45	85			288	-58
417	-73	46	-62			294	54
433	-60	262	77			316	53
434	-63	282	-67			408	-53
496	-63	434	60			526	62
498	64	457	64				
504	60	465	64				
596	66	468	71				
600	-68	494	65				
600	-70	496	63				
601	74						
601	71						
602	-66						
602	-75						
608	63						
608	66						
609	-68						
612	-71						

456	-50
466	-53
468	57
471	-49
488	-59
551	72
558	49
596	51
4	73
5	75
19	81
20	92
21	81
22	62
24	-60
33	64
41	66
42	63
43	74
46	77
51	55
54	63
108	49
172	-66
191	62
204	72
259	-48
260	55
263	57

Table C.2 (continued)

Dream Variable	Ages 3–5 Correlate	r	Ages 5–7 Correlate	r	Ages 7–9 Correlate	r	Ages 9–11 Correlate	r	Ages 11–13 Correlate	r	Ages 13–15 Correlate	r
			613	−67							362	53
			613	−76							433	−62
			629	−73							468	−49
			638	60							481	53
			646	−68							488	53
			651	−69							535	72
											547	52
											550	−52
											551	−59
Active participation (NREM)					12	57	15	−53	6	47	22	62
					51	−65	40	66	179	67	36	−60
					52	55	58	−55	246	−75	42	60
					493	73	68	56	443	−72	97	−60
					571	88	159	−56	461	−51	125	−58
					572	75	169	−62			180	56
							170	−74			339	−53
							237	−77			454	−53
							287	−62			483	54
							290	−56			535	55
							376	58			596	63
							400	70				
							451	54				
							576	−60				
Active participation (sleep-onset)					51	−72	5	−72	37	50	8	52

Setting distortion (REM)

Upper block:

No.	dist.	No.	dist.	No.	dist.	No.	dist.
172	61	21	−63	247	−62	16	64
184i	−99	22	78	409	82	27	−72
203	82	24	−73	411	−79	50	55
415	−93	32	−68	419	−79	55	54
433	−62	42	86	420	−72	95	52
		46	−72	435	61	113	61
		108	−66	461	−65	191	61
		223	64	513	−61	340	53
		286	61	514	−55	353	−60
		298	−66			354	−62
		378	64			360	53
		467	62			363	58
		596	66			428	−59
						434	52
						543	60
						547	−69
						549	57

Lower block:

No.	dist.	No.	dist.	No.	dist.	No.	dist.	No.	dist.	No.	dist.
13	−57	4	59	29	−57	19	−59	64	−59	3	−55
18	−61	23	−61	42	−59	23	72	71	72	5	46
24	−73	25	72	56	44	37	−58	108	−58	36	−62
160	56	26	63	175	56	42	−65	123	−65	51	64
193	−60	44	74	198	−80	54	−51	295	−51	72	−49
238	64	49	−74	199	−57	110	63	404	63	119	60
400	−63	164	67	241	−56	184	−54	421	−54	120	52
		174	−65	429	−49	185	−57	423	−57	205	54
		175	−62	445	65	222	61	450	61	340	−58
		184	67	506	82	238	53	515	53	397	48
		185	65			466	−57	533	−72	401	−72
		195	65					596	52	423	52
		223	58							471	50

Table C.2 (continued)

Dream Variable	Ages 3–5		Ages 5–7		Ages 7–9		Ages 9–11		Ages 11–13		Ages 13–15	
	Correlate	r	Correlate	r	Correlate	r	Correlate	r	Correlate	r	Correlate	r
			502	61								
			599	64								
			614	66								
			615	67								
			628	71								
			644	−86								
Longitudinal *decrease* in setting distortion (REM)			13	−60	6	63			3	−74	5	−55
			25	−74	7	65			19	−60	17	−51
			32	−60	23	−63			52	−55	19	−50
			49	65	25	70			54	−66	27	−73
			184	−70	26	63			114	−68	33	−51
			185	−66	31	64			120	−62	46	−48
			644	72	44	70			121	−56	214	−49
					49	−78			178	−60	215	50
					174	−86			222	57	229	48
					176	−67			318	54	311	52
					187	68			450	62	333	−51
					191	68			523	75	341	60
					226	61			596	−58	437	51
					422	73					468	51
					500	65					481	−53
					506	−59					547	−53
					565	70					589	52
					567	74					591	52

Setting distortion (NREM)

568	71	3	−70	22	−57	593	54
570	76	7	−68	42	−58	594	55
573	69	55	68	315	67	17	−54
241	68	61	−74	415	51	448	−53
241	70	171	−60	443	80	459	−57
446	67	235	56			535	56
458	−60	239	54				
461	59	288	−67				
462	62	289	60				
465	60	449	−55				
		457	−79				

Setting distortion (sleep-onset)

16	−59	4	67	20	−63	6	−55
17	−59	6	60	24	58	17	53
42	−81	8	67	26	−48	22	−54
44	71	18	−89	30	56	36	64
61	−63	21	72	88	51	37	−54
150	−72	25	68	187i	−84	69	−52
198	−77	51	72	315	68	72	−54
236	−58	77	−70	450	−52	101	−60
279	59	94	−63	526	55	104	52
285	−63	104	−63			105	52
399	−75	161	−63			108	−62
401	74	169	−68			123	54
403	76	173	−78			262	59
449	76	290	−71			334	53
455	67	297	77			340	−63
456	72	463	69			423	51

Table C.2 (continued)

Dream Variable	Ages 3–5		Ages 5–7		Ages 7–9		Ages 9–11		Ages 11–13		Ages 13–15	
	Correlate	r	Correlate	r	Correlate	r	Correlate	r	Correlate	r	Correlate	r
Character distortion (REM)					458	−70	467	−68			485	56
	33	−68	23	−70	5	50	575	−75	22	−70	22	54
	36	−66	44	59	17	−46	577	−71	42	−54	120	−63
	43	−70	161	−66	32	−51	16	−66	79	63	179	−56
	56	−81	164	76	156	−64	45	64	81	48	249	59
	58	69	184	74	157	−59	55	−75	83	53	371	49
	164	64	185	83	158	−64	172	52	84	−48	411	−48
	167	66	189	65	186	−56			105	49	445	−54
	238	62	195	66	263	48			123	67	468	−55
	427	−65	237	64	571	−59			184i	−93	539	56
	430	−73	408	58					267	49	551	−54
	433	−76	410	−58					269	−51	591	−50
	599	65	491	63					315	64		
	608	65	495	66					384	60		
	609	65	499	−74					385	62		
	612	−71	502	60					386	52		
	613	−76	610	−66					387	62		
	613	−77	614	60					388	77		
	626	75	627	64					389	50		
	626	75	628	75					390	63		
	627	77							391	67		
	627	75							392	65		
	628	75							393	−58		

Longitudinal *decrease* in character distortion (REM)

ID	Value		ID	Value		ID	Value		ID	Value
630	−70		30	−72		23	−67		400	−52
632	65		164	−76		174	−68		405	46
634	74		184	−68		176	−68		522	−47
634	78		186	−63		192	60		527	60
638	87		188	−75		244	61			
			189	−71		403	−61		45	76
			190	−68		458	70		267	−71
			234	−78		573	61		292	−58
			240	−63					320	63
			408	−64					442	60
			409	−78					444	60
			410	73					450	59
			411	76					514	−71
			418	66					516	69
			419	80					517	−70
			420	78					528	68
			499	75					579	58
			507	74						
			610	68						
			642	69						

ID	Value
7	−56
19	−52
20	−56
22	−71
34	−57
42	−60
71	−51
120	54
249	−60
304	−51
332	49
333	−48
468	54
483	−52
535	−61
540	−57
591	56

Character distortion (NREM)

ID	Value		ID	Value		ID	Value		ID	Value		ID	Value
35	−52		6	58		15	−54		38	−65
51	63		11	−65		18	−72		51	−72
170	53		18	−67		47	−64		52	−56
236	−56		109	−65		106	−61		68	−55

Table C.2 (continued)

Dream Variable	Ages 3–5		Ages 5–7		Ages 7–9		Ages 9–11		Ages 11–13		Ages 13–15	
	Correlate	r	Correlate	r	Correlate	r	Correlate	r	Correlate	r	Correlate	r
					399	−59	159	−59	180	−75	125	−54
					452	61	170	−65	266	−58	232	−57
					456	79	399	55	267	56	302	−53
					458	−88	427	57	269	−67	307	57
					572	−78	428	65	392	66	332	−62
							431	−75	395	60	354	57
							436	57	425	58	356	52
							465	−61	426	58	406	−54
							575	−83	439	68	413	−54
							577	−83	448	−68	439	−58
									457	−80	556	59
									468	−59	563	55
Character distortion (sleep-onset)					5	67	7	−95	22	−67	15	58
					17	−90	9	−86	29	−58	44	−55
					22	−75	55	85	42	−67	57	−62
					39	−66	93	−73	48	68	64	58
					51	64	109	−84	56	−59	67	−74
					147	−95	171	−71	60	67	69	−59
					148	−83	184	86	77	63	71	−52
					149	−95	185	69	101	−61	72	−68
					172	−91	186	68	288	51	117	−62
					231	−88	224	−90	292	59	130	55
					232	−91	288	−82	381	65	248	−55
					233	−89	378	−81	383	54	253	−77

399 −76
415 87
417 84
505 96

575 −79
577 −82

384 67
385 77
388 54
391 66
393 −72
398 −61
401 76
429 −53
431 −57
453 −55
455 55
460 57
465 −56
510 −70
521 75
527 73
530 −59

311 −53
341 −63
431 54
432 61
436 −54
441 −53
446 54
485 64
487 54

Verbal, either/locomotor,
either

1 −46
12 −54
25 −46
30 −47
52 −46
184i 79
185i 79
194 52
227 61
228 69
230 62
258 64

14 −61
24 56
117 −52
179 73
209 52
301 58
310 50
312 51
335 −50
355 52
367 58
409 −52

Table C.2 **(continued)**

Dream Variable	Ages 3–5 Correlate	r	Ages 5–7 Correlate	r	Ages 7–9 Correlate	r	Ages 9–11 Correlate	r	Ages 11–13 Correlate	r	Ages 13–15 Correlate	r
					259	–48					411	53
					442	59					417	–56
					447	50					419	53
					450	67					431	53
											432	56
											434	56
											436	–56
											441	–49
											446	49
											482	49
											483	–57
											486	72
											539	–66
											551	55
											585	–54
Sensory, either/motor, either					18	53					14	–61
					35	46					113	62
					148	60					114	63
					149	57					335	50
					151	62					337	64
					175	–65					397	71
					237	47					401	–80
					241	56					415	66
					241	65					451	49
					243	57					461	65

Cognitive, either/motor, either

243	61	475	70
245	68	477	−61
398	−56	480	53
433	−45	486	−58
566	56	488	−48
		557	−50
22	47	1	−68
37	53	7	−70
52	−51	19	−59
174	−63	20	−54
187	62	22	−76
191	60	34	−71
198	68	38	−54
230	56	42	−67
231	77	49	53
232	73	52	−51
233	56	53	−55
234	48	55	−54
237	49	63	−48
506	−66	69	−65
565	65	84	−53
567	67	87	−53
568	60	89	−56
569	46	91	−55
570	61	108	−54
574	61	124	−52
		127	70
		159	67
		160	62

Table C.2 (continued)

Dream Variable	Ages 3–5		Ages 5–7		Ages 7–9		Ages 9–11		Ages 11–13		Ages 13–15	
	Correlate	r	Correlate	r	Correlate	r	Correlate	r	Correlate	r	Correlate	r
											161	60
											170	56
											172	63
											173	56
											204	−54
											205	−50
											212	55
											217	49
											218	58
											250	63
											259	53
											260	−53
											271	64
											301	53
											333	−55
											354	51
											367	55
											433	61
											443	−68
											453	−52
											464	61
											469	−56
											487	66
											489	52
											490	58

Maximum social or object motive (either) minus maximum organic motive (either)

48	-61	540	-56
50	-44	551	51
61	50	552	-51
234	-47	5	54
238	59	9	59
240	-57	35	60
242	66	46	54
281	45	75	57
401	-62	76	49
445	-67	80	64
456	-57	83	48
		101	-63
		339	-52
		357	-53
		365	56
		449	49
		553	-58
		590	-52

Male stranger (any) minus female stranger (any)

1	59	4	55
27	52	5	85
45	-51	20	66
187	-49	21	60
201	76	38	55
202	-56	46	69
258	-56	51	54
399	52	87	62
433	-56	91	52
437	68	106	-53
438	65	114	-75

Table C.2 (continued)

Dream Variable	Ages 3–5		Ages 5–7		Ages 7–9		Ages 9–11		Ages 11–13		Ages 13–15	
	Correlate	r	Correlate	r	Correlate	r	Correlate	r	Correlate	r	Correlate	r
					441	−59					171	−67
					444	−57					172	−53
					447	−57					173	−63
					450	−59					204	70
					452	−69					212	−53
					454	−56					215	49
					502	−61					217	−54
					508	58					218	−49
											259	−80
											260	78
											263	48
											357	−68
											367	−54
											411	−50
											419	−50
											433	−51
											435	56
											436	52
											446	−52
											487	−55
											539	61
											547	55
											551	−64
											553	−65
											598	−76

Maximum known (Any: M or F) *minus* maximum family (Any: M or F)

32	−48	18	54
39	51	23	52
48	56	30	49
50	60	57	−73
154	−68	59	56
155	−68	66	62
196	−62	81	52
198	62	83	48
199	65	88	58
230	61	105	69
231	72	107	−63
232	61	122	70
424	63	169	61
426	67	179	−60
459	51	251	−58
		329	59
		334	53
		424	−52
		474	−49
		478	−54
		484	−64
		486	−60
		586	61
		588	58
		596	51

Name Index

Subject Index